Die Jugend und ihre Zukunftschancen
Herausgeber: Johannes C. Welbergen

D1935729

DIE JUGEND UND IHRE ZUKUNFTSCHANCEN

Ein Symposium mit Jugendlichen und Vertretern aus Wissenschaft, Wirtschaft, Politik und Verwaltung

vom 26. bis 28. 6. 1978
auf Schloß Gracht bei Köln

2,65
WEL
Inventar Nr. 2618

Jugendwerk der Deutschen Shell

ECOLE DES AFFAIRES DE PARIS
– Niederlassung Düsseldorf –
c/o Universität Düsseldorf
4 Düsseldorf
Universitätsstraße 1
Gebäude 25,12
Telefon (02 11) 34 70 51

CIP-Kurztitelaufnahme der Deutschen Bibliothek

Die Jugend und ihre Zukunftschancen
(Hrsg. J. C. Welbergen), Hamburg, 1979
ISBN 3-922245-005
NE: Welbergen, Johannes C. (Hrsg.)

Herausgeber:	Johannes C. Welbergen Deutsche Shell Aktiengesellschaft Überseering 35, 2000 Hamburg 60
Satz:	Heinz E. Mänz, Hamburg, IBM-Composer
Umschlag:	Monica Herkewitz, Hamburg
Fotos:	Hans E. Müller, Hamburg
Druck:	von Stern'sche Buch- und Offsetdruckerei, Lüneburg

INHALT

Vorwort 9

1. Gesellschaftspolitische Aspekte

Begrüßung durch den Tagungsleiter **W. R. Schürer**, Delegierter des Verwaltungsrates der MS Management Service KG, St. Gallen 13

Eröffnung des Symposiums durch **J. C. Welbergen**, Vorsitzender des Vorstandes der Deutschen Shell AG 15

The Prospects of Youth in the Post Industrial Society 19
Prof. D. Bell, Dep. Sociology Harvard University

Arbeitsgruppe Bell 29

Humane Wirtschaftsdemokratie als Chance der Jugend 41
Prof. Dr. O. Šik, Lehrstuhl für Wirtschaftswissenschaften Hochschule St. Gallen

Aussprache über die Referate Bell und Šik 54

Zukunftschancen der Jugend unter politischen Aspekten 76
Prof. Dr. K. Deutsch, Internat. Institut für vergleichende Gesellschaftsforschung, Berlin

Arbeitsgruppe Deutsch 94

Sicherung von Zukunftsinteressen in der parlamentarischen Demokratie 117
Prof. Dr. K. Biedenkopf, Stellvertr. Vorsitzender der CDU, Bonn

Aussprache 131

Die Politik der Bundesregierung zur Sicherung der Zukunftschancen der Jugend 141
K. F. Zander, Staatssekretär im BM für Jugend, Familie und Gesundheit, Bonn

Aussprache 152

2. Die Orientierung der jungen Generation

Orientierungskrise – sozialer Wandel als intellektuelle und politische Herausforderung 169
Prof. Dr. H. Lübbe, Lehrstuhl für Philosophie und politische Theorie Universität Zürich

Der junge Mensch auf der Suche nach Sinn 180
Prof. Dr. V. E. Frankl, Lehrstuhl für Neurologie und Psychatrie Universität Wien

Das Leben ist nicht sinnlos im Jahre 2000 – Vom Sinn der Arbeit 192
Pater Dr. H. B. Streithofen, Institut für Gesellschaftswissenschaften Walberberg

Aussprache über die Referate Lübbe, Frankl, Streithofen 200

Jugend und sozialer Wandel 218
Prof. Dr. L. Rosenmayr, Lehrstuhl für Soziologie Universität Wien

Arbeitsgruppe Rosenmayr 236

3. Zukunftschancen – bildungspolitische und wirtschaftliche Perspektiven

Gedanken zum Problem der Jugendarbeitslosigkeit aus der Sicht eines Unternehmens 253
Johannes C. Welbergen, Vorsitzender des Vorstandes der Deutschen Shell AG

Neue Anforderungen an die Bildungspolitik? 264
Dr. P. Glotz, Senator für Wissenschaft und Forschung, Berlin

Aussprache über die Referate Welbergen, Glotz 271

Die wirtschaftliche Perspektive für die 80er Jahre – Ansätze zur Überwindung der Wachstumsschwäche und der Arbeitslosigkeit 279
Prof. Dr. N. Walter, Institut für Weltwirtschaft Universität Kiel

Statement zur Frage beruflicher Ausbildung aus gewerkschaftlicher Sicht 294
H. Rappe, stellvertr. Vorsitzender der IG Chemie, Hannover

Aussprache über das Rappe Statement und das Referat Walter 299

Schlußwort:
Zukunftschancen der Jugend – Versuch eines Resümmes 322
W. R. Schürer

4. Anhang

(Vor Beginn des Symposiums hielt Prof. Blücher eine Einführung in die Shell-Jugendstudie, die anschließend diskutiert wurde.)

Die Eingliederung der Jugend in der Welt der Erwachsenen – Einführung in die 7. Shell Jugendstudie 330
Prof. Dr. V. Graf Blücher, Lehrstuhl für Soziologie Universität Bern

Aussprache 351

Teilnehmerverzeichnis 354

Veröffentlichungen der Deutschen Shell AG

Vorwort

Im Juni 1978 fand auf Einladung des Jugendwerks der Deutschen Shell auf Schloß Gracht bei Köln ein dreitägiges Symposium mit dem Thema ,,Die Jugend und ihre Zukunftschancen" statt.

Mit der Einladung von jugendlichen und älteren Vertretern aus verschiedenen gesellschaftlichen Bereichen, nämlich aus Wissenschaft, Politik, Wirtschaft, Verwaltung, Gewerkschaften, Schule, Universität, Kirche, Jugendarbeit und Bundeswehr, sollte eine möglichst umfassende und vielseitige Erörterung der Frage nach den Zukunftschancen gewährleistet werden.

Die Symposien des Jugendwerks sind Bestandteil der Jugendarbeit unseres Unternehmens und verstehen sich als Weiterführung der Jugendstudien, die in unserem Auftrag erstellt werden. Wir sehen diese Arbeit auf dem Gebiet der Jugendforschung als Ausdruck der gesellschaftspolitischen Verantwortung, die wir mit der Formulierung des Unternehmensziels ,,Beachtung der Belange des Gemeinwesens" übernommen haben.

Mit dem Symposium wollten wir einen Lösungsansatz zur Frage nach der Zukunft der jungen Generation ermöglichen und denjenigen, die an Entscheidungen in diesem Bereich – als Agierende oder Betroffene – beteiligt sind, die Gelegenheit zur Begegnung schaffen. Ein Versuch, der angesichts der Komplexität der Fragestellung und der vielschichtigen Zusammensetzung des Teilnehmerkreises sicher ein Risiko bedeutete.

Die Teilnehmer des Symposiums waren stellvertretend für Gruppen zugegen, die für die Erörterung der Zukunftschancen der Jugend Bedeutung haben. Um aber die verschiedenen Beiträge dieser Klausurtagung einem breiten Interessentenkreis zugänglich zu machen, sind alle Referate, Diskussionen und Ergebnisse der Arbeitsgruppen in diesem Buch zusammengestellt worden.

Wir hoffen, mit der Veröffentlichung neue Impulse für die Sicherung der Zukunftschancen der heute jungen Generation zu erbringen.

Der Herausgeber

P.Glotz

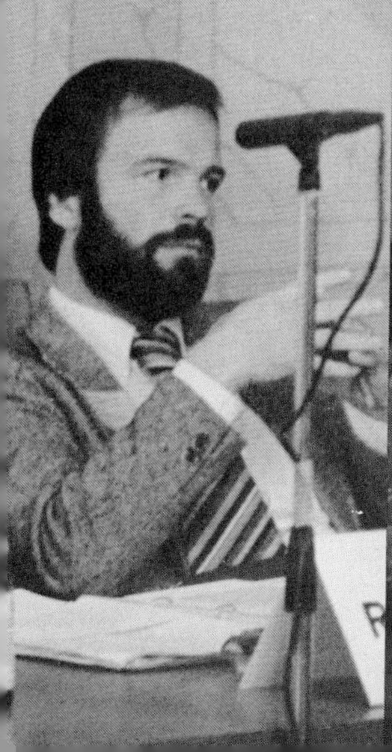

Begrüßung

Wolfgang R. Schürer

Meine sehr verehrten Damen und Herren,

ich begrüße Sie anläßlich der Eröffnung des 2. Symposiums des Jugendwerks der Deutschen Shell zum Thema „Die Jugend und ihre Zukunftschancen".

Ich möchte Herrn Welbergen bei seinen Ausführungen zur Eröffnung nicht vorgreifen, sondern mir die Freiheit eines sehr persönlichen Wortes nehmen. Diese Tagung ist wegen ihrer Thematik außerordentlich wichtig. Sie kann nur dann zum Erfolg führen, wenn auf der einen Seite gewisse faktische Grundlagen bekannt sind und erörtert werden, auf der anderen Seite die kontroverse Diskussion zustandekommt.

Ein persönliches Wort erscheint mir aber aus einem ganz anderen Grund angebracht. Es ist in der Tat selten, daß sich Unternehmen mit diesem Thema nicht nur intern auseinandersetzen – dafür gibt es viele zwingende Gründe –, sondern darüber hinaus zu einer öffentlichen Erörterung einladen. Als einer der vielen jüngeren Leute hier freue ich mich, mit Ihnen zusammen die nächsten drei Tage als Ihr Tagungsleiter gestalten zu können.

Zuerst möchte ich den Referenten besonders herzlich dafür danken, daß sie der Einladung gefolgt sind, und Ihnen dafür, daß Sie sich freiwillig entschieden haben, zu dieser Klausur zusammenzukommen.

Erlauben Sie mir aber auch, ein Wort des persönlichen Dankes an Herrn Welbergen und Herrn Hoffmann. Ich glaube, es ist nicht symptomatisch – ich hoffe, Sie werden mir das nachsehen –, daß ein Großunternehmen eine solche Tagung zustandebringt, sondern hier manifestiert sich ein starkes persönliches Anliegen. Es ist die Erkenntnis aufgrund mehrjähriger Jugendarbeit, daß die Themen wichtig sind und wir alle, die wir hier zusammensitzen, im Grunde genommen wissen, daß es die Lösung mindestens bisher nicht gibt. Aus dieser Einsicht und dem inneren Engagement folgte die Bereitschaft, eine Veranstaltung durchzuführen, um zu versuchen, neue Impulse zu finden, den Dialog zu fördern, die Kontroverse zu suchen und festzustellen: stimmen überhaupt die Voraussetzungen, von denen wir glauben, daß sie so valide sind? Das ist ein klein wenig Ausdruck dessen, was – wie ich persönlich meine – zum Engagement des Unternehmers oder Managers Johannes Welbergen gehört. In diesem Sinne möchte ich ihm danken, daß er mir die Gelegenheit gegeben hat, dieses Symposium mitzugestalten. Ein zweites Wort des Dankes möchte ich an Herrn Hoffmann richten. Er ist in der Deutschen Shell u.a. verantwortlich für die Bereiche Gesellschafts- und Wirtschaftspolitik, und er hat mir die Möglichkeit gegeben, zusammen mit ihm in den letzten vier, fünf Monaten bei der Vorbereitung ein bißchen geistiges Sparring zu üben. Er hat manchmal eine kontroverse Position gegenüber meiner eingenommen, dann haben wieder andere uns beide hinterfragt. Wir hoffen, daß die Kontroverse und die Vielfalt der Meinungen in diesem Programm sichtbar werden, und wir hoffen, daß Sie wie gestern abend begonnen, heute weitermachen. Wir wollen wirklich versuchen, kontrovers in die Dinge einzusteigen. In diesem Sinne freue ich mich, daß ich Ihnen zur Verfügung stehen darf. Nun darf ich Sie, Herr Welbergen, bitten, das 2. Symposium des Jugendwerks der Deutschen Shell zu eröffnen.

Eröffnung des Symposiums durch Johannes C. Welbergen

Albert Einstein hat einmal gesagt: „Ich denke niemals an die Zukunft – sie kommt früh genug."

Sie kommt früh genug, sie steht uns unmittelbar bevor, denn tiefgreifende Veränderungen gesellschaftlicher Normen und Wertvorstellungen prägen unser heutiges Leben in immer schnellerer Folge. Der Wandel äußerer, z.B. technologischer Bedingungen, findet zeitgleich mit dem Wandel dieser inneren Bedingungen statt.

Kennen wir die Richtung der Veränderung?

1. Verantwortung für die Zukunft

Basis für die Veränderungen ist das, was die vielen Generationen bis heute geschaffen haben. – Der Ist-Zustand!

Unbestreitbar prägt das Handeln – prägen die Entscheidungen – derjenigen, die heute Verantwortung tragen, das Geschehen von morgen – und damit auch die Zukunft der heute jungen Menschen.

Im Rahmen dieser Konstellation tragen die Älteren ein besonders hohes Maß an Verantwortung gerade für die Zukunft der jungen Generation.

Ich frage mich oft, ob die zahlreichen Entscheidungen, die heute in Politik, Gewerkschaft, Kirche, Wirtschaft und anderen Institutionen gefällt werden, überhaupt an Soll-Vorstellungen für die Zukunft orientiert sind? Und wenn ja, von welchen Soll-Vorstellungen? Oder verfolgt nur jede Gruppe etwa ihr eigenes Ziel?

Wir können uns heute die Feststellung nicht länger leisten: „Ich denke niemals an die Zukunft."

Ich meine, wir sollten sie ständig im Auge behalten, dies ist die Voraussetzung, uns der Verantwortung für morgen „qualifiziert" zu stellen. Die Verantwortung für morgen ist eine gemeinsame. Die Jugend trägt eine ganz erhebliche Verantwortung für ihre eigene Zukunft. Die Frage nach dieser Verantwortung wird sicherlich noch einen breiten Raum in der Diskussion einnehmen.

Ich möchte diese Verantwortung in zwei Fragen zum Ausdruck bringen:

1. Welche Chancen geben wir, die Älteren, der Jugend für die Zukunft?
2. Welche Chancen erkennt die Jugend selbst, und ist sie gewillt, sie zu nutzen?

Doch zuerst eine Antwort auf eine Frage an uns als Gastgeber:

2. Warum befaßt sich ein privatwirtschaftliches Unternehmen wie die Shell mit Jugendfragen?

Warum wendet die Shell erhebliche Kräfte und Mittel auf, z.B. für
– Jugendverkehrserziehung,
– Jugendstudien,
– Jugendsymposien?

Kritiker könnten einen Werbetrick vermuten, Profilierungssucht einzelner Unternehmen unterstellen oder schlicht von Geldverschwendung sprechen – denn, was bringt das alles?

Dieser Kritik haben nicht nur wir uns zu stellen, zahlreiche Unternehmen sind in ähnlicher Weise wie wir aktiv.

Daher möchte ich hierzu einige grundsätzliche Bemerkungen machen: Ich sprach eingangs von den Veränderungen der Wert- und Normvorstellungen. Auch das Verhältnis von Wirtschaft und Gesellschaft unterliegt diesem ständigen Wandel.

Dies zeigen zum Beispiel die vielfältigen Beiträge in der öffentlichen Diskussion über die Stellung des Unternehmens in der Gesellschaft. Diese Diskussion ist in den letzten Jahren immer intensiver geführt worden – stärker als jemals zuvor. Als Stichworte mögen genügen
– „Umweltschutz",
– „Humanisierung des Arbeitslebens",
– „Soziale Sicherheit".

Sie verdeutlichen, wie umfassend die gesellschaftspolitische Verantwortung der Unternehmen heute ausgelegt wird.

Wir haben seit einigen Jahren erkannt, daß auch an die Unternehmenspolitik heute neue Anforderungen gestellt werden.

Mit vielen anderen Unternehmensführern bin ich der Meinung, daß eine Unternehmenspolitik, die die sozialen Belange der Gemeinschaft außer Acht läßt und sich einseitig auf das Erreichen ökonomischer Ziele ausrichtet, zum Scheitern verurteilt ist. – Ja, sie wäre sogar schädlich für unser gesamtes freiheitliches Wirtschaftssystem. Eine solche Unternehmenspolitik wäre Wasser auf die Mühlen derjenigen, die sich zum Ziel gesetzt haben, den unternehmerischen Handlungsspielraum immer weiter einzuengen.

Eine im letzten Jahr vom „Managermagazin" durchgeführte Untersuchung über das soziale Engagement deutscher Industrieunternehmen läßt erfreulicherweise darauf schließen, daß der bei weitem überwiegende Teil der Unternehmen sich ihrer sozialen Verantwortung nicht nur bewußt sind – sondern auch dementsprechend handeln.

Das sind unter anderem die Gründe, die uns zu unseren weitergehenden Aktivitäten veranlaßt haben.

Man kann natürlich darüber diskutieren, für welchen speziellen Zweck man Mittel einsetzt, auf welchem Gebiet man sich engagiert. – Wir haben uns für Jugendfragen entschieden.

3. Warum dieses Symposium auf Schloß Gracht?

In vielen Fragen und Antworten unserer 7. Jugendstudie klingt die Frage nach den Zukunftserwartungen, den Zukunftschancen der Jugend an.

Das 1. Symposium des Jugendwerks vor zwei Jahren in Haus Rissen hat uns ermutigt, an ein weiteres Symposium zu denken.

Dieser Grund und das starke Interesse verschiedener Gruppen an der Studie waren schließlich ausschlaggebend für die Idee, in einem weiteren Symposium die einzelnen Interessengruppen zusammenzuführen und ein gemeinsames Gespräch über das Kernproblem – die Zukunftschancen – zu ermöglichen. Deshalb haben wir diesen Rahmen gewählt, um Ihnen in freiwilliger Klausur die Gelegenheit zum Gedankenaustausch zu geben.

Wir glauben, daß die Idee richtig ist, ob sie sich bewährt, ob sie Früchte trägt, müssen wir abwarten.

4. Teilnehmer aus verschiedenen Interessengruppen

Ein wichtiger Gesichtspunkt bei der Einladung der Referenten und der Teilnehmer war für uns, das Problem kontrovers zu diskutieren, und zwar unter gesellschaftlichen, politischen, technologischen und wirtschaftlichen Aspekten.

Ich.glaube, wenn Sie das Teilnehmerverzeichnis durchblättern, werden Sie feststellen, daß die Anwesenheit von älteren und jugendlichen Vertretern aus Politik, Wirtschaft, Wissenschaft, Gewerkschaft, Kirche und der Jugendarbeit eine gute Voraussetzung ist, die uns gemeinsam berührende Problematik vielschichtig zu diskutieren.

Schon die Themenformulierung durch die Referenten allein läßt erkennen, wie vielschichtig die Betrachtungsweise ist.

Chancen für die junge Generation schaffen, heißt Vorbereitungen für die zahlreichen Herausforderungen der Zukunft treffen.

Was auch immer hier an Lösungsansätzen für diese Vorbereitungen erarbeitet wird – ich bin sicher, die Durchführung ist Aufgabe aller Gruppen unserer Gemeinschaft. Darum sollten Vertreter dieser Gruppen auch bei Diskussionen über das Thema vertreten sein.

Wir haben uns bemüht, für Gespräche viel Zeit einzuplanen. Ich sagte schon, daß wir dieses Symposium als eine Fortsetzung unserer Jugendstudie ansehen.

Wie mit dieser Studie wollen wir auch mit dem Symposium einem möglichst großen Kreis die Gelegenheit geben, an den Beiträgen jedes Einzelnen teilzunehmen. Wir möchten deshalb die Referate und die Diskussionen aufzeichnen und sie Ihnen und weiteren Interessenten in Form eines Buches zur Verfügung stellen.

Ob wir Lösungsansätze finden werden zu der Frage *Welche Zukunftschancen hat die Jugend,* wird sich in den nächsten Stunden und Tagen zeigen.

In diesem Sinne eröffne ich das Symposium und wünsche uns allen fruchtbare Gespräche auf Schloß Gracht.

The Prospects of Youth in the Post Industrial Society

Prof. Dr. Daniel Bell

Es tut mir leid, aber Sie müssen entschuldigen, daß ich auf Englisch sprechen werde. Ich bin in New York geboren und habe als Knabe ein bißchen Jiddisch, Plattdeutsch und ein bißchen Schwyzertütsch gelernt; Hochdeutsch jedoch ist sehr schwer. Es ist daher besser, daß ich Englisch spreche, als daß ich Ihnen „Quatsch" erzähle.

I've explained, why I have to speak in English: in order to be more intelligible to a serious subject. And talking about the nature of youth in the post-industrial society I want to sketch a series of questions and put them in context.

The more immediate context is essentially a demographic one. When one talks of the chances of youth or the future of youth, to some extent in Germany at least, the problem really is of one decade, of ten years. As many of you know, actually the birthrate in Germany is going down and over time the total German population is going down. I'm told, there is a magical thing called „der Pillenknick", and as a result of this „Pillenknick" there is a change in the contours of German population.

It is quite clear that in about ten years from now there probably will be shortages of skilled labour and of the intellectual professions. Unfortunately, those who are of the present generation in their twenties and thirties, are in, what we call „the bulge" and therefore this is now the real problem. In ten years from now it will be a very different kind of problem.

There is however a second context, which is for the next thirty years probably more important. It is basically that we call the north-south-confrontation and the relation of the advanced industrial countries to the southern world. I am sometimes tempted – and perhaps it is useful to overdramatise the situation – by saying that there was written about two years ago a new Communist Manifesto. When people think of the Communist Manifesto, they think of Marx, they think of 1848, they think of the rhetoric and the very flaming language of the Communist Manifesto, and sometimes because they become confused by history, or perhaps the way, in which history gives them a wrong impression, when they think of revolutions, they look for similar kinds of manifestoes. They read Che Guevara, they read Frantz Fanon, or they read Baader-Meinhof or they read the „Red Brigades", and think this is the new Communist Manifesto. Those are not. That is old utopianism in many ways. The new Communist Manifesto is typical of a new age. It is written in stiff, bureaucratic prose, in heavy economic language and goes under the title of „The Required Restructuring of the World's Manufacturing Output". It is in fact the statement of the United Nations' Commission on

Referat Bell

Trade and Development. The new Communist Manifesto, if I can call it so, is a statement, which is officially adopted at the United Nations; which is very strange to have the United Nations adopt, what I would call a Communist Manifesto. The declaration was first put forth in a place called Lima Peru, and it's called the Lima Target. I don't know, how many of you know about the Lima Target. But this is a document, makes explicit economic and political demands on the Western World. The specific figures were put forth last year in Nairobi, in Africa. And it says that by the year 2000, 22 years from now, 25 per cent, or one fourth, ein Viertel, of the world's manufacturing output should be in the hands of the Third-World countries.

This may be very desirable. But apart from that it is a very fundamental political demand on the part of what is an „external proletariat". Today only about seven per cent of the world's manufacturing output is in the hand of the new nations. There is now a demand by, what Lin Piao called the external proletariat, that 25 per cent of the world's manufacturing output be shifted this way.

It would take about eleven per cent a year growth in world's manufacturing output to reach that figure without substantial redistribution. That is impossible. So by combination of political demands and market demands there will be a huge tug of war, a huge confrontation in this respect.

Most particularly, what this means is that the old kind of industrial production – shoes, .textiles, ship-building, steel – will move out of the western world and be relocated in Mexico, Brazil, South-Korea and various parts of the world. In fact, in the next 25 years we will begin to see a **new international division of labour**.

Every western country is going to face huge problems of industrial readjustment. There are some countries, like Great Britain, which will be in a more difficult position, even though there is now North-Sea-oil. England faces a problem with an old fashioned steel-industry, an old fashioned shipbuilding-industry, an old fashioned textile-industry. In other words: there is a very great problem.

Whether there can be a peaceful transition, a new adjustment, depends on what can be called the Third Industrial Revolution, a change, which derives from post-industrial society.

Now, the important thing is that Germany was one of the leaders in the Second Industrial Revolution. The First Industrial Revolution was a revolution of steam-power creating the large industries such as textiles and such. The Second Industrial Revolution in 1870, was a revolution in chemistry and electricity, just about a hundred years ago. And German with Siemens, with Rathenau, with the large chemical firms, the leader in that Second Industrial

Revolution. It became so by being one of the first countries to establish industrial research laboratories and „Technische Hochschulen", which in a sense created the research foundations or this change. England fell behind. And today it faces the consequences in many cases of that falling behind.

The Third Industrial Revolution is essentially a revolution whose leadership is in the science-based industries. This leadership is basically in the areas of electronics, optics, computers, polymers and such. And it derives from a radical principle, a very new radical principle, in the nature of this Third Industrial Revolution, which is the foundation for what I call a post-industrial society.

Let me take three dimensions of a post-industrial society to illustrate, what may come. I am not saying that it **will** come; it **may**. The ability for it to come depends upon the kind of political balance and economic readjustment; in part because of the energy situation and the new course of the western world, in part, because there is a new international division of labour. But if a post industrial society does come – and it is moving slowly, its pace of change is adjustable to the political situation – it has these features:

The first, and the one, which is most obvious, but perhaps less important, but still quite dramatic, is a change from a goods producing society, from fabrication to a service society, the „Dienstleistung". If I take the United States today; what is most striking is: there are only 17 per cent – 17 Prozent – of the labour force, and the labour force of the United States is about 95 million people who are industrial workers. Only 17 per cent are workers. When one thinks of the proletariat and the dreams of the old Marxian vision, it is quite striking that only 17 per cent today are industrial workers.

By the year 2000, only **ten** per cent of the American labour force will be industrial workers. Now, if this seems extraordinarily small to you, consider the fact that **today** less than four per cent of the labour force is in agriculture, and this four per cent – about 3,5 million people – produce enough food for the whole country as well as for large numbers of exports beside.

You find a situation in the United States today, where about 70 per cent of the labour force is in services. And most, 25 per cent, one out of every four persons, are professional and technical and managerial. There is, of course in the United States a lot of poverty, because it is a huge country and there are large numbers of people given the inequality of the system and who suffer. But what people don't see is that at the other end of the scale there are 25 per cent, one out of every four persons, who are professional, technical and managers. And this number is increasing, while the number of industrial proletariat decreases in the country.

So there is a basic change from goods to services. But these services are also different in the kind of services in a pre-industrial and in an industrial economy. In a pre-industrial economy most of the services are house-hold services, domestic services. In an industrial economy most services are auxiliary to industry – transportation, utilities, or finance. In an post-industrial society most services are professional services, such as computer services, and human services – social services, health, education and the like. So this is one of the first, of the major changes in the character of the post-industrial society.

Now, the same process occurs in Europe as well: at a lesser pace. What is most striking is that in Europe, large portions of Europe only went through major industrialisation **after** World War II. People think of Europe as being an industrial country, or an industrial society long ago. For large parts of England and Germany, it was some more true. But France and Italy really became industrialized only after World War II, which is, when you had your expansion of the working class. And it is only now, that you begin to get the beginning of a post-industrial change in European economy.

But the second and most crucial aspect of the post-industrial world is not this manifest or striking element of a change from goods to services, but a new principle. A new principle, of innovation in the society. And this principle, what I call here the „axial princip" is the codification of theoretical knowledge.

Now, every society has always existed using knowledge. But, it is only in the last thirty years that we have a new relationship, in which the codification of theoretical knowledge becomes directive of change. For illustration let me take the relation between science and technology. If you look at the major industries we still have – steel, automobiles, aviation, electricity, telephone – these are all 19th century industries, even though steel begins in the 18th century, aviation in the 20th century. These are 19th century industries, because they were all created by, what we call in English idiom „talented tinkerers", inventers, people, who worked with their hands, skilled mechanics – people like Siemens or Henry Ford or Thomas Edison –, but who lacked any theoretical knowledge of science, Thomas Edison, who created the electric lamp or the gramophone or the motion picture or Siemens, who created the dynamo or Henry Ford or Renault, who created automobiles, knew very little or nothing of the work of scientists, such as Maxwell and Faraday, who created electric magnetism. Marconi, who created the wireless, knew almost nothing of the word of Hertz on radio-waves. They were making things with the hands.

The first modern industry is chemistry, because you have to have a theoretical knowledge of the properties of the macro-molecules in order to know how to rearrange these. And essentially it is the new relationship of physics and chemistry, of solid state physics, which give you the theoretical formulations of the properties of nature, the properties of matter, which allow you now to advance fundamentally in areas such as electronics or computers or optics and such.

So it is basically for the first time that work in theoretical knowledge, which becomes directive of change in economic and social innovation. This is now producing, what I would call a Third Industrial Revolution. I do not have the time to really develop, what is to me (and it is the subject of a new book of mine) a very fascinating set of changes, which are now beginning in what we call now – it's a very heavy English word – compunications*). Compunications is a mixture of computer with communications. It is a merging of the two. It's the basis of a whole new revolution in a society.

I can perhaps put it this way: every society is tied together, is held together, by three different kinds of infrastructures. The oldest is transportation: roads, rivers, canals, etc. Every major city, we know is located on water, because water was the main way of transportation. Transportation is the oldest of all ways, in which exchange in commerce between cities take place. The second infra-structure is energy: water systems, electricity grids, water pipelines, gas pipelines etc. The third system is communication: The oldest form postal services, then telegraph, telephone and now a huge new set of merging communications – computers, television, facsimile, microwaves, a whole series of technical terms –. But what they're producing is basically a whole set of networks between people in which knowledge and information is being tied together to new systems and exchanges taking place in this way.

All this comes hand in hand with a second development, which for the first time makes possible real automation; and these are microprocesses. Many of you know in a general way about, what these are: microprocesses are little chips of silicon about the size of my thumb-nail, literally. And on it you can make, and it costs you perhaps 10 Marks, you can make a chip, which has 16 K, sechzehn, sixteen thousand bits of memory. These can be dropped into numerical control machine-tools to make different kinds of parts in this respect. So for the first time one has the possibility having compiterized automatic machine-tools under instructions, to begin to make a large variety of products.

Now, this has true large scale implications. Again, it would take a considerable time to spell out. Let me take one, which is important to those of you, who are interested in economics. The modern cooperation is really about 70 or 80 years old.

We've always had **business** activities. But the modern cooperation was created to coordinate men, materials nad markets for the mass production of goods.

---

*) In France Simon Nora calls this telematique.

It created huge, vertical integration, large cooperations in order to have economics of scale.

Where you have the new kind of communication's devices, and with varied production, that kind of vertical integration becomes dysfunctional for the rapid movements of technical change. One will have to see a new kind of adaptive economic structures, a new kind of organisational form to meet these new kinds of technologies. The modern cooperation was created for the mass production systems. We have now with microprocesses a means of moving from that kind of mass production system into **customized**, individual production of short runs of different kinds. And one will have to have a very different kind of organisational structure for the new kind of markets, for the new kinds of technologies, which will be arising from these technological changes.

I have tried to sketch very briefly some of the major outlines of the fundamentals of this new technological changes: changes, which involve where and how people work; a change away from factory work to various kinds of service and analytical work; a new importance for theoretical knowledge; a shift in the character of infra-structures: the computers and communication, and the way, in which society gets tied together. That it seems to me is the baseline, the „Grundlagen", from which one has to begin to look at the question: of what kinds of ways can one prepare for this world? And this is therefore the problem of the young people. Your are going to live more and more in a post-industrial world (if we gain political stabilization); if we have a new international division of labour, which creates a possibility for a new relationship for the world's economy. I leave these as a big „If". These are political questions outside my frame of reference. But assuming that, if we look ahead for the next thirty years: you will be living in a new kind of a post-industrial, new kind of tele-communications, new kind of compunications' world as your parents and grandparents were living in a different kind of factory and industrial civilization, a world itself different from the older agrarian civilizations.

Let me take three aspects, which are important for the problem of young people. One is in the change of character of the kinds of knowledge. Just as labour and capital were central to an industrial society, so information and knowledge become the strategic resources of post-industrial world. (And let me say, although there are large political differences, this is not simply a matter of the western capitalistic world; the Soviet world calls it the scientific and technical revolution. They claim that only they can implement it. I think that the Soviet Union is a disadvantage in implementing a scientific and technological revolution, because it is too bureaucratic as society. The very nature of a scientific and technological revolution requires a greater degree of flexibility to change and a world, which is heavily bureaucratic resists that kind of change. There are large elements of bureaucracy, state bureaucracy and business bureaucracy in the western world as well. I think, in the Soviet world there is a heavily politicalized state bureaucracy, which inhibit the change which they call the scientific and technological revolution.)

Central to all of this, however, is this emphasis on information and knowledge. Let me take two dimensions of it: one is the increasing importance of, what I call an intellectual technology. When one uses the word technology, people think of machines; but technology is **not** just the machine. Technology is a way of thinking, it's a way of systematic thinking, it's a way of the systematic organisation of technical knowledge. And the new kind of intellectual technology involves system theory, mathematical analysis, linear programming, decision theory, in all of the devices for the ordering large areas of the organized complexity of the world. Increasingly this is a world, because it becomes larger, it becomes more interdependent. There are many more variables one has to take into account, and one has to have a systematic way dealing with these large number of variables. So you have an increase, an exponential increase in organized complexity. And we have to have ways of dealing with this, and this in the role of the new intellectual technology.

The second aspect of knowledge, which is more subtitle, is that the world becomes, what I call a game between persons, „ein Spiel zwischen Personen". And this is in one sense very new in human civilisation. What I mean is this: in most parts of the world, in Africa, Asia, Latin America, a pre-industrial world, people work on the land, the „Landwirtschaft, Bergbau, Fischerei, Holz, Öl, Gas". It's a game against nature, „der Kampf gegen die Natur", in which you have to live with the vicissitudes of nature. In an industrial world you have a game against fabricated nature, in which you have the man – machine relationship. In a post- industrial world nature is excluded, things are excluded. It is a world between people.

Now there have always been societies, where small groups of people, particularly on the top, have to work and live with one another; but if work is the basis of character – and we do believe that work is the basis of character – we now live in a world, where most people live **not** against nature, or with things, but with one another; the doctor and patient, the teacher and student, the research team, organisational structure, in the office, in the bureau, in the government organisation. And learning to live with one another is very difficult. There are deep sources of aggression within the human beings, deep sources of desire for domination, deep sources of desire for power. There is an humanistic psychology talk about the need of self-realization, but most humanistic psychology forgets, there is also a deep desire and a deep drive for domination and for power, and even – if you want a quite old-fashioned word – evil that is there in human life. And when you have a world, which you only deal with one another, the problem of sensitivity, the problem of psychological awareness of learning how to live with one another in a human relationship becomes very, very difficult. Yet increasingly this is the problem we all have, that we don't work together against nature or against things, but we have to learn to live in the nuances of these psychological relationships. It's quite often difficult to two people to live together. Look at the large incidences of divorce. And how much more difficult it is for people to work together in larger organisations. So this becomes one of the major consequences of a post-industrial world organised arount knowledge. These two dimensions, then, cover the first topic.

Let me take a second topic of the three I want to deal with: „Bildung", the crucial character of education, because a new kind of „Bildung" becomes necessary to learn how to live in a post-industrial world. If the problem is to learn how to manage organized complexity the central theme for the foundation of knowledge becomes more and more epistomology. Not a discipline, not even economics or sociology or engineering, but epistomology: the principle of intellectual apperception, how to learn how to think about thinking, the principles of thinking, how to learn how to reorganize in a sense of thinking.

The worst education is to be educated narrowly in one single subject. In the Soviet Union, for example, there is a huge expansion in the number of engineers. But that knowledge quickly becomes useless as the whole plot of technology changes. One has to in a fact make a distinction: one will learn a subject matter on a **job**, whereas in a university, one does not learn a subject, but one learns epistomology, a way of thinking about relationships between disciplines, between subjects.

It was Kant who once said: knowledge is the imposition of the logical order on a factual disorder. And there are different kinds of logics, one can establish, depending on one's standpoint. Let me take one simple illustration: the way we look at geographical maps. If I ask you to imagine the map of the world, most of the ways in which we draw maps are drawn from a 19th century „scientistic" way of thinking. In the center is Northamerica, below is Southamerica. To the right there is Europe, below that Africa. To the west is Japan, then is South-East-Asia. Yet, if you look at strategy-maps, Europe from the viewpoint of Boston has a very different configuration than Europe from the standpoint of Northafrica. **Where you stand gives you a different configuration.** The outline of Europe is not a fixed outline. From the United States there is one configuration; from North-Africa there is another. And this is what every military-map, what every strategy-map can show you.

In the same way, thinking about the world is a matter of understanding, which standpoint one is using; so that fundamentally knowledge has to go back to problems of epistomology. The ways of knowing and the ways of reorganizing knowledge, to see new relationships in this way. This is the after all fundamental to all kinds of knowledge. When Isaac Newton said that there is a relationship between an apple falling from a tree and the tides of the water, people said: you must be crazy. What is the relationship of something like an apple falling from a tree and the rising and falling of tidal water? And he found a common underlying law, which is obviously the law of gravitation.

These are the problems of the ways of reorganizing knowledge: to look for underline relationships. And in the codification of theoretical knowledge, which is crucial here, this is the rootproblem. The whole structure of „Bildung" has to be a foundation in conceptional thinking. When I use the word **„Bildung"**, I realize all the difficulties with the term, as between „Bildung" and „Ausbildung", or even of „Berufsbildung" or „Berufsausbildung". In dealing with conceptual knowledge, it might have been easier to talk of „Wissenschaft". But today, „Wissenschaft" becomes too allied with technique. Since „Bildung" retains the English idea of „cultivation" – in the humanistic sense – I want to retain that word. The applications of „Bildung" would be in the work you do. More and more organisations will take over the instruction (Erziehung) on the job. The United States today, large cooperations spend as much money in education as the major universities; they provide specific training. And they want a training which is applicable to the kinds of work they do. So that in universities, at best, you'll learn basically **ways of knowing** rather than specializing in subjects. In this respect the whole structure of education itself one has to be thought through again.

Finally let me come to the third aspect as it deals with philosophical dimension of a post-industrial society: I've said that the first aspect is basically the learning of an intellectual technology and of understanding work as a game between persons. The second aspect is this problem „Bildung" of learning ways of knowing, the epistomological problems of the society and of knowledge. The third is fundamentally a semi-philosophical problem. There is first a tendency in these matters, let us call it the technocratic mentality. One finds even in intellectual work too much specialisation. Many years ago the Hans Magnus Enzensberger wrote, what I thought was a very useful essay, on the industrialization of the mind. There is a danger in this respect of the industrialization of the mind. I remember a few years ago I met a young economist at Harvard and I said to him: „What are you doing?" And he said: „I am the zinc-led-man in the Leontieff input-output-tables." My colleague Professor Leontieff had created input-output-tables, which is a matrix of 64 cells by 64 cells. On the one side you have inputs, such a steel, rubber, zinc, and on the other side you have outputs, which are finished goods. This man had specialized task to fill in the zinc and lead inputs. This was a form of intellectual specialization as mechanistic or industrial work. This is a risk, and a very difficult one in a post-industrial society.

Within this third aspect, there is another danger: more and more a distinction between an elite and the mass. Every society has always had a problem of the elite and mass. This is still one of the difficult problems of all political organization. Here we have a new aspect, in which a **technical** elite becomes fact the key-group in the society. On the other hand you have the problem of structural unemployment, of people, who are incapable of mastering, the kind of complexity necessary to manage and understand this kind of world.

How do we bring the mass of people into the society – for understanding, for participation – particularly, when decisions become more and more technical ones.

And the third aspect too, which has been crucial and increasingly so in the western world is: what sources of idealism can one have? Young people especially? Most people have drawn from different sources of idealism. The oldest form is religion in which one had a kind of religious attachment to the world. Or one had secular religions, such as communism or fascism, which gave one a kind of emotional outlet and attachment. A capitalistic society and a post-industrial society are basically utilitarian; they are basically instrumental. In and of themselves they provide no foundations, exept for few people, who are organizers or scientists. But economic provides no source of fundamental values or goals for the society. In fact, it increasingly creates more and more, what Max Weber called: the specialist without heart, the sensualist without spirit.

People will find a source of ideals in which to attach the kind of new technical powers, which a post-industrial society can bring. And that I would regard as the **outermost**, yet most crucial of problems.

Here we have the growth of technical and intellectual powers. Technical and intellectual powers far beyond what every civilisation so far has been able to make. And yet those intellectual and technical powers lack – if you will, here is an oldfashioned word – the spiritual dimension. Where is that spiritual dimension to come from?

That, it seems to me, is the large unanswered question of a post-industrial society.

Arbeitsgruppe Bell

Leitung: Wolfgang R. Schürer

Schürer:

Die erste Frage an Herrn Professor Bell lautet: Was wollen Sie mit der Jugendarbeitslosenreserve in einer Zeit machen, in der die Jugendarbeitskräfte noch nicht gebraucht werden?

Bell:

It depends on what kind of training of the youth you have. One of the things we find is – seriously enough – that we do not have enough of *technical training*, for the younger people. Let me put it into this context: If one looks ahead for to next twenty years, a new revolution is beginning; it takes place in the area of telecommunication and in, what I call intellectual technology. In this areas we will see heavy shortages in the next ten or fifteen years. We will find a very difficult situation, in which by 1985 there will be a lot of tasks to be fulfilled and a smaller number of people. The new area of expansion is a big gap in the curriculum of sociology.

The other question about what will happen to those who do not have technical training is a much more difficult question. I gave a brief, perhaps inadequate answer this morning.

Teilnehmer:

Die Technik kann doch letzten Endes auch dazu führen, daß weniger und weniger Menschen ein bestimmtes Produkt herstellen oder eine bestimmte Dienstleistung erbringen. Trotzdem sind Sie optimistisch, daß die dann in den 80er und 90er Jahren und danach Beschäftigung finden, obwohl die Bevölkerung dann abnimmt, wie es zum Beispiel auch in der Bundesrepublik der Fall ist.

Bell:

It is quite true, that the kind of system doing the mass production is the more capitalistic system. Therefore this production needs fewer und fewer workers. But one has to consider the absolute and relative numbers. Fewer and fewer workers *per* unit are looked for. But new units arise. There is another crucial point; I also spoke about it this morning. I said that in the next thirty years the most important development is a new international division of labour. In this new international division of labour the traditional manufacturing will be taken over by the developing countries: Brazil, Mexico, Algeria, Singapore and others. The comparative advantage of the western world will be a highly technical one. If you want to have special advantages in the next twenty years the extraordinary market is these technical areas. Take one of the markets: telephones. It is only 15 or 20 years ago that the majority of persons in Germany were able to have their own telephone. Think of the need of telephone-systems for the Iran or Iraq, Egypt, Brazil or Mexico etc. These people do not have the possibility to create such systems. It's not just the employment in this countries, but the tremendous expansion on the world market. I have to give you another information: I would assume that in about twenty years from now those countries like Iran, Algeria etc. will develope their own educational systems. I would assume further that in the next twenty years students of the Third World will come to us for graduate study, because they can't afford having „Hochschulen" and „Universitäten". As the birthrate goes down, more and more foreign students will go into our universities. It is something like a symbiosis between the western world and the non-western world. It is a classical relationship between those countries. They need trained help, trained in sciences, engineering and high technology. They provide a kind of advanced expectation. Therefore I am not pessimistic at all but optimistic.

Teilnehmer:

I think, the expectations of this revolution will turn out great problems during the next fifteen years. How, do you think will people solve these problems?

Bell:

Well, that is a difficult problem. Let me show it with the help of the blackboard.

If you have 1000 Dollar income per person in the western world and 100 Dollar income in the Third World, the gap between both is about 900 Dollar. If a person in the western world gains 5 % it is now 1050 Dollar. If the person in the Third World earns ten Dollars more, he has improved his income with *ten* percent to 110 Dollar, but the absolute gap is larger, even though the *relative* gain has been greater in the Third World. The Third World develops itself today twice as fast as the western world does it – but it is the *initial* gap that presents the problem.

Teilnehmer:

I think of the problem inside the Western world like Canada, the United States of America. What can tell us about the difficulties about finding a job in those countries?

Bell:

Well, this question is basically a generational one. You can't blame your parents, whether your mother has wanted you or not. Most of the children are wanted in that way.

When I pick out a firm in America and consider the machinepaid jobs I see that only 15 % of the workers work are machinepaid jobs. You have an increase of automation. 25 % of the labour-force is professional and technical nature. The greatest gains have been and will be in the professional and technical fields.

Teilnehmer:

It seems to me that the period in the United States of America between 1968 and 1971 was a period of greatest occupation opportunity and of great political instability. But yet I have still some optimism left to say, that although the economic situation may well improve that this is no guarantee at all that the social stability will fall on it. The political and social problems may be very important and difficult to be managed.

Bell:

Let me draw the attention to the following consideration:

Namely, the way selective attention by the media distort perceptions – particularly if you wish to interpret the nature of social stability.

The medias have dramatized unusual situations. If an event or a movement attracts a million persons, say, they blow up and one thinks something-extraordinary is going on. Yet, actually, a million persons are only one-half percent of the population.
It is all a matter of proportions. A few years ago, a young colleague of mine began to write a book on the dissolution of the family – because the media was full of stories about the rise in the divorce rate, or because „many" young people were living together without being married. She published the book this past year. It is called: The Family is here to stay. When she looked at the *total magnitudes*, she found a very different picture. True, more than two out of five marriages were ending in divorce; but a few years ago, it was extremely difficult to get a divorce in the States and more often than not one had desertions. When the laws were liberalized the statistics jumped. Was there a real change?

Or take the youth unrest in the 1960s. On reason for it – a condition, not a cause – was the sudden increase in the cohort of young people in the society in that decade. From 1940 to 1950, there was no increase in the proportion of young people. Similarly from 1950 to 1960 there was no increase. From 1960 to 1968 it jumped 54 percent in eight years – creating the basis for the turmoil. Yet, if one compares the unrest in the sixties to that of the 1930s, one sees how little there was, on a comparative basis.

Arbeitsgruppe Bell

I do not often make „predictions", since it is difficult to specify exact events. Yet about 1962 the head of the Ford foundation asked me to provide some examples of predictions – since we were interested in funding future studies.

I said, well: in 1964 there will be an election for President in the U.S., in 1968 there will be an election, in 1972, in 1976, in 1980, in 1984, and probably 1988. That is a „trivial" prediction, he said. Perhaps, I replied, but of the 150 countries in the world, of how many can you, with confidence, make such a prediction! What I am saying is that, clearly, there are institutional rules and stability underneath the system in the U.S.

Teilnehmer:

This morning you spoke about a new kind of elite; it is the technological elite which is part of the political elite. The other elite was the democratic one. Do you see any problems in communication between those two? Are you optimistic or worried about that?

Bell:

Well, I would say, this is an old problem with new players. The role of the technical elite is the essential question. The technical elite can frame the question, but only the politican can say „yes" or „no". The technical elite can never do that. I do not think that the technical elite will become a new class. The best illustration in the United States of America in the last 25 years was the fact that increasingly all military problems were technical ones; yet the basic decision were made by the politicans.

When Oppenheimer came, a bureaucratic war developed between the scientists and the military. The scientist lost this fight; this, I think happens to every technical elite.

Teilnehmer:

This morning you spoke of the distinction between elite and mass. Then you put the question: What sources of idealism does one have?

My question to you is: What kinds of idealism would you give to the mass, to the „Handwerker", who do not have the technical mentality?

Bell:

Well, I would say, the technocratic mentality does not provide idealism. It provides not only technocratic work. The whole society is a problem of idealism. The *mass* has, what a friend of mine, Steven Marcus predicted years ago „Porno topia". That is quick joy, quick fun, you can find it in sexshops, you can find it in airports. But in the end it is unsatisfying.

Things like that are the indicators of the failures of idealism. I think that

there is no society, which can exist without some conception of religion or the sacral. If you would go back to the thinkers of the „Aufklärung". They thought that the religion would disappear from Kant to Marx. Their conception of religion was interesting, it was evolutionary.
Hegel thought of the religion as the childhood of the human race. Marx also believed in fetishism as the mode of primitive belief. I think that the human race has reached a level, where today everthing is profane and flat. Yeat a change will come.

If one looks ahead thirty years, the very nature of production will have changed. Few units will have more than 500 people in one place. If you look at big factories, automobile factories or this big Shell you see that they employ many thousand people, concentrated in one place. In the future the unit of work will be small. Further there is the fact that life will not be „ein Kampf zwischen Menschen", sondern „ein Spiel zwischen Menschen"! They will work together in the university, in a hospital, in small production units. And they will have „ein Spiel oder einen Kampf".

The national state has become too big for the small problems of life. The national state of the 18./19. century is no more useful in this sense. So that is the big problem. The scale of institutions must be responsible for the solution.

Teilnehmer:
The Discussion did not touch the following problem yet. On the one hand the „Rohmaterial" gets smaller and smaller, and on the other hand the destruction of the environment is blown up. Does this fact play any role in the picture of the future?

Bell:
This motion is „purer Quatsch". I have spent several years on working out that problem. There is no shortage of physical material in the world. TheClub of Rome predicted certain shortages. Look at the business with copper. From 1972 to 1976 the price of copper went up 40 to 60 pence per pound. As a result countries like Zaire, Panama and others found old copper sources. With the new methods and at the new price it was more effective to produce this material. So those countries could stand the competition with the other countries. But at the price, there was substitution, and the price balance. The oil of Canada is enough to fill the earth for another hundred years. The only problem is that the production of it costs a lot. If you have now such countries and if you want to get your oil, you are willing to pay the higher price.

I want to come to the other example: In some countries of the world food is not a resource problem. It is a problem of social and political organization. In south-east Asia Burma was the biggest exporting country. It is even bigger than China. But because of a military socialist dictatorship the economy dropped down. Burma become a rice importing country.

The Soviet Union is as large as the United States and Canada. A third of the labour-force is employed in the agriculture. But nevertheless one has to import grain. None of the other countries has to do this, neither the Polish nor the Rumanians etc. The logic is for simple reason: controling is system.

To come to another point: ,,Rohmaterial" is free good, that is the opinion of many people. But one has realized that they become rare and with this expensive. But still some state that things like water and air should be free. They ask: How could we charge the air? If something is free, we misuse it. If you charge people for resources that is economize. If you know it will cost you something you'll be more careful using it.But primarily one can see that it is a matter of resources and economic production in this way.

Teilnehmer:

When you closed your contribution you focused on the cultures. Could you comment on this?

Bell:

Well, that goes back to very basic problems, which is the fact that increasingly the very nature of interdependence is growing. You have to sign and begin to think of a problem and look for some connexions. My crucial point is that there is not just one way to think of a problem. This is very much the 19th century's way of thinking. But to think else shows you different configurations. The real problem of the social analysis is to know, which kinds one can have. And there is not just one way you can do that. You can also do it in another way. And this depends on what your point of view is.

Marxism has a ,,Spiegelbild" view of knowledge. Now, the ,,Spiegelbild" knowledge is wrong. The real problem in ,,Bildung" is epistomology. That is, what I understand by ,,Erkenntnistheorie" and ,,Wissenschaftslehre". And the whole problem of ,,Erkenntnistheorie" and ,,Wissenschaftslehre" is the problem of combining and recombining.

Perhaps I should give an example to you. If you have a twelve-year-old child and say to it: You have a wale and an elephant. What is the difference? It'll say they are both mammoths. Although the one has a ,,Rüssel" and the other breathes, they have a common underlying structure. And the conceptional thinking is: what shall I select out? What property of the resources would you collect out and group together? It is a problem of comparison and variety And again there is not one fixed way. You can have different qualifications. Therefore the conceptional thinking is the art of selection. If you think of the problem of flexibility it is basically the art of conceptual thinking. It is also the relationship between concrete and abstract.

The same problem exists in physics. The theory of difference needs another way of considering a problem. Things get more complex. In earlier times you had just the electron and the proton in the atom-model, nowadays you can look at hundreds and hundreds of new particles. When Heisenberg tried to deal with it, it became obvious that he was, that the 19th century kind of thinking was oldfashioned. The whole question of conceptual thinking is the whole foundation of teaching people to be able to look at problems from different points of view. It is also the principle, why we select out.

Teilnehmer:

You spoke from the fact that people have to have correspondence. Yet it seems to me that we have the right to have it. But there is no indication that there is any correspondence at all. It almost heard people demanding more correspondence; they also demand their lifes and I don't see, where this increasing sense of responsibility comes from.

Bell:

Well, what I only said is this: optimism is a philosophy and pessimism is character trait. One has to understand, why the other is optimistic or pessimistic. This is again a matter of classification.

Teilnehmer:

Is it not the action itself in relation to life? To keep my life away from somebody's life?

Bell:

No, I think it's fairly enough a different thing. The question is: Do I use my money well? There is the opinion that taxes are the creation of services that people can buy for themselves, which is true. Now, I think, the reaction is: What do we get for our money? If you think you're right, you'll say: I'm only optimistic.

I want to tell you another story. Two angels were dancing and celebrating. The one asked the other one: Are you optimistic or pessimistic? The other said: Well, I am optimistic. But why are you crying then, was the answer of the first. Well, said the second, I am not sure, whether my optimism is justified.

Teilnehmer:

Ich habe eine Frage zur Technologie. Es ist eine enorme Entwicklung vom Handwerk zur intellektuellen Technologie. Was aber passiert mit dem Menschen? In der Zeit des Handwerks konnte dieser sich selbst bestätigen. Er tat das im Handwerk als Handwerker. In bezug auf die intellektuelle Technologie können vergleichsweise weniger Menschen folgen. Das ist das eine.

Arbeitsgruppe Bell

Zerfällt die Menschheit dann in zwei Klassen, in die eine der Intellektuellen und in die andere, die Klasse derjenigen, die sich aufgrund ihrer Anlagen und dieser zukünftigen Welt nicht mehr verwirklichen können? Das Ganze hat ja schon angefangen. Der größte Teil der Arbeitslosen sind ja unqualifizierte, unausgebildete Menschen, die auch selbst durch ein besseres Schulsystem nicht alle diese Qualifikationen erwerben können.

Zum anderen Punkt: Ist es überhaupt wünschenswert, daß das jetzt Besprochene bereits in der Ausbildung, in den normalen Schulen überbewertet wird? Die intellektuelle Schulbildung vergleichsweise kann eigentlich der persönlichen Entwicklung eines Intellektuellen nicht förderlich sein, sondern vielleicht sogar schaden. Wie sehen Sie dieses Problem?

Bell:

I can't be responsible for the second part of your question, because I don't know very much about it; I don't know enough about your school system. Let me speak to the first part, which is the problem of what the mass of people do, who work, when more and more work becomes technological. Let me say: people do not have the sense of multiplicationship in kind of work.

In the United States there is something called the dictionary occupational type; different kinds of occupations. In the United States there are 22.000 different kinds of occupations, and there were 10.000 only about twenty years ago. The huge expansion of services in some societes can't be neglected.

When I came from the airport to „Schloß Gracht" we saw miles and miles of caravans and looked for the nationalities. Most of them were Dutch and Danish. We said to them: it's lovely that you came here in June. With the word camping one combines recreation. All services expand. Also the sector of medicine expands. If you have a larger variety of services you have a larger variety of thinking on the people. We have more magazines than before. Television as well has expanded. We have larger expansion on the whole area of recreation, so that the area of services is not shut. Also the area of high technology is not shut, the development is still going on. After all the people were working in previous times sixty hours a week, 40 hours a week, and now they do just 35 hours a week. The reduction of the work leeds to expansion of social services, to a variety of new kinds of jobs. But that is primarily a more general problem and not one of technical function. And here I have to accept the warning that optimism is not automatic in this respect. It is a true question of economic and social policy.

Teilnehmer:

This morning you said that the kind of spiritual dimension of the post industrial society is not yet known. My first question is: What is the spiritual dimension like and what would it be like and how could it contribute to the educational system?

Bell:

Well, that is the most difficult question to that reason. You cannot manufacture the spiritual dimension. You can manufacture a product and a policy; many people do manufacturing. There is an American advertisement about headache remedies, which promise: quick, quick, quick relief, and then it says: quick, quick, quick, quick, belief. You get quick relief, you also get quick disbelief.

I believe that a spiritual thing enlarges very much. It grows to much importance to you. Therefore you cannot design an advance.

I have again another speculation: what could the sources be?

I have a question to Max Weber, because he was a great sociologist in religion; how, if you look at Weber's religion, you see that new religions arise against old institutions, by individuals with personal charisma. Jesus, Luther and Calvin had the force to tear down instructions. When I think about it, I ask myself: What is nowadays to be torn down? Each person judges the world for himself. He is antinomian.

If I go to a person and ask him: Who are you? He will answer: I am I. If you ask yourself, what happened to the generation of 1968 you'll get a result. What did they feel? They felt free. And then they had children. And the children ask: Daddy, what did you do in the war of 1968?

I tore everything down. I didn't want that condition.

You tore everything down? What did happen then?

Now let us try to speak in generational terms about what happened then. Who are we? Who am I? I am a son of my father and of his father. And it looks like on more psychological force on an ancient obligation. I think that if new religions arise, they will not be charismatic, but return to the pieties of the past – to emphasize tradition and continuity.

In the moment we are in a kind of clearing. But by the fact that we are in a kind of clearing we say that none of the old ways are satisfying. There is a hunger for some new kinds. I think that is a way on which the sense of a new spirit will come.

Teilnehmer:

But my second question was: How could you describe education. You know that this might be like an institution, people might not have any religion or philosophy.

Arbeitsgruppe Bell

Bell:

Well, it comes back – you see – to the perception that natural work emphazises relationships.

Most of the post industrial work essentially emphazises personal relationships. This is the institutional part. The worst thing, which could happen is that the irrationality comes up. Deep sources of aggression would appear ... . People say that human beings were duplex: On the one hand he does the murder, on the other hand he deals with love.

Teilnehmer:

Meine Frage lautet: Sie haben vorhin gesagt, daß für Sie die wichtigsten Probleme auf dem politischen und sozialen Gebiete zu suchen seien und nicht auf dem Gebiete der Rohstoffverknappung.

Nun sind aber die Rohstoffe für die Länder der Dritten Welt die einzige Einnahmequelle, oder zumindest die größte. Sie haben auch darüber gesprochen, in welche Schwierigkeiten diese Länder kommen, z.B. dadurch, daß der Kupferpreis gefallen ist, und nun würde ich gerne von Ihnen wissen, wie Sie für das Jahr 2000 die Beziehungen zwischen den Industrieländern und denen der Dritten Welt in struktureller Hinsicht sehen.

Bell:

The copper-situation was just an illustration and not so much a total picture of the mechanism of the market. Now, if one thinks of the relationship between the industrial society and the Third World – which I do think is the most important problem – it will come out of the demand for a new international division of labour. This was also said in a declaration of the United Nations. It was adopted in Nairobi. Now, I think, whether a new international division of labours is possible, which means that the old methods of manufacturing move out of the western world. And that means that the traditional industry loses its function in the technology ... On this respect the computer industry begins to expand. The difficulty is there: they have to accept each other. Lots of people are used to say we don't want a change. In the future we could lose jobs. Therefore we should do something against it: protectionism. England for example is without protection. It is the country which is hit as hard as no other country. Already 20 % of the technical needs are imported. I think, one should protect those industries. It is very understandable. Let me give you another illustration: British steel lost last year four billion marks. The most logical thing would be to shut this industry because of inefficiency. But the actual, real world stood against the economic rationality. So this industry is still producting. 70 % of British ship-building industry needs support. It is no efficient enough. Now, which German industry needs protection? I don't know one.

The countries of the Third World have to buy systems like computers, television, telephone and others. The American telephone system is now totally new organized. Computers are used on many sectors. For every purpose now they can choose a special mechanism.

There is a name for those systems, which is: super-conductivity, which means that electricity is transmitted on wire without friction. We have advertisers for those telephone systems. Now the American asks a person from the Third World: Look, we have a very good electronic technology? I want to have the best technology. That is, why we will have difficulties for the next fifty years.

But to come back to first question: there is an answer, which is the new international division of labour; it is difficult to manage, but it is the principle answer.

Zusammenfassung Arbeitsgruppe Bell

Die Diskussionsgruppe mit Prof. Bell kann man insoweit weniger als Arbeitsgruppe bezeichnen, als es sich hier nicht darum handelte, daß in der Diskussion neue Aspekte und Perspektiven erarbeitet wurden.

Es wurden vielmehr aus dem Teilnehmerkreis gezielte Fragen zu dem vorgetragenen Referat gestellt,und Prof. Bell bekam Gelegenheit, unklar gebliebene Gesichtspunkte zu erläutern, Gedankenvorgänge zu vertiefen.

Die Fragen bezogen sich ohne Ausnahme – und hier sieht man das starke Interesse der Zuhörer – auf Bells optimistische Zukunftsversion.

Die Jugendarbeitslosigkeit betrachtet Bell als kurzfristiges Problem. In naher Zukunft wird seiner Meinung nach die technologische Entwicklung einen großen Bedarf an technisch ausgebildeten Arbeitskräften schaffen. Auch im sozialen Bereich sieht er einen zunehmenden Arbeitskräftebedarf.

Industrieländer und Dritte Welt sieht er einander näherkommen. Studenten der Dritten Welt werden zunehmend in Universitäten der westlichen Welt ausgebildet werden, Menschen aus Industrieländern werden Arbeitsplätze in der Dritten Welt einnehmen und die technische Entwicklung dorthin tragen.

Unlösbare soziale Probleme dieser Entwicklung befürchtet Bell nicht:

„I know very few social forces, which come up and cannot be stopped."

„There is an answer, which is the new international division of labour; it is difficult to manage, but it is the principle answer."

Humane Wirtschaftsdemokratie als Chance der Jugend

Prof. Dr. Ota Šik

Nach der exakten Redezeit von Daniel Bell ist es ein schweres Unterfangen, hier in einem kurzen Vortrag gewisse Hauptgedanken näherzubringen, die wir in einem eben beendeten Buch festgehalten haben, das den gleichen Titel trägt, den der angekündigte Vortrag hat: „Humane Wirtschaftsdemokratie – ein dritter Weg". Es sind Ergebnisse einer Forschungstätigkeit, die vor ungefähr 15 Jahren oder noch länger in der Tschechoslowakei begonnen hat, die dann durch eine praktische politische Tätigkeit unterbrochen wurde und die ich nun in der Schweiz mit Hilfe eines kleinen Forschungsteams – vom Schweizer Nationalfond finanziert – in diesen Tagen beenden konnte. Das Buch hat 1100 Seiten und soll im nächsten Frühjahr publiziert werden.

Ich muß hier natürlich auf die ganze Analyse verzichen, aus welcher die Vorstellungen eines neuen Wirtschaftssystems – als humane Wirtschaftsdemokratie bezeichnet – entstanden sind. Es war nicht unser Ziel, eine neue ideale Wirtschafts- und Gesellschaftsform auszudenken, sondern unsere Modellvorstellung entstand aufgrund bestimmter erkannter grundliegender Probleme und Entwicklungsschwierigkeiten der beiden heute existierenden Systeme, des westlichen sogenannten kapitalistischen martkwirtschaftlichen Systems und des östlichen kommunistischen Planungssystems.. Die aufgrund dieser Analyse ausgearbeiteten Hauptprinzipien eines eventuellen neuen Wirtschaftssystems beruhen auf erstens einer makroökonomischen Verteilungsplanung, zweitens auf der Entwicklung eines von uns so genannten „neutralisierten Kapitals" und drittens auf einer Regulierung des Marktmechnismus.

Die **makroökonomische Verteilungsplanung** soll die in den westlichen marktwirtschaftlichen Systemen auftretenden Schwierigkeiten und Entwicklungsprobleme überwinden. Es ist meine tiefe Überzeugung, daß auf der heutigen Stufe der Entwicklung ein mehr oder weniger reines marktwirtschaftliches System nicht imstande ist, folgende Entwicklungsprobleme erfolgreich zu lösen:

1. die Existenz einer **zyklischen Wirtschaftsentwicklung**; einer Entwicklung, die charakterisiert ist durch beständige, periodisch eintretende inflationäre Hochkonjunkturen, die immer wieder durch Rezessionen oder auch allgemeinere Wirtschaftskrisen abgelöst werden,
2. die Tendenz einer **wachsenden Bürokratisierung** der Wirtschaftsentscheidungen; einer Bürokratisierung, die besonders stark in den großen mamutartigen Wirtschaftskonzernen zu verzeichnen ist, und in noch stärke-

rer Weise sich in der Verquickung der Wirtschaft und des Staates abzeichnet,

3. die **Einseitigkeit der Konsumtionsentwicklung**; d.h. einer übertriebenen Steigerung der privaten Konsumtion, bei ungenügender Beachtung und Befriedigung immer bedeutenderer gesellschaftlicher Bedürfnisse,
4. schließlich in dem ungemein stark hervortretenden Konsumtionsinteresse der breiten Massen der Bevölkerung bei ihrem völligen Desinteresse für die Investitions- und Kapitalentwicklung, für die Sicherung der Wirtschaftsbasis.

Ich möchte nur kurz diese Probleme streifen, um aufzuzeigen, daß man sie höchstwahrscheinlich ohne eine bestimmte Makroplanung nicht lösen kann.

Die **zyklische Entwicklung** in der Marktwirtschaft ist nicht nur und nicht vor allem das Ergebnis von strukturellen Änderungen der Bedürfnisse und der Nachfrage. Im Gegenteil, ich würde sagen, daß der Marktmechanismus allein fähig ist, mit strukturellen Änderungen der Produktion und ihrer flexiblen Anpassung an die Änderungen der Bedarfs- und Nachfragestruktur leicht fertig zu werden und dies besser, als eine dirigistische, zentrale Planung. Bei einer beständig steigenden allgemeinen Nachfrage, bei einem mehr oder weniger kontinuierlichem Wachstum der Einkommen und der Nachfrage von seiten der Bevölkerung ist auch die Produktion ohne besondere Schwierigkeiten imstande, sich den mit dieser steigenden Nachfrage zusammenhängenden strukturellen Änderungen der Nachfrage anzupassen.

Was Schwierigkeiten hervorruft, sind die immer wieder auftretenden Disproportionen zwischen den durch Verteilungsprozesse geschaffenen großen Einkommensgruppen mit wesentlich unterschiedlicher Verwendungsart. Ich habe hier im Sinn: erstens die Lohneinkommen im breiten Sinne des Wortes als vornehmlich konsumtiv ausgerichtete Einkommen, zweitens die Kapital- oder Gewinneinkommen als vornehmlich investiv ausgerichtete Einkommen und drittens die Staatseinkommen als jene Einkommen, ohne welche heute die Befriedigung der gesellschaftlichen Bedürfnisse schwer vorstellbar ist. Die Entwicklung dieser großen Einkommensgruppen ist nicht das Ergebnis bestimmter planmäßiger Zukunftsberechnungen, sondern reines Ergebnis eines Verteilungskampfes, heute eines Verteilungskampfes zwischen im Grunde monopolistischen Interessengruppen, zwischen den Unternehmerverbänden, den Gewerkschaften und dem Staat. Die Ergebnisse dieses Aufteilungskampfes rufen eine solche Entwicklung dieser großen Einkommensgruppen hervor, die notwendigerweise immer in bestimmten Momenten mit der Produktionsentwicklung und mit den Bedürfnissen einer optimalen Produktionsentwicklung in Widerspruch kommen.

Kurz gesagt: die Perioden eines schnellen technischen Fortschritts, verbunden mit schnellen Produktivitätssteigerungen, führen gewöhnlich auch zu schnellen Steigerungen der Gewinneinkommen und zu einer relativ langsameren Entwicklung der Lohneinkommen sowie Senkung der Konsumquote. Die Steigerung der Produktivität würde aber eher das Gegenteil verlangen.

Genauso würden die Etappen einer sinkenden Grenzproduktivität, vor allem der sinkenden Kapitalgrenzproduktivität, eine Verlangsamung der Konsumquote und Vergrößerung der Gewinnquote verlangen. Auch hier sehen wir in der Realität eher die gegenteilige Verteilungsentwicklung.

Immer wieder entstehen so Entwicklungsstörungen dadurch, daß in bestimmten Momenten die Konsumtionsentwicklung entweder zu langsam oder dann wieder zu schnell wächst, daß die Gewinnentwicklung und aus ihr die Investitionsentwicklung in bestimmten Perioden zu schnell, in anderen zu langsam wachsen. Das Endergebnis der Disproportionen zwischen der Einkommensentwicklung und der Produktionsentwicklung bedeutet jedesmal Reduzierung der Investitionstätigkeiten, Reduzierungen, die sich dann schnell auf die gesamte Wirtschaftsproduktion übertragen und zu Rezessionen und auch schwerwiegenden Krisen führen.

Die Beibehaltung dieser zyklischen Entwicklung ruft wachsende soziale Probleme hervor. Sie muß meines Erachtens – besonders natürlich in den Ländern, in welchen diese Störungen sehr tief verlaufen und große Arbeitslosigkeit mit sozialer Unsicherheit hervorrufen – zu politischen Radikalisierungen führen. Aus ihr erwachsen vor allem kommunistische Entwicklungsforderungen und Entwicklungsgefahren oder – um diesen vorzubeugen – faschistische Entwicklungen.

Die **Bürokratisierung** ist das notwendige Ergebnis der ungemein schnell wachsenden Konzentration der Produktion und des Kapitals. Sie ist aber auch das Ergebnis der immer schwerer zu bewältigenden Wirtschaftsprobleme und -schwierigkeiten, die dann eben auch verstärkte Eingriffe des Staates hervorrufen. Diese werden jedoch durch eine im Grunde unverantwortliche, anonyme Bürokratie durchgeführt. Die Bevölkerung wird nicht zum Nachdenken über ihre Zukunftsentwicklung gebracht, und sie kann auch nicht mitentscheiden. Vielmehr sind die Entscheidungen der Staaten der Bevölkerung gegenüber immer mehr entfremdet; sie werden durch ökonomisch unverantwortliche, anonyme Apparate gefällt. Es sind in wachsendem Maße Apparate, die die Resultate ihrer Entscheidung nicht an der eigenen Stellung, kurz gesagt an den eigenen Einkommen, der eigenen Tasche verspüren. Darin sehe ich besonders auf Grund der östlichen Erfahrung die Grundcharakteristik bürokratischer Entscheidungsfällungen. Meines Erachtens wird es immer stärker notwendig, daß die breiten Schichten der Bevölkerungen auf demokratischem Wege über ihre Zukunftsentwicklung mitentscheiden können und auch bestimmte Lernprozesse in der Sphäre der makroökonomischen Entscheidungsfällung durchmachen können. Dies wiederum ist ohne eine bestimmte Planmäßigkeit der Bestimmung der zukünftigen Entwicklung nicht möglich.

Die **einseitige Konsumtion** – ich würde sagen private Überkonsumtion – ist das typische Ergebnis einer reinen marktwirtschaftlichen Entwicklung. Die Produktion hat die Tendenz, diese Konsumtionsentwicklung übermäßig zu steigern und in einem gewissen Sinn zu manipulieren. Andererseits ist die Bevölkerung vornehmlich an der Deckung jener Bedürfnisse interessiert, die durch private Einkommen gesichert werden. Dabei wachsen aber notwendigerweise auch in sehr schnellem Tempo die Bedürfnisse, die nicht aus privaten Einkommen gesichert werden können. Nach meiner Ansicht ist es eine Illusion, zu glauben, diese Probleme dadurch lösen zu können, daß man eine Menge der heutigen Bedürfnisdeckungen, die aus gesellschaftlichen, vor allem staatlichen Fonds gesichert werden, in Bedürfnisdeckungen aus individuellen, privaten Einkommen zu verwandeln. Das kann sich meines Erachtens in der Praxis nicht durchsetzen.

Eher ist folgendes zu erwarten: Die wachsenden Schwierigkeiten der Lebensbedingungen der Menschen, die Probleme der Städtesanierungen, eines erforderlichen neuen Städtebaus, immer bedeutendere Transportprobleme, die Probleme des Umweltschutzes, die steigenden Anforderungen an eine neue Bildungsentwicklung, wachsende sozialmedizinische Bedürfnisse usw. können, langfristig gesehen, nur aus gesellschaftlichen Fonds gesichert werden und verlangen seitens der Gesellschaft eine entsprechende Beachtung.

Bei der Einseitigkeit des reinen marktwirtschaftlichen Systems werden aber diese gesellschaftlichen Bedürfnisdeckungen von der Bevölkerung selber als etwas ihr Fernliegendes angsehen, etwas mehr oder weniger Fremdes. Die Bevölkerung spürt zwar die Notwendigkeit der Lösung dieser Probleme immer wieder am eigenen Sein, aber die Art der Entscheidungsfällung und die steuermäßige Finanzierung dieser Bedürfnisdeckung ist ihren Interessen entfremdet. Die Menschen haben keine Möglichkeit, über diese Entwicklung tiefer nachzudenken, Alternativentwicklungen zu sehen. Sie werden ihnen nicht vorgelegt. Sie haben nicht die Möglichkeit, über alternative Entwicklungen zu entscheiden. Deshalb stehen sie auch den Forderungen nach Steuervergrößerungen feindlich gegenüber, obzwar sie als Mitglieder der Gesellschaft die Mängel in diesen Sphären immer stärker zu spüren bekommen.

Mit alldem ist natürlich die ungemein starke Konsuminteressiertheit der heutigen Bevölkerung in den industriell entwickelten Ländern und zugleich ihr Desinteresse an der Entwicklung der Basis dieser Konsumbefriedigung, an der Entwicklung des Kapitals, den Investitionen, der Wirtschaftserweiterung überhaupt, verbunden.

Die Menschen fühlen sich für diese Entwicklung nicht verantwortlich. Jahrhundertelang ist es Sache einer relativ schmalen Schicht der Gesellschaft gewesen. Früher hat die Entscheidungsfällung durch die relativ kleine Schicht der Kapitaleigentümer und der Unternehmer genügt, um die notwendige Investitions- und Kapitalentwicklung abzusichern. Heute genügt dieses Interesse allein nicht mehr. Es wird zusehends schwächer im Vergleich zu den wachsenden Lohn- und Konsumtionsforderungen.

In vielen industriell entwickelten Ländern, z.B. in Großbritannien, Italien u.ä. sind die ungenügenden Mittel, die für die Investitionstätigkeit zur Verfügung stehen, die Grundursache des immer langsameren Wachstums der Nettoinvestitionen des technischen Fortschrittes und der Produktivität. Dies ruft ein langsameres Wachstum des Nationaleinkommens per capita hervor, und infolgedessen verlangsamt sich auch das Wachstum der Konsumtion. Das führt jedoch zu noch stärkeren Kämpfen um die Umverteilung, zu noch stärkeren gewerktschaftlichen Forderungen, die in ihrem Ergebnis die Investitionsentwicklung weiter erschweren. So kommt die Gesellschaft in einen Teufelskreis hinein, aus dem man in vielen Ländern heute nicht heraus weiß. Diese Probleme können nicht gelöst werden, solange die breite Masse der Bevölkerung, die Lohnempfänger, der Investitionstätigkeit und der Kapitalentwicklung fremd gegenüberstehen werden und in der Form von einseitigen Lohn- und Konsumforderungen nur die Hand hinhalten, ohne sich für die Entwicklung der Investitionen und ihrer Wirtschaftsbasis verantwortlich zu fühlen.
Aus diesen kurz zusammengefaßten Erkenntnissen entwickelten wir die Vorstellung einer **Makroverteilungsplanung**. Das Ziel dieser Planung darf nicht die Planung der Produktions- und Investitionsentwicklung sein. Das ist die grundlegende Erkenntnis aus dem östlichen Planungssystem. Hier kennen wir das Desinteresse der Betriebe an einer hocheffektiven Produktions- und Investitionsentwicklung, ihr völlig pervertiertes Interesse an der rein quantitativen Erfüllung der Produktions- und Investitionsentwicklung, ihr völlig pervertiertes Interesse an der rein quantitativen Erfüllung der Produktions- und Investitionspläne, an dem globalen Wachstum der Produktion. Das ruft derartige Effektivitätsverluste hervor, daß dieses Wirtschaftssystem keines seiner einst theoretisch-ideologisch aufgestellten Ziele wirklich realisieren kann. Es hat einfach nicht genügend Mittel zur Hand, und bleibt in seiner Effektivität weit hinter dem westlichen, marktwirtschaftlichen System zurück.

Die Erkenntnisse aus diesen Effektivitätsverlusten führen dazu, daß die Entscheidungen über die konkrete Produktions- und Investitionsentwicklung in den Händen der Betriebe, der Unternehmen bleiben müssen, in den Händen jener, die einzig und allein die Resultate dieser Entscheidungsfällung an der eigenen Einkommensentwicklung zu verspüren bekommen. Ihre Entscheidungen sind daher qualitativ effekttiver und verantwortlicher als die Entscheidungsfällungen anonymer, bürokratischer Kommissionen oder Institutionen.

Die Planung soll daher nicht versuchen, den Marktmechanismus zu ersetzen, sondern sie soll jene Einkommensentwicklung absichern, die sich durch den Marktmechanismus nur mit Hilfe schwerwiegender makroökonomischer Störungen durchsetzen kann. Es ist eine Planung der Sphäre, in welcher der Marktmechanismus sozusagen ungenügend funktioniert bzw. notwendigerweise von schwerwiegenden Störungen begleitet ist. Es ist eine Planung der Aufteilung der Einkommen auf die großen Einkommensgruppen.Deshalb spreche ich von einer „Makroverteilungsplanung“ . Diese Planung erfolgt nicht in absoluten Größen, sondern mit Hilfe einer Quotenplanung, mit Hilfe der Planung der Lohneinkommensquote als Anteil der Lohnsumme am Bruttoeinkommen.Lohneinkommen sind im breiten Sinne des Wortes zu verstehen: Löhne, Gehälter, Stipendien, Sozialversicherung und ähnliches, also jene Einkommen, die vorwiegend konsumtiv genutzt werden. Mit einer Planung der Gewinnquote wird in erster Linie die benötigte Investitionsquote abgesichert. Die Staatseinkommensquote ist, wie es heute bereits in den Budgets geschieht, weiter aufgeteilt auf die Hauptsphären der gesellschaftlichen Bedürfnisdeckung: die Bildungsphäre, die sozialmedizinische Sphäre, die kulturelle Sphäre, den Umweltschutz, den öffentlichen Transport und ähnliches.

Die Planung sollte mit Hilfe von zwei Gruppen von Planungskommissionen durchgeführt werden, nicht also durch einen bürokratischen Apparat. Erstens mittels der Gruppe von Konsumtionskommissionen, zusammengesetzt aus Experten, die zugleich unterschiedliche Interessengruppen vertreten. Zweitens durch eine Gruppe von Produktionsbranchenkommissionen, in welchen die Vertreter der Unternehmen und Branchenforschungsinstitute teilnehmen würden. Die Aufgabe dieser Branchenkommissionen ist die Ausarbeitung von Prognosen der zu erwartenden Produktionsentwicklung und überhaupt die Aufdeckung grundlegender Produktivitätsmöglichkeiten der nächsten Jahre.

Es ist bekannt, daß besonders die größeren Firmen heute alle langfristig ihre Produktionsentwicklung vorausplanen müssen, auf viele Jahre voraus, also auch ihren Kapitalbedarf, ihren Bedarf an Arbeitskräften voraussehen können, und vor allem die technische Entwicklung vorausbestimmen, aufgrund welcher wieder die mehr oder weniger zu erwartende Produktivitätsentwicklung verläßlich vorausberechnet werden kann.

Es sind nicht die Schwächen der Produktivitätserfassung, die meist dazu führen, daß die heutigen Wirtschaftsprognosen in der Praxis selten eingehalten werden. Sondern es sind eben die Schwierigkeiten im Voraussehen der zukünftigen Verteilungsprozesse, die unvoraussehbaren Änderungen der Lohn-, Preis- und Gewinnentwicklung, die größtenteils auch zu einer Negierung der aufgestellten Wirtschaftsprognosen führen. Demgegenüber können sozusagen die reinen Voraussagen der zu erwartenden Entwicklung der

Technik und Hauptproduktionsfaktoren mit Hilfe von Branchenanalysenkommissionen relativ verläßlich durchgeführt werden.

Gleichzeitig muß auf der anderen Seite die Gruppe der Konsumtionskommissionen arbeiten.Wir nennen sie breiter „Lebensqualitätskommissionen" –, weil es hier zwar in erster Linie um die Fixierung der langfristigen und grundlegenden Konsumtionsentwicklung geht, aber nicht nur um dies, sondern auch um solche Bestimmungen, wie die der grundlegenden Richtung unseres Lebens überhaupt, unserer Lebenserwartung, die Festsetzung der Arbeitszeitentwicklung, damit zusammenhängend der Freizeitentwicklung und der eventuellen neuen Freizeitgestaltung u.ä.. Dies sind breitere Probleme und nicht nur allein Konsumtionsprobleme. In dem Sinne spreche ich von „Lebensqualitäts-Zielfixierungen". In den Lebensqualitätskommissionen, untergliedert nach den Hauptbereichen der zukünftigen Makrosphären der Lebensqualität, sollten Vertreter aller großen Interessengruppen mitwirken; jeweils fachlich ausgerichtete Experten, aber zugleich Vertreter der großen politischen Parteien, der Gewerkschaften, der Bauernverbände und ähnliche.

In diesen Kommissionen müßte es zur Diskussion und Konfrontation der unterschiedlichen Lebensvorstellungen, -erwartungen und Entwicklungsvorschlägen kommen. Auf Grund der Diskussion dieser verschiedenen Wünsche und Vorstellungen, sowie bestimmter Kompromisse würde die Ausarbeitung von zwei oder drei komplexen Alternativentwicklungen folgen. Alle Alternativziele müßten natürlich immer mit den Möglichkeiten der Produktion ausbilanziert sein.Das heißt, daß die Ziele in einer beständigen Zusammenarbeit mit den Produktionskommissionen in mehreren Iterationen, Annäherungen, aufzustellen sind, so daß jede der vorgeschlagenen, grundlegend unterschiedlichen Entwicklungsalternativen nicht reine Wunschträume darstellen würde, sondern jeweils von der Produktionsentwicklung abgesichert werden könnte. Eine jede Produktionsentwicklung müßte natürlich immer dem geplanten Umfang an Investitionen, daher auch der benötigten Gewinnquote und der dieser wieder entsprechenden Lohnquote entsprechen.

Zwei oder drei Alternativpläne müßten dann der Bevölkerung zur breiten Diskussion übergeben werden, und zwar verbunden mit den politischen Wahlen, jeweils in Abständen von fünf Jahren. Wenn die neue Regierung gewählt wird, würde gleichzeitig die Auswahl dieser oder jener Entwicklungsalternativvorstellung erfolgen. Die politischen Parteien würden gemäß ihren bereits in den Kommissionen durchgesetzten und in dieser oder jener Alternative fixierten Entwicklungsvorstellungen für diese oder jene Planalternative um Stimmen werben.

Dies könnte auch zu einer Versachlichung in der Politik führen. Ihre Schwäche besteht heute vor allem darin, daß sie die grundlegenden Entwicklungsfragen beiseite lassen muß, daß sie über die Wirtschaftsentwicklung langfristig und komplex nicht entscheiden kann; und daß man in erster Linie nur Machtinteressen, politische Karrieren verfolgt, weniger jedoch die wirkliche Lösung herangereifter und wachsender gesellschaftlicher Probleme vor Augen hat.

Die Realisierung der Pläne wäre mit Hilfe von grundlegenden wirtschaftspolitischen Instrumenten möglich. Dabei würde die Einkommenspolitik die entscheidende Rolle spielen, was die Überwindung des heutigen Verteilungskampfes erfordert.

Wenn auch in den unterschiedlichen Alternativplänen mit unterschiedlichen Entwicklungen gerechnet würde, so würde es doch jeweils eine planmäßig fixierte Steigerung der Lohneinkommen darstellen. Es wäre die Planung eines Lohnwachstums, das eine realistische Konsumentwicklung absichern sollte, also weder inflationsantreibende Überkonsumtionsentwicklungen noch rezessionsbedingende Konsumtionsverlangsamungen hervorrufend, sondern solche Lohnsteigerungen, die bei dem erwarteten Wachstum der Produktivität und der Konsumgüterproduktion zu einer optimalen Konsumtion führen würden.

Es handelt sich um eine verbindliche Entwicklung der Lohnquote mit einem jeweils damit verbundenen gesamtwirtschaftlichen Lohnkatalog, der sich natürlich jeweils aus differenten Branchenlohnkatalogen zusammensetzt. Die Einhaltung der Lohnquote wäre für die Unternehmen verbindlich; aber ich betone: als Quote, d.h. als Prozentsatz.Mit anderen Worten: es untergräbt nicht das Marktinteresse der Unternehmen. Je größer die Bruttoeinkommen des Unternehmens aus seiner Leistung sind, desto größer ist auch entsprechend und absolut die Lohnsumme bei Einhaltung der Lohnquote. Damit sind gleichzeitig die benötigten Investitionsmittel abgesichert. In die Lohnquote gehört noch die Gewinnbeteiligungsquote hinein, von welcher ich im weiteren sprechen werde.

Neben der planmäßigen Lohnpolitik sind noch die Kreditpolitik und die Steuerpolitik als weitere wichtige Instrumente zur Realisierung des jeweils akzeptierten Makroverteilungsplanes zu sehen.

Dies sind in Kürze – stenografisch ausgedrückt – die Hauptvorstellungen, was die Planung betrifft. Selbstverständlich ist es nicht möglich, hier in jene Details zu gehen, die ich im Buch auszuarbeiten versucht habe. In diesem werden die Planungsmethoden, die Planungsorganisation, die Möglichkeiten der Erfassung benötigter Daten und Informationen, die Möglichkeit der Regulierung aller Umverteilungsprozesse usw., dargestellt.

Ich gehe nun zu der **zweiten Säule** dieses Systems über, deren Realisierung als Voraussetzung der angestrebten Verteilungsplanung zu sehen ist. Es ist meine tiefe Überzeugung, daß solange die Kapitalentfremdung der Lohnempfänger existieren wird – und aus ihr hervorgehend das einseitige Lohn- und Konsuminteresse – solange auch ein Verteilungskampf existieren muß. Aber solange es einen Verteilungskampf gibt, solange hat die Gesellschaft nicht die Möglichkeit, ihre zukünftige Wirtschaftsentwicklung zielbewußt anzustreben. Es geht also um die Überwindung des Verteilungskampfes, was vor allem die Entstehung eines Kapitalinteresses bei allen arbeitenden Menschen, ihres realen Interesses an der Kapital- und Gewinnentwicklung und an der Investitionsentwicklung voraussetzt. Mittels eines starken Kapitalinteresses kann das einseitige Lohninteresse überwunden werden. Damit könnte es zu einem Ausgleich der kurzfristigen Konsumtionsinteressen und der langfristigen Entwicklungs- und Kapitalinteressen kommen.

Aber ein solches Interesse bei allen arbeitenden Menschen zu schaffen, ist nicht mit Hilfe einzelner Aktienverkäufe, wie es manche Firmen versuchen, möglich. Eine tiefergehende Untersuchung hat uns gezeigt, daß auf diese Weise das Problem realistisch nicht zu lösen ist. Bei der großen Masse der Lohnempfänger ist es nicht möglich, das Kapital unter alle Lohnempfänger individuell aufzuteilen. Wenn dies überhaupt in einer Extremvorstellung möglich sein sollte, käme auf jeden Lohnempfänger ein derart kleiner Teil des Kapitalwertes, daß es heute schon existierende Ersparnisse von Lohnempfängern nicht übersteigen würde. Es wäre nichts anderes als das Interesse an gewissen Ersparnissen und den Zinsen daraus. Dies würde die Einstellung der Lohnempfänger gegenüber ihrer Firma überhaupt nicht ändern. Das Interesse an der Lohnentwicklung wäre weiterhin entscheidend und hätte den Lohnkampf zur Folge. Deshalb sehe ich auf diesem Wege nicht die mögliche Lösung.

Auch die existierenden Vorstellungen der Schaffung überbetrieblicher Vermögensformen sind meines Erachtens keine Lösung des Problems. Denn sie hätten zweierlei zur Folge: Erstens gäbe es zwischen den Fonds und den arbeitenden Menschen eine solche Entfremdung, daß diese Lösung im Grunde einer Verstaatlichung gleichkäme. Die Bürokratisierung solcher Vermögensfonds läßt es unmöglich erscheinen, daß das Interesse und die Einstellung der arbeitenden Menschen zu den Unternehmen sich ändert. Zweitens bedeutet es die Abschöpfung von Mitteln aus den Firmen, und das würde in größerem Umfang Schwierigkeiten schaffen, die für eine Wirtschaftsentwicklung nicht denkbar sind.

Teilnehmer:

Ich weiß nicht, ob es mir allein so geht, und ich weiß nicht, ob es sinnvoll ist, die Veranstaltung in diese Richtung laufen zu lassen. Ich frage mich: was hat dieses Thema mit der Frage zu tun, welche Chancen die Jugend sieht?

Referat Šik

Schürer:

Ich würde einen anderen Vorschlag machen: daß wir die Zeit auf fünf Minuten terminieren und die Frage dann nach einer kurzen Pause in die anschließende Diskussion direkt mit einbeziehen. Ich wäre dankbar, wenn Sie versuchten, in etwa fünf Minuten die weiteren Thesen zusammenzufassen.

Rosenmayr:

Die Sache ist aber doch etwas hart. Hier werden grundlegende gesellschaftspolitische Dinge für die Zukunft besprochen.
Daß man ausreden lassen muß, das ist mein Standpunkt!

Schürer:

Dann schlage ich Ihnen vor, daß wir die Pause verschieben und nachher nachholen, aber den Referenten ausreden lassen.

Šik:

Ich kann natürlich jetzt nicht darlegen – ich möchte es der Diskussion überlassen –, ob dies für die Jugend wichtig ist oder nicht. Meines Erachtens ist es wichtig, eine Lösung der heute heranwachsenden Probleme zu suchen. Nur Vorschläge, die aus der Analyse gegenwärtiger Probleme hervorgehen, können überhaupt bestimmte Möglichkeiten einer Zukunftsentwicklung aufzeigen.

Die Entstehung eines Interesses der Mitarbeiter an der eigenen Kapitalentwicklung bzw. an der Entwicklung des Kapitals der eigenen Firma sehe ich darin, daß man eine Form des Eigentums anstrebt, die ich als Neutralisierung des Kapitals bezeichne. Das neutralisierte Kapital ist Kapital, das nicht mehr aufteilbar auf einzelne Personen, auf einzelne Mitarbeiter ist, auch nicht nach Abgang der Mitarbeiter von der Firma. Eine jede Aufteilung des Kapitals würde den benötigten flexiblen Arbeitsmarkt erschweren. Wir brauchen aber die Flexibilität des Arbeitsmarktes. Ein neutralisiertes Kapital, ist also ein Kapital, das immer nur der Firma gehört, von einem Vermögensverwaltungsrat treuhänderisch verwaltet wird und der Firma für ihre Entwicklungszwecke, für ihre Produktionsbedürfnisse zur Verfügung gestellt wird.

Es ist natürlich nur eine grundlegende Idee, daß die Zukunft zwei Interessenmomente miteinander verbinden muß. Der Marxismus hat bisher den grundlegenden Fehler gemacht, daß er das private Interesse, das Interesse einzelner Menschen, das Interesse von Unternehmern total unterschätzt und ignoriert hat. Die ganze Erfahrung zeigt, daß es ohne dieses Unternehmerinteresse nicht geht. Deshalb hier der Versuch einer Verbindung der Existenz eines privaten Unternehmerinteresses, sowie privater Unternehmeraktivität mit der Existenz eines neutralisierten Kapitals aller Mitarbeiter.

Dies würde wahrscheinlich die Entstehung von drei Haupteigentumssektoren bedeuten. Ich glaube, daß die Unternehmerinitiative dort erhalten bleiben muß, wo sie auch heute ihre wirtschaftliche Funktion hat. Das ist aber im Grunde nicht in den großen Kapitalgesellschaften der Fall. In großen Kapitalgesellschaften ist die Unternehmeraktivität auf das Management übergegangen, während die Kapitaleigentümer im Grunde aufgehört haben, Unternehmer im eigentlichen Sinne des Wortes zu sein. Daher soll in den großen Kapitalgesellschaften die allmähliche, programmierte Verwandlung dieser Gesellschaften aus Aktiengesellschaften, also Gesellschaften, die sich in einem fremden Aktieneigentum befinden, in sogenannte Mitarbeitergesellschaften stattfinden. Die allmähliche, programmierte Verwandlung wäre hier ohne Enteignungen möglich. Sie wäre auf dem Wege des programmierten Zurückkaufens von Aktien durch die Firma in einer Reihe von Jahren möglich. Aufgrund dessen könnte die Verwandlung des Kapitals, sowohl des alten als auch des aus den Gewinnen neugeschaffenen, in das neutralisierte Kapital der Mitarbeiter erfolgen.

Den zweiten Sektor würden die mittleren Unternehmen bilden, in welchen das Privateigentum der privaten Unternehmer erhalten bleiben muß, aber daneben sich aus den Gewinnen das neubildende Kapital ab einer fixierten Größe der Gewinne in neutralisiertes Kapital verwandeln würde. Hier würde in den mittleren Gesellschaften das private Eigentum zusammen mit dem neutralisierten Kapital der Mitarbeiter wachsen, und es würde ein immer stärkerer Gleichlauf der Interessen der privaten und der mitarbeitenden Eigentümer entstehen.

Der dritte Sektor wäre schließlich der, der kleinen Unternehmen, der Handwerker, der kleinen Dienstleistungsunternehmen und ähnlichen, so weiterhin privates Eigentum erhalten bleiben sollte.

Dies ist die Vorstellung von drei Sektoren, innerhalb welcher die Mitarbeitergesellschaften das größte Gewicht in der ganzen Zukunftsentwicklung hätten. Das neue Eigentum der Mitarbeiter würde sich in folgendem äußern: 1. in der Verfügungsgewalt über die Nutzung des Kapitals, 2. in der Aneignung von einem Teil der Gewinne als Resultat der Kapitalnutzung..Dabei wäre die Verfügungsgewalt, so wie heute, über einen Aufsichtsrat realisiert, nur mit dem Unterschied, daß dieser sozusagen aus den mitarbeitenden Miteigentümern gewählt wäre. Der Aufsichtsrat wäre ungefähr mit den gleichen Befugnissen wie heute ausgestattet, als Kontrollorgan über dem Management stehend. Ansonsten läge aber die volle Verantwortung für die konkreten Produktions- und Investitionsentscheidungen in den Händen des Managements.

Das wichtigste ist nun die Gewinnbeteiligung der Mitarbeiter. Aus der Gewinnbeteiligung soll das Interesse der Mitarbeiter an einer möglichst effektiven Entwicklung der Firma, an einer effektiven Investitions- und Produktionsentwicklung entstehen. Die Beteiligung an den Gewinnen soll aber gleichzeitig einer der Faktoren der Maktroverteilungsplanung sein, d.h. der Makroplanung, die die Einkommensentwicklung zu bestimmen hat. Der Plan würde nicht nur die Quote der Grundlöhne aus dem Bruttoeinkommen der Unternehmen bestimmen, sondern auch die Quote der Gewinnbeteiligung aus den Gewinnen, wieder nur als Prozentsatz, als Quote! Daraus müßte das Interesse an einer optimalen Steigerung der Gewinne, auch als Grundlage des persönlichen, individuellen Interesses der Mitarbeiter entstehen.

Der andere Teil der Gewinne wäre dann für die Kapitalerweiterung, für die Investitionen, für die Schaffung und Erweiterung des neutralisierten Kapitals bestimmt. In den mittleren Gesellschaften müßte neben der Quote der Beteiligung der Mitarbeiter für das neutralisierte Kapital natürlich auch die Quote des privaten Unternehmergewinnes seinem Privatkapital entsprechend gesichert sein. Die Anwendung der geplanten Quoten in den Unternehmen könnte relativ leicht sein und – ohne daß ich jetzt auf Details eingehe – auch unterschiedliche Kapitalzusammensetzungen einzelner Branchen, ja sogar unterschiedliche Umschlaggeschwindigkeiten des Kapitals in verschiedenen Branchen berücksichtigen.

Auf diese Art und Weise wäre sowohl die Motivation der Unternehmertätigkeit als auch das Interesse der Mitarbeiter an der Gewinnsteigerung gesichert. Das sind die Grundgedanken, die es ermöglichen würden, den langwierigen und langandauernden Kampf um die Umverteilung zu überwinden und die Interessen einer Unternehmertätigkeit und die Interessen der arbeitenden Menschen miteinander zu verbinden.

Die dritte Säule – ich kann sie nur andeuten, da sie nicht in so kurzer Zeit zu erklären ist – ist die **Sicherung des Marktmechanismus.** Es geht nicht nur um seine Fortdauer, sondern vor allem um die mögliche Vertiefung des Marktmechanismus. Dabei wird eine zielbewußte Wettbewerbsförderung, die ich aufgrund von Analysen ausgearbeitet habe, verfolgt. Es geht ebenfalls um eine gewisse Regulierung der Gewinnspanne. Damit soll erreicht werden, daß die Gewinne sich zwar differenziert – gemäß unterschiedlicher Leistungen der Unternehmen – entwickeln, aber gewisse Spannen nicht überschreiten. In der Überschreitung dieser Spannen sehe ich den Ausdruck monopolistischer Stellungen und Marktbeherrschungen. Es wird – ohne es hier näher erklären zu können – mit einer gewissen Monopolgewinnsteuer gerechnet. Diese gäbe die Möglichkeit, die differente Entwicklung der Gewinne zwar abzusichern, und damit das Interesse an den Effektivitäts- und Leistungssteigerungen in den Firmen aufrechtzuerhalten, aber gleichzeitig sollten gewisse Raten nicht überschritten werden, denn diese müßten die angestrebte Gewinnbeteiligung untergraben.

Die Notwendigkeit einer solchen regulierten Gewinnspanne entspricht der Erfahrung aus dem jugoslawischen System, das eine solche Art der Verteilungsplanung und Marktregulierung nicht kennt. Die großen Differenzen zwischen den Gewinnen dort sind Ausdruck dessen, daß die schwächeren Firmen, die nicht in monopolitischer Situation sind, nicht solche Gewinnquoten erreichen können wie die größeren oligo- und monopolistischen Unternehmen. Daraus entsteht der Kampf der Arbeiter in den schwächeren Unternehmen um Lohnsteigerung, um Anpassung ihrer Löhne an die großen Firmen, dem dann niemand widerstehen kann. Die Lohnsteigerungen setzen sich sogar auf Kosten der Investitionsentwicklung durch. Damit wird erstens eine ungemeine Inflationsentwicklung angeheizt, und zweitens hat dies eine ungenügende Investitionsentwicklung zur Folge. Diese muß wieder zur Arbeitslosigkeit führen. Beides ist für Jugoslawien charakteristisch.

Eine Gewinnbeteiligung kann also nur bei einer gewissen Regulierung des Marktmechanismus, bei der Förderung des Wettbewerbs und bei zielbewußten antimonopolistischen Maßnahmen realisiert werden.

Das sind die Grundzüge der Vorstellung eines Wirtschaftssystems, die nicht auf utopischen Erwartungen aufgebaut ist. Sie rechnet mit den Menschen so, wie sie eben sind, mit ihrem Egoismus, mit ihren selbstbezogenen Interessen. Das neue Wirtschaftssystem gäbe aber den Menschen in wachsendem Maße die Möglichkeit, auch über ihre gemeinschaftlichen Entwicklungsziele bewußter und demokratisch zu entscheiden. Es gäbe ihnen die Möglichkeit in den Unternehmen, in der Mikorsphäre mitzuentscheiden, aber dies als kapitalinteressierte und nicht als nur einseitig lohninteressierte Menschen.

Es würde ihnen die Möglichkeit gegeben, auch in der Makrosphäre demokratisch mitzuentscheiden und ihre Zukunft aufgrund von Lernprozessen immer zielbewußter zu beeinflussen.

Aussprache über die Referate Bell und Šik

Leitung: Wolfgang R. Schürer

Schürer:

Ich möchte kurz auf die beiden Referate eingehen. Die Chance, die ich in diesen Ausführungen sehe, und das Problem, das diese Ausführungen aufwerfen, sind folgende. Wenn man kurzfristig auf die Frage „Was können wir zum Problem der Arbeitslosigkeit der Jugend im jetzigen Moment machen?" eine Antwort erwartet, dann wird sicherlich ein Mehr an Fragen offenbleiben, als Antworten gegeben werden können. Wenn man aber davon ausgeht, daß wir über eine Dauer von Jahren bestimmte Probleme immer wieder vor uns her wälzen – verschoben im Hinblick auf Konstellationen von Wachstumsraten, die heute nicht mehr da sind und über deren zukünftige Existenz man eher Zweifel anmelden muß –, dann, glaube ich, wird das Grundsätzliche in den vorangegangenen beiden Referaten klar.

Mir liegt folgende Frage an Professor Šik vor:

Wie soll der Bürger an der Festlegung der Quoten durch den „Sachverständigenrat" beteiligt werden?

Šik:

An der Festlegung der Quoten kann der Bürger natürlich nicht direkt beteiligt werden. Bei einer so großen Zahl Beteiligter kann einfach kein volkswirtschaftlicher Plan aufgestellt werden.

Der Bürger kann nur in folgender Weise Einfluß nehmen. Erstens kann er an seine Vertreter, sei es in politischen Parteien oder anderen großen Interessenorganisationen, mit Vorschlägen in der Phase der Vorbereitung von Plänen herantreten. Das heißt, daß die Bürger verschiedene Entwicklungsalternativen bereits vorher diskutieren sollten. Die Planungskommissionen sollten dann die unterschiedlichen Vorstellungen innerhalb der Bevölkerung zusammenfassen, und in die Pläne einzubauen versuchen. Zweitens hat der Bürger natürlich die Möglichkeit, an der Auswahl aus den unterschiedlichen Alternativen in politischen Wahlen direkt demokratisch teilzunehmen.

Bei der Aufstellung der Verteilungsquoten kann man keine direkte Demokratie erwarten, aber man kann sozusagen über die Repräsentanten auf die Zielfixierung Einfluß nehmen und über diese auf die Quoten.

Teilnehmer:

Ich würde sagen, die Probleme entstehen heute, weil der Jugendliche feststellt – nicht nur den Eindruck hat, sondern es ist auch so –, daß er an der Gestaltung seiner Umwelt in einer Gesellschaft nicht spürbar mitwirken kann, sondern nur in geringem Maße. Ich glaube, wenn ein Sachverständigenrat die Quoten festlegt, dann entsteht wieder eine große Bürokratie, die die gleiche Eigentätigkeit entwickeln wird, die Sie vorhin beschrieben haben. Der Jugendliche ist wieder an einer Grenze und sagt: Entscheidende Sachen kann ich wieder nicht beeinflussen, denn mir sind so enge Grenzen gesetzt, daß eine wirkliche Mitbestimmung gar nicht möglich ist.

Šik:

Es gibt keine Möglichkeit einer direkten Bestimmung, einer Mitwirkung durch die Bevölkerung, alle können einfach nicht in den Plankommissionen mitarbeiten. Aber hier ist ein Unterschied gegenüber heute. Erstens kann der Bürger und daher auch der Jugendliche, überhaupt aus drei wesentlich unterschiedlichen Alternativen wählen, und zweitens sind die Mitarbeiter und die Mitglieder der Planungskommissionen keine Beamten. Es soll nicht einen beständig gleichen Apparat geben (der eigentliche Apparat ist klein).
Die gewählten Vertreter werden nach einem Schlüssel sozusagen von unten in die Kommission geschickt. Auch Vertreter von Minderheiten, die mit entsprechenden Vorschlägen in Massenmedien auftreten oder mit anderen Vorschlägen kommen, können in die Planungskommission einbezogen werden. Die Aufstellung der Planungskommissionen von unten her mit den verschiedensten Vorstellungen und aus verschiedenen Interessengruppen gibt der Bevölkerung die Möglichkeit auf die Zielfixierung einzuwirken.

Eine andere, weitergehende Lösung kann ich mir einfach nicht vorstellen. Nicht jeder einzelne Mensch aus der großen Gesellschaft kann Forderungen aufstellen, wie die Entwicklung aussehen soll. Es muß immer eine Verallgemeinerung geben. Aber sie ist trotzdem noch demokratischer als heute, wo es für die Bevölkerung keine Alternativauswahlen gibt, zweitens die Proportionen zwischen privater und gesellschaftlicher Konsumtion überhaupt nicht planmäßig bestimmt werden und die steuerliche Deckung der gesellschaftlichen Bedürfnisse eine reine Sache des bürokratischen Apparates ist. Es sind Entscheidungen über das bürokratisch vorbereitete Budget, das die Abgeordneten im Grunde nie mehr wesentlich ändern können und ohne die Möglichkeit einer Alternative mehr oder weniger akzeptieren müssen.

Teilnehmer:

Nun habe ich heute noch die Parteien im Auge, ich kann unter den Parteien wählen. Diese Möglichkeit hätte ich beim „Sachverständigenrat" nicht, wenn ich das richtig verstanden habe, und der „Sachverständigenrat" wäre noch wesentlich anonymer als die heutigen Parteien.

Aussprache Bell, Šik

Šik:

Das muß ein Mißverständnis sein. Ich sagte ja: Parteien sind weiter wichtig. Die Parteien entsenden ihre Vertreter in die Planungskommissionen. In normalen Wahlen werden dann nicht nur gewisse Programme von Parteien, sondern vorgeschlagene planmäßige Alternativentwicklungen geboten, hinter denen die Parteien stehen. Die Parteien werden versuchen, für diese oder jene Alternative zu werben. Die Parteien existieren also durchaus weiter. Von der Partei, die die Mehrheit bekommt, wird dann sozusagen auch der Alternativplan mit akzeptiert. Er ist dann verbindlich für die neue Regierung, für die Realisierung ihrer Wirtschaftspolitik, die sie mit Hilfe eines Wirtschaftsrates – als operativem Organ – durchführen kann. Aber sie ist dem Parlament und der Bevölkerung für die Realisierung der akzeptierten Entwicklungsziele verantwortlich.

Schürer:

Herr Bussiek hat an Professor Šik die Frage gestellt, wie der Unternehmensegoismus verhindert werden soll.

Bussiek:

Ich darf das vielleicht kurz erläutern. Zunächst möchte ich sagen, daß ich es sehr verdienstvoll finde, daß ein Stab von Leuten Ideen entwickelt hat. Das ist erfreulich und anerkennenswert in einer Zeit, in der Ideenlosigkeit herrscht. Aber ich sehe, Herr Sik, eine strategische Gefahr, die mit dem Stichwort da vorne angedeutet worden ist. Wenn Sie den Hebel bei der Einkommensquote ansetzen und damit die volkswirtschaftlichen Daten in Gang setzen wollen, ist noch ein inhaltliches Problem zu lösen.

Ich darf es an einem Beispiel verdeutlichen. Die Krux an der heutigen Mitbestimmung ist doch, daß die Arbeitnehmervertreter im Aufsichtsrat von Daimler-Benz beispielsweise freudig zustimmen werden, wenn es darum geht, die Lastwagenproduktion auszuweiten. Aber sie denken mit keinem Gedanken daran, daß dadurch Arbeitsplätze bei Magirus-Deutz gefährdet werden, weil Daimler-Benz ihnen auf dem Lastwagenmarkt Konkurrenz macht. Das heißt, die Investitionsplanung geht doch an den Interessen der Menschen völlig vorbei. Wenn das dem Markt überlassen bleibt, dann werden eben bei Magirus-Deutz Leute entlassen; ganz egal, wer die Entscheidungsträger sind, die Makroplanung wird beibehalten.

Vielleicht steht das, was Sie dazu sagen könnten, auf den 1100 Seiten Ihres Buches. Sie konnten es ja nicht ausführlicher darstellen. Ich wäre dankbar, wenn Sie dazu noch einen Satz sagen könnten.
In diesem Zusammenhang ein zweiter Gesichtspunkt. Wenn Sie den Einkommenshebel benutzen, befürchte ich, daß dieser Hebel bei breiten Interessen-

kreisen im marktpolitischen Gefüge natürlich wohlwollend aufgenommen wird. Aber wie soll es beispielsweise geschehen – um konkret zu werden –, daß Sie der Shell AG klarmachen, daß sie sich zu einer Mitarbeitergesellschaft umwandeln soll? Ich fürchte, die Einkommensquote wird verwirklicht werden, aber die Umwandlung einer großen Kapitalgesellschaft in eine Mitarbeitergesellschaft wird nicht erfolgen.

Šik:

Man kann das Eigeninteresse der Firmen an einer möglichst effektiven Investitionsentwicklung einfach nicht beseitigen. Wenn ich es beseitige und die Entscheidung über Investitionen gewissen bürokratischen Kommissionen übertrage, dann entsteht das, was in den Ostblockstaaten zu verzeichnen ist. Wenn Sie nicht eine höchst effektive Ausnutzung der Produktionsfaktoren haben, können Sie kein gesellschaftliches Problem lösen, weder eine humanere Gesellschaftsentwicklung noch eine besser gesicherte humanmedizinische Versorgung oder eine längere und bessere Freizeitgestaltung herbeiführen. Sie können kein großes gesellschaftliches Problem mit einer uneffektiven Wirtschaft lösen. Das ist die Grunderkenntnis. Davon gehe ich aus. Das ist mit meinen Erfahrungen in den Ostblockstaaten aus allen Sphären unterlegt. Auch in der Sphäre der Medizin, der sozialen Versorgung, der sozialen Sicherung, bleibt die Entwicklung im Osten hinter den Industriestaaten zurück, weil man einfach nicht genügend Mittel hat, die man hier zuteilen könnte.

Ich kann das Problem nicht lösen, indem ich die Investitionsentscheidungen den Betrieben aus der Hand nehme. Wenn ich Ihnen erzählen könnte – die Zeit reicht leider nicht –, wie die Investitionsentscheidung in einer bürokratischen Kommission, bei staatlicher Regulierung aussieht, dann würden Sie sich vor Lachen biegen. Jeder Vertreter der Ministerien kommt mit einem Papier, aus seinem Ministerium damit ausgestattet, dann läuft die Diskussion Stunden und Tage, und dann sind alle müde. Sodann versuchen die Bürokraten, die Entscheidung schnell herbeizuführen, egal wie sie ausfällt. Denn sie tragen ja keine Verantwortung und können überhaupt auch nicht zu einer Verantwortung herangezogen werden. Die Verluste sind so immens, daß man sie sich gar nicht vorstellen kann.

Deshalb kann ich das Problem nur durch eine Makrosteuerung zu lösen versuchen. Ich kann nur sagen, in welcher Richtung sich die Grundausrichtung der Wirtschaft bewegen soll. Wie schnell soll z.B. die Produktion wachsen? Soll sie soundsoviel Prozent jährlich wachsen oder weniger? Wie groß soll der Investitionsumfang sein? Soll er kleiner sein? Aber über die Struktur aller Investitionen soll tatsächlich der Marktmechanismus im Rahmen der großen makroökonomischen Zielfixierung entscheiden. Da hat man die Möglichkeit, größere oder kleinere Investitionsquoten zu bestimmen, eine Beschleunigung der privaten Konsumtion oder der gesellschaftlichen Bedürfnisdeckung; das ist ja das, was die Menschen vor allem interessiert und wo sie mitentscheiden müssen.

Sie fragen nach der Entstehung der Mitarbeitergesellschaften.

Hier geht es um nichts anderes als um einen Alternativvorschlag, – um für das ganze System eine andere Entwicklung, als sie heute das marktwirtschaftliche oder das kommunistische System darstellt zu gewährleisten. Jeder Vorschlag kann sich unter demokratischen Bedingungen aber nur durchsetzen, wenn er genügende politische Unterstützung erhält. Er könnte nur mit Hilfe gewisser Gesetze realisiert werden, die unter bestimmten politischen Bedingungen entstehen könnten. Ein Gesetz, das meinetwegen sagen würde, daß aus den Gewinnen – von einer bestimmten Größe der Gewinne an, mit einer Quote von soundsoviel und mit einer bestimmten Schnelligkeit – das neutralisierte Kapital entstehen soll. Die Entstehung eines solchen Gesetzes oder einer entsprechenden wirtschaftspolitischen Anordnung ist vollkommen denkbar. Die Bestimmung, wie schnell es geschieht, hängt von politischen Bedingungen ab. Man könnte für die großen Unternehmen, wenn die politischen Bedingungen eine Beschleunigung möglich machten, anordnen, daß nicht nur die Nettoinvestitionen, sondern sogar die Bruttoinvestitionen sich in neutralisiertes Kapital verwandeln sollten, womit das Ganze wirklich beschleunigt würde.

Ich bin nun einmal Anhänger von demokratischen politischen Entscheidungen. Uns schwebt vor, daß sich nicht eine einzige Partei hinter solche grundlegende gesellschaftliche Änderung stellen sollte, sondern eine breitere Front mehrerer Parteien.

Deshalb sehe ich das Ganze nicht als eine Sache von Morgen an, sondern eine eventuelle Realisierung bedarf noch einer längeren Vorbereitung. Ich bin sogar, ehrlich gesagt, ein bißchen skeptisch. Ich habe die Befürchtung, daß die Entwicklung nicht eher eintritt, bis noch stärker als bisher den Menschen die Notwendigkeit einer volkswirtschaftlichen Zukunftsbestimmung vor Augen tritt. Ich habe die Befürchtung, daß noch weit größere Katastrophen als bis heute in der westlichen Welt und überhaupt in der ganzen Welt auf die Menschen zukommen werden. Erst unter dem Druck weiterer negativer Erfahrungen wird sich stärker das Verlangen durchsetzen, in dieser oder jener Form die wirtschaftliche Entwicklung vorauszubestimmen. Die Bürgerinitiativen, die heute schon entstehen, sind ein Symptom dafür, daß die Menschen die wirtschaftliche Entwicklung nicht einfach den Politikern überlassen wollen, sondern versuchen, aktiv bei den sie am meisten bedrohenden Entwicklungsmomenten einzugreifen. Ich glaube, diese Entwicklung wird sich ungemein steigern, in den folgenden Jahren bzw. im nächsten Jahrzehnt.

Schürer:

Herr Professor Bell wollte kurz etwas sagen zum Thema Jugendarbeitslosigkeit und welche Chancen zu ihrer Überwindung gesehen werden.

Bell:

I don't want to interrupt the technical discussion of Mr. Šik's plan, but I did think that the question of youth-unemployment should receive some discussions, although my friend, Mr. Schürer, said that it is too complicated for such short period of time. Let me deal with two points. I tried to indicate that this is primarily, in the west, a demographic problem, and that within ten years from now there will be a **shortage**, a very heavy shortage of intellectually trained persons in a society. Particularly in a post-industrial society, which will require more and more intensive intellectual training. For the moment there is a surplus or a relative surplus. There is a simple logic: if we have a resource and if we know that in the future there may be a problem of a shortage of resources, we use a policy of, what in English is called„technically stock-piling". What is this translated?
(Lagerhaltung)
Now, if one is to do stock-piling, one can plan the same thing for human resources: to have a bank which would in a fact subsidize kinds of training and retraining, necessary to maintain the skill of people, because, as I say, in ten years the situation will be reversed. It would be a pity – a tragedy – to lose the talents of a generation.

But I'd like to broaden the question to show that in ten years from now, there's going to be a very different situation in other parts of the world. And we are going to have a huge problem of imbalance between the western world and the socalled „third world".

Let me call your attention to the fact that in all of Latinamerica with exception of Argentina, all of Asia, all of Africa, the proportion of young people under 17 years of age is between 40 or 50 percent of the population. In all of the United States, Japan, Europe and the European part of the Soviet Union the proportion of young people today under 17 is less than 25 percent of the population. In other words, we have a situation, in which these third world countries the proportions of the young people are double the proportion of the West. Let me take one country for illustration, which is similar in many respects to Germany, for one reason, and that is Mexico.
Mexico, which is just south of the American border. It may surprise you to learn, today Mexico has more people than Germany. Mexico today has 64 million people and the west-German population is about 62 million. In Mexico today, 48 percent, almost half the population is under 17 years of age. It is a country, in which you have now a 20 percent inflationrate, in which you have a 12 to 15 percent industrial productionrate and in which you have a high urbanisation of the population. In other words: within the next ten years you're going to get a tidal wave of young people coming of age

in that country as in all of Latinamerica.
(Africa is lesser the problem, because it's a dimly populated area). In Latinamerica you're going to have a real problem. In other words: in about ten years from now or less, there'll be a problem of international emigration; on a scale very different to the last ten years.
In Europe in the last ten years, you had a large number of „Gastarbeiter" from Turkey, Greece, Yugoslavia, southern Italy at a time, when you had expanding economy. In the next ten years there will be either a contracting economy or on the same level. This is true the entire world economy, which will not grow at the rate it did of the last 25 years.

The problem of youth-unemployment is a momentary problem in Germany and in western Europe, and will pass quickly in the next five years, but the question of youth-unemployment is a very real and even double severe problem in **other parts of the world.** And the question comes in: „What will happen, when you have this young population come, I would say like a tidal wave to the rest of the world?"

Will we have an international emigration policy? Will there be a policy, in which the advanced industrial countries will now take in the youth? And what happens, when you have the differences of language and the differences in education? There is, where your real youth problem will be in the next ten years.

Teilnehmer:

Der Analyse, die Herr Šik vorgetragen hat, kann ich weitgehend folgen. Aber die Alternativen, die Sie vorgeschlagen haben, sind doch weitgehend problematisch. Sie gehen davon aus, daß eine Entfremdung weiter Teile der Bevölkerung von der wirtschaftlichen Basis ihrer Existenz vorhanden ist; das kann man wohl sagen. Sie wollen eine Harmonisierung, eine andere Groborientierung, eine Kapitalorientierung herbeiführen. So, wie Sie es im Modell vorschlagen, scheint es mir, daß Ihre Harmonisierung nur auf dem Wege über die Einsetzung einer Expertokratie durchgeführt werden kann. Denn es ist für den einzelnen kaum möglich, auf die Globaldaten der wirtschaftlichen Planung Einfluß zu nehmen.

Eine solche Lösung könnte den Entfremdungsprozeß nicht aufheben. Der Entfremdungsprozeß ist ja auch ein psychologisches Problem. Es kann nur dann gelöst werden, wenn der einzelne nicht nur über die Stimmabgabe beispielsweise über eine Alternative entscheiden kann – wie wir es in der parlamentarischen Demokratie sowieso schon haben –, sondern wenn er konkrete Möglichkeiten der Mitbestimmung und Selbstbestimmung hat. Das aber habe ich bei Ihrem Modell nicht feststellen können. Ich habe eher den Eindruck, daß Ihr Modell einer Vorstellung von einer globalen Utopie anhängt, die dazu führt, daß schließlich sogar die Konsumtion des einzelnen von Experten geplant wird. Da muß ich ehrlich sagen: dann ist es mir doch lieber, daß es noch Gewerkschaften gibt, wo ich mich organisieren kann und und wo ich meine eigenen Interessen vertreten kann. Solange die gesellschaftlichen Verhältnisse nicht so gestaltet sind, daß Interessenunterschiede überwunden sind – und die sind meines Erachtens nicht überwunden –, kann ich mich damit schwer anfreunden.

Noch ein Wort zu der globalen Utopie! Ich meine, daß Ihre Vorstellung, wie Sie den Entfremdungsprozeß aufheben können, zu wenig auf informationstheoretische Fragestellungen Rücksicht nimmt, nämlich insofern, als die Möglichkeit der Beteiligung an gesellschaftlichen Prozessen nur besteht, wenn eine gewisse Transparenz vorhanden ist, wenn auch wirklich konkrete Einflußmöglichkeiten für den einzelnen bestehen. Diese Möglichkeiten sind aber nur in relativ überschaubaren Gruppen gegeben. Ich orientiere mich da an Ausführungen von *Milton Friedmann* in seinem Buch *„Machbare Utopie"*. Danach gibt es kritische Gruppen, die, wenn sie überschritten sind, die Transparenz unmöglich machen. Insofern wird von ihm auch klargemacht, daß globale Utopien, wie Sie sie sich vorstellen, nicht möglich sind, jedenfalls nicht mit Vorstellungen von Demokratie vereinbar sind.
Daher jetzt meine Frage an Sie: Wie stellen Sie sich eine Harmonisierung von Kapitalinteressen, Kapitalorientiertheit und Einkommensorientiertheit vor? Wie kann nach Ihrer Meinung diese Harmonisierung herbeigeführt werden, indem der einzelne die Möglichkeit erhält, konkret an der Veränderung seiner Arbeitsbedingungen beteiligt zu werden? Wie stellen Sie es sich vor, daß der einzelne an Rationalisierungsmaßnahmen und, was ich sehr wichtig finde, an der Gestaltung von Forschungsvorhaben in der Technologie beteiligt werden kann?

Šik:

Es ist immer sehr schade, wenn wir gleich so sehr verallgemeinernde Bezeichnungen benützen – wie „globale Utopie". Ihnen ist doch klar, daß ich über alle Sachen hier nicht sprechen konnte. Das Referat hat schon eine Stunde gedauert, und man hatte schwerlich die Möglichkeit, alle Grundideen zu bringen. Ich habe weitere eingehendere Vorstellungen beiseite lassen müssen.

Wir haben natürlich die Vorstellung einer Vertiefung der konkreten Mitbestimmung und Selbstbestimmung, vor allem natürlich in der Mikrosphäre. Denn in der Mikrosphäre des Informationsprozesses, über eine größere Einschaltung der Massenmedien zur Diskussion der Entwicklungsmöglichkeiten, über eine Einbeziehung gewisser Gruppenvertreter in die Planung. Sonst bleibt es ein Prozeß, der in einer zu breiten Gruppe durchgeführt werden muß. Wenn er nicht durchgeführt wird, bleibt natürlich die ganze Wirtschaftsentwicklung weiterhin Entscheidungssache einer kleinen Machtelite. Hier geht es vor allem gegen die Gefahr der immer stärkeren Bürokratisierung, wie in den östlichen Ländern, vorzugehen. Dann kommt es überhaupt nicht mehr darauf an, unter welchen Vorzeichen – kommunistischen oder nichtkommunistischen Vorzeichen – die staatsbürokratische Entscheidungsfällung sich so ungemein verbreitet. Dagegen muß ich einen Weg suchen. Ich sehe ihn in einer Demokratisierung der Pläne. Aber Sie haben recht: die Entscheidungsfällung bleibt in einem ungemein breiten Rahmen.

Hier geht es nur um die Entscheidung: was ist besser? Wer sich für die bürokratische Entwicklung entscheidet, wird mit meinen Ansichten überhaupt nicht einverstanden sein. In der Mikrosphäre kann ich dagegen Wege einer Vertiefung der demokratischen Mitbestimmung viel stärker realisieren. Wir haben hier einen viel tieferen Ansatz genommen, als ich ihn überhaupt zeigen konnte. Wir befassen uns mit der Einseitigkeit der ökonomischen Theorie, die nur den homo oeconomicus und nur das Vorteildenken vor sich sieht. Wir wenden uns aber zugleich gegen wirklich utopische Vorstellungen, die das Vorteildenken ganz beseitigen möchten, die also die Vorstellung „Sein statt Haben“ heute als die Lösung der Probleme sehen. Wir glauben, daß das eine Utopie bleibt. Denn das war ja die Grundvorstellung der ganzen kommunistischen Entwicklung, die in der Praxis versagt hat.

Wir müssen also sozusagen gegen die ökonomische Einseitigkeit kämpfen, aber auch gegen die andere utopische, extreme Entwicklung, die den ökonomischen Vorteil, das ökonomische Denken ganz beiseite lassen will. Wir sehen die Lösung in den Betrieben in einer Bildung von autonomen Arbeitsgruppen. Wir haben versucht, uns mit den skandinavischen Experimenten tiefergehend zu befassen. Wir glauben, daß hier eine reale Entwicklungsmöglichkeit besteht: in der Überwindung des autoritativen Führungsstils, in seiner Ersetzung durch einen demokratischen Führungsstil, durch die bekannten Prozesse des „Job Enrichment“ und des „Job Enlargement“ innerhalb der autonomen Arbeitsgruppen, d.h. das Wechseln von einer Arbeitstätigkeit zur anderen, die Schaffung noch kreativerer Arbeitsbedingungen, die Möglichkeit sogar der Wahl des Vorarbeiters oder Meisters – oder wie immer er bezeichnet wird – durch die Arbeitsgruppe, die Selbstbestimmung über die konkrete Organisation des Arbeitsprozesses innerhalb der von oben gegebenen Produktionsaufgaben. Das alles ist natürlich von uns durchgearbeitet und konkretisiert worden; ich konnte es hier wegen Zeitmangels nicht erwähnen.

Wir sehen sogar eine Möglichkeit – aufgrund weiterer Erfahrungen und Experimente –, daß von unten her eine Erweiterung in der genannten Richtung in den ganzen Betrieb hinein erfolgen könnte. Wir heben natürlich die Notwendigkeit der Bildung von kleinen Profitzentren hervor, so daß für den Mitarbeiter kleinerer Produktionseinheiten eine Überschaubarkeit der ökonomischen Entwicklung dieser Einheit entsteht, wollen aber nicht die Aufhebung großer Konzerne und großer Unternehmen; das würden wir für eine Utopie ansehen, denn es würde einen ungemeinen Abstieg in der Produktivität bedeuten. Wir sehen es realistisch. Uns geht es um die Stärkung der Dezentralisierungsprozesse, um die Vertiefung des Informationsflusses innerhalb der überschaubaren Einheiten, um häufigere Rechenschaftsabgabe des gewählten Aufsichtsrates den Mitarbeitern gegenüber. Aufgrund der so wachsenden Interessen und Erfahrungen im ökonomischen Gebiet kann eine Vertiefung der ökonomischen Schulung vor sich gehen, damit die Mitarbeiter verstehen, wovon die Entwicklung des Betriebes abhängt, wofür sie sich interessieren und worüber informieren sollten.

Das alles ist ausgearbeitet. Ich konnte leider über die Sache nicht sprechen. Ich möchte nun noch einmal betonen, daß man nicht Bezeichnungen, die man schnell zur Hand hat, verwenden sollte, um bestimmte Ideen abzustempeln – mit „Expertokratie" und „globaler Utopie" –, sondern man sollte versuchen, aufgrund konkreter Probleme konkrete Lösungen zu suchen. Entweder sage ich: ich will keine Lösung und mache es weiterhin ohne jede Vertiefung der Wirtschaftsdemokratie, und dann sollte ich auch ganz offen sagen: ich will eine stärkere Elite für Entscheidungsfällungen über Gesellschaftsentwicklung in der Makrosphäre und in der Mikrosphäre. Oder ich halte dies für eine grundlegende Gefahr für die Gesellschaft und sehe in der Schaffung einer vertieften Demokratie eine Hauptwaffe gegen diese Gefahr. Ich bin aufgrund der östlichen Erfahrungen zu dem letzteren gekommen. Im Osten hat man auch mit der Utopie angefangen, den Menschen zu verbessern, den Menschen an den Interessen der Gesellschaft stärker auszurichten, sein Bewußtsein in dieser Richtung zu fördern. Dann ist das Ganze gescheitert, da man das **ökonomische Interesse** der einzelnen Menschen und der Betriebskollektive unterschätzt hat. Man ist zwar auf gewisse materielle Linien zurückgegangen, aber ohne dem Menschen eine wirkliche Entscheidungsmöglichkeit in der Mikro- und Makrosphäre zu geben. De facto ist man zu einer ungemeinen Stärkung der Machtbürokratie gelangt, die ihre Stellung nur durch immer stärkere repressive Methoden gegen die Gesellschaft erhalten kann.

Teilnehmer:

Ich nehme an, daß dies ein normatives Modell ist. Da möchte ich mal eine Frage an Sie richten. Nehmen wir einmal an, dieses demokratische oder kommunistische Wirtschaftssystem hätte sich in einem Lande etabliert, etwa bei uns, und die Wirtschaftslage ändert sich wieder. Man machte einen neuen Plan und kommt darauf, daß man weniger Akademiker braucht. Man hat vorher gesagt: die Bildung muß höher sein. Die Anforderungen werden also höher. Man will größere Bildung und will in die Hochschulen hinein. Jetzt aber haben Produktions- und Qualitätskommissionen gesagt: Nein, wir brauchen mehr Facharbeiter. Trotz des höheren Bildungsniveaus müssen die Leute also unqualifiziertere Ausbildung in Kauf nehmen. Das Ganze wird dann qua Marktentscheid abgesegnet und legitimiert.

Aussprache Bell, Šik

Dazu habe ich eine Frage: Diese Absegnung erfolgt durch Leute, die den Plan nicht gemacht haben. Ihre Interessen werden mehrheitlich vertreten, durch legitimierte Demokraten, würde ich sagen. Aber für die Minderheit ist es natürlich eine undemokratische Entscheidung, weil die Versprechungen, die ihnen gemacht worden sind, nicht eingelöst werden. Was macht das System, wenn diese Minderheiten jetzt versuchen, Mehrheiten zu mobilisieren und Entscheidungen zu verweigern, also streiken oder sich etwas anderes einfallen lassen, wie z.B. 1968? Denn es ist ja nicht gesagt, daß mehrheitliche plebiszitäre Entscheidungen qualifiziert sein müssen.

Šik:

Das ist wahr. Aber sie sind für mich immer entscheidender als Minderheitsentscheidungen, als Entscheidungen, die eine Minderheit der Mehrheit aufzuzwingen versucht. Ich habe keine andere Form der Entscheidung für bestimmte allgemeine volkswirtschaftliche Entwicklungen gefunden als die Entscheidung durch die Mehrheit. Ich halte dies auf jeden Fall für fortschrittlicher als eine Entscheidung durch eine anonyme bürokratische Minderheit, wenn Sie so wollen. Denn das ist ja für die Ostblockstaaten charakteristisch.

Ich kann mir keine ideale Gesellschaft ausdenken, in der es keine Interessenwidersprüche gibt. Ich will ja nur eine bessere Lösungsform als die heutige. Das heißt, die Minderheit kann nur die Möglichkeit bekommen, sich in eine Mehrheit zu verwandeln. Sie kann versuchen, auch mit Detailvorschlägen – das ist das Anliegen dieses Modells – die Minderheitenansichten publik zu machen, bei den Planaufstellungen zu diskutieren und durch Erlangung einer Mehrheitsunterstützung durchzusetzen.

Teilnehmer:

Um es konkret zu sagen: Das geht nicht. Man hat 3 % Studenten, denen versprochen worden ist: höhere Bildung, höhere Position. Diese laufen jetzt bei uns herum, das ist gelaufen. Wenn man Ihr System jetzt nimmt, die Mehrheit mit 70 %, wieviel das kostet, die Ausbildung an Universitäten, und dann entscheidet man: Nein, es gibt keine Ausbildungsplätze mehr bzw. es gibt auch keine Stellen für Akademiker. Man hat es den Leuten erst versprochen, weil die wirtschaftliche Entwicklung eben gut war. Auch in diesem System kann es Umstrukturierungen geben. Wie reagiert das System dann?

Wir haben in unserem jetzigen System gestern abend keine Lösung gefunden, wie man arbeitslose Akademiker in großem Stil integrieren kann. Aber ein System, das aufgrund einer Mehrheitsentscheidung den Leuten sozusagen am Anfang qua demokratischer Legitimation den Hals abschneidet, ist doch noch viel unheimlicher als ein offenes System, das den Leuten noch Alternativen der freien Auswahl läßt. Also: nicht Globalsteuerung innerhalb des Systems, daß man sagt: Ihr müßt jetzt etwas anderes machen, weil das sonst nicht klappt.

Šik:

Gut. Ich weiß jetzt wirklich nicht, was besser ist: Wenn ich den Leuten verspreche „studiert und kommt in die Wirtschaft", und dann lasse ich sie arbeitslos oder wenn ich aufgrund viel tiefergehender Analysen als sie heute denkbar sind, auch die Überwindung von zyklischen Schwankungen und eine kontinuierliche Beschäftigungsentwicklung erreiche. Man kann eine solche Entwicklung der Einkommensgruppen durchsetzen, mit denen eine Überproduktion oder eine Krisenentwicklung gar nicht entstehen muß. Es geht doch darum, solchen großen Schwankungen vorzubeugen. Gerade die großen Schwankungen bringen doch die Probleme mit sich, und nicht vor allem die strukturellen Änderungen in der Produktion.

Um konkret zu sein: Man hat gesehen, daß 1972 die Kapitalproduktivität und sogar noch vorher die Grenzproduktivität des Kapitals sinkt, und man hat jetzt festgestellt, daß dann ab 1972 sogar die Gesamtproduktivität, d.h. berechnet auf das Kapital und auf die Arbeit, gesunken ist. Dadurch war ein ungemein schnelles Sinken der Gewinnquote zu verzeichnen. Aufgrund dieser beiden Prozesse ist aus der folgenden Verlangsamung des Wachstums der Realkonsumtion, sowie aus den immer kleineren Motivationen für die Investitionstätigkeit die Krise ausgebrochen. Aber im heutigen System kann man ja nicht die Produktivitätsentwicklung voraussehen und in der Einkommensverteilung rechtzeitig auf diese reagieren. Es gibt ein Wechselwirkung zwischen Inflation, die durch die Überkonsumtion entstanden ist, und der Wirtschaftskrise. Die Motivationen für den technischen Fortschritt sind ja während der Inflation immer kleiner geworden, und damit hat sich auch das Wachstum der Produktivität verlangsamt. Wegen des immer langsameren Fortschritts kam es schließlich zu einer Stagnation der Produktivitätsentwicklung. Man hätte im Gegenteil eine Verlangsamung der Konsumtionsentwicklung in diesen Zeiten benötigt, ferner eine Beschleunigung der Gewinnquotenentwicklung und aus ihr heraus frühere Investitionstätigkeiten in Richtung der Modernisierung der Produktion. Aufgrund dessen hätte es zu einer Wandlung der Produktivitätsentwicklung kommen können. Es hätte also überhaupt nicht zu der Wirtschaftskrise kommen müssen. Wir versuchen die Beweisführung auch durch eine konkrete Analyse z.B. der Wirtschaftsentwicklung in der Bundesrepublik zu erbringen.

Ich kann natürlich nichts anderes sagen als dies: die und die Wirtschaftsentwicklung ist realer, bei einer solchen Entwicklung der Einkommensgruppen zu erwarten, und aufgrund dieser realergesicherten Wirtschaftsentwicklung ist es möglich, diese und jene Einreihung weiterer Arbeitskräfte zu garantieren, eventuell auch ihre Struktur (hochqualifizierte oder weniger qualifizierte etc.) besser vorauszusehen.

Das sind die Prozesse, die voraussehbar sind und reguliert werden können. Ich glaube, das kann der Jugend mehr helfen, als wenn man eine vollkommen spontane Entwicklung der Wirtschaft erhält. Dann stehe ich zuerst immer vor einer Hochkonjunktur, vor einer sich übersteigenden Inflationsentwicklung, der aber auch immer periodisch eine Rezession, eine Krise folgt. Kein Mensch hat noch 1972 geahnt, daß wir vor einer solchen Rezession, vor einer so plötzlichen Reduzierung des ganzen Wirtschaftswachstums stehen. In dem vorgeschlagenen System sind die Makroprozesse voraussehbar. Wir haben versucht aufzuzeigen, nicht nur wie die Pläne aufgestellt werden könnten, sondern auch wie der Zusammenhang der Wirtschaftspolitik mit der Planung sich durchsetzen kann: wie man in bestimmten Momenten – wenn das Vorausgesehene nicht eintritt – mit Hilfe von Änderungen in den wirtschaftspolitischen Instrumenten darauf möglichst schnell reagieren kann. Aber wenn ich keinen Plan habe, kann ich nicht einmal nötige Wandlungen in der Wirtschaftspolitik rechtzeitig realisieren. Die fiskalische Konjunkturpolitik, wie sie allgemein vertreten wird, ist ja in der Praxis völlig gescheitert. Ich bin überzeugt, es gibt keine Möglichkeit einer realen Einwirkung auf die Zyklus-Entwicklung, weil man überhaupt nicht sehen kann, wann der entscheidende Moment kommt, in dem ich gewisse fiskalische Instrumente so oder so ändern und benutzen sollte.

Teilnehmer:

Vor meiner Frage möchte ich eine Vorbemerkung machen. Sie sind in Ihrem Referat davon ausgegangen, unser System zu analysieren, und haben einige Problemkreise herausgebrochen: Die Existenz einer zyklischen Wirtschaftsentwicklung, die Bürokratisierung der Wirtschaftsentscheidungen, die einseitige Konsumtionsentwicklung und andere Problemkreise. Als Vorschlag zur Überwindung dieser Probleme haben Sie Ihre makroökonomische Verteilungsplanung vorgetragen. Dazu möchte ich jetzt meine Meinung sagen.

Ich glaube, mit einer Verteilungsplanung wird man die zyklische Wirtschaftsentwicklung nicht in den Griff bekommen können. Auch in den Reinkulturen, in den staatsmonopolistischen Ländern des Ostblocks ist es nicht gelungen, soweit ich informiert bin, und bei uns haben wir es nach meiner Meinung auch nicht schaffen können. Die Bürokratisierung scheint mir bei der vorgeschlagenen makroökonomischen Verteilungsplanung eher stärker zu werden denn geringer. Auch ist die Frage, ob eine Konsumtionsentwicklung steuern kann.

Auf der anderen Seite hat mir Ihre Entwicklung des neutralisierten Kapitals sehr gut gefallen. Deshalb stelle ich dazu folgende konkrete Frage. Ist es von Ihrem Ansatz aus möglich – sozusagen als Modell und herausgenommen aus dem Konzept –. ein solches sozialistisches Kapital konsequent zu installieren, also ohne die makroökonomische Verteilungsplanung? Wäre das Ihren Intentionen zufolge möglich oder durchführbar, aus dem Zusammenhang herausgerissen?

Šik:

Mit solchen Stellungnahmen kann man immer sehr schwer etwas anfangen. Ich lehne es ab, wenn gesagt wird: der Zyklus kann nicht bewältigt werden, die Bürokratie wird stärker, die einseitige Konsumtionsentwicklung beseitigen wir auch nicht. Das sind solche schnellgefaßten Kurzschlüsse, daß man sie nicht mehr diskutieren kann. Ich bitte Sie, nehmen Sie wenigstens zur Kenntnis – ich sage ja immer, ich will niemanden unsere Vorstellungen aufdrängen, und sie brauchen von niemandem akzeptiert zu werden –, aber man sollte nicht immer von vornherein in dieser Weise etwas ablehnen, wenn dahinter eine Arbeit von ungefähr 15 Jahren steht, die versucht, alle Vor- und Nachteile der verschiedenen Entwicklungen und Experimente zu erfassen und auch Mittel und Wege zu finden. Man sollte wenigstens sagen: Gut, ich bin skeptisch, ich will mich erst näher überzeugen, wie die Sachen dargestellt werden und ob sie realisierbar sind. Ich bin der Überzeugung, daß man natürlich so etwas wie das neutralisierte Kapital ohne weiteres schaffen kann. Aber es besteht die Gefahr, daß eine Entwicklung in der Richtung, die nur ein stärkeres Interesse und Beteiligung der Mitarbeiter in der Mikrosphäre in den Unternehmen schafft, nicht die erwarteten Resultate bringt, wenn die ganze Entwicklung der Investitionen und Löhne, also der Gewinne und Löhne wieder nur den Betrieben überlassen wird. Sie schaffen tatsächlich nur so etwas wie eine geistige Mitentscheidung, ein Miteigentumsgefühl bei den Mitarbeitern. Aber kein Unternehmen allein kann darüber entscheiden, wieviel es investieren soll und wie schnell die Löhne steigen sollen. Das ist und bleibt nun einmal ein volkswirtschaftlicher Zusammenhang, ein volkswirtschaftliches Problem.

Die Lohnentwicklung hängt mit der Konsumgüterproduktentwicklung in der ganzen Volkswirtschaft zusammen, nicht mit der Produktion des einzelnen Betriebes. Und die Entwicklung der Investitionen hängt zusammen mit der Investitionsgüterproduktion in der ganzen Volkswirtschaft. Und diese Investitionsgüterproduktion hängt, wenn sie optimal sein soll, wieder mit der Konsumgüterproduktion zusammen. Das sind nun einmal volkswirtschaftliche Zusammenhänge. Sobald man innerhalb der partiellen Teile der Volkswirtschaft darüber entscheiden wird oder gar in einem Interessenkampf darüber entscheidet, in dem Augenblick müssen in der Volkswirtschaft Widersprüche entstehen.

Sie können nicht mit dem Ostblock argumentieren, abgesehen davon, daß dort die Zyklen einen ganz anderen Charakter haben. Wenn dort so etwas wie ein Zyklus überhaupt existiert, so sind es ausgesprochen Fehler in der Investi-

tions- und Produktionsplanung, die ich ja ablehne. Es sind solche Planvorstellungen, die rein politische Ziele verfolgen: eine ungemein schnelle Stärkung der militärischen Macht, eine Produktion der Schwerindustrie, der Rüstungsindustrie mit einem völligen Zurückbleiben der Konsumgüterindustrie. Bedenken Sie nur die Tatsache, daß im Durchschnitt in den Ostblockstaaten 80 % der gesamten Industrie Investitionsgüterproduktion ist, nur 20 % sind Konsumgüterproduktion. Bedenken Sie, was allein aus dieser Struktur für Probleme erwachsen müssen, und daß hier völlig andere Gründe für eine Inflationsentwicklung gegeben sind. Abgesehen davon, daß das Interesse der Betriebe sich in dieser Richtung noch weiter verstärkt, weil die Betriebe einfach weiterhin lohninteressiert sind und ihre Mitarbeiter konsuminteressiert sind. Diese können die Löhne erreichen, wenn sie den Plan erfüllen und formell das Wachstum erzielen. Je leichter sie dies erfüllen wollen, desto mehr geht es auf Kosten der Effektivität, auf Kosten der Wirtschaftlichkeit, auf Kosten der benötigten Strukturentwicklung. Daraus entstehen die ungemeinen Schwierigkeiten des Ostblocks.
Die ganze Vorstellung ist doch nicht nur auf einer Analyse des westlichen Systems, sondern auch auf einer tiefgehenden Analyse des östlichen Systems aufgebaut worden. Hinzu kommt die Erkenntnis, daß man Marktimpulse und -kriterien mit einer Makroplanung koppeln muß. Aber die Koppelung kann eben nur die Koppelung über die Verteilungsprozesse sein.

Ich wiederhole noch einmal: Ich will das niemandem aufdrängen, aber ich bitte Sie einzusehen, daß dahinter langjährige Überlegungen stehen, mit denen ich mich etwas näher bekanntmachen muß, wenn ich darüber urteilen will. Hier sollte es nichts anderes als gewisse Denkimpulse bringen, und wenn das erreicht ist, haben wir schon viel erreicht.

Frau Haenchen:

Um von den Denkimpulsen zu sprechen, brauchen wir eigentlich nur einen Satz von Daniel Bell zu wiederholen: „A problem of sensivity in the human relationship". Denken Sie daran, daß am Eingang des Uttweiler Institutes steht: „Im Mittelpunkt der Mensch!" Wir sprechen immer von Wirtschaft, von Markt, von Demokratie, aber ich meine, daß das Menschenbild mal wieder ins Gespräch kommen sollte.

Rosenmayr:

Es geht ein bißchen in diese Richtung; es ist sozusagen ein Vermittlungsschritt zwischen dem Wirtschaftssystem und dem Konzept, das zu einem Menschenbild führen kann, und zwar möchte ich bei Professor Bell's Frage nach dem Ausbildungsideal einsetzen: Sie haben eigentlich die Notwendigkeit eines Universalisten entworfen und zwar eines Universalisten in der höheren Bildung, die sich so ausdrückt, daß er hauptsächlich das Lernen und die Vielseitigkeit der Verwendbarkeit lernen muß. Daß er sich also eher für eine abstrakte, allgemeine Bildung auf höchster Stufe hingibt, die eine gewisse Vielseitigkeit, so scheint mir der Verwendung garantieren soll. Nun möchte ich Sie fragen, ob diese Tendenz – daß man diese allgemeine Bildung in den Schulen, in den höheren Schulen und auf den höchsten Bildungsgängen ausführt –, ob sie wirklich so generell durchgehalten werden soll. Denn die Firmen können auch Mittel für solche Lehrgänge ausgeben. Es gibt sehr viele Zweige – nicht nur in der öffentlichen Verwaltung, sondern überhaupt in dem sich weiterentwikkelnden öffentlichen System der Bedürfniswahrnehmung, der Sozialarbeit, der von Ihnen auch genannten medizinischen Dienste usw. –, wo dann die Frage auftaucht: „Wer soll die konkrete Ausbildung für anwendbares Wissen wirklich übernehmen?" Ich bemerke in den Hochschulen Tendenzen – besonders in den Sozialwissenschaften –, die vieles an dem alten Akademismus in Frage stellen mit dem Konzept, daß anwendbares und verwendbares Wissen vermittelt werden soll, ohne daß dabei diese, die das vertreten, Kurzschlüsse begehen.

Teilnehmer:

Ist die nachindustrielle Gesellschaft wirklich eine Gesellschaft ohne Werte? Sind wir nicht hier, um Grundlagen für neue Wertsysteme – ich betone: neue – zu erarbeiten? Wie müßte nach Ihrer Meinung ein solches Wertsystem aufgrund dessen, was Sie als gesellschaftliche Analyse dargelegt haben, aussehen?

Bell:

The question falls together with the comments of Miss Haenchen and of Mr. Rosenmayr. It seems to me important to except the fact that every economy and technology does not have a full value component. To put it most simply: economics and technology haben eine Zweckrationalität und keine Wertrationalität. One of the difficulties in the contemporary world is that the „Zweckrationalität" became an end in itself. And these are the modern problems of bourgeois society. So one should accept the fact that economy and technology including a post industrial society do not have a value-system of its own, es hat keine Wertrationalität.

However – and this, it seems to me, is the crucial point – there is now **an increasing possibility**, in the nature of the new communications's patterns, in the new revolution in communications, to create a genuine **decentralisation** of work, a genuine **decentralisation** of place. One of the very natures of an industrial economy – as I tried to indicate it – was to create large scale-organisations, in order to maximize output and production, within an enterprise. Therefore there has been a tendency in all industrial system for large scale-organisations and this gets reinforced by the political tendencies to its domination and bureaucracy. I am not saying that the elements of a post-

industrial society necessarily will create decentralisation. I say, it has the possibilities. It also has the possibilities to create more centralisation, because it creates everything within a larger network. And more and more centralisation always creates more and more power. There is an old Russian joke, which says: „Who is Stalin? And it says: Stalin is Dschingis-Khan with a telephone at one end".
That is centralisation in this way. But what a post-industrial society allows, what to do, is to create decentralisation. Now, Mr. Sik has pointed out: there are efforts to break out of the patterns of work, to allow combinations of job-changes and such. It is now possible – **because of the very nature of the new technologies** – to break away form mass production, to allow more individual variation, to be more responsive to the consumer, to make the market a genuine element of variation an of individual variation to give people what they want.

So, what I will say is this: in so far as people want a sense of more control over their lifes, what is happening incontemporary society is the spread of bureaucracy. If I can put it in a different context: if the national state, which is our unit of politics, has become too small for the big problems of life (which is in the international system) it has become too big for the small problems of life, because of the variations that exist in local places.

It is now possible to begin to break off the large scale-organisations in order to be more responsive to smaller and smaller units. We have a new basis for new values to arise. New values cannot arise out of thin air. One cannot simply manufacture values. Genuine values arise out of shared experience, which are meaningful for the people. When they engage in activities, which have meaning to them, then something sacred, something holy begins to emerge. It is a matter of restoring the scale on which economic and social organisations can function to be more responsive to human beings. Then the new experiences of people, can provide something, which is more genuine to them. I can only say that a post-industrial society allows one to do, is to provide the possibility, for the first time –– given the new elements of microprocessors, given the new elements of tele-communications –– to provide for a decentralisation of a society and therefore to bring things back to the control of smaller groups in the areas of work and the areas of social life.

Bell:

The question was: in what sense is youth itself conscious of taking part in the industrial revolution? I think, it's a crucial question in two very different ways. The extraordinary point is that nobody was conscious of taking part in the First Industrial Revolution. It didn't occur at a particular period of time. In fact, the phrase – Industrial Revolution – was first coined by Arnold

Toynbee (the father of the historian Toynbee) in 1883.

He gave a series of lectures, in which he said: „For the last hundred years, if we look back, we've been living through a revolution. We havent't been conscious of it."

The important point is this that as regards economic changes until now, nobody voted in the industrial revolution. Here was a change, which through factory organization, urban living etc. transformed life. Yet nobody met together and said: „Do we want it, or do we not want it?" Political revolutions are voted in. There was an American revolution for liberty, there was a French revolution for fraternity, there was a communist revolution presumingly for equality; these were political acts. The industrial revolution was a process and nobody voted it in, nobody was conscious at a time that a revolution is taking place.

What is different now is the fact of consciousness. People are aware of changes taking place and now they start controlling. In a curious way these elements of post industrial revolution are in one sense primarily the products of youth, but not in the way we sometimes think of it. When **I say that it is the product of youth** it is this: most of the advances in science and technology are created by young scholars. Mathematicians flourish at the age between 17 and 25 and then they are outmoded. They are „finished" the age of 25. Their creativity, that is diminished.

Science and technology come out of young people, because science is primarily a young persons's game. What we old people only have is history and criticism, where living in a past has some gain. And the past allows you as a ground of analysis.

Since most of science and technology and mathematics are abstract puzzles, they're done much better by young people, whose minds are still more flexible. So the curious fact is that most of the changes in science and technology are primarily those of young scientists and most of the greater studies are made by younger people. People today are much more conscious of these changes and therefore they try to control them.

Teilnehmer:

Jugendarbeitslosigkeit scheint mir kein „rein statistisches Problem zu sein". Für die „Intelligenzjugend" werden die Probleme wohl kleiner. Was aber passiert mit den Jugendlichen, die den immer höher werdenden Ansprüchen der Ausbildung – aus welchen Gründen auch immer sei dahingestellt – nicht ganz oder überhaupt nicht gerecht werden können und deren möglichen Arbeitsplätze wegrationalisiert werden?

Aussprache Bell, Šik

Bell:

Well, here I must unfortunately refer to Professor Šik's reiterated opening statements: „It's very complicated, it's very difficult, it's very hard to answer, because the subject is more complex". Clearly, where you have people, who have very particular skills, who have education and training, it is easy to find some places for them. There is unfortunately a large problem with those who do not have those skills. And this goes back to one of the points, I was making. It is not just problem of the press. It's a recurrent problem. It's a problem, which I referred to towards the end of my talk about the relationship between the elite and the mass. You have now a **new** relationship between the elite and the mass, in which the **new** elites are basically technical elites. You can „save" some of those technical elites, who for the moment are unemployed by means of a „resourcebank" or some way doing that. But the other large number of youths remain as a problem. Essentially, it seems to me, of finding a social policy which is going to produce some useful employment for them, paid the state. I see no other way out. In the United States during the time of Franklin Delano Roosevelt, we created a youth corps to go and do socially useful tasks like conservation, preservation or work in the fields and the parks and such. Unfortunely, there are too much of echoes of this in what the National Socialists did in the thirties, with that kind of youth-policy. Yet one has to go and find a set of special projects. Let me say one further word along that line: there is in every society a large number of human needs, which are usually not filled, because there's nobody to pay for it. These are in hospitals, in the parks, in the pollutions-areas and such. If you link social policy with employment policy it is accepted as a social course and therefore as a social benefit for the society.

Teilnehmer:

Bei der Darstellung Ihrer Idee, Prof. Šik, haben Sie sich sicherlich Gedanken gemacht, welche Möglichkeiten Sie sehen, Menschen zu befähigen,

1. Wirtschaft und Zusammenhänge, z.B. Lebensqualitäten transparent zu machen und diese überhaupt verstehen zu können.
2. Haben Sie bestimmte Vorstellungen und Forderungen an unsere Erziehungs- und Bildungseinrichtungen, z.B. an die Schulen, die Verbände, organisierte Gruppen, Gewerkschaften, Arbeitgeber etc.?

Šik:

Das ist eine breitgefächerte Frage, und ich bin froh, daß ich jetzt darauf antworten kann, denn es ist ja verschiedentlich in einigen Beiträgen in dieser Richtung schon angesprochen worden. Selbstverständlich unterschätze ich nicht die ganze Erziehungstätigkeit, die Bildungsentwicklung der Menschen.

Aber man muß sich nun die Frage stellen, ob ich den Menschen in einer relativ kurzen Zeit einfach grundlegend verändern kann. Ich muß natürlich diese Frage mit „Nein“ beantworten. Ich kann versuchen, die Erziehung der Menschen so zu beschleunigen, daß sie fähiger sein werden, wichtige gesellschaftliche Zusammenhänge tiefergehend zu erkennen und zu verstehen. Aber ich kann das Interesse bei den Menschen, an den gesellschaftlichen Problemen und den großen gesellschaftlichen Fragen unserer Zeit nur wecken, wenn ich ihnen die Erfahrung gebe, daß sie auf diese Entwicklung, wenigstens in einer gewissen Weise einwirken können.
Sie können doch aus den verschiedesten Beispielen sehen, daß die breite Öffentlichkeit noch in gewissen Momenten und besonders, wo das öffentlich zum Ausdruck kommt, sogar bildungsfeindlich ist, weil sie einfach überhaupt noch nicht versteht, wozu mehr und höhere Bildung nötig ist.

Viele Menschen verstehen nicht, was Bildungsvertiefungen dem Volk oder der Gesellschaft bringen können. Ich glaube, nur dort, wo die Bevölkerung beginnt, aufgrund institutioneller Einrichtungen und Absicherungen über große gesellschaftliche Zusammenhänge nachzudenken und es die Erfahrung gewinnt, daß es auf diese einwirken kann, wird sich auch seine Einstellung in dieser Richtung ändern. Ich habe hier ganz konkret an die letzte Abstimmung in der Schweiz über die Hochschulförderung, die ja von der Bevölkerung abgelehnt wurde, gedacht.

Gleichzeitig sehe ich in der Schweizer Demokratie einen ungemein wichtigen Ansatz für das, was mir vorschwebt, nämlich demokratische Wahlen von Planalternativen. Aber ich betone, eben nur einen Ansatz. Einstweilen ist diese Entscheidungsfällung noch zu beschränkt und diese Beschränktheit hat sogar negative Folgen. Es wird immer nur über einzelne Maßnahmen abgestimmt – auch über einzelne wirtschaftspolitische Maßnahmen, ohne diese in den breiten Zusammenhängen zu sehen. Es wird z.B. abgestimmt über die Probleme einer Sozialversicherungsentwicklung, ohne den Zusammenhang mit dem Wirtschaftswachstum, mit der Lohnentwicklung, mit den Investitionen zu sehen. Das nächste Mal wird wieder über Hochschulförderung, ohne den Zusammenhang mit der Investitions-, Einkommens-, Arbeitsentwicklung usw. zu sehen, abgestimmt. Es sind alles nur Teilmaßnahmen und nicht eine komplexe Entwicklung, über die abgestimmt wird. Ich bin der Überzeugung, daß erst dann, wenn Makropläne existierten ein wirklicher Vorteil dieser direkten Demokratie bestünde. Bei der Abstimmung über diese Pläne könnte das Volk die verschiedenen Entwicklungsprozesse in ihren großen Zusammenhängen sehen.

Bei der Auswahl aus verschiedenen Planalternativen würde das Volk nicht immer nur die Alternative der schnellsten Lohnsteigerung anstreben. Wenn eine andere Alternative zwar ein langsameres Wachstum der privaten Konsumption, dafür aber eine schnellere Lösung der Transport- oder Umweltprobleme aufzeigen würde, könnte sie in bestimmten Momenten eine stärkere Unterstützung erhalten. Es ist heute gar nicht mehr so eindeutig, daß die Menschen sozusagen immer nur für die Alternative des schnellen Wachstums der individuellen Konsumption votieren würden.

Aber natürlich muß diese Planung Hand in Hand gehen, nicht nur mit institutionell gesicherten Wahlmöglichkeiten, sondern auch mit der ganzen Erziehung und mit der öffentlichen Informationsvermittlung. In dem Sinne ist es tatsächlich eine komplexe Gesellschaftsreform. Aber dies bedeutet nicht, einer Utopie zu unterliegen, gemäß welcher man die heutigen Probleme dadurch lösen könnte, daß man die Menschen zu Bedürfnissenkungen und Konsumptionsentsagungen erzieht. Ich halte das für unrealistisch. Natürlich kann man eine solche Forderung theoretisch aufstellen, ich halte sie aber einfach für nicht realisierbar. Alle Erfahrungen aus dem Ostblock zeigen es doch eigentlich. Die Bedürfnisse und Konsumentwicklungen des Westens wirken auf die Menschen des Ostens so stark, daß man heute, obwohl man es überhaupt nicht wollte, die Produktion von Coca Cola oder die Produktion von Jeans einführen bzw. Importe in dieser Richtung erhöhen muß. Die Bedürfnisse der Menschen haben sich real so entwickelt. Und wenn Sie sich heute die Bedürfnisentwicklung der unterdurchschnittlichen Einkommensgruppen in den höchstentwickelten Industrieländern ansehen, dann können Sie nicht erwarten, daß sie diese von ihren wachsenden materiellen Konsumansprüchen abbringen können. Sie können ihnen nicht einfach sagen: „Ihr solltet nicht mehr konsumieren“; das halte ich wirklich für eine Utopie.

Wir kommen zwangsläufig zu der Schlußfolgerung, daß eigentlich nur in ganz kleinen Gemeinschaften, die sich völlig von der übrigen Gesellschaft isolieren, es möglich ist, die Bedürfnisse der Menschen zu beschränken, nicht aber in den großen industriellen Staaten. Bei der Betrachtung der kleinen landwirtschaftlichen Gemeinschaften, Kommunen, stellt sich aber immer noch die große Frage, wie lange das hier anhält.

Tatsache ist, daß die Menschen ihre wachsenden Bedürfnisse durchsetzen werden, und deshalb muß man Vorstellungen ablehnen, gemäß welcher das Wachstum der Produktivität in Zukunft nicht nötig sei. Senkungen der Produktivität würden Aufruhr und Rebellion in der großen Masse der Bevölkerung hervorrufen. Das zeigen uns auch die Beispiele der Entwicklung in der Sowjetunion und des Ostblocks überhaupt: das Wirtschafts-System der Ostblockstaaten hat zu einer relativen Senkung der Produktivität geführt, und die Folge ist eine beständig wachsende Unzufriedenheit der Bevölkerung.

Ich glaube, man muß so reformieren, daß das System nicht grundlegend, revolutionär verändert wird, sondern so, daß es der Bürokratisierung entgegenwirkt. Der Prozeß der Entbürokratisierung würde sich erheblich beschleunigen, wenn die Menschen die Möglichkeit sähen, wirklich auf die Entscheidungsfällung einwirken zu können. Mir schwebt nicht eine Ummodelung des

Menschen vor, sondern der Gedanke, den Menschen zu nehmen wie er ist und dort anzusetzen, wo es um die neuen Bedürfnisse und Interessen der Menschen und ihre schnellere Durchsetzung mit Hilfe institutioneller Änderungen geht.

Zukunftschancen der Jugend unter politischen Aspekten

Prof. Karl Deutsch

Wir befassen uns mit den Zukunftschancen der Jugend. Da ist es vielleicht nützlich, mit der Frage anzufangen, was wir mit den Begriffen meinen, die wir verwenden.

Was ist eigentlich Zukunft? Es gibt eine wunderschöne Radierung eines Franzosen aus dem 19. Jahrhundert, Honore Daumier, die die Begegnung mit der Zukunft zeigt. Was man da sieht, ist ein riesengroßer, riesenstarker Ringkämpfer mit einer Kapuze, die sein Gesicht verhüllt. Man sieht nur, seine gewaltigen Arme und seinen mächtigen Körper. So steht dieser verkleidete Ringer vor dem Beschauer: Die Zukunft ist riesenstark, aber wir kennen sie nicht.

Soweit der Künstler. Was sagen die Wissenschaftler? Der Physiker und Nobelpreisträger Bridgman sagte: Die Zukunft ist ein Programm. – Ich schlage vor, es genauer zu sagen: Die Zukunft ist das Ergebnis heute existierender Gegebenheiten und Programme.

Wir sind im Juni 1978. Wenn ich angeben sollte, wo und wie das deutsche Volk wahrscheinlich seine Ferien im August verbringen wird, müßte ich fragen: Wo sind die Erholungsgebiete, die Ferienorte, wo stehen die Gaststätten, wo gibt es Ferienwohnungen oder kleine Häuschen, die man mieten kann, wo liegen die Autobahnen, wer hat welche Transportmittel zur Verfügung, wieviel deutsche Familien haben wie viele Kinder, und wieviel deutsche Gattinnen sind heute bereits berufstätig und haben außerdem noch den Haushalt und sind bereit, auch in den Ferien zu kochen, wie steht es mit der Einkommenslage, wer kann sich ein bescheidenes Hotel leisten, und wer muß eben doch kochen?

Übrigens kann man im Jahre 1978 schon fragen: Wieviel deutsche Gatten sind bereit, beim Geschirrwaschen mitzuhelfen?

Aus all diesen Dingen ergibt sich dann ein Bild der Ferienverteilung. Ich habe Neckermann ausgelassen und die Gruppenflüge nach Ceylon, Mallorca oder Nepal. Aber Sie werden schon sehen, daß die Verteilung nicht die Zukunft der einzelnen Familie, sondern die Verteilung des deutschen Ferienverkehrs zu einem gewissen Grade voraussehbar macht.

Ähnlich: Ich weiß nicht, wie viele von Ihnen, die heute unverheiratet sind, die Absicht haben, im nächsten Juli, ein Jahr ab heute, zu heiraten. Aber ich weiß, daß etwa im Oktober die deutschen Warenhäuser, ähnlich wie die amerikanischen die Möbelbestellungen der jungen Paare einplanen, die im nächsten Juni anfangen werden, einen eigenen Haushalt zu gründen. Im Budget der Stadt Berlin sind bereits die Übersiedlungsbeihilfen und die Haushaltsbeihilfen für jene jungen Paare eingeplant, die auf die Idee kommen könnten, nach Berlin zu ziehen.

Das heißt, man kann sehr viel von der Zukunft voraussehen, und zwar im ganzen leichter als im einzelnen. Aber da gibt es Irrtümer. Es könnte im August eiskalt oder fürchterlich heiß werden, es könnte die Politik durcheinanderkommen; das wissen wir nicht. Aber die Wahrscheinlichkeiten sind da, und man irrt sich nicht allzu oft, wenn man sich an die Wahrscheinlichkeiten hält, obwohl auch das passieren kann. Sagen wir vielleicht:

Die Zukunft ist die Menge der möglichen Ereignisse. Da gibt es eine erste Einsicht, ausgedrückt in einer schönen deutschen Redensart: „Das ist doch nicht drin.“ Wenn Sie ein deutsches Kartenspiel haben und sehen sich um nach der schönen österreichischen Tarockkarte, dem Spieß, werden Sie im Kartenspiel vergeblich suchen: er ist nicht drin. Oder wenn Sie schon etwas gespielt haben und die vier Könige sind schon gefallen, dann können Sie sicher sein, daß in einem ehrlichen Spiel niemand mehr mit einem fünften König aufwartet.

Dann gibt es noch eine Aussage: Das ist möglich, das könnte doch passieren. Ferner gibt es die Aussage: Das ist wahrscheinlich; wenn nicht etwas ganz Ungewöhnliches geschieht, dann wird das wohl so kommen. Die Aussage: „Das ist wahrscheinlich“ ist oft übertrieben. Sie kennen vielleicht das Lied von Wolf Biermann, das den Kehrreim hat: „So wird es sein“. Es gibt ein amerikanisches Lied von George Gershwin aus seiner Oper „Porgy and Bess“ mit dem entgegengesetzten Kehrreim: It aint necessarily so – Genauso muß es nicht notwendigerweise kommen. Zwischen diesen beiden „So wird es sein“ und „Gerade so muß es nicht unbedingt kommen“ liegt irgendwo die Wirklichkeit.

Dann gibt es noch die Aussage: Das wünsche ich, so soll es sein. Dann fragen wir: Was sind die Dinge, die wir uns wünschen? Vielleicht eine bessere Welt, vielleicht ein wertvolleres, sinnvolleres, ein erfüllteres persönliches Leben für uns selbst und für andere Menschen, an denen uns etwas liegt? Und dann fragen wir: Ja, was kann ich denn dazu tun?

Wenn wir fragen, was man für die Zukunft tun kann, dann gibt es vielleicht drei ganz grob angedeutete Möglichkeiten. Die erste heißt, bereit sein. Will ich mich irgendwie bereit machen, bin ich bereit, auf die Herausforderung der Zukunft zu antworten. Hier kommt der verhüllte Ringer wieder. Habe ich die Fähigkeiten dazu? Wenn die große Flut kommt, bist du bereit, ins Wasser zu springen? – Jawohl. – Einen Augenblick Denkpause: Hast du schwimmen gelernt?

Es genügt nicht, bereit zu sein. Man muß Kenntnisse, Fähigkeiten, Fertigkeiten entwickelt haben, damit man diesen Willen auch ausführen kann. Die Jugend ist eine Zeit der Werterwerbung, der Sinnstiftung, der Willensbildung und des Erwerbs von Fähigkeiten. Man kann Jugend als Verzögerungszeit empfinden und sagen: Es ist doch schrecklich; früher waren die Jungen mit 14, 15 Jahren schon ausgebildet, sie gingen in die Lehre, sie verkauften Zeitungen, sie putzten Schuhe, sie taten irgend etwas, waren Schusterjungen oder Handelslehrlinge, Kommis in irgendeinem Unternehmen und verdienten ihren Lebensunterhalt. Selbständige Leute waren sie. Im Wilden Westen hatten die Jungen schon mit 15 ihr Schießeisen. Schrecklich, wie sich das alles heutzutage in die Länge zieht und verzögert.

Aber die gleichen Leute, die von der Jugend als Verzögerung sprechen, sprechen von der moderen Industrie als Umwegproduktion. Man geht eben nicht mehr in den nächsten Sumpf, holt ein Stück Eisenerz heraus und beginnt, es mit Hilfe eines Holzkohlenfeuers zu schmelzen und zu schmieden. Man schickt heute Schiffe nach Kanada, holt Erz und schickt es durch ziemlich umständliche Förderanlagen, Hochöfen usw. hindurch; aber man bekommt auch beträchtlich mehr Eisen.

Wir haben heute eine Umwegproduktion der Fähigkeiten und Fertigkeiten. Es dauert länger, bis die jungen Leute ausgebildet sind, aber dafür sind einige nachher Versicherungsmathematiker, und andere können Auto fahren wie Niki Lauda. Einige können fliegen, und einige erklettern die unwahrscheinlichsten Berge, neuerdings sogar ohne Sauerstoff. Die Leistungsfähigkeit, die Fähigkeiten und Fertigkeiten der Menschen nehmen ganz beträchtlich zu. Als ich in meiner Schülerzeit die Leichtathletikrekorde verfolgte, war ein Zwei-Meter-Hochsprung eine Sensation. Heute liegt der Weltrekord, glaube ich, bei 2,31 m.

Irgendwer hat also irgend etwas dazugelernt. Diese Umwegproduktionen haben doch wohl dafür gestanden. Man soll also die Verzögerungszeiten nicht völlig unterschätzen; es ist auch etwas dafür erworben worden.

Wir sagen immer noch: bereit sein. Ja, wofür denn? Wir sagen: bereit sein für den Erwerb von Fähigkeiten und Fertigkeiten in einer Welt, in der die Komplexität der menschlichen Beziehungen zunimmt. Wer von den Älteren hat erwartet, mitten in Berlin Tür an Tür mit Türken zu wohnen? Heute ist das in Berlin-Kreuzberg normal, es heißt im Volksmund „Klein-Ankara". Wer hat erwartet, daß man in der Stadt, in der ich lebe, in Boston, jetzt auch Plätze nach spanischem Muster einrichtet oder daß es in meinem Stadtbezirk Volksschulunterricht auf Spanisch und Portugiesisch gibt, neben der größten Zahl der Klassen, die weiterhin auf Englisch unterrichtet werden? Aber es ändert sich eben etwas in der Welt. Die menschlichen Beziehungen werden wichtiger. Sie sehen es schon an den Frauen. Es wird schwerer und schwerer, mit ihnen auszukommen.

Erst wollten sie Anstellungen, und jetzt wollen sie auch noch befördert werden. Was wird ihnen nächstens noch einfallen? Womöglich die volle Gleichberechtigung!

Von den Beziehungen zu den Kindern will ich gar nicht sprechen, die sind noch verwickelter. Aber das haben Sie noch vor sich. Sie sind verwickelter, aber sie sind es auch wert. Im gleichen Maße, in dem die menschlichen Beziehungen schwieriger werden, werden sie manchmal sogar um vieles schöner. Denken Sie daran, wie Peter Handtke das Leben der Generation seiner Mutter unter dem ausdrucksvollen Titel „Wunschloses Unglück" beschreibt. Es sind doch heutzutage etwas weniger Leute bereit, ihr Leben unter einem solchen Titel zu verbringen.

Daneben müssen Sie stellen, daß die Welt auch wissenschaftlicher wird. Diese Fertigkeiten braucht man auch. In Cambridge (Mass.) gibt es einen großen Supermarkt, wo die Käufer mit ihren Warenkarren einkaufen können und an der Kasse abrechnen. Da das lange dauert, wenn die Hausfrauen für eine ganze Woche einkaufen, gibt es eine Expreßspur, die man mit nur sechs Waren benutzen kann. Da erscheint in dieser Spur ein junger Mann mit hochgetürmtem Wagen. Die Verkäuferin fragt ihn: Kommen Sie von Harvard, wo man nicht zählen kann, oder von M.J.T. (der größten technischen Universität Amerikas), wo man nicht lesen kann?

Die Welt wird von Ihnen verlangen, daß Sie zählen und rechnen können, daß Sie Ziffern und Buchstaben beherrschen, daß Sie etwas von der Wissenschaft und von wissenschaftlichen Verfahren verstehen und von dem, was Daniel Bell heute früh und auf dem schönen Flugblatt, das er verteilte, das Systemdenken und das Modelldenken genannt hat – und daß Sie etwas von der Vielfalt, dem Reichtum und der Tiefe der menschlichen Beziehungen verstehen, so wie sie große Kunst und große Literatur vermitteln können. Auch das wird das Leben von uns verlangen.

Man kann es auch prosaischer ausdrücken: Im Durchschnitt werden die jungen Leute, die heute mit 25 Jahren voll ins Berufsleben eintreten, etwa 40 Jahre vor sich haben, wenn es nicht einen Krieg gibt und die Kernphysiker die Geschichte radikal ändern. Aber wenn es keinen Vernichtungskrieg der Menschheit gibt, die Menschheit keinen Selbstmord verübt, dann müssen Sie mit 40 Jahren Berufsleben rechnen. Aber in sehr vielen Berufsformen wird heute beobachtet, daß die Lebenserwartung eines Berufs etwa 20 Jahre ist. In den Zeiten der alten Römer sagte man: Das Leben ist kurz, die Kunst ist lang. Damit meinte man den Ärzteberuf von damals. Die Ärzte von damals hatten nicht sehr viel gelernt, also auch nicht sehr viel umzulernen. Aber heute ist das Leben länger als der Beruf, heute überleben die Menschen ihre Berufe, so wie bereits in der letzten Generation, sagen wir zwischen 1940 und 1970, die Mehrheit der Menschen ihre Regierungen überlebt hat. Früher haben die Staaten und die Dynastien lange gedauert, und das Leben der Menschen war kurz. Aber zwischen 1940 und 1970 waren die Regierungen, die

Monarchen, die Regierungssysteme und die Kolonialreiche alle kurzlebiger als die Menschen.

Sie müssen sich also überlegen, daß Sie, vielleicht sogar mit einer gewissen Wahrscheinlichkeit, Ihren Beruf mindestens einmal wechseln müssen. Es kann noch passieren, daß die Staatsform wechselt. Es kann passieren, daß manche Wirtschaftsgesetzgebungen oder Reformen wechseln. Es könnte sogar sein, daß ein größerer Teil der Kultur- oder Sozialordnung wechselt. 40 Jahre sind eine lange Zeit. Gehen Sie von heute zurück, und überlegen Sie, wie Europa und Amerika 1938 aussahen und wie sie heute aussehen.

Da Sie sich auch nach Ihrem Eintritt in den Ruhestand nicht sofort umbringen wollen, werden Sie wahrscheinlich noch mindestens 10 Jahre und womöglich länger leben wollen. Das ist ein halbes Jahrhundert. Gehen Sie 50 Jahre in die Zukunft. Überlegen Sie sich, wieviel Umlernen jeder von Ihnen brauchen wird. Ich kann auf keine 50 Jahre mehr rechnen, aber ich habe allerhand Umlernen durchgemacht und werde wahrscheinlich noch einiges mit Umlernen unternehmen können. Denken Sie also einmal, was Ihnen jetzt schon als Zukunft in die Augen sieht; Berufswechsel ist nur ein Punkt.

Der andere Punkt heißt: Bereit sein zum Gewohnheitswechsel. Die Welt ändert sich in ganz beträchtlichem Ausmaß und mit ganz beträchtlicher Geschwindigkeit. Um in dieser Welt durchzukommen, müssen wir als Individuen, als Gemeinschaften, als Völker, als Staaten, als soziale Gruppen, auch übrigens als Religionsgemeinschaften, uns anpassen oder irgendwie die ständige Änderung bewältigen. Es kann auch passieren, daß diese Änderungen die Kommunikation zwischen den Generationen abschneiden.

Ich bin froh, daß Prof. Rosenmayr und auch Graf Blücher finden, daß es nicht ganz so schlimm ist. Ein amerikanischer Autor, John R. Platt, schrieb, das Tempo der Veränderungen sei wie ein Messer zwischen die Generationen gefallen. Eine Anthropologin, Margaret Mead, sagte etwa:

> Wenn sich die Gesellschaft fast gar nicht ändert, ist es viel besser, alt zu sein als jung. Dann hat man nämlich viel mehr gesehen, und alles, was man gesehen hat, ist noch anwendbar. Wenn sich die Welt ein wenig ändert, dann ist noch viel von den Erinnerungen der älteren Generationen anwendbar. Aber es ist schon genug verschieden geworden, so daß die Jungen auch schon etwas wissen, und das macht das Gespräch zwischen den Generationen interessanter. Wenn sich die Welt aber sehr schnell ändert, dann könnte es passieren, daß sehr viel von dem, was die älteren Leute noch für normal halten, der Jugend bereits absonderlich vorkommt.

Ich kenne einen Nobelpreisträger, einen Volkswirtschaftler, der steif und fest glaubt, daß die ökonomische Welt von 1910 normal war, und der immer noch ein wenig darauf wartet, daß die Welt zu diesem Zustand der Normalität zurückkehrt. Ich schätze ihn sehr hoch: Er ist ein glänzender Volkswirtschaftler, hat große Leistungen vollbracht – und er verhilft mir dazu, mich jung zu fühlen.

Aber überlegen Sie einmal, wieviel Dinge eine Generation, eine Altersgruppe noch für selbstverständlich hält und wieviel andere Dinge eine andere Altersgruppe schon für selbstverständlich hält. Es ist nicht so weit gegangen, daß der Familienzusammenhang ganz zerrissen ist; er ist noch da. Aber es ist ein Problem, auf das Sie achtgeben müssen, und das führt uns zur dritten Form des Bereitseins:

Bereit sein zum gemeinsamen Handeln als Mitglieder in einer Familie, als Mitbürger im Ort, in der Stadt, im Land, in der Nation, im Staat, als Kollegen im Betrieb und sonstwo, überhaupt als zusammenarbeitende Menschen in Politik, Wirtschaft und Kultur. Das bedeutet, die Koalitionsfähigkeit behalten, und das ist schwer und kostspielig. Denn wenn das Leben zu kompliziert wird, tun wir mit ihm, was manchmal Mathematiker mit einer komplizierten Gleichung tun. Wenn sie in einer Gleichung zu viele Unbekannte haben und damit nichts Rechtes anfangen können, dann gibt es noch einen Trick: Setzen Sie einige Unbekannte gleich null und, wenn Sie wollen, einige andere gleich unendlich; was übrig bleibt, ist eine Gleichung, die Sie lösen können. Da die Mathematiker eher ehrliche Leute sind, nennen sie allerdings eine solche Gleichung eine degenerierte Gleichung. Viele Menschen sind versucht, wenn das Leben zu kompliziert wird, es mit Hilfe degenerierter Gleichungen zu bewältigen. Viele indiskutable Dogmen und Theorien sind solche degenerierten Gleichungen, wo man eben kurz entschlossen viele Lücken läßt und dann sagt: So einfach ist das alte, und nun man feste druff. Das kann in der Politik von rechts kommen, das kann von links kommen.

Wenn wir sagen: das ist vielleicht nicht gut genug, dann fragen wir: Was wird die Welt von uns verlangen? – Da Sie hier drei Tage haben und zahlreiche Fachleute hier sind, will ich mich auf mein besonderes Gebiet beschränken. Ich will Ihnen für den Rest der Aussprache von meiner Seite die Frage vorlegen: Was wird in den nächsten 20 und 40 Jahren die Welt von uns verlangen? Was wird die Welt von uns fordern? Welche Tatsachen kommen sichtbar heute schon auf uns zu?

Das erste, was auf uns zukommt, sind etwa 4 Milliarden Mitmenschen. Nach den gegenwärtigen Raten der Bevölkerungszunahme werden wir im Jahre 2010 ungefähr 7 Milliarden Menschen sein. Es könnte passieren, daß das bis 2020 dauert. Die Demographen sagen die Weltbevölkerung voraus. Ich habe ihre Voraussagen seit den dreißiger Jahren verfolgt. Sie haben eine Neigung, die Zukunft in ihren Voraussagen ein bißchen der augenblicklichen Gegenwart anzupassen.

Referat Deutsch

In den dreißiger Jahren sagten die Demographen eine geringe Bevölkerungszunahme der Vereinigten Staaten voraus. In den späten vierziger Jahren sagte man phantastische Bevölkerungszuwachsraten voraus. In den sechziger Jahren gab es große Aufregung über die Explosion der Weltbevölkerung. Jetzt, wo wir die Depression, eine Art Krise, haben, revidiert man die Projektion wieder herunter. Wenn die Wirtschaft wieder ein bißchen in Gang kommt, werden Sie sich wundern, wieviel Babies man voraussagt.

In Wirklichkeit nimmt die Geburtenhäufigkeit in den hochentwickelten Ländern ab, aber die Dörfler in Afrika, in Südasien, in Lateinamerika und in den arabischen Ländern werden die Gewohnheiten des Ehelebens nicht schnell ändern. Das ist eine Sache, die wir mit einer gewissen Sicherheit voraussagen können. Die Babies in Asien, Südamerika und Schwarzafrika werden weiterhin in Scharen geboren werden, aber da die Mütter in all diesen Ländern genauso wie die Mütter hierzulande ein engstirniges Vorurteil in dem Sinne haben, daß sie wollen, daß ihre Kinder überleben, werden sie darauf bestehen, daß man öffentliche Maßregeln trifft und medizinische Hilfen und Gesundheitsfürsorge einführt. Das geschieht überall in der Welt. Was man dann bekommt, ist der bekannte demographische Übergang.

In der traditionellen Gesellschaft sind die Geburten- und Sterberaten hoch, ungefähr gleich groß, und die Bevölkerung nimmt nicht oder wenig zu. Nun beginnt die Gesundheitsfürsorge, und daraufhin beginnt die Sterberate zu sinken bis zu einer bestimmten Höhe; denn unsterblich kann uns die Medizin noch nicht machen. Inzwischen geht aber das Eheleben weiter und damit eine gewaltige Zunahme der Bevölkerung. Nach einiger Zeit aber bemerken die Eltern, daß ihre Kinder am Leben bleiben. Man sagt, es wäre vielleicht besser, weniger Kinder zu haben und mehr für sie zu tun; man könnte sie sogar besser kennenlernen. Dann beginnt die Geburtenziffer zu sinken, und nach einer gewissen Zeit liegen Geburtenzahlen und Sterberaten wieder ziemlich nahe beisammen. Der Bevölkerungszuwachs geht also wieder zurück. Wenn Sie das Ganze sehen, dann sehen Sie einen demographischen Übergang.

Das Ganze hat einen kleinen Haken. Der Haken ist, daß die Zeit, in der die Bevölkerung stark zunimmt, etwa 100 Jahre dauert, und in dieser Zeit kann sich die Bevölkerung etwa vervierfachen, in manchen Fällen könnte sie sich verachtfachen. Die ganz hohen Fruchtbarkeitsziffern gibt es allerdings eher auf kleinen Inseln, auf den Antillen und sonstwo. Mexiko hat heute noch einen Bevölkerungszuwachs von 35 pro 1000; es ist wirklich mitten im Übergang. Da gibt es jetzt 64 Millionen Mexikaner, und man schätzt noch 7 Millionen illegal in den Vereinigten Staaten. Diesen Übergang kann man nicht kurzfristig durch Regierungsintervention stoppen oder ändern.

Die wichtigste Änderung, die wir kennen, ist, daß die Bevölkerung lesen und schreiben lernt, und zwar zu über 80 %. Ich kenne kein Land, das mehr als 80 % Lese- und Schriftkundige hat, in dem es in den fünfziger oder sechziger

Jahren mehr als 30 Geburten pro 1000 der Bevölkerung gab. Des Rätsels Lösung ist nicht, daß Druckerschwärze geburtenverhindernd wirkt, sondern daß die Frauen lesen und schreiben lernen. Die Frauen gelten bei allen Meinungsforschern als eher konservativ, und das ist auch richtig. Aber wenn die Frauen sich ändern, dann ändert sich die Welt. Wenn die Frauen in einem Lande anfangen, lesen und schreiben zu lernen, dann ändern sich die Familiengewohnheiten, und dann ändert sich etwas in diesem Lande ganz beträchtlich.

Wir müssen damit rechnen, daß wir zwischen 7 und 8 Milliarden Menschen haben werden, bevor sich das Gleichgewicht der Weltbevölkerung einpendelt. Es könnte sogar passieren, daß das in einigen Regionen der Welt weitergeht und die Weltbevölkerung nicht vor etwa 12 Milliarden Menschen zum Stillstand kommt. Vor einigen Jahren hat man sogar bis 16 Milliarden gerechnet, aber ich glaube, heute ist es realistisch, 12 Milliarden als Obergrenze anzunehmen. Man hat bis vor kurzem angenommen, daß das Bevölkerungswachstum auf dem Erdball etwa 2075 zum Stillstand kommt, plus/minus 25 Jahre. Heute kann man hoffen, daß wir das Gleichgewicht bereits im Jahre 2050 erreichen, wieder plus/minus 25 Jahre. Manche Kollegen erwarten einen früheren Stillstand, manche sagen, das geht noch eine Weile weiter. Diese Menschen müssen essen. Nehmen wir an, wir bekommen nicht mehr als 8 Milliarden Menschen und wir haben sie im Jahre 2020, also ungefähr gerade dann, wenn Sie 40 Jahre Berufstätigkeit hinter sich haben und bereit sind, in den Ruhestand zu gehen. Das heißt, daß für jeden Menschen, der heute zu essen bekommt, dann noch ein anderer etwas zu essen bekommen muß, möglicherweise dreimal am Tag. Wo soll das herkommen?

Das heißt, daß man die Nahrungsmittelproduktion der Welt verdoppeln muß. Kurzfristig scheint das gar kein Problem zu sein. In vielen Ländern gibt es noch ein bißchen Land, das man unter den Pflug nehmen könnte. Es gibt noch Verbesserungen der Landwirtschaft. Man könnte noch etwas mehr Getreide vor den Ratten schützen, man könnte noch etwas mehr Kunstdünger auf die Reisfelder legen. Aber die Nahrungszufuhr verdoppeln, das ist eine andere Geschichte. Es wird gehen. Wir haben ganz neue, sehr ertragreiche Sorten von Wunderweizen, Wunderreis und besonders fruchtbare Sorten von Mais, die die Hektar-Erträge ohne weiteres verdoppeln. Bevor ich „ohne weiteres" sage: Mit reichlicher Zufuhr von Wasser, mit viel mehr Kunstdünger, als je zuvor verwendet wurde, d.h. also mit viel mehr Aufwand.

Woher soll das Wasser kommen? Es regnet nicht immer dann und nicht immer dort, wo man es braucht. Man muß Staudämme, Kanäle, Bewässerungssysteme bauen, man muß riesige Massen von Erde auf allen Kontinenten bewegen, um die Bewässerung zu sichern.

Man muß viel mehr Kunstdünger erzeugen als je zuvor, und nicht alles wird aus Petroleum kommen können. Ganz soviel Petroleum wird es vielleicht in

20 oder 40 Jahren nicht geben. Man muß Stickstoff aus der Luft holen, und das bedeutet großen Aufwand an Energie und Fabriken für die Nitrogen-Fixierung, wie das technisch heißt. Das kostet alles Energie und Kapital, und man müßte noch für die Übergangszeit vorsorgen.

Es werden heute in der Welt etwa 400 Millionen Tonnen Brotgetreide geerntet, vor allem Weizen. Nach einer Studie des Wissenschaftszentrums Berlin könnte man mit etwa 6 Millionen Tonnen in Reserve beinahe garantieren, daß es in 99 von 100 Fällen keine große Hungersnot irgendwo geben wird. Wenn wir bereit wären, einmal in 20 Fällen Hungersnot zu dulden, brauchen wir weniger. 60 Millionen Tonnen sind ungefähr 14 % oder ein Siebtel der Welternte eines Jahres; das sollte möglich sein. Die Anweisungen, daß das gut wäre, stehen schon in der Bibel. Aber bisher haben mehr Regierungen die Politik der Frau Potiphar imitiert als die Nahrungsmittelpolitik des Josef. Als erstes müßten die hochentwickelten Länder Amerika, Kanada, England, die Bundesrepublik, die Schweiz, Frankreich, ein Scheunenprogramm einführen, eine Technologie, die tropensichere, ungeziefersichere, fäulnissichere Lagerstätten für große Mengen von Getreide schafft. Man könnte so den Entwicklungsländern helfen, zumindest einen Teil des Weltvorrats dort zu lagern. Denn wenn es eine Hungersnot in Bangladesh gibt, dann ist es gar nicht so leicht, all die Frachtdampfer aufzutreiben, um das Getreide dorthin zu bringen. Wenn man aber einen Teil des Getreides in den wahrscheinlichen Notstandsgebieten lagert, wird es etwas leichter.

Man könnte natürlich sagen: Das ist doch unklug, Getreide ist eine Waffe. Denkt doch daran, was für glänzende politische Konzessionen man aus den hungernden Völkern herauspressen könnte, wenn wir das Getreide für uns behalten. – Der erste Haken ist, daß die Russen das auch können. Denn die russische Getreideeinfuhr gilt heute den Hühnern und Schweinen. Die Leute essen dort auch lieber Fleisch als nur Kohl und Hirsebrei. Aber wenn es auf die Politik ankommt, kann die russische Regierung auch immer wieder ein paar Millionen Tonnen herbeischaffen; das hat sie in den vergangenen Jahren mehrfach getan. Außerdem, wenn man ein hungerndes Land mit Nahrungsmittellieferungen erpreßt, so bekommt man vielleicht Zugeständnisse, aber Liebe und Dankbarkeit bekommt man nicht. Der Wucherer in Notzeiten wird gehaßt, und der Nahrungsmittelwucherer in Hungersnöten wird noch mehr gehaßt als jeder andere Wucherer.

Ich glaube, daß es politisch unklug wäre, Getreide in Notzeiten als politische Waffe einzusetzen. Herbert Hoover hat 1920 Getreide nach Sowjetrußland geschickt, obwohl er den Bolschewismus des Lenin sehr verabscheute. Aber er dachte doch: Wenn Menschen verhungern, hilft man, und über Politik redet man später. Ich glaube, Hoover hat Recht gehabt. Wir können etwas tun, um schon bestehende Hungersnöte zu lindern oder wenigstens große Hungersnöte zu verhindern.

Aber die Dinge, die ich erwähnte, kosten Energie. Zugleich werden Rohstoffe knapp, und wir werden auf die Dauer noch weiterhin viel mehr Kapital brauchen. Man muß die Rohstoffe aus tieferen Lagen herausholen, oft vom Meeresboden. Man muß das Öl von dort holen. Man muß Kernkraftwerke bauen, und die müssen mit immer kostspieligeren Entsorgungs- und Sicherheitsmaßnahmen versehen werden. Man muß dafür sorgen, daß die Dampfleitungen nicht so leicht brechen und daß die automatischen Sicherungsgeräte nicht so leicht abgeschaltet werden können. All das kostet Geld. Es wird mehr Kapital in der Form von Metallen und ähnlichen Dingen und unsichtbares Kapital in den Köpfen der Menschen: einerseits in der Kenntnis von neuen Prozessen, neuen Forschungen, neuen Fertigungsmethoden, neuen Ersatzstoffen, neuen Technologien, andererseits im Trainieren der Menschen, so daß sie, wenn eine Rohrleitung bricht, besser wissen, was zu tun ist.

Man wird also die Qualifikation der Arbeitskräfte erhöhen müssen. **Wir müssen mehr produzieren**, wenn in der Welt der Zukunft, in der Sie leben werden, nicht Millionen verhungern sollen. Das erscheint mir völlig unausweichlich.

Bisher habe ich nur von Menschen, Tonnen Getreide und Kilowatt Energie gesprochen. Ich kann Ihnen sagen, wenn Zahlen Sie interessieren, daß der Energieverbrauch, der heute auf etwa 7 Terrawatt beziffert wird, bis zur Mitte des nächsten Jahrhunderts auf ca. 35 Terrawatt ansteigen wird; das ist der fünffache Energiebedarf. Vergessen Sie nicht, alle diese Dinge werden nicht heute oder morgen als sichtbar in der Zeitung stehen, im Gegenteil, es wird manchmal gegenläufige Entwicklungen geben. Plötzlich wird Getreide billig sein. Gelegentlich wird es zuviel Öl geben. Gelegentlich werden sich die Weizenhändler beschweren, daß es zuviel Weizen gibt. Aber die kleinen Wirbel sind nicht der große Strom. Man kann in Wirbeln sogar ersäuft werden, aber wenn Sie Ladungen verschiffen wollen, müssen Sie wissen, wo der Strom hingeht.

Ich sprach bisher von materiellen Tatsachen. Aber vergessen Sie nicht, daß sich die **Art** der Menschen in der Welt geändert hat und vor unseren Augen weiter ändert. Ich habe für diesen riesigen Veränderungsprozeß den Ausdruck „soziale Mobilmachung“ vorgeschlagen. Was ist das, Mobilmachung? Beim Militär heißt das, daß jeder Mann aus dem Haushalt herausgezogen wird. Da steht er nun mit seinem Koffer und muß zum Bahnhof, und dann ist er verfügbar für die Generalität oder für die Regierung, die ihn überall hinschicken kann, wo sie will; er ist mobil.

Man kann natürlich Leute auch für nichtkriegerische Zwecke mobil machen. Man macht sie heute in der Gesellschaft mobil für neue Produktionsweisen und neue Verhaltensweisen. **Soziale Mobilmachung** heißt also Loslösen von alten Gewohnheiten und alten Verhaltensmustern und zum Teil Loslösen von verhaltensmäßig starren Sozialbindungen. Das beginnt mit der Mobil-

machung der menschlichen Meinungsbildung. Jedes Kind, das je ein Flugzeug gesehen hat, ist ein bißchen anders als ein Kind, das nie eines sah; denn es weiß, daß Menschen fliegen können. Jeder Dörfler, der ein Lastauto vorbeidonnern hörte und sah, daß sich Menschen schneller bewegen können als Kamele, weiß mehr als seine Vorfahren wußten. Solche **Demonstrationseffekte** erfassen heute wahrscheinlich bereits die beträchtliche Mehrheit der Menschheit.
Um Ihnen nur vom Fernsehen her Zahlen zu geben: Man sagt, daß bei der Fußballweltmeisterschaft 650 Millionen Menschen, also ein Siebentel der Menschheit, zugesehen haben. Als die amerikanischen Kosmonauten auf dem Mond landeten und dort ihre staatsbeamtlichen Stiefelabdrücke hinterließen, haben 950 Millionen Menschen zugeschaut. Das heißt, ungefähr jeder vierte Mensch der Welt kann heute etwas im Fernsehen miterleben. Bertrand Russell sagte: Die modernen Demonstrationseffekte geben allen Menschen einen Begriff der möglichen Macht der Menschen, die es nie vorher in der Geschichte gegeben hat.

Keine Generation hat je gedacht, daß Menschen auf dem Mond spazieren gehen können. Man merkt nun, was getan werden kann. Das Radio, das Kino, das Fernsehen, die Presse, die Flugblätter, die Bücher, die Zeitungen, alle tragen dazu bei; die Ausdehnungsraten sind gewaltig. Seit der Erfindung der Schrift ist 1955 zum erstenmal in der Geschichte der Welt die Mehrheit der Menschen lese- und schriftkundig geworden; heute sind es über zwei Drittel der Menschheit, am Ende des Jahrhunderts werden es 85 oder 90 % sein. Alle 10 Jahre wechseln 7 Prozent der Menschen von den Analphabeten zu den Schriftkundigen. Da die Menschheit zahlenmäßig zunimmt, muß die Zahl der Analphabeten für einige Zeit nicht absolut abnehmen, aber relativ nimmt sie schon lange ab.

Dann gibt es das tägliche Verhalten. Drei Viertel der Welt benutzt heute Geld. Das war früher auch nicht so häufig. Die Leute haben heute an vielen Plätzen wöchentlich Märkte, wo es früher keine Märkte oder nur einen Markt im Jahr gab. Das deutsche Wort Jahrmarkt sollte Sie noch daran erinnern. Natürlich könnte man, wenn man wollte und das Geld hätte, täglich einkaufen. Aber Märkte haben sich ungeheuer ausgebreitet.

Steuern werden heute von neun Zehnteln der Menschheit erhoben. Etwa nur ein Drittel oder ein Viertel der Menschheit zahlt direkte Steuern, aber irgendwie werden Steuern heute überall gesammelt.

Der Militärdienst erfaßt ungefähr ein Viertel der Welt, d.h. ein Viertel der jungen Männer sind irgendwie der Verpflichtung zum Wehrdienst unterworfen, auch wenn man nicht alle tatsächlich einzieht.

Etwa die Hälfte der Kinder der Welt im Schulalter gehen heute tatsächlich zur Schule.

Bei Wahlen einer oder der anderen Art machen etwa zwei Drittel der Menschheit mit, wenn nicht mehr. Nun gibt es natürlich Wahlen, wo es, wie in Rußland, nur eine Kandidatenliste gibt, oder, wie in Brasilien, wo es eine Regierungspartei und eine Opposition gibt; wie mir ein brasilianischer Freund erklärte: Die eine sagt zur Regierung ja, und die Opposition sagt jawohl – aber dennoch sagen auch dort die Wahlen dem Staatsbürger: Deine Stimme wird gewünscht, auf Deine Stimme kommt es an. Das hat kein türkischer Sultan seinen Bauern und Schafhirten in der Vergangenheit gesagt. Heute wird es überall auf der Welt den Menschen in steigendem Maße gesagt.

Dann kommt der Auszug aus der Landwirtschaft. Alle 10 Jahre ziehen im Weltdurchschnitt 7 % der Beschäftigten der ganzen Welt aus der Landwirtschaft ab. Die Mehrheit der Menschen ist heute nicht mehr in der Landwirtschaft beschäftigt, das erste Mal seit Erfindung des Ackerbaus.

Die Beschäftigung der Menschen ändert sich. Ein Drittel oder ein Viertel der Welt ist heute in Lohnarbeit, viele davon in Fabrikarbeit. Ein berühmter Soziologe, Alex Inkeles, sagt uns, daß, wenn jemand 10 Jahre in der Fabrik arbeitet, sich seine Ansichten, seine Verhaltensmuster, die Dinge, die er für selbstverständlich hält, ziemlich gründlich ändern. Sein Buch heißt „**Becoming Modern**“ und ist 1974 erschienen, auf einer Studie von sechs Ländern aufgebaut.

Es gibt überall auf der Welt Verstädterungen. Heute lebt vielleicht schon die Mehrheit der Menschen nicht mehr in Dörfern, sie lebt in Kleinstädten, Mittelstädten und Städten. Es gibt riesige Wanderungen. Viele davon erscheinen nicht in den internationalen Statistiken, weil es Binnenwanderungen sind. Aber dennoch finden diese Wanderungen statt.

Wenn Sie all das zusammennehmen, können Sie sagen, daß der Mittelwert all dieser Mobilisierungsprozesse etwa 7 % in 10 Jahren oder 3/4 % pro Jahr beträgt. Wenn man das in Rechnung stellt, dann sieht man, daß die Mehrheit der Menschheit am Ende dieses Jahrhunderts ziemlich gründlich mobilisiert sein wird.

Aber mobilisiert sein heißt neue Nöte und neue Hoffnungen haben, neue Ansprüche empfinden. Die neuen Nöte: Wenn man nicht in der traditionellen Großfamilie auf dem Dorf lebt, ist Gesundheitsfürsorge eine politische Frage. Wenn man nicht mehr irgendwo in einem Wald lebt, dessen Bachwasser man ungestraft trinken zu können glaubt, dann ist die Trinkwasserbereitung und die Wasserreinhaltung eine politische Frage.

Dinge, die früher nicht politisch waren, werden heute politisch. Modernisierung heißt Politisierung des täglichen Lebens. Das ist eine unerhörte Änderung, in den Dingen, die die Menschen brauchen.

Wenn man in der Großfamilie lebt und sehr alt wird, sollen sich die Kinder und Enkel um einen sorgen. Das ist übrigens ein Grund, warum in der traditionellen Gesellschaft die Geburtenraten so hoch sind. Wenn man nicht mehr in der Nähe der Familie lebt oder wenn man weniger Kinder hat, dann muß man sich über Renten und Alterspensionen den Kopf zerbrechen. Die Sanierung der Renten ist nicht nur ein deutsches Problem. Ein Freund von mir hatte die Altersversicherung in einem Land eingerichtet, wo es keinen Familiennamen gab und ungefähr jeder dritte junge Mann Achmed hieß. Da mußte man den Leuten Nummern geben, um ihre Sozialfürsorgekonten in Ordnung zu halten. Aber es ging; die Leute haben heute eine Sozialversicherung, wenn auch eine einfache.

Die Welt ändert sich, sie wird politisch, und zugleich sehen die Menschen, was sie versäumen. Die Welt ist ungleich und arm, aber sie ist noch mehr ungleich, als sie arm ist. Innerhalb eines Landes wird eine Ungleichheit von etwa 10:1 als leicht tragbar empfunden, also der Unterschied vom Reichsten zum Ärmsten der Bevölkerung. Eine Ungleichheit von 15:1 wird noch ohne Weiteres ertragen, eine Ungleichheit von 20, 30, 40:1 ist schon schwierig. In der Welt ist der Grini-Index der Ungleichheit berechnet zwischen den Staaten über 80:1, nach der Bevölkerung gewichtet über 60:1. Das heißt, die Welt ist so ungleich wie nur einige der allerschlechtest regierten Länder. Kein Wunder, daß die Welt unstabil ist.

Zuleich gibt es dabei noch die Ausbreitung der Wehrfähigkeit. Überall auf der Welt bringt man den Leuten bei, wie man schießt. Das machen die Regierungen und die Staaten. In Europa hat man das allgemeine Schießenlernen der Bevölkerung im 19. Jahrhundert eingeführt, d.h. die allgemeine Wehrpflicht. In Frankreich fing es mit der Revolution an, in Preußen machten es Scharnhorst und Gneisenau, nachher Bismarck und die preußische Monarchie. Und wie doch der Zufall spielte: als man allen Männern des Volkes das Schießen beibrachte, kam auch bald der Wohlfahrtsstaat. Man kann nicht der ganzen Bevölkerung das Schießen beibringen und dann erwarten, daß sie still verhungert. Das geht nicht über Nacht, aber wir nähern uns der Zeit, wo das auf dem Erdball nicht gehen wird. Einerseits lernen die Völker, mit konventionellen Waffen umzugehen, und der militärische Vorsprung der hochentwickelten Länder ist sehr zusammengeschrumpft. Englische Kanonenboote können nicht mehr auf den Yangtse-Fluß fahren; das letzte solche Boot entkam mit knapper Not im Jahre 1947. Man kann heute nicht mehr eine Handvoll Soldaten in ein Araberland schicken und sagen, nehmt euch doch die Ölquellen. Der Kampf, der herauskäme, wäre zu teuer, und nicht viele Ölbrunnen würden ihn überleben. Nachdem in Amerika einige Politiker 1973 davon sprachen, hat man es dann schleunigst aufgegeben. Israel ist ein modernes Land, Ägypten war es nicht. Aber 1973 haben sich die beiden Länder gegenseitig ganz beträchtlichen Schaden zugefügt. Das geht jetzt auf der ganzen Welt so. Überall auf der Welt verschwindet der Machtvorsprung bestimmter Länder, und dabei breiten sich nicht nur die konventionellen Waffensysteme aus, sondern ungefähr alle 11 Jahre hat sich bisher die Zahl der Atomwaffen besitzenden Länder verdoppelt. Heute haben wir offiziell 7 Länder, von denen das bekannt ist. Vielleicht gibt es ein achtes oder neuntes, das sie schon im stillen hat; das wissen wir nicht. Gegen Ende des Jahrhunderts werden es vielleicht 15 sein. Im Jahre 2020 werden es 50 oder mehr sein. In keinem dieser Länder können wir uns leisten, das Volk zur völligen Verzweiflung zu bringen.

Die Zeit der Kolonien ist schon vorbei. Die Unhaltbarkeit der direkten Rassendiktatur ist fast überall offenkundig gewesen. In Rhodesien und in Südafrika gibt es Überreste, in Mozambique und Angola sind sie schon verschwunden. Es gibt andere Übelstände in diesen Ländern, aber die Rassenherrschaft ist nicht mehr da, und ich glaube nicht, daß sie jemals wiederkommen wird. Es war das Unglück des deutschen Volkes, daß eine Nazi-Regierung einem Volk eine Rassenherrschaft als begehrenswert angeboten hat gerade zu einer Zeit, wo sie auf dem ganzen Erdball unhaltbar wurde.

Denken Sie einmal an ein Staatsgespräch im Jahre 2000. Der indische Premierminister, nennen wir ihn Desai-Gandhi, kommt nach Bonn und spricht mit dem deutschen Bundeskanzler, Herrn Schmidt-Kohl, und sagt: Sehen Sie, wir sind eine sehr gemäßigte, vernünftige, verfassungsmäßige indische Regierung, aber es droht uns eine furchtbare Hungersnot. Wir brauchen dringend Wirtschaftshilfe, und die 0,29 % des deutschen Volkseinkommens – ihr gegenwärtiger Beitrag – helfen da wirklich nicht sehr viel. Wir brauchen viel mehr Wirtschaftshilfe. – Darauf sagt Herr Schmidt-Kohl: Das würden doch die Leute meiner Partei – welche immer das wäre – nicht mitmachen, und die Wähler machen das auch nicht mit, die sind ganz dagegen. Die sind damit beschäftigt, daheim das verbesserte Modell des Farbfernsehens einzuführen, und wir können nicht für verhungernde Inder noch soviel Geld verschwenden. – Ja, sagt Herr Desai-Gandhi, das verstehe ich schon. Aber leider gibt es in meinem Land eine furchtbar radikale Partei, das sind die Revolutionär-Konservativen, geführt von einem Mann, der erzreligiös ist, dem im Traum die Göttin Kali, die Göttin des Todes, erschienen ist. Wenn wir keine Hilfe bekommen, würde meine Regierung selbstverständlich gestürzt, denn leider hat der Verehrer der Göttin Kali viele Anhänger unter den jüngeren Offizieren des indischen Heeres, der Luftflotte und der Unterseeboot-Streitkräfte. Wenn das passiert, wird meine Regierung gestürzt, und wir bekommen ein Regime von Desperados, die vor nichts zurückschrecken. Möchten Sie dann die Verantwortung dafür übernehmen? Ich kann es nicht. – Was soll Herr Schmidt-Kohl antworten?

Denken Sie an ein ähnliches Gespräch im Weißen Haus, sagen wir bei Jimmy Carter-Ford. Würde er es verantworten? – Ich glaube, wir nähern uns einer Zeit, wo man keine großen Gruppen von Menschen, keine große Bevölkerung mehr zur Verzweiflung treiben kann. Es ist merkwürdig, aber die Verzweiflung großer Gruppen können wir uns nur dann noch leisten, wenn sie keine

Kernwaffen oder keine anderen Waffen der Massenvernichtung haben. Aber mit der Ausbreitung der modernen Wissenschaft und Technologie ist es unvermeidlich, daß auch diese Waffen früher oder später in die Hände der Menschen kommen. Wir können es verlangsamen, und das ist gut so. Aber ganz verhindern können wir es nicht.

Dann gibt es noch die Gefahren von Kriegen. Ich spreche von den Gefahren der Hungerkriege, den Gefahren der Einwanderungskriege. Was passiert, wenn ein Inder sagt: Amerika ist halbleer, und wenn die Chinesen sagen: Sibirien ist halbleer; warum wandern wir nicht dort ein? Es könnte sogar sein, daß irgendein hungriges Volk sagt, daß in der Eifel noch viel Platz wäre, und die Tibetaner könnten ihre Augen auf die Schweiz werfen.

Hungerkriege sind eine Gefahr, Glaubenskriege sind eine zweite. Im Augenblick haben wir keine wirklich fanatisch-kriegerische Religion. Es gibt keine Kreuzzüge mehr, und die Protestanten und Katholiken töten einander auch nicht mehr außerhalb Nordirlands. Aber irgendwie ergibt sich die Gefahr der Glaubenskriege ohne Gott. Die Leute, die nicht an Gott glauben, könnten sich massenweise wegen der richtigen Planung von Fabriken umbringen. Das nennt man Kapitalismus und Kommunismus. Prof. Šik hat Ihnen gezeigt, daß sie beide nicht sehr gut funktionieren, aber die Leute sind noch bereit, sich für diese Unterschiede umzubringen. Das wird eine Riesenaufgabe: die Verhinderung der Glaubenskriege der Gläubigen und der Glaubenskriege der Hoffnungslosen.

Lassen Sie mich zusammenfassen. Was vor uns liegt, ist ein Weg durch Engpässe. Ich nannte als ersten Engpaß das Bevölkerungswachstum und die Nahrungsmittelknappheit, als zweiten Engpaß die Knappheit von Energie und Kapital auf der einen Seite und, damit verbunden, die Schwierigkeit, daß, wenn mehr Menschen so leben wollen wie der Mittelstand, das bedeutet, daß sie mehr an Material und Energie verbrauchen.

Ein Demograph, Professor Nathan Keygitz, hat ausgerechnet, daß, wenn sich die Menschheit verdoppelt und sie alle wie arme asiatische Bauern leben wollen, es kein Problem wäre, für sie Platz und zur Not Nahrung aufzutreiben. Aber wenn sie wie Mittelständler leben wollen, dann gibt es nicht oder kaum genug Kupfer und andere Dinge. Wir haben aber den Menschen überall in der Welt eine Annäherung an die Lebenshaltung dieses Mittelstandes versprochen. Das war die große Antwort des Westens auf die Klassenkampf-Idee des Karl Marx und seiner Nachfolger.

Wenn sich aber herausstellt, daß es gar nicht so einfach ist, eine mittelständische Lebenshaltung für alle zu ermöglichen, dann gibt es wirklich Probleme, dann werden die Leute wieder auf die Klassenkampf-Ideen zurückkommen. Was können wir da tun?

Wir finden, es könnte zur Not gehen. Wir finden nach einer Studie am Wissenschaftszentrum Berlin, daß, wenn man ein pessimistisches Weltmodell des Club of Rome als Ausgangspunkt nimmt, sich herausstellt: wenn es gelänge, Energie- und Rohstoffprobleme um 3 % pro Jahr zu verbessern, erstens dadurch, daß man neue Quellen auftreibt, zweitens, daß man die Techniken, welche Rohstoffe und Energie verwenden, effizienter macht, drittens dadurch, daß man Substitut-Materialien entwickelt, Fiberglas statt Stahl, Kernkraft und später Sonnenkraft an Stelle von Petroleum – dann geht es. Ob man jeweils eine 3prozentige Verbesserung pro Jahr erreichen kann und für wie lange, wissen wir heute nicht, aber eine unserer Studien zeigt, daß es nicht unmöglich sein sollte.

Ähnlich steht es mit dem Engpaß der Umweltbelastung. Wenn die Umweltverschmutzung entsprechend der Industrieproduktion wächst, dann brauchte man etwa 2 % pro Jahr Verbesserung der Umwelttechnologie, um diese Gefahr zu bannen. Mit der 3prozentigen Verbesserung bei Rohstoffen und Energie und der 2prozentigen Verbesserung der Umweltbelastung ist das nächste Jahrhundert in ziemlich guter Form zu überstehen. Am Ende dieses Jahrhunderts hätte dann die Menschheit im Durchschnitt ungefähr den Lebensstandard, den heute Westeuropa hat, und in Westeuropa – das werden Sie mir vielleicht zugeben – läßt sich immerhin noch leben.

Es gibt einen Engpaß der **Solidarität**. Wenn man der Welt heute sagt: es ist nicht genug von allem da, was wir brauchen, und wenn die Menschen Solidarität empfinden, dann sagen sie: gut, dann werden wir die Dinge einteilen, den eigenen Verbrauch beschränken und den anderen helfen. Wenn sie aber keine Solidarität empfinden, dann sagen sie: jeder ist sich selbst der Nächste, das Hemd ist mir näher als der Rock, mein Volk vor allen anderen, mögen die anderen verhungern. – Da die anderen das auch sagen, gibt es dann die Vernichtungskriege der hungernden Völker gegeneinander, wie sie übrigens in seinem primitiven Denken Adolf Hitler in „Mein Kampf" vorausgesagt hat. Darin steht, daß die Zahl der Menschen blind zunehmen wird – er wußte noch nichts vom demographischen Übergang –, daß die Nahrungsmittelproduktion nicht einfach erhöht werden kann, daß die verhungernden Völker einander ausrotten werden und darum Hitler mit seinem Volk den Anfang machen müßte, die anderen auszurotten. – Es ist ein mörderisches Buch, aber es wurde damals in großen Auflagen verkauft.

Der Engpaß an Solidarität heißt, daß wir versuchen müssen, dafür zu sorgen, daß die Menschen lernen, etwas mehr ihre Schicksalsverbundenheit, ihre gegenseitige Abhängigkeit und ihre gegenseitigen Bedürfnisse nach Hilfe in ihre Denkgewohnheiten, in ihr Denken und Fühlen einzubauen. Ich glaube, so wie man von den Dörfern zur Nation kam, müssen wir in unserem Denken und Fühlen von den Nationen zur Menschheit kommen.

Referat Deutsch

Das wirtschaftliche Wachstum kann nicht aufgegeben werden. Die Lehre vom Nullwachstum ist heute eine Lehre für Völkerkriege und Bürgerkriege. Wir kommen in den hochentwickelten Ländern nicht ohne etwa 2 % Wachstum pro Jahr im Durchschnitt des Pro-Kopf-Einkommens weiter, denn sonst können wir die Versprechen sozialer Besserung an unsere arbeitenden Schichten nicht erfüllen. In den Entwicklungsländern wird man wahrscheinlich 4 % brauchen. Das kommt dann beim Volksvermögen der Erde auf etwa 3 % im Durchschnitt heraus.

Es ergibt sich ein Engpaß von Krieg und Frieden, den ich bereits erwähnt habe. Um diesen zu bewältigen, haben wir einen Engpaß von Forschung und Innovation, nicht aus Luxus, sondern aus Notwendigkeit. Wir können die 3 % Verbesserung an Rohstoffen und Energie nicht mit den alten Technologien herausholen. Wir brauchen neue Technologien, neue Substitute, neue Energieformen, von der Sonnenenergie angefangen. Das heißt aber, daß wir Intellektuelle brauchen.

Was ist ein **Intellektueller**? Das ist jemand, der bereit ist, in abstrakten Begriffen außerhalb seines Gebietes der Berufsspezifizierung zu denken. Nach diesen Begriffen gibt es seit Hans Sachs Schuster, die Intellektuelle sind, und es gibt Steuerberater, die keine Intellektuellen sind, weil sie nur die Steuervorschriften abstrakt im Griff haben, aber sonst nichts. Intellektuell ist der Mensch, der geübt ist, zwischen den Fachgebieten zu arbeiten, Fachgebiete miteinander in Verbindung zu bringen. Jedes Fachgebiet hat doch die Eigenschaft, daß die Entdeckungen, die in seiner Mitte angesiedelt werden, meist schon gemacht wurden und daß die möglichen Neuentdeckungen in Grenzgebieten sind. Neuentdeckungen und Intellektuelle aber sind nicht ein Luxus, sie sind eine Notwendigkeit für die Zukunft.

Dann haben wir den Engpaß der **Kohärenz**, der **Sinnstiftung**. Wir haben so viele Spezialprobleme, so viele Spezialaufgaben, so viele Spezialvergnügungen. Wie hängt das alles zusammen? Vor Jahren schrieb Kästner:

Die Spezies Mensch ging aus dem Leime, und mit ihr Haus und Hof und Welt. Ihr wollt, daß ich es zusammenreime, und glaubt, daß es dann zusammenhält.

Die modernen Dichter sagen es nicht mehr in Versen, aber sie sagen es ähnlich. Die Bezugslosigkeit, die Zusammenhanglosigkeit, die Gefahr des Sinnverlusts steht vor uns, und auch das ist eine geistige Aufgabe allererster Ordnung, nicht nur für Wissenschaftler, auch für die Künstler.

Dann gibt es den Engpaß der Anpassung und des **Entwerfens neuer gesellschaftlicher Einrichtungen**. Heute vormittag haben Sie Dr. Šik gehört. Es ist so, daß Gesellschaftsordnungen von oben gegeben sind, von einer Vorsehung oder von unserem Landesschicksal. Aber es ist auch nicht so, daß Gesellschaftsordnungen natürlich, organisch wachsen wie Kartoffeln. Sogar Kartoffeln kann man heutzutage verbessern. Man kann Gesellschaftsordnungen modifizieren, durch Denken und Handeln ändern. Was wir heute im Kampf der Ideologien von rechts und links haben, sind Konflikte zwischen Formen ungeduldiger Unwissenheit. Wir haben noch lange nicht angefangen, zu begreifen, wieviel man wahrscheinlich noch aus dem Marktsystem und dem Privatunternehmen herausholen kann, wieviel man auch Planungsmechanismen verbessern und vermenschlichen kann, welche Kombinationen noch machbar und möglich sind. Das wird ein gefährlicher Engpaß. Wir können uns in diesen Glaubenskriegen, von denen ich sprach, umbringen, oder wir können entdecken und lernen: die Zukunft ist offen, wenn wir durch die Engpässe durchkommen.

Wir werden in den nächsten 30 Jahren wahrscheinlich einige Hungerkatastrophen erleben, einige furchtbare soziale Umwälzungen, einige Bürgerkriege in Asien und Afrika, einige konventionelle Kriege zwischen kleinen Staaten. Ich glaube nicht, daß wir uns Kernwaffenkriege leisten können. Wir werden eine Zeitlang ein zweigleisiges Friedenssystem haben: Kriege zwischen den Ohnmächtigen und den Kleinen und knurrenden Frieden zwischen den Grossen. Aber schließlich werden wir, so glaube ich, durchkommen. Es gibt ein schönes Theaterstück von dem amerikanischen Dichter Thornton Wilder mit dem Titel „Gerade noch davongekommen". Nach Katastrophen, Engpässen, großen Sorgen, und in vielen Teilen der Welt nach furchtbaren Leiden, werden wir vielleicht auch noch sagen können: Gerade noch davongekommen.

Wenn Sie das für Optimismus halten, können Sie es ruhig tun. – Ich danke Ihnen.

Arbeitsgruppe Deutsch

Leitung: Volker Hoffmann

Hoffmann:

Ich begrüße Sie zu unserer Arbeitsgruppe von Professor Deutsch. Die Diskussion in der Arbeitsgruppe ist keine formelle Sache, Vorträge haben Sie heute schon reichlich gehört. Wir wollen deshalb den Versuch machen, ein offenes Gespräch zu führen, ohne von einer Leitung zu sehr bestimmt zu werden. Ich lade Sie also ein: fragen Sie! Sie sollen hier Gelegenheit haben, selber eine Aussage zu machen, sich vom Geist der Ausführungen des Referenten anregen zu lassen. Ich bin sicher, daß Sie aus dem Referat zahlreiche Aspekte aufgegriffen haben, die Sie nun vorbringen und vertiefen wollen.

Teilnehmer:

Ich kann es im Moment nicht anders formulieren, aber meine Frage läuft darauf hinaus, wie Sie die Lernfähigkeit des Weltsystems als Projektion in die nächsten 50 oder 100 Jahre beurteilen. Ich meine nicht die kurzfristigen Erscheinungen, sondern das, was notwendig an Innovationen ist, um die Stabilität zu erhalten.

Deutsch:

Im allgemeinen könnte man die Lernfähigkeit eines großen politischen oder sozialen Systems auf nationaler oder internationaler Ebene danach schätzen, wieviel operationale Reserven da sind, d.h. Reserven, die nicht festgefroren sind. Das Bild kommt aus dem Militärwesen. Wenn die Linien der Truppen sich nicht mehr bewegen, sondern fest sind, nimmt ein General eine Einheit als operationale Reserve, mit der man unerwartet neue Linien besetzen kann. Für die Welt als Ganzes müssen Sie also fragen: was sind operationale Reserven? Ich würde sagen: die Studenten der westlichen Länder zählen dazu. Aber seien Sie bereit, daraus auch die Konsequenzen zu ziehen!

Zuruf:

Aber wenn man nicht erkennt, daß die Reserve gebraucht wird?

Deutsch:

Ein vernünftiges Management läßt die Reserven nicht verkommen!

Zuruf:

Was macht man in der Zwischenzeit, während die Reserven lagern?

Deutsch:

Menschen kann man nicht lagern wie Kohlrüben. In Amerika gab es nach 1938 zehn Millionen Arbeitslose. Ich war damals erstaunt, daß die Regierung des Präsidenten Roosevelt ein System hatte, die Menschen zu motivieren. Es gab ein Bundestheater, da spielten Arbeitslose, arbeitslose Regisseure führten die Regie, arbeitslose Beleuchter sorgten für die Beleuchtung usw. Ähnlich wurden andere Künstler beschäftigt. Damals gab es viele vorwärtsweisende soziale Experimente in Amerika. Und jetzt, wo wir wieder eine Krise haben, wird es, fürchte ich, noch einige Jahre dauern, bis wir uns erinnern, was es schon alles einmal gab. Wichtig ist: man darf die Fertigkeiten der Leute nicht verkommen lassen.

Teilnehmer:

Glauben Sie, daß es eine Akademikerschwemme gibt, und wenn ja, glauben Sie, daß man mit Akademikern ein solches Beschäftigungsmodell machen kann wie in Amerika?

Deutsch:

Ich glaube nicht, daß es ernsthaft eine Akademikerschwemme geben wird, denn es gibt zu viele Dinge, die getan werden müssen. Aber wir haben eine Vorstellung, daß die hergebrachten Beschäftigungen und Positionen mit Recht aus öffentlichen Geldern finanziert werden können. Was da nicht hineinpaßt, soll auf den Wohlfahrtssektor gehen. Jedoch beklagt man sich dann über die Wohlfahrtskosten.

Zweitens fragten Sie nach dem wirklichen Bedarf. In Amerika hat die normale Schulklasse 25 bis 28 Kinder. Welches sind die Ziele der Schule? Daß die Kleinen ruhig sitzen und nicht zu lebhaft sind. Was geschähe, wenn die Schulklasse nicht 25 Kinder hätte, sondern nur 12 bis 18? Jedes Kind wäre dem Lehrer sofort mit dem Namen bekannt. Hier sehen Sie den Bedarf.

Hoffmann:

Darf ich eine Frage aufwerfen? Das Minderbegabtenproblem ist in der Diskussion noch nicht herausgekommen. Was geschieht mit denjenigen, denen Fähigkeiten und Begabungen fehlen?

Deutsch:

Ich habe da eine Erinnerung. Es war eine Fakultätsversammlung in einer der anspruchsvollsten Hochschulen der Vereinigten Staaten, in California. Im Jahr 1947 rief der Präsident uns alle zusammen: Er hatte festgestellt, daß der Leistungsdurchschnitt in allen Bereichen deutlich gestiegen war. Was war da los? Können Sie raten, was geschehen war? Die Veteranen waren zurück. Sie waren etwas älter. Sie hatten allerhand gesehen und erlebt. Die meisten waren

ECOLE DES AFFAIRES DE PARIS
– Niederlassung Düsseldorf –
c/o Universität Düsseldorf
4 Düsseldorf
Universität

verheiratet. Sie lebten in Wohnwagen und Blechhütten und hatten daheim eine Frau und ein Baby. Sie hatten eine beträchtliche Motivierung. Das war der Grund. Deshalb war der Durchschnitt beträchtlich besser.

Das zeigt doch, daß ein Teil des Studienerfolges die Begabung ist, ein Teil ist die Kultur von daheim, die Motivation. Wer zuhause ein Pfarrerssohn ist, hat gelernt, Bücher zu lesen. Wenn mein Vater Arzt war, habe ich Präparate in der Hand gehabt und gesehen, was im menschlichen Körper eine Rolle spielt. Wenn ich der Sohn eines türkischen Gastarbeiters bin, kann ich die gleichen Grundzellen, ein Erbgut von gleichguter Qualität haben, aber bis ich zuhause ein Buch finde und bis ich den Vater dazu bringe, es mit mir konzentriert zu lesen, kann ich lange warten.

Ein Wort zu dem letzten Punkt! Wir geben in Amerika und in Deutschland 2,3 % des Nationaleinkommens für die Forschung aus. Es wäre schön, wenn wir in 20 Jahren die Sonnenenergie hätten. In diesem Falle müßte der Forschung mehr geholfen werden. Was könnte nicht alles geschehen, wenn wir 4 % in die Forschung steckten? Für manche Sachen braucht man aber Genies. Man kann einen Einstein nicht auf das Budget eines Ministeriums setzen und sagen: „Werde ein Genie!".
Aber man kann, um eine Entwicklung zu beeinflussen, einige neue Tatsachen schaffen, auch vielleicht einige ungewöhnliche. Als es in Deutschland noch Tausende von Familien gab, die Hausmusik machten, als es Hunderte von Orgeln und den lutherianischen Kirchengesang gab, da gab es auch einen Johann Sebastian Bach.

In den Ländern, wo jeder Fußball spielt, ist auch mindestens die rein theoretische Wahrscheinlichkeit für einen Weltmeister.

Teilnehmer:

Sie haben vorhin in der Zusammenfassung Ihres Referates gesagt, man müsse eine auf Grundsätze festgelegte, aber flexible Grundhaltung haben, und es müsse über die Welt reflektiert werden. Wie stellen Sie sich das vor? Ich bin der Meinung, daß die Leute bei uns sehr materialistisch eingestellt sind, sehr auf ihren persönlichen Vorteil bedacht. Wie wollen Sie das dann realisieren?

Deutsch:

Man muß bedenken, Deutschland ist ein Land, das zerschlagen wurde. Ich habe die Trümmer gesehen. Aber ich habe auch gesehen, daß die inneren Verwüstungen größer waren als die äußeren. Jeder Mensch wollte zunächst wieder ein Haus haben, das ist immer die erste Sache, die Konzentration auf den engsten Kreis.

Vergessen Sie auch nicht: die Menschen haben viele Freunde, aber Ihre Frau hat nur einen Mann, und Ihr Kind hat nur einen Vater und eine Mutter. An diesen Stellen sind die Menschen unersetzlich. Das ist cin Unterschied. Es wäre schlimm, wenn man sich zwar für die Menschheit begeistern, aber für den Menschen selber nichts tun könnte.

Ein Wort zur Frage des Reflektierens, des Denkens. Es gab eine Zeit, da kannte man eine säuberliche Teilung zwischen sogenannten Kulturwissenschaften auf der einen Seite und den Naturwissenschaften auf der anderen Seite. Hegel hat darüber Gedanken entwickelt. Da gab es einen menschlichen Geist und eine Wirklichkeit, und der Mensch war auch ein Stück Natur. Inzwischen hat es eine Änderung in vielen Ländern gegeben. Mir fällt dazu ein Beispiel ein. Es gab einen Riesenkrach in Berlin um die revolvertragenden Anwältinnen, die in das Gefängnis kamen. Man überlegte, ob man einen Senator zum Rücktritt zwingen und ob man ein neues Gesetz machen solle. Ich war damals aus Amerika gekommen und habe gesagt: wenn man ein Gerät hat, das „piep-piep" macht, wenn ein großes Metallstück versteckt ist, dann hätten die Damen zwar mit ihrem Gesetzbuch durchkommen können, aber nicht mit dem Revolver. Das wäre so einfach gewesen.

Wir brauchen also einen Verbund zwischen Theorie und Praxis. Tiefgründigkeit und Abstraktionsvermögen, diese Fähigkeiten haben wir nicht verloren, und man braucht sie dringend, aber ein bißchen von einer gewissen Praxis könnte man auch gebrauchen, vor allem weniger doktrinären Inhalt.

Teilnehmer:

Sie haben einige mögliche Entwicklungen aufgezeigt. Mich würde interessieren: wie sehen Sie die Entwicklungen zu den Menschheitskatastrophen? Sehen Sie Möglichkeiten, den Menschen zu beeinflussen, dieser Entwicklung vorzubeugen?

Deutsch:

In unserer Zeit der Massenmedien haben wir gewissenhafte und anregende Schriftsteller, die beschreiben alle Katastrophen, die man nicht verhindert hat. Würde ein Journalist einmal ein Buch schreiben über die Katastrophen, die verhindert worden sind, er würde damit Geld verdienen. Auch Kriege, die verhindert oder schnell beendet wurden, gab es. Ich glaube, davon wird mehr noch in die Zukunft hineinwirken müssen, und je schneller das geschieht, desto besser.

Zuruf:

Aber sind wir dazu in der Lage?

Deutsch:

Man fängt irgendwo an. Jede Vorsorge, die getroffen wird, ist nützlich. Zum Beispiel haben die Schweizer ihre Landschaft sehr ordentlich geschützt. Sie haben nicht gewartet, bis sie kaputt war.

Arbeitsgruppe Deutsch

Es hat einmal ein Radikaler im 19. Jahrhundert gesagt, jede Zeit habe ihre Aufgaben und ihre Menschen, die sie lösen könnten. Das ist fast wahr. Es gibt eine ganze Menge von Fragen, die, einmal gestellt, von vornherein zu beantworten sind. Wir werden da auch weiterkommen. Wir müssen bessere Fragestellungen ausarbeiten. Wir werden mehr Mittel und Zeit aufwenden und mehr Aufmerksamkeit auf Arbeiten und Versuche richten müssen, die Lösungen bringen.

Teilnehmer:

Sie hatten vorhin in Ihren Ausführungen gesagt, daß die Welt in zwanzig Jahren höhere Anforderungen an die Menschen stellt. Glauben Sie, daß die Menschen eigentlich genügend darauf eingestellt sind, mit dem Leben auf den von Ihnen aufgezeigten Wegen fertigzuwerden? Ist es nicht so, daß auch heute schon Ansätze gefunden werden müssen, um morgen darauf vorbereitet zu sein?

Deutsch:

Das ist schon wahr. Das ist ein Punkt, den Herr Bell heute vormittag angesprochen hat, daß oft Sinn und Glück und Fortschritt nur in kleinen Gruppen erlebt wird. Aber Sie können Ihr eigenes Leben immer nur selber gestalten. Eine Zeitlang kann eine Gruppe Geborgenheit vermitteln. Aber der Mensch hat ein Gedächtnis. Er weiß, daß er geliebte Menschen verlieren kann. Er weiß, daß Liebe aufhören kann. Er weiß, daß nicht auf alle Verlaß ist. Er fürchtet, daß er nicht davon verschont bleibt. Das macht die Menschen unsicher.

Die jungen Menschen, die einander gern haben und sagen: „Wir müssen uns aufeinander verlassen können", die können ein Stück Glück und eine Sicherheit empfinden, aber sie müssen sich immer fragen: Wann kommt die nächste Alternative? Es gibt Augenblicke, wo man nicht kritisch sein darf, wenn man das Glück in der Hand hat. Sie können Ihr Glück überall suchen, in Spielautomaten oder in einer Sinfonie. Die Erfahrung zeigt, daß das Glück in einer Sinfonie haltbarer ist.

Sie können auch die Natur nehmen. Niemand hat beim Anblick eines Sonnenunterganges ein Gefühl des Unglücks empfunden. Es gibt sehr viele solcher Beispiele. Man kann da ganz beruhigt sein.

Teilnehmer:

Ich möchte einmal bei folgender Frage einhaken. Ich finde Ihre Ausführungen sehr idealistisch und sehr schön. Aber ich bin nicht so optimistisch wie Sie. Sehen Sie sich einmal an, wie die Schüler heute, z.B. wegen des Numerus clausus, hart herangenommen werden. Die sollen noch Sinfonien hören, obwohl sie für ihr Fach den Musikunterricht gar nicht mehr brauchen, wenn sie nicht gerade Musik studieren.

Sie haben geschildert, wie Künstler vor 30 Jahren beschäftigt worden sind. Aber sie können doch nicht hunderttausend arbeitslose Künstler im Theater beschäftigen. Wir haben heute die Situation, daß hunderttausend Jugendliche vor der Ausbildung bereits arbeitslos sind. Sie finden keine Lehrstellen. Das Problem ist heute nicht so einfach zu lösen wie damals.

Ich finde, nicht viele Verantwortliche haben eine solche Einstellung wie Sie. Ich habe solche Antworten wie von Ihnen von Politikern nicht gehört.

Deutsch:

Dann sollten die Politiker von Ihnen lernen. Warum warten Sie auf die Politiker? Sie sind jung, Sie wissen doch, wo der Schuh drückt.

Sehen Sie im Numerus clausus mal etwas Angenehmes. Wenn Sie das Fach wählen wollen, das Sie gern haben, muß er Sie nicht unbedingt hindern. Wenn Sie nicht Rot und nicht Blau bekommen können, dann nehmen Sie doch Violett! Vielleicht wird jemand dann Pharmakologe oder Biochemiker. Man muß auch lernen, seine Ausbildung nach den bestehenden Möglichkeiten einzurichten. Die Diktatoren – von Hitler angefangen – haben Ihre Studienpläne doch noch ganz anders verdorben. Damals haben doch unheimlich viele Leute umgesattelt.

Teilnehmer:

Ich glaube, man muß das Problem von der anderen Seite sehen. Sie haben immer gesagt, das idealistische Denken sei sehr wichtig. Das ist das Problem, vor dem wir stehen. Die Jugendlichen sind einem totalen Leistungsstreß unterworfen. Bestimmte Leistungen müssen erbracht werden. Wir haben die Regelstudienzeit, da wird man nur auf einem engen Pfad sein Wissen produzieren und dafür ein Diplom kriegen. Das ist doch nicht das, was Sie wollen!

Deutsch:

Die Prüfungsnoten sind normativ, man kann sie nicht weglassen. Sie sind eine Art Konsumentenschutz. Im Geschäftsleben brauchen Sie so etwas auch, wenn Sie ein Hühnerei der Güteklasse IA als großen Luxus verkaufen oder kaufen wollen. Auch beim Zahnarzt gibt es Qualitätsunterschiede; das haben wir alle einmal erlebt.

Ich glaube, die Studenten könnten einmal eine bessere Methode ausarbeiten, wie man Leistungen richtig identifiziert. Man könnte neue Noten für Prüfungen schaffen, einmal für die schriftlichen Arbeiten, wenn man sie als Ganzes bewertet, und zum anderen für die gefürchteten amerikanischen „objektiven Tests“. Diese haben einen Vorteil: Die Studenten lesen die Bücher, die sie interessieren. Bis zum Prüfungstag haben sie vieles gelesen, nur nicht das, was vorgeschrieben war. Das stellt man schnell fest. Beim objektiven Test nützt ihnen alles, was sie gelesen haben. Der objektive Test ist der Freund des Eigenbrötlers. Das habe ich immer wieder festgestellt. Ich habe auch festgestellt, wie wichtig es ist, keinem Auswahlverfahren zu trauen. Viele Prüfungsmethoden bieten deshalb die Möglichkeit, nach jeder Stufe eine zweite oder dritte zu machen und zu zeigen, daß man es doch kann. Das ist viel wert. Man traut nie einer einzigen Methode.

Zuruf:

Also sind Sie der Meinung, daß man es in der Bundesrepublik ändern sollte?

Deutsch:

Sie leben ja hier, schlagen Sie es vor!

Sie können doch sagen: Wir wollen eine menschlichere Studienordnung, eine flexiblere Prüfungsordnung, eine zweite und dritte Chance, und Sie bekämen das. Es ist doch Ihre Universität. Sie sind doch hier. Sie sind eine Million Leute.

Teilnehmer:

Sie haben wahrscheinlich die Entwicklung im Auge, wie es in Deutschland zur Zeit ist, mit der Regelstudienzeit. Ich streite nicht ab, daß man auf diese Weise ein Studium machen kann. Aber nach den acht Semestern hat man eine Prüfungsordnung mit mathematischen Methoden. Ich kenne Referendare, die haben an vier Unis studiert, in den USA und überall. Das ist für uns heutzutage unmöglich.

Deutsch:

Jeder Student, der seine Regelstudienzeit in acht Semestern schafft, kriegt zwei Semester, in denen er studieren kann, was er will. Das halte ich für richtig, denn es ist ein Unterschied, ob man Gelder für Leute ausgibt, die Leistungen zustande bringen oder die erst anfangen.

Ich hatte mal einen Bekannten, der ging zum Dekan und sagte: Da ist ein Student, der berechtigt zu Hoffnungen, geben Sie ihm eine Chance. – Die Antwort lautete: Wenn Sie die acht Semester hinter sich haben, gehen Sie zum Guerilla-Theater und studieren Sie Dramatik, wenn Sie es können.

Teilnehmer:

Aber im Moment ist es ja so, daß von vornherein die Initiative untergraben wird, weil die Leute sagen: Ich muß in der Regelstudienzeit fertigwerden, weil die Firmen mich nur bis zum 28. Lebensjahr einstellen.

Deutsch:

Mein Ratschlag: Überlegen Sie, was kann ich aus dieser verdammten Situation noch herausholen, was kann ich lernen, was mir oder anderen Menschen helfen könnte? Das geht, wenn ich ungefähr weiß, was ich kann und was ich nicht kann. Um das herauszufinden, braucht man eine gewissen Zeit. Versuchen Sie 'mal, das in der Regelstudienzeit herauszukriegen! Wenn die Studienzeit unbegrenzt lang wäre, würden die Menschen alles mögliche andere machen. Das geht nicht. Das kann man den Leuten, die acht Stunden am Tag in der Fabrik sind, nicht zumuten.

Teilnehmer:

Ich will nicht sagen, daß es unmöglich wäre, so etwas zu machen. Aber die Tendenz geht dahin, daß die Leute weniger studieren und auch weniger Initiative zeigen. Aber Sie haben gesagt: Wir brauchen viel mehr Initiative und einen weiteren Blick.

Deutsch:

Wenn Sie einen konkreten Plan haben, ist das eine Sache, die Sie Ihrer Regierung vorschlagen können.

Zuruf:

Das ist ein Vorschlag, aber wird er realisiert? Das ist doch die Frage!

Deutsch:

Sicher! Denn Parteien brauchen Stimmen. Schlagen Sie es einmal vor! Wenn man Sie nicht umbringt, werden Sie vielleicht für die deutsche Politik tätig sein. Eine Partei, die auf Sie nicht Rücksicht nimmt, wäre sehr unintelligent. Nur, wenn Sie Dinge vorschlagen oder verlangen, die ein Gewerkschaftssekretär nicht verstehen kann, ist es sehr schwer, sich bei ihm durchzusetzen. Die Studenten sollen schon mitreden. Aber es geht nicht, daß man sagt: Ich will möglichst viele Scheine für möglichst wenig Kenntnisse bekommen.

Teilnehmer:

Ich finde, das Problem entsteht schon am Anfang des Studiums. Da taucht eine unheimliche Schwierigkeit auf, was die Literatur angeht. Man steht vor dem Problem, aus einer ungeheuren Komplexität auszuwählen. Das ist für den einzelnen unüberschaubar. Deshalb wäre es meines Erachtens notwendig, erst ein Orientierungsstudium zuzulassen, ein Studium, bei dem man zunächst einmal in die Sache hineinriecht, auch praktisch. Das Studium generale ist verlorengegangen.

Arbeitsgruppe Deutsch

Deutsch:

Das kommt hinzu. Die Orientierung ist zum großen Teil dem einzelnen überlassen. Sie können nicht einen Zusammenhang von der Fakultät her erwarten, den sie nicht gelernt hat herzustellen. Es gibt viele Kollegen von mir, die alle glänzende Fachleute sind, aber darunter sind nur wenige, die einen solchen Sinnzusammenhang herstellen können. Einen großen Teil müssen Sie selber machen.

Teilnehmer:

Herr Professor Deutsch, ich glaube nicht, daß die Frage der Regelstudienzeit das zentrale Problem der Jugend ist. Wir sprechen nur von den Hochschulabsolventen, aber nicht von dem Problem der Arbeitslosigkeit. Für Sie existiert das Problem nicht, oder es läßt sich einfach lösen.

Ich frage mich, was mit den Nicht-Hochschülern geschieht bzw. mit denen, die einen Ausbildungsplatz suchen. Welche Beschäftigungsmöglichkeiten haben diese Jugendlichen nach ihrer Ausbildung? Darüber hinaus stellt sich die Frage, die Herr Hoffmann vorhin schon angesprochen hat: Was geschieht mit den Jugendlichen, die noch nicht einmal berufsreif sind, die also keinen Schulabschluß haben, die Sonderschüler, die Problemgruppen des Arbeitsmarktes? Welche Zukunftsperspektiven haben diese Schüler?

Teilnehmer:

Ich meine, das ganze Dilemma kommt daher, daß in einem so starken Maße Kenntnisse vermittelt werden, die als Wissen abgefragt werden, und daß viel zu wenig versucht wird, ein beschränktes Maß an Informationen zu ermitteln, die in der Praxis verwertet werden können. Was in dieser Beziehung in Deutschland den jungen Leuten beigebracht wird, ist recht gering hinsichtlich der Anwendbarkeit.

Deutsch:

Fertigkeiten sind stets schwieriger und teurer zu vermitteln als bloße Gedächtnishilfen. Aber die akademische und nichtakademische Arbeitslosigkeit sollte man nicht als nebensächlich abtun. Es gibt sehr viel mehr Leute, die gern Schauspieler würden, als es Schauspielplätze an den Theatern der Bundesrepublik gibt. In Amerika gibt es mehr junge Leute, die Journalisten werden wollen, als es im Fernsehen und bei den Zeitungen Stellen für sie gibt. Das ist die Frage der Verteilung der Wünsche, der Ausbildungsplätze und der möglichen Arbeitsplätze. Wenn man die Leute fragt, welche Hoffnungen und Wünsche sie haben, kann man schon sehen, wie sie fröhlich werden: Mein erster Wunsch wäre dieser oder jener Arbeitsplatz, der zweite ist der, und der dritte der.

Denken Sie daran, wieviel Sie tun könnten! Es gibt eine Art Beruf, die ist eine

Berufung. Wenn ich diesen Beruf bekomme, ist es gut. Wenn ich ihn nicht bekomme, bin ich unglücklich. Wenn ich ihn aber bekomme und er mir nicht gefällt, bin ich noch unglücklicher. Das kann man den Leuten ein bißchen beibringen, indem man von vornherein sagt, wie die Arbeitsplatzsituation ist. Aber dann müßte auch die Regierung dafür verantwortlich sein und sagen: wir können nicht jedem den Arbeitsplatz garantieren, den er gerne hätte. Aber es müßte genügend Arbeitsplätze geben. Das könnte man schon verlangen. Ich könnte mir vorstellen, daß die jüngeren Jahrgänge in einer Stadt oder in einer Region sich zusammensetzten, um zu sehen: wie bringen wir die Wünsche und die Ausbildungsplätze und die Arbeitsplätze unter einen Hut? Es ist schwer, solange nicht alle es einsehen.

Teilnehmer:

Ich habe gerade das Abitur gemacht, in einem Hamburger Gymnasium. Ich habe es am eigenen Leibe erlebt, was es heißt, eine Berufsplanung nicht verwirklichen zu können. Ich habe von vornherein auch eingesehen, daß man immer mehrere Alternativen haben muß. Aber das zweite Berufsziel hat auch nicht funktioniert. Deswegen kann ich mir vorstellen, daß man mit Ihrem Vorschlag nur eine wahnsinnige Mittelmäßigkeit erreicht, weil die Leute Berufe ergreifen, für die sie sich nicht berufen fühlen.

Deutsch:

Es muß keine Mittelmäßigkeit sein. Ich hoffe, es klingt nicht wie eine hohle Phrase: Man kann es versuchen. Es gibt Leute, die sagen: Wenn ich 40 Jahre lang etwas gemacht habe, dann mache ich es gut. Man kann den Willen haben, es gut zu machen. Es kann sein, daß Sie, statt Sozialpolitik zu studieren, gelernt haben, Kinder zu betreuen. Vielleicht können Sie das ganz besonders gut. Man sollte sich zunächst von sich selber ein Bild machen. Vielleicht meint man, man könne nur eine Sache machen. Aber ich kann Ihnen sagen, daß die Leute in vielen Berufen vor starken Änderungen stehen, in Facharbeiterberufen und anderen. Auch wenn sie gerade für diesen Beruf eine Berufung hatten. Das ist zwar eine Gefühlslage, die ich respektiere, aber sie entspricht einer Welt, in der Berufe länger dauerten als Menschen. Das war damals. Heute ist es umgekehrt. Da gibt es einen Beruf, aber die Leute werden ihn überdauern. Sie sind da und die Welt ist da. Deshalb sollte man den Leuten das Beste geben, was sie brauchen. Aber es kann in verschiedenen Jahren sehr verschiedenes sein.

Teilnehmer:

Eine höherwertige Ausbildung wird immer Leute verdrängen, die eine geringere Ausbildung hatten. Was soll man zu denen sagen, die ihre Probleme nicht artikulieren können, die es nicht gelernt haben, auch in den veränderten Verhältnissen fit zu sein, wie Sie in Ihrem Vortrag gesagt haben?

Arbeitsgruppe Deutsch

Deutsch:

Die Leute in dieser Stufe, die sich nicht fit halten können, sind heute Randgruppen, z.B. Gastarbeiter und ...

Zuruf:

Die Gastarbeiter können es erst recht nicht, aber es gibt große Teile der Bevölkerung, die sich immer noch nicht artikulieren können!

Deutsch:

Man kann nicht jemanden in einen Betrieb schicken: „mach das" und dann ist er glücklich. Dazu ist ein Prozeß erforderlich. Es kann lange dauern, und es wird mühsam sein. Aber Sie können wirklich das Leben in die Hand nehmen. Sie können sich fragen: was kann ich mit meiner Zeit, mit meinen Fähigkeiten, mit meinen Kräften tun, damit ich nicht der Gefangene meines Berufes, meiner Arbeit bin? Es ist auch nicht so, daß ich selbst nicht den Weg finden könnte. Einigen steht eine klare Berufslaufbahn bevor. Die wissen in jedem Augenblick, wohin sie wollen. Man hat Beschränkungen, man hat unfaire Hindernisse im Weg. Aber Sie sind nicht Sklaven dieses Systems. Ich bin sicher, Sie werden schon etwas finden.

Teilnehmer:

Ich würde Ihnen in einem großen Bereich Ihrer Ausführungen zustimmen. Aber es tauchen Probleme auf, wenn eine ganze Nation nur noch verwaltet wird. Wir kurieren nicht mehr etwa an Symptomen, sondern nur noch an der Oberfläche. Da muß man nach den Lösungen fragen, die die Politiker empfehlen.

Deutsch:

Sie können in Ihrer Lage von der Politik mehr verlangen als nur, daß wir eine Vollbeschäftigung haben. Die alten Leute hätten auch lieber stabile Preise statt einer Inflation. Da ist der eine 25, der andere 60, aber beide haben ein großes Interesse daran, daß es Vollbeschäftigung und stabile Preise gibt. Aber wenn die Alternative zu einer chronischen Arbeitslosigkeit das Schwächen und Schädigen der Arbeitsmotivation einer ganzen Generation junger Menschen ist, dann, glaube ich, müßte man ernstlich an der Entwicklung verzweifeln.

In Süddeutschland gab es vor vier Wochen einen Streik, weil die Gastwirte überhaupt niemanden mehr kriegen konnten, der im Gastgewerbe helfen wollte. Trotz der großen Arbeitslosigkeit. Meine Tochter war Kellnerin in Amerika während ihres Studiums. Sie hat es sich damit finanziert. Bei uns gibt es nicht die Meinung, daß es eine unehrenhafte Arbeit wäre. Aber bei uns gibt es manches an Arbeit, was nicht der Brahmanenkaste entspricht. Da haben wir die deutschen Brahmanen! Gibt es überhaupt unzumutbare Berufe?

Körperliche Arbeit ist nichts Schlimmes. Jemand kann sein ganzes Leben lang Kellner bleiben. Man kann auch für einige Zeit alles mögliche ausprobieren. Es gibt viele Sparten, in denen Bedarf herrscht. Es kann auch sein, daß Sie zur Regierung gehen, wo die Vollbeschäftigung geplant wird. Aber Sie können die Vollbeschäftigung nicht ernsthaft diskutieren, ohne die Beschäftigungstour zu kennen, auch die Zumutbarkeitsfrage. Man kann nicht zu den Brahmanen gehen und sagen, ich muß als Brahmane höherwertig beschäftigt werden. Das geht nicht einmal in Indien.

Teilnehmer:

Ich möchte ein bißchen wegführen aus dieser Diskussion. Wenn man Ihnen, Herr Professor, zuhört, meint man, es sei alles vielleicht nicht in bester Ordnung, aber es geht schon, wenn man sich bemüht. Soweit ich sehe, ist aber besonders in der Studentenschaft die Initiative weitgehend verschwunden. Jeder schaut auf seine eigenen Hände. Er sieht zu, daß er drankommt. Das gesellschaftsbewegende Bewußtsein ist großenteils verschwunden.

Deutsch:

Wenn das der Fall ist, warum sind Sie dann hier? Seien Sie froh! Im Bewußtsein seines Wertes sitzt der Kater auf dem Dach.

Sie haben als Student in Ihrem Umkreis viele Gelegenheiten. Es ist schon besser, man hat Freunde und Kollegen, kann mit ihnen die Dinge besprechen und anpacken. Das hilft sogar für die Prüfungen; man kann miteinander wiederholen und sich auf das Examen vorbereiten.

Aber das Problem, das Sie hinsichtlich der Studenten angeschnitten haben – daß sie von einem Ausbildungsplatz verdrängt werden oder daß sie andere verdrängen –, das gibt es für alle jungen Leute. Eines ist sicher: keine Gesellschaft kann es sich leisten, große Mengen der jungen Generation ohne Ausbildung und ohne Arbeit zu lassen. Das kann sich auch die unsere nicht leisten. Das muß man mit der Vollbeschäftigung schaffen. Daran ist wirklich nichts zu ändern.

Teilnehmer:

Wenn man Sie hört, muß man die Meinung bekommen, daß alles in bester Ordnung sei. Das ist so, als wenn man einem Ertrinkenden rät, sich am eigenen Schlips herauszuziehen. Sie sagen: Dann muß die Regierung helfen.

Deutsch:

Wer ist denn die Regierung?

Teilnehmer:

Die Regierung sind wir auch, sicher. Aber die Machtkonstellationen sind doch wohl ein bißchen anders verteilt.

Deutsch:

Dazu kann ich Ihnen nur sagen: Macht beruht vor allem auf der Billigung der Macht durch die Beherrschten. Macht kann ich nur ausüben, wenn die anderen mitmachen. Macht entfremdet. Wird sie von außen her aufgezwungen, ist sie ein schlechtes Mittel, eine Ordnung herzustellen oder zu erhalten. Die Gefahren sind akut, und sie werden mit der Zeit noch schlimmer. Das habe ich heute nachmittag zu sagen versucht. Es kann schauerlich gefährlich werden. Aber man kann etwas tun. Es gibt immer etwas, was man tun kann. Wir haben dazu die Demokratie und das Grundgesetz. Was haben die Leute für einen Heidenschreck bekommen durch die Grünen Parteien! Aber was geschähe, wenn es eine „Vollbeschäftigungs-Partei" gäbe? Oder wenn die Leute sagten: Wir wollen stabile Preise, wir wollen eine Anti-Inflations-Partei!

Auch Arbeitsplätze kann man nur durch eine ausgewogene Politik bekommen. Es geht nur, wenn die Betroffenen sich selber auf die Hinterbeine stellen. Die Arbeitslöhne und die Arbeitsgesundheit würden besser, aber auch die Karrieren würden besser.

Teilnehmer:

Sie sagten, der Unschuldige wird aufgehangen. Diesen Satz möchte ich einmal auf die Kinder übertragen. Die Kinder werden doch so erzogen, wie die Erwachsenen es wollen. Wie können sie sich denn da verteidigen?

Deutsch:

Wir haben immer wieder gesehen, daß es eine nicht zu unterschätzende Resistenz der jungen Menschen gibt. Die Eltern können alle möglichen Dummheiten machen, aber meist sind die Auswirkungen bei den Kindern gering, manchmal sogar positiver als man denkt. Sie erholen sich von den Torheiten ihrer Eltern, sie erholen sich auch von den Torheiten ihrer Lehrer – und von den Lügen ihrer Regierung.

Teilnehmer:

Aber wie ist es denn mit denen, die das nicht erreichen? Die kennen doch ihr Schicksal nicht!

Deutsch:

Ich kann nur sagen: So viel Sie können, helfen Sie! Man kann den geistigen und seelischen Widerstand wecken. Wo Sie es nicht können, besteht keine Chance, daß das moralische und geistige Leben gehalten werden kann. Aber heute gibt es noch Hunderte von Chancen.

Tun Sie, was Sie können. Sie können nicht alle retten. Aber retten Sie so viele, wie Sie können! Wenn Sie das Optimismus nennen, stimmt es vielleicht sogar, aber es ist wirklich so: Sie müssen durchkommen. Das ist alles, was Sie tun können. Bringen Sie so viele Zeitgenossen durch, wie Sie können.

Teilnehmer:

Sie haben gesagt, wir müssen etwas tun. Aber soweit ich blicken kann, bietet die heutige Jugend dazu gar keine Ansätze. Wenn man von der Jugend spricht, stellt man zunächst einmal fest, sie ist in zwei große Gruppen geteilt. Die einen sind die, die Weltflucht begehen mit Rauschgift oder irgendwelchen Sekten. Die anderen sind die, die sich anpassen und die Angst um ihren Arbeitsplatz haben.

Deutsch:

Aber das sind doch zwei Extreme, die Sie da geschildert haben. In allen Zeiten haben sich Leute dem Alkoholismus ergeben und sind auch den Sekten nachgelaufen. Die Sektiererei ist meist das letzte Mittel für die armen Teufel, die nicht mit dem Leben fertigwerden.

Anpassung ist nicht Gleichschaltung. Die Studenten, die Jura studieren, passen sich an. Die werden in der Regelstudienzeit fertig. In Amerika müssen Sie es, weil es nicht anders geht wegen der Prüfungen. Und sie wenden eine Extrazeit als Studenten auf und verraten ihren Mitmenschen, wie sie sich gegen Schwindeleien, gegen Ratenagenturen, gegen Hausbesitzer usw. schützen können. Vielleicht machen sie später eine Anwaltsfirma oder Steuerberatungspraxis auf. Um weiterzukommen, arbeiten sie einen Tag in der Woche für das öffentliche Wohl. Sie gehen nicht einem Beruf nach, aber sie tun etwas. Man kann also ordentlich seinen Lebensunterhalt verdienen.

Eines ist ganz sicher, und das gilt auch für Sie. Wenn Sie in den vier Jahren Studienzeit Jura gelernt haben, wissen Sie etwas. Aber wenn Sie nur die verschiedenen Drogen ausprobiert oder nur die verschiedenen Sekten durchstudiert haben, dann wissen Sie nach vier Jahren nicht viel mehr als vorher und können den anderen Menschen wenig nützen.

Teilnehmer:

Darin stimme ich Ihnen voll zu. Aber die Realität sieht anders aus. Es ist so, daß geradezu eine Flucht begangen wird.

Deutsch:

Ich weiß das, aber ich kenne noch mehr Leute, die weder Drogensüchtige noch vollkommene Egoisten geworden sind. Die sich mit Anstand ihren Lebensunterhalt verdienen, sich sogar noch um ihre Familien kümmern und zugleich für den Frieden und nicht für den Krieg sind. Leute, die darüber hinaus gelernt haben, ihre Ressentiments nicht aufzubauen, sondern abzubauen, sich um soziale Dinge zu kümmern und darum, wie man die Städte schöner und anständiger macht. Ich kenne eine Menge solcher Leute. Sie setzen sich für das ein, was sie für gut und wahr und richtig halten.

Es gibt doch Möglichkeiten zu arbeiten, ohne die Integrität und die Aktivität zu verlieren. Da kann man immer einiges machen. Wenn Sie in einer entsetzlichen Diktatur lebten, wäre es schwer. Aber in der Bundesrepublik sind Sie nicht so eisern umklammert, es ist doch ein Rechtsstaat.

Teilnehmer:

Vielleicht sollte man einmal folgendes überlegen. Es gibt doch eine große Gruppe, die nicht betroffen ist, die ihre Ausbildung beendet hat und inzwischen im Erwachsenenstadium ist. Man sollte überlegen, ob man von dieser Seite nicht etwas machen kann. Die Situation sieht doch bedrohlich aus: Die Jugendarbeitslosigkeit, die Orientierungslosigkeit, das ist bedrohlich. Man sollte überlegen, ob man nicht von einer anderen Seite Werte und Ziele vorgeben kann.

Deutsch:

Es könnte ja sein, daß in Deutschland die älteren Menschen sagen: Diese Jugendarbeitslosigkeit kann nicht unbegrenzt weitergehen. Die Politiker sagen es uns auch. Ich muß ihnen glauben, daß der Umfang des Problems so groß ist, wie er dargestellt wird. Das ist psychologisch ganz bedrückend.

Teilnehmer:

Ich glaube, alles, was hier angesprochen wurde, betrifft das Problem der Flexibilität. Man hat früher versucht, Probleme der Studenten an den Hochschulen innovativ zu lösen. Heute muß der Student reflektieren, was in den Skripten steht. Es gilt als tugendhaft, möglichst viel daraus zu lernen. Wer den Inhalt der Skripten am besten reproduziert, schreibt die besten Arbeiten. Die Professoren erkennen nicht einmal, daß die Studenten Innovationsprobleme haben. Neue Inhalte können sie nicht einmal einfügen, es paßt überhaupt nichts, weil man sich an den Schemata orientieren muß, die in den Skripten standen. Wir stellen doch fest, daß einfach die Möglichkeit nicht mehr da ist, die notwendige Flexibilität auszuüben, nicht einmal, diese Flexibilität zu erkennen.

Deutsch:

Sie meinen, das sei eine neue Erscheinung. Keineswegs. Das hat es schon vor hundert Jahren gegeben. Man kennt doch all die unruhigen Köpfe aus dem 19. und der ersten Hälfte des 20. Jahrhunderts. Sie kamen alle aus Universitäten, wo man nach Skripten studieren mußte. Ich kann mir nicht vorstellen, daß es eine Universität in Europa gäbe, wo die Leute innovativ lernen.

Teilnehmer:

Herr Professor, ich wollte deutlich machen, daß eine Tendenz dazu vorhanden ist, daß die Schüler bereit sind, einen ungeheuren Aufwand zu erbringen, in acht Semestern fertig und gute Fachleute zu werden, daß sie dazu ihre Skripten gut auswendig lernen. Aber sie lernen nicht, zwischen den Zeilen zu lesen und innovativ Probleme zu lösen.

Deutsch:

Ich frage mich, wie kann man dieses Wunder fertigbringen, junge Leute so zu beschränken, daß sie wirklich beschränkt werden? Beschränkte Prüfungsmethoden hat es seit 100 Jahren gegeben. Ich höre zum erstenmal, man müsse die Beschränkung auch innerlich annehmen.

Letzter Punkt: Mikroprozessoren! Man kann doch die Mikroprozessoren verwenden, um unfähige Leute herauszuwerfen, zu überwachen oder zu unterdrücken. Man kann sie auch noch auf andere Weise verwenden. Stellen Sie sich vor, daß es einen Büroschalter mit drei Knöpfen gibt, die ein Besucher nach der Erledigung seines Anliegens betätigen muß. Der eine Knopf besagt: Die Bedienung war mittelmäßig. Der andere Knopf besagt: Die Bedienung war sehr schlecht. Der dritte Knopf besagt: Die Bedienung war ungewöhnlich gut, ich war sehr zufrieden. Der Mikroprozessor nun schreibt die Ergebnisse auf. Wenn ein Beamter als zu unangenehm empfunden wird, kommt jemand und schaut nach. Wenn ein Beamter gut war, kommt auch jemand und prüft, ob der Beamte nicht Freunde hinbestellt hat, um diesen Knopf zu drücken.

Ich versuche Ihnen bewußt zu machen, daß es unglaubliche Möglichkeiten für den Menschen gibt, daß noch in jeder Situation Ansätze für gute Lösungen vorhanden sind.

Teilnehmer:

Das ist theoretisch vielleicht machbar. Aber Sie sehen nicht die praktische Seite! Daß Jugendliche dazu in der Lage sind, muß nicht selbstverständlich sein. Auch die Generation, die vor uns war, war ja nicht dazu in der Lage.

Deutsch:

Wenn Sie nicht gemerkt haben, daß ich versuchte, Ihnen einige Ziele und Werte vorzuschlagen, haben Sie nicht viel gemerkt. Vielleicht meinen Sie die grossen Ziele: Abschaffung des Krieges, Abschaffung der Hungersnöte. Es gibt nicht gerade einen Mangel an großen Zielen. Wenn einem daran liegt, Zielen zu dienen, dann ist kein Ziel unwichtig. Wie sorge ich für die Leute, die von mir abhängig sind? Wie kann ich Menschen helfen, die zum Glücklichsein meine Hilfe brauchen?

Ich erinnere an Buchenwald, Dachau und Meidanek. Wer jemals einen dieser

Orte gesehen hat, wer weiß, was der Mensch den Menschen angetan hat, der muß sich doch fragen: was wäre aus der Welt geworden, wenn Hitler zehn Jahre länger Atombomben gebaut hätte!? Stellen Sie sich vor, was Heinrich Himmler und Göbbels mit Atombomben gemacht hätten!

Und ich sage Ihnen: Was heute auf uns zukommt, ist vielleicht ein bißchen besser, aber nicht viel. Ich hoffe, es wird nicht so schlimm wie im Dritten Reich oder im Zweiten Weltkrieg. Aber es kommen ganz schwere, ganz gefährliche Zeiten, in denen man Sie unerhört brauchen wird.

Sie stehen vor dem Problem, Ihr eigenes Leben in einer höchst unvollkommenen Demokratie so einzurichten, daß Sie durchkommen, ohne Ihre eigene Dignität zu verlieren und ohne Ihre Solidarität verkümmern zu lassen. Aber man muß durchkommen. Wenn Sie nicht durchkommen – und anderen nicht helfen können –, würde Ihre Integrität versteinern und wirkungslos bleiben. Sie müssen Fertigkeit und Fähigkeit dazu entwickeln. Es geht nicht anders. Vielleicht haben Sie an diese kleinen Dinge nicht gedacht, aber sie sind nicht zu klein. Denken Sie an die phantastischen Probleme, die auf uns zusteuern. Sie werden unerhört gebraucht! Aber es hat keinen Zweck, dies von jenen Leuten zu verlangen, die mit knapper Not durch die damalige Krise gekommen sind.

Das Merkwürdige ist: bis 1930 kam es nicht so sehr darauf an, was eine Generation von Leuten machte. Es lief alles ziemlich automatisch. Die Dampfmaschinen wurden verbessert, die Eisenbahnen wurden gebaut. Aber seit 1930 ist das Schicksal der Welt immer wieder auf des Messers Schneide gewesen. Ich fürchte, es wird in den nächsten 40 oder 50 Jahren immer wieder auf des Messers Schneide stehen.

Teilnehmer:

Sie müssen aber davon ausgehen, daß es eine breite Masse von Jugendlichen gibt, die einfach nicht die Sicherheit hat, von sich aus etwas zu tun, die einfach zu unsicher sind. Es ist einfach gesagt: Ihr müßt das machen, ihr müßt ausbrechen und eigene Initiativen zeigen. Es wird zwar eine gewisse Schicht geben, und die meisten, die hier sind, werden diese Initiative zeigen, aber es gibt einen großen Prozentanteil in der Jugend, der die dazu erforderliche Sicherheit nicht hat.

Deutsch:

Das ist ein Stück der großen Kulturänderung. Jung sein, heißt unsicher sein; heißt aber auch, große Möglichkeiten haben. Ich hoffe, daß es Ihnen gelingt, auch Ihren Kollegen. Es wird nicht bei allen gelingen, aber bei einigen.

Wichtig ist dabei, daß Sie die Solidarität mit den Schwächeren nicht aufgeben. Die Integrität und die Solidarität scheinen mir zwei ganz wichtige Dinge zu sein. Wichtig ist auch, daß Sie die Jagd nach Posten und Beförderung nicht überbewerten. Wofür lebt man denn eigentlich, wenn nicht für andere Menschen? Wenn man nicht für andere Menschen leben kann, kann man auch nicht sehr glücklich sein.

Teilnehmer:

Sie sagen immer wieder, daß man im Kleinen etwas ändern kann. Das ist aber nicht das Ausschlaggebende, das die Zukunft beeinflußt. Darin sehe ich das vordringliche Problem: Man muß sich gegen die Bürokratie durchsetzen, möglicherweise gegen Gewalt.

Deutsch:

Ich habe den Vorschlag gemacht, Rückkopplungskreise anzulegen: von den Beherrschten oder den Klienten hin zum Bürokraten. Ich habe einen elektronischen und einen menschlichen Weg vorgeschlagen. Dann gibt es demnächst Beurteilungsformulare, die die Studenten ausfüllen und darin ihre Lehrer beurteilen. Das wäre eine primitive Form einer Rückkopplung.
Aber dazu gehört auch die Frage, wie man dezentralisiert. Wieviele Schalter soll man in Dienststellen öffnen? Es gibt eine Warteschlangentheorie. An der Harvard-Universität hat es eine mathematische Untersuchung über die Bürokratisierung gegeben. es gibt eine Menge Literatur, auch Manuskripte. Der Ansatz ist da, und damit ist zu arbeiten. Die Frage ist aber auch hier wieder: Wir haben so viele Politologen, Soziologen und Psychologen, die hervorragende Leitartikel schreiben. Aber wir haben sehr wenige, die sagen: Wie kann man etwas ändern? Wir brauchen mehr „Designer". Wie entwirft man das? Irgendjemand hat einmal erfunden, daß man die Steuern zahlt. Irgendjemand hat das Bundestheater erfunden. Es gibt so viel Raum für Erfindungen. Wir sprechen immer von „Schöpferkraft". Zum Kuckuck, versuchen wir sie doch! Man soll es nicht als Bastler mit Kleinigkeiten versuchen. Aber die großen Änderungen, z.B. hinsichtlich der Vollbeschäftigung, die sind wichtig.

Teilnehmer:

Das ist einfach eine Frage zwischen Risiko und Sicherheit. Die Studenten wählen heutzutage die Sicherheit. Sie wollen in acht Semestern fertigwerden. Deshalb meine Frage: Sind es nicht die Studenten, die durch Verzicht auf das Risiko eben diese Situation schaffen und hinnehmen müssen?

Deutsch:

Es gibt auch eine andere Art, sein Studium zu planen. Ich weiß nicht, wo es in der Studienordnung steht. An den großen amerikanischen Universitäten z.B. haben sie alle die Regelstudienzeit. Das ist vollkommen normal. Die Studenten bleiben zwei Jahre, vier Semester. Dann sagt mancher: es wird zuviel, und er kommt und möchte ein Jahr Urlaub nehmen. Er geht nach Arizona als Landvermesser und kehrt sonnengebräunt zurück. Er hat sein Brot halbwegs verdient. So macht man das in Amerika. Man kann Urlaub nehmen, man kann das Studium unterbrechen; oder man kann sagen: ich mache acht Semester.

Versuchen Sie doch etwas anderes! Wir haben es im Augenblick schwer, Bewerber für die guten amerikanischen Stipendien zu kriegen, weil die Leute zu ängstlich sind. Da kann man studieren, was man will. Das ist notwendig. Sie müssen sich nicht alles gefallen lassen. Der Versuch ist es wert. Entweder kann ich in acht Semestern nicht mein Mindestpensum schaffen, oder ich kann nicht schöpferisch denken. Dann kann ich auch nicht frei studieren. Somit stehen Sie vor einer falschen, unerträglichen Alternative. Aber Millionen Leute haben es erfahrungsgemäß fertiggebracht. Leute wie Sie sind unfähig zu sagen: Du kannst nicht in acht Semestern fertigwerden. Oder: Du kannst dir nicht die Integrität und die Schöpferkraft erhalten. Das scheint mir eine unbrauchbare Alternative zu sein.

Teilnehmer:

Sie erkennen nicht, daß Sie die junge Generation nicht mehr verstehen, und sie Sie auch nicht.

Sie sehen alles so unproblematisch. Sie sagen so ein bißchen: es wird schon weitergehen. Aber wie soll ich mich in eine andere Richtung bewegen, ohne gleichzeitig das Ziel ändern zu müssen? Da muß ich doch Widerstände bekommen.

Deutsch:

Sicher. Ich habe Ihnen das zu sagen versucht. Arbeiten Sie auf der gesellschaftlichen Ebene, das kann die Gemeinde, das kann der Staat, das kann die Weltpolitik sein. Versuchen Sie, soweit Sie können, die Dinge zu ändern, die schlecht sind. Das müssen Sie tun! Das ist wirklich wichtig! Eine unpolitische Welt gibt es nicht. Zugleich dürfen Sie nicht vergessen, daß Sie auch Ihre eigene Ausbildung betreiben müssen, daß Sie Ihre eigenen Fertigkeiten entwickeln müssen. Das ist eine schwierige Balance. Das heißt nicht, daß Sie ein amerikanischer Selfmademan werden müssen. Ich habe auch versucht, Ihnen etwas über Solidarität zu sagen.

Zuruf:

Das ist etwas, was es in der Jugend nicht gibt!

Deutsch:

Ist das wahr, daß Sie einander nicht mehr helfen?

Teilnehmer:

Das gibt es nur in kleinem Kreise. Aber sich nach außen zu artikulieren, das ist sehr schwer. Wer die Studenten da oben vertritt, das sind doch ideologische Gruppen. Ein Student, der sich um solche Sachen wie Arbeitsplätze Gedanken macht oder über ein anderes Studium, der ist dort völlig fehl am Platze. Er gibt nach kurzer Zeit auf.

Teilnehmer:

Die Studenten übernehmen einfach den Begriff der Verdrängung, der so einfach nicht stimmt. Es wird niemand verdrängt. Sondern was stattfindet, ist eine Auslese. Wir haben die vorgegebene Anzahl von Ausbildungsplätzen nicht nur in den Betrieben, sondern auch an den Hochschulen. Das ist eine Größe, die ist vorgegeben. Das hat dazu geführt, daß man sich bei der Auswahl für eine bestimmte Gruppe entscheidet. Was stattfindet, ist nicht eine Verdrängung, sondern eine Auslese.

Teilnehmer:

Vorhin hieß es, daß die Ausgangsbedingungen Schuld seien. Jetzt ist es die Auslese. Dazu muß man sagen, daß es historisch gesehen immer einen Wettbewerb gegeben hat. Auch wenn die konditionalen Ausgangspositionen annähernd egalisiert sind, wird sich die Pyramide aus Know how, Technologie und Intelligenz nicht wie eine Säule nach oben fortpflanzen, sondern sich verdünnen. Wenn aber nicht alle die gleichen Ausgangsbedingungen haben, wie sollen sie dann die gleichen Endpositionen erreichen?

Teilweise merkt man auch hier die Mentalität einiger Studenten, die schon unzufrieden sind, wenn sie nicht sofort eine Staatsposition auf Lebenszeit bekommen. Sie möchten bis zum 60. Lebensjahr ihren Schreibtisch haben, sie brauchen dann nicht mehr nachzudenken und unterliegen keiner großen Auslese in einem freien System. Wenn sie aber keinen Job bekommen, resignieren sie. Dazwischen auf die Idee zu kommen, irgendetwas zu verkaufen oder eine Würstchenbude aufzumachen, eine eigene Idee zu verwirklichen, das ist bei vielen nicht mehr drin. Oder sie denken nicht daran. Das ist das verbreitete Versorgungsdenken, daß der Staat für alles da ist, daß der Staat bei jedem Problem angegangen werden kann. Vom Staat wird gefordert, daß er die Probleme löst. Das ist eine gefährliche Entwicklung. Deshalb wird es wahrscheinlich immer weniger Eliten geben.

Teilnehmer:

Ich meine, wir machen es uns zu leicht, wenn wir sagen, es müssen andere Wege gefunden werden. Wenn da von Studenten geredet wird, die unzufrieden seien, warum kann man die denn nicht zu einer Minderheitengruppe mobilisieren?

Arbeitsgruppe Deutsch

Teilnehmer:

Die kann man nicht mobilisieren!

Zuruf:

Du bist doch kritisch! Warum kannst du deine Kritik nicht mobil machen?

Deutsch:

Sie haben die Auslesefrage angesprochen. Es gibt verschiedene Arten der Beschäftigung, die dabei unterschieden werden müssen. Es gibt Arbeiten, bei denen die Qualitätsunterschiede sehr stark und auch sehr folgenschwer sind. Lesen und schreiben kann jeder. Das zu erlernen, ist vollkommen möglich. Aber für bestimmte Berufe gibt es Auslesen. Es wäre eine Denkarbeit für Sie, festzustellen, wo und wann ein Ausleseverfahren im Interesse derjenigen notwendig ist, die sich einer bestimmten Dienstleistung anvertrauen, und wo ein Ausleseverfahren Unfug ist, weil es gar nicht notwendig ist. Weil es sich um eine Sache handelt, die jeder können sollte. Ich glaube, damit kämen Sie weiter als mit der allgemeinen Verdammung des Ausleseverfahrens.

Zusammenfassung Arbeitsgruppe Deutsch

Die Arbeitsgruppe mit Prof. Deutsch war gekennzeichnet von einer äußerst lebhaften und freien Diskussion. Das lag zum größten Teil an dem völlig „unprofessoralen“ Verhalten von Prof. Deutsch, der es verstand, eine harmonische, fast freundschaftliche Arbeitsatmosphäre zu schaffen, in der Zurückhaltungen oder gar Hemmungen gar nicht erst aufkommen konnten.

Zum anderen Teil brannten die angesprochenen Problemkreise den Teilnehmern auf den Nägeln. Das wurde sehr schnell deutlich. Es ging ja auch zum großen Teil um Themen wie „Akademikerschwemme“, Regelstudium, Numerus clausus, fehlendes Orientierungsstudium oder mangelhafte Prüfungsmodalitäten; Themen also, die die jungen, vorwiegend akademischen Teilnehmer veranlaßten, die tagtäglich auf sie zukommenden Schwierigkeiten darzustellen und anzuklagen. Prof. Deutsch konnte zuhören und verstehen. Seine Antwort aber verblüffte, ja schockierte seine jungen Zuhörer und rief zum Teil lebhaften Widerspruch hervor.

Immer wieder rief er die Jugend auf, initiativ zu werden, ihre Probleme selbst in die Hand zu nehmen, unzumutbare Verhältnisse zu ändern, berechtigte Forderungen anzumelden und auch durchzusetzen. Demokratie und Grundgesetz böten zahlreiche Mittel dazu, und Politiker müßten darauf hören, denn sie seien auf jede Wählerstimme angewiesen.

Unüberhörbar steckte der Vorwurf hinter seinen Worten, die Jugend von heute sei bequem und wenig risikobereit.

„Jung sein heißt unsicher sein, aber auch große Möglichkeiten haben.“ „Sie können Ihr eigenes Leben immer nur selber gestalten.“ „Warum warten Sie auf die Politiker? Sie sind jung, Sie wissen doch, wo der Schuh drückt!” „Melden Sie sich mit Ihren Vorschlägen!”

Auf der anderen Seite wies er seine jungen Zuhörer darauf hin, flexibel zu sein und Ideen zu entwickeln. Beschränkungen hätte es zu jeder Zeit gegeben und es sei wichtig, auch innerhalb der gegebenen Grenzen neue Möglichkeiten zu finden.

„Wenn Sie nicht rot und auch nicht blau studieren können, versuchen Sie es doch 'mal mit violett!” „Ich versuche, Ihnen bewußt zu machen, daß es unglaubliche Möglichkeiten für Menschen gibt, daß noch in jeder Situation Ansätze für gute Lösungen vorhanden sind.”

Aber auch Umdenken forderte Prof. Deutsch und entsetzte damit manchen jungen Studenten.

„Körperliche Arbeit ist nichts Schlimmes. Jemand kann sein ganzes Leben lang Kellner bleiben. Man kann auch für einige Zeit alles mögliche ausprobieren. Es gibt viele Sparten, in denen Bedarf herrscht.”

Zusammenfassung Arbeitsgruppe Deutsch

Diesen Grundtenor behielt Prof. Deutsch bei, als die Diskussion über die rein studienbezogenen Themen hinaus auf allgemein-gesellschaftliche Probleme unserer Zeit wuchs. Jugendarbeitslosigkeit, Minderbegabtenprobleme, Generationsprobleme bis hin zu den großen Menschheitskatastrophen: Prof. Deutsch sieht die Gefahren.

„Es kommen schwere Zeiten und es kann schauerlich gefährlich werden." „Seit 1930 ist das Schicksal der Welt immer wieder auf des Messers Schneide gewesen. Ich fürchte, es wird in den nächsten 40 oder 50 Jahren immer weiter auf des Messers Schneide stehen." „Ich hoffe, es wird nicht so schlimm wie im Dritten Reich oder im Zweiten Weltkrieg. Aber es kommen ganz gefährliche Zeiten, in denen man Sie unerhört brauchen wird."

Initiative, Handeln der Starken und Solidarität mit den Schwachen, das ist die Antwort von Prof. Deutsch.

„Tun Sie, was Sie können, Sie können nicht alle retten. Aber retten Sie so viele, wie Sie können." „Sie stehen vor dem Problem, Ihr eigenes Leben in einer höchst unvollkommenen Demokratie so einzurichten, daß Sie durchkommen, ohne Ihre eigene Dignität zu verlieren und ohne Ihre Solidarität verkümmern zu lassen. Aber man muß durchkommen!"

Sicherung von Zukunftsinteressen in der parlamentarischen Demokratie

Prof. Dr. Kurt Biedenkopf

Ich habe es übernommen, einige Gedanken zur Frage der Zukunftssicherung in der parlamentarischen Demokratie vorzutragen und möchte vorausschikken, daß das notwendigerweise nur einige Gedanken sein können. Ich kann hier weder eine Gesamtkonzeption entwickeln, noch würde ich mich in Anwesenheit so vieler bedeutender Kollegen trauen, das zu tun.

Ich möchte einige Überlegungen vortragen, die wir sowohl im Bereich der Arbeit in der Grundsatzkommission meiner Partei angestellt haben, wie aber auch darüber hinaus im Zusammenhang mit dem, was wir schon seit längerem als die allgemeine Parlamentarismuskritik bezeichnen.

In der Einführung zu dem Papier „Die Jugend und ihre Zukunftschancen" steht die Feststellung, daß jede Entscheidung, jede Maßnahme, die man in der Gegenwart trifft, auch die Bedingungen der Zukunft berührt, und daß es deshalb Zukunftshandeln in einem abstrakten Sinne eigentlich nicht gibt. Statt dessen entfaltet jede politische Entscheidung Zukunftswirkungen, gleichgültig, ob diese Zukunftswirkungen in den Entscheidungshorizont der Betroffenen eingehen oder nicht. Aus dieser unbestreitbaren und unausweichlichen Tatsache, aus diesem unausweichlichen Zusammenhang wird zu Recht in der Beschreibung der Konzeption die Schlußfolgerung gezogen, daß deshalb die Generation, die heute Verantwortung trägt, diese Verantwortung nicht nur für die Gegenwart, sondern auch für die Zukunft trägt.

Das zentrale Problem lautet: Wie kann diese auf die Zukunft hin orientierte Verantwortlichkeit derer, die heute Verantwortung tragen, in den Entscheidungshaushalt Eingang finden? Wer macht diese Zukunftsbedürfnisse geltend? Wie können sie gegen die jeweiligen Anforderungen der Gegenwart durchgesetzt werden? Nach welchen Kriterien wird die Abwägung in der Gegenwart geltend gemachter Bedürfnisse gegen die Notwendigkeiten zukünftiger Gestaltung vorgenommen? Welches sind die Sanktionen, die sicherstellen, daß Zukunftsbedürfnisse in der Gegenwartsentscheidung berücksichtigt werden?

Die parlamentarische Demokratie – um das sehr vereinfacht zu sagen – geht davon aus, daß sich alle Staatsgewalt, d. h. die Gewalt staatlichen Handelns, auf das Volk zurückführen läßt. Sie geht davon aus, daß das Volk seine umfassende Souveränität durch Repräsentanten zur Geltung bringt, daß diese Repräsentanten für das Volk politisch entscheiden – der klassische Ort für diese Entscheidungen ist das Parlament – daß diese Repräsentanten durch die Erteilung eines Mandats entscheidungsbevollmächtigt werden. Das Mandat des Parlamentariers ist theoretisch für die Dauer der Erteilung ein unabhängiges

Mandat, d. h. der einzelne entscheidet laut Verfassung nach seinem Gewissen.

Aber die parlamentarische Demokratie sieht einen ganz entscheidenden Kontrollmechanismus vor, eine Sanktion, nämlich die Notwendigkeit der regelmäßigen Mandatserneuerung. Derjenige, der zur Entscheidung beauftragt wird, muß sich in regelmäßigen Abständen dem Volkssouverän stellen, konkret gesprochen, den Delegiertenversammlungen der Parteien, den Auswahlgremien, die ihn wieder aufstellen oder nicht wieder aufstellen. Er muß Rechenschaft über die Handhabung des Mandates ablegen, und er muß sich um eine Erneuerung seines Mandates bewerben. Dieser Sanktionsmechanismus, nicht wieder gewählt zu werden, betrifft natürlich nicht nur den einzelnen Mandatsträger, sondern auch seine politische Partei. Sie betrifft insbesondere die Chance der jeweiligen politischen Partei oder der Parteien, die Macht im Staate auszuüben oder auf die Oppositionsbänke verwiesen zu werden. Es gibt also eine ganze Reihe von politisch relevanten Sanktionsmechanismen für den Fall, daß die Mandatsträger den Willen derer, die das Mandat erteilt haben, nicht vollziehen.

Also müßte man eigentlich zu dem Ergebnis kommen: Da der Volkssouverän sich aus vielen Generationen zusammensetzt, ist die Auswahl der Mandatsträger bereits ein Ergebnis der Abwägung von Gegenwarts- und Zukunftsbedürfnissen. In der Praxis jedoch ist es nicht so. Die Praxis zeigt, daß der politische Entscheidungsprozeß – so wie wir ihn in der modernen Industriedemokratie entwickelt haben – eine außerordentliche Präferenz für die Befriedigung von Gegenwartsbedürfnissen entwickelt. Das ist keineswegs auf unser Land beschränkt, und keine politische Partei – meine eigene nachhaltig eingeschlossen – ist von dieser Praxis ausgenommen. Der politische Entscheidungsprozeß hat außerdem außerordentliche Schwierigkeiten, den Zukunftsbedürfnissen angemessen Rechnung zu tragen.

Ein Feld, in dem dies in den letzten Jahren sehr nachhaltig zum Ausdruck gekommen ist, ist der Umweltschutz. Es handelt sich speziell um die Verwendung natürlicher Ressourcen, von denen wir glauben, daß sie mehr oder weniger nicht beliebig vermehrbar wären. Wir haben es in den letzten Jahren verstanden, unsere Ressourcen, seien es natürliche Rohstoffe, Energien, Wasser oder Luft, zu begrenzen. Wir haben gelernt, daß solche Ressourcen nicht unbegrenzt zur Verfügung stehen oder deshalb auch nicht im Sinne beliebiger Zugängigkeit oder beliebiger Verbrauchbarkeit kostenlos sind. Denn eine Sache, die beliebig zur Verfügung steht, hat keinen Tauschwert, weil sie ja beliebig erneuert und vermehrt werden kann. Sie hat allenfalls den Wert dessen, was es kostet, ihn zu vermehren. Diese Begrenztheit unserer Ressourcen ist uns inzwischen deutlich geworden, wir haben ja auch politische Diskussionen darüber. Es ist uns aber bisher nicht gelungen, diese Beschränktheit unserer Ressourcen, die ja eine Beschränkung der Zukunftschancen und damit auch der Zukunftschancen der Jugend zur Folge hat, im politischen Entscheidungsprozeß zum Ausdruck zu bringen. Der politische Entscheidungsprozeß in der parlamentarischen Demokratie ist noch nicht dahin fortgeschritten, daß diese Begrenztheit voll erkannt und umgesetzt wird.

Wir haben aber keineswegs nur in diesem Bereich ein Ungleichgewicht zwischen der Befriedigung von Gegenwartsbedürfnissen und von Zukunftsinteressen. Wenn wir unsere augenblickliche gesellschaftliche Situation analysieren, müssen wir vielmehr feststellen, daß dieses Ungleichgewicht zwischen der Befriedigung von Gegenwartsbedürfnissen und der Bevorratung von Zukunftsnotwendigkeiten fast überall auftritt. Dieses Ungleichgewicht wiederum muß sehr viel stärker, als es vielleicht in der allgemeinen Diskussion draußen deutlich wird, auch ein strukturelles Problem sein. Auch hier wiederum unterscheidet sich keine der politischen Parteien in der Bundesrepublik von der anderen wesentlich in ihrer Leistungsfähigkeit, Zukunftsbedürfnisse zu sichern.

Es gibt eine Reihe von Indikatoren in unserer gesellschaftlichen Entwicklung, die deutlich machen, daß wir die Zukunftsbedürfnisse nicht ausreichend befriedigen. Wenn ich jetzt einige dieser Indikatoren aufzähle, dann sind sie willkürlich ausgewählt. Man könnte auch andere heranziehen, aber diese sind besonders plastisch. Im wirtschaftlichen Bereich ist die Eigenkapitalbildung Ausdruck der ausreichenden Zukunftsvorsorge. Es handelt sich hierbei um die Abzweigung eines Teiles des jeweiligen laufenden Bruttosozialproduktes für langfristige Investitionen. Wir können ja alle Bedürfnisse, die wir in der Gegenwart befriedigen wollen, im Prinzip immer nur aus dem befriedigen, was an laufendem Bruttosozialprodukt erzeugt wird. Eine Volkswirtschaft kann ihre Bedürfnisse nicht, jedenfalls nicht wesentlich aus der Verzinsung von investiertem Kapital befriedigen. Die wesentlichen Bedürfnisse werden aus dem jeweiligen Bruttosozialprodukt befriedigt, in das die Verzinsung mit eingeht, aber nur eine ganz untergeordnete Rolle spielt. Die Wertschöpfung dessen, was allgemein erarbeitet worden ist, ist die Grundlage für die Bedürfnisbefriedigung. Es muß also in den Verteilungsprozessen, die eine Gesellschaft beherrschen und die zum wesentlichen Teil durch den politischen Willensbildungsprozeß beeinflußt und gestaltet werden, ständig entschieden werden: Was wird aus dem laufenden Bruttosozialprodukt für die Befriedigung von Gegenwartsbedürfnissen verwendet, was wird für das Abtragen von Verpflichtungen verwendet, die aus der früheren Befriedigung von Bedürfnissen entstanden sind, und was wird für die Sicherung der Zukunft verwendet?

Diese zunächst sehr einfach skizzierte Schematisierung der Verteilungsfragen läßt sich nun vielfältig aufgliedern. Im Rahmen dessen, was für die gegenwärtige Bedürfnisbefriedigung zur Verfügung gestellt wird, findet nun wieder eine ganze Fülle von Verteilungsproblemen oder Verteilungskonflikten statt, die befriedigt werden müssen. Ein ganz wichtiger Verteilungskonflikt ist: Wie soll das, was wir in der Gegenwart gewissermaßen als konsumtive Einnahmen verbrauchen, verteilt werden? Was soll der Staat bekommen, was soll der öffentliche Dienst bekommen, was soll das Bildungssystem bekommen, was sollen die Arbeitnehmer bekommen, was sollen die Unternehmen an laufendem Unternehmerlohn bekommen usw.?

Wir haben für Entscheidung dieser Verteilungskonflikte eine ganze Reihe von Verfahren entwickelt. Wir haben die Verteilung des Einkommens aus dem allgemein erzeugten Bruttosozialprodukt durch Wettbewerb entwickelt. Wer eine hohe Leistung im Markt erbringt, bekommt eine höhere Vergütung. Was Leistung ist, entscheidet der Markt. Wir disponieren über einen wesentlichen Teil des Bruttosozialproduktes durch politische Entscheidungen. In der Bundesrepublik Deutschland sind es ungefähr die Hälfte. Ungefähr die Hälfte des Bruttosozialproduktes in der Bundesrepbulik Deutschland wird unter politischen Gesichtspunkten verteilt. Die sogenannte Staatsquote von etwas mehr als 47 % bringt das zum Ausdruck.

Politisch verteilt heißt das: Entweder der Staat nimmt diesen Teil des Bruttosozialproduktes in Anspruch – über Steuern, Abgaben, Einkommen von öffentlichen Unternehmen oder auf andere Weise – und verteilt dieses Geld dann entsprechend der in den staatlichen Haushalten festgelegten Verteilungsformen aufgrund politischer Entscheidungen im Sinne der Ausgaben. Durch die Tarifautonomie haben wir einen wichtigen Verteilungskonflikt im Lande gelöst. Wir haben also denjenigen, die als Lohn- und Gehaltsempfänger einen Anspruch gegen das Bruttosozialprodukt auf Einkommen stellen, die Unternehmen gegenübergestellt und im Tarifkonflikt eine Entscheidung darüber herbeigeführt, welcher Teil des gemeinsam Erwirtschafteten in Lohn und Gehältern ausgezahlt wird und welcher Teil des gemeinsam Erwirtschafteten im Unternehmen bleiben soll. Ich möchte das jetzt nicht im einzelnen vertiefen.

Wir treffen über den Teil dessen, was wir in der Gegenwart verbrauchen wollen, ununterbrochen politische Entscheidungen. Das geht auch gar nicht anders, denn in der arbeitsteiligen Volkswirtschaft, die ja keine autarken Einzelwirtschaften darstellt, sondern eine Summe von hochgradig voneinander abhängigen Einzelwirtschaften, müssen diese Verteilungsprobleme gelöst werden. Die Verteilungskonflikte entstehen dadurch, daß das zur Verteilung Anstehende kleiner ist als die Ansprüche. Es werden sehr viel mehr Ansprüche an das Bruttosozialprodukt geltend gemacht, als verteilt werden können. Also entsteht ein Stau, und dadurch kommt der Konflikt zustande. Die Arbeitnehmer erwarten eine achtprozentige Lohnerhöhung; die Unternehmer sagen: Es ist überhaupt kein Geld in der Kasse. Wenn überhaupt etwas in der Kasse ist, brauchen wir das für Investitionen.

Es ist zunächst einmal eine Überforderung, wenn ich die Ansprüche addiere. Aus dieser Überforderung muß ein Kompromiß gefunden werden. Nun gibt es zwei Wege, diesen Kompromiß zu erleichtern: Der eine Weg ist, daß man den

Anteil dessen, was man verteilt, zu Lasten der beiden anderen Anteile, von denen ich gesprochen habe, erhöht; d. h. daß man den Anteil, den man in der Gegenwart verteilen kann, erhöht, indem man das, was man für die Zukunft vorbehält, verringert. Die andere Möglichkeit ist die, daß man das, was man zu verteilen hat, nominell vermehrt, indem man Inflation zuläßt. Man erhöht den zahlungsmäßigen Wert des zur Verteilung Stehenden dadurch, daß man den Wert inflationiert. Ich möchte den zweiten Weg zunächst außer Betracht lassen, weil es die Sache zu kompliziert macht.
Wir haben also eine Situation, in der wir Verteilungskonflikte auf die vielfältigste Weise zu lösen haben. Diese Verteilungskonflikte sind schwierig zu lösen. Immer ist irgend jemand betroffen, der weniger bekommt, als er eigentlich wollte, oder gar nichts. Derjenige, der weniger bekommt, als er eigentlich wollte, oder gar nichts, wird dann seine Möglichkeiten der politischen Einflußnahme geltend zu machen versuchen, um den Verteilungskonflikt zu seinen Gunsten zu verändern. Es entsteht eine Fülle von Einwirkungen auf den Verteilungsprozeß. Diejenigen, die nun die Verteilungsentscheidungen treffen wollen, auf welchen Ebenen und auf welche Weise auch immer, versuchen, diesem Druck auszuweichen, indem sie den Kuchen vergrößern. Da der Kuchen sich aber insgesamt nicht vergrößern läßt, versuchen sie, den Anteil dessen, was sie jetzt verteilen müssen, zu vergrößern. Das geht dann zu Lasten der Zukunftsbedürfnisse.

Wir können feststellen, daß die Eigenkapitalquote der deutschen Unternehmen in den letzten zehn Jahren ständig zurückgegangen ist; 1968 lag der Eigenkapitalbetrag über 30 %, heute beträgt er nur noch 22 %. Wir können feststellen, daß der Anteil der öffentlichen Mittel, die in den Haushalten für Investitionen ausgegeben werden, zurückgegangen ist. Die Investitionsrate des Bundeshaushaltes liegt heute unter 10 %. Die Schätzungen schwanken etwas, weil die Abgrenzung zwischen konsumtiven und investiven Ausgaben der Haushalte Schwierigkeiten macht. Unbestritten aber ist, daß die Investitionsrate zurückgegangen ist.

Gleichzeitig stellen wir ein drittes Phänomen fest, nämlich einen weiteren Weg, die Verteilungsprobleme zu vereinfachen, und das ist die Verschuldung. Wir erhöhen das zur Verfügung Stehende, was wir verteilen können, dadurch, daß wir Schulden machen; d. h. dadurch, daß wir das, was wir verteilen, mit der Aufnahme von Krediten finanzieren, die wir Jahre später einmal zurückzahlen müssen. Wir machen also einen Vorgriff auf das Sozialprodukt von Morgen in der Erwartung, daß das Sozialprodukt weiter wächst und diese Vorgriffe sich aus dem Wachstum teilweise finanzieren lassen.

In dem einen Fall vergrößern wir den Kuchenteil, der für die Gegenwart zur Verfügung gestellt wird, zu Lasten des Zukunftsteiles. In dem anderen Fall machen wir für Bedürfnisse Schulden, die wir in der Gegenwart befriedigen – wohlgemerkt nicht für Investitionen, die in die Zukunft reichen –, und wir

erwarten von zukünftigen volkswirtschaftlichen Einnahmen die Abdeckung der Schulden. In beiden Fällen verringern wir die Zukunftschancen zugunsten der Gegenwart. Mit anderen Worten: Wir belasten in beiden Fällen zukünftige Generationen. Nicht nur diese wirtschaftliche Entscheidung ist eine Belastung der Zukunftschancen zugunsten der einfacheren Befriedigung von Gegenwartsbedürfnissen; wir haben auch sonst eine wachsende Präferenz für Gegenwartsbedürfnisse und eine immer geringere Durchdringlichkeit der Notwendigkeiten der Zukunft im gegenwärtigen Entscheidungsprozeß. Ich habe das hier mit allen damit verbundenen Risiken ganz bewußt außerordentlich vereinfacht.
Meine Überzeugung ist jedoch – und das ist eine These, die ich aufstellen möchte –, daß das gegenwärtige demokratische Entscheidungsprinzip, d. h. die Gegenwartsstrukturen, nach denen wir politische Entscheidungen treffen, aus einer Reihe von Gründen eine immer stärkere Präferenz der Gegenwartsbedürfnisse zu Lasten der Zukunftsinteressen mit sich bringt. Daraus kann eine Gefährdung der Demokratie erwachsen, jedenfalls des Vorganges der demokratischen Willensbildung, den wir in der Bundesrepublik als Demokratie zu bezeichnen gewohnt sind. Die Gefährdung kann daraus erwachsen, daß ein über einen längeren Zeitraum konstant beibehaltenes Verhalten, welches Zukunftsbedürfnisse zugunsten von Gegenwartsansprüchen unbefriedigt läßt, die Glaubwürdigkeit und die Legitimität eines solchen Entscheidungsprozesses in Frage stellt.

Ich möchte ein ganz einfaches Beispiel anführen: Die meisten von Ihnen, die hier sitzen und bereits einer Berufstätigkeit nachgehen, zahlen Beiträge in die Rentenversicherung. Dieses Zahlen von Beiträgen in die Rentenversicherung bedeutet, daß Sie eine gegenwärtige Leistung in Erwartung einer zukünftigen Gegenleistung erbringen. Mit Ihren Beiträgen finanzieren Sie das Alterseinkommen derer, die vor Ihnen diese Beiträge gezahlt haben. Sie arbeiten heute nicht mehr und erwarten, daß aus dem laufenden Bruttosozialprodukt als Gegenleistung für die ebenso erbrachte frühere Leistung heute ein Teil abgezweigt wird, um die Alterseinkommen derer zu finanzieren, die nicht mehr arbeiten.

Sie zahlen diesen Beitrag aufgrund der gesetzlichen Zusicherung, daß sie, wenn Sie einmal aus dem Berufsleben ausscheiden, einen ebensolchen Anspruch gegen die dann erwerbstätige Bevölkerung haben. Sie erwarten, daß dieser Anspruch gesichert ist, den Sie gegen zukünftige Generationen haben. Gesetzlich ist dieser Anspruch heute gesichert. Gesetzliche Ansprüche kann man verändern; d. h. wenn sich in zwanzig oder dreißig Jahren Mehrheiten bilden, die in diesen Anspruch eingreifen und ihn verändern, auch zu Ihren Lasten verändern, ist das jedenfalls prinzipiell nicht unzulässig.

Wenn aber die Veränderungen einen Umfang erreichen, der Sie in einen akuten Stand der Not versetzt, würde die verfassungsrechtliche Grenze des

Einflusses erreicht sein. Die Veränderung des angemessenen Besitzstandes im Rahmen eines angemessenen Umstandes wäre natürlich möglich. Sie gehen als selbstverständlich davon aus, daß nicht nur Ihr Beitrag als Beitrag zum Generationsvertrag im Rahmen des Gesetzes heute als Verpflichtungsbeitrag honoriert wird, sondern daß Sie auch in Zukunft Ihre Gegenleistung erhalten. Daß Sie Ihre Gegenleistung erhalten, ist davon abhängig, daß in Zukunft ein vergleichbares Bruttosozialprodukt erzeugt werden kann. Die Voraussetzungen dafür, daß in Zukunft ein vergleichbares Bruttosozialprodukt erzeugt werden kann, werden heute gelegt, bzw. in absehbarer Zeit und nicht erst zu dem Zeitpunkt, zu dem Sie in Rente gehen.

Wir müssen also heute – ich spreche von der Gegenwart als einer Zeitspanne von einigen Jahren – dafür Vorsorge treffen, daß die von uns heute begründete Verpflichtung zu Ihren Gunsten und zu Lasten zukünftiger Generationen einlösbar ist.

Das setzt voraus, daß die dann arbeitenden Generationen ausreichend mit Eigenkapital ausgestattet sind. Das setzt vor allen Dingen voraus, daß die jetzigen Generationen überhaupt dazu beigetragen haben, daß die zukünftigen Generationen, die wir bereits verpflichten, existieren. Und bereits diese Frage ist jedenfalls in der Bundesrepublik Deutschland heute nicht mehr selbstverständlich beantwortbar. Der wesentliche Rückgang der Geburtenraten in den letzten zehn Jahren ist, wenn er sich demographisch fortsetzt, geeignet, die Belastungen zu der Zeit, in der Sie in Rente gehen, so anwachsen zu lassen, daß auf zehn Beitragszahler sieben Rentner fallen. D. h., daß zehn Mitglieder der erwerbstätigen Bevölkerung praktisch sieben Menschen mit ernähren müssen, die keine Einkommen mehr haben. Das tritt nach den jetzigen demographischen Projektionen bei gleichbleibender Geburtenrate etwa im Jahre 2015 bis 2020 ein. Das ist etwa zu der Zeit, in der Sie ins Rentenalter kommen.

Das ist auch ein Problem der Zukunftschancen der Jugend. Wir können nämlich das Problem der Zukunftschancen der Jugend nicht einfach so definieren, daß es nur um die Frage geht, ob die Jugend Chancen hat, solange sie Jugend ist. Das eigentliche Problem der Zukunftschancen der Jugend sind die Zukunftschancen der jungen Menschen, wenn sie älter werden, d. h. für die Gestaltung des eigenen Lebens. Wenn wir feststellen, daß im politischen und im gesellschaftlichen Entscheidungsprozeß, der natürlich auch politische Relevanz hat, die Zukunftschancen unberücksichtigt bleiben oder nachhaltig vernachlässigt werden, dann müssen wir uns fragen: Wie können wir das ändern? Wir können es sicher nicht in der Weise ändern, daß wir die Menschen mit staatlichen Mitteln anhalten, mehr Kinder zu haben. Ganz abgesehen davon, daß das unserem Freiheitsverständnis, unserem demokratischen Verständnis, unserem Verständnis von der menschlichen Autonomie diametral entgegengesetzt wäre, ist es auch rein von der praktischen Seite her fast unmöglich.

Natürlich kann man mit enormen finanziellen Aufwand das Haben von Kindern ökonomisch belohnen. Aber selbst da bestehen nicht nur erhebliche politische, sondern auch ethische und moralische Bedenken. Nach meiner Auffassung zeigt sich aber in der Entwicklung der Geburtenrate eine Resonanz der Einzelnen, der Ehepaare, der Familien, vor allem der jungen Frauen auf die gegenwärtige politische und gesellschaftliche Einstellung in unserem Lande bezüglich des Konfliktes Gegenwart und Zukunft. Auch das ist nämlich eine Präferenz für die Gegenwart, wenn die Gesellschaft die Sicherung der Generation benachteiligt, d. h. diejenigen benachteiligt, die die Generation in der Zukunft sichern, und diejenigen bevorzugt, die zu der Dauerhaftigkeit des Generationsvertrages nur einen Beitrag leisten, der aber nicht in die Zukunft zeigt.

Diese Diskriminierung ist nachhaltig. Eine Frau, die vier Kinder auf die Welt bringt und großzieht, hat keinen eigenen Rentenanspruch, weil sie nicht arbeiten kann und deshalb keine Beiträge gezahlt hat. Die Frau, die keine Kinder hat und arbeitet und Beiträge zahlt, hat einen Rentenanspruch. Der Rentenanspruch der zweiten Frau richtet sich gegen die Kinder der ersten Frau. Die eigene Mutter hat gegen ihre Kinder, wenn sie später einmal erwachsen sind, keinen gesicherten gesetzlichen Anspruch auf Alterssicherheit. Die Nachbarin aber, die keine Kinder hat, hat diesen Anspruch. Das spricht sich herum.

Es spricht sich herum, daß man sich in der Gegenwart ein schönes Leben machen kann, wenn man die Belastungen einer Familie vermeidet und trotzdem einen Alterssicherungsanspruch an die Kinder der Nachbarin hat. Indem sich das herumspricht und diese Verhaltensweise allgemein wird, wird genau die Prämisse für diese Erwartungen gefährdet, weil nicht mehr genug Kinder da sind. Wenn diese Kinder dann einmal mehrheitsfähig sind, weil sie als Erwachsene die politischen Entscheidungen treffen, werden sie sich der Verpflichtungen entledigen, die frühere Generationen ihnen aufgebürdet haben und die überhaupt nicht einlösbar sind, weil die früheren Generationen die Voraussetzungen für die Einlösbarkeit vernachläßigt haben. Das ist in meinen Augen das Kernproblem unserer gegenwärtigen Situation.

Nun ist es außerordentlich schwierig, diesem Kernproblem mit institutionellen Regeln zu Leibe zu rücken. Eine drastische Maßnahme wäre z. B., daß man bei jeder Entscheidung im Parlament, die eine Vergütung über das laufende Bruttosozialprodukt darstellt, nach den langfristigen Auswirkungen dieser Verfügung fragt und die parlamentarische Entscheidungsfähigkeit konstitutionell, d. h. auf Verfassungswegen, einschränkt. Ich meine, daß man der Zerstörung von Zukunftschancen durch Gegenwartsentscheidungen einen verfassungsrechtlichen Riegel vorschiebt. Man hat dies schon etwas versucht im Artikel 112 des Grundgesetzes, indem man die Verschuldung des Bundes, des Bundeshaushaltes begrenzt hat. Aber wie schwierig das Einhalten solcher Begrenzungen unter Belastungen praktischer politischer Probleme ist, haben wir in den letzten Jahren erlebt. Auch meine eigene Partei hat in den letzten Jahren immer wieder Forderungen entweder nach zusätzlichen staatlichen Ausgaben oder nach Entlastungen von Steuern oder Beiträgen gefordert, ohne die jeweilige Äquivalenz in ausreichender Weise zu sichern, ohne daß Zukunftschancen berührt worden wären.

Was ist die Ursache dafür? Die Ursache wird von vielen darin gesehen, daß die Mandatserteilung in zu kurzfristigen Räumen erneuert werden muß. Die Ursache wird darin gesehen, daß diejenigen, die ein Mandat durch Wahl erhalten, im Grunde nur ein bis zwei Jahre relativ unabhängig entscheiden können. Dann steht die Wiederholung der Mandatserteilung ins Haus, dann kommen die Wahlkämpfe, und dann kann man nicht gut denen, von denen man gewählt sein will, Belastungen zumuten. So sieht jedenfalls die generelle Denkstruktur aus. Wenn jeder so denkt, dann verhält man sich auch so. Der Gegenbeweis ist deshalb bisher nicht angetreten worden, weil kein Mensch den Versuch gemacht hat, ihn anzutreten; weil man insbesondere nicht versucht hat, festzustellen, ob eine Veränderung der Prioritäten, etwa die ausdrückliche Betonung von Zukunftsbedürfnissen zu Lasten in der Gegenwart geltend gemachter Ansprüche nicht vielleicht auch mehrheitsfähig ist. Ich bin überzeugt davon, daß wir jedenfalls auf dem Wege zu einer Entwicklung sind, in der eine solche Veränderung des Verhältnisses von Gegenwarts- und Zukunftsbedürfnissen mehrheitsfähig werden könnte. Aber bisher ist noch keine der politischen Parteien bereit, das Risiko eines solchen Testes auf sich zu nehmen.

Das ist im übrigen in meinen Augen einer der Gründe dafür, daß sich, wenn auch in geringfügiger Weise, aber möglicherweise mit einem großen Entwicklungspotential, neue politische Gruppierungen außerhalb der traditionellen Parteien bilden, weil die Menschen das Gefühl haben, daß im politischen Entscheidungshaushalt ein nachhaltiges Ungleichgewicht eingetreten ist, über dessen Charakter sie nicht im einzelnen reflektieren, dessen Gefährdung sie aber empfinden. Die Gefährdung, die von diesem Ungleichgewicht ausgeht, wird empfunden.

Eine zweite Möglichkeit wäre es, daß man die Möglichkeit der Verschuldung der öffentlichen Haushalte ebenfalls auf konstitutionelle Weise drastisch reduziert. Eine andere Möglichkeit, die keinerlei Sinn im Sinne schon ausgereifter Vorschläge hat, könnte an dem Umstand ansetzen, daß die Zukunftsgenerationen im parlamentarischen Willensbildungsprozeß keine Stimme haben. Denn Kinder haben keine Stimme und Ungeborene erst recht nicht. Deshalb gibt es im parlamentarischen Entscheidungsprozeß keine Antwort auf die Bedürfnisse der Stimmlosen, weil die Stimmlosen keine Sanktionsmöglichkeiten haben. Sie können nicht Einfluß auf die politische Willensbildung nehmen.

Referat Biedenkopf

In einem System, in dem der Abgeordnete mit einer hochgradigen Sensibilität auf die jeweiligen Tageswünsche derer reagiert, die ihn wählen, ist die zentrale Frage: Wie kann ich die noch nicht stimmberechtigten Interessen, d. h. die Interessen der Jugendlichen, der Kinder und vor allem der nichtgeborenen Generationen, in den Entscheidungsprozeß einbringen? Nach meiner Überzeugung kann ich das nicht allein auf die institutionellen Vorkehrungen schaffen, die die Parlamente daran hindern Mehrheiten zu sichern, indem sie ihren vorhandenen Mehrheiten zusätzliche Wohltaten versprechen. Das ist einer der wesentlichen Gründe dafür, daß wir ein solches Ungleichgewicht haben.

Ich bin davon überzeugt und meine das überhaupt nicht resignativ, daß sich das gegenwärtige parlamentarisch-politische Verhalten der etablierten Parteien nur dadurch ändert, daß die Bevölkerung ihrem Wunsch nach stärkerer Berücksichtigung der Risiken im politischen Willensbildungsprozeß Ausdruck verleiht. Wenn die vorhandenen politischen Parteien diesen Wunsch nicht aufnehmen und ihre Verhaltensstrukturen nicht ändern, dann ist es der einzig richtige und pausible Weg, den vorhandenen Strukturen neue entgegenzustellen. Diese stellen das, was sie bisher etabliert haben in Frage, und durch dieses In-Frage-Stellen lösen sie einen Wettbewerbsdruck aus, der dann die vorhandenen Parteien entweder zwingt ihre Verhaltensweisen zu ändern, oder neue Mehrheiten bildet.

Es ist die Chance des parlamentarischen Systems, daß die etablierten Parteien die Wahrnehmung solcher Chancen mit der allergrößten Skepsis beobachten. Umgekehrt aber, was ja ganz charakteristisch ist, unterstützen die Medien, die elektronischen Medien und auch die Presse, die Wahrnehmung solcher Chancen nachhaltig. Daß damit die Eintrittsschwierigkeiten für den Newcomer in den Markt der politischen Parteien wesentlich verringert werden, ist eine Hoffnung der Lebendigkeit des parlamentarischen Systems.

Die Zukunftschancen der Jugend im parlamentarischen System hängen, wenn wir an diesem System festhalten wollen, von der Fähigkeit ab, in der gegenwärtigen Entscheidungspraxis eingebaute Präferenzen der Gegenwartsbedürfnisse zu Lasten der Zukunftsinteressen zu ändern. Dort, wo diese Präferenzen jedenfalls in den Augen vieler eine gefährliche Natur annehmen, wie z. B. beim vorzeitigen Ressourcenverbrauch, beim Umweltschutz oder in der Kernenergie, haben sich Gegenbewegungen bereits manifestiert.

Wir haben politisch gesehen kein Interesse daran, daß diese Gegenbewegungen zu einer Zersplitterung des Parteiensystems führen. In Zukunft hätten wir dann Parteien im Parlament, die nur noch ganz bestimmte Teilinteressen vertreten. Wir haben aber ein Interesse daran, daß die Stabilität der politischen Willensbildung erhalten bleibt, und dazu sind Organisationen wie größere politische Parteien notwendig. Aber dieses Interesse an der Stabilität darf nicht als Alibi dienen für die Zerstörung von Zukunftsbedürfnissen und Zukunftserwartungen durch eine Überforderung des Bruttosozialproduktes für Gegenwartsinteressen. Deshalb ist Stabilität ein wichtiger Wert, aber kein Wert an sich. Wenn es nicht möglich ist, die jetzt eingeschliffenen Präferenzen für Gegenwartsinteressen zu Lasten der Zukunftsbedürfnisse in einem geordneten Prozeß der Konfliktbewältigung zu ändern, dann wird die Gewinnung eines neuen Gleichgewichts mit großen Instabilitäten verbunden sein.

Das neue Gleichgewicht ist ein Gleichgewicht, welches die Zukunftsinteressen stärker berücksichtigt, als das heute der Fall ist. Das will ich überhaupt nicht ausschließen. Denn es ist für einen 25jährigen, der rechnen kann, der Zeitung lesen kann und der sich hinsetzt und über seine eigenen Zukunftschancen nachdenkt, heute eine Provokation, wenn er feststellen muß, daß im politischen Entscheidungsprozeß die Bedürfnisse, die für ihn auftreten, wenn er 40 Jahre alt ist, überhaupt keine Rolle spielen. Es ist für ihn untragbar, daß die Ansprüche an das Bruttosozialprodukt, die heute gestellt werden, nicht nur über das hinausgehen, was wir insgesamt produzieren, sondern, weil sie trotzdem befriedigt werden, ihn mit seinen Chancen, die er hat, wenn er 40 Jahre alt ist, noch zusätzlich belasten. Er ist belastet dadurch, daß sie tatsächlich zurückgezahlt werden und damit seinen Lebensstandard verringern, sei es dadurch, daß er unter den Konsequenzen fehlender Vorsorge leiden muß. Dadurch muß er jetzt gewissermaßen die doppelte Leistung erbringen.
Natürlich können wir so argumentieren – ich möchte das zum Abschluß sagen, – daß sich eine ganze Reihe von Konflikten zwischen Gegenwart und Zukunft lösen werden, weil wir in fast blindem Vertrauen auf die Möglichkeit des technologischen Fortschrittes davon ausgehen, daß die Produktivität ungeheuer steigt. Wir gehen ferner davon aus, daß immer weniger Menschen immer mehr erzeugen können und daß sich deshalb die jetzt abzeichnenden Konflikte in Wohlgefallen auflösen. Das ist die Erfahrung, die wir in der Zeit nach dem zweiten Weltkrieg gemacht haben. Wir haben die Erfahrung gemacht, daß die Überforderung des laufenden Bruttosozialproduktes problemlos ist, weil es ständig steigt.

Außerdem war es möglich, aus dem Zuwachs des Bruttosozialproduktes über das hinaus, was man schon versprochen hatte, noch weiteres zu versprechen und zu verteilen. Wenn man Politik im wesentlichen unter dem Gesichtspunkt der Verteilungskompetenz sieht, dann bedeutet das: Politik ist möglich, solange es etwas zu verteilen gibt. Wenn es nun nichts mehr zu verteilen gibt, wäre die Konsequenz: Politik ist unmöglich. In der Tat gibt es eine breite Meinung, die sagt: Ohne ein ständiges Wachstum unserer Volkswirtschaft ist Politik unmöglich. Man formuliert das nicht so dramatisch, aber man sagt: Ohne ein ständiges Wachstum unserer Volkswirtschaft ist z. B. Stabilität, soziale Sicherheit, soziale Befriedigung in unserem Lande nicht möglich, was auf dasselbe hinausläuft.

Das bedeutet, daß wir in die Erfüllung der politischen Aufgaben eine Prämisse, nämlich ständig wesentliches Wachstum, einfügen, die, wenn sie wegfällt, dann die ganze Lösung der politischen Aufgaben unmöglich macht. Ich bin überzeugt davon, daß wir unsere Zukunftsprämissen nicht auf einer solchen blinden Erwartung aufbauen dürfen. Wir können uns zwar anstrengen, das zu leisten; wir können uns anstrengen, mehr Wachstum zu erzeugen. Ich halte es auch für richtig, daß wir das tun. Aber ich halte es für lebensgefährlich, den Erfolg oder Mißerfolg der politischen Gestaltung einer befriedeten Gesellschaft von der Erfüllung der Prämisse abhängig zu machen.

Ich bin der Meinung, daß es noch einen weiteren Grund gibt, warum es lebensgefährlich ist, die politische Gestaltung einer freien und sozial befriedeten Gesellschaft von dieser Prämisse abhängig zu machen: Die Entwicklung und Veränderung der Weltwirtschaftsordnung. Weltweit gesehen befinden wir uns heute in der Situation des reichen Fabrikanten, der in der zweiten Hälfte des 19. Jahrhunderts im Ruhrgebiet das Ärgernis und den politischen Widerstand der armen Arbeiterschaft hervorgerufen hat. Die Verhältniszahlen sind nicht ganz die gleichen, sie ähneln sich aber in etwa. Die rund 60 Millionen Deutschen leben in einer Welt von jetzt über 4 Milliarden Menschen in einer Situation, die, gemessen an den Lebensstandards und Zukunftserwartungen von 2/3 der Menschheit nur als paradiesisch beschrieben werden können. Das, was wir für dringende Bedürfnisse halten, sind bei der überwiegenden Mehrheit der Menschheit nicht einmal denkbare Bedürfnisse. Wenn überhaupt, dann sind es marginale, das Leben verschönernde, aber seine Substanz überhaupt nicht berührende Bedürfnisse. Diese Diskrepanzen sind nach meiner Überzeugung auf die Dauer nicht durchzuhalten.

Wir werden einen Teil dessen, was wir gemeinsam erarbeiten und erwirtschaften, in Form von Steuern, die ganz neuartige Formen annehmen werden, an die Weltgemeinschaft abliefern müssen. Wir werden bisher nur in ganz bescheidenem Umfang besteuert. Bisher werden wir besteuert durch höhere Rohstoffpreise, durch Rohstoffonds und durch höhere Ölpreise. Das sind noch keine Steuern im normalen Sinne, denn es gibt noch keine Weltrechtsordnung, die eine geordnete Besteuerung der Reichen zugunsten der Armen ermöglicht. Es ist noch mehr das Steuersystem zur Zeit des Raubrittertums, wo jemand am Wege lagert und den Transport des Reichen belastet, weil er ihn sonst nicht durchläßt. Der Transport des Reichen sind z. B. die Ölschiffe, und der Kampf in Afrika ist nichts anderes als der Kampf um Positionen, von denen aus man die Schiffe kontrollieren kann, wenn ich es einmal ganz vereinfacht formuliere. Wir müssen uns daran gewöhnen, daß wir auf diese Weise in Anspruch genommen werden.

Aber ich würde das gar nicht einmal so negativ sehen, denn mit dieser Inanspruchnahme eröffnen sich natürlich auch enorme Chancen für die jüngeren Menschen, an der Gestaltung dieser Weltwirtschaftsordnung mitzuwirken. Aber das war nicht mein Thema, ich habe das nur als einen Exkurs erwähnt.

Mein Thema war die Zukunftssicherung der parlamentarischen Demokratie. Meine Antwort lautet: Sie ist möglich, wenn Sie die Mittel und die Möglichkeiten der parlamentarischen Demokratie nutzen.

Wenn es notwendig ist, müssen wir die oligopolitische Parteistruktur durch Newcomer aufbrechen, aber nicht im Sinne der Diskussion der Vierten Partei, um hier überhaupt keine Mißverständnisse aufkommen zu lassen. Der Gedanke der Vierten Partei ist nichts anderes, als denselben Produktinhalt in zwei verschiedenen Verpackungen zu verkaufen, um auf diese Weise den Marktanteil für das Produkt insgesamt zu erhöhen. Davon rede ich nicht, sondern ich rede hier von dem echten Newcomer, der in den Markt eindringt und ein vom Markt vernachlässigtes Bedürfnis so nachhaltig zur Geltung bringt, daß die Wettbewerbssituation der vorhandenen Anbieter beeinträchtigt wird. Dieser Newcomer zwingt die vorhandenen Anbieter, ihr Angebot zu verändern, um in der Marktterminologie zu bleiben, die ja angesichts des Veranstalters sicher gestattet ist.

Was auf diese Weise geltend gemacht werden muß, wenn es sich innerhalb der vorhandenen Parteistruktur nicht geltend machen kann, ist das Zukunftsinteresse. Es ist für mich überhaupt keine Überraschung gewesen, als ich im niedersächsischen Wahlkampf feststellte, daß ein wesentlicher Teil derer, die engagiert in den Grünen Listen mitgearbeitet haben, junge Leute waren, so wie Sie hier sitzen. Denn hier wird ein ganz bestimmtes Zukunftsinteresse mit einer großen Immanenz, vielleicht auch verzerrt, geltend gemacht. Und es ist immer der Fall, wenn man in eine verfestigte Struktur eindringt, daß man dann nur mit großem Lärm eindringen kann, wenn es überhaupt Erfolg hat. Genau dies geschieht zur Zeit.

Ich bin überzeugt, daß die parlamentarische Demokratie die Möglichkeiten bietet. Aber lassen Sie mich das als letzten Satz sagen: Es wäre ein verhängnisvoller Irrtum zu glauben, daß die Möglichkeiten der parlamentarischen Demokratie bereits gleichbedeutend sind mit der Problemlösung. Das Wesen einer freiheitlichen Gesellschaft besteht darin, daß sie Angebote macht. Sie macht Angebote, indem sie Möglichkeiten und Chancen zur Mitwirkung begründet. In dem Augenblick, in dem man die Sicherung der Zukunftschancen von den staatlichen Entscheidungsprozessen als immanente Leistung erwartet, hat man den demokratischen Staat überfordert. Man geht nicht davon aus, daß man zur Geltendmachung dieser Zukunftsinteressen selbst aktiv werden muß, sondern man glaubt, daß gewissermaßen der Staat diese Reformleistung aus sich selbst, aus seinen Institutionen selbst leisten könnte.

Nur ein Staat kann das, der den Bürger dann auch entmündigt, denn die parlamentarische Demokratie reagiert im wesentlichen auf die gesellschaftlichen und politischen Strömungen in der Bevölkerung. Leute, die alle vier Jahre wiedergewählt werden wollen, müssen, nachdem sie sich dazu entschlossen haben, zum Berufsparlamentarier überzugehen, auch damit rechnen, daß die Nicht-Wiederwahl erhebliche wirtschaftliche Sanktionen zur Folge hat. Diese Männer und Frauen reagieren mit großer Sensibilität auf das, was sie für die augenblickliche öffentliche Meinung halten. Das Zukunftsinteresse muß deshalb in dieser öffentlichen Meinung zur Geltung gebracht werden, damit es in den politischen Entscheidungsprozeß Eingang findet. Ich bin der Auffassung, daß die Chancen dafür günstig sind. Ich glaube ferner, daß die politischen Parteien, und zwar die beiden großen politischen Parteien vor allem, längst wissen, daß diese Asymmetrie besteht und daß sie dringend überwunden werden muß. Ich bin sicher, daß es im wesentlichen des Anstoßes der Newcomer im Markt bedarf, um auch das Verhalten der Etablierten in die neue Richtung zu ändern. Deshalb habe ich immer wieder betont, daß ich das Auftreten dieser Newcomer, so desorganisiert, so unkonventionell, so völlig unüblich sie auch sonst sein mögen, nicht nur als ein Symptom für eine Asymmetrie, sondern auch als ein Signal willkommen heiße, das für die großen Parteien notwendig ist, um ihre Orientierungsrichtungen zu korrigieren.

Aussprache über das Referat Biedenkopf

Leitung: Johannes C. Welbergen

Welbergen:

In der gestrigen Zusammenkunft haben wir auch schon über den Verteilungskampf gesprochen, und Ota Šik hat dazu seine Ideen entwickelt. Wir haben es sehr bedauert, daß wir Sie, Herr Biedenkopf, gestern nicht hier haben begrüßen können. Denn ich kann mir vorstellen, daß wir eine ganz interessante Konfrontation gehabt hätten. In der Fragestellung an Herrn Professor Biedenkopf sollte vielleicht auch ein bißchen das berücksichtigt werden, was wir bereits von Daniel Bell gehört haben, damit wir versuchen können, einen Faden zu finden.

Hier ist die erste Frage: Ota Šik sah in dem Verteilungskampf einen konjunkturlösenden Störfaktor. Wie beurteilen Sie diese These? Was wird mit „konjunkturlösender Störfaktor" bezeichnet?

Biedenkopf:

Sie meinen: für den Konjunkturzyklus, für die sich jetzt abzeichnenden Erscheinungen der Konjunktur? Ich bin überzeugt, daß da Zusammenhänge bestehen, aber ich würde keine singuläre Kausalität akzeptieren.

Teilnehmer:

In den letzten Tagen wurde hier viel über die Probleme der Bildung, der Arbeitslosigkeit, der Mobilität usw. gesprochen. Sie haben in Ihrem Vortrag den Begriff „Zukunftschancen" nach meinem Eindruck rein materiell verstanden. Sie haben Politik praktisch als Verteilungskompetenz definiert, als die Möglichkeit, bestimmte Ressourcen materieller Art auf irgendwelche Gruppen zu verteilen.

Ich betrachte alle Probleme, mit denen wir konfrontiert worden sind, und frage: wie muß Bildung aussehen und verbreitert werden, damit die Jugendlichen als Personen in ihrer Zukunft noch Chancen haben? Ich wäre dankbar, wenn Sie noch darauf eingehen könnten.

Biedenkopf:

Diese Frage, die Sie angesprochen haben, möchte ich in drei Teilaspekte aufgliedern. Erstens: Was kann der Staat tun, was kann die Politik tun hinsichtlich des Bildungsproblems? Zweitens: Was muß von der Gesellschaft geleistet werden, also im nichtstaatlichen Bereich? Der dritte Aspekt: Was muß der einzelne selber dazu beitragen?

Aussprache Biedenkopf

Um mit dem Dritten anzufangen: es wäre sicherlich eine völlige Verkennung der Möglichkeiten eines freiheitlichen Gemeinwesens, wenn man glaubte, daß dieses Gemeinwesen den Beitrag des einzelnen zur Gestaltung seiner Zukunft wesentlich entlasten könnte. Dem steht die andere Meinung gegenüber, daß man gewissermaßen dem Jugendlichen eine Zukunft wie ein Warenhausangebot anbieten könne. Wir haben in Bochum solche Angebote gegeben, und zwar an junge Menschen, die von der Hauptschule ohne Abschluß abgegangen sind. Die jungen Leute haben keinen Gebrauch davon gemacht.

Welche Ursachen gibt es dafür? Eines ist sicher: sie haben Schwierigkeiten, eigene Initiative zu entfalten, um von solchen Angeboten Gebrauch zu machen. Umgekehrt: würde man auf die Idee kommen, die Leute zu verpflichten, von dem Angebot Gebrauch zu machen, würde die Hölle losgehen. Wir sind also darauf angewiesen, die jungen Menschen zu einem Minimum eigeninitiativer Fähigkeiten zu erziehen.

Zweitens: Wir müssen im gesellschaftlichen Bereich eine stärkere Initiative bekommen. Ich spreche nun wieder von meinem Wahlkreis, weil er typische Elemente dieser Probleme enthält. Es ist ein Industriewahlkreis mit relativ hoher Arbeitslosigkeit – höher als im Bundesdurchschnitt –, mit etwa 12.000 Arbeitslosen; das sind knapp 7 %. Bei der Vermittlung von Chancen müssen wir eine stärkere Mitwirkung der gesellschaftlichen Einrichtungen haben als bisher. Es hat sich gezeigt, daß die staatlichen Einrichtungen, insbesondere die Arbeitsämter, nur in begrenztem Umfang eine individuelle Behandlung leisten können. Individuelle Behandlung wird woanders geleistet: durch die Kammern, durch die Gewerkschaften, durch private Initiativen von Einrichtungen der Bürger usw.

In den letzten Jahren hat es – wiederum in der Stadt Bochum – eine sehr interessante Bewegung gegeben. Frauen haben für junge Menschen, die keinen Hauptschulabschluß hatten und die durch alle „Ritzen" fielen, Patenschaften übernommen. Sie haben die jungen Leute an die Hand genommen, wollen Arbeitgeber suchen usw. Diese Leistung staatlich zu ersetzen, ist unmöglich.

Der dritte Punkt betrifft die Aufgabe des Staates. Ich habe diese Problematik absichtlich von hinten nach vorn aufgerollt aber nicht, um Ihrer Frage auszuweichen. Ich bin der Meinung, daß wir eher zuviel staatliche Bildungspolitik als zuwenig haben, und daß man eine Fülle von Mitentscheidungsträgern im gesellschaftlichen Bereich mit ganz entscheidenden Initiativen ausläßt, weil man sich an die Vorstellung gewöhnt hat, der Staat sei für alles zuständig.

Mir sagen beispielsweise Handwerksmeister: Wir gehen nicht mehr zum Arbeitsamt, weil das nichts bringt; die schicken uns doch immer falsche Leute, und wir müssen nur Formulare ausfüllen. – Das ist ein Indiz dafür, daß die Eigeninitiative auf beiden Seiten – auf der Seite der Lehrlinge und auf der

Seite derer, die die Lehrlinge einstellen – unterentwickelt ist. Wir müssen nach dem Warum fragen. Wir dürfen nicht glauben, daß durch eine Vermehrung der staatlichen Aktivitäten das Problem lösbar sei.

– Das Arbeitsamt ist für die Lösung von Aufgaben in typischen Fällen eingerichtet. Wenn es sich nicht mehr um typische Fälle handelt, sondern immer stärker um individuelle Fälle, ist die administrative Vermittlung nicht mehr geeignet, diese Probleme zu lösen. Da müssen andere Anstöße kommen, ermunternde Initiativen von Gruppen, z. B. von karitativen Gruppen, kirchlichen Institutionen, von den Gemeinden, den Kammern usw.; sie alle sollen mit anpacken. Aber dazu muß man erst einmal der Vermittlungsmonopol der Arbeitsämter korrigieren, damit derartige Gruppen überhaupt wirksam werden können. So sieht die Praxis aus.

Teilnehmer:

Herr Prof. Biedenkopf, Ihre Kernaussage war die, daß das gegenwärtige Sozialprodukt für die Zukunftssicherung überfordert sei. Sie haben 3 Mechanismen angeführt: Tarifwettbewerb, Autonomie, politische Entscheidungen. Der Wettbewerb funktioniert gut, nach meiner Auffassung viel zu gut. Sehen Sie sich als Ergebnis die Rendite an! Wir haben in der Industrie eine Nettorendite von 2 %. Das ist viel zuwenig. Bedenken Sie, daß in Amerika die Umsatzrendite das Zweifache beträgt, fast das Dreifache. Somit bleiben die Tarifautonomie bzw. der Staat und die politischen Entscheidungen übrig.

Bei der Tarifautonomie sind 85 % lohnabhängig und unterliegen in irgendeiner Form den Tarifverträgen. 70 % beträgt die Lohnquote. Ein ganz wesentlicher Grund, warum wir heute überkonsumieren oder zu hohe Ansprüche an das Sozialprodukt stellen, sind doch die Tarifverträge.

Deshalb meine Frage an Sie: ist es nicht an der Zeit, zu überlegen, ob nicht der Arbeitsmarkt genauso wie alle anderen Märkte in das System von Bindung, in das System der freiheitlich-staatlichen Wettbewerbsordnung einbezogen werden sollte?

Biedenkopf:

Ich möchte Ihre letzte Frage einen Augenblick zurückstellen. Daß die Tarifautonomie einen wesentlichen Einfluß auf die Verteilung des Sozialproduktes hat, ist unbestritten. Eines der wesentlichen Probleme, das ich in der Tarifautonomie sehe, ist, daß der Konflikt falsch dargestellt wird. Er wird als Konflikt zwischen Kapital und Arbeit dargestellt. Ich kann aber Arbeit und Kapital nicht vergleichen. Arbeit ist immer wichtiger als Kapital, wenn man sie als Wert betrachtet und ein Tarifkonflikt ist daraus noch nie entstanden. Heute geht es um die Frage: Was von dem gemeinsam Erwirtschafteten soll investiert werden, und was von dem gemeinsam Erwirtschafteten soll als Konsum ausgezahlt werden?

Aussprache Biedenkopf

Das Problem ist, daß die investierten Mittel nach unserer Gesellschaftsordnung und nach unserer Rechtsordnung im wesentlichen den Eigentümern der schon vorhandenen Investitionen zukommen. Deshalb entsteht hier ein Verteilungsproblem. Man kann es nicht dadurch lösen, daß man keine Investitionen mehr zur Verfügung stellt, weil man dann die anschließenden Probleme nicht mehr lösen kann. Was man hier macht, ist: man schüttet das Kind mit dem Bade aus. Man weist die zur Verfügung gestellten Mittel als Unternehmereinkommen aus. Das ist falsch. Denn die Mittel dienen zwei völlig verschiedenen Zwecken.

Die Sachverständigen zur Begutachtung der gesamtwirtschaftlichen Lage haben seit Jahren darauf hingewiesen, daß die Ungleichgewichtigkeit im Tarifkonflikt dazu führt, daß nicht ausreichend investiert und daß zu viel zum Konsum zur Verfügung gestellt wird.

Nun könnte man sagen: das ist doch nicht schlimm, die Arbeitnehmer können ihr Geld durch den Konsum wieder in die Wirtschaft investieren. Aber sie tun es nicht, sie tragen es zur Sparkasse. Dorthin tragen sie zur Zeit 15 % ihrer durchschnittlichen Einkommen. Die Unternehmer müssen in Fremdmittel ausweichen. Dadurch entsteht eine immer größere Verzerrung hinsichtlich der Beweglichkeit, eine immer geringere Flexibilität und eine ständige Abnahme der Risikobereitschaft.

Dieser Circulus vitiosus setzt sich laufend fort. Man kann ihn nur durchbrechen, indem man deutlich macht, daß der Tarifkonflikt eine ganz andere Frage entscheidet als den Verteilungskonflikt zwischen Kapital und Arbeit. Wenn man deutlich macht, daß diese beiden unterschiedliche gesellschaftliche Interessen vertreten und nicht ihre eigenen.

Die andere Frage ist die nach dem Wettbewerb. Da bin ich nicht Ihrer Meinung, daß wir zuviel Wettbewerb haben. Ich bin auch nicht der Meinung, daß die Rendite der Ausdruck von zuviel Wettbewerb ist. Wettbewerb gibt es in Amerika auch. Die geringe Rendite ist Ausdruck der falschen Verteilung des Bruttosozialprodukts. Diese kommt dadurch zustande, daß der Konsument in der Bundesrepublik nicht bereit ist, höhere Preise für seine Bedürfnisse zu zahlen, als er zahlt. Auch wird der Ertrag aus dem Preis falsch verteilt. Wir nehmen dem Unternehmen zuviel für den Staat und zuviel für den Konsum weg. Deshalb bleibt der Rest als zu geringe Rendite übrig. Das ist das Problem.

Ich glaube nicht, daß Sie durch eine Änderung der Wettbewerbsverhältnisse die Bereitschaft der Kunden verändern, andere Preise zu zahlen. Abgesehen davon, daß in der Bundesrepbulik angesichts der Offenheit unserer Märkte für Importe eine solche autarke Preispolitik gar nicht möglich wäre.

Teilnehmer:

Die Existenz der Grünen Listen ist doch ein Zeichen dafür, daß offenbar immer mehr das Vertrauen zu den etablierten Parteien schwindet. Ich halte es für sehr gefährlich, wenn diese Tendenz so anhält, zumal wegen der 5-%-Klausel diese Gruppen – im Moment wenigstens – nur die Möglichkeit haben, sich außerparlamentarisch zu bewegen.

Deshalb folgende Frage: was müßten die Parteien tun, um diese Gruppen – Sie sagten selber: in erster Linie geht es um die junge Generation – ein bißchen mehr zu integrieren? Denn hier geht es ja auch um die Frage der Zukunft der Jugend.

Sind Sie nicht auch der Ansicht, daß man als etablierte Partei ein bißchen mehr Kompromißbereitschaft zeigen müßte, z. B. in Fragen des Umweltschutzes, weil es ein existentielles Problem der Zukunft ist?

Ferner hätte ich noch gern gewußt, wie Sie dazu stehen, daß gerade in Ihren Reihen der Herr Gruhl ein bißchen mit dem Maulkorb belegt worden ist.

Biedenkopf:

Wenn Sie im zweiten Teil nicht diese Frage gestellt hätten, hätte ich Herrn Gruhl als Beispiel dafür genommen, was ein Außenseiter zustande bringen kann, der eine bestimmte Idee hat und von seiner Organisation selber nicht verstanden und gefördert wird, deshalb ausbricht, um seiner Idee als Newcomer Geltung zu verschaffen. Herr Gruhl ist ein praktisches Beispiel dafür, daß jemand eine gute Idee hat, aber sie ohne Kompromißbereitschaft so hoch bewertet, daß die Partei nicht in der Lage ist, ihre Prioritäten zugunsten neuer Fragestellungen zu ändern. Er verlangt von der CDU, daß sie ihre politischen Aussagen unter dem Gesichtspunkt „Umweltschutz" verändert, also bereit ist, Dinge zu beschließen, die sie wegen des ausbalancierten Kompromisses zwischen allen gesellschaftlichen Interessen, nicht beschließen kann.

Wenn ich irgendwo etwas verändere, verändert sich in dem Interdependenzsystem eine ganze Menge mit, unter anderem auch die Besitzstände. Wenn ich Umweltschutz machen will, muß ich bei den Besitzständen anfangen. Das gilt glückerlicherweise für fast alle, und zwar überparteilich.

Nun zur 5-%-Klausel. Sie ist kein Hindernis. Wenn eine Parteigruppierung in 12 Wochen 3 % zusammenbringt, ist es eine unglaubliche Sache. Wenn dazu die Medien noch mithelfen, haben diese Minderheitengruppen schon fast eine gleiche Wettbewerbschance. Denn die Medien sind zur Zeit dabei, Wettbewerbsnachteile kleinerer Gruppen durch außerordentliche Publizitätspräsenz auszugleichen. Diese Möglichkeit des Ausgleichs ist eine positive Sache. Sie liegt durchaus im eigenen Interesse der Medien, die an nichts anderem als an Konflikten interessiert sind. Denn das ist die beste Nachricht.

Daß es diese Gruppen gibt, halte ich nicht für eine Gefahr. Ich glaube, daß ihre Existenz sich schon jetzt vermindert hat. Es gibt Risiken, die mit einer solchen Bewegung verbunden sind. Die müssen wir in Kauf nehmen. Es gibt keine Innovation ohne Risiko, und es gibt auch keine Erneuerung oder Reform ohne Risiko. Man kann keine risikolose Parteistruktur haben und eine dauernde Reform dazu; das ist ausgeschlossen. Folglich muß man immer solche Umbruchsituationen in Kauf nehmen. Wenn eine Demokratie diese nicht verkraften kann, ist sie nicht wert, daß man sie vertritt.

Teilnehmer:

Wir haben von Herrn Prof. Deutsch gehört, daß die Zukunftsaussichten der Jugend entscheidend von der Einzelinitiative abhängen. Auch Sie, Herr Prof. Biedenkopf, haben das erwähnt. Aber ist es im Moment nicht so, daß die Eigeninitiative eingeschränkt wird?

Biedenkopf:

Ich kann Ihnen eine relativ kurze Antwort geben. Prüfen Sie, in welche Länder Sie fahren können, und vergleichen Sie das Ergebnis mit der Zahl derjenigen Länder, in die wir zu unserer Zeit ohne Risiko fahren konnten. Sie haben heute viel größere Chancen als früher. Aber Sie haben eine gesellschaftliche Umwelt, in der Sie ständig von allen Seiten ermutigt werden, diese oder jene Angebote anzunehmen. Das empfinden Sie als eine Einschränkung von Chancen. Machen Sie sich von gesellschaftlichen Angeboten unabhängig, und schaffen Sie sich selber welche! Sie haben heute eine Menge Möglichkeiten.

Sie können nicht beides haben: ein abgesichertes Leben, für das die Gesamtheit immer geradesteht, oder eine Palette solcher vielfältigen Angebote. Das ist unmöglich. Sie können sich gesellschaftlich betreuen lassen. Aber dann müssen Sie in den gesellschaftlichen Strömen mitschwimmen, die vorhanden sind. Sie können auch aus der gesellschaftlichen Betreuung ausbrechen und ein gewisses Eigenrisiko auf sich nehmen. Dadurch können Sie eine Menge Chancen ausschöpfen. Das ist genau das, was Karl Deutsch sagte.

Daß die Bereitschaft zur Selbständigkeit in der Gesellschaft zurückgegangen ist, stimmt. 17 % der Erwerbstätigen haben es 1976 gesagt. Aber die Chance, die Sie haben, besteht immer darin, aus dem allgemein gebahnten Weg auszusteigen. Das können Sie heute stärker als je zuvor. Sie sollten sich nich einreden lassen, es gäbe heute keine Chancen.

Teilnehmer:

Ich möchte an diesem Punkt anknüpfen. Es geht um die Einbeziehung der Jugendlichen in den Entscheidungsprozeß. Dieses Problem soll institutionell geregelt werden. Wir haben es diskutiert. Wenn aber die Einbeziehung der Jugend in den Verantwortungsprozeß in Zweifel gezogen wird, ist davon die Glaubwürdigkeit solcher Aussagen betroffen.

Ich kann dazu Beispiele anführen. Wir machen mit großem Engagement Programme für die Durchführung von Seminaren, für Schulungsmaßnahmen, um die Jugendlichen auszubilden. Die Bildungsreferenten müssen laut Erlaß vom Kultusminister nachweisen, welche Bücher sie lesen zur Vorbereitung auf die Teilnahme.

In der Bundesrepublik Deutschland gibt es eine große Bewegung fast aller demokratischen Jugendorganisationen, die u. a. an den 11. Weltjugendfestspielen in Kuba teilnehmen wollen. Da versucht man die Teilnahme in ein bestimmtes Licht zu rücken. Es gibt weitere Initiativen, die Jugendlichen und Kindern dienen und wo von Seiten der politischen Parteien versucht wird, dafür zu sorgen, daß sie sich nicht durchsetzen können.

Biedenkopf:

Sie meinen, daß Sie keine öffentlichen Mittel bekommen?

Teilnehmer:

Es geht nicht um öffentliche Mittel. Es geht um die Verbote gegen die Einrichtung von Kindergärten, um den Ausbau, die Öffnung oder Schließung von Jugendhäusern.

Biedenkopf:

Sie sind Mitarbeiter in einem Jugendverband? Ohne Arbeit? Gut, dann haben sie ein eigenes Interesse daran. Da sollte man einmal deutlich folgendes sagen. Die Jugendlichen in der Bundesrepublik sind noch nie mit so viel Geld alimentiert worden wie in der heutigen Zeit.

Das ist eine Feststellung. Der Politiker ist dem Steuerzahler Rechenschaft schuldig, was er mit dem Geld tut. Also können die Parlamente als Repräsentanten der Steuerzahler verlangen, zu erfahren, was in der Ausbildung mit diesem Geld gemacht wird.

Wir wissen, daß die Verbände an der Eigeninitiative der Jugendlichen etwas weniger interessiert sind. Sie haben ja ein Angebot. Sie bieten an, den Jugendlichen zu helfen. In jeder möglichen Weise bilden Sie sie aus usw. Sie sind natürlich daran interessiert, daß die Nachfrage nach diesem Angebot möglichst groß ist und daß die öffentlichen Mittel, die dafür zur Verfügung gestellt werden, möglichst umfangreich sind. Deshalb habe ich große Zweifel, ob eine ganze Reihe von Organisationen ernsthaft darum bemüht ist, junge Leute zur Selbständigkeit zu erziehen. Das, was ich gesehen habe, als ich mir die Verbände selber angesehen habe, muß diese Zweifel bestärken.

Sie haben die Festspiele in Kuba erwähnt. Ich habe nichts dagegen, daß Sie dorthin reisen, aber ich habe etwas dagegen, daß Sie es mit meinem Steuergeld tun. Jeder kann zu Festspielen reisen. Aber öffentliche Mittel dafür in

Anspruch zu nehmen, um einer Organisation ein Forum zu bieten, deren politische Ausrichtung festliegt, unterliegt der politischen Entscheidung der Parlamente.

Zuruf:

Also Kontrolle von staatlicher Seite!

Biedenkopf:

Durch die Parlamente, und die Parlamente kontrollieren durch ihre Mehrheiten. Wer die Minderheit hat, übt die Kontrolle aus.

Welbergen:

Ich möchte Sie bitten, die weiteren Fragen zu straffen und keine parteipolitischen Diskussionen zu führen.

Teilnehmer:

Habe ich Sie richtig verstanden, daß Sie Berufsparlamentarier bejahen?

Biedenkopf:

Nein.

Teilnehmer:

Sie haben von der Eigeninitiative gesprochen. Besteht da nicht eine gewisse Gefahr, wenn die Eigeninitiative in der Gegenwart durch Beschlüsse für die Zukunft insoweit eingeschränkt wird, daß ich für meine Zukunft keine große Initiative mehr entwickeln kann, weil ich schon festgelegt bin?

Biedenkopf:

Zunächst einmal ist die Entfaltung von Eigeninitiative nicht nur eine Frage des Geldes. Soweit dies politisch beeinflußt wird, spielt die materielle Seite eine erhebliche Rolle, aber auch nicht nur.

Zweitens ist der Spielraum Ihrer Eigeninitiative zunächst einmal durch Ihre eigenen Möglichkeiten bestimmt. Diese sind im Schnitt in den letzten 20 Jahren besser geworden.

Heute hat man z. B. die Möglichkeit, wenn man einen Beruf A ergriffen hat und möchte lieber den Beruf B ergreifen, sich aus öffentlichen Mitteln für den Beruf B ausbilden zu lassen. Ich verweise auch auf das BAFöG. Als Beispiel erwähne ich eine 28jährige Sekretärin, die studieren will und einen Unterhaltsanspruch gegen ihre Eltern hat.

Ich bin nicht Ihrer Auffassung, daß die Möglichkeit zur Eigeninitiative geringer wird. Allerdings ist bezüglich bestimmter Eigeninitiativen ein zunehmendes Maß von administrativen Hemmnissen festzustellen, vor allem wenn man sich selbständig machen will. Das ist eine ungewöhnlich schwierige Sache.

Zum anderen gibt es ein Bewußtsein des immer engeren Eingebundenseins in die Gesellschaft, das die subjektive Fähigkeit zur Eigeninitiative lähmt. Wir müssen zwischen subjektiver Fähigkeit zur Eigeninitiative und objektiven Chancen zur Eigeninitiative klar unterscheiden. Deshalb habe ich vorhin gesagt, daß die Bildungspolitik eine zentrale Rolle spielt. Die subjektive Fähigkeit zur Eigeninitiative muß gefördert werden. Sonst nützen die Angebote überhaupt nichts.

Rosenmayr:

Wie sehen Sie die plebiszitären Möglichkeiten hinsichtlich des Umweltschutzes? Ich verweise auf Österreich und die Schweiz.

Biedenkopf:

Für mich geht es wesentlich um das Problem der Größe der Entscheidungseinheiten. In der Schweiz sind Entscheidungseinheiten sehr klein. Deshalb wurde eine plebiszitäre Entscheidung über Atomkraftwerke abgelehnt. In Amerika waren die Entscheidungseinheiten sehr groß. Man hat nicht abgelehnt, sondern zugestimmt, weil es so weit weg war, daß man es nicht als ein persönliches Risiko empfunden hat. Ich meine, daß die gegenwärtigen Möglichkeiten in unserem Land bis zur quasi-plebiszitären Geltendmachung politischer Issues ausreichen. Eine Erweiterung von Volksabstimmungen sollte nicht über das hinausführen, was wir z. B. in der Verfassung von Nordrhein-Westfalen mit dem Volksbegehren schon jetzt haben.

Welbergen:

Die letzte Frage!

Teilnehmer:

Sie sagten bezüglich der jungen Wähler, daß sie den Zukunftsinteressen von sich aus zum Durchbruch verhelfen müßten. Ich sehe aber eine Gefahr: Die jungen Leute haben doch bereits resigniert, was man an der äußerst geringen Wahlbeteiligung bei den Kommunalwahlen in Schleswig-Holstein – im Extrem unter 50 % – gemerkt hat.

Biedenkopf:

Das können Sie nicht verallgemeinern. Die Wahlbeteiligung der jungen Menschen in der Bundesrepublik Deutschland liegt weltweit an der Spitze – wenn Sie von denjenigen Ländern absehen, die Wahlpflicht haben.

Aussprache Biedenkopf

Die Wahlbeteiligung in der deutschen Bevölkerung ist bei den jungen Menschen nicht wesentlich anders als bei den Erwachsenen. Es mag sein, daß bei Kommunalwahlen solche Erscheinungen aufgetreten sind. Woanders sind es über 70 % gewesen.

Ich sehe das Problem etwas anders. Die jungen Leute, die sich engagieren, sind nicht resigniert. Auch die großen Wählerzahlen sind nicht resigniert. Die „Marschierer" gehen auch wählen. Das Engagement ist nicht Sache von Mehrheitsbewegungen, sondern Engagement ist eine Sache von relativ wenigen. Initiativen werden normalerweise nicht von Mehrheiten, sondern von Minderheiten ergriffen, die etwas ändern wollen. Deshalb kann ich aus einer Wahlbeteiligung noch keine Rückschlüsse auf die Fähigkeit zur Innovation im Bereich der Jugendlichen ziehen.

Ich habe die begründete Hoffnung, daß eine ganze Reihe von Jugendorganisationen – auch die meiner eigenen Partei – solche Themen aufgreifen werden, und zwar sehr viel schneller als die ganze Partei. Dann wird es wieder zu Konflikten kommen, die ich außerordentlich begrüßen würde. Denn ein Konflikt läßt auch das Generationsproblem erkennen. Zusammenfassend: ich bin wesentlich optimistischer, als Sie in Ihrer Fragestellung zum Ausdruck gebracht haben.

Die Politik der Bundesregierung zur Sicherung der Zukunftschancen der Jugend

Karl Fred Zander

Den Überblick über die politischen Anstrengungen der Bundesregierung für junge Menschen möchte ich mit der Frage beginnen, von welchen Zielvorstellungen diese Politik ausgeht. Dabei verstehe ich unter dem Begriff Jugend eine große Zahl von Gruppen junger Menschen, die unter sehr unterschiedlichen individuellen, sozialen, ökonomischen und kulturellen Bedingungen leben und mit sehr eigenen, persönlichen und gruppenspezifischen Reaktionen auf eben diese Bedingungen.

Einige Zahlen können dies deutlich machen, auch ohne den Anspruch, ein komplettes soziologisches und demographisches Bild vermitteln zu wollen.

Wir haben es in der Bundesrepublik mit rund 15 Millionen Kindern und Jugendlichen unter 18 Jahren zu tun. Die Zahl der 14- bis 21jährigen beträgt 6 Millionen.

Jedes 12. Kind lebt in einer unvollständigen Familie, wächst also entweder ohne Vater oder ohne Mutter auf.

Vier Millionen Kinder unter 18 Jahren , also ein Viertel dieser Altersgruppe, sind Einzelkinder.

Im Schuljahr 1975 besuchten rund 10 Millionen Schüler allgemeinbildende Schulen. Das stärkste Kontingent stellen mit 6,4 Millionen Jugendlichen die Schüler von Grund- und Hauptschulen. Knapp 400.000 besuchten Schulen für Behinderte, 1,2 Millionen Realschulen und rund 1,9 Millionen Gymnasien. Etwa ein Drittel der Schulabgänger erreichte den Hauptschulabschluß nicht.

Unter den 1974 ermittelten 1,6 Millionen Schülern an Berufs- und Berufssonderschulen befanden sich 1,4 Millionen Auszubildende und Praktikanten mit Vertrag sowie über 54.000 Schüler ohne Beruf oder Erwerbstätigkeit.

Im April 1974 gab es nach der amtlichen Statistik 358.000 behinderte Kinder unter 16 Jahren, 17 Prozent dieser Kinder lebten in Heimen. Über drei Viertel wuchsen in vollständigen Familien auf.

Je ein Drittel der Jugendlichen lebt in Dörfern, in kleineren und mittleren Städten sowie in großstädtischen Ballungsräumen.

Schon diese wenigen Zahlen belegen, daß es beachtliche Unterschiede und Ungleichheiten im Blick auf die Lebens- und damit die Zukunftschancen unserer jungen Menschen gibt.

Bei allen Unterschieden gibt es selbstverständlich viel Gemeinsames. Darum scheint es mir wichtig zu sein, sich die grundsätzlichen Aufgaben von Jugendpolitik immer wieder ins Gedächtnis zu rufen, weil jede jugendpolitische Aktivität daran gemessen werden muß, in welcher Weise sie zu der Erfüllung unserer Ziele schließlich beiträgt.

Eine jede Gesellschaft, ob in der Vergangenheit, Gegenwart oder Zukunft, muß ihr Fortbestehen durch Erziehung und Bildung sichern.

Für den Fortbestand der Gesellschaft müssen Erziehung und Bildung drei grundlegende Befähigungen für die heranwachsenden Bürger gewährleisten:

Es sind dies:

1. Die Fähigkeit zur gemeinsamen, doch individuell differenzierten Arbeit und Leistung, durch die die Voraussetzungen und Möglichkeiten unseres individuellen und gemeinschaftlichen Lebens geschaffen werden.
2. Die Fähigkeit zur sozialen und politischen Kooperation der Menschen untereinander und zur Übernahme politischer Verantwortung, durch die, um es mit den Worten Bertold Brechts zu sagen, „der Mensch dem Menschen ein Helfer“ werden kann.
3. Die Fähigkeit zur Beteiligung am kulturellen Leben der Gesellschaft, denn in der Kultur gewinnt eine Gesellschaft ihr Selbstbewußtsein wie auch das Bewußtsein ihrer künftigen Möglichkeiten. „Der Mensch lebt nicht vom Brot allein“.

Bitte verstehen Sie das bisher Gesagte nicht so, als ob Erziehung und Bildung keinen anderen Auftrag hätten, als die heranwachsenden jungen Menschen an die ökonomischen sozialen, politischen und kulturellen Verhältnisse dieser Gesellschaft anzupassen, sie entsprechend auszubilden, auszurichten und zu integrieren. Auf eine gängige Formel gebracht also „Erziehung zur Anpassung“.

Es kann aber keinen Zweifel darüber geben, daß die **eine** Hauptaufgabe der Erziehung und Bildung unserer Gesellschaft tatsächlich darin besteht, daß junge Menschen lernen, den erreichten Stand der gesellschaftlichen Arbeitstellung zu beherrschen. Sie müssen sich in der Vielfalt sozialer und politischer Kooperationsmöglichkeiten und Zusammenhänge einer immer komplizierter werdenden Massengesellschaft auskennen. Damit erst werden sie sozial und politisch handlungsfähig und in die Lage versetzt, die ökonomische Fortentwicklung – die ja Grundlage unserer gesellschaftlichen Existenz ist – mitzutragen.

Junge Menschen müssen diese Gesellschaft in ihrer ganzen Breite und Mannigfaltigkeit kennenlernen, um mitbestimmen und Möglichkeiten und Gefahren künftiger Entwicklungen sehen und beeinflussen zu können.

Wer von der Aneignung dieser Fähigkeiten ausgeschlossen ist oder wird, verliert die Möglichkeiten der Selbst- und Mitbestimmung.

Mit dem Ziel, Selbst- und Mitbestimmung zu lernen, hängt aber zugleich die zweite Hauptaufgabe der Erziehung und Bildung zusammen. Mit dem Wissen um die gegebenen Zusammenhänge muß die Fähigkeit zur Kritik dieser Zusammenhänge und die Fähigkeit, Alternativen dazu zu entwerfen, vermittelt werden.

Kreativität ist eben nicht unpolitischen musischen Inseln vorbehalten, sie gehört vielmehr ins Zentrum der demokratischen Willensbildung. Ohne sie tritt auch die Demokratie auf der Stelle, das heißt Staat und Gesellschaft sind in Gefahr zu verkrusten.

Ich kann mir diese Gesellschaft nicht anders vorstellen, als geprägt durch ein ständiges Ringen um mehr Freiheit und Demokratie, mehr soziale Sicherheit und Gerechtigkeit, mehr persönliches und gemeinschaftliches Glück und Erfüllung.

Diese Ziele verlangen aber, daß Erziehung und Bildung nicht nur die Reproduktion des Bestehenden leisten, sondern frei machen für die Kritik des Bestehenden und für eine kreative Veränderung des Bestehenden, wo dies notwendig erscheint, damit sich Gesetz und Rechte nicht wie eine ewige Krankheit forterben.

Erziehung und Bildung müssen also auch die Voraussetzungen dafür schaffen, daß der Prozeß des Fortschritts dieser Gesellschaft in Gang gehalten bleibt.

In einer demokratischen Gesellschaft, wie der der Bundesrepublik Deutschland, darf die erneuernde und kritische Kraft der Jugend nicht in die – sicher notwendigen – Qualifikationsanstrengungen des Einzelnen „wegintegriert" werden.

Der Einladung zu dieser Tagung haben die Veranstalter als Diskussionsrahmen ein Papier unter der Überschrift *„Perspektiven 2000"* beigefügt. In ihm wird einerseits zutreffend auf die zunehmende internationale Verflechtung verwiesen, der mehr und mehr auch bislang autonome Bereiche der nationalen Politik unterliegen.

Andererseits kann ich nicht zustimmen, wenn in diesem Papier gesagt wird, „daß die Grenzen und Konflikte innerhalb unserer Gesellschaft und zwischen den Völkern und Nationen nicht geringer, sondern eher größer werden".

Haben die Ergebnisse der 7. Jugendstudie des Jugendwerkes der Deutschen Shell nicht wieder einmal demonstriert, daß, wie eine frühere Untersuchung von Leopold Rosenmayr feststellte, „es einen Normen- und Wertkonflikt zwischen den Generationen im wesentlichen nicht gibt" *(Seite 64 und Seite 66 Band III).* Und kommt nicht die vorliegende Untersuchung, deren großes Verdienst es ist, der zunehmenden internationalen Wechselwirkung durch eine entsprechend angelegte Forschung zu entsprechen, zu dem die Forscher verblüffenden Ergebnis, daß es in der Jugend europäische Wertmaßstäbe bis in die Details hinein gibt? *(S. 67 Band III)*

Man rufe sich die Gegensätze der politischen Einstellung auch der jungen Menschen in Europa bis zum Ende des 2. Weltkrieges hin ins Bewußtsein, um die Bedeutung einer Aussage zu würdigen, wie sie am Schluß des 3. Bandes zu finden ist: Ich zitiere: „Nirgendwo chauvinistische Einstellung, sondern überall eher Besonnenheit, ein nur begrenzt ausgedrückter Nationalstolz stand einer breit zum Ausdruck gebrachten Gleichgültigkeit entgegen; das kann man auch als Offentheit gegenüber einer europäischen Entwicklung interpretieren."
Angesichts einer solchen Ausgangslage wird die Bundesregierung die jugendpolitische Zusammenarbeit sowohl bilateral als auch im Rahmen der EG und des Europarats, durch die Förderung des Jugendaustausches weiter intensiv fördern. Die erwähnten Einstellungen sind auch Ergebnis der intensiven Förderung der internationalen Jugendarbeit.

Die Ostpolitik der Bundesregierung hat auch die Chance eröffnet, einen Prozeß der Zusammenarbeit und Verständigung mit der Jugend der Staaten Osteuropas in Gang zu bringen, wenngleich dabei erhebliche Schwierigkeiten überwunden werden müssen. Vor allem dem Austausch mit Polen gelten derzeit unsere besonderen Anstrengungen. Grenzen und Konflikte werden also im Gegensatz zur Aussage des Textes Perspektive 2000 nicht eher größer, sondern sie lassen sich eher überwinden und austragen.

Dabei vergesse ich nicht, daß den Beziehungen zu den wirtschaftlich wenig entwickelten Ländern, speziell auch zu den rohstoffreichen Ländern, auch auf jugendpolitischem Gebiet eine andere Qualität zukommt als etwa entsprechende Beziehungen zu Industrienationen.

Ich wehre mich aber dagegen, nur unsere Verwundbarkeit zu sehen und darüber unsere Verpflichtung zu einer Gesamtpolitik aus dem Auge zu verlieren, die auch diesen Ländern Perspektiven einer nicht mehr durch Not, Elend und einseitiger Abhängigkeit gekennzeichneten Zukunft gibt.

Ich sehe, daß viele junge Menschen dabei sind, Wege zu suchen, auf denen sich ein neues, durch wirkliche Partnerschaft zu den Ländern der Dritten Welt gekennzeichnetes Verhältnis finden läßt. Die Jugendpolitik der Bundesregierung wird sie dabei unterstützen und gleichzeitig um ihre Einbettung in eine entsprechende Politik gegenüber den Ländern der Dritten Welt insgesamt besorgt sein.

Natürlich sehen wir auch unsere Interessen. Ihre erfolgreiche Vertretung kann aber nicht mehr über berechtigte Interessen der Länder der Dritten Welt hinweggehen. Dies ist der Ansatz der unter dem Vorsitz von Willy Brandt arbeitenden Nord-Süd-Kommission und dies ist wohl auch der Kern dessen, was Carl Friedrich von Weizsäcker unter der künftig zunehmend notwendigen „Weltinnenpolitik" versteht.

Der neue international vergleichende Ansatz in der Reihe der Jugenduntersuchungen der Deutschen Shell und Akzente im Problempapier zu dieser Tagung haben mich veranlaßt, zunächst einmal Fragen der international ausgerichteten Jugendpolitik anzusprechen.

Die von mir dargelegten grundsätzlichen Aufgaben der Jugendpolitik sind aber vor allem innenpolitisch von Bedeutung. Ich möchte daher mit einem Seitenblick auf das, was jugendpolitisch von der Bundesregierung getan wurde aufzeigen, welche Probleme der Gegenwart und der Zukunft erkennbar sind.

Die sozialliberale Bundesregierung hat der Jugendpolitik in ihrem gesellschaftspolitischen Konzept von Anfang an einen hohen Stellenwert eingeräumt. Wir haben, um nur einige Beispiele zu nennen,
- das Wahlalter und das Volljährigkeitsalter herabgesetzt
- die Reform des Jugendhilferechts in Angriff genommen und vorangetrieben (auf diesen Punkt komme ich gleich noch zurück)
- das Adoptionsrecht und das Adoptionsvermittlungsrecht reformiert
- das Hochschulrahmengesetz, das Ausbildungsförderungsgesetz und das Ausbildungsplatzförderungsgesetz geschaffen
- die Reform des gesetzlichen Jugendarbeitsschutzes verwirklicht
- im Betriebsverfassungs- und im Personalvertretungsgesetz jungen Arbeitnehmern mehr Chancen und mehr Rechte auf Mitbestimmung und Mitverantwortung eingeräumt
- die Reform des elterlichen Sorgerechts eingeleitet
- den Bundesjugendplan seit 1970 laufend den neuen Entwicklungen angepaßt und auch finanziell besser ausgestattet.

Gegenwärtig macht das Feld Ausbildung und Beruf für junge Menschen uns die größten Sorgen. Dabei ist auf diesem Gebiet seit Ende der sechziger Jahre auch vieles verbessert worden.

Ich darf in diesem Zusammenhang an folgende Tatsachen erinnern:

1. 1965 besaß jeder elfte Jugendliche, der eine Berufsschule verließ, keine abgeschlossene Berufsausbildung. Heute sind es nur noch 6 von Hundert.

2. Die Chancen eines Arbeiterkindes, eine Hochschule zu besuchen, sind heute achtmal so groß wie noch vor 15 Jahren – allerdings immer noch nur ein Viertel so groß wie bei einem Kind eines Beamten oder Selbstständigen.

3. Jeder fünfte junge Erwachsene erwirbt heute die Hochschulreife. 1965 hatte nur jeder Elfte eine Studienchance.

4. Der Rückstand der Mädchen bei den Bildungschancen im Schul- und Hochschulbereich hat sich verringert: 1965 waren 35 Prozent der Abiturienten weiblich, 1975 waren es 45 Prozent – und zwar von einer erheblich größeren Gesamtzahl.

5. Die Klassen in den Schulen sind kleiner geworden. Allein seit 1970 ist die Zahl der Lehrer um über 100.000 angewachsen. Zwergschulen sind heute kein Thema mehr.

Auf diesem Hintergrund sehe ich auch die Ergebnisse der 7. Jugendstudie des Jugendwerkes der Deutschen Shell, wonach die deutschen Jugendlichen, was die Überprüfung ihres elementaren Wissens angeht, am besten abschneiden oder mit den Worten der Verfasser der Studie: „das reformierte Schulsystem in Deutschland offensichtlich vergleichsweise recht gute Wirkung zeitigt".

Ich verkenne nicht, daß wir noch für einige Jahre vor beträchtlichen jugendpolitischen Problemen stehen:

- Noch immer verläßt jeder sechste Hauptschüler seine Schule ohne Abschluß.
- Noch immer fallen zahlreiche Unterrichtsstunden aus.
- Noch immer unterliegen etwa 12 Prozent der Studienplätze an wissenschaftlichen Hochschulen dem Numerus clausus.
- Noch immer findet nicht jeder Jugendliche den Ausbildungsplatz, den er sich wünscht, und junge Menschen, die ihre Ausbildung abgeschlossen haben, treffen auf eine Arbeitswelt, in der es schwieriger geworden ist, eine angemessene Beschäftigung zu finden. Viele Jugendliche sind ohne Arbeit.

Ganz besonders bedrückend ist die Lage der Jugendlichen, die weder einen Ausbildungs- noch einen Arbeitsplatz erhalten.

Für Jugendliche, die am Beginn ihres Arbeitslebens stehen, ist Arbeitslosigkeit besonders schwerwiegend:

Sie bedeutet für den Einzelnen, daß er weder eigenes Einkommen noch volle sozialrechtliche Ansprüche hat, daß er nicht an den Erfahrungen seiner Altersgruppe teilnehmen und seine Lebenspläne nicht verwirklichen kann.

Auch die nicht unmittelbar betroffenen Jugendlichen fürchten, selbst arbeitslos zu werden. Dies behindert die freie Entfaltung ihrer Persönlichkeit und belastet das Lehren und Lernen in allen Bereichen des Bildungs- und Ausbildungssystems.

Gelingt es nicht, die Jugendarbeitslosigkeit zu überwinden, so wird dies nachteilige Folgen für die politische und soziale Stabilität haben.

Die jungen Menschen haben Anspruch darauf, beruflich und sozial in die Gesellschaft eingegliedert zu werden. Die Gesellschaft braucht die Mitarbeit und das Engagement der jungen Generation.

Hinzu kommt, daß eine hochindustrialisierte Volkswirtschaft, wie die der Bundesrepublik, hochqualifizierte Nachwuchskräfte benötigt, wenn sie im internationalen Wettbewerb bestehen will. Hier darf es auch dann keinen Engpaß geben, wenn die Zahl der Arbeitskräfte gegen Ende der 80er Jahre aufgrund der dann ins Erwerbsleben tretenden geburtenschwächeren Jahrgänge zurückgehen wird.

Jugendarbeitslosigkeit ist ein Teil der allgemeinen Arbeitslosigkeit und hat zuerst auch dort ihre Ursachen.

Jugendliche sind jedoch besonders benachteiligt, weil
- sie in der Regel Berufsanfänger sind und ihnen damit praktische Berufserfahrung fehlt,
- sie nicht im gleichen Maße wie ältere Arbeitnehmer sozial- und arbeitsrechtlich geschützt sind,
- die Tendenz der Arbeitgeber festzustellen ist, keine zusätzlichen Arbeitskräfte mehr einzustellen, so daß gerade neu auf den Arbeitsmarkt drängende Jugendliche benachteiligt werden,
- und in wirtschaftsschwachen Regionen nach wie vor ein erheblicher Mangel an Ausbildungsplätzen besteht.

Die großen bildungspolitischen Ausbauleistungen der letzten Jahre waren insbesondere auf die Schulen und Hochschulen ausgerichtet. Die Bundesregierung hat daher zur Verbesserung und Weiterentwicklung der beruflichen Bildung im Interesse der Jugendlichen und der gesamten Volkswirtschaft eine Kurskorrektur in der Bildungspolitik eingeleitet, die sich vor allem auf folgende Schwerpunkte konzentriert:

1. Sicherung eines ausreichenden Angebotes qualifizierter Ausbildungsplätze für alle Jugendlichen.

   Dazu sind in den letzten Jahren wichtige Handlungsvoraussetzungen und ein aufeinander abgestimmtes Handlungsinstrumentarium konkreter Maßnahmen geschaffen worden:

   - Das Ausbildungsplatzförderungsgesetz mit einer Finanzierungsregelung, die die Erhebung einer Umlage für den Fall eines unzureichenden Lehrstellenangebots vorsieht. Da die Wirtschaft 1977 die vom Gesetz geforderten zusätzlichen Ausbildungsplätze bereitstellte, konnte auf diese Finanzierungsregelung bisher verzichtet werden.

   - Das Schwerpunktprogramm der Bundesregierung zur Förderung überbetrieblicher Ausbildungsstätten mit einem Finanzvolumen von 1 Milliarde DM. Mit diesem Geld sollen vorhandene überbetriebliche Ausbildungsstätten ausgebaut und neue Einrichtungen errichtet werden. Es wurden die Voraussetzungen dafür geschaffen, daß allein in den Jahren 1974 bis 1976 19.000 Ausbildungsplätze entstanden.

   - Ich verweise insbesondere auch auf die gemeinsam von Bund und Ländern beschlossenen Stufenpläne sowie das Programm zur Minderung von Beschäftigungsrisiken Jugendlicher, mit dem zusätzliche Ausbildungsmöglichkeiten für 300.000 Jugendliche in der beruflichen Bildung geschaffen werden sollen.

2. Ein zweiter Schwerpunkt wird die Weiterentwicklung der Ausbildungsqualität sein, um die beruflichen und persönlichen Zukunftschancen der Jugendlichen auch künftig zu sichern. Dazu gehört insbesondere die Modernisierung der Ausbildungsordnungen.

3. Die Bundesregierung bietet zur Verbesserung der Ausbildungschancen und zur Minderung der Jugendarbeitslosigkeit nicht nur finanzielle Mittel an, sondern sie leistet auch selbst einen eigenen unmittelbaren Beitrag zur Steigerung des Ausbildungsplatzangebotes im öffentlichen Bereich. So wurden z. B. bei Bundespost und Bundesbahn im Jahre 1977 rd. 5.000 Jugendliche über den tatsächlichen Bedarf hinaus ausgebildet. Auch im Bereich der Bundeswehr wurden seit 1975 zusätzliche Ausbildungsplätze geschaffen. Dabei geht es uns vor allem darum, für solche Berufe auszubilden, die eine berufliche Mobilität über den öffentlichen Dienst hinaus vermitteln.

4. Besondere Aufmerksamkeit widmet die Bundesregierung auf dem Ausbildungsstellenmarkt den Problemgruppen, zu denen die lernschwachen Jugendlichen und leider immer noch auch die Mädchen zählen.

   Die Bundesanstalt für Arbeit führt gegenwärtig Lehrgänge durch, die Jugendlichen, die keinen Ausbildungsplatz gefunden haben und noch nicht die Voraussetzungen für eine Lehre erfüllen, helfen sollen. In diesen Lehrgängen befinden sich insgesamt ca. 30.000 Jugendliche.

Einen besonderen Schwerpunkt in der von der Bundesregierung vorangetriebenen Politik der Öffnung des Bildungswesens bildet das gemeinsame Aktionsprogramm, auf das sich die Regierungschefs von Bund und Ländern am 4. November 1977 in Bonn geeinigt haben. Es umfaßt die ganze Bandbreite der bildungs- und beschäftigungspolitischen Fragen – vom Ausbau der beruflichen Bildung über den Abbau des Numerus clausus, die finanziellen Hilfen für die Hochschulen einschließlich der Förderung des wissenschaftlichen Nachwuchses sowie die Studienreform und die Bildungs- und Berufsberatung bis hin zu den Konsequenzen für das Beschäftigungssystem. Ich will auf die Einzelheiten nicht näher eingehen und möchte nur als Stichworte erwähnen:

– den Abbau der Zulassungsbeschränkungen zum Hochschulstudium
– die Verbesserung für über 600.000 Schüler und Studenten durch die Erhöhung der Leistungen nach dem Bundesausbildungsförderungsgesetz
– den Rahmenplan für den Hochschulbau, wonach rund zwei Milliarden DM für den Ausbau der Hochschulen eingeplant sind. Bei entsprechender personeller Ausstattung der Hochschulen kann Anfang der achtziger Jahre das Studienangebot für mindestens eine Million Studenten gewährleistet werden.

Alle diese Jugend- und bildungspolitischen Entscheidungen und Anstöße zeigen, daß neue Grundlagen geschaffen worden sind, um zu mehr Chancengleichheit für alle Jugendlichen in der Bildungspolitik zu kommen. Diesen Weg wird die Bundesregierung in den kommenden Jahren fortsetzen.

Es liegt in der Natur der Sache, daß die bildungs- und arbeitsmarktpolitischen Aspekte der Jugendpolitik gegenwärtig im Vordergrund des öffentlichen Interesses stehen. Jugendpolitik, die auf die Sicherung der Zukunftschancen der Jugend gerichtet ist, erschöpft sich jedoch keineswegs nur in gezielten bildungs- und arbeitsmarktpolitischen Initiativen. Sie erstreckt sich u.a. auch auf den Bereich der Jugendhilfepolitik.

Ein überaus wichtiger Schwerpunkt unserer jugendpolitischen Arbeit in dieser Legislaturperiode ist die Reform des Jugendhilferechts.

Jugendhilfe ist ein allzuoft vor der Öffentlichkeit verborgenes Arbeitsfeld, von dem viele erst Notiz nehmen, wenn Jugendliche auffällig werden, wenn Jugendkriminalität, Drogenabhängigkeit oder ähnliche schwere Fehlentwicklungen zu beobachten sind. Deshalb darf auch die Reform des Jugendhilferechts nicht mehr nur Diskussionsthema für Fachleute bleiben.

Das neue Jugendhilferecht ist der wichtigste Schritt auf dem Wege zu besseren Entwicklungsmöglichkeiten von Kindern, Jugendlichen und Heranwachsenden.

Es wirkt für den Laien trocken und spröde, aber hinter den oft formalistisch wirkenden Paragraphen verbergen sich dramatische Probleme junger Menschen.

Die Reform des Jugendhilferechts ist seit langem überfällig. Immer noch gilt das Jugendwohlfahrtsgesetz von 1922, das damals ein großer Fortschritt war, heute aber, trotz verschiedener Novellierungen, den Ansprüchen eines modernen Jugendhilfegesetzes nicht mehr genügt. So war zum Beispiel die damals noch einseitig obrigkeitsstaatlich geprägte Verwaltungsrechtswissenschaft nicht in der Lage, das Gesetz in der Form eines echten Leistungsgesetzes zu gestalten. Dies zeigt augenfällig die Verwendung des damals vorherrschenden Begriffeinstrumentariums wie „Maßnahmen", „Maßregel", „Überwachung", „Aufsicht", etc. Noch wichtiger aber ist, daß dem Gesetz ein Leistungskatalog als Kernstück und ordnendes Prinzip fehlt, die Terminologie unsystematisch ist und die Bereiche Jugendpflege und allgemeine Förderung der Familienerziehung kaum angesprochen sind.

Kein Wunder, daß dieser unbefriedigende rechtliche Zustand heute zunehmend zur Fessel für die Entfaltung einer modernen und umfassenden Jugendhilfe geworden ist.

Wir haben bei der Abfassung unseres Entwurfes sehr darauf geachtet, daß die **praktische Hilfeleistung** im Mittelpunkt steht. Die Fachwelt braucht einen

Entwurf, der sich an den praktischen Problemen der Jugendhilfe orientiert. Vor allem aber brauchen die betroffenen Kinder und Jugendlichen Hilfe und nicht Ideologie.

Nun hat allerdings das Jugendhilferecht eine magische Anziehungskraft auf Ideologen von links wie von rechts.

Die Analyse der ersten Reaktionen in der Öffentlichkeit zeigen, daß die alten ideologischen Schlachten wieder geschlagen werden sollen – teilweise werden dabei dem Gesetz Absichten unterstellt, die im Gegensatz zum Gesetzestext stehen.

Der sensibelste Bereich ist die Frage des Elternrechts, dabei vor allem die Frage von Eingriffen gegen den Willen der Eltern.

Nach dem Entwurf ist Jugendhilfe grundsätzlich freiwillig. Eltern und junge Menschen sollen entscheiden, ob sie von Angeboten der Jugendhilfe Gebrauch machen wollen. Dies ist auch geltendes Recht.

Im künftigen Recht soll der Grundsatz der **Freiwilligkeit** jedoch **stärker betont** und in § 2 besonders verankert werden. Ein wesentliches Reformziel ist, das Jugendamt von dem Geruch der Eingriffsverwaltung in der Nähe von Gericht und Polizei zu befreien und zu einer Instanz der Leistungsverwaltung zu machen.

Nun weist das Grundgesetz in Artikel 6 Abs. 2 Satz 2 der staatlichen Gemeinschaft die Aufgabe zu, über die Betätigung des Elternrechts und der Elternpflicht zu wachen. Es gab deshalb früher und wird auch in Zukunft Fälle geben, in denen Jugendhilfe gegen den Willen der Eltern eingreifen muß. Eine solche Anordnung kann sowohl nach geltendem Recht als auch nach künftigem Recht **nur das Vormundschaftsgericht** treffen, nicht eine Verwaltungsbehörde.

Nach geltendem Recht gibt es dafür zwei Grundlagen: die allgemeine des § 1666 BGB und für die Fürsorgeerziehung die Spezialvorschrift des § 64 JWG, die ein Einschreiten unter etwas leichteren Voraussetzungen als § 1666 BGB erlaubt.

Nach künftigem Recht wird es **nur noch die Grundlage des § 1666 BGB** geben, dies erhöht die Eingriffsschwelle.

Fazit: Das neue Recht wird weniger Eingriffsmöglichkeiten in das Elternrecht kennen als das geltende!

Im Mittelpunkt unserer Reformüberlegungen steht die Entwicklung des jungen Menschen: er hat ein Recht auf freie Entfaltung seiner Persönlichkeit, das – wie das Bundesverfassungsgericht entschieden hat – die Richtschnur des Jugendhilferechts sein muß. Das neue Recht will deshalb die Rechtsstellung des jungen Menschen verbessern und ihn stärker als bisher zum Träger eigener

Rechte und Pflichten machen.

Jugend hat viele Probleme – Jugendpolitik ist daher ein weites Feld der Politik. Viele Vorhaben und Probleme muß ich unerwähnt lassen. Zum Beispiel unsere Bemühungen um eine kinderfreundlichere Umwelt, die Vorarbeiten zum internationalen Jahr des Kindes oder die vielfältigen Anstrengungen zum Ausbau und zur Qualifizierung der Erziehungs-, Jugend- und Familienberatung, die neuen Jugendreligionen oder der internationale Jugendaustausch mit seinen Kontroversen, die sich an der Teilnahme unserer Jugendverbände in den Weltjugendfestspielen wieder gezeigt haben. Es muß bei dieser Erwähnung bleiben. In diesem weiten Feld darf man die Orientierung nicht verlieren, wenn man politisch wirksam sein will. Die Orientierung der Bundesregierung wollte ich deutlich machen:
Wir arbeiten:
- für mehr Erziehungschancen
- für mehr Bildungschancen
- für mehr Chancen für ein Aufwachsen ohne materielle Not, ohne ökonomischen Mißbrauch und in körperlicher und seelischer Gesundheit
- für mehr Mitwirkungschancen.

Die Ziele der Jugendpolitik können nicht allein durch die Politk der Bundesregierung oder überhaupt staatliche Maßnahmen allein erreicht werden, sondern auch durch Inhalt und Stil des Verhaltens, den die Erwachsenen und die Institutionen dieser Gesellschaft gegenüber den jungen Menschen an den Tag legen. Dem dient auch dieses Symposion und die wichtige Untersuchung *„Jugend in Europa"*, die ihnen als Ausgangsbasis dient. Ich benutze die Gelegenheit für beides herzlich zu danken.

Aussprache über das Referat Zander

Leitung: Johannes C. Welbergen

Welbergen:

Vielen Dank, Herr Staatssekretär. Sie sehen, die Fragen häufen sich. Die erste Frage lautet: Worin liegt Ihrer Meinung nach der Grund dafür, daß zwei Drittel der Arbeitslosen weiblich sind?

Zander:

Das liegt daran, daß erstens die Ausbildung von Mädchen hinsichtlich der Qualität immer noch weit hinter der Ausbildung von Jungen zurückbleibt. Es liegt aber auch sehr daran, daß das Beschäftigungsspektrum in unserer Wirtschaft über 300 Berufe vorsieht und weit über 90 % der Mädchen und Frauen nur in einem guten Dutzend dieser Berufe tätig sind. Die überwiegende Mehrzahl der Berufe unserer Wirtschaft ist in den Augen der Eltern und der Mädchen selbst nicht für junge Mädchen geeignet.
Hier ist ein sich gegenseitig verschärfender und zum Nachteil der Mädchen ausgehender Kreislauf. Man nimmt an, daß überhaupt nur ein Dutzend Berufe in Frage kommen. Man rechnet damit, daß junge Mädchen heiraten und aus dem Erwerbsleben ausscheiden. Man beachtet nicht die Notwendigkeiten einer Berufsausbildung, und steht dann wiederum mit dem Ergebnis eines solchen verkürzten Bildungsprozesses nur vor einem kleinen Spektrum von Berufen, für die man geeignet ist. Hier muß also sowohl auf Seiten der Wirtschaft als auch auf Seiten der Eltern und der jungen Mädchen einiges an ihrer Einstellung verändert werden.

Dies Ganze fußt natürlich auch im traditionellen Rollenverständnis in unserer Gesellschaft über die Rolle der Frau.

Welbergen:

Stimmt es überhaupt, daß zwei Drittel der Arbeitslosen weiblich sind?

Zander:

Ja, der Jugend.

Welbergen:

Die nächste Frage: Die Jugendorganisation Ihrer Partei fordert in ihrem Aktionsprogramm die Abschaffung des dualen Bildungssystems. Wie stellt sich die Bundesregierung zu dieser Forderung? Gibt es eventuell Alternativen?

Zander:

Die Bundesregierung lehnt eine Abschaffung des dualen Systems ab. Ich würde das – und die Bundesregierung würde das ebenfalls – für einen schweren Fehler halten, weil das duale System in unserer Berufsausbildung die Probleme des Übergangs zwischen Bildungssystem und Beschäftigungssystem nachweislich besser löst, als es andere Systeme der Berufsausbildung tun. Die Bundesregierung hielte die Abschaffung des dualen Systems auch deshalb für einen Fehler, weil es unserer Meinung nach kein System der beruflichen Bildung gibt, das so flexibel den Innovationen in der Wirtschaft folgen kann, auch hinsichtlich der Anforderungen an die Qualifikation, wie es das duale System tun kann. Mit diesen beiden Grundsatzaussagen will ich natürlich nicht sagen: dieses duale System, wie wir es in der Bundesrepublik vorfinden, ist in seiner Ausprägung ideal; aber vom Prinzip her halten wir es für ein vorzügliches Berufsbildungssystem.

Allerdings gibt es eine Reihe von notwendigen Verbesserungen und Ergänzungen. Ich habe bei dem Bereich der überbetrieblichen Ausbildung, bei der Modernisierung von Ausbildungsordnungen einige dieser Probleme erwähnt. Es ist die Frage des Zehnten Pflichtbildungsjahres, es ist die Frage des Berufsgrundbildungsjahres in der Diskussion. Es ist nicht so, als wäre dieses System perfekt. Aber es ist vom Prinzip her ausgezeichnet, insbesondere wegen der beiden Vorteile, die ich eingangs genannt habe.

Welbergen:

Eine weitere Frage lautet: Ein wesentlicher Grund für die hohe Jugendarbeitslosigkeit sind die Kündigungsschutzvorschriften für ältere Arbeitnehmer. Wie will die Bundesregierung darauf reagieren?

Zander:

Ich glaube, es wäre völlig falsch, und das könnte keiner wünschen, wenn wir auf diesem Felde anfingen, die Generationen gegeneinander auszuspielen. Ich wage überhaupt nicht abzuwägen, was sozialpolitisch nachteiliger ist: wenn etwa ein älterer Arbeitnehmer plötzlich entlassen wird – auch mit allen sozialen Problemen für seine Familie, trotz der Arbeitslosenunterstützung –, oder ob es schwerwiegender ist, wenn ein junger Mensch nicht hineinkommt.

Was wir tun müssen, ist, insgesamt die Zahl der angebotenen Arbeitsplätze zu vermehren. Das geht auf zwei Wegen. Entweder kann ich durch mehr Wachstum dafür sorgen, daß mehr Arbeitsplätze angeboten werden. Andererseits kann ich, wenn es lange Zeit bei einer strukturell bedingten Arbeitslosigkeit zum Nachteil der Jugend bleiben sollte, überlegen, wie man die vorhandene Arbeit in dieser Gesellschaft anders aufteilt. Da sind ja eine Fülle von Überlegungen in der Diskussion, angefangen von der Altersgrenze bis zur längeren Ausbildung vor dem Berufseintritt bis hin zur Wochenarbeitszeit. Ich weiß, daß diese Fragen in der Wissenschaft und zwischen Arbeitgebern und Gewerkschaften diskutiert werden. Ich möchte hier keine Lösungsvorschläge machen, aber ich meine, unsere Anstrengungen müssen in die beiden Richtungen gehen: Wachstum und damit insgesamt mehr Arbeitsplätze, und die verbleibende strukturelle Arbeitslosigkeit muß künftig durch eine andere Verteilung der Arbeit in der Gesellschaft behoben werden.

Den Abbau erreichter sozialer Sicherungen halte ich für ein ungeeignetes Mittel, weil dies natürlich insgesamt auch zu einem Abbau der sozialen Sicherung der Gesellschaft insgesamt beiträgt und eine verhängnisvolle Entwicklung einleiten würde.

Welbergen:

Ein Teilnehmer bittet noch einmal zu erläutern, warum die Bundesregierung nicht vorschlägt, das Ausbildungsförderungsgesetz zurückzuziehen.

Teilnehmer:

Ich möchte das kurz erläutern. Sie haben in Ihren Ausführungen das Gesetz als eine Maßnahme zur Verbesserung der Ausbildungsstellensituation sehr stark gelobt. Ich bin da etwas anderer Meinung. Ich sehe, daß dieses Ausbildungsplatzförderungsgesetz Risiken in sich birgt, die es eher zu einem Ausbildungsplatz-Verhinderungsgesetz werden lassen.

Die Unsicherheit in der Wirtschaft über dieses Ausbildungsplatzförderungsgesetz ist doch sehr groß. Sie birgt auch die Gefahr, daß es jetzt, solange die Finanzierungsregelung noch nicht in Kraft getreten ist, zu einer Ausbildungsplatzverminderung kommt, um sie später wieder zu steigern, falls es doch einmal kommt. Darin liegt eine Gefahr.

Zweitens: Selbst wenn die Finanzierungsregelung in Kraft gesetzt würde, bestehen Gefahren darin, daß die Verteilung der Mittel aus dem Ausbildungsplatzförderungsfond, der dann geschaffen würde, sehr starke Eingriffsmöglichkeiten für das Bundesministerium für Bildung und Wissenschaft böte, und es könnte eine ganz gelenkte Verteilung der Mittel einsetzen.

Zander:

Ich will einmal meine Meinung zu diesem Thema ganz offen sagen. Wir haben in der Bundesrepublik seit 1969 – das war das Jahr des Inkrafttretens des jetzt noch gültigen Berufsbildungsgesetzes – einen Rückgang der Zahl der Ausbildungsplätze. Diesen konnten wir in der Hochkonjunktur und damals noch auf dem Hintergrund der geburtenschwachen Jahrgänge verkraften. Aber der Rückgang der Zahl der Ausbildungsplätze kam in dem Moment in eine gefährliche Größenordnung, als kein Überschuß an Ausbildungsplätzen insgesamt rechnerisch mehr da war, die Zahl der Ausbildungsplätze gerade noch so hoch war wie die Zahl der Jugendlichen, die einen Ausbildungsplatz suchten, ja sogar darunter abzusinken drohte.

In dieser Situation konnte der Staat nach meiner Überzeugung nicht zusehen, wie durch Verweigerung der Bereitstellung von Ausbildungsplätzen durch die Wirtschaft versucht wurde, staatliche Reformpolitik zu stoppen. Diesen Versuch hat es ja gegeben.

Aber es mußte etwas geschehen, um diese Tendenz umzukehren. Nun ist aus dem ganzen großen Anlauf zur Reform der beruflichen Bildung nur das Ausbildungsplatzförderungsgesetz übriggeblieben. Ich weiß aus vielen Erklärungen: die Unternehmer in der Bundesrepublik scheuen die Anwendung des Ausbildungsplatzförderungsgesetzes wie der Teufel das Weihwasser. Von ihrem Standpunkt aus völlig zu Recht, denn es ist ja nicht zu übersehen: wenn ich dieses Gesetz anwende, werden sich seine Mängel sehr schnell herausstellen, und der Wunsch nach noch größerer Umlage und nach noch perfekterer Handhabung dieses Systems wird laut. Dann könnte in der Tat eine Gefahr auftreten, die das duale System tangieren würde.

Seit aber das Gesetz da ist, gibt es nun plötzlich mehr Ausbildungsplätze, sogar in der Rezession. Im vergangenen Jahr waren es rund 90 000 mehr, in diesem Jahr wird es noch einmal eine ähnliche Größenordnung sein, nach allem, was wir im Augenblick wissen. Das heißt, diese Drohung des Ausbildungsplatzförderungsgesetzes, das Schwert an der Wand, hat die Entwicklung des Ausbildungsplatzangebotes in der Bundesrepublik umgekehrt, und zwar rechtzeitig, im Interesse unserer Jugendlichen. Wenn ich die Entwicklung der nächsten Jahre überblicke, dann vermute ich, daß wir dieses Gesetz nie werden anwenden müssen. Aber ich glaube, es war dringend erforderlich, es zu schaffen, als ein Instrument in einer Zeit, in der die Wirtschaft selber nicht mehr in der Lage war, aus eigener Kraft genügend Plätze bereitzustellen.

Damit beantwortet sich auch die Frage, ob beabsichtigt ist, dieses Gesetz abzuschaffen. Es ist auf absehbare Zeit nicht beabsichtigt, es abzuschaffen.

Welbergen:

Ich sah, daß jemand den Kopf schüttelte, während Ihrer Ausführungen, vielleicht können wir demjenigen zwischendurch mal das Wort geben.

Teilnehmer:

Herr Staatssekretär, sind Sie wirklich der Ansicht, daß die Zahlung von 5000 DM für einen zusätzlichen Ausbildungsplatz angesichts von Kosten von 35.000–45.000 DM – man kann bis 50.000 DM gehen – für eine qualifizierte Ausbildung wirklich einen Anreiz bietet, zusätzliche Ausbildungsplätze zu schaffen? Oder war es nicht vielmehr das allgemeine Bewußtsein, das sich in der Bevölkerung und in der Wirtschaft breitgemacht hatte, hier nun zusätzlich etwas zu tun?

Aussprache Zander

Zander:

Was ich behauptet habe und wobei ich bleiben möchte, ist das folgende. In der Wirtschaft gibt es eine große Sorge: daß es bei diesem Gesetz, wenn es angewandt wird – eben weil die Beträge gemessen an den Kosten der Ausbildung so bescheiden sind –, daß es dabei nicht bleiben wird. Die Sorge der Wirtschaft besteht darin, daß es der Einstieg sein wird in eine viel umfangreichere und umfassendere Finanzierung.

Davor, nicht vor den relativ bescheidenen Umlagen, die das Gesetz vorsieht, ist die Besorgnis da. Darauf habe ich auch meine These gestützt, daß wieder mehr Ausbildungsplätze bereitgestellt worden sind. Es steht für mich außer Frage, daß viele Unternehmen auch aus Sorge um die damit zusammenhängenden politischen Gefahren und Instabilitäten mehr ausgebildet haben. Ich weiß aber auch, daß das andere Element eine Rolle gespielt hat, insbesondere bei dem sehr starken Engagement der Kammern.

Teilnehmer:

Ich habe noch eine Frage zu diesem Komplex. Eigentlich muß man doch davon ausgehen, daß die Wirtschaft daran interessiert ist, Ausbildungsplätze bereitzustellen und dadurch ausgebildete Kräfte zu schaffen, weil sie diese später braucht. Wenn das nicht der Fall ist, muß es irgendwelche Ursachen haben. Sollte man nicht besser versuchen, diese Ursachen herauszufinden und zu ändern, statt irgendwo an den Symptomen herumzukurieren und einfach einen Erpressungsversuch zu starten?

Zander:

Ich räume Ihnen gern ein, daß einiges von dem, was Sie als Ursachen vermuten, eine Rolle spielt. Aber die entscheidende Tatsache sind doch die Kosten. Bei aller Ausbildungsbereitschaft kann ein Betrieb sich doch sagen: wozu soll ich denn die 30.000 DM aufbringen, laßt doch die anderen ausbilden, die qualifizierten Fachkräfte hole ich mir dann auf dem Arbeitsmarkt. Eine solche Entwicklung hatten wir. Wir waren in der Bundesrepublik vor dem Ausbildungsplatzförderungsgesetz so weit, daß nur noch 16 % der Betriebe ausgebildet haben, aber 100 % Betriebe natürlich ausgebildete Kräfte beschäftigt haben.

An diesem Punkt setzte die naheliegende Überlegung ein: dann sollen doch über einen Fond zu den Kosten alle Betriebe beitragen, und denjenigen Betrieben, die eine qualifizierte Ausbildung machen, werden die Kosten – jedenfalls zu einem gewissen Teil – ersetzt werden. Dies war ein Ausfluß der Tatsache, daß die Zahl der Betriebe, die ausgebildet haben, immer weiter zurückging.

Welbergen:

Warum haben nur noch 16 % der Betriebe ausgebildet. Ging es da nur um die Kosten, oder waren es die gesetzlichen Anforderungen, die viele Betriebe nicht mehr erfüllen konnten?

Zander:

Es hat um die Ausbildereignungsverordnung Klagen gegeben. Da sind wahrscheinlich auch aus der Vorstellung der Fachleute in den Betrieben die Normen unter Umständen etwas zu hoch gesetzt worden.

Es hat sicher dort einige Ursachen gegeben. Möglicherweise haben auch andere Fragen, z.B. der bürokratische Aufwand, eine Rolle gespielt. Ich bin aber davon überzeugt, das Dominierende waren die gestiegenen Kosten der Berufsausbildung.

Teilnehmer:

Ich darf dort gerade mal anschließen, Herr Zander: Wenn Sie die duale Ausbildung wollen, dann darf das Ausbildungsplatzförderungsgesetz dieses System nicht beeinträchtigen. Sie sagten mit Recht: der Hauptgrund, weswegen nicht in ausreichendem Maße ausgebildet wurde, ist die Höhe der Kosten gewesen. Tatsache ist auch, daß die Zukunftschancen, die beruflichen Chancen eines jungen Menschen umso schlechter sind, je häufiger er den Beruf wechseln muß.

Bekanntlich hat die Edding-Kommission, die seinerzeit die Kosten der Berufsausbildung untersucht hat, festgestellt, daß z.B. im Handwerk die Kosten durchaus erträglich sind, bzw. daß die Ausbildung in erheblichen Bereichen sogar einen Gewinn für den Handwerksbetrieb abwirft. Andererseits kostet die Ausbildung z.B. in Großunternehmen, Industriebetrieben, immense Summen. Wenn jetzt also eingeführt wird, per Ausbildungsumlage 5.000 DM für den ausbildenden Betrieb zu zahlen, dann wir das den, der 35.000 DM aufwenden muß, aller Wahrscheinlichkeit nach nicht dazu veranlassen, mit einer Ausbildung zu beginnen. Aber der Handwerksbetrieb hat den Vorteil. 71 % aller im Handwerk Ausgebildeten verlassen den handwerklichen Bereich und gehen in die Industrie oder in den Dienstleistungsbereich. 71 %, das bedeutet eine immense Zahl von Fehlausbildung.

So bekommt man zwar vordergründig die Schulabgänger von der Straße, aber man bekommt sie in den verkehrten Ausbildungszweig hinein. Es wäre nach meiner Vorstellung doch wesentlich sinnvoller, ein Förderungssystem über steuerliche Entlastungen zu schaffen, das den Ausbildungsbetrieb, eventuell nach Branchen gegliedert, entsprechend der Höhe der tatsächlichen Kosten der Berufsausbildung entlastet. Denn in dem Maße würden dann die größeren Industriebetriebe zur Ausbildung veranlaßt, und ein hohes Maß an Fehlausbildung würde verhindert.

Zander:

Es ist sicher sehr reizvoll, über ein Gesetz, das noch nie angewandt wurde, und seine Wirkungen zu spekulieren; ich sage einmal: zu spekulieren.

Die Alternative, die Sie vorgeschlagen haben, nämlich steuerliche Entlastungen, halten wir für falsch. Ich will nur zwei Gründe nennen. Erstens ist eine solche Regelung mittelstandsfeindlich, und zweitens benachteiligt sie alle lohnintensiven Betriebe. Ich halte das für eine unglückliche Alternative zu diesem Ausbildungsplatzförderungsgesetz.

Teilnehmer:

Herr Staatssekretär, ist Ihnen bekannt, daß aufgrund der Ausbildungsordnungen in einer Vielzahl gerade auch von Großbetrieben nicht mehr ausgebildet werden kann, weil bestimmte Ausbildungsinhalte dort nicht mehr geboten werden? Wäre es deshalb nicht sinnvoller, eventuell aus den Mitteln des Ausbildungsförderungsgesetzes überbetriebliche Ausbildung zu fördern?

Zander:

Ich gebe Ihnen recht, hier befinden wir uns in einem Dilemma. Einerseits bedarf es qualifizierter Ausbildung. Andererseits sagen Sie zu Recht, es gibt eben eine Reihe von Betrieben, deren Ausbildungsmöglichkeiten diesen Anforderungen nicht mehr nachkommen können. Um diese Schwierigkeiten zu beheben, bedarf es aber gar nicht der Mittel aus dem Ausbildungsplatzförderungsgesetz. Ich habe Ihnen vorhin gesagt, daß die Bundesregierung für die Förderung überbetrieblicher Ausbildungsstätten eine Milliarde bereitgestellt hat. Diese Ausbildungsstätten werden meist von einer Innung oder einer Kammer getragen, manche auch mit Beteiligung der kommunalen Gremien. Es gibt ganz unterschiedliche Trägerkonstruktionen. Sie werden bereits heute von der Bundesregierung sehr intensiv gefördert.

Deutsch:

Ich habe zwei undezente Fragen an den Herrn Staatssekretär. Wie lange ist ein junger Arbeitsloser im Durchschnitt arbeitslos? Ist das ein ziemlich kurzes Durchgangsstadium, in das immer neue junge Leute eintreten, oder ist das für eine größere Anzahl junger Menschen eine lang andauernde Sache? Macht da die Berufsausbildung einen Unterschied, so daß die Leute, die ausgebildet sind, schneller zu Arbeit kommen als die anderen? Wenn das Letzte zutrifft, ist dann nicht jede Berufsausbildung für junge Menschen nützlich, so daß man nicht von Fehlausbildung sprechen kann, auch wenn der junge Mensch nachher seinen Beruf wechselt? Wenn es Leute gibt, die ohne Ausbildung bleiben müssen und die lange arbeitslos sind, ist das nicht eine unsichtbare Form der Verschuldung an die Zukunft?

Ich weiß nicht – das müssen Sie hier im Raum besser wissen –, was Ihnen größere Sorgen macht: Vollbeschäftigung heute oder die Altersrente im Jahre 2020? Glauben Sie, daß im wesentlichen die Jugendarbeitslosigkeit auf dem Bildungswege abgeschafft oder entscheidend reduziert werden kann? Oder braucht man auch andere Maßnahmen zur Vollbeschäftigung?

Zander:

Über die statistischen Angaben kann ich nur aus meiner Erinnerung – nicht mit dem Anspruch, daß sie präzise sind – folgendes sagen: Die Dauer der Arbeitslosigkeit der Jugendlichen ist eindeutig unterdurchschnittlich, verglichen mit der Dauer der Arbeitslosigkeit insgesamt.

Die Zahlen beruhen, wenn ich das richtig im Kopf habe, auf der Altersgrenze von 21 Jahren. Aber ich habe die Statistik nicht hier vorliegen, um das genau sagen zu können. Ich kann nur über die Tendenz sagen: ich weiß, daß die Arbeitslosigkeit der Jugendlichen unterdurchschnittlich ist. Ich weiß allerdings auch, daß eine hohe Dunkelziffer bei der Jugendarbeitslosigkeit vorhanden ist, die das auch wiederum relativiert, was ich gesagt habe.

Aber der entscheidende Punkt Ihrer Frage ist ja: wie sieht das mit der Qualifikation und der Sicherheit des Arbeitsplatzes aus? Da ist die Aussage ganz eindeutig: je besser jemand qualifiziert ist, desto größere Chancen hat er, einen Arbeitsplatz zu finden und ihn auch zu behalten.

Wenn Sie meinen, daß geringere Qualifikation eine Art Vorgriff auf zukünftige Belastungen ist, dann muß ich Ihnen in dem Sinne recht geben, daß Jugendliche, die heute nicht ausgebildet werden, diejenigen sein werden, die bei jeder wirtschaftlichen Rezession zuerst wieder aus den Betrieben herausfliegen und zuletzt wieder in die Betriebe hineinkommen. Diese Jugendlichen sind dazu programmiert, während ihres ganzen Arbeitslebens mehrfach von der Arbeitslosigkeit betroffen zu werden und auch immer wieder der Arbeitslosenversicherung zur Last zu fallen.

Allerdings müssen wir die Dinge auch in der Relation sehen. Meines Wissens gibt es kein Industrieland in Westeuropa, in dem der Anteil der jungen Menschen unter 21 Jahre mit einer abgeschlossenen Berufsausbildung so hoch ist wie in der Bundesrepublik Deutschland. In fast allen anderen Ländern ist der Anteil derjenigen, die keine Berufsausbildung haben, größer als bei uns. Dies ist übrigens sicher auch ein Vorteil des dualen Systems. Trotz unserer Probleme – für die Bundesregierung ist jeder einzelne arbeitslose oder ausbildungsplatzlose Jugendliche einer zuviel – müssen wir sehen, daß wir in einem internationalen Vergleich recht gut dastehen. Aber damit darf sich niemand beruhigen, wegen des Individuums, wegen des Einzelnen, nicht wegen der Statistik.

Aussprache Zander

Teilnehmer:

Wir sagen, wir müssen die Berufsausbildung qualitativ permanent verbessern, aber es gibt Gruppen von Jugendlichen, die diesen Abschluß gar nicht schaffen können, weil sie z.B. lernbehindert oder schulbehindert sind – darunter fallen auch die Kinder von Gastarbeitern –, und dann werden solche Berufsabschlüsse nicht mehr erreicht.

Weshalb gibt es nicht mehr Stufenausbildung, damit diese Jugendlichen die Chance haben, wenigstens den praktischen Teil eines Berufses zu erlernen – was bei vielen Berufen möglich ist –, um nicht mehr nur Hilfsarbeiter zu sein, sondern doch einen Berufsabschluß zu haben?

Zander:

Es steht außer Frage, daß solche Gruppen von lernbehinderten Jugendlichen besonderer Förderung bedürfen. Sie muß aber zum Teil – nehmen Sie die Kinder von Ausländern als Beispiel – sogar schon im Vorschulalter einsetzen.

Ich sage das nicht, um die Bundesregierung freizusprechen, die keine Kompetenz auf diesem Gebiet bei uns hat. Vielmehr ist dies eine gesellschaftspolitische Aufgabe im Hinblick auf die zweite Ausländergeneration. Sie wird, wie ich annehme, in unserer Gesellschaft sehr große Spannungen mit sich bringen, wenn wir dieses Problem nicht lösen. Denn es zeigt sich, daß diese Kinder zu einem sehr großen Teil schon den Hauptschulabschluß nicht schaffen. Gerade sie bilden die Gruppe, die keine Chance bekommt, eine Berufsausbildung zu erlernen.

Ich würde es für richtig halten – ohne daß ich hierzu aus politischer Verantwortung qua Amt etwas sagen kann –, wenn sich die Länder eine sehr viel intensivere Förderung schon in der Vorschulklasse einfallen ließen. Hier beginnen, wenn Sie so wollen, schon die Sonderschul-Karrieren. Außerdem gibt es einen weiteren Teil von Jugendlichen in Problemgruppen. Lernbehinderte ist ein weiteres Stichwort. Die Behinderung kann vielfältige Ursachen haben.

Hier haben wir eine Mitverantwortung. Wir haben von unserem Ministerium aus eine Reihe von Maßnahmen über die Jugendhilfe eingeleitet, für berufsunreife, lernschwache Jugendliche, die nicht nur eine Förderung durch die Bundesanstalt für Arbeit brauchen, mit deren Hilfe sie den Schulabschluß nachholen können, sondern die zum großen Teil erst durch individuelle Betreuung in die Lage versetzt werden müssen, die Angebote wahrnehmen zu können, die es gibt. Die Bundesanstalt und das Arbeitsförderungsgesetz stellen ja großartige Angebote dar. Hier haben wir mit Mitteln der Jugendhilfe gezielt eingesetzt. Sicherlich müßte der Umfang wesentlich erweitert und vergrößert werden.

Daß Stufenausbildungssysteme große Vorteile haben, ist unbestritten. Nur eignen sich eben nicht alle Berufe dazu, eine Stufenausbildung zu organisieren. Auch nicht alle Betriebe eignen sich dazu. Wenn ich diesen Teil zu sehr formalisiere, gerate ich in die Gefahr, daß viele Betriebe den Anforderungen einer Stufenausbildung nicht gerecht werden können. Ich muß die Vielfalt der Betriebe und ihrer Probleme sehen. Wo ich das nicht mit überbetrieblichen Ausbildungsstätten kompensieren kann, kann ich eben in bestimmten Berufen keine Stufenausbildung konzipieren. Im Prinzip muß man diesen Weg gehen, aber nicht dogmatisch, nicht überall, sondern da, wo sich ein Beruf dafür besonders eignet.

Welbergen:

Die nächste Frage lautet: Wie sehen Sie im Rahmen des Jugendhilferechts Möglichkeiten und Bedeutung der in die Länderkompetenz fallenden Jugendbildungsgesetze und die Möglichkeiten der Bildungsgesetze für die Chancen der Jugendlichen? Wann werden solche Gesetze kommen?

Zander:

Für die Damen und Herren, die mit dem Thema nicht speziell vertraut sind, möchte ich vorweg folgendes sagen. Ich habe davon gesprochen, daß wir ein Jugendhilferecht konzipieren. Die Jugendhilfe umfaßt nach unserem Verständnis auch die außerschulische Jugendhilfe. Der Bundesgesetzgeber hat nach dem Grundgesetz eine Gesetzgebungskompetenz, die er bei dem Jugendhilferecht ausschöpft. Diese Gesetzgebungskompetenz leitet sich aus Artikel 74 des Grundgesetzes ab. Da steht: Der Bund hat die Gesetzgebungskompetenz für die öffentliche Fürsorge. Wir regeln aber in dem Entwurf des Jugendhilferechtes auch Fragen wie etwa politische Bildung, musische Bildung, sportliche Jugendbildung. Hier taucht der Begriff „Bildung", wie wir meinen, nicht in dem Sinne auf, wie es föderalistisch in der Regelungskompetenz den Ländern vorbehalten ist, sondern als ein Teil des Gesamtkomplexes „Sozialisation eines jungen Menschen", die auch Erziehungs- und Bildungselemente beinhalten. Deshalb meinen wir, daß der Bundesgesetzgeber dazu die Regelungskompetenz hat. Aber die wird uns von den Ländern bestritten. Im Laufe des Gesetzgebungsverfahrens wird mindestens die Bayerische Staatsregierung mit Sicherheit widersprechen. Dort bestreitet man ja überhaupt, daß der Bund eine Regelungskompetenz hat. Aber darüber wird es zwischen den Verfassungsjuristen während des Gesetzgebungsverfahrens mit Sicherheit zu einem Streit kommen. Wie weit er führt und mit welchen Ergebnissen er abgeschlossen wird, kann ich nicht vorhersagen. Wir meinen, wir haben eine Regelungskompetenz.

Was eine Durchführungsverordnung zum Jugendwohlfahrtsgesetz angeht, muß ich sagen: darüber weiß ich nichts. Wenn es jemandem sehr auf den Nägeln brennt mit dieser Information, müßte ich sie aus unserem Hause einholen und schriftlich nachliefern. Ich weiß das einfach nicht.

Teilnehmer:

Ich möchte für eine Gruppe sprechen, die hier überhaupt nicht eingeladen ist, die hier gar nicht vertreten ist. Es sind die 75 % unorganisierten Jugendlichen.

Es geht um die Frage, ob es möglich sein wird, daß das neue Jugendwohlfahrtsgesetz den jungen Menschen auch irgendwelche Möglichkeiten bietet, ein Recht auf Hilfe in der Freizeit zu bekommen. Wir haben die Erfahrung gemacht, Freizeitstätten von Jugendverbänden, von Kirchen und von Kommunen als prophylaktische Arbeit zu sehen. Das ist eine unschätzbare Arbeit, die bisher immer so verstanden worden ist: Jugend von der Straße, ein bißchen Schach spielen, ein bißchen Tischtennis, und es gibt keine Unruhe in der Bevölkerung.

Zander:

Ich habe jetzt – es ist immer gut, wenn man sich an etwas orientiert – noch einmal einen Blick in den Text „Perspektive 2000" geworfen. Da lese ich ziemlich am Ende: „Staat und Gesellschaft müssen vor einer ausufernden Betreuung des Bürgers bewahrt bleiben." Ich weiß nicht, ob Ihre Frage bezüglich der Regelung für das Freizeitangebot darunterfällt. Aber das will ich mal nicht annehmen.
Das Problem ist dabei folgendes. Diese Freizeitangebote spielen sich naturgemäß da ab, wo die Jugendlichen wohnen, d.h. wo ihre Wohnung, wo ihre Ausbildungs- oder Arbeitsstätte ist. Das wiederum heißt, solche Freizeiteinrichtungen müssen von den Kommunen bereitgestellt werden, die es ja auch jetzt schon tun: die vielen Jugendheime, Sportstätten, die Häuser der Offenen Tür und vieles mehr, die zielen ja in diesen Bereich. Hier hat die Bundesregierung nach unserer Verfassung keine Möglichkeit, per Gesetz die Gemeinden zu verpflichten. Dennoch meinen wir, daß dieser ganze Bereich ein sehr wichtiger ist, der zunehmende Bedeutung erlangen wird, wenn wir etwa von Perspektiven möglicher Arbeitszeitentwicklungen ausgehen. Wir werden im Jugendhilferecht einige Normen haben, die beschreiben, wie ein solches Angebot aussehen müßte. Ich bin sicher: mit den Vorschriften, die wir schaffen, werden wir die Entwicklung auch in der Richtung beeinflussen, daß künftig dieses Angebot stärker von den Gemeinden bereitgestellt wird.

Eine Bemerkung zu Ihrem Hinweis auf die unorganisierte Jugend. Es gibt bei den jungen Menschen in der Bundesrepublik eine Tendenz, sich nicht mehr allzusehr zu organisieren. Es gibt eine gewisse Zurückhaltung, aber zugleich ein großes Interesse und eine Bereitschaft, an Angeboten der Jugendarbeit teilzunehmen. Hierauf haben ja auch die Jugendverbände durchaus reagiert, die sehr intensive Angebote auch der offenen Jugendarbeit bereitstellen. Ich glaube, wir brauchen beides. Denn ich habe sehr oft festgestellt, daß eine solche freie Jugendinitiative, die sich um wenige Personen gruppiert, versandete, wenn diese Personen, die das getragen haben, verschwunden waren. Da war dann die Arbeit tot.

Dann besinnt man sich dankbar darauf, daß auch noch organisierte Jugendverbände da sind, die dann wieder ein Angebot machen können. Ich meine also, hier ist sowohl eine Überbetonung des einen wie des anderen von Schaden.

Teilnehmer:

Ich möchte die Gewährleistungsverpflichtung ansprechen. Ich höre mit Interesse von Ihnen, daß der Rechtsanspruch des Kindes auf eine Kindertagesheimerziehung zurückgenommen worden ist. Ist es tatsächlich so? Denn die Gewährleistungsverpflichtung ist im neuen Referentenentwurf noch verstärkter enthalten als im alten Gesetz.

Die zweite Frage: Das alte Jugendwohlfahrtsgesetz geht davon aus, die Förderung bis zum 25. Lebensjahr durchführen zu können. In dem neuen Referentenentwurf wird aber das 18. Lebensjahr angesprochen. Darüber hätte ich gern eine Auskunft.

Zander:

Also zum Ersten: Gewährleistungsanspruch. Wir haben nie in einem Entwurf einen Gewährleistungsanspruch auf allgemeine Jugendarbeit gehabt. Aber selbstverständlich haben wir, was Kindertagesstätten angeht und entsprechende Einrichtungen, nach wie vor einen solchen Anspruch im Gesetz konstituiert, und dabei werden wir auch bleiben. Dieses Problem hat sich sehr dadurch entschärft, daß wir heute ein fast flächendeckendes Angebot an Kindertagesstätten zur Verfügung haben, so daß auch wir bei der Konzipierung dieses Gesetzentwurfes von ganz anderen Teilzahlen und Kosten ausgehen konnten.

Die zweite Frage betraf die Altersgrenze: Wir haben die Frage diskutiert, ob wir nicht für die Jugendförderung Konsequenzen aus der Tatsache ziehen müssen, daß wir die Volljährigkeit und das Wahlalter auf 18 Jahre heruntergesetzt haben. Es war die Frage, ob die Förderung für junge Menschen, die mit 18 Jahren erwachsen sind, bis 25 Jahre weitergehen muß. Wir sind zu dem Ergebnis gekommen: Ja, weil diese jungen Erwachsenen ja teilweise schon ihrerseits die Empfänger der nach diesem Gesetz viel breiter gefächerten Angebote der Familienunterstützung sind. Sie sind ja teilweise schon junge Familien, junge Eltern. Als Teilnehmer einer internationalen Jugendbewegung sind sie uns genauso willkommen wie auch als junge Eltern. Es muß sich also um einen Irrtum handeln, wenn Sie annehmen, wir würden die Leistungen für die Jugend bis 18 Jahre begrenzen.

Welbergen:

Aussprache Zander

Angesichts der fortgeschrittenen Zeit und des etwas speziellen Themas möchte ich die Diskussion hier abbrechen und zu der nächsten schriftlich gestellten Frage kommen: Wie Sie sagten, ist es das vorrangige Ziel der Erziehung, allen Jugendlichen eine qualifizierte Berufsausbildung zu geben. Ist es nicht heute viel akuter, das Problem der Überqualifikation von Akademikern zu lösen? Die daraus resultierende Arbeitsplatzverdrängung ist meines Erachtens nicht sehr fortschrittlich, zumal die Betroffenen ihrerseits gezwungen werden, sich unsolidarisch zu verhalten.

Zander:

Zu Ihrer Bemerkung, Herr Welbergen, daß das ein spezielles Thema sei, möchte ich etwas sagen: Unsere Gesellschaft ist geneigt, bis zu 5.000 DM im Monat für die Heimunterbringung eines deliquenten Jugendlichen aufzubringen, aber sie ist nicht bereit, ein Zehntel dieser Summe für vorbeugende Hilfen in der Familie bereitzustellen. Weil dies ein grundsätzliches Problem des Verständnisses von Jugendarbeit in unserer Gesellschaft ist, möchte ich Sie sehr dringend bitten, die Bedeutung dieser Lebenshilfereform nicht zu unterschätzen.

Eine Bemerkung zu der Frage: akademische Berufe. Ein Blick auf die Statistiken der Arbeitslosen zeigt, daß die akademischen Berufe ganz unterschiedlich von Arbeitslosigkeit betroffen sind. Bei einer allgemeinen Arbeitslosenquote von rund 4 % haben wir eine Akademikerarbeitslosenquote von 2,2 bis 3 %. Bei uns ist dies ein besonderes Problem, weil wir es natürlich auf dem Hintergrund der geburtenstarken Jahrgänge sehen. Andere europäische Industriestaaten haben diese großen Bevölkerungsschwankungen nicht. Daher wird dieses Problem dort auch als eine ganz stetige und gleichmäßige Entwicklung gesehen, während wir hier immer noch diskutieren: Wie wird dann der Übergang von Akademikern ins Beschäftigungssystem sein? Mit einiger Sicherheit wird der Bedarf an Absolventen unserer Hochschulen im öffentlichen Dienst, das läßt sich jetzt schon absehen, nicht mehr so stark wachsen wie bisher. Das liegt daran, daß der Staat in der Vergangenheit expandiert hat und daß viele Beschäftigte auch in relativ jungen Jahren dort arbeiten, so daß die Abgangsquote an Bedeutung verlieren wird. Auf der anderen Seite gehen wir davon aus, daß die private Wirtschaft einen etwas steigenden Bedarf an akademisch ausgebildeten Absolventen oder Erwerbstätigen haben wird.

Natürlich ist diese Frage auch eine der Verfassungsfragen. Selbst wenn ich es wollte, könnte ich keine Steuerungssysteme in unser Bildungssystem einbauen, die die Quote der Absolventen von Hochschulen und Ausbildungsgängen bewußt geringer hält als es die Teilnehmer unseres Bildungssystems selbst wünschen.

Zur Frage, inwieweit hier eine Verdrängung gegenüber denen, die weniger qualifiziert sind, da ist: Ich glaube, darauf werden wir uns einstellen müssen.

Es wird insgesamt, auch für Akademiker selbst, einen größeren Wettbewerb um qualifizierte Funktionen in dieser Gesellschaft geben. Ich glaube, das kann man aufgrund der Zahlen und der Erwartungen jetzt schon vorhersagen.

Welbergen:

Herr Staatssekretär, noch eine letzte Frage: Gibt es in Ihrem Ministerium Zukunftsperspektiven bezüglich der Weltinnenpolitik und über Export von Fachkräften in Entwicklungsländer? Gibt es andere Überlegungen um Planungsansätze in Richtung internationaler Integration Jugendlicher, die heute etwa für das Jahr 2000 projiziert werden? Ich glaube, man kann die Frage hinzunehmen: Welche Rolle spielt die Fortsetzung der Entspannungspolitik der Bundesregierung für die Zukunft der jungen Generation? Welche Schwerpunkte setzt die Bundesregierung?

Zander:

Was den ersten Bereich angeht: Entwicklungspolitik, Wirtschaftspolitik, muß ich meine Inkompetenz anmelden. Dieses wird in einem anderen Ressort, wirtschaftliche Zusammenarbeit, behandelt. Im Bundesministerium für Jugend, Familie und Gesundheit gibt es keinerlei Planungen.

Ich glaube, daß es, was die Entspannung angeht, keinerlei Alternative in der Politik gibt, es sei denn, man will wieder Verschärfung der Spannungen. Denn wenn es wieder zu kriegerischen Auseinandersetzungen kommt, gerade auf dem Hintergrund atomarer Waffen, ist über Zukunftsaussichten, über Berufsperspektiven, überhaupt nicht mehr zu reden und zu diskutieren. Unser Ressort unterstützt diese Politik möglichst auf Gegenseitigkeit basierend auch durch eine intensive Förderung des Jugendaustausches. Wir haben noch nicht mit allen Staaten, z.B. den Warschauer-Pakt-Staaten, erreicht, daß genausoviel Jugendliche von dort in unser Land kommen, wie Jugendliche von unserem Land in diese Länder gehen. Wir entwickeln das aber schrittweise weiter. Wir tun es gestützt auf die Jugendstruktur, die wir in unserem Land haben, die ja zum Teil auch verschieden von der in anderen Ländern ist. Es gibt wohl kaum ein Land mit einer solchen Vielzahl verschieden strukturierter Jugendverbände. Wir unterstützen sie bei ihren Aktivitäten, auch wenn sie nach Havanna zu den Weltjugendfestspielen fahren. Gerade auch mit Blick auf die vielen Staaten der Dritten Welt halte ich es für unverzichtbar, daß sich dort in Havanna auch demokratische Jugendverbände artikulieren können. Das ist der Grund, warum wir meinen, daß auch Steuergelder für diesen Zweck gerechtfertigt sind. Aber ich räume gerne ein, daß das ein umstrittenes Thema ist. In diesem Sinne unterstützen wir vom Jugendministerium her die Entspannungspolitik. Ich habe vorhin einen Schwerpunkt angedeutet: Polen. Angesichts der historischen Belastung, der das Verhältnis zu Frankreich, Israel und Polen ausgesetzt war, fände ich es gut, wenn wir für die jungen Menschen in unseren Ländern eine Jugendbegegnungsstätte errichten würden. Das deuteten schon der Bundeskanzler und auch der Parteichef Gierek in einer gemeinsamen Erklärung an. Ich glaube, das Feld der Entspannungs- und Jugendpolitik ist ein Feld, dem man nicht genügend Aufmerksamkeit widmen kann. Schönen Dank.

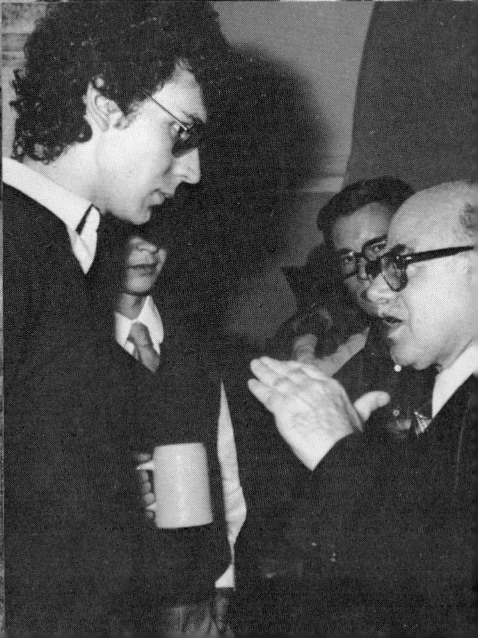

Orientierungskrise – sozialer Wandel als intellektuelle und politische Herausforderung.

Prof. Dr. Hermann Lübbe

In unserer kulturellen Gegenwart ist eine auffällige Zuwendung zur Vergangenheit zu beobachten. Ich zähle einige der Symptome auf, an denen sich dieser Bestand ablesen läßt.

1. Wir wurden kürzlich von Wellen der Nostalgie überspült, und diese Wellen haben sich keineswegs schon verlaufen. Das Pathos der Reformen, die laute Philosophie der evolutionären, ja revolutionären Erneuerung, wurde plötzlich von einer Stimme übertönt, die Ansprüche aufs Schmecken der Süße macht, die auch mit derjenigen Liebe verbunden ist, die wir als Liebe zu alten Zeiten kennen. Selbst sozialdemokratische Stadtväter, die sich doch auf eine Politik progressiver Reformen verpflichtet wissen, überbieten sich gegenwärtig in Bemühungen, in ihren Kommunen Flohmärkte zur Institution zu machen, und nicht zuletzt das Engagement Jugendlicher verhilft ihnen bei diesen Bemühungen zum Erfolg. Abgelegte Gebrauchsgegenstände werden massenhaft in den Adelsstand von Antiquitäten erhoben, und deren Preise steigen überproportional im Verhältnis zum Anstieg der Masseneinkommen.

2. Die Historisierung und Musealisierung unserer kulturellen Umwelt macht rasche Fortschritte. Wir haben ein internationales Denkmalschutzjahr hinter uns, und die Ansätze in den entsprechenden Kapiteln unserer öffentlichen Haushalte wiesen, jedenfalls vor dem gegenwärtigen Konjunktureinbruch, überproportionale Steigerungsraten auf. Auch der Abstand der Zeiten, die wir in die Kultur des historischen Bewußtseins einbeziehen, wird immer kürzer. Selbst Industriebauten der dreißiger Jahre sind längst denkmalsfähig geworden – von der längst abgeschlossenen Historisierung des architektonischen Historismus gar nicht zu reden.

3. In Hessen gab es einen kulturrevolutionären Versuch eines ehemaligen Kultusministers, den Geschichtsunterricht in den weiterführenden Schulen ausschließlich, wie es hieß, am Maßstab gegenwärtiger, zukunftsbezogener Handlungsinteressen auszurichten. Dagegen erhob sich, landauf, landab, ein Elternprotest, der sich meßbar in Wahlstimmenverlusten für die Partei des Ministers niedergeschlagen hat. Das war eine eindrucksvolle Belehrung darüber, was heute den Bürgern die Vergangenheit wert ist. Der Massenansturm bei der Eröffnung des eindrucksvollen Römisch-Germanischen Museums gleich neben dem Dom zu Köln demonstriert uns dasselbe, und der Bestsellererfolg von Popularhistorien über die Phönizier, die Kelten und selbst über die alten Germanen desgleichen. Man erinnert sich, daß auch das erste deutsche Nachkriegsbeispiel der litera-

tursoziologischen Gattung „Bestseller" ein Werk populärer Laienarchäologie war, nämlich Ceram's *„Götter, Gräber und Gelehrte"*. – *„Asterix"* ist von diesem Trend die gemeineuropäisch erfolgreiche Comic-Version.

Bereits an dieser Stelle, bevor wir uns mit weniger schönen Dingen beschäftigen, möchte ich einen Versuch machen, die angedeuteten, uns allen wohlbekannten Phänomene zu erklären und sie damit in ihrem Zusammenhang sichtbar zu machen. Sind wir, wie alte Leute, dabei, das Prinzip Hoffnung durch das Prinzip Erinnerung zu ersetzen? Bescheidener darf man vermuten, daß die angedeuteten Phänomene Symptome von Schwierigkeiten sind, die wir haben, ein historisch beispielloses Tempo des sozialen Wandels zu verarbeiten. Tempo des sozialen Wandels, und zwar ein im ganzen sich immer noch steigerndes Tempo des sozialen Wandels – das ist nichts, was bloß im Zerrspiegel subjektiver Eindrücke existierte. Anwachsendes Tempo des sozialen Wandels – das ist ein objektiver, meßbarer, von den makrosoziologischen Theoretikern des sozialen Wandels tatsächlich auch längst vermessener Bestand, der sich in optisch eindrucksvollen Verlaufskurvenarrangements graphisch darstellen ließe – von der global unverändert exponentiell anwachsenden Population des homo sapiens bis zur absinkenden Halbwertszeit wissenschaftlicher Literatur, und von der Steigerung unserer beruflichen Mobilität bis zum Rückgang des Hauptschüleranteils an unseren schulpflichtigen Jahrgängen.

Materiell neue Erkenntnisse habe ich über solche Prozesse hier nicht mitzuteilen. Es soll lediglich geltend gemacht werden, daß wir Anzeichen dafür haben, das Tempo des sozialen Wandels könnte, jenseits ungewisser Grenzen, unsere Orientierungsstabilität gefährden. Es ist trivial zu vermuten, daß unsere individuellen und institutionellen Kapazitäten zur orientierungspraktischen Verarbeitung von Veränderung Grenzen haben. Nicht trivial ist es zu vermuten, daß wir uns im Bereich dieser Grenzen längst bewegen. Die geschilderten Nostalgie- und Erinnerungsexzesse deute ich als Symptome entsprechender Schwierigkeiten. Angesichts einer Welt, die vor unseren eigenen Augen zur fremden wird, verschaffen wir uns Entlastung durch ästhetisch-retrospektive Vergegenwärtigung einer Vergangenheit, die die Verheißung hat, ein Mehr an Orientierungssicherheit geboten zu haben. Wir unternehmen Versuche, unser Bewußtsein durch Wiedererkennungserlebnisse zu stabilisieren. Wenn unsere Städte pro Jahr mehr als 2,5 bis 3 % ihrer Bausubstanz erneuern, so vermutet ein Zürcher Professor für Städtebau, verlieren sie für ihre Bewohner die Anmutungsqualität der Vertrautheit. Sie werden tatsächlich vor unseren eigenen Augen zu Fremden. Nicht nur die Bewohner des Frankfurter Westends haben diese Erfahrung machen können, und es ist evident, daß genau auf diese Erfahrung die aktuellen Bemühungen der Restaurateure Wilhelminischer Stuckfassaden kompensatorisch bezogen ist.

Kompensation ist das entscheidende Stichwort. Wir haben es, in allgemeiner

Formulierung, zu tun mit vergangenheitsorientierter Kompensation eines änderungstempobedingten Vertrautheitsschwundes.

Eine ernstere Folge des erreichten Tempos des sozialen Wandels ist es, daß ein zwangsläufiger Rationalitätsschwund unseres administrativen und politischen Handelns eintritt. Rationales Handeln setzt die Kalkulierbarkeit von Realitätsbedingungen voraus. In unsere Entscheidungen gehen stets Annahmen über die Wirklichkeit ein, und die unseren Entscheidungen folgenden Handlungsabläufe werden sogleich sehr kompliziert, wenn die Annahmen über die Wirklichkeit, die wir ihnen zugrunde gelegt hatten, sich gleichsam unter der Hand als unzutreffend erweisen. Genau das ist aber unser Fall. Unter den Bedingungen des anwachsenden Tempos wissenschaftlichen und sozialen Wandels ändern sich die Realitätsprämissen unseres Handelns nicht selten schneller als wir informations- und organisationstechnisch in der Lage sind, diese Veränderungen in unserem Handeln zu berücksichtigen.

Bedarf es der Beispiele? Ich bringe ein selbsterfahrenes. Es handelte sich um die Errichtung einer neuen Universität – immerhin keine Kleinigkeit. Was macht die Verwaltung zur Rationalisierung fälliger Entscheidung? Sie fragt bei Entscheidungen solcher Größenordnung Experten. Diese erklärten damals die Campus-Idee zum konzeptionellen Non-plus-ultra des Universitätsbaus – die nach innen gewandte geistige Konzentration in der Gemeinschaft der Lehrenden mit den Lernenden, unterstützt durch architektonisch gewährleistete Zonen kommunikativer Verdichtung. So jedenfalls lauteten die Worte der planerischen Verheißung. Einige Zeit später hatte sich die Hochschularchitekturtheorie geändert, und statt der Zonen kommunikativer Verdichtung galt nun das Konzept der urbanen Verflechtung. Inzwischen waren aber die ersten Universitätsbauten fertiggestellt, und da standen sie nun für Jahrzehnte als betongewordene Denkmäler unseres administrativen Irrtums.

Was tun, wenn unter Bedingungen beschleunigten wissenschaftlichen und sozialen Wandels die Konstanz unserer Annahmen über die Wirklichkeit geringer wird und damit die Rationalitätschancen unserer Entscheidungen abnehmen? Als eine der Antworten auf die Herausforderung dieser Frage will ich die sogenannte Futurologie erwähnen. Auch diese Antwort ist ersichtlich eine kompensatorische. Die sogenannte Zukunftsforschung ist der Versuch, anwachsenden Zukunftsgewißheitsschwund zu kompensieren. Das bedeutet: es wäre ein komplettes Mißverständnis, die Zukunftswissenschaft, das heißt das interdisziplinäre Bemühen zur Nutzung der Prognose potentialer theoretischer Wissenschaften für Handlungszwecke, für eine Kunst zu halten, endlich den Vorhang beiseite zu schieben, der die Zukunft vor unseren Blicken so lange verborgen gehalten hätte. In unserem Zeitalter der Zukunftsforschung wissen wir nicht mehr, sondern weniger als je zuvor über die Zukunft. Oder umgekehrt formuliert: zu jeder früheren Zeit wußte man einfach deswegen mehr über die Zukunft, weil die Wahrscheinlichkeit ungleich größer war, daß die

Zukunft der Gegenwart in wesentlichen Zügen gleichen werde. Die Zukunft wird unkalkulierbarer, wenn, wie es der Fall ist, die Menge der unsere Situation strukturell verändernden Ereignisse und Vorgänge pro Zeiteinheit anwächst. Genau dazu verhält sich die Zukunftsforschung kompensatorisch. Sie ist ein Versuch, mit künstlichen Mitteln der Wissenschaft sozusagen Schneisen ins dichter werdende Dickicht der Zukunft zu schlagen, um die Kalkulierbarkeit von Realitätsbedingungen unseres Handelns jedenfalls eine Strecke weit wiederherzustellen.

Man erkennt, daß die gewisse Euphorie unserer Zukunftsforscher, die wir noch aus den sechziger Jahren in Erinnerung haben, auf einem elementaren Mißverständnis beruht. Unsere gegenwärtigen prognostischen Künste repräsentieren zwar einen Fortschritt. Aber der Segen dieses Fortschritts gleicht bestenfalls dem Glück des Kurzsichtigen, der seine Brille bekommt.

Ganz analog wäre es auch ein Mißverständnis, unser unverändert in Blüte stehendes wissenschaftliches Beratungsdienstleistungswesen für eine Einrichtung zu halten, die den Zweck hat, endlich Elemente wissenschaftlicher Rationalität in das System unseres administrativen und politischen Handelns einzuspeisen, die bislang nicht darinnen gewesen wären. Die Sache verhält sich genau umgekehrt. Wissenschaftliche Politik- und Verwaltungsberatung erfüllen eine Prothese-Funktion. Diese Prothese repräsentiert den Versuch, den fortschreitenden Kompetenzverlust des politischen common sense zu kompensieren. Common sense – das ist ja nichts anderes als eine Instanz, die die Orientierungspotentiale einer Tradition bewährter Erfahrung nutzt, um die Rationalitätschance fälliger Entscheidungen zu erhöhen. Unter Bedingungen beschleunigten sozialen Wandels ist es eben ungleich schwieriger, solche Traditionen bewährter Erfahrung auszubilden. Traditionen altern heute sehr rasch. Insofern ist es wahr, daß uns für aktuelle Handlungszwecke relikthafte Traditionen oft hindernd im Wege stehen, und Akte der Befreiung von ihnen sind fällig. Aber kein Prognose-Institut ist in der Lage, die Orientierungsstabilität wiederherzustellen, die einst durch funktionierende Traditionen gesichert war. Der Minister, der sich heute ein wissenschaftliches Gutachten bestellt, bekommt nicht nur etwas, was noch keiner bisherigen Administration zur Verfügung stand. Er bekommt vor allem auch etwas, was früher keine Administration brauchte.

Das anwachsende Tempo des wissenschaftlichen und sozialen Wandels hat uns orientierungspraktisch eine Situation beschert, in der die Menge des praxisrelevanten Wissens größer ist als je zuvor, aber geringer als je zuvor in Relation zum angebbaren Wissensbedarf. Genau diese sich verschlechternde Relation repräsentiert die Realität des Traditionsverfalls. Es erübrigt sich zu sagen, daß es sinnlos wäre, demgegenüber Traditionsrestauration zu empfehlen. Unser Problem ist ja gerade dieses, daß unser handlungsrelevantes Wissen rascher veraltet als wir in der Lage sind, unsere tatsächlich praxisleitenden Orientierungssysteme umzubilden.

Wenn Erfahrungen rascher veralten als sie sich bilden und konsolidieren lassen, so verliert der common sense seine öffentliche, politische Kompetenz. Es ist evident, daß das für die Funktionsfähigkeit demokratisch organisierter politischer Systeme potentiell bedrohlich ist. Exakt diese Bedrohlichkeit spiegelt sich in den Aktivitäten mancher unserer frei im politischen Raum agierenden Bürgerinitiativen. Protestaktion gegen den Abriß eines Altbaus hier, Dauerbesetzung des Geländes für einen Chemie- oder Kernkraftwerkbau dort –: bezeugt das endlich erwachten kritischen Bürgersinn, Willen zur Mitbestimmung, demokratische Kompetenz, Reife des politischen Urteils? Politpädagogische Zuversicht legt es in der Tat nahe, diese Phänomene, die unseren verantwortlichen politischen Instanzen ja zumeist sehr lästig sind, in solcher mutmachenden Weise zu deuten, und es wäre unbillig, diese Deutung generell als illusionär zu verwerfen. Aber gerade in den spektakulären Fällen am Rhein entlang von Kaiseraugust über Wyhl bis nach Orsoy erhob sich nicht nur common-sense-orientierter Bürgersinn gegen Willkür von Bürokraten und Kapitalisten. Es manifestierte sich hier auch die Weigerung, überhaupt noch etwas zu tun angesichts einer Situation, die so komplex ist, daß die Folgen und Nebenfolgen anstehender Entscheidungen sich nicht mehr zu rationalen Urteilen über ihren Nutzen und Nachteil bündeln lassen. Die Politiker selbst reden in solchen Fällen, zielgruppenabhängig, mit mehrfach gespaltener Zunge, und aus dem Komplex von Arbeitsplatzbeschaffung und Energiesicherung, technologischer Evolution und Oekologie, Landschaftsschutz und Oekonomie ist ein Schluß, der ebenso richtig wie allgemein verständlich wäre, kaum noch zu ziehen. Ist die Situation einschließlich des Fernsehens dann da, beeilt sich vom Energiekonzernsprecher bis zum Ministerpräsidenten jedermann zu versichern, man habe offensichtlich Aufklärungspflichten versäumt. Beim Versuch, das nachzuholen, merkt dann endgültig jeder, daß Aufklärung eine Aufgabe darstellt, die heute objektiv schwieriger geworden ist, und dem Leser der regierungsamtlichen einschlägigen Postwurfsendungen bleibt nicht verborgen, daß die hinzugezogenen Public-Relations-Experten schließlich nichts anderes tun als den rhetorischen Schein der Einfachheit dessen zu erzeugen, was objektiv höchst kompliziert geworden ist.

Anwachsendes Tempo des sozialen Wandels läßt unsere Erfahrungen entsprechend schneller veralten. Die geschilderte neue Geltung des Prinzips Erinnerung entspricht dem, wissenschaftspraktisch die Zukunftsforschung desgleichen und politisch die Hoffnung auf gelingende Kompensation manifesten Erfahrungsmangels durch die Beratungsdienstleistungen eben dieser Wissenschaft.

Ich möchte jetzt noch mit einigen wenigen Hinweisen deutlich zu machen versuchen, daß die wandlungstempobedingte Orientierungskrise nicht nur ihre öffentliche Seite hat. Sie schlägt bis in die individuelle Existenz durch und konfrontiert uns mit historisch beispiellosen individuellen Lebensproblemen. Auch für diesen Bestand bringe ich eine kleine Reihe signifikanter Exempel.

1. Wir brauchen unbeschadet ungewisser Grenzen stets ein Minimum an Zeit, um Erfahrungen machen zu können. Eben diese Zeit steht nicht mehr zur Verfügung, wenn die Verhältnisse rascher sich ändern als wir Zeit hatten, unsere auf diese Verhältnisse sich beziehenden Erfahrungen konsolidieren zu können. Die Lasten dieses Vorgangs hat in unserer Gesellschaft in erster Linie das Alter zu tragen. In relativ stabilen Gesellschaften genießt das Alter den Vorzug, seine anwachsende physische Schwäche sozial durch ein Mehr an konsolidierter Erfahrung, durch Ratgeberkompetenz also kompensieren zu können. Demgegenüber ist unsere Lage dadurch charakterisiert, daß wir mit dem altersbedingten Schwund unserer Anpassungsfähigkeit jeweils morgen stets ein wenig mehr von gestern sein werden. So enden wir in unserer Welt nicht nur physisch, sondern nun auch lebensorientierungsmäßig als ein Fall gerontologisch unterstützter Sozialfürsorge. Die Altersforschung wird heute überall in modernen Gesellschaften schwerpunktmäßig gefördert. Es steht nichts entgegen, das als einen Fortschritt zu rühmen. Man darf nur nicht übersehen, daß auch dieser Fortschritt partiell Kompensationscharakter hat. Man merkt das an dem überständigen Ton, den in unseren Ohren das mit „Alter" korrelierende Wort „Weisheit" angenommen hat. – Auch dieses für Zustände raschen sozialen Wandels charakteristische Altersproblem läßt einen Durchblick auf politische Verhältnisse zu. Die Gerontokratie, deren politische Chancen trotz des Sonderfalls Adenauer bei uns generell rückläufig sind, ist heute eine Spezialität totalitärer Länder, Chinas zumal. Wieso das? Es hat vor allem zwei Gründe. Erstens sind in totalitären Ländern die Prozesse des personellen Führungswechsels schwerer zu bewältigen als in liberalen Systemen. Zweitens definieren totalitäre Systeme ihre Identität durch eine integrale Doktrin, deren Wahrheiten kanonisch und ewig sind. Als Repräsentanten solcher Wahrheiten eignen sich wieder die Alten vorzüglich. Bei uns indessen verfügen wir über solche Wahrheiten von öffentlicher Geltung ersichtlich nicht mehr, und die Alten werden entsprechend auch als ihre Repräsentanten nicht mehr benötigt.

2. In der pädagogischen Bewegung unserer Zeit sind die bekannten Stichwörter *„life-long-learning"*, *„education permanente"* etc. gelegentlich von einem euphorischen Glanz umgeben. Es ist begreiflich, daß insbesondere unsere Pädagogen sich von dieser Euphorie anstecken lassen. Immerhin wird ja, wenn wir zum lebenslangen Lernen verurteilt sind, ihre Zuständigkeit, die bislang an der Schwelle des Erwachsenenalters endete, auf das Ganze unseres Daseins ausgedehnt. Die Lehrer ziehen insofern endlich mit den Absolventen der oberen Fakultäten, nämlich

mit den Priestern, Staatsanwälten und Ärzten gleich, mit denen wir es ja immer schon bis ans Lebensende zu tun hatten, und entsprechend findet auch ein Aufstieg der Lehrer in die einschlägigen Gehaltsklassen statt. Pädagogischer Fortschritt also? Gewiß! Aber auch in diesem Fall ist, was als Fortschritt gefeiert wird, nichts als ein Versuch der Kompensation erhöhter Geschwindigkeit des Veraltens einmal erworbenen Wissens. Die Schule wird zur Lebenseinrichtung auf Dauer, und wir müssen auf die Freuden des Tages Verzicht üben lernen, an welchem wir früher endlich die Schule definitiv hinter uns hatten.

3. Wenn das nutzungsfähige Schulwissen mit wachsendem Tempo des wissenschaftlichen und sozialen Wandels immer rascher veraltet, verlieren unsere Lehrprogramme auf allen Stufen ihren Charakter aufmerksamkeitsunbedürftiger kultureller Selbstverständlichkeit. Genau dieser Situation entspricht die Curriculumreform als pädagogisch-kulturpolitisches Dauerthema. In der Konsequenz wird die Schule der Kinder den Eltern zu fremden. Die kulturelle Homogenietät des sozial verbreiteten Wissens nimmt zu. In der Spiegelung des individuellen Bewußtseins bedeutet das, daß die Vertrautheit der kulturellen Umwelt abnimmt. Der Satz „*Ich verstehe die Welt nicht mehr*“, mit dem im 19. Jahrhundert Hebbel ein Bürgerliches Trauerspiel beschloß, wird ein Satz von erwachsenenpädagogisch nur schwach überdeckter Dauergeltung.

In einem weiteren Durchgang möchte ich jetzt noch ein paar spektakuläre Erscheinungen unseres öffentlichen Lebens in Erinnerung bringen, die man in euphorischer Gestimmtheit zunächst gern als politische Erscheinungen gedeutet hat. Ich halte es demgegenüber für angemessener, die gemeinten Erscheinungen als sozialpathologische Protuberanzen der Unfähigkeit zu interpretieren, eine wandlungstempobedingte Orientierungskrise zu ertragen. Ich zähle exemplarisch auf:

1. Wir erlebten in den letzten zehn Jahren eine Renaissance des politischen Utopismus, insbesondere in der internationalen neuen Jugendbewegung. Dieser Utopismus wurde, wie wir uns erinnern, politpädagogisch frohgemut als neue Orientierung einer Generation begrüßt, die nicht mehr in der von Schelsky beschriebenen politischen Skepsis unserer fünfziger Jahre verharrt, vielmehr zu neuen Ufern aufbricht und den Mut zur Veränderung, zum Wandel und zur Bewegung hat. – Mir will demgegenüber scheinen, daß der in der Tat unübersehbare Neoutopismus der späten sechziger und frühen siebziger Jahre mit exakt entgegengesetztem Richtungssinn interpretiert werden muß. Denn was ist, seit alters, das entscheidende Charakteristikum der Utopie? Die Utopie zeigt uns das Bild eines gesellschaftlichen Zustands, der, indem er vollendet ist, sich nicht mehr wandelt. Im strukturellen Stillstand aller Dinge kontrastiert die

Utopie zu unserer Gegenwart stärker als zu jeder früheren, und genau das macht ihre kompensatorische Attraktivität heute aus. Man hat die ewigen Änderungs- und Anpassungszwänge, denen wir in einer sich wandelnden Welt unterliegen, satt; man will nicht mehr werden – man will endlich *sein*.

2. Von Kalifornien bis zu den Niederlanden hat sich in unserer hochkomplexen mobilen Gesellschaft eine jugendbewegte Subkultur der Verweigerung etabliert. Auch diese Subkultur ist eine Erscheinung der Flucht aus desorientierender Gegenwart. Der Utopist flüchtet in die Ferne einer stillgestellten Zukunft; der Verweigerer flüchtet in die Ruhe ferner Vergangenheiten. Was gibt es da? Urproduktion auf ländlichen Hippiekommunen; Reisen nach Nepal und Goa im Verlangen nach Früchten östlicher Meditationskultur; schließlich die Immediaterlösung aus allen objektiven Orientierungsschwierigkeiten durch den subjektiven Frieden, den die Droge verschafft.

3. Es gibt eine zunächst verblüffende intellektuelle Renaissance alter Lehren aus dicken, im Original längst verstaubten Büchern des 19. Jahrhunderts. Wieso das? Es ist doch zunächst einmal angesichts der unleugbaren Fortschritte der Wissenschaften höchst unwahrscheinlich, daß wir aus Flugschriften des Vormärz und aus hundertjähriger Politökonomie sonderliche Aufschlüsse über unsere Gegenwart zu gewinnen vermöchten. Wieso steht gleichwohl der Name Karl Marx im Licht der Verheißung? Eine Antwort – die in unserem Zusammenhang wichtigste Antwort – ist diese: der Marxismus ist heute in einem Drittel der Welt eine Lehre von kanonischer Geltung, aus der geschulte Interpreten auf jede gestellte Frage eine verbindliche Antwort abzuleiten vermögen, und eine Lehre, die eben dieses leistet, ist in Orientierungskrisenzeiten gefragt. Das wirksame Faszinosum heißt Weltvereinfachung, Komplexitätsreduktion, Zugang zu Wahrheiten, die zwischen zwei Buchdeckeln eines politökonomischen Katechismus Platz haben. Man greift nach Lehren, die die Verheißung haben, in ihrer Geltung ein für alle Mal festgestellt zu sein.

Was ist in einer historischen Lage raschen sozialen Wandels mit seinen geschilderten orientierungskritischen Folgen zu tun? Auf diese komplexe Frage will ich abschließend drei Antworten zu geben versuchen. Diese Antworten haben keinerlei technischen Sinn. Es handelt sich um Antworten zur Verbesserung unserer Verständigung über die Lage, in der wir uns befinden. Diese Antworten haben insofern lediglich einen orientierungspraktischen Sinn. Es sind zugleich Beiträge zur Rekonstruktion des common sense unter erklärten Bedingungen.

1. Wir müssen lernen, die dominanten Schwierigkeiten unserer Lage, statt als Fortschrittshemmungen, als Schwierigkeiten der Steuerung eines Fortschritts zu verstehen, der längst im Gang ist. Man erkennt dann, daß

selbst noch das eine zeitlang großmächtig wirkende Pathos einer Politik der Reformen nichts anderes ist als ein rhetorisches Relikt geschichtsphilosophischer Orientierungsmuster des längst vergangenen 18. Jahrhunderts. Welche Sorte von Fortschritt wird denn eigentlich reformpolitisch durchgesetzt, wenn wir ökologische Krisen meistern und wenn wir die Sichttiefe des Rheins tatsächlich um einige Zentimeter verbessern? In welche Zukunft brechen wir auf, wenn es uns gelingen sollte, in quantitativ interessanten Dimensionen Substitution für traditionelle Energieträger herbeizuschaffen? Welche Reaktion haben wir eigentlich niedergekämpft, wenn es uns gelungen ist, durch gesundheitsministerielle Trimm-Dich-Aktionen die Herztodquote um meßbare Prozente zu senken? In welchem Sinne verbessert sich unsere Lebensqualitätsbilanz, wenn wir die längst komplett gewordene Auflösung des sozialen Schutzraums der Großfamilie durch ausreichende Wohnheimkapazitäten für preziös sogenannte Senioren kompensiert haben? – Mit Fragen dieser Sorte könnte man endlos fortfahren. Ich behaupte nicht, das sei die einzige Sorte von Fragen, mit denen wir es gegenwärtig praktisch zu tun haben. Aber unverkennbar handelt es sich um sehr wichtige Fragen, die auch auf Wahlplattformen jeglicher Parteien herausgestellt werden, und insoweit das zutrifft, ist nicht der aufgehaltene, sondern der stattfindende Fortschritt unser Problem, und hilfreich ist insoweit nicht die Intensität progressiver Gesinnung, sondern der Pragmatismus an der Politik der Kompensation kritischer Fortschrittsnebenfolgen.

2. Wenn wir verstanden haben, in welchem Umfang wir die Schwierigkeiten unserer Lage prekären Fortschrittsnebenfolgen zuzuschreiben haben, werden wir auch resistent sein gegen die Verheißungen derer, die sich uns als ideologische Experten für neue Zielsetzungen anempfehlen. Es ist verblüffend, in welchem Umfang unsere wissenschaftliche, technische, ökonomische und administrative Intelligenz in den letzten Jahren sich durch den ideologischen Vorwurf der Zielblindheit hat einschüchtern lassen. Hat diese Intelligenz tatsächlich Dienstleistungen für Zwecke erbracht, die ihr unbekannt oder gleichgültig gewesen wären, und wäre das der Grund für unübersehbare Mißlichkeiten unserer Lage? Wenn diese Deutung zuträfe, so wäre es in der Tat konsequent, die technisch orientierte Intelligenz endlich unter Kuratel zu stellen und sie einer Schulung durch ideologisch versierte Zielreflexionsexperten zu unterwerfen. Ein Technik-Soziologe hat tatsächlich drucken lassen, was die zu fordernde Konsequenz wäre, zum Beispiel: Elektrizitäts-, Gas- und Wasserwerker, die, statt unsere Versorgung zu sichern, uns mit dem Griff nach dem Abstellhebel politisch erpressen, damit wir uns endlich auf den Weg der höheren politischen Einsicht begeben. – In Wirklichkeit ist diese ganze Rede von der angeblichen Zielblindheit der technologisch versierten,

pragmatisch orientierten Intelligenz ein politisch gezieltes Märchen zur Rechtfertigung des von Helmut Schelsky analysierten ideologischen Machtanspruchs von Teilen unserer räsonnierenden Intelligenz. In Wirklichkeit liegen die Dinge so, daß die großen Zielorientierungen unseres politischen und sozialen Lebens, anstatt im Nebel verschwunden zu sein, unverändert ihren jedermann erkennbaren Ort auf der Gemeinplatzebene haben. Um welche Ziele handelt es sich denn? Ich zähle einige wenige auf: Entlastung des Menschen vom physischen Zwang niederdrückender Arbeit, Steigerung der Produktivität unserer Arbeit, entsprechend Mehrung der Wohlfahrt und durch Mehrung der Wohlfahrt Sicherung des sozialen Friedens. – Nicht Alternativen zu solchen Zielen brauchen wir. Vielmehr brauchen wir eine zusätzliche praktische Orientierung an dem zusätzlichen Gemeinplatz, daß der Verwirklichung der genannten Ziele wie ihrer Vereinbarkeit bei Strafe prekärer Fortschrittsnebenfolgen Grenzen gesetzt sind. Für den Zweck von Debatten in akademisch geschulten Zirkeln will ich dasselbe auch noch einmal weniger schlicht formulieren: die transparent gewordene partielle soziale Dysfunktionalität technisch-industrieller Prozesse sowie des ganzen sozialen Wandels indiziert nicht fehlende Führungsgrößen, sondern defiziente Regelkapazitäten zur Kompensation von Systemstörungen durch nicht-prognostizierte sekundäre Effekte, und sie indiziert außerdem die Inkompatibilität des angestrebten Systemzustands mit Bedürfnissen, die in das sich entwickelnde soziale System als Führungsgrößen bislang noch gar nicht eingegeben waren. – Ob man es einfach oder kompliziert formuliert –: es ist wohl deutlich geworden, daß wir zur Beschreibung der Schwierigkeiten, die uns gegenwärtig bedrängen, nicht auf das denunziatorische Märchen zurückzugreifen brauchen, unsere technisch-administrative Intelligenz lege in der Beschränktheit ihrer instrumentellen Vernunft der Frage keine Bedeutung bei, ob die Ziele, denen sie dient, auch als solche vernünftig sind.

3. Wenn somit feststeht, daß unsere wandlungstempobedingte Orientierungskrise nicht eine Zielkrise ist, vielmehr eine Steuerungskrise, so steht auch fest, daß wir, um im Bilde zu bleiben, diese Steuerungskrise nicht meistern können, indem wir das Steuer abrupt herumwerfen und die Geschwindigkeit unserer Fortbewegung gleichzeitig noch einmal steigern. Das Rezept muß vielmehr lauten: Spur halten und vorsichtig drosseln. Metaphernfrei formuliert würde das die Orientierung, statt an neuen Zielen, an einer Verfahrensregel bedeuten, die primär die Neuerung statt der Erhaltung, mit der Pflicht zum Nachweis ihrer Fälligkeit und Notwendigkeit belasten. Gerade der Gemeinplatzcharakter unserer geltenden Ziele von der sozialen Sicherheit bis zum Frieden ist es, der uns eine realistische, panikfreie Gefahreneinschätzung erlaubt. Wir kennen dann insoweit die Übel, die uns drohen, und die pragmatische Orientierung an zu ver-

hindernden angebbaren bekannten Übeln ist politisch stets sicherer als die ideologische Orientierung an Vorstellungen unbekannten künftigen Glücks.

Der junge Mensch auf der Suche nach Sinn

Prof. Dr. Viktor E. Frankl

Es ist jetzt ein bißchen mehr als ein halbes Jahrhundert her, daß ich in Wien und dann in sechs anderen Städten Mitteleuropas sogenannte Jugendberatungsstellen für junge Menschen in seelischer Not gegründet habe. Sie konnten sich ohne Namensnennung, ohne einen Groschen zahlen zu müssen, unter Zusicherung vollster Diskretion an die Jugendberater in deren Privatwohnungen wenden. Ich habe dann ein paar Jahre später eine Arbeit über die statistischen Ergebnisse in einer psychoanalytischen Zeitschrift publiziert. Da hat sich herausgestellt, daß die jungen Leute sich hauptsächlich wegen sexueller Fragen an uns gewendet hatten. Etwa ein halbes Jahrhundert später überreicht mir ein Fachlehrer in Wien ebenfalls eine Statistik. Er hatte seine Schüler, 13- bis 14jährige, eingeladen, ihm schriftlich und anonym Fragen zu stellen, welche auch immer sie auf ihren Lippen haben mögen. Das Spektrum begann mit der Frage „Gibt es Leben auf fremden Planeten?“ über Drogenabhängigkeit, Sexualfragen usw. Wissen Sie, was die meistgestellte Frage war? Selbstmord! 13- bis 14jährige!

Sie sehen, die Szenerie hat sich in diesem halben Jahrhundert gewandelt. Sie müssen auch bedenken, daß an der Idaho State University 60 Studenten, die Selbstmord versucht hatten, psychologisch gescreent wurden, und das Ergebnis war, daß in 85 % der Selbstmordversuch aus einem Gefühl kompletter Sinnlosigkeit des Daseins erfolgt war. Ich komme auf diese Statistik noch zurück.

Ich hoffe, Sie werden jetzt verstehen, warum ich nicht müde werde, seit den vierziger Jahren zu sagen, zumindest vorherzusagen, daß heute nicht mehr wie zur Zeit von Sigmund Freud die sexuelle Frage im Vordergrund steht bzw. verdrängt wird, sondern die Sinnfrage, daß heute längst nicht mehr wie zur Zeit von Alfred Adler das Minderwertigkeitsgefühl die Patienten zu uns Psychiatern treibt, sondern ein abgründiges Sinnlosigkeitsgefühl, verbunden mit einem Leeregefühl, verbunden mit dem, was ich im Jahre 1955 das existentielle Vakuum genannt habe.

Das ist keineswegs auf unsere Gesellschaftskreise, unsere Gesellschaft, unsere Länder, unsere Staaten beschränkt, sondern Brünner Psychiater haben längst nachgewiesen und in kommunistisch-psychiatrischen Zeitschriften publiziert, daß dieses von den Logotherapeuten so bezeichnete existentielle Vakuum, das Sinnlosigkeitsgefühl, sich bereits in den kommunistischen Ländern bemerkbar macht, und dasselbe haben ein Neurologe von der Universität Olmütz und Christa Kohler von der Karl-Marx-Universität in Leipzig schon in Buchform publiziert. Es beschränkt sich nicht einmal auf die Erste und Zweite, sondern dehnt sich auf die Dritte Welt aus. Längst schon haben amerikanische Professoren Arbeiten über das existentielle Vakuum in Tansania und in anderen Entwicklungsländern publiziert. Vor allem ist es so, wie der polnische Marxist Adam Schaff, der auch Gastprofessor in Wien ist und in dessen Marxismus-Seminar ich wiederholt Gelegenheit hatte, auf seine Einladung über diese Dinge zu sprechen, in einem eigenen Kapitel über das existentielle Vakuum in seinem Buch über Entfremdung als soziales Problem kürzlich publiziert hat, – Sie wissen, welche Bedeutung Adam Schaff in bezug auf die Humanisierung des Kommunismus zukommt. Er schreibt:

> „Das Gefühl des Menschen, den Sinn seines Lebens verloren zu haben, ist eine Erscheinung, die vor keinem bestimmten System, vor keiner bestimmten Gesellschaftsklasse halt macht. Wer das nicht zur Kenntnis nehmen will, der versperrt sich auch die Möglichkeit, die Ursachen solcher sozialen Erscheinungen, wie Jugendkriminalität, Alkoholismus, Rauschgiftsucht usw. zu erkennen, wenn diese gesellschaftlichen Charakter annehmen."

Was heißt das? Auch wenn Sie Marxisten sind, dürfen Sie sich das heute nicht mehr so leicht und bequem machen, daß Sie sagen: Alles hat sozioökonomische Ursachen; es ist die gesellschaftliche Lage, es sind die gesellschaftlichen Bedingungen. Damit ist überhaupt kein Hund hinter dem Ofen hervorzuholen. Umgekehrt müssen Sie es machen, so wie Adam Schaff, der große Marxist.

Jetzt fragen Sie mich: Woher kommt das existentielle Vakuum? Ich habe eine kurze, ganz schematische Antwort bereit; ich kann nur immer wieder darauf zurückkommen. Sie lautet: Im Gegensatz zum Tier sagen dem Menschen heute keine Instinkte und Triebe, was er **muß**. Im Gegensatz zum Menschen in früheren Zeiten sagen ihm heute keine Traditionen und durch Traditionen tradierten Werte mehr, was er **soll**. Weder wissend, was er muß, noch was er soll, weiß er anscheinend überhaupt nicht mehr, was er eigentlich **will**.

Das Ergebnis: Entweder will er nur das, was die anderen tun. Da haben Sie den Konformismus. Oder, umgekehrt, er tut nur das, was die anderen wollen, von ihm wollen. Da haben Sie den Totalitarismus. Daß an dieser Hypothese etwas sein muß, ergibt sich daraus, daß die Statistiken in aller Welt nachweisen, daß in der jungen Generation das existentielle Vakuum am meisten verbreitet ist. Gegenprobe: Marshal in New York hat nachgewiesen, daß unter den unter 30jährigen am meisten die Leute wegen eines Sinnlosigkeitsgefühls in seine Klinik kommen. Also am meisten unter der Jugend, und unter der Jugend an neurotischen oder pseudoneurotischen Erscheinungen am meisten die Sinnlosigkeitsgefühle.

Soviel zur Ätiologie; jetzt fragen wir nach der Symptomatologie. Wie zeigt sich das zunächst bei der Jugend? Da hat einmal die Studentenschaft der Universität of Georgia in Athens von mir verlangt, ihnen einen Vortrag unter dem Titel zu halten *„Is the New Generation Mad?"* – *„Ist die Jugend von heute*

verrückt?". Ich habe mich mit Händen und Füßen dagegen gewehrt; nein, der Titel mußte so lauten. Ich fliege nach Atlanta, will nach Athens weiterfliegen, Gewitter, der Flug wird abgesagt, ich muß mir ein Taxi nehmen. Ein alter entzückender Neger fährt das Taxi und fragt: „Was machen Sie bei dem Wetter in Athens?" – „Ich muß einen Vortrag halten." – „Einen Vortrag. Worüber sprechen Sie?" – „Is the New Generation Mad?" – Er lacht. Ich sage: „Lachen Sie nicht. Ich mache Ihnen einen Vorschlag":
„Ich übernehme den Wagen, Sie übernehmen den Vortrag". – „Das könnte ich niemals tun," – „Warum nicht? Sie halten doch sozusagen die Hand am Puls der Zeit. Sie kennen die amerikanische Jugend besser als ich. Sagen sie mir: Is the new generation mad?" – Wie aus der Pistole geschossen sagt er mir: „Of course they are. – They kill themselves, they kill each other, and they take dope." – Sie töten sich selbst, sie töten einander, und sie nehmen Drogen. – Das war die Antwort dieses alten Neger-Taxidrivers, wie aus der Pistole geschossen. Das können Sie nennen: Die massenneurotische Trias der Jugend: Selbstmord, erhöhte Aggressivität, Drogenabhängigkeit.

Das sind nicht bloß Anekdoten. Daß die Drogenabhängigkeit mit dem Sinnlosigkeitsgefühl zu tun hat, ist empirisch erwiesen. Es gibt heute vier logotherapeutische Tests, den Purpose-in-Life-Test von Crumbaugh and Maholick, den Seeking-of-Noetic-Goals-Test von Crumbaugh, den Logo-Test von Elisabeth Lukas, die wir das Vergnügen haben, heute unter uns zu wissen, und den Attitudinal-Value-Scale-Test von Dansart. Damit kann man messen, quantifizieren, sozusagen den Pegel der Sinnerfüllung in einem Individuum. Längst ist das Ergebnis der Korrelationen da; das wurde erwiesen. Eine Dissertantin von mir in Kalifornien hat erwiesen, daß diese Abhängigkeit ganz durchgängig ist.

Sie konnte nachweisen, daß der Drug-Involvement-Index, also das Maß der Versuchung, sich mit Drogen zu befassen, mehr als doppelt so groß ist bei jenen, die einen niedrigen PIL-Test aufgewiesen haben, die also Sinnlosigkeitsgefühle haben. Ich sage es jetzt ganz plump, damit Sie wissen, worum es geht. Wenn jemand ein Sinnlosigkeitsgefühl hat, dann hat er einen Drug-Involvement-Index von 8,9, und wenn er kein Sinnlosigkeitsgefühl hat, hat er einen Drug-Involvement-Index von 4,25, also weniger als die Hälfte.

Jemand, der nicht bei mir dissertiert hat, den ich persönlich gar nicht kenne, ein bekannter Psychiater aus New York, hat ganz unabhängig von diesen Dingen erwiesen, daß unter drogenabhängigen Jugendlichen das Sinnlosigkeitsgefühl zu 100 % verbreitet war.

Daß Hilfe geboten werden kann, können Sie natürlich auch erweisen. Einer meiner Schüler hat in Kalifornien ein Rehabilitationszentrum für Drogenabhängige. Der Durchschnittserfolg liegt in Amerika bei 11 %; er hat mit einer sinnorientierten Therapie 40 %. Elisabeth Lukas hat zusammen mit dem Direktor des Kalifornischen Logotherapie-Instituts erst vor einem Jahr eine Publikation in den „Drug Survival News“ gehabt. Sie hat hier in Europa eine eigene Technik entwickelt und wird uns vielleicht darüber erzählen können; sie hat hervorragende Resultate. Das gleiche gilt auch für schweren Alkoholismus. Eine andere Dissertantin von mir, die heute in Honolulu praktiziert, hat zeigen können, daß unter den chronischen Alkoholikern in schweren Fällen 90 % an einem abgründigen Sinnlosigkeitsgefühl gelitten haben. Soviel zur Drogenabhängigkeit.

Bei der Aggression haben Sie genau dieselben Verhältnisse. Mit dem PIL-Test haben die Leute in Neuseeland gearbeitet. Sie haben gezeigt, daß der Durchschnitt der Bevölkerung in Neuseeland – da gibt es anscheinend noch viel Sinn – 115 PIL-Scores ist, der Durchschnitt in den Gefängnissen ist 86.

In bezug auf die Jugendkriminalität haben Sie wieder die Erfolge eines anderen Schülers von mir, der in vier Monaten den PIL-Index von 86 auf 103 anheben konnte. Der Durchschnitt der Rückfallquote in den Vereinigten Staaten ist 40, in seinem Rehabilitationszentrum ist er nicht 40, sondern 17.

Die Depression äußert sich in den eingangs erwähnten Suizidgefährdungen der heutigen Jugend. Ich weiß nicht, ob es hierzulande bekannt ist; Sie müssen verzeihen, aber ich doziere hauptsächlich in Kalifornien, weniger in Wien, geschweige denn hier. In Amerika ist unter den Studenten der Selbstmord als Todesursache an zweiter Stelle, gleich nach den Verkehrsunfällen. Die Selbstmordversuche unter Studenten in Amerika sind fünfzehnmal häufiger. Von der Dunkelziffer wird lieber nicht gesprochen.

Ich weiß nicht, ob Sie wissen – darüber wird ja hier nicht gesprochen –, welche Verantwortung die Massenmedien auf diesem Gebiet haben. In Detroit ist die Selbstmordquote plötzlich ganz brüsk abgesunken, für sechs Wochen unten geblieben und nach sechs Wochen ebenso plötzlich wieder angestiegen. Während dieser sechs Wochen war ein kompletter Zeitungsstreik in Detroit. Jetzt werden Sie verstehen, was das heißt, zu behaupten, es sei das Recht oder die Pflicht, um jeden Preis alles zu sagen. Wenn ich einem Patienten den Blutdruck messe und er hat 160, und ich sage ihm, der Blutdruck ist leicht erhöht, dann hat er schon nicht mehr 160, sondern 180, weil er sich vor dem Schlaganfall fürchtet. Wenn ich ihm auf seine Frage, wie der Blutdruck ist, sage: „Praktisch normal“, dann sagt er: „Gott sei Dank, ich habe schon gemeint, ich bekomme einen Schlaganfall“, und hat gar nicht mehr 160, sondern 140, wirklich einen normalen Blutdruck. – Man muß nicht alles sagen; das ist ein Mißverständnis, meine Damen und Herren. Sie werden verstehen, daß es mir als Arzt näher liegt, einem Menschen zu helfen, als ihm um jeden Preis irgendeine Wahrheit zu sagen, die existentiell in dem Augenblick, kraft der Paradoxie des Wahrheit-Sagens, in eine Lüge umschlägt.

Halten Sie mich nicht für so naiv, daß ich jetzt sagen will, jeder Selbstmordversuch oder Selbstmord ist auf ein Sinnlosigkeitsgefühl zurückzuführen. Ich

sage nicht, daß die Selbstmorde, um die es sich da handelt, immer aus einem Sinnlosigkeitsgefühl heraus unternommen wurden. Aber sehr wohl wage ich zu behaupten, daß sie unterblieben wären, wenn so ein Mensch um etwas gewußt hätte, das seinem Leben Sinn zu geben vermag, oder wie es C. G. Jung einmal in seinen Erinnerungen gesagt hat: Sinn macht vieles, vielleicht alles ertragbar – dafür, daß das gilt, stehe ich ein auf Grund von drei Jahren Erfahrungen in Auschwitz und zwei Filiallagern von Dachau. Dort ist diese Wahrheit erhärtet worden.
Sie werden verstehen, wenn ich auf dem Standpunkt stehe, so banal er auch klingen und nach heiler Welt aussehen mag: Was der junge Mensch in erster Linie braucht, sind Aufgaben, die Spannung, die sich aus der Anforderung, dem Anspruch heraus ergibt, eine Aufgabe zu erfüllen, eine selbstgewählte oder zumindest bejahte Aufgabe. Die amerikanische Soziologin Sherif hat einmal nachgewiesen – ein berühmtes Experiment: Psychologen, hineingeschmuggelt in ein Pfadfinderlager, waren dort imstande, Aggressionen zwischen Gruppen aufzubauen, interessanterweise dadurch, daß sie Sportwettbewerbe gemacht haben. Nachdem die Aggressionen aufgebaut waren, haben sie beobachten können, daß ein einziges Mal alle gegenseitigen Gruppenaggressionen verschwunden waren: Als nach einem Unwetter der Karren, der ihre Lebensmittel ins Lager bringen sollte, steckengeblieben war und alle Gruppen miteinander herbeigeholt werden mußten und sich gemeinsam der Aufgabe widmen mußten, den Karren wieder aus dem Dreck herauszubringen. Eine gemeinsame Aufgabe hatte sie geeint, und das bedingte den Fortfall der Gruppenaggressionen.

Das können Sie auch auf die Jugendkriminalität anwenden. In Oslo hatten vor Jahren solche jungen Leute, die man hier Halbstarke genannt hat, Statuen in öffentlichen Parks zertrümmert, die Lederbezüge in der Straßenbahn aufgeschlitzt. Die Polizei hat sie geschnappt und aus ihnen freiwillige Brigaden gemacht, die nun die halbe Nacht herumgefahren sind und verhindert haben, daß andere junge Leute dasselbe gemacht haben. Sie haben eine Aufgabe gefunden und waren geheilt, ohne jede weitere Bestrafung selbstverständlich. Junge Menschen brauchen eine Aufgabe, und noch etwas:

Das klingt wiederum nach heiler Welt, ich weiß. Sie brauchen eine Aufgabe und das Vorbild von Menschen, die ihre Aufgaben erfüllen. Sie brauchen das Vorbild, sie brauchen ein Beispiel. Denn wir können nur das Beispiel geben; Werte geben, erzeugen, fabrizieren, Sinn rezeptieren, das können wir nicht. Wir müssen froh sein, wenn der Sinn nicht genommen wird durch Massenmedien, durch gewisse künstlerische Intentionen.

Ich habe die Ehre gehabt, den Internationalen Pen-Club bei seiner Jahrestagung vor zwei Jahren mit einem Vortrag zu adressieren: „*A Psychiatrist Looks at Modern Literature*“. Ich habe diese berühmten Schriftsteller und Nobelpreisträger an ihre soziale Verantwortung erinnert: Wenn ihr schon nicht fähig seid, die Chance der Literatur zu nutzen und Therapie auf kollektiver Ebene zu bieten, wenn ihr schon nicht imstande seid, die Leute angesichts des heutigen existentiellen Vakuums gegen den Nihilismus zu immunisieren, dann infiziert sie doch um Gottes Willen nicht noch mit eurem eigenen Nihilismus und Zynismus. Es gibt heute Theater, die man nicht nur nicht als moralische Anstalt im Sinne von Schiller bezeichnen kann, sondern wenn Sie hineingehen, glauben Sie, Sie sind in einer psychiatrischen Anstalt. Das ist die Situation, die im allgemeinen verschwiegen wird, weil es gerade in ist, Selbstdarstellung der eigenen Leere, der eigenen Nichtigkeit, des eigenen abgründigen Sinnlosigkeitsgefühls. Aber man darf es nicht dabei belassen, und Sie müssen mir schon zubilligen, daß ich als Arzt es wage, das in diesem Sinne auszusprechen.

Eine erste Hilfe gibt es natürlich in Fällen von existentiellem Vakuum bei jungen Menschen. Vor allem muß man ihnen klarmachen, daß diese Depression gar keine Krankheit ist. Ich habe einen Buchtitel geschaffen: *„Das Leiden am sinnlosen Leben"*. Das ist ein Leiden, aber keine Krankheit, das ist keine Neurose.

Jetzt möchte ich auf die Selbstmorde an der Idaho State University zurückkommen. 93 % derjenigen, die das aus Sinnlosigkeitsgefühl gemacht hatten, waren psychisch gesund, physisch gesund, in guten familiären Verhältnissen, in guten sozioökonomischen Verhältnissen, hatten akademische Erfolge und waren sozial engagiert. Das heißt, sie waren in jeder Hinsicht gesund, aber sie haben um keinen Lebenssinn gewußt. Sie wußten nicht, wozu das alles. Das ist keine Krankheit, das gehört zum Menschsein. Nur dem Menschen ist es vorbehalten, die Frage nach dem Sinn zu stellen, nein, mehr als das: Den Sinn des Lebens sogar in Frage zu stellen. Das macht keine Biene, die Karl von Frisch studiert hat, das macht keine Graugans, die Konrad Lorenz studiert hat, so etwas macht eben nur der Mensch. Es ist nicht ein Zeichen von seelischer Krankheit, sondern von geistiger Mündigkeit.

Der junge Mensch lehnt es ab, aus den Händen der Tradition die Werte entgegenzunehmen. Der junge Mensch will selber und selbständig den Sinn seines Lebens finden. Wir müssen nur eines wünschen: Daß dieser Mut gepaart werde mit Geduld, mit der Geduld, auch zu warten, bis ihm früher oder später Sinn dämmert, und nicht einfach das Leben wegzuwerfen, wie an der Idaho State University. Das heißt, es hat überhaupt keinen Sinn, das aus der Stimmung heraus zu tun.

Was gegen den Selbstmord spricht, ist: Wenn mir eine Situation noch so aussichtslos erscheint – wenn nur in einem einzigen Fall, was immer wieder geschieht und von uns Neurologen beobachtet wird, jemand ein paar Wochen, Monate, Jahre später darauf gekommen wäre, daß es doch noch eine Lösung gab, daß ihm doch noch ein Sinn aufgegangen ist, in einem einzigen Fall unter tausend – wér garantiert mir, daß es nicht in meinem Fall auch so sein wird?

Eines Tages wird es anders sein. Aber diesen einen Tag muß ich erleben, auf den muß ich mich aufsparen und darf nicht einen Schritt unternehmen, den ich nie wieder gutmachen kann. Das spricht gegen Selbstmord, nicht das, was die Psychoanalytiker sagen (ich zitiere aus der *„Psyche"):*

> „Bei Selbstmordabsichten läßt sich feststellen, daß es sich immer darum handelt, daß ein unbewußter Mordimpuls gegen irgend jemanden da ist. Der wird umgewendet gegen das eigene Ich und wird abreagiert am eigenen Ich, und dadurch kommt es zum Selbstmord."

Locken Sie einen Hund mit so etwas hinter dem Ofen hervor, nämlich in einem Fall, wo es sich nicht um den Ödipus-Komplex handelt, sondern zur Abwechslung einmal um das existentielle Vakuum.

Soviel zur Therapie. Aber jede Therapie basiert auf einer Theorie. Solange Sie gebunden, indoktriniert sind, in dem Sinne, daß Sie sagen: Der Mensch ist ein Wesen, das hat Triebe und Instinkte, die müssen abreagiert werden, damit die Homöostase wiederhergestellt wird, und die ganze Welt, die Sachen, denen man dient, die Partner, die man liebt, sind gut genug, um diese Abreaktionen vorzunehmen, mit so einem Menschenbild kommen Sie nicht weiter. Wenn Sie dann sagen, der Mensch ist nicht ein abreagierendes, sondern ein reagierendes Wesen, ein Wesen, das immer auf Reize reagiert, dann kommen Sie damit auch nicht weiter. Der Mensch ist weder abreagierendes, noch reagierendes, sondern ein sich selbst transzendierendes Wesen.

Was heißt Selbsttranszendenz? (So wie ich das Wort gebrauche, hat es mit Religion überhaupt nichts zu tun.) Unsere Augen möchte ich nennen selbsttranszendent. Das heißt, die Fähigkeit meines Auges, zu sehen, ist unabdingbar mit seiner Unfähigkeit verbunden, sich selbst zu sehen.

Wann sieht mein Auge etwas von sich selbst? Wenn ich einen Grauen Star habe, dann sehe ich Wolken; das ist meine Linsentrübung. Wenn ich den Grünen Star habe, dann sehe ich Regenbogen um die Lichter, das ist der erhöhte Druck in der Vorderkammer in meinem Auge. Dann sieht das Auge etwas von sich selbst. Das normale Auge sieht die Welt, und nur deshalb, weil es nichts von sich selbst wahrnimmt. Genauso ist der Mensch mit seiner Selbsttranszendenz. Der Mensch ist ganz er selbst und ganz Mensch in dem Maße, in dem er über sich selbst hinauslangt. Menschsein heißt, über sich selbst hinausweisen auf einen Sinn, den es zu erfüllen gilt, oder auf einen anderen Menschen, dem man liebend begegnet.

Das heißt, in dem Maße, in dem der Mensch sich selbst übersieht oder vergißt, wird er eigentlich ganz er selbst. Das steht nicht im Widerspruch mit der Selbstverwirklichungstheorie. Selbstverwirklichung ist nur durch Selbsttranszendenz möglich. In den letzten drei Jahren seines Schaffens hat der verstorbene große Maslow, der Begründer der Humanistic Psychology, diese meine Kritik an seiner ursprünglichen Selbstverwirklichungstheorie vollkommen unterschrieben, auch in seinen Publikationen. Oder um mit Karl Jaspers zu sprechen: Was der Mensch ist, das ist er durch die Sache, die er zur seinen macht.

Die beiden Aspekte dieser Selbsttranszendenz sind also: Im Dienste an einer Sache oder in der Liebe zu einem Menschen werde ich ganz Mensch. Der erste Aspekt wird in der Logotherapie mit dem motivationstheoretischen Begriff des Willens zum Sinn umrissen. Willen zum Sinn nenne ich das Bestreben des Menschen, nicht nur in seinem Leben, sondern in jeder einzelnen ihm begegnenden Lebenssituation einen Sinn zu sehen und ihn zu erfüllen. Sieht er einen solchen Sinn, dann ist er bereit, Verzichte auf sich zu nehmen, Opfer auf sich zu nehmen, dann ist er bereit, sein Leben zu opfern. Wenn er keinen Sinn sieht, dann ist er nahe daran, dieses sein Leben wegzuwerfen, denn dann pfeift er auf sein Leben. Das ist der Mensch.

Er wirft sein Leben weg inmitten des Wohlstands und inmitten der Wohlfahrtsgesellschaft, und zwar deshalb, weil die Industriegesellschaft darauf aus ist, ihm jedes Bedürfnis von den Augen abzugucken und zu befriedigen. Die Konsumgesellschaft ist sogar darauf aus, Bedürfnisse zu erzeugen, damit sie sie endlich befriedigen kann. Aber ein Bedürfnis wird ignoriert und frustriert: Das Grundbedürfnis des Menschen, in seinem Leben einen Sinn zu finden. Das wird von der Gesellschaft frustriert und von der Wissenschaft ignoriert.

Denken Sie doch nur an einen Begriff, der in Mode und in aller Munde ist: Midlife-Crisis, ein altbekanntes Phänomen, was uns Psychiater anlangt. In der Mitte des Lebens, d.h. auf der Höhe der Karriere, haben die Leute endlich genug, wovon sie leben können, und kommen plötzlich darauf, daß sie nichts haben, wofür sie zu leben vermöchten. Die Midlife Crisis ist eine Sinnkrise, und unmittelbar hat das gar nichts mit dem Absinken der Potenz usw. zu tun. Mein Assistent in Harvard hat nachgewiesen, daß von den Harvard Graduates, die in 20 Jahren wunderbare Karrieren als Rechtsanwälte, Industrielle, Chirurgen, Psychoanalytiker gemacht haben, ein unglaublicher Prozentsatz nicht gewußt hat, wozu das überhaupt gut war. Dasselbe gilt für die Arbeitnehmer. Von einem verhaltenstherapeutischen Zentrum in Amerika, also gar nicht beeinflußt von Logotherapie, sinnorientierter Therapie, ist eine Statistik erarbeitet worden, die besagt, daß die meisten Arbeitnehmer klagen: Sie haben einen Posten, sie haben Erfolg in ihrem Beruf, aber sie möchten sich das Leben nehmen, weil sie keinen Sinn zu sehen vermögen.

Das Gegenstück, das Negative, haben sie dann, wenn die Arbeit aufhört: Am Sonntag, am Wochenende, dann bekommen sie die Sonntagsneurose. Das Allensbacher Institut für Demoskopie hat nachgewiesen, daß in einer Reihe von Jahren in letzter Zeit der Prozentsatz derer, die nicht wissen, was sie mit ihrer Freizeit am Sonntag anfangen können, von 26 auf 37 % hinaufgeschnellt ist.

Nun können Sie auch verstehen, wie es kommt, daß ich im Jahre 1933 in der Sozialärztlichen Rundschau – es ist eine ganze Weile her – etwas beschrieben habe, was jetzt wiederum gesagt wurde, ganz unabhängig von mir. Ich habe die Arbeitslosigkeitsneurose beschrieben und konnte nachweisen, daß diese jungen Leute – das war ein Auftrag der Arbeiterkammer in der Aktion „Jugend in Not" – so deprimiert und verzweifelt waren – nicht wegen der Arbeitslosigkeit an sich, sondern aus einem ganz anderen Grund: Weil sie geglaubt haben, Arbeit ist Sinn, Arbeitslosigkeit meint Sinnlosigkeit. Beweis: Ich habe diese jungen Leute in Jugendorganisationen, Volkshochschulen geschickt, sie haben ehrenamtlich, freiwillig gearbeitet. Das Ergebnis: Die Depression ist geschwunden, der Magen hat genauso vor Hunger geknurrt, aber sie haben eine Aufgabe und einen Lebenssinn finden können; die Depression war weg.

Das ist jetzt in einem Buch bestätigt worden: Aktuelle Ergebnisse der sogenannten Arbeitslosenforschung, *„Vom Schock zum Fatalismus"*. Die Leute „fühlen sich nutzlos und überflüssig". In einer alten Studie von Arbeitern in Marienthal ist das vielfach vorweggenommen worden, aber nicht mit dieser stringenten Deutung.

Heute ist die Arbeitslosigkeit nicht mehr durch die Weltwirtschaftskrise bedingt, sondern durch die Energiekrise. Die Energiequellen sind erschöpft. Aber der Sinn ist unerschöpflich. Bis vor kurzem war es so, daß die Leute sich hauptsächlich um die Lebens-Mittel gekümmert haben, die Mittel, die man braucht, um zu leben, im weitestens Sinne des Wortes. Sie haben Geld gescheffelt, sie wollten Erfolg haben, waren arbeits-, leistungszentriert usw. Die Chance der Energiekrise liegt darin, daß immer weitere Kreise den Akzent von den Lebens-Mitteln zum Lebenszweck verpflanzen. Das geht auch trotz Arbeitslosigkeit, trotz eingeschränkten Wirtschaftswachstums. Daß das keine Phantasterei von mir ist, geht daraus hervor, daß in den Ländern mit Massenarbeitslosigkeit der Bücherkauf und das Bücherlesen hinaufgeschnellt sind, trotz allem.

Es ist also die Problematik der Freizeitgesellschaft, des Überflusses an Freizeit. Wie können wir die sinnvoll auswerten? Ich wiederhole: Im Gegensatz zu den Energiequellen sind die Sinnmöglichkeiten unerschöpflich.

Sie sind es deshalb, weil man nicht nur einen Sinn finden kann, indem man eine Tat setzt oder ein Werk schafft, sondern auch indem man etwas erlebt in Kunst, Wissenschaft, Wahrheit, Forschung, indem man etwas in der Natur draußen erlebt oder indem man nicht etwas, sondern jemanden erlebt, in seiner Einmaligkeit, Einzigartigkeit, d.h. ihn liebt. Wir können einen Sinn im Leben finden in der Arbeit und in der Liebe, ganz plump gesprochen; das versteht der Mann von der Straße.

Wir können noch etwas vom Mann auf der Straße lernen: Daß es noch immer einen Sinn darüber hinaus gibt. Wenn wir das hilflose Opfer einer hoffnungslosen Situation sind, wenn wir mit einem Schicksal konfrontiert sind, das wir nicht ändern können, mit einem unheilbaren Leiden, einem nicht mehr operierbaren Krebs, dann kann der Mensch wie sonst nie zeigen, was an ihm ist, er kann Zeugnis ablegen von der spezifisch menschlichen Fähigkeit, ein Leiden in eine menschliche Leistung umzuprägen, eine persönliche Tragödie in einen Triumph zu verwandeln.

Jetzt sagen Sie: Ja, aber das soll Ihnen einmal jemand vormachen, das ist alles leicht gesagt. – Es vergeht kaum eine Woche, kaum ein Tag, wo ich nicht solches Material aus aller Welt bekomme. Lassen Sie mich das aus der Kasuistik herausgreifen:

Eine Studentin von mir ist in Kalifornien Krankenschwester, Sozialbetreuerin. Der Fall betrifft einen 31jährigen Mann, einen Mechaniker, der in das Spital, wo sie arbeitet, eingeliefert wurde. Sie wurde ihm als Special Nurse zugeteilt. Der Mann hatte einen Starkstromunfall, und von den Knien und den Ellenbogen ab waren alle vier Extremitäten brandig und mußten amputiert werden. Während der Amputationsoperation sind den Chirurgen, dem Anästhesisten und der Operationsschwester nur so die Tränen aus den Augen geflossen. Es war meiner Studentin vorbehalten, diesem jungen Mann beim Erwachen aus der Narkose mitzuteilen, daß ihm sämtliche vier Extremitäten amputiert wurden. Im Laufe von Wochen gelang es ihr, einen Funken von Sinnmöglichkeiten in ihm zu erwecken, dank logotherapeutischer Techniken.

Sie hat mit ihm ein Buch von mir, das drüben in jedem Spital und in jeder Haftanstalt aufliegt, durchgesprochen. Sie hat ihn im Laufe von Wochen sogar so weit gebracht, daß er sich von sich selbst distanzieren konnte, wie wir das in der Logotherapie nennen. Er hat sogar Humor aufgebracht. Er hat erkannt, daß er im Sinne der Selbsttranszendenz anderen dienen konnte. Er hat sich eines vom Genick abwärts vollkommen gelähmten anderen jungen Mannes angenommen. So ging es weiter. Er hat gelesen, und aus diesem Buch von mir – das gibt es sogar in Deutsch, *„Trotzdem ja zum Leben sagen“* heißt es – hat er sich immer wieder vorgesagt: Der Mensch, der einer wird – es handelt sich um einen Gefangenen im Konzentrationslager –, ist das Resultat einer persönlichen Entscheidung; im Grunde kann jeder Mensch aber unter allen Bedingungen und Umständen bestimmen, was aus ihm wird, psychisch und geistig. Er kann seine menschliche Würde bewahren, auch in solchen Grenzsituationen, und alles kann man ihm nehmen, aber diese Freiheit kann ihm niemand nehmen, und die ist das, was Menschenleben sinnvoll macht.

Er war dann nach einem halben Jahr so weit, daß er ein Geschäft führen konnte, seine Familie erhalten konnte, seine Familie auf einen Urlaub nehmen konnte, in einem besonderen Auto, das er dann bekommen hat, vom Atlantik zum Pazifik, und dann hat er ihr eines Tages folgendes geschrieben: „Ich war innerlich ganz ausgehöhlt vor dem Unfall. Ich war immer besoffen gewesen und zu Tode gelangweilt“. Dann schreibt er – ohne vier Extremitäten! –: „Jetzt erst weiß ich, was Glück heißt“.

Referat Frankl

Das sind die Realitäten, meine Damen und Herren. Das sind keine Philosopheme, das sind harte klinische Tatsachen. Das ist das, was wir von unseren Patienten lernen können. Ich bin in der glücklichen Lage, Sie mit einer taufrischen Befragung zu konfrontieren. Das Imas-Institut in Linz hat tausende von Menschen gefragt, wovor sie am meisten Respekt haben. Das waren nicht die Politiker, das waren nicht die Sportler, das waren nicht die Forscher, das waren nicht die Künstler, das waren nicht einmal die Astronauten, sondern das war mit großem Abstand ein Mensch, der unter großen Opfern anderen hilft, und gleich danach ein Mensch, der ein schweres Schicksal meistert, ohne zu klagen. Das ist das, was der Mann von der Straße denkt, der nicht jahrelang auf psychoanalytischen Couchen herumgekugelt ist und nicht jahrelang auf den Campussen reduktionistischer Universitäten indoktriniert wurde. Das ist das, was der Mensch als solcher denkt. Das müssen wir von ihm lernen, damit wir es andere lehren können.

Wir können also nicht einem Menschen sagen, was der Sinn des Lebens ist, aber sehr wohl können wir ihm sagen, daß das Leben einen Sinn hat und ihn bedingungslos bis zum letzten Atemzug behält. Das ist nicht die Privatansicht von Herrn Frankl, obwohl ich zugebe, daß ich diese Dinge als Teenager entwickelt habe; aber inzwischen sind sie empirisch verifiziert worden. Keine Angst, ich werde es Ihnen nicht aufzählen; es sind genau 20 wissenschaftliche Arbeiten, die auf Grund von Statistiken und Tests an tausenden und abertausenden Personen ergeben haben, zwischen Polen und Neuseeland, daß der Mensch einen Sinn finden kann nachweislich unabhängig von seinem Alter, unabhängig von seinem Geschlecht, unabhängig vom Intelligenzquotienten, unabhängig vom Ausbildungsgrad. Natürlich ist eines leichter als das andere, aber er kann einen Sinn finden grundsätzlich unabhängig von der Charakterstruktur, unabhängig von der unmittelbaren Umweltsituation, auch in Haft, unter allen Umständen, irgendeinen Sinn zu finden vermag er. Das heißt nicht – Sie brauchen mir nicht zuzumuten, daß ich so kurzschlüssig denke: Gehen wir alle in Haft, dort kann man am besten einen Sinn finden. So primitiv denken wir ja alle nicht. Ich habe einmal nachzuweisen versucht, daß auch in Auschwitz die Leute noch vor dem Eingang der Gaskammern einen Sinn gefunden haben und in den Gaskammern. Wenn ich so etwas sage, heißt das nicht: Gehen wir alle Arm in Arm in die Gaskammern von Auschwitz. Sie müssen eine grundsätzliche Frage von der praktischen Frage unterscheiden.

Ich habe gesagt: Im Leiden einen Sinn zu finden, ist nur möglich, wenn ein unaufhebbarer, schicksalhafter Tatbestand da ist, oder, wie es einmal in einem Inserat in einer deutschsprachigen Zeitschrift in New York heißt: „Was der Himmel dir beschieden, trage mit Geduld hienieden. Doch bei Wanzen greife ein, wende dich an Rosenstein." – Eine Wanzenvertilgungsfirma. Ein unnötiges Leiden hat also keinen Sinn. Eine Gesellschaft unverändert zu lassen, hat keinen Sinn. Aber es soll nun einmal auch Dinge geben, wo man nicht weiter kann, es soll unheilbare Krankheiten geben, und angeblich soll sogar der Tod auf jeden von uns warten und nicht auf einzelne unglückliche Personen . . .

Es gibt eine Reihe von Arbeiten unter den 20, die nachweisen konnten: Sinn zu haben ist für jeden Menschen grundsätzlich unabhängig davon, ob er religiös ist oder nicht. Wenn er religiös ist, ist es unabhängig davon, welcher Konfession er angehören mag. Pikanterweise ist das letztere ein Ergebnis aus der Forschungsarbeit von katholischen Priestern in Kanada bzw. Polen.

Meine Damen und Herren, ich schließe mit einem Zitat aus einer Arbeit in der *„Sozialwirtschaftlichen Korrespondenz – Zeitschrift für Sozial- und Wirtschaftspolitik"*, die vor wenigen Wochen erschienen ist. Dr. Christoph Günzl schreibt:

> „Wenn wir die Massenmedien als Indikatoren nehmen, werden wir finden, daß dort eine Vokabel auftaucht, die vorher kaum zu hören oder zu lesen war, und diese Vokabel lautet „Sinn". Es scheint also, daß die Frage nach dem Sinn des Lebens virulent zu werden beginnt. In der Tat ist, wie Viktor E. Frankl zeigt, einem großen Prozentsatz unserer Zeitgenossen der Sinn des Lebens fraglich geworden. Dieser Umstand gewinnt nun auch politische Bedeutung."

Jetzt steige ich den Politikern vom Nachmittag ins Kraut.

> „Die Frage nach dem Lebenssinn hat plötzlich parteipolitische Relevanz bekommen. Wenn in der Vergangenheit einmal Wirtschaftsordnungsprobleme das Geschehen determinierten und später Fragen der Gesellschaft und der gesellschaftlichen Struktur das politische Klima bestimmten, so beginnt nun offensichtlich eine Entwicklungsphase, die von der Sinnfrage beherrscht wird, und das politische Geschehen wird von der Faszination bestimmt sein, die aus diesem Fragenkomplex kommt. Und jene politische Gruppe oder politische Partei, die hierauf Antworten zu geben vermag oder wenigstens Beiträge zur Lösung dieser Problematik liefert, wird von dieser Faszination profitieren."

Sie werden jetzt verstehen, wie es kommt, daß der österreichische Gewerkschaftsbund bei seinem letzten großen Kongreß die These aufgestellt hat und darüber abstimmen ließ: „Was die Jugend braucht, ist ein Lebensinhalt". Sie werden auch verstehen, daß der österreichische Bundeskanzler in einem Zeitungsinterview bereits gesagt hat: „Eigentlich scheint mir das Wichtigste zu sein, sich gegen die Vorstellung von einer Sinnlosigkeit des Lebens zu stellen."

Das Leben ist nicht sinnlos im Jahre 2000
– Vom Sinn der Arbeit –

Dr. Heinrich Basilius Streithofen

Die Frage nach dem Sinn des Lebens und besonders der Arbeit wird in diesem Jahrzehnt immer wieder gestellt. Zukunftsforscher machen uns glauben, daß im Jahre 2000 nur noch wenige Menschen arbeiten müssen. Ihren Optimismus teile ich nicht. Die Arbeit gehört zur conditio humana. Sie ist auch ein konstitutives Element des menschlichen Glücks.

Jahrhunderte träumte das Menschengeschlecht von einem göttergleichen Leben ohne Arbeit mit viel Muße und Genuß. Bisher gab es dieses Leben für die meisten Menschen nicht. Der Gedanke eines von Arbeit befreiten Lebens ist nicht neu. In den Sozialutopien der Neuzeit taucht er immer wieder auf.

Wird nun durch den technischen Fortschritt ein göttergleiches Leben im Jahre 2000 verwirklicht? Ich bezweifle es.

Auf die Fragen, Sorgen und Probleme der Arbeitswelt im Jahre 2000 weiß ich keine schlüssige Antwort. Was es an Antworten gibt, wird jeden Tag und überall von Menschen praktisch gegeben. Sofern es sich um faktische Lösungen von Problemen handelt, sind diese eine Sache der Politik und der Wirtschaft.

Was ich hier und heute zu leisten vermag, ist eine Art Besinnung, eine Meditation über den Sinn der Arbeit.

Arbeiten zu können gehört zur menschlichen Wesensverfassung. Das Tier kann nicht arbeiten. Es hat auch kein Verhältnis zu Zeit und Raum. Nur weil der Mensch arbeiten kann, darf, muß, weil er ein Verhältnis zu Zeit und Raum hat, können wir über den Sinn oder die Sinnlosigkeit der Arbeit im Jahre 2000 reden.

Dieses faszinierende Jahr 2000 kommt schnell. In 22 Jahren ist es da. Wird sich da noch viel verändern in der Forschung, der Industrie, in der Politik? Ich weiß es nicht. Vielleicht in der Technologie. Aber schauen wir uns einmal die letzten zweitausend Jahre an. Blicken wir zurück und lernen aus der Vergangenheit, um die Zukunft meistern zu können.

1. „Klassische“ Aussagen über den Sinn der Arbeit

Das vielleicht älteste Buch der Welt, die Bibel, erzählt, daß zur Strafe für die Sünde der ersten Menschen die Arbeit, vorher eine Lust und Freude, zu einer Last wurde. Es ist, als hätten die alten Völker geahnt, daß auf der Arbeit, wie sie nun einmal an den Menschen herantritt, ein Fluch liege.

Es geht wie eine Empörung durch die Antike, die Flucht vor der Arbeit, die Verachtung der Arbeit. Das Feuer, die Vorbedingung jeder Kulturarbeit, ist nicht von den Göttern mildreich den Menschen gegeben, sondern von **Prometheus** den Göttern abgetrotzt.

Herakles, der antike Mensch schlechthin – wie **Faust** der moderne Mensch – wird von den Göttern durch arbeiten gequält und zermalmt, arbeiten zu müssen, ist sein Leiden.

Was diese Sagen in grandiosen Bildern ausgesprochen haben, hat in der ganzen antiken Welt, in ihrer Kultur Widerhall gefunden. Alle körperlichen Arbeiten sahen die Griechen als von den Barbaren entlehnt an und verachteten sie entsprechend, wie sie die Barbarei verachteten.

Schon bei **Homer** murrt **Agamemnon** gegen **Zeus**, weil dieser ihm das Gesetz der Arbeit auferlegt hat. Der Grund seines Murrens ist der, daß es ihm und dem **Menelaos** Mühe macht, des nachts ihre Leute einzeln aufzurufen *(Ilias X, 70)*. Der Historiker **Herodot** glaubt die Quellen dieser bei den Griechen notorischen Arbeitsscheu und Arbeitsverachtung noch bei älteren Kulturvölkern zu finden. Er spricht von den ägyptischen Priesterkasten, welche nicht arbeiten, sondern nur das Kriegshandwerk ausüben, und bemerkt dann: „Ob nun die Hellenen auch dies von den Ägyptern übernommen haben, kann ich nicht entscheiden. Ich sehe, daß auch bei den Thrakern, den Skythen, den Persern, den Lydern und fast allen anderen Barbarenvölkern die Handwerker und ihre Abkömmlinge in geringerer Achtung stehen als die übrigen Bürger. Wer von körperlicher Arbeit befreit ist, gilt für edler, namentlich wer sich der Kriegskunst widmet. Das haben sämtliche Hellenenstämme übernommen, am meisten die Lakedaimonier. Am wenigsten verachtet sind die Handwerker in Korinth" *(Herodot, Historien, II, 167, Deutsche Gesamtausgabe, Stuttgart 1959, 173)*.

Die Großen unter den griechischen Philosophen haben diese Ansicht geteilt und verteidigt. Der historische **Sokrates** geht ständig in den Werkstätten umher, um dort den Banausen zu beweisen, daß sie nicht das Recht hätten, einen Gedanken, ein Urteil zu wagen, das über die Sphäre ihrer harten, gewöhnlichen Arbeit hinausgehe.

Von **Sokrates** stammt das harte Wort über den Demos, das Volk, das uns von **Xenophons** berichtet wird, von „den Unverständigsten und Schwächsten", von Walkern, Schustern, Zimmerleuten, Schmieden, Bauern, Kaufleuten, die sich nie um Staatsgeschäfte gekümmert haben *(vgl. Xenophon, Erinnerungen an Sokrates, Leipzig 1883, III, 7, 5–7)*.

Bei **Plato** finden sich manche sympathische Ausführungen über die Behandlung der Arbeiter, Tagelöhner und Sklaven. Aber man kann sich beim Lesen seiner Texte nicht des Gefühls erwehren, daß sein Verständnis von Mitleid geprägt ist, nicht aber vom Rechtsbewußtsein. Bei **Plato** ist der Arbeiter ein Mensch von geringem Verstand, ein Unfreier, der seine Kräfte gegen Lohn verkauft *(vgl. Plato, der Staat, II, 371)*.

Schärfere und verächtlichere Ausführungen über Arbeit und Arbeiter finden wir bei **Aristoteles.** Er kennt im Grunde keinen Unterschied zwischen dem Sklaven und dem Arbeiter. „Unter denen, welche die unentbehrlichen Arbeiten leisten, waltet nur der Unterschied ob, daß, wer sie nur für einen verrichtet, Sklave ist; wer sie aber für das gesamte Publikum verrichtet, wird Handwerker oder Tagelöhner genannt“ *(Aristoteles, Über die Politik, III, 2).*

Aus diesem Grunde muß auch dem Handwerker die politische Tätigkeit verschlossen bleiben; denn er ist unfrei wie der Sklave, weil er ja für andere arbeitet; auch macht ihn seine Arbeit engherzig und für große Interessen unempfindlich *(vgl. Aristoteles, Über die Politik, VIII, 2).*

Und hier wiederum liegt der Ausgangspunkt zu den exorbitanten Sätzen, daß Arbeit und Bildung sich gegenseitig ausschließen, daß bei der Arbeit die Tugend nicht sein könne *(vgl. Aristoteles, Über die Politik, IV, 9).*

Die verhängnisvolle Wirkung dieser Ansichten der geistigen Stimmführer des griechischen Volkes über die Arbeit konnte nicht ausbleiben. Die Folge war eine ungeheure Arbeitsscheu. Schon im 4. Jahrhundert gab es in Griechenland eine Volksschicht, die um keinen Preis arbeiten wollte.

Rom besiegte militärisch Griechenland. Das griechische Denken, d.h. seine Philosophie, unterjochte die Römer. Der Grieche brauchte aber dem Römer die Verachtung der Arbeit nicht erst zu lehren.

Nichts ist bezeichnender, als das mit ein und demselben Wort „labor“ in der römischen Sprache sowohl die Arbeit, wie die Mühsal bezeichnet wird. Damit war die Arbeit gebrandmarkt. Der Gedanke, daß sie auch ein Segen sein könnte, war ausgeschlossen. Und darin lag schon auch die stumme Aufforderung, der Arbeit zu entfliehen und, wo dies nicht möglich sei, sie auf ein Minimum zu beschränken.

Bis in die Zeit der Könige und Kaiser geht die Verachtung der Arbeit. Zur Zeit des **Augustus** konnte der gebildete Mann die Mißachtung, die er der Arbeit entgegenbrachte, damit begründen, daß schon **Romulus** die Handwerker von der Teilnahme am Staatsdienst ausgeschlossen habe.

In seinem Werk über die Pflichten legt **Cicero** in klassischer Weise dar, wie die Römer über Erwerbstätigkeit gedacht haben. Er sagt hier nicht seine persönliche Meinung. Manchmal wurde das behauptet. Diese Stelle möchte ich Ihnen nicht vorenthalten. „Über die Künste und Gewerbearten, welche von ihnen anständig, welche gemein seien, gilt bei uns ungefähr Folgendes. Erstlich, alle Gewerbe werden mißbilligt, die verhaßt machen, zum Beispiel die der Zöllner und der Wucherer. Unanständig ferner und gemein sind die Gewerbe alle Tagelöhner, deren Arbeit und nicht deren Kunst man bezahlt. Denn bei ihnen ist der Lohn nichts als ein Handgeld zur Knechtschaft. Für gemein müssen auch die gelten, welche zum Verkauf im kleinen von Kaufleuten Waren einhandeln.

Denn sie können durchaus nicht fortkommen, wenn sie sich nicht sehr auf's Lügen einlassen. Nichts aber ist schändlicher als solche Marktschreierei. Auch die Handwerker treiben eine gemeine Kunst. Denn eine Werkstätte kann nichts Edles hegen. Am wenigsten indes kann man die Beschäftigung billigen, welche Dienerin des Vergnügens sind: die Salzfischer, Fleischer, Köche, Fischer und Wurstmacher, wie Terenz sagt; dazu, wenn man will, die Salbenhändler, Tänzer und alle Arten von Glücksspielern. Die Künste hingegen, welche entweder einen höheren Grad von Einsicht verlangen, oder nicht geringen Nutzen stiften, zum Beispiel die Arzneikunst, die Baukunst, den Unterricht in anständigen Dingen, alles dies ist für diejenigen, deren Stand es angemessen ist, anständig. Der Handel im kleinen muß für gemein gelten. Wird er hingegen im großen und in bedeutendem Umfange betrieben, führt er viele Waren aus allen Ländern ein und verschafft vielen den Genuß derselben ohne Marktschreierei, so verdient er eben nicht besonderen Tadel. Ja, ich glaube, er kann sogar mit dem vollsten Recht gelobt werden, wenn der Kaufmann, gesättigt oder vielmehr zufrieden mit seinen Gewinnen, wie vorher oftmals von dem hohen Meere in den Hafen, so am Ende aus dem Hafen selber auf Ländereien und Besitzungen sich zurückzieht. Von allen Erwerbsarten aber ist keine besser als der Ackerbau, keine angenehmer, keine eines Menschen, keine eines freien Mannes würdiger" *(Cicero, de officiis, I, 42).*

Fragt man sich, wie die Antike zu dieser für uns noch kaum zu begreifenden Verachtung der körperlichen Arbeit kommen konnte, so scheinen drei Gründe von Gewicht zu sein: die Sklaverei, die Überschätzung des Staatsideals und die Überschätzung der rein geistigen Arbeit.

2. Die Aussagen der Theologen

Einen radikalen Bruch mit der antiken Auffassung von der Arbeit vollzog der hl. **Augustinus.** Er war, bevor er Christ wurde, Professor an den drei großen Zentren antiker Bildung, in Karthago, Rom und Mailand. Er war Schüler **Ciceros** und **Plotins,** die letzte große Erscheinung der antiken Geisteswelt. Dieser Mann wurde Christ, bestieg einen Bischofsstuhl, wurde der tiefsinnigste Verteidiger christlicher Glaubenssätze und Mitbegründer einer neuen Zeit. Die mittelalterliche Theologie und Philosophie sind ohne **Augustinus** nicht denkbar.

„Die Erdendinge sind eine Stufe, auf denen man zur himmlischen Gerechtigkeit aufsteigt" (in terrenis rebus fit gradus ad caelestem justitiam), dies ist ein allgemeiner Lebensgrundsatz des **Augustinus.** Er wandte ihn auch auf die Arbeit an. Sie ist ihm ein Mittel zu Gott zu gelangen.

Schon in einer seiner frühesten Schriften, in dem Werke de quantitate animae, spricht er diesen Gedanken aus. Er sagt: „Die zahlreichen Künste, die mit der Hand geübt werden, die mannigfaltigen Bepflanzungen der Äcker, die Gründungen der Städte, die Wunderwerke der Baukunst, die Erfindungen sinnvoller Zeichen in Schrift und Rede, in der Tonwelt, Malerei und Bildnerei, die vielen Sprachen und Einrichtungen der Völker aus alter und neuer Zeit, die Unzahl der Bücher und sonstigen Denkmäler zum Festhalten des Geschehens, die ausgedehnte Sorge für die Nachwelt, die Stufenleiter der bürgerlichen, militärischen und priesterlichen Ämter, die Großtaten des Denkens und Erfindens, die Ströme der Beredsamkeit, die Fülle der Dichtungen, die bunte Welt des Spieles und des Scherzes, die Fertigkeit im Musizieren, die Genauigkeit im Messen, der Scharfsinn im Rechnen, die Erschließung des Vergangenen und Zukünftigen aus der Gegenwart, das alles ist groß, und des Menschen wahrhaft würdig *(Augustinus, de quantitate animae, 72).*

Diese gleichwertige Nebeneinanderstellung von körperlich-mechanischer und geistiger Arbeit ist für die geistesstolze Antike etwas Ungeheuerliches. Alle diese Arbeiten sind des Menschen wahrhaft würdig; des Menschen schlechthin, also nicht mehr nur derjenigen, „deren Stand sie entsprechen", wie **Cicero** meinte.

Alle Arbeiten, auch die geringsten, sind etwas Großes. Sie sind Mittel, zu Gott zu gelangen, zeitliche und ewige Werte zu schaffen. So kann **Augustinus** feststellen: „Die Weltmenschen arbeiten aus irdischen Motiven; du arbeite aber nicht aus irdischer Liebe, sondern der ewigen Ruhe wegen, die Gott verspricht". Die ewige Ruhe ist die letzte Vollendung des Menschen.

Die Arbeit ist keine Strafe für **Augustinus.** In seinem Kommentar zur Genesis betont er ausdrücklich, daß Gott dem Menschen schon ursprünglich, gleich bei der Erschaffung, den Befehl gegeben habe, zu arbeiten. Er habe ihm das Paradies übergeben, „damit er es bewache und bebaue". Schon vor dem Sündenfall habe die Pflicht zur Arbeit bestanden. Jedoch wäre die Arbeit weder Last noch Mühsal, sondern Lust gewesen. Nach **Augustinus** gehören Mühseligkeit und Schweiß nicht notwenig zur Arbeit.

Thomas von Aquin geht von einem ganz anderen Ansatzpunkt aus, um den Sinn der Arbeit und des Arbeitens zu erklären.

Die Ethik des **Thomas** ist eine Ethik des Handelns. Als solche steht sie in einem Gegensatz zu jeder Ethik, die im Untätigsein, in der geruhsamen Unbewegtheit ein Ideal sieht.

Für **Thomas** gilt der Grundatz: „Jedes Ding ist wegen seiner Tätigkeit und seiner eigenen Vervollkommnung da". Damit verbindet er einen anderen Grundsatz: „Das Handeln folgt dem Sein". Jedes Ding ist entsprechend seiner Natur tätig. Es soll und muß sich in einer Weise beschäftigen bzw. betätigen, die mit seinem Wesen, seiner Seinsbeschaffenheit übereinstimmt.

Thomas anerkennt den Menschen als Person und zählt ihn damit zu dem, was er als das Vollkommenste in der ganzen Natur bezeichnet. Die Person ist ein geistiges, bzw. geistbegabtes Wesen. Der Person gebührt ein Eigenwert, der den Wert aller ungeistigen Dinge schlechthin überragt. Nur die Person ist imstande, sich dem Guten erkennend hinzugeben. Niemals können Sinn und Aufgabe der Person darin aufgehen, Nutz- und Gebrauchswert für andere zu sein, auch nicht für andere Personen. Die unvernünftigen Dinge haben die naturhafte Bestimmung, für die Zwecke und Notwendigkeiten von Personen in Dienst genommen zu werden. Wer das von einer Person verlangen oder ihr zumuten würde, würde sich an der Ordnung der Natur vergreifen bzw. des Schöpfers.

Alles menschliche, d.h. alles überlegte und freie Tun des Menschen hat an diesem personhaften Selbstwert unmittelbaren Anteil. Es trägt die beiden maßgeblichen Merkmale des Personhaften an sich: es ist selbstmächtiges und selbstzielhaftes Handeln.

Weil der Mensch Person ist und Arbeiten wesentlich zu seiner Existenz gehört, widerstreitet es der inneren seinshaften wie ethischen Bewandtnis der Arbeit, daß sie als Ware angesehen und angeboten wird. Die menschliche Arbeit ist kein marktgängiges Tauschgut, das wie ein Gebrauchsgegenstand im Handel nachgefragt und gekauft wird. Es ist unrecht und entspricht nicht der Menschenwürde, die Arbeit in erster Linie mit Boden und Kapital als „Wirtschaftsfaktor", als „Kostenelement" zu betrachten und dementsprechend unter dem Gesichtspunkt von Gewinn und Verlust rein rechnerisch zu erfassen. Eine solche Rechnung kann niemals aufgehen.

Selbstverständlich kann der Lohn, der für die Arbeitsleistung des Menschen als Entgelt gezahlt wird, rechnerisch eingesetzt und mitgeführt werden. Abgesehen davon, daß bereits die ganzen Fragen um Lohnhöhe usw. nicht sinnvoll und gerecht entschieden werden können, ohne den personalen Charakter der menschlichen Arbeit zu beachten und einzubeziehen, liegt die Problematik der gegenwärtigen Anschauungen darin, daß der „Marktwert" den ersten und wirtschaftlich allein geltenden Maßstab für die Beurteilung und den Einsatz der menschlichen Arbeit darstellt.

Vollziehen wir hier eine gedankliche Zäsur. Versuchen wir einen anderen Zugang, um das Problem über den Sinn der Arbeit zu klären.

Für **Thomas** ist Gott lauterste Tätigkeit, Tun und Schaffen in Person. Nicht das untätig ruhende Geschöpf ist und wird ihm am meisten ähnlich, sondern das tätige, das sich regt und bewegt, das arbeitet. Nicht die ungeistige Kreatur, die trotz aller Bewegtheit nur in Triebgebundenheit dahinlebt, ist das getreue Abbild Gottes, seines ewig-tätigen Wesens, sondern die geistbegabte Kreatur, der Mensch, der sinnverstehend und darum Sinn zu deuten mächtig ist, der sich in freiem Entscheid selbst bestimmt und bewegt.

Thomas hat versucht, den Sinn der Arbeit zu deuten. Er gibt ihr eine persönliche, soziale, kosmische und religiöse Bedeutung.

Referat Streithofen

Die menschliche Arbeit ist die Quelle des Wohlstandes, der Kultur und des Fortschrittes unter den Menschen. Sie ist nicht der Zweck, der Inhalt, der Sinn des menschlichen Lebens. Sie kann niemals Selbstzweck sein, sondern muß immer höheren Zielen und Zusammenhängen zu-, ein- und untergeordnet sein.

Die Arbeit hat einen persönlichen Sinn, weil sie dem arbeitenden Menschen und seiner Familie den Lebensunterhalt verbürgt und sichert. Sie ist Erwerbstitel, Grundlage der wirtschaftlich-beruflichen Existenz.

Die Arbeit ermöglicht es dem Menschen, seine Kräfte, Fähigkeiten, Anlagen und Talente auszubilden und auszuwirken. Sie gibt ihm tagtäglich vielfältige Gelegenheit zu ethischer Bewährung. Sie ist Lern- und Übungsschule moralischer Verhaltensweisen – der Gelehrigkeit, der Geduld, der Ausdauer, der Härte gegen sich selbst –; sie vermittelt Freude, Zufriedenheit; sie fordert Rücksichtnahme auf Menschen, sie ist gemeinschaftsbildend.

Der soziale Sinn der Arbeit zeigt sich darin, daß sie das erste und wichtigste Erzeugungsmittel – „Produktionsfaktor" – ist, von dem die wirtschaftliche Ergiebigkeit, der materielle Wohlstand des Volkes abhängt.

In der Arbeit erleben die Menschen ihre gegenseitige Abhängigkeit, ihre Angewiesenheit aufeinander. Nur einmütiges bzw. partnerschaftliches Zusammenwirken von Kapital und Arbeit überwindet bzw. entschärft den Klassenkampf.

Die Arbeit hat auch einen kosmischen, d.h. weltallbezogenen Sinn. Die Welt mit ihren unermeßlichen Möglichkeiten ist dem Menschen von Gott zur Herrschaft und Nutzung anvertraut. Sie soll durch den Menschen zur Vollendung emporgeführt werden. Der Weg dazu ist die Arbeit. Durch sie werden die Kräfte der Natur erschlossen und gebändigt, Wärme und Kälte, Sturm und Wasserfluten in menschliche Dienste gezwungen, die materiellen Güter der Erde nutzbar gemacht, das Atom gebändigt. Die Arbeit ist da, damit Mensch und Universum immer stärker miteinander verbunden werden, damit der Geist sich immer mehr mit dem Stoff vereine. Der Mensch ist der Herr des Weltalls, Mitarbeiter an der Schöpfung, Nutznießer und geistiger Baumeister der Natur. Die Menschheit braucht für ihr Leben und für ihre Vollendung den Kosmos.

Der religiöse Sinn der Arbeit zeigt sich darin, daß der Mensch in der Arbeit seine Kräfte betätigt. Die Arbeit macht ihn in besonderer Weise Gott ähnlich, insofern Gott „reine Tätigkeit in Person", actus purus ist.

3. Ausblick auf das Jahr 2000

Die Bücher und Artikel über den Sinn der Arbeit im Jahre 2000, über die Folgen der Automation, sind zahllos. Oft vermitteln sie den Eindruck, als werde eine ganz neue geschichtliche Ära eröffnet. Nun, bisher galten die „Mechanisierung", die „Rationalisierung" und die „Automatisierung" als moderne Methoden zur Steigerung der Produktion, zur besseren Verteilung der Güter und zur besseren Organisation der Arbeitskräfte in den Unternehmen. Mit neuen technologischen Erfindungen verbinden sich neue Hoffnungen. Die Menschen glauben, daß sich ihr Leben grundlegend ändern könnte. Bei der Beurteilung der Zukunft gibt es Optimisten und Pessimisten in bezug auf den Menschen und die Welt des Jahres 2000. So entsteht das Gefühl, daß man mit ihr etwas zu schaffen vorhat, was die Mechanisierung, die Rationalisierung und Automatisierung wesentlich übertrifft. Selbst die Tatsache, daß zum Beispiel die Automatisierung nicht der praktischen Erfahrung, sondern den theoretischen Kenntnissen der modernen Naturwissenschaften entstammt, kann an sich nicht den Eindruck von etwas vollständig Neuem im Rahmen der gegenwärtigen Bemühungen um die Bedeutung des Jahres 2000 wecken. Wenn aber die Futurologen und Zukunftsdeuter glauben, daß eine völlig neue Periode in der Geschichte der Menschheit eingeleitet wird, so ist es klar, daß man den Naturwissenschaften eine ganz neue Rolle in der Bildung des menschlichen Lebens zuweisen will. Man möchte ihnen eine Schlüsselstellung einräumen, eine Stellung, die sie bisher mit anderen Wissenschaften teilen mußten. So kommt es zu der Behauptung, daß mit der Automation eine neue Welt beginnt, die ausschließlich vom Menschen gemacht sei, und daß der von den exakten Wissenschaften erleuchtete Mensch heute zum ersten Mal Demiurg und autonomer Herr der Welt geworden sei.

Die Automation, die Entwicklung der Elektronik, werden dem Menschen noch viel helfen. Sie machen die Muskeln, die Nerven und auch das Hirn für manche Produktionsvorgänge überflüssig. Selbstverständlich kann man sich eine Fabrik ohne Menschen ausdenken oder erträumen, die irgendein Produkt hervorbringt. Das alles ist möglich. Aber daß der technische Fortschritt als solcher, als neuer Typ der Organisation der materiellen Produktionskräfte, allein imstande sein soll, das Leben der Menschen und der Gesellschaft grundlegend zu ändern, das bezweifle ich. Auch für das Jahr 2000. Dies können nur Zeitgenossen behaupten, die mit dem Marxismus fälschlicherweise der technischen Seite des menschlichen Lebens, der sinnfälligen Seite des Arbeitsvorgangs, eine grundlegende und ausschlaggebende Bedeutung beimessen.

Die Technologie wird dem Menschen manche Erleichterungen bringen. Aber er wird arbeiten müssen im Jahre 2000 und später. Der persönliche, der soziale, der kosmische und der religiöse Sinn der Arbeit werden auch im Jahre 2000 für den Menschen von Bedeutung sein.

Aussprache über die Referate Lübbe, Frankl, Streithofen

Leitung: Johannes C. Welbergen

Welbergen:

Meine Damen und Herren!

Wir haben von Orientierungslosigkeit und Sinnlosigkeit gehört. Gibt es hier einen Zusammenhang? Ich glaube, das ist etwas, was man sich fragen muß. Wir haben sowohl gestern wie auch heute wieder über die Bereitschaft zur Zusammenarbeit gehört; das ist hervorgehoben worden. Wir haben über Motivation und den Sinn der Arbeit gehört. Ich glaube, wir sollten nicht Einzelfaktoren heraussuchen, sondern wirklich versuchen, den roten Faden in den verschiedenen Beiträgen zu finden,um über die Gesamtheit zu reden. Wir haben hier zwei Wortmeldungen, die schon schriftlich abgegeben worden sind.

Frankl:

Vielleicht darf ich die Fragen vorlesen? – Wie sieht die Logotherapie praktisch aus? Wie wird der Sinn gegeben?

Was die erste Frage anlangt: Ich kann nur wiederholen, was der Schöpfer des uralten Begriffes der Neurasthenie einmal gesagt hat: „ Wenn ein Arzt zwei Fälle von Neurasthenie gleich behandelt, dann hat er mindestens einen falsch behandelt.“ Das sage ich deshalb, weil man in der Psychotherapie und besonders in der Logotherapie nicht genug individualisieren kann; von Augenblick zu Augenblick muß man auch improvisieren können. Nun kann man aber auch dieses Individualisieren und Improvisieren lernen. Allerdings ist es unmöglich im Rahmen einer Fragenbeantwortung, das würde ungefähr zwei Semester dauern.

Es gibt ein paar Dutzend Bücher über Logotherapie, in denen hauptsächlich Kasuistik beschrieben wird, d.h. Sie können anhand von einzelnen ganz konkreten Fällen sehen, wie die logotherapeutischen Prinzipien verwirklicht werden. Allerdings muß ich darauf aufmerksam machen, daß das, was ich Ihnen heute zu bieten versucht habe, nur ein Blitzlich auf **einen** Aspekt der Logotherapie ist. Die Logotherapie ist ja darüber hinaus eine psychiatrische Behandlung von Angst-, Zwangs- und Sexualneurosen. In denen kommt die Sinnproblematik praktisch überhaupt nicht vor. Das sind Dinge, bei denen die Logotherapie ganz bestimmte Techniken entwickelt hat, die heute in hohem Ansehen hauptsächlich bei den Verhaltenstherapeuten stehen. Aber diese Techniken der Behandlung von Phobien usw. sind ja gar nicht angeklungen.

Die 2. Frage: Besteht nicht die Gefahr einer unpolitischen Haltung, wenn ich **überall** Sinn sehe, in Situationen der totalen Entmündigung, z.B. auch?

Nun, dazu möchte ich folgendes sagen: Ich habe ausdrücklich, und zwar ganz scharf ein zweites Mal darauf hingewiesen, daß nur ein Leidenszustand, der unabhängig ist oder für eine gewisse Zeit unabänderlich bleibt, eine Sinnmöglichkeit im Sinne der Gestaltung einer Tragödie in sich birgt. Es behält also die Sinnmöglichkeit Nr. 1, d.h. eine Tat zu setzen oder ein Werk zu schaffen – die Wirklichkeit zu verändern – Priorität, d a s ist der primäre Sinn. Es ist also zunächst die Sinnmöglichkeit eine schöpferische. Nur dort, wo es nicht geht, muß diese Priorität zurücktreten. Erst, wenn wir wirklich nicht mehr anders können, wenn wir mit einer unabänderlichen Situation konfrontiert sind, z.B. in einem Kriegsgefangenenlager, in einem Konzentrationslager, in unheilbarer Krankheit und am Sterbebett, erst dann tritt die Frage in ihr Recht: Was kann ich jetzt noch machen?

Zunächst wird logotherapeutisch ein Patient qua Sinnmöglichkeiten so behandelt, daß er nicht zuletzt auch politisch aktiviert wird, auch einen Sinn, einen zusätzlichen Sinn, vielleicht den Hauptsinn seines konkreten Lebens darin sieht, politisch etwas zu ändern. Das ist nicht nur nicht ausgeschlossen, sondern das kann ja sogar die Präferenz sein. Aber es gibt nun Situationen, in denen auch der Politiker nichts machen kann. Es kommt sogar bei führenden Politikern vor, daß sie in einer konkreten Situation nichts tun können, und erst dann kommt die Frage, Einstellungswerte zu verwirklichen. Die Logotherapie ist also von vornherein nichts, was einen Menschen ins unpolitische Dasein hineinlocken würde.

Lukas:

Die Frage ist: Bei wem, glauben Sie, liegt die Verantwortlichkeit für das Fehlverhalten der Jugendlichen?

Ich bin ganz froh, daß diese Frage nach Verantwortungsbewußtsein überhaupt gestellt wird, denn gerade die Psychologen, gerade wir Fachleute haben in den letzten Jahrzehnten immer wieder diese „Frage nach Verantwortung" vom Menschen selbst abgeschoben. Die Fachleute erklären ihn immer wieder für nicht verantwortlich für etwas: Er kann ja gar nicht anders handeln, weil seine Kindheit so schief gelaufen ist, weil seine Eltern, die Umwelt oder die Gesellschaft ihn falsch erzogen haben. Irgendwie ist das Wissen verlorengegangen, daß der Mensch selbst **auch** für das verantwortlich ist, was er tut. Genauso ist er verantwortlich für die Frage, ob er sein Leben wegwirft oder nicht. Ebenfalls ist er verantwortlich dafür, ob er aus seinem Leben etwas macht bzw. seinen unglücklichen Zustand beendet, oder ob er einfach aufgibt. Für all das ist man letzten Endes selbst verantwortlich.

Natürlich ist das Abschieben der Verantwortung auch sehr bequem. Ich muß sagen, die Hauptschuld tragen eigentlich Kollegen aus meinen eigenen Reihen, aus der Psychologie, weil man vorwiegend ein Menschenbild geboten hat, in dem der Mensch gar nicht mehr mündig entscheidet über sein Tun und Lassen, sondern einfach ein Ergebnis von irgendwelchen Umständen, von Erbmasse, Umwelt, sozialer Struktur usw. ist. Dadurch hat man ihm aber viel von seinem Wert als Menschen genommen. Erst durch die modernen Motivationstheorien der letzten Jahre kommt man wieder auf das ganz natürliche Wissen zurück, daß die Menschen ja auch selbst verantwortlich sind.

Dann wurde hier die Frage gestellt: Welches Verhalten zeigen die betroffenen Jugendlichen? Welchen Appell richten sie an die Politiker oder an die Erzieher?

Nun, ich arbeite in einer Erziehungsberatungsstelle. Ich kann die Frage nach dem Appell an die Erzieher eigentlich besser beantworten als die Frage nach politischen Forderungen. Durch die Fachleute ist sehr viel Verunsicherung bei den Eltern entstanden. So erlebe ich immer wieder, daß Eltern bei mir sitzen und sagen: „Wir haben überall etwas anderes gehört. Wir waren schon bei anderen Beratungsstellen. Die Verhaltenstherapeuten sagen etwas anderes, die Ärzte sagen etwas anderes, die Schulen sagen etwas anderes, überall hören wir etwas anderes." Im Grunde genommen sind die Erzieher heute furchtbar verunsichert. Wie sollen sie überhaupt ihre Kinder erziehen? Auch die Erziehungsarten ändern sich ständig, die Meinungen der Fachleute ebenfalls, manche sprechen für eine autoritäre, manche für eine antiautoritäre Erziehung. Die pädagogischen Modeströmungen ändern sich, während die Eltern verunsichert sind und die Kinder ihnen „über den Kopf wachsen". Es sind also enorme Konflikte und Differenzen zwischen Eltern und Kindern vorhanden.

Ich glaube, daß auch in dieser Hinsicht sehr viel geändert werden müßte. Diese Eltern-Generation hier in Deutschland hat ja unheimlich viel geleistet, sie hat aus einem kriegszerstörten Land ein blühendes Wirtschaftsparadies aufgebaut, aber sehen Sie, aufbauen ist schöner als erben. Wenn man aufbaut, hat man ein Ziel vor Augen, und man sagt sich: Ich tue das aus dem oder jenem Grunde, also für etwas Bestimmtes. Ich setze meine ganzen Kräfte für dieses Ziel ein. Man kann das Ziel selbst natürlich in Frage stellen, aber es ist jedenfalls etwas da, wofür man sich einsetzt. Wenn man erbt, fällt einem das Erbe in den Schoß, und es hat z.B. für die Jugendlichen, die alles von ihren Eltern übernommen haben, gar keinen eigentlichen Sinn, gar keinen Wert mehr. Sie können nicht ihr Lebensideal an das schwer abgezahlte Eigenheim der Eltern hängen, und das hätte man den Eltern auch sagen müssen. Man muß die Eltern beraten, den Kindern auch Werte aufzuzeigen und Möglichkeiten offenzulassen, selbst eigene Werte zu finden und sich dafür einzusetzen. Gerade dieser wichtige Faktor wurde vernachlässigt, daß der heranwachsende Mensch sich nach Sinn und Werten orientieren muß, wenn er in das eigene Leben hineintritt. In der Logotherapie sind Ansätze dafür gegeben, wie man den Eltern in dieser Richtung helfen kann.

Dann ist hier noch eine dritte Frage: Welchen Sinn des Lebens soll ein junger Mensch finden, wenn es ihm verwehrt ist, sein Berufsziel zu erreichen, z.B. durch Lehrstellenknappheit oder Numerus clausus?

Auch das ist eine sehr schwierige Frage, die wir in der Beratungssituation immer wieder vorfinden. Denn hier handelt es sich ja schließlich um ein unabänderliches Schicksal. Ein Ziel wurde gesetzt, und dieses Ziel zu erreichen, ist also jetzt verwehrt. Ich kann als Therapeut nun nicht sagen: das oder jenes sollen Sie jetzt machen; ich kann überhaupt kein konkretes Angebot machen, weil ich diesen Menschen auch nicht so gut kenne. Es geht ausschließlich darum, seine Einstellung zu dieser Tatsache, daß er an irgendeinem Punkt mit seinen Vorstellungen und Zielen gescheitert ist, diese Einstellung in eine gesunde zu retten. Therapeutisches Anliegen ist, daß er jetzt nicht alles hinschmeißt und sagt: „Also gut, ich habe das Ziel nicht erreicht, also können Sie mich gern haben! Der Staat ist schuld, die Politiker sind schuld, ...“ und was weiß ich, was alles noch schuld ist. Es ist ja sehr bequem und sehr verlockend zu sagen, ich mache jetzt nichts mehr, aber daran scheitert er dann erst wirklich.
Es ist meine Aufgabe als Therapeut, ihm das zu ersparen; er soll eine gesunde Trotzmacht entwickeln, so daß er sich sagt: „Schön, das ist schiefgegangen, aber jetzt zeige ich, daß ich trotzdem etwas aus meinem Leben machen kann“. Dann überdenkt er die Möglichkeiten, die er hat, und was er daraus verwerten könnte. Er soll beweisen, was in ihm steckt. Wenn ich nur das einem jungen Menschen vermitteln kann, fühle ich mich zufrieden, auch wenn er zunächst einmal nicht das erreichen konnte, was er ursprünglich wollte. Diese Einstellungsmodulation ist, so glaube ich, ein Hauptaspekt der Logotherapie, nämlich daß eine ungesunde, unglückliche Einstellung in eine gesunde transformiert wird.

Welbergen:

Ich glaube, daß Ihre Einstellung „Selbstarbeiten ist schöner als erben“ ein bißchen auch mit den Theorien von Herrn Dr. Streithofen zusammenhängen. Vielleicht sollten wir am besten bei diesem Thema bleiben.

Teilnehmer:

Ich frage mich, ob nicht zugleich mit dem Leben auch dem Tod ein Sinn abgewonnen werden müßte? Ich frage mich weiter, ob die von Ihnen aufgezeigten Sinnlosigkeiten diese Frage abdecken.

Meine zweite Frage lautet: Es steht ja wohl das Sinnlosigkeitsgefühl am Ende einer Suche nach dem Sinn. Haben Sie erkannt, wonach in Ihrer

Arbeit gesucht worden ist und was gefunden worden ist? Kann das unter Umständen mit dem ersten Teil meiner Frage zusammenhängen?

Frankl:

Es ist natürlich so, daß das Leben letzten Endes sinnlos würde, wie Sie richtig angedeutet haben, wenn nicht **auch der Tod** einen Sinn hat, das Leben **trotz des Todes** einen Sinn hat, trotz seiner wesentlichen Vergänglichkeit. Diese Sache wird ganz ausführlich im Rahmen des Systems der Logotherapie abgehandelt. Wir stehen auf dem Standpunkt, daß die Vergänglichkeit dem Sinn des Daseins keinen Abbruch tun kann. In dem Augenblick, wo eine Sinnmöglichkeit verwirklicht wurde, ist sie ein für allemal verwirklicht worden. Laotse hat einmal gesagt: „Eine Aufgabe erfüllt zu haben, heißt ewig sein." Ich möchte sagen, wir haben diese Sinnmöglichkeit hineingerettet in das Vergangensein, wo sie gerade vor der Vergänglichkeit bewahrt ist. Gewöhnlich sieht der Mensch nur die Stoppelfelder der Vergänglichkeit, aber wenn er näher hinschaut, sieht er auch die vollen Scheunen der Vergangenheit, in die er schon längst die Ernte eingebracht hat.

Wir müssen uns der Tatsache des Todes und der eigenen Sterblichkeit stellen. Nur so können wir die Sinnträchtigkeit des Lebens überhaupt in den Griff bekommen. Das ist unbedingt notwendig. Aber nicht nur das, sondern auch, daß die Bedingungslosigkeit der Sinnhaftigkeit des Lebens ja erst dann wirklich zur Vollendung gelangt, wenn wir uns der Tatsache nicht verschließen, daß nicht nur Leidenssituationen, sondern auch das Sterben die letzten Möglichkeiten aus dem Menschen herausholen kann. Das heißt, durch Leiden können wir sogar noch im Tod reifen und wachsen, sogar über uns hinauswachsen.

Lübbe:

Ich würde mich gerne auf diese Frage nach dem Tod beziehen, obwohl das ja sozusagen fachlich nicht meine Zuständigkeit ist. Ich würde einen Schritt weitergehen, und sagen: Sinn hat das Leben nicht nur trotz des Todes, sondern auch der Tod selbst hat Sinn. In diesem Sinne verlangt auch der Tod, damit Leben sinnvoller sein kann, eine Zustimmung. Man braucht nur in die religiöse Tradition einschließlich ihrer Gegenwart hineinzugehen, und dann fallen einem die Formeln ein, in denen genau dieses geleistet wird. Es sind alles diese Strophen aus Psalmen, Kirchenliedern, die Sie kennen. Man stirbt alt und um es mit einem Satz des alten Testaments auszudrücken: Mit Fried' und Freud' fahr ich dahin. Das sind die Formeln, die genau das ausdrücken, und es ist selbstverständlich, daß so etwas nicht als eine individuelle Leistung erbracht werden kann.

Wie die Menschen sich verhalten, das ist im wesentlichen eine Frage der Kräftigkeit und der kulturellen Lebendigkeit der Institutionen und ihrer rituellen

Reden über dergleichen, an dem man sich dann orientieren kann. So etwas kann man nicht als individuelle Lebensleistung erbringen. Wenn Sie individuelle Lebensleistung erbringen wollen – und darauf kommt es ja letzten Endes an –, braucht man dafür die Leistung und Angleichung kultureller Möglichkeiten, die durch funktionierende religiöse Institutionen geleistet werden. Es ist kein Geheimnis, daß moderne Gesellschaften durch eine abnehmende kulturelle und institutionelle Kräftigkeit der religiösen Lebensorientierung gekennzeichnet sind. Die kompensatorische Reaktion darauf ist ersichtlich:

Man kann die massenhafte Etablierung religiöser Randgruppen und Subkulturen in modernen Gesellschaften beobachten, am kräftigsten natürlich, weil es die fortgeschrittenste Gesellschaft ist, in den Vereinigten Staaten von Amerika, aber auch in Europa. Unsere Soziologen haben die einschlägigen Phänomene längst gezählt. Wenn man einem Überblick über die Dinge im ganzen nimmt, darf man mit einigem Risiko die soziologisch gemeinte Prognose wagen, daß wir in Gesellschaften von der Struktur der Bundesrepublik eine Erneuerung, eine Erkräftigung, eine Neubelebung des religiösen Lebens finden werden. Das stellt natürlich eine Herausforderung an die etablierten Kirchen dar, und es ist keineswegs sicher, ob die etablierten Kirchen mit dieser Herausforderung fertig werden. Es liegt aber sehr viel daran, daß sie damit fertigwerden, weil sonst das religiöse Leben, wenn es etabliert ist, auch eine zerstörende Kraft entwickeln könnte.

Frankl:

Ich als Arzt muß darauf bestehen, daß man dieser Frage auch eine säkuläre Wendung gibt. Ich würde sagen, daß für den nicht religiös eingestellten Menschen der Tod einen Sinn behält. Wenn es keinen Tod gäbe, wenn wir unsterblich wären, würde ja das Leben sinnlos werden, denn wir könnten alles ins Unendliche aufschieben. Es bestünde nie ein Grund, den Augenblick zu nützen, um eine Sinnmöglichkeit zu erfüllen. Für den säkulär eingestellten Menschen ist der Tod auch an sich noch etwas Sinnvolles.

Streithofen:

Mir fällt es schwer, dazu etwas zu sagen, denn ich habe in den letzten Wochen sehr viele Menschen sterben sehen, gläubige Menschen und nicht gläubige Menschen. Ihre Frage ist: Sinn des Todes. Mich hat immer die physische Konstitution bei Frommen und Nichtfrommen beeindruckt. Bleiben wir zunächst bei den Frommen. Ich kann kein Werturteil fällen. Es gibt Leute, die ausgesprochen demütig sterben – Fromme und Unfromme. Man merkt das auch am Sterbebett. Das ist die eine Seite, wo man noch merkt, daß es vielleicht Hoffung hat, daß es nach dem Tode weitergeht. Es kommt dann immer – damit möchte ich abschließen – die Einsamkeit des Sterbens eines Menschen, wo Sie an einem Bett sitzen und nichts mehr tun können und die Familie aufhört, die Hand zu halten. Wenn man dann als Mensch wieder nach Hause geht, ist man mitunter sehr nachdenklich. Ich habe Ihnen eine sehr ehrliche Antwort gegeben, und man lebt mit vielen Zweifeln, die auch nie lösbar sind.

Teilnehmer:

Es ist eine unheimliche Gefahr, daß in der Medizin die technische Entwicklung immer weiter darauf hinarbeiten wird, daß man immer wieder nach der Ursache für den Tod fragt und dann irgendwann ein Krankheitsbild ermittelt, so daß der Tod praktisch als provisorisch unheilbare Krankheit verstanden wird. Man kann irgendwann sogar einmal zu einer unheimlichen Euphorie in den biologischen Wissenschaften kommen, so daß man sagt: Wir schieben das Alter immer weiter hinaus, vielleicht wird es uns gelingen, alle Krankheiten zu beseitigen. Ich frage mich, ob man nicht, wenn man sich so sehr auf die Technik stützt, Gefahr läuft, durch die provisorische Krankheit am Menschen vorbeizugeben.

Frankl:

Wenn die heutige Medizin etwas weiß, dann weiß sie, daß der Mensch niemals unsterblich werden wird. Vielfach wächst die Technik dem Mediziner über den Kopf; das sieht man ja allenthalben, und man muß sich fragen, ob der technische Aufwand berechtigt ist. Er ist nur dann bedingungslos berechtigt, wenn man für den Sinn des Lebens das Leben selbst hält. In dem Augenblick, wo Sie mit dem Begriff der Selbsttranszendenz ernst machen, ist es ganz klar, daß, wenn das Elektroenzephalogramm keinerlei Kurven mehr zeigt, in diesem Augenblick praktisch ja nicht mehr davon die Rede sein kann, daß da Leben existiert. Das ist gewiß kein menschenwürdiges Leben, weil es kein menschliches Leben ist; das nicht nur vital existiert, sondern auch sich selbst transzendiert. Selbsttranszendenz heißt, Menschsein weist immer über sich selbst hinaus auf etwas oder auf jemanden, auf eine Sache, der es dient, oder auf einen anderen, den man liebt.

Lübbe:

Ich möchte zum Thema Tod und Gesellschaft eine etwas riskante These formulieren. Diese These lautet: Mit Stabilität der Gesellschaft korreliert immer die Präsenz des Todes und Präsenz der Toten. Je mehr die Präsenz des Todes verschwindet, und je mehr wir uns auf die Gegenwart der Toten beziehen können, um so instabiler werden Gesellschaften. Es ist klar, daß unsere Gesellschaften solche sind, die den Tod sozial isolieren. Er findet ja sozusagen nicht mehr zu Hause statt, und daher verfallen auch unsere Möglichkeiten, uns zu dieser Realität zu verhalten.. Insofern lassen wir den Tod aus der Gesellschaft verschwinden.

Die Mobilität der Gesellschaft ist identisch mit dem Schwinden der Präsenz der Toten, d.h. wer lebt noch an dem Ort, an dem seine Eltern und Großeltern begraben sind? Sie können das auch daran sehen, daß die Zahlen für die Belegungsfristen immer kürzer werden. Heute begräbt man schon ab 30 Jahren, und ich möchte Sie fragen: Wer von Ihnen hat heute noch Gräber, die 80 Jahre alt sind? Ich brauche Ihnen wohl nicht zu beschreiben, daß es eher simple sozialpsychologische Mechanismen sind, die aber sehr tief in den Menschen hineinreichen. Dadurch sollen die Gesellschaften noch einmal mit der Präsenz des Todes und der Präsenz der Toten stabiler werden. Deswegen gehört es selbstverständlich zum rituellen Zubehör totalitärer Gesellschaften, daß sie gewisse Tote ganz öffentlich einbalsamieren, in Bergen gegenwärtig halten; und unentwegt und endlos ziehen die Lebenden an ihnen vorbei. Das ist sehr eindrucksvoll. Fahren Sie einmal nach Moskau, wenn Sie das sehen wollen.

Rosenmayr:

Zuerst möchte ich etwas zum Letzten sagen. Ich glaube nicht, daß die Grabpflege ein Indikator dafür ist, wie man mit den Verstorbenen, zu denen man eine Beziehung hatte, lebt. Ich glaube, daß es gerade dadurch, daß wir mit mehr Bewußtsein und mit mehr Selbstreflektion leben, dazu führen kann, daß wir erkennen, daß wir auch mit jemandem, der verstorben ist, Jahre und Jahrzehnte weiterleben, auch wenn wir nicht auf den Friedhof gehen. Ich würde da schon vorsichtig sein und nicht diese traditionellen Formen von Verräumlichung als eine solch unabdingbare Voraussetzung angeben.

Ich wollte Sie eigentlich etwas fragen zu Ihren Gedanken über die Flucht aus der desorganisierten Gegenwart und über die kompensatorischen Effekte, die Sie sehen. Nämlich die Frage: Wo sind die Kriterien für Flucht? Was ist Flucht und was ist nicht Flucht?

Ich möchte das gerne am Beispiel der Nostalgiewelle deutlich machen. Ich komme aus einem schrecklich traditionalistischen Land, aus Österreich, und aus seiner noch viel traditionalistischeren Stadt, aus Wien. Daher bin ich von dieser Seite her leicht einseitig vorbelastet. Aber wenn jemand vom Flohmarkt etwas nach Hause bringt, ein altes Stück vielleicht, dann ist möglicherweise der Ansatz gegeben, daß man über dieses alte Stück ein Gespräch beginnt. Es ist möglich, daß in die Geschichte zurückgegriffen wird und daß vielleicht auch die Großmutter oder irgendein anderer alter Mensch in seiner lebensgeschichtlichen Bedeutung zurückgreift und somit neue Anknüpfungspunkte entstehen. Ich meine also: Steckt nicht hinter der Nostalgiewelle ein Bedürfnis, sich selbst lebensgeschichtlich zu verstehen? Das wäre z.B. eine Frage.

Dann frage ich mich, ob das, was Sie über Altersforschung sagen, als kompensatorischer Effekt durchgängig stimmt? Denn die Notwendigkeit für die Alten, eine neue Funktion zu finden, ist doch sicher ein sehr reales Problem. Es dreht sich also darum, daß man nach Wegen sucht, auf denen der Sinnverlust für die Alten wiedergefunden werden kann. Das wäre ein wichtiges Thema der Altersforschung.

Ich habe eine Frage an Viktor Frankl: Wie kann der Unterschied zwischen Sinn und Pseudosinn gefunden werden? Wie kann im Konkreten die Bestimmung ausgesprochen werden? Etwas trivial gesagt: Wie bin ich sicher, daß ich mehr Sinn erfülle, daß ich der Sinndiskussion hier beiwohne, statt zu Hause bei mir am Institut den sich gegen Semesterende auftürmenden Schreitisch abzuräumen? Wie hilft mir in der konkreten Entscheidung dieses Problem? Wie kann ich Mut finden, wenn ich nicht ganz genau weiß, ob ich hierbleiben soll oder nach Hause fahren soll? Wenn ich ganz genau weiß, daß ich es tun soll, wie kann ich mir dabei helfen, die Hemmungen und Ängste, die ich habe, um das zu tun, zu überwinden? Wie kann ich Mut finden, oder wie kann ich mich überhaupt über diese immer wieder erlebten Hemmungen hinwegsetzen?

Das letzte: Sie haben über die erfolgreichen Ärzte und Rechtsanwälte in einer Studie gesprochen. Haben denn diese in einer frühen Phase ihres Lebens nicht sehr viel Sinn empfunden? Haben sie sich denn nicht in ihre Familien, in ihre Ehen, in ihre Berufe mit ungeheuer viel Elan und Erfülltheit hineingestürzt? Sie werden vor diese Frage gestellt, anders als diejenigen, die mit 40, 50 oder noch später oder nie darauf kommen. Wie also komme ich zu einer Revision von einmal erfahrenem Sinn, und wie unterscheide ich vor allem Sinn und Pseudosinn?

Teilnehmer:

Ich möchte eine andere Dimension zu diesem Sinn- und Pseudosinnproblem aufzeigen: Wie unterscheide ich den Sinn, der mir vermittelt wird – der Sinn, der für mein Leben und meine persönliche Entfaltung sinnvoll ist – von dem Sinn, der mir aufgepfropft wird und den ich irgendwie fressen muß? Dieser dient nur dazu, mich zu benutzen und zu manipulieren, meine Arbeitskraft auszunutzen. Soweit „Sinn" bei Ihnen auftauchte, erschien das Wort immer austauschbar. Deshalb möchte ich doch darauf drängen, daß man das auch etwas mit Inhalt füllt.

Frankl:

Die Unterscheidung zwischen Sinn und Pseudosinn muß getroffen werden. Aber auf keinen Fall kann sie getroffen werden von einem Psychiater, von einem Psychotherapeuten, von einem Psychologen und auch nicht von einem Logotherapeuten! Ich habe einmal gesagt, man scheint die Logotherapeuten zu verwechseln mit der Schlange aus dem Paradies. Es war nämlich die und nicht ein Logotherapeut, der den Leuten gesagt hat: Ich werde euch weise machen, und ich werde euch zeigen, was gut und was böse ist, was sinnvoll und was nicht sinnvoll ist, was wertvoll und was wertlos ist. Das kann kein anderer entscheiden, denn Sinn kann nicht gegeben werden. Sinn muß gefunden werden, und zwar von einem selbst. Der Mensch verfügt über etwas, das man nicht ein Sinnesorgan, sondern das Sinn-Organ nennen könnte, das identisch ist mit dem, was die Menschheit seit Jahrtausenden das persönliche Gewissen nennt. Aber auch das Gewissen wird Ihnen nie mit absoluter Gewissheit sagen können, ob es sinnvoll ist, hier bei den Vorträgen zu sitzen oder zu Hause zu arbeiten. Man kann von Ihnen nur verlangen, daß Sie Ihrem Gewissen lauschen und dann hingehen und eben mutig das tun, was das Gewissen Ihnen aufgetragen hat. Dann natürlich kann unter Umständen ein Logotherapeut helfen, Ihnen, Herr Rosenmayr, helfen, das, was das Gewissen Ihnen vorschreibt, durchzuführen. Aber wenn Sie sagen, Ihr Gewissen sagt Ihnen, daß Sie das tun sollten, aber Sie haben nicht die Courage dazu, brauchen Sie nicht einmal einen Logotherapeuten, es kann ein Individualpsychologe nach Alfred Adler sein: die haben nämlich die Ermutigung des Menschen auf ihre Fahne geschrieben.

Aber auch das Gewissen kann Ihnen nie mit absoluter Gewissheit sagen: Das ist der Sinn deines Lebens oder deiner Situation.

„Ignoramus et ignorabimus" hat Du Bois-Reymond gesagt in bezug auf das psychophysische Problem, und ich sage hier: Wir werden bis auf unser Sterbebett nicht 100 %ig sicher sein können, ob das wirklich der Sinn unseres Lebens war, was uns unser Gewissen vielleicht nur vorgegaukelt hat. Wir können nichts anderes machen als lauschen und dann hingehen und es tun. Niemand hat das schöner in Worte gefaßt als Gordon Allport von der Harvard University, der einmal gesagt hat: „We can be at one and the same time half-sure and whole-hearted." D.h., wir können gleichzeitig einer Sache nur halb sicher sein und trotzdem mit vollem Herzen hingehen und es tun. Es ist auch in Ihrer Theologie so – ich selbst bin nicht katholisch, ich bin nicht einmal Christ –, daß kein Rückzug vor dem Gebot Ihres persönlichen Gewissens möglich ist. Das ist die letzte Instanz, der Sie sogar in Fragen des religiösen Bekenntnisses zu gehorchen haben.

Was aber diese Harvard-Studenten betrifft, so muß ich sagen, daß sie sich niemals gefragt haben, was der Sinn ihres Lebens sei. Sondern die Sinnfrage ist erst aufgebrochen, als es ihnen gut ging, als sie Erfolg hatten. Das ist ja genau die heutige Situation. Schauen Sie sich die Verhältnisse in Ihrer Bundesrepublik doch einmal an. Vom Jahre 1946 an geht es den Leuten immer besser und besser bis zum Jahre 1978, und die Selbstmorde steigen immer weiter und weiter bis zum Jahre 1978. Sie haben keine Erfüllung, sondern die Befriedigung von Bedürfnissen. Ich bin ja davon ausgegangen, daß ich gesagt habe, die heutige Gesellschaft befriedigt Bedürfnisse, erzeugt sie sogar, nur das Grundbedürfnis befriedigt sie nicht: dieses Problem konfrontiert uns heute in Wohlstand und Überfluß.

Jetzt frage ich Sie, meine Damen und Herren, woher kommt es, daß auf der einen Seite die Sinnfrage in den Konzentrationslagern von Auschwitz und Dachau aktuell und akut war – dafür lege ich Zeugenschaft ab –, und daß auf der anderen Seite dort, wo es den Leuten gut geht, diese Frage wieder an Bedeutung gewinnt? Es gilt nicht, was Bert Brecht gesagt hat: „Erst kommt das Fressen, dann kommt die Moral." Die Leute haben heute genug zu fressen und schmeissen ihr Leben weg. Die Menschen in Auschwitz hatten einen Dreck zu fressen und sind in die Gaskammern eingetreten mit dem jüdischen Kaddisch-Gebet oder mit dem Vaterunser.

Das ist nur zu erklären, wenn man weiß, daß die Maslow'sche Bedürfnishierarchie nicht gilt. Es ist nicht so, daß erst die biologischen und sozialökonomischen Bedürfnisse befriedigt werden müssen und man dann erst Zeit hat, die weiteren Bedürfnisse wie Sinn in Betracht zu ziehen. Es gilt nicht „primum vivere, deinde philosophari", zuerst leben und dann anfangen zu philosophieren, sondern wir haben es immer wieder gesehen, daß es umgekehrt ist: „Primum philosophari, deinde mori", d.h. erst sich Rechenschaft ablegen über den Sinn oder Unsinn dieser menschlichen Existenz, und dann erst kann man wirklich hingehen und auch als Mensch sterben.

Welbergen:

Vielen Dank, Herr Prof. Frankl. Jetzt muß ich Herrn Prof. Lübbe die Möglichkeit geben, noch auf die Frage von Herrn Prof. Rosenmayr einzugehen.

Lübbe:

Die Antwort lautet: Ich habe die von mir analysierten Phänomene der Nostalgie, der Historisierung unserer kulturellen Umwelt, der Rücklenkung der Vergangenheit, der Ästhetisierung der Vergangenheit nicht als Fluchtphänomene bezeichnet, sondern als Kompensationsphänomene charakterisiert; Kompensation ist systemerhaltungsdienlich. Eine Flucht z.B. sehe ich bei Hippiekommunen, den religiösen Randgruppenkulturen und den Drogenkulturen. Das Kriterium dafür ist immer: Flucht ist eine Bewegung, die das, was sie zurückläßt, entweder zerstört oder sich zu ihr nassauerisch und parasitär verhält. Das gilt fast ausnahmslos für die Randgruppenkulturen mit ganz wenigen Elementen, die die Chance haben, Elemente unserer allgemeinen Kultur zu werden. Die Rückkehr zur Vergangenheit ist keine Flucht, sondern sie hat den Charakter der Kompensation. Um es mit einem sehr hochgestochenen Terminus zu sagen: Sie kompensiert die Rückwendung zur Vergangenheit und die sozialpsychologische, aber auch individuelle Gefahr einer temporalen ... Diffusion, d.h., sie verhindert die fortschreitende Unmöglichkeit, eigene Vergangenheit als eigene zu erkennen und als zugehörig anzuerkennen.

Welbergen:

Vielen Dank. Von den zwei Themen möchte ich dieses zuerst an die Reihe nehmen. Ich habe hier drei Fragen, die zusammenhängen.

Hängt der Sinn der Arbeit nicht auch von der subjektiven, individuellen Einstellung zur Arbeit ab? Sind wir in unserer Gesellschaft nicht auf dem Wege, den Sinn der Arbeit über die innere subjektive Einstellung des einzelnen zu entleeren? Verbunden damit ist die Frage: Herr Dr. Streithofen hat Arbeit als den Sinn des Lebens bezeichnet. Frau Dr. Lukas sprach von „Abfinden mit der Situation".

Sollte man die Jugend – auch unter dem Gesichtspunkt der Selbstverantwortung der Jugendlichen – in die Lage versetzen, für eine Veränderung der Verhältnisse einzutreten?

Ich glaube, die dritte Frage, die wir hier mit hineinnehmen können, lautet: Dr. Streithofen hat gesagt: Glückliche Arbeit ist der stabilste Faktor einer menschlichen Welt. Nun ist die Arbeitszeit sehr kurz; und sie wird wohl auch noch kürzer werden. Reicht das Glück, das während der Arbeit gewonnen wird, aus, um auch in der arbeitsfreien Zeit glücklich zu sein? Müssen hier nicht stabilisierende Hilfen gegeben werden? Wenn ja, wer sollte diese geben und koordinieren?

Ich werde die etwas provokative Frage, ob wir ein Ministerium für Freizeit brauchen, hier aus der Diskussion weglassen; wir werden sie morgen früh behandeln. Ich glaube, hier gibt es ein paar Fragen, die ineinander übergehen.

Teilnehmer:

Wenn Sie es mir erlauben, würde ich gern ein kurzes Statement geben. Ich glaube, daß die Antworten noch etwas profilierter würden – weil ich etwas Böses will: ich will nämlich die Rolle der Schlange spielen, die die Menschen gegen ihren Gott ausgespielt hat. Ich möchte gerne Herrn Frankl gegen Herrn Streithofen ausspielen ...

(Zuruf: Das schaffen Sie nicht, aber versuchen Sie es ruhig!)

Ich darf bei dem anknüpfen, was Sie, Frau Dr. Lukas, gesagt haben. Die Älteren haben eine Welt in sehr harter Arbeit aufgebaut, die Jüngeren haben sie geerbt und können nichts damit anfangen; sie suchen vergebens nach einem Sinn, wenn ich das einmal aufs Extreme bringen darf. Andererseits heißt es aber: Was Du ererbt von Deinen Vätern hast, erwirb es, um es zu besitzen!

Herr Frankl hat uns eine ganz andere Antwort als Herr Streithofen auf die Sinnfrage gegeben. Herr Frankl ging aus von der anthropologischen Grundvoraussetzung, daß der Mensch ohne Instinkte auf sich allein gestellt ist bzw. auf das, was die Welt zusammenhält; es handelt sich dabei um die gleiche Logik in allen Weltkörpern, um gleiche Elemente, um gleiche Grundprinzipien für Weltall und Mensch. Der Mensch hat sich an Stelle der Instinkte, die dem Tier Sicherheit verleihen, Institutionen geschaffen. Diese Institutionen stammen von gestern, aus der Zeit, in der die Arbeit höchster Sinn war. Ich kann nicht sagen, daß ein einziger Tag in dieser harten Arbeitszeit sinnlos war.

Jetzt müssen wir uns nach neuen Sinngebungen fragen; alte Institutionen taugen nichts mehr für neue Entwicklungen. Auch der Wandel von der Antike zur christlichen Arbeitsethik ist vollzogen worden. Protestantische Ethik und Geist des Kapitalismus, siehe Max Weber, haben den Sinn dieser Arbeitsorientierung, der vor 20 oder 30 Jahren hochgradig gegeben war, vertrieben. Jetzt gilt, was uns Herr Bell gestern gesagt hat. Jetzt gilt es, sich in einer Welt einzurichten, die ganz anders wird. Wir bringen die Menschen zu neuer Frustration, wenn wir den Sinn nicht in den Dingen selbst suchen und finden.

Herr Frankl hat uns von den Untersuchungen berichtet, nach denen Freizeit für den und den sinnlos sei. Warum? Das kommt deshalb, weil die Institutionen nicht dementsprechend eingerichtet sind. Es kommt deshalb, weil wir eine falsche Arbeitsethik in die Stände gesetzt haben, in der die Mehrzahl der Menschen nun einmal gezwungen ist, ihren Sinn in der Freizeit zu suchen. In der fremdbestimmten Arbeit kann man diesen Sinn nicht finden; das ist unmöglich. Infolgedessen ist es notwendig, im Sinne der Selbstgestaltung der Umwelt durch die Menschen den Ort zu finden, wo es überhaupt nur sein kann, nämlich in der realen Existenz, so wie sie nun einmal ist, ob wir es wollen oder nicht.

Lukas:

In meiner Dissertation habe ich Tausend Leute auf der Straße gefragt: „Was ist für Sie der Sinn Ihres Lebens, für Sie ganz privat, persönlich, individuell? Was würden Sie als das Wichtigste, als das Wertvollste in Ihrem Leben bezeichnen?“

Die Antworten waren sehr unterschiedlich. Es war nicht nur die Arbeit oder der Beruf; es gab auch eine ganze Reihe verschiedener Antworten. Ich habe sie in neun Kategorien zusammengefaßt. Ich hätte natürlich auch mehr daraus machen können, das hängt ganz davon ab, wie man die Antworten einteilt.

Die großen sinngebenden Kategorien betrafen tatsächlich die Arbeit, also den Beruf; aber auch z.B. ein Hobby, irgendetwas, das die Freizeit erfüllt, etwas, das man einfach gerne macht. Oder aber manche wollten einfach für die Familie da sein, sich mit den Kindern beschäftigen und der Familie eben eine entsprechende Basis bieten. Man könnte z.B. arbeiten, aber nicht aus Freude an der Arbeit, sondern um es den Kindern zu ermöglichen, zu studieren. Eine andere Sinn-Möglichkeit wäre es, sich selbst zu verwirklichen bzw. die Arbeit an sich selbst aufzunehmen, um sich weiterzubilden oder zu verändern. Man kann sich als Sinn-Möglichkeit auch das Engagement an einer Sache im religiösen oder im politischen Sinne vorstellen; oder einfach ein Erlebnis, auch ein Naturerlebnis, z.B. wenn ein Bergsteiger am Gipfel die untergehende Sonne betrachtet, auch das wäre geeignet, als sinngebender Lebensinhalt zu fungieren.

Es gibt einfach verschiedene Arten, Sinn zu finden und Sinn zu erfüllen, die gleichzeitig vorhanden sein können. Sie können aber auch mit Akzenten und Schwerpunkten behaftet sein.

Es gibt eine sehr interessante Arbeit von Prof. Kratochril, der folgendes sagt: *Diejenigen Menschen, die viele Inhalte in ihrem Leben finden, die also viele Sinnmöglichkeiten erfüllen, sind psycho-hygienisch viel stabiler und gesünder als Personen, die ein sogenanntes „pyramidales" Wertsystem haben. Die ersteren nennt er „parallel" gesichert, weil sie viele gleiche, also parallele Werte in ihrem Leben finden. Bei den zweiteren steht ein Wert an der Spitze, z.B. die Arbeit, und alle anderen Werte sind dem untergeordnet wie bei einer Pyramide.*

Er folgert daraus: *Der Mensch fällt leicht in tiefe Verzweiflung, wenn er ein pyramidales Wertsystem hat und sein oberster Wert fällt. Z.B. kann es ja sein, daß jemand an einem anderen Menschen im höchsten Maße hängt und dieser stirbt. Oder jemand findet nur in seinem Glauben Sinnerfüllung, und aus irgendwelchen Gründen zweifelt er plötzlich. Die anderen Werte, die er besitzt, sind dann nicht stark genug, um ihm noch genügend Sinnerfüllung im Leben zu geben. In dem Fall ist er wirklich gefährdet. Hat er aber viele Sinnmöglichkeiten, an denen er sich orientieren kann, viele Interessen, die ihm offenstehen und etwas bedeuten, dann ist es nicht so schlimm, wenn ein Wert ausfällt. Die anderen Werte halten ihn psycho-hygienisch stabil und er kann die Krise leichter überwinden.*

Herr Prof. Kratochril hat noch etwas festgestellt, nämlich, daß Menschen, die eine pyramidale Werteinstellung haben, oft sehr fanatisch sind und andere Menschen, die nicht den gleichen Wert wie sie an die Spitze stellen, nicht verstehen können. Sie verachten leicht die Mitmenschen, die vielleicht eine andere Sinnerfüllung haben. Wenn z.B. eine Mutter nur für ihr Kind da ist, nur für ihr Kind lebt und alles andere in den Schatten stellt, während auf der anderen Seite eine Mutter berufstätig ist und sich voll der Arbeit widmet, dann ist es für die erste schwer, die andere zu verstehen. Vielleicht läßt sie sich sogar dazu hinreißen, die andere zu verurteilen. Daher ist die Kommunikation zwischen parallel-gesicherten Menschen leichter, und es ist mehr Verständnis zwischen denjenigen Menschen, die selbst viele Werte besitzen, weil sie dann ein fremdes Wertsystem besser akzeptieren und respektieren können; es paßt immer in ihre eigene Vielseitigkeit hinein.

Soweit ein Beitrag, der zeigen soll, daß die Arbeit nicht allein als einzige Möglichkeit existiert, um Sinn im Leben zu finden und zu erfüllen.

Frankl:

Wir leben – wie schon angedeutet – in einer Leistungsgesellschaft, die die schöpferische Leistung vergötzt, und das nicht nur im Arbeitsbereich, sondern auch im Genußbereich. 70 bis 80 % der Potenzstörungen – der Fälle von Impotenz, mit denen wir es zu tun bekommen – sind darauf zurückzuführen, daß auch auf sexuellem Gebiet das Leistungsprinzip übertragen wurde. Je mehr es dem Manne darauf ankommt, seine Potenz unter Beweis zu stellen, desto sicherer ist er impotent. Je mehr die Frau ihre Orgasmusfähigkeit beweisen will, um so mehr ist sie dazu verdammt, mit Frigidität zu enden.

Das ist das Wichtige – ich weiß nicht, was Sie, Herr Professor, dazu sagen werden –, warum ich glaube, daß heute nicht nur die vita activa, sondern auch die vita contemplativa wieder in die Rechnung hineinkommen muß.

Wir werden mit einer immer größeren Freizeit in der Gesellschaft konfrontiert und müssen uns rechtzeitig nach neuen Formen einer Freizeitgestaltung umsehen, die nicht zentrifugal ist, also vor sich selbst flieht, sondern zentripetal ist, daß man zu sich selbst findet.

Streithofen:

Vielen Dank, Herr Professor, für das, was Sie gesagt haben. Ich darf nur noch ergänzen und auf Ihre Frage von vorhin zurückkommen.

Es wird ja viel diskutiert; ich habe mich neulich einen ganzen Abend mit Norbert H. unterhalten. Sie müßten einmal sehen, wie in konfessionellen oder nicht konfessionellen Krankenhäusern mit Toten umgegangen wird. Ich will keine Beispiele bringen. Ich könnte sie Ihnen erzählen; es ist grauenhaft, wie sie im Badezimmer abgestellt werden oder wie bei Menschen, wenn sie tot sind, die Würde von den Toten in deutschen Krankenhäusern, in denen wunderbare medizinische Geräte vorhanden sind, weggenommen wird. Man fragt sich auch nach der Humanität dieser Gesellschaft. Aber das steht hier nicht zur Diskussion.

Ich möchte mal auf die Fragen, so wie ich sie mir notiert habe, im Telegrammstil Antwort geben.

Natürlich habe ich gesagt: Arbeit ist ein stabiles Element für das Glücksbefinden des Menschen und kann nur sinnvoll sein. Natürlich ist die Arbeit nur ein Teilsinn. Sie können nicht sagen: Es gibt Sinn, sondern es gibt viele Sinne im Leben, wie Herr Prof. Frankl das gesagt hat. Mich erschüttert immer wieder, daß alle Kreise, mit denen Sie diskutieren – gleichgültig, ob es Wirtschaft, Bundeswehr oder sonst wer ist – immer nach Leitbildern fragen. Fragen Sie doch mal ausgewachsene Generäle, fragen Sie Vorstandsvorsitzende großer Gesellschaften; sie werden Ihnen antworten: Welche Leitbilder haben wir für die Jugend? Das Leitbild gibt es nicht. Es gibt vielleicht viele Ideale, für die sich ein junger Mensch überhaupt einmal begeistern kann. Aber dann müssen wir wieder sagen: Früher war das anders. Dann können wir wieder sagen: Dann richten wir doch wieder einen Reichsarbeitsdienst ein. Es gibt nicht den Sinn allein und ausschließlich. Das zeigt uns ja auch die Religionsgeschichte. Warum gibt es im Christentum verschiedene Interpretationen der confessio? Den Sinn gibt es nicht.

Aber ich glaube, daß es auch im Jahre 2000 für den Menschen, für sein Glück sinnvoll ist, arbeiten zu können. Dabei möchte ich gerne auf das vierte Jahrhundert zurückkommen: ora et labora. Das war die Rede des heiligen Benedikt: Bete und arbeite. Heutzutage haben wir keine Muße mehr. Wir können nicht mehr entspannen. In meiner Gottesfurcht habe ich neulich etwas Erschütterndes erlebt: Es kamen die Ideologen der drei Parteien im deutschen Bundestag, FDP, SPD und CDU, DGB und DAG, um ihre neue Freizeitideologie auf die Menschen herabzulassen. Die werden dann auch wieder beschäftigt. Was Frau Doktor neben mir eben sehr wissenschaftlich gesagt hat, das möchte ich jetzt etwas anschaulicher darstellen.

Ich darf das mal aus der Erfahrung heraus schildern. Wir sind hier im Braunkohlegebiet und machen mit der evangelischen Kirche zusammen sogenannte Staubkohleexerzitien, Besinnungstage für die Meister und Direktoren im Braunkohlegebiet. Wir hatten Arbeiter und Vorarbeiter da, und es gab auch die sogenannten Freizeitideologen. Es hat da einer vollkommen verständnislos gesessen und gesagt: „Warum wollt ihr mich denn beschäftigen? Wenn ich abends nach Hause komme, sehe ich meine 35 Kaninchen – und ich weiß nicht, wieviele davon Rammler sind –, dann versorge ich die Kaninchen, setze mich mit meiner Frau abends hin, trinke ein Kölsch und beobachte diese Tiere; meine Damen und Herren, ich bin gut zufrieden.“ Wissen Sie, dieser Mann hatte die Ruhelosigkeit überwunden.

Es gibt natürlich – und da bekommen Sie eine Teilantwort – Arbeit. Wozu? Sicherlich auch, um Muße und Ruhe zu haben. Ich meine, das sollte man jedem einzelnen überlassen und man sollte die Menschen möglichst wenig bevormunden. Es gibt ja schon genügend Trimm-Dich-Pfade, die die Landschaft genügend verunstalten, weil das politisch notwendig ist. Man sollte die Leute ruhig auffordern, sich zu trimmen. Ich war leider gestern nicht hier und kenne also auch nicht die Veröffentlichungen von Herrn Prof. Bell. Es wurde auf den Beitrag von Herrn Prof. Bell hingewiesen und darauf, daß eine Veränderung der Verhältnisse kommt. Ich bedaure sehr, sagen zu müssen, daß ich allen Prognosen, wie die Gesellschaft im Jahre 2000 aussieht, ausgesprochen skeptisch gegenüberstehe. Ich bin immer wieder erstaunt, woher die Prognostiker das so genau wissen. Das fällt für mich nämlich bereits in den Bereich der Theologie und des Glaubens, und dafür bin ich wieder zu rational eingestellt. Selbst wenn wir die 35- oder 30-Stunden-Woche haben, gibt es genügend zu tun.

Ich war kürzlich bei einem leitenden Beamten des Postministeriums zu Besuch. Er hat sich einen Garten zugelegt, und das war für ihn ein Gedicht. Früher war er so etwas wie ein Staatssekretär in Düsseldorf, heute züchtet er Radieschen in der Nähe von Bonn. Er war ganz stolz. Auch die höheren Beamten haben mehr Zeit im Staatsdienst. Er hat zig Quadratmeter Garten. Ich habe dort Radieschen und Lauchgemüse aus dem eigenen Garten gegessen. Der Stolz dieses ausgewachsenen höheren Beamten kam deutlich zum Ausdruck als er sagte: „Herr Pater, probieren Sie doch auch mal dieses hier." Um dem Mann eine Freude zu machen, habe ich den ganzen Abend danach ... (Gelächter). Aber dieser Mann hat eine Freizeitbeschäftigung, und jetzt auf einmal leidet er mit der Witterung. Man soll eine These nicht einfach aufstellen, sondern man sollte sie auch diskutieren. Ich möchte noch einmal sagen, daß es **den** Sinn der Arbeit nicht gibt. Soweit es möglich war, sich auf diese Tagung vorzubereiten, habe ich am Sonntagnachmittag meine private Meinungsumfrage gemacht. Ich habe sie nach der berühmten Wickert-Methode gestaltet.

Auf dem Klosterparkplatz standen drei junge Leute. Ich hatte eine Cordhose an, bin zu ihnen hingegangen und habe gesagt: „Verzeihung, darf ich einmal eine Frage stellen?" – „Ja, bitte schön." – Ich fragte: „Was machen Sie?" – „Wir wollten zum See, wir wollten etwas schwimmen gehen. Vielleicht gehen wir auch in das Phantasieland." – „Ich habe da noch weitere Fragen: Was sind Sie von Beruf, und macht Ihnen Ihre Arbeit Spaß, und was machen Sie überhaupt?"

Der erste hatte eine Gesellenprüfung als Metzger gemacht. Daraufhin habe ich ihn gefragt: „Warum sind Sie Metzger geworden?" „Ja", sagte er, „warum sind Sie Pater geworden? Es macht einfach Spaß." Er konnte das vielleicht nicht besser artikulieren. Wir haben uns darüber unterhalten, und wir sind zu dem Schluß gekommen, daß der Junge mit Leidenschaft Metzger ist. Die Eltern wollten ihn etwas Besseres werden lassen und haben sofort vorgesorgt und wollten ihn Elektrotechniker werden lassen. Daraufhin hat er gesagt: „Da war ich eine Nummer, in der Metzgerei bin ich etwas."

Der zweite hat das Abitur gemacht und geht zur Zeit zum Bund, wie man so sagt. Ich fragte ihn, was er dann mache. Er antwortete: Landwirtschaft, und er möchte irgendwo Verwalter auf einem Hof werden.

Den dritten traf ich per Zufall, und ich mußte sehr lachen, als er mir antwortete: „Was machen Sie denn?" Und er gab mir die verschrobenste und verstellteste Antwort: „Ich möchte gerne katholische Theologie studieren." – „Warum denn?" – „Ja", sagt er, „um den Menschen die frohe Botschaft zu verkünden." Das ist zu respektieren, aber ich finde, das war eine nicht mehr so natürliche Antwort, sondern eine gestellte.

Meine Damen und Herren, die Menschen sind doch teilweise viel vernünftiger, als man das hier hört. Und da liegt vielleicht der Dissens zwischen Herrn Frankl und mir.

Es ergibt sich die Frage: Gehen wir nicht zu sehr von Randerscheinungen aus? Ich kann nur sagen, daß mir viele Alkoholiker und Drogenabhängige begegnen. Ich möchte mit dem folgenden Beispiel schließen. Ich habe mal einen Jungen bei einem Spaziergang am Rhein gefragt, warum er Drogen nehme. Ich war damals durch eine befreundete Familie angesetzt und kenne auch seine Eltern. Sie sind ein hochverdientes Arztehepaar, er ist Gynäkologe, sie ist Kinderärztin. Sie machen sich gut in einer mittelrheinischen Großstadt. Plötzlich sagt der 17jährige Peter zu mir: „Ich habe mal meine Eltern kennengelernt. Ich möchte nur einmal am Tag eine Stunde lang glücklich sein." Daraufhin konnte ich nichts mehr sagen. Ich habe fast selber geheult. Ich sagte ihm: „Komm, Peter, gehen wir essen." Dann sind wir in Bonn essen gegangen. Es ist die Frage an das Elternhaus, ob das das Normale ist. Das ist nur eine Frage, Herr Frankl, und keine Beurteilung dessen, was Sie vorgetragen haben. Ich spreche von meiner Erfahrungswelt.

Welbergen:

Meine Damen und Herren! Mich freut eigentlich, daß die Diskussion so rege war. Ich bin aber etwas betrübt, daß wir eine ganze Anzahl von Fragen nicht beantwortet haben. Besonders betrübt bin ich, daß wir die Schlußfrage, die ich mir bis zum Schluß aufbewahrt habe, mit Rücksicht auf die Pilger nicht beantwortet haben.

Die Frage lautet: Wie muß, um die Krise zu überwinden, Ihrer Meinung nach auf die Orientierungslosigkeit reagiert werden? Die anderen Fragen sind jetzt sehr ähnlich. Ich glaube, es wäre vermessen, jetzt um Antwort zu bitten. Deshalb werde ich auch keinen der Podiumsteilnehmer bitten, hierzu das Wort zu ergreifen. Das ist die Frage, die unbeantwortet bleibt. Ich glaube, keiner von uns, der an der Organisation dieses Symposiums mitgearbeitet hat, hat eigentlich gedacht, daß wir die Antwort auf alles finden werden. Wir wollten Denkanstöße geben, an denen wir weiter arbeiten können. Ich glaube, die Denkanstöße haben wir bekommen. Die Antworten hingegen haben wir noch nicht bekommen.

Vielleicht können wir beim Mittagessen versuchen, uns in Grüppchen zusammenzusetzen, damit wir auf diese Fragen etwas mehr im Detail eingehen können. Es dreht sich um die Probleme der Sinnlosigkeit und der Orientierungslosigkeit. Wie gehen wir diese Frage an? Das ist eine der Fragen, die uns wieder zum Thema „*Die Chancen der Jugend*" zurückbringt. Danke schön.

Jugend und sozialer Wandel

von Prof. Dr. Leopold Rosenmayr

Ich setze mir zum Ziel, die Ergebnisse der neueren soziologischen Forschung[1]) auf die Frage nach der **Rolle der Jugend im sozialen Wandel** zu beziehen; dabei beschränke ich mich auf die mitteleuropäische Situation der Gegenwart.

Unter sozialem Wandel verstehe ich nicht nur die Veränderungen in den Produktionsformen und in den politischen Strukturen, sondern auch den Wandel in den Lebensformen des persönlichen und privaten Bereichs.

Die Frage lautet auch: inwieweit trägt diese Jugend heute dazu bei, bei all ihrer Abhängigkeit und Gebundenheit an ihre Herkunft, neue politische Haltungen und einen neuen Lebensstil mit neuen Bedürfnissen und neuen Werten zu schaffen? Eine solche Veränderung, ein Beitrag zum sozialen Wandel, wäre auch ein Schritt in Richtung auf die Gestaltung ihrer eigenen **Zukunftschancen.**

1. Ansätze und Probleme der Jugendsoziologie

Der gegenüber dem Journalisten und Politiker viel schwerfälligere Wissenschaftler glaubt oft, daß es notwendig sei, die Voraussetzungen darzulegen und die Sprache zu erläutern, in der er über sein Thema spricht.

Vielleicht ist es daher erforderlich, daß ich im Sprechen über Jugend die Legitimierung problematisiere, die ich diesem Thema gegenüber zu haben glaube. Man kann eine solche Legitimierung selber kaum beurteilen, aber man kann die Motive offenlegen, aus denen heraus man sich mit einer Frage befaßt.

Ich finde Jugendforschung deswegen so fesselnd, weil sie zeigt, wie der Mensch sich in seinen Überzeugungen und Zielsetzungen konstituiert. Persönlich empfinde ich – zusätzlich zu diesem Erkenntnis-Ziel – eine wenn auch etwas vage Verpflichtung, die Bedingungen zu verbessern, unter denen eine neue Kohorte ihre gesellschaftliche Arbeit und Transformation unternimmt, und mir liegt auch daran, daß Werte, die mir wichtig sind, dabei zum Tragen kommen, obwohl es mir im einzelnen sehr schwer fiele, diese Werte genau zu bestimmen und auszudrücken. Man kann das als einen paternalisierenden Zugang bezeichnen. Ich bin als Hochschullehrer immer wieder mit neuen Kohorten (Gruppen von Altersjahrgängen), deren Entwicklung ich beobachte, konfrontiert und bei meiner Entscheidung für die Jugendsoziologie hat auch meine Rolle als Vater von 4 Kindern mitgewirkt.

Ich fasse deshalb dieses Symposion so auf, daß es dazu dienen soll, mit Praktikern der Jugendpolitik und der Jugendarbeit, mit Vertretern der Jugendverbände, mit Erziehern im weitesten Sinn über Ergebnisse der neueren Forschung zu sprechen. Wir sollten uns aber auch der Grenzen unseres Wissens bewußt sein und **nicht nur über Jugend, sondern auch mit ihr sprechen.** Für die Forschung hätte das z.B. zur Konsequenz, daß man vom thematischen Ansatz her versucht, Jugend an der über sie zu veranstaltenden Studie mit zu interessieren und zu involvieren.

Vielleicht sollte man von vornherein eingestehen, daß die Jugendforschung unübersichtlich und voller Mängel ist und daß durch sehr verschiedene Formen theoretischen und ideologischen Verständnisses der Konsens in ihrem Bereich geringer ist, als dies in einigen anderen soziologischen Forschungsbereichen der Fall ist. Daß die von Herrn Blücher vorgestellte Studie in mehreren europäischen Ländern gleichzeitig durchgeführt wurde und daß innerhalb der „Jugend" noch ganz bewußt nach Altersgruppen differenziert wird, halte ich bereits für einen wichtigen Fortschritt. Die Zukunft wird überdies in starkem Maße die Ergänzung der Umfrageforschung durch Tiefeninterviews, Gruppengespräche, Situationsanalysen- und Beobachtungen auch im Hinblick auf konkrete Einzelvorhaben, (z.B. die Entwicklung von Jugendzentren) erfordern.

2. Zur inneren Differenzierung des Jugendbegriffs

Zwar brauchen wir weiterhin den Begriff **Jugend**, doch muß er aufgegliedert werden, wenn er für unser Verständnis im einzelnen dienlich sein soll. So müssen wir zwischen Jugendlichen oder Adoleszenten auf der einen Seite und jungen Erwachsenen auf der anderen unterscheiden; eine junge verheiratete Arbeiterin ist keine Jugendliche mehr, auch wenn sie eben erst 18 geworden ist und Studenten, selbst wenn sie von den Eltern finanziell abhängig sind, sind keine „Jugendlichen", und doch sind sie ein weit über ihre zahlenmäßige Bedeutung hinaus sehr wichtiges Element der Gesamtjugend.

Neue Untersuchungsergebnisse scheinen es nötig zu machen, zusätzlich eine Phase der **Früh**adoleszenz zu unterscheiden. Das Durchschnittsalter, in dem die ersten heterosexuellen Erfahrungen gewonnen werden, hat sich im letzten Jahrzehnt, vielleicht am stärksten im letzten Jahrfünft vorverlagert. Die Bereitschaft eines manchmal gezielten, manchmal mehr unbewußten Experimentierens mit sich selbst in und durch sexuellen Verkehr kann als eine Zäsur gegenüber einer früheren Lebensphase betrachtet werden. Es wird sehr häufig als Abschied von einer mehr **vorbildorientierten** Phase zu einer der **Selbstbehauptung** und **Entscheidungsfähigkeit** aufzufassen sein.

Sexualität ist heute vielleicht mehr denn je auch ideologisch als Emanzipationssymbol, besonders für die jungen Mädchen emotional besetzt. Der sogenannte doppelte Standard für die beiden Geschlechter verschwindet; noch vor 15 bis 20 Jahren wurden einem jungen Mann vor der Eheschließung sexuelle Erfahrungen auch mit mehreren Mädchen zugebilligt, den jungen Mädchen jedoch weit weniger Erfahrungen mit Männern. Man gewinnt den Eindruck, daß die weibliche Jugend beim doppelten Standard nicht mehr mitspielt.

Referat Rosenmayr

Noch vor einem Jahrzehnt war voreheliche Sexualität vor allem bei der weiblichen Jugend hauptsächlich auf einen Partner fixiert; neue Daten zeigen, daß sich die eheartigen Partnerschaften vermehren, aber auch die „wechselnden Verhältnisse“, selbst in jungen Jahren. Es ist (noch) nicht zu entschlüsseln, ob die Zunahme der Partner-Instabilität auf Egozentrismus (oder positiver ausgedrückt: auf „Ich-Stärke“) oder auf Konsumismus mit Zwang zum Wechseln zurückgeht. Oder führt eine zunehmende „Sensibilisierung“ zur Unfähigkeit, sich zu Bindungen zu bekennen und an ihnen festzuhalten?

Ganz außerordentlich wichtig wären sogenannte **Längsschnitt- oder Verlaufstudien:** z.B. 15jährige heute zu befragen und die Befragung der gleichen Personen in 5 Jahren und in einem Jahrzehnt oder in 15 Jahren zu wiederholen, so daß man sie als 20-, 25- bzw. 30-jährige wieder antrifft. Das erst wären echte Kohortenuntersuchungen.

Wenn wir nämlich zum gleichen Zeitpunkt 15-jährige mit 30-jährigen vergleichen und finden, daß die 15-jährigen wesentlich weniger von Zuverlässigkeit und Pünktlichkeit halten als die 30-jährigen, so wissen wir nicht, ob diese 30-jährigen durch die Lebenserfahrung im Beruf einfach darauf gestoßen wurden, daß gewisse Aspekte der Verläßlichkeit notwendig sind, **also ihre Einstellungen geändert** haben, oder ob sie aus einer „früheren Welt“, aus einer anderen Mentalität heraus **schon von ihrer Kindheit an** auf mehr Verläßlichkeit und Pünktlichkeit hin erzogen worden sind. **Altersvergleiche ohne Verlaufsstudien beantworten leider die Frage nicht, ob sich der Zeitgeist geändert hat oder ob sich junge Menschen der von ihnen erfahrenen Wirklichkeit angepaßt haben.**

Eine Schwierigkeit, die im Gespräch zwischen Wissenschaftlern und Praktikern immer wieder auftaucht, ist, daß die Umfrage-Industrie mehr Ergebnisse produziert als sie selbst – ganz zu schweigen von den Wissenschaftlern – zu verarbeiten im Stande ist. Ich will das an einem Beispiel anschaulich machen: Aus einer international vergleichenden Studie[2)] wurde z.B. hervorgehoben, wie **positiv von den Jungen das Verhältnis zu ihren Eltern beurteilt wird.** Mit Hilfe der Umfragedaten wird die soziale Wirklichkeit rekonstruiert und die Familienspannungen ins Reich der „Literatur“ verwiesen. Eine Jugend, wie sie Thomas Bernhard oder Peter Handke erlebt haben, ist eben dann die schwierige Jugend der Literatur. Oder?

3. Beziehungen zwischen den Generationen in der Familie – ein Basisproblem der Jugendforschung

Man muß hier Argumente zur Interpretation des positiven Befundes der Familienbeziehungen einführen. Emotionale Einstellungen zu den Eltern sind immer ambivalent. Daß bei Befragungen die positiven Seiten hervortreten – und dies nicht nur in der von Herrn Blücher präsentierten Studie – ist nicht falsch, aber es zeigt **nur die eine Seite** des gesamten Einstellungskomplexes. Aus der

Psychoanalyse wissen wir, wie groß die Widerstände sind, bloß vor uns **selbst** die Gefühle der Ablehnung gegenüber Personen einzugestehen, mit denen wir eng verbunden oder von denen wir abhängig sind. Noch ein zweites: auch emotional wenig geöffneten, mit sich selbst beschäftigten Eltern gegenüber kann man und muß man sich zumindest bis zur frühen Adoleszenz herauf identifizieren. Da bleibt kaum eine andere Wahl.

Wenn wir uns die Elterngenerationen der 45- bis 60-jährigen vergegenwärtigen, so müssen wir die Verbindung von deren Lebensgeschichte mit dem wirtschaftlichen Aufstieg von 1955–1970 uns vor Augen führen. Es handelt sich um eine Elternkohorte mit Phänomenen einer Ethik der harten Zweckmäßigkeit, einer enterotisierten Leistungsbetonung und der Gefahr entleerter persönlicher Verhältnisse.

Versuchen wir kohortenspezifisch zu interpretieren: Eltern aller Schichten, aber besonders Eltern, die einen Aufstieg mitgemacht haben, der sich auch materiell in dem Erwerb eines Heims, von Fahrzeugen, in kostspieligen Urlauben usw. niederschlug, sind im Nachkriegsabschnitt von 1950 bis 1965 vielfach außerordentlich stark mit eben diesem sozioökonomischen Aufstieg beschäftigt gewesen. Als sie in diesen Jahren Kleinkinder oder Schulkinder aufzogen, waren sie vom Drang und Zwang zum materiellen Fortschritt erfüllt, waren an Rekonstruktion bzw. Ausbau des Bestehenden fixiert, an Aufstieg oder Festigung ihrer Position im System. Jedoch wurde mehr als ihre Zeit und ihre Energie damit aufgebracht; ihre gefühlshafte Verausgabung, ja Erschöpfung ließ sie die Möglichkeit von Bruchlinien im Verhältnis zur Kindergeneration übersehen und sie vermochten es dann nicht mehr, sich selber in Frage zu stellen. Bei den heute 45- bis 60- bzw. 65-jährigen, die als Eltern von Adoleszenten und jungen Erwachsenen die Phase der Auflehnung ihrer Kinder mitgemacht haben, müßte genauer festgestellt werden, in welchen Schichten, Berufsgruppen, unter welchen Voraussetzungen ihres persönlichen und beruflichen Erfolgsstrebens sie eine besonders starke „Ethik der harten Kontinuität“ vertreten, bzw. in enterotisierten und entleerten persönlichen Verhältnissen und Beziehungen auch ihre Familien als Arbeitsfeld aufgefaßt hatten; wieweit sie sich von ihrer „Moral“ her in ihrer Haltung als legitimiert erachteten, als sie plötzlich vom Schock in der Privatsphäre durch die antiautoritäre Propaganda einerseits und den Sex-Boom andererseits „erfaßt“ wurden.

Zur Geschichte dieser besonderen Elterngeneration gehört der Umstand, daß bei der Konzentration der Kräfte auf den enormen sozialen und wirtschaftlichen Aufstieg zwischen 1950 und 1970 gleichzeitig eine relative Isolierung der Familien mit ihren spezifischen Problemen entstand. Eine Kommunikation, das Bedürfnis über Probleme zu sprechen, scheiterte an der geringen Verfügbarkeit emotionaler Ressourcen und an der Schwäche zum Durchbrechen der genannten Isolierung. Waren zuerst die **Familien** als solche isoliert, so blieben bzw. bleiben beim Heranwachsen der Kinder nun die **Eltern** isoliert und zurück; denn die Kinder versuchten, dieser Isolierung rasch zu entkommen. Dabei mag zweitrangig gewesen sein, ob nun der Vater oder die Mutter oder beide real oder nur psychisch „abwesend" waren.

Aufklärungsprozesse und Gedanken bezüglich einer Reform der Erziehung hatten diesem historischen Typus von Elterngeneration nicht grundsätzlich gefehlt. Vor allem bestimmte neue Aspekte der Kleinkindererziehung: Ernährung, fundamentale Fragen der Pflege des Kinder, zum Teil auch neue Auffassungen hinsichtlich der Reinlichkeitsgewöhnung usw., wurden in reformistischer Absicht aus den sich rasch ausbreitenden Sachbüchern, Zeitschriftenartikeln usw. rezipiert. Jedoch ist eine Aufklärung und eine neue **Eltern-Pädagogik für die späteren Jahre der heranwachsenden Kinder ausständig geblieben.** Gerade die schwierigen Aufgaben der Erziehung, die Hilfeleistungs- und Beratungsfunktionen hinsichtlich der Konstituierung der Persönlichkeit, des Ausblicks auf das künftige Leben der Kinder in Beruf und Freizeit, die Sexual- und Partnerschaftsfragen waren Eltern anheimgestellt, die sich in diesen für sie neuartigen Problemen zu wenig zurechtfinden konnten. Eine sozial-pädagogische Aufarbeitung der Situationen, in die sie mit ihren Jugendlichen gerieten, ist für diese Elterngeneration nicht oder kaum erfolgt. Sie hätte bei **einer Reflexion über die Gesamtstruktur der Elterngeneration** ansetzen und zu einer Haltung hinführen müssen, von der aus man bereit ist, **sich selbst oder gewisse eigene Grundannahmen in Frage zu stellen.** Nun haben die Jugendlichen selbst die Initiative ergriffen und sind der weit nachhinkenden Erziehung ihrer Eltern davongeeilt. Vielleicht wäre es unter anderen Voraussetzungen gelungen, das Toleranzpotential zwischen den Generationen stärker auszubilden.

4. Die Familie mit der Elterngeneration des Wohlstandsaufschwungs

Die aus den verschiedenen Untersuchungen berichteten Ergebnisse lassen auf viel tiefere Unfähigkeit zur Toleranz einerseits und auf einen Mangel an Bereitschaft und Fähigkeit zum entschlossenen Vertreten von Positionen andererseits schließen. In das Bild der durch Kommunikationsarmut oder -unfähigkeit gestörten und durch sie behinderten Generationenbeziehung gehören verschiedene Phänomene, die im Licht kohortenspezifischer Interpretation einsichtiger werden.

Zum Typus der Familie, wie sie sich in der Phase des Wohlstandsaufschwungs entwickelt hat, gehört auch die Gesetzmäßigkeit der sozialpsychologischen Verspätung der Eltern ihren Kindern gegenüber. Diese läßt sich am Zärtlichkeitsverhalten einsichtig machen. Gerade in ihrem Bedürfnis, den Kindern ihre Sympathie und ihre Gefühle und die darin enthaltene Zuwendung zu zeigen, tendieren Eltern gegenüber ihren adoleszenten Kindern dazu, diese um 2–4 Jahre „verspätet" zu behandeln. Sie regredieren darin sehr häufig auf eine frühere Phase, da der junge Mensch noch „klein", kindlich war, wogegen sich der junge Mensch nur mit einer gewissen reaktiven Härte abschirmen kann. Ein Form der Reaktion Jugendlicher gegen die sozialpsychologische Verspätung, die in der faktischen oder perzipierten aufdringlichen Zärtlichkeit der Eltern sichtbar wird, ist jene, die eigenen **Eltern zu depersonalisieren.** Das Distanzierungsstreben bewirkt, daß man den erwachsenen Elternteil sozusagen als Maske „des" Vaters, „der" Mutter sieht; und dies wiederum potenziert die Distanzierung. Dieser an sich für den Jugendlichen notwendige Schritt könnte jedoch fruchtbarer gestaltet und vor allem könnten Spannungsverhältnisse zwischen den Generationen in der Familie erträglicher gemacht werden, würde eine Fähigkeit entwickelt, den jeweiligen „Rollenzustand" zu revidieren. Wenn es den einzelnen Mitgliedern einer Familie gelingt, ihre Positionen und Beziehungen zueinander neu zu definieren und sie dadurch zu verlebendigen, kann der Sprung in eine neue Phase des Familienlebenszyklus gemeinsam unternommen werden. Eine auf diese Weise gewonnene Kommunikation und Solidarität könnte an die Stelle von konfliktueller Verhärtung treten.

Die traditionalistische Familie ist bezüglich ihrer jeweiligen Positionen fixiert; meist ist sie auch noch durch falsche Erfüllungswünsche belastet. Hier ist die Gefahr gegeben, daß im zwischenmenschlichen Verhältnis zwischen den Eltern und ihren Kindern von seiten der Eltern der Versuch unternommen wird, die in der eigenen Psyche ungelösten Probleme am Kind und durch das Kind zu „lösen". Man will sich die eigenen unerfüllten Träume mit dem Kind bzw. Jugendlichen erfüllen, die auf einen bestimmten Beruf, auf eine selber nicht erreichte „Sehnsuchtserfüllung" hin gedrängt werden. H. E. Richter spricht von der geheimen Ausbeutung von Kindern und Jugendlichen zu „narßistischen Zwecken".[3)]

Ein klassisches Beispiel der genannten und oben skizzierten sozialpsychologischen Verspätung in den Einstellungen von Eltern gegenüber ihren Adoleszenten, die häufig zur konfliktuellen Verhärtung führt, ist die Frage des „Nach-Hause-Kommens" besonders der Töchter. In diesem Bereich kristallisiert sich – meist ganz dysfunktional hinsichtlich der Erreichung der wie immer gesetzten moralischen oder erzieherischen Ziele der Eltern – ein Konfliktfeld, bei dem es schließlich hauptsächlich um die **Einhaltung der von der Eltern gesetzten, zumeist äußerlichen Normen** geht, und damit um die Selbstbestätigung ihrer Autorität.

Bei neueren Untersuchungen über die Einstellungen von Jugendlichen gegenüber ihren Eltern tritt dementsprechend das Problem der Aufrichtigkeit, mit der Eltern die von ihnen gesetzten Normen vertreten, besonders hervor. Jugendliche nehmen besonders Anstoß daran, wenn Eltern **mehr am günstigen Eindruck** liegt, den das Verhalten ihrer Kinder in der Nachbarschaft, bei Bekannten usw. macht, **als an ihrem tatsächlichen Verhalten**: d.h. wenn ihnen scheint, den Eltern sei mehr an der Meinung der Nachbarschaft, von Bekannten und Freunden, hinsichtlich einer „vorbildlichen“ Aufführung ihrer Kinder gelegen, als an deren tatsächlicher Lebensweise und realen Problemen.

Wir haben mit diesen Beispielen versucht, für den Bereich der Beziehungen zwischen Eltern und Jugendlichen in der Familie Konfliktstoffe und Reibungsflächen darzustellen, um damit ein Bild des intergenerativen Verhältnisses der Familie zum Zeitpunkt des Jugendalters der zweiten Generation zu ergänzen.

Ist dieses Bild von einer Gemeinsamkeit von Werten und Normen in Grundfragen geprägt? Neuere Urteile über das Verhältnis der Generationen in der Familie scheinen zu harmonistisch, wenn sie zu leugnen suchen, daß es „crosspressures“ zwischen Peer-Einfluß und Eltern-Einfluß bzw. Peer-Beziehung und Eltern-Beziehung für Jugendliche gibt. J. P. Hill z. B. behauptet,[4] die Gelegenheiten für Konflikte seien relativ selten, weil die verschiedenen Rollen der Jugendlichen – einerseits die Sohn- und Tochterrollen, andererseits die Peer-Rollen – in **verschiedenen Situationen zum Tragen** kämen. Außerdem meint er, daß die Peers ohnehin entsprechend dem Geschmack und den Wertsystemen der Eltern gewählt würden.

Mit der zunehmenden Mobilität, der Fragmentierung der Nachbarschaften, mit zunehmender multipler Loyalität, der Fähigkeit, sich an Personen verschiedener Wertsysteme gleichzeitig zu binden, dürfte jedoch diese saubere und klaglose Rollenteilung, wie sie Hill beschreibt, nicht in dem von ihm erwarteten Maß funktionieren.

5. Die Konsequenzen von Beziehungen

Soziologische Untersuchungen über Beziehungen von Eltern und Jugendlichen geraten in Gefahr, durch den richtig erhobenen Bestand grundsätzlich positiver Beziehungen, die sich in der relativen Gewißheit für die Jugendlichen, unterstützt zu werden, in schwierigen Situationen Hilfe zu erhalten, sich den Elternpersonen grundsätzlich emotional nahe zu fühlen usw., ein einseitiges Bild zu bieten. Diese Untersuchungen haben nämlich die Tendenz, **in der Analyse von Beziehungen diese selber und nicht deren Konsequenzen zu erfassen.** Beziehungen mögen eng sein, sie mögen als stützend, emotional, nahe usw. erlebt werden, haben aber oft dennoch die **Wirkung,** daß sie **neurotische Strukturen oder zumindest psychische Störungen bei der nachwachsenden Generation hervorrufen bzw. begünstigen.** Was selbst bei projektiven Tests verbal als „Nähe“, Unterstützungsbereitschaft des Vaters oder der Eltern von seiten der Jugend positiv bezeichnet wird, mag einer mehr oder weniger unbewußten Registration eines Dominierungsverhaltens des Vaters bzw. der Eltern Hand in Hand gehen, welches als Zwang erlebt und dementsprechend durch Unsicherheit oder unbewußtes Abwehrverhalten beantwortet wird. Dies vermag sich in Verhaltensstörungen, wie z.B. teilweisem Nicht-

Erfüllen der eigenen Pflichten, Nicht-Aufstehen-Können am Morgen, Zuspätkommen etc., äußern, als ablehnendes Verhalten und Kommunikations-Verweigerungen gegenüber Lehrpersonen und später auch gegenüber den Eltern selber.

Jugendsoziologie im Rahmen einer intergenerativen Theorie der Altersgruppen, der Sozialisationstheorie und einer Theorie sozialen Wandels, muß sich auf eine innere Verbindung zu sozialpsychologischen und tiefenpsychologischen Theorien sowie zu Fragestellungen der Arbeitswissenschaften, der Politologie und anderer Disziplinen stützen. Die weitere Entwicklung kann unseres Erachtens nur in einer **pluridisziplinären Verflechtung der Jugendsoziologie** liegen, die in dieser – auf der Basis ihres eigenen theoretischen Selbstverständnisses – eine bedingte Selbständigkeit behält.

Als Hauptakteure einer solchen intergenerationellen Betrachtungsweise mit pluridisziplinärer (auch die Tiefenpsychologie einbeziehender) Grundlage müssen die **Eltern** in die Jugendsoziologie ebenso einbezogen werden wie die Kinder. Wenden wir uns also den Eltern zu:

Oft reichen die bisherigen begrifflichen Grundlagen der Soziologie, z.B. hinsichtlich des Rollenbegriffes, nicht aus, um innere Spannungen und Konflikte in den Elternpersönlichkeiten zu erfassen, welche für die Gestaltung der Beziehungen selber, aber auch für die oben geforderte Analyse der Konsequenzen ausschlaggebend erscheinen können. Die Rollentheorie vermag nicht in jene innerpsychologische Ambivalenz einzudringen, welche die Widersprüchlichkeit von intendiertem und realem Verhalten zur Folge hat.

Gefühle der Verpflichtung gegenüber bestimmten Normsystemen legen selbst für reflektierende, sich der Probleme der Erziehung bewußte Eltern einen bestimmten Bereich von Verhaltensweisen fest. Aus einem sich auf direkte Anweisungen beziehenden und ständig Rechenschaft verlangenden Erziehungsstil von Eltern werden nicht nur Ängste und Unselbständigkeit in den Kindern gefördert, es ergeben sich auch **Streßsequenzen für die elterlichen Akteure selber.** Je schutzloser die Eltern diesem Streß ausgesetzt sind, desto stärker reagieren sie mit regressivem Verhalten. Im Regreß kommt häufig spiegelbildlich das an sich selbst erlebte Verhalten der eigenen Eltern zutage; die vor Jahrzehnten vermutlich noch stärker verbreiteten körperlichen Gewaltanwendungen liegen dann zwischen den Generationen gleichsam in der Luft. Aus eigenen Untersuchungen ging hervor[5]), daß das Angebrülltwerden der Jugendlichen durch den Vater gegenüber den Ohrfeigen zwar im Vordergrund stand, daß aber das Erleben gewalthafter Erziehungsmittel sowohl bei der ehedem erfolgten Sozialisation der Eltern durch die vorhergehende Generation wie, wenn auch in geringerem Maß, im Verhältnis der heutigen Eltern- und Kindergenerationen einen beträchtlichen Platz einnimmt.

Der Regreß ist jedoch nur eine, wenn auch die am radikalsten realisierte Möglichkeit der Ambivalenz der Eltern. Aufklärungsliteratur über Erziehung, allgemeine aus den Medien aufgegriffene Empfehlungen gegen Strenge im Erziehungsverhalten haben die Einsicht verbreitet, daß das traditionelle Bestehen auf Normen durch „harte" Maßnahmen gegenüber Jugendlichen nicht optimal sei. So ergibt sich bei den Eltern die Bereitschaft, milder, verständiger zu sein, die Erziehung auf der Basis von Aussprachen und im Rahmen einer bestimmten Mitwirkung der heranwachsenden Kinder in Haushalt und Familie durchzuführen.

Hier können sich nun, einerseits durch im Grunde unüberzeugtes Nachgeben, andererseits durch Rückfälle von den für sich selbst gesetzten neuen toleranteren Standards in der Erziehungsgestaltung Schuldgefühle bei den Eltern ergeben. Die Wahrscheinlichkeit, daß Schuldgefühle über das eigene Versagen auftreten, ist um so häufiger, je eher die Eltern selber hohe Ansprüche an sich und damit auch an ihre Kinder stellen.

Die Chance einer Diskrepanz zwischen intendiertem und realem Erziehungsverhalten nimmt mit der Unsicherheit bezüglich des Erziehungsstiles natürlich zu; weicht das reale Verhalten allzusehr vom intendierten ab, ergibt sich eine Art Zick-Zack-Kurs voller Unstimmigkeiten, der nicht nur zur Enttäuschung der Eltern gereicht, sondern auch von den Jugendlichen als inhomogen wahrgenommen wird und **nicht** dazu beiträgt, das Verhältnis zu den Eltern in irgendeiner Weise positiv zu profilieren.

Probleme, wie wir sie hier darzustellen versucht haben, wären Gegenstand differenzierter Untersuchungen sozialpsychologischer und soziologischer Art im Überlappungsbereich von Familiensoziologie und Jugendsoziologie und von zentraler Bedeutung für die Erziehungswissenschaften.

Hierzu sind eine Menge technischer und methodischer Gesichtspunkte zu bedenken, da man Elternbeziehungen nicht so einfach erforschen kann wie man einen routinemäßigen Intelligenztest durchführt – auch diesem gegenüber sind nicht nur die Personalchefs, sondern auch die Testpsychologen selber skeptischer geworden.

Bezüglich der **Auslegung** und **Bewertung** der Ergebnisse über Elternbeziehungen gibt es noch große Unsicherheiten, und die theoretischen Erklärungsversuche sind kontrovers. Es ist aber gelungen, die sozialhistorischen Konzeptualisationen in die Analyse mit einzubeziehen. Im Verhältnis der Jugend zu ihren Eltern sind Probleme von großer Tragweite involviert, es spiegelt sich darin nicht nur die Kultur, sondern die Ausprägung von Mitmenschlichkeit in dieser Kultur.

6. Jugend als Faktor gesellschaftlicher Reproduktion und Transformation

Erwin Scheuch hat vor einigen Jahren eine Abhandlung unter den Titel gestellt: **Die Jugend gibt es nicht**[6)].

Max Kaase hat 1968 gezeigt, daß es damals in der BRD bemerkenswerte Unterschiede zwischen den Studenten einerseits und der nichtstudierenden Jugend andererseits gab. In vielerlei Hinsicht war die **nicht**-studierende, (vorwiegend die Arbeiter-Jugend), politisch den Erwachsenen dieser Periode sehr viel ähnlicher als die Studenten[7]. Die Emnid-Studie von 1975[8] hebt hervor, daß politische Mobilisierbarkeit die Bereitschaft zu Demonstrations-Protest und Solidarisierung in politischen Gruppen bei allen, die betrieblich und beruflich festgelegt sind, wesentlich geringer ist als unter jenen, die des Freiraums Schule oder Hochschule teilhaftig werden.

In den Vereinigten Staaten dürften sich nach Untersuchungen von K. Jennings[9] gewisse Protesthaltungen auch über das College hinaus allgemein verbreitet haben. Wenn man den Studien von D. Yankelovich vertrauen darf[10], haben in den USA in den frühen siebziger Jahren die unteren sozialen Schichten der Jugend die Einstellungen zur Sexualität zu **übernehmen** begonnen, welche die College-Jugend ein schwaches Jahrzehnt vorher bereits entwickelte. Den oberen Schichten einer Großkohorte (einem Jahrgangsbündel von 10 – 15 Jahren) kommt also viel eher – eher im doppelten Sinn: früher und mit höherer Wahrscheinlichkeit – die Kraft zur **Transformation**, zum sozialen Wandel zu als den unteren Schichten ihrer Altersgenossen, da diese sowohl sozial unfreier sind und auch weniger direkten Zugang zu neuen Ideologien haben. In manchen wirtschaftlichen und politischen Hinsichten ist die soziale Klassenzugehörigkeit somit ausschlaggebender als das Lebensalter, besonders an den Extremen der Einkommensverteilung. Dies ist im Auge zu behalten, wenn man an die Ausbildung eines Lebensstils, an jugendliche Konsuminteressen, an die indirekte Wertvermittlung durch Film und Zeitschriften, die Vorbildwirkung bestimmter Sportler, Sänger oder Musik-Heroen denkt. Sicher gibt es über die einzelnen Gruppen der Jugend hinaus **gemeinsam charakterisierende Vorlieben**; der Umfang dessen, was wir „jugendliche Subkultur" nennen, ist jedoch je nach Lebens- und Erlebensgebieten gesondert abzustecken und natürlich auch zeitgeschichtlich zu bestimmen.

Einheit oder **Vereinheitlichung** ist bei einem sozialen Phänomen immer dann umgreifend, wenn entweder starke äußere Zwänge vorliegen oder bestimmte Triebkräfte eine Bewegung hervorrufen, die dieses Phänomen in seinem Zusammenhang erscheinen lassen. (Die Frauenbewegung der letzten Jahre ist ein Beispiel dafür.)

Einerseits ist an der inneren Differenzierung des Jugendbegriffs festzuhalten und weiterzuarbeiten. Andererseits sollte man den Jugendbegriff als solchen zur inneren Überprüfung, wo und wodurch Einheit vorhanden ist, nicht fahren lassen.

Jugend ist zu sehen als ein für den Menschen spezifisches und, seit dem 18. Jahrhundert, von der ihrer selbst sich bewußt werdenden Polit- und Erziehungsgesellschaft systematisch hervorgebrachtes Phänomen der **Verzögerung des Eintritts in die Produktions**- und Reproduktionsprozesse.

Jugend trat als **Freiheitssymbol** in die Welt. Der Westen hat seit den Erziehungs- und Revolutionstheorien J. J. Rousseau's, aber auch der von Rousseau z.B. in der „Nouvelle Héloise" geprägten Empfindsamkeit Jugend idolisiert. Die Figur des Jünglings erschien nicht nur den deutschen, sondern auch den russischen Romantikern als Heilbringer, von Hölderlins Hyperion bis zu Dostojewskis Aljoscha. Erinnern Sie sich an den Glauben, den Ernst Bloch in Rudi Dutschke setzte? Und es ist noch gar nicht so lange her, daß J. P. Sartre auf der Suche nach Heroen in Deutschland Gefängnisbesuche bei Baader-Meinhof machte.

Der Jugendbegriff als solcher hat immer ideologische Dimensionen besessen; man muß sie jeweils neu zu verstehen suchen, wie immer man sich zu ihnen einstellen mag. Die Studentenbewegung der späten 60er Jahre hat sich allerdings – im Unterschied zur Jugendbewegung der Jahrhundertwende – nie als Bewegung **der** Jugend **für** die Jugend, sondern eigentlich als **gesellschaftsverändernde** Kraft verstanden; Bernd Rabehl (geb. 1938), einer der seinerzeitigen Führer der Bewegung, definiert die Studentenbewegung rückblickend durch „Antiimperialismus, Antifaschismus, Antiinstitutionalismus und direkten Aktionismus", wodurch sie „auf andere Schichten und Klassen gewirkt habe".

Man muß aber neben dem **ideologischen** Aspekt immer auch den **soziologischen** sehen: Jugend darf nicht gleichsam statisch und für sich betrachtet werden (das ist die Gefahr jeder Diskussion über Jugend), sondern sie ist als **historisches Moment im Prozeß der Reproduktion** (also der Wiederholung vorhandener Sozialformen) und der **Transformation** (also der Veränderung dieser) zu sehen. Bei aller Plötzlichkeit, mit der Jugendprotest und Revolte aufzutreten vermögen, die Voraussetzungen dafür sind doch jeweils vorher schon im Gesellschaftssystem vorhanden. **Die Gruppen der Jugend tragen immer den Stempel der gesellschaftlichen Arbeitsteilung und der Ausbildungssysteme, welche dieser Arbeitsteilung und Produktionswelt mehr oder minder gut zugeordnet sind.**

7. Jugend, politische Sozialisation und politischer Wandel

Die Doppelbetrachtung von Jugend als Transformation einerseits und Reproduktion andererseits läßt sich an Forschungsmaterialien exemplifizieren. Wir hatten aufgrund der Anlage einer internationalen Studie die Möglichkeit, die Verhaltensweisen der Jugendlichen **mit denen ihrer Eltern zu vergleichen.** Diese Untersuchungsanlage erlaubte uns nachzuweisen, daß vieles, was man manchmal als typisch jugendliche Kritik bezeichnet, in Wirklichkeit auch bei anderen Altersgruppen in gleicher Weise ausgesprochen wird.

In ganz ähnlicher geringer Weise nehmen Erwachsene wie Jugendliche an, daß die Politiker wirklich berücksichtigen, was „Leute wie wir" denken; die Mehrzahl von ihnen glaubt, daß die Abgeordneten zum Bundestag im allgemeinen den Kontakt zur Bevölkerung sehr schnell verlieren. Die Behauptung, daß die Parteien nur die Stimme der Wähler bekommen wollen, ohne sich für deren Meinung zu interessieren, wird von einem großen Teil der befragten Jugendlichen **und** Erwachsenen **gleichermaßen** vertreten. Daß die Politiker, die Abgeordneten zum Bundestag oder die Minister im allgemeinen die Wahrheit sagen, wird nur von einer sehr geringen Minderheit der befragten Jugendlichen wie der Erwachsenen angenommen.

Die Unterschiede zwischen Erwachsenen und Jugendlichen scheinen nicht so sehr in der Bewertung der politischen Situation zu bestehen, als in der Tatsache, daß – nach den Untersuchungen von 1974 – sich die Jugendlichen sehr viel besser als die Erwachsenen eine andere Situation vorstellen können, daß sie zukunftsoffener sind. Jugendliche erwarten eine Möglichkeit der Durchsetzung in der Politik, wenn überhaupt, durch ad hoc geformte Gruppen, durch Demonstration, Opposition außerhalb der etablierten politischen Parteien, während die Erwachsenen eher auf den Apparat vertrauen.

Interessant ist, daß bei **regionalen** Wahlen, wo die ideologischen Unterschiede weniger ins Gewicht fallen, die Unterschiede zwischen den Altersgruppen geringer sind (d.h. die Wahrscheinlichkeit, daß Vater und Sohn die gleiche Partei wählen, größer ist) als bei Bundestagswahlen. **Nationale** Wahlen enthalten mehr Transformationsappell oder enthielten ihn jedenfalls in der Bundesrepublik noch in den frühen 70er Jahren. Allerdings fällt auch bei den Bundestagswahlen der Apfel nicht weit vom Stamm. Es sind die Mechanismen der politischen Sozialisation (intrafamilial und auch außerhalb der Familie), die bei den Jugendlichen dazu beitragen, die zwischen Eltern und Kindern festzustellenden Unterschiede im Wahlverhalten relativ gering zu halten. Verglichen mit anderen Verhaltensbereichen, z. B. der Freizeit, scheint im intrafamilialen Bereich der Trend zur politischen Konformität mit dem jeweiligen Milieu, dem der Jugendliche ausgesetzt ist, größer zu sein. Dies führt, was „die Präferenz einer Partei" betrifft, zu bedeutenden Übereinstimmungen zwischen Eltern und Kindern.

Es gibt allerdings Bereiche politischer Einstellungen und Verhaltensdispositionen, in denen sich Unterschiede zwischen den Jugendlichen und jungen Erwachsenen einerseits und den der älteren Erwachsenen – jeweils als Aggregate gemessen – zeigen lassen. Hierzu gehören vor allem die Bereiche der generellen politischen Ziele, der grundsätzlichen Billigung von weniger konventionellen Formen politischer Partizipation und die Einstellung zu repressiven Maßnahmen seitens einer Regierung, sowie die Art und Weise, in der Mitarbeit an politischen Themen ins Auge gefaßt wird.

Bei Jugendlichen steht die politische Arbeit im Rahmen einer informellen

Gruppe oder einer Organisation häufiger im Vordergrund als bei Erwachsenen.

Trotz der Ergebnisse einer erkennbaren Verschiebung in einer Reihe politischer Einstellungen zwischen Jugendlichen und Erwachsenen läßt sich zeigen, daß die Vorstellung eines massiven, innerfamilialen Generationskonfliktes nicht zutrifft. Auch ist **politische Aktivität von Jugendlichen nicht das Produkt eines in der Familie erlebten und auf die Gesellschaft projizierten Konfliktes zwischen den Generationen.** Es besteht wenig Zusammenhang zwischen der Meinung der Kinder über ihre Eltern und dem Ausmaß des zwischen den Aggregaten (den Eltern als Gruppe und den Kindern als Gruppe) gemessenen Unterschiedes.

Man könnte aus all dem vielleicht folgern, daß **elterliche Sozialisation mehr reproduktive Folgen hat als transformative** und annehmen, daß über Bildung und Medien Motivation und Gehalte, die zu sozialem Wandel führen, eher eingebracht werden als über die Familien. Aber so einfach läßt sich soziale Wirklichkeit nicht einteilen.

Wir können sehr wohl zeigen, daß elterliche Sozialisation sich auch in einer **unterschwelligen Ermutigung zur Abweichung** auswirken kann, was wiederum auf Wertähnlichkeit verweist. Ich greife damit auf den schon früher herangezogenen Gedanken der Ambivalenz zurück.Vor über 15 Jahren hat James Coleman [11)] bei einer amerikanischen Jugenduntersuchung auf den Primat des Lernerfolges (gegenüber den sportlichen Leistungen im College) hingewiesen, den Eltern behaupten und verlangen, aber insgeheim doch ersehnen, daß die Kinder primär **Sporterfolge** haben, da diese den Kindern **mehr Popularität erbringen** als der Lernerfolg; explizit oder implizit, jedenfalls durch Identifizierung mit den Kindern „partizipieren" die Eltern dann an deren Popularität.

Unsere empirischen Daten zeigen, daß das Ausmaß,in dem sich Kinder immateriellen, z. T. utopischen Werten zuwenden, davon abhängen dürfte, inwieweit die Eltern in ihre, wenn auch praktisch-materialistische Wertstruktur bereits einige ‚utopische' Wertkomponenten aufgenommen haben. Unter der Voraussetzung höherer Schulbildung sowohl der Eltern als auch der Kinder ergibt sich, daß die emotionalen Beziehungen **nicht** wesentlich getrübt werden, wenn die Kinder politisch abweichen. Es muß also tendenziell eine gewisse Ermutigung zu dieser Abweichung bei den Eltern oder eine „innere Toleranz" dieser Devianz vorliegen, so als würden die Eltern eine sich selber nicht zugestandene Selbsterfüllung im Radikalismus der Kinder erleben.

Sehr merkwürdig sind auch die von uns zwar nicht beobachteten, aber aus den Daten vermuteten Prozesse – wir hatten leider keine **Verlaufsdaten** zur Verfügung – die auf ein **Wieder-Einmünden in die Verhaltensweisen der Eltern im Lebenslauf deuten.** Vermutlich finden Lernprozesse auf den verschiedensten Ebenen statt, die nicht leicht zu durchschauen bzw. voneinander zu trennen sind. Prozesse der Imitation, der Identifizierung in der Kindheit, führen zur Übernahme von Verhaltensstilen, die auch durch Ablösungs- und Verselbständigungsprozesse (samt der Ablehnung der Eltern) und dem z. T. schon bewußten **Aufgreifen neuer Werte außerhalb der Familie** während der Adoleszenz **zwar überdeckt aber nicht ausgelöscht** werden. Wirksame Identifizierungen werden also in das System der Handlungsstrukturen aufgenommen und es kommt zu einem post-edukativen Durchbruch elterlicher Lebensstile und Verhaltensweisen. Wertprävalenz während der Adoleszenz, die zur Innovation von Zielen und Motiven führt, schließt das Wiederauftauchen von älteren (d.h. **früher** im Lebensablauf grundgelegten) Über-Ich-Strukturen nicht aus.

Ist das vielleicht die „List der Vernunft" (Hegel) zur Erhaltung von sozialer Kontinuität?

8. Psychische und soziale Introversion – Kennzeichen einer neuen Jugendgeneration?

Ich möchte zum Abschluß noch den Versuch machen, einige Beobachtungen und Spekulationen zu Tendenzen in der Jugend heute zu formulieren, um daran einige wenige Hinweise zu Jugendarbeit und Jugendpolitik zu knüpfen.

Herr Blücher hat eine Reihe von wichtigen Jugendproblemen benannt, die, wie er sich ausdrückte, forschungsmäßig nicht **operationalisierbar**, d.h. durch Untersuchungen – und er hatte dabei vor allem Befragungen im Auge – nicht faßbar seien.

Ich stimme ihm zu: es gibt einen, wenn auch nicht lineraren, Zusammenhang zwischen Komplexität, Relevanz und Erforschbarkeit. Leider ist dieser Zusammenhang negativ.

Deswegen möchte ich einen Versuch über „Tendenzen" der Entwicklung vorlegen, die ich durch einige von mir für exemplarisch gehaltene Beobachtungen rechtfertigen kann. Ein solcher Versuch einer Gegenüberstellung der Protestgeneration der späten 60er Jahre und frühen 70er Jahre mit Tendenzen in der Jugend heute, also mit Generationssegmenten der später 70er Jahre, die der Protestgeneration vergleichbar sind, ist im Grunde genommen fällig. Ich beziehe mich dabei hauptsächlich auf die akademische Jugend und die letzten Klassen der höheren Schulen bzw. die ästhetisch und politisch wacheren Gruppen anderer Milieus.

Die Protestgeneration hat die Kluft zwischen der Erziehungschance und der Wirklichkeit beruflicher und politischer Institutionen sehr wohl empfunden.

Auch Shmuel N. Eisenstadt[12)] hat übrigens von der **„growing dissociation between the values of educational institutions and future occupational and parental roles and responsibilities"** gesprochen.

Referat Rosenmayr

Die Protestgeneration definierte die Universität als ihren Freiraum und Aktionsraum und **okkupierte** sie, in der utopischen Erwartung, von **dorther** das Establishment nicht nur als solches zu entlarfen, sondern (dies allerdings nur sehr vage) auch ersetzen zu können. Die Anweisung zum ,,langen Marsch durch die Institutionen" (R. Dutschke) ist eigentlich schon eine resignative Formel; sie wurde geprägt, als der utopische Geist schon auszurauchen begann.

Vielleicht läßt der Unterschied zwischen der **Protestgeneration** und der heutigen Tendenz der Ernüchterung und der **Introversion von Opposition** sich in der verschiedenartigen Auslegung eines Satzes zeigen, der 1968 an der Sorbonne in Paris angeschrieben stand. Wie so vieles damals war dieser Satz eine Frage: „Gibt es ein Leben vor dem Tod?"

Die Antwort, die in dieser Frage 1968 mitschwang, war ein **Ja**, oder richtiger der Aufruf, dieses **Leben** von den Barrikaden her zu erzwingen. Über Protest und Revolte zu Partizipation und Kreativität und damit zum „Leben" zu finden, das war die Vorstellung von 1968.

Aus der heutigen Tendenz einer ernüchterten Jugend klingt die Frage nach dem „Leben vor dem Tode" hart und traurig. Warum?

Die Kohorten an den Universitäten der späten 60er Jahre, innerhalb derer die virulenten Stimmen des Protestes und der Partizipation laut wurden, welche Geschichte deuteten und z.T. auch dadurch machten, wollten sich mit **Utopien** auseinandersetzen, deren Kennzeichen war, sich mit einem bestimmten Anspruch auf **Vernunft** zu artikulieren. Marcuse und Habermas (wenn auch letzterer mit Einschränkungen gegenüber dem ersteren) vertraten die Hoffnung auf eine neue synthetische Vernunft, welche die emotionalen Bedürfnisse nach Selbstdeutung durch ,,Kommunikation" erfüllen und die innere Festigung durch Findung einer ,,Identität" leisten würde.

Eine solche „Vernunft" scheint mir jedoch heute der Sinnkohärenz im großen umspannenden Rahmen zu entbehren, jedenfalls ist sie nicht mehr glaubhaft genug. Vielleicht waren die späten 60er Jahre paradoxerweise das letzte Aufflackern der Idee einer humanistischen Universität. Das sich differenzierende Wissen tritt nun, – wie auch Eisenstadt meint – aus der gesamten Kulturordnung heraus. Es wird Sache der spezialisierten „Labors" und Werkstätten, es entgleitet einem kommunikativ-kontemplativen Freiheitsraum, weil sowohl die Wissenschaft andere Voraussetzungen braucht, als auch die vervielfachte Zahl der eingeströmten Studenten. Die ästhetischen, religiösen und meditativen Funktionen, die noch im 19. Jahrhundert mit der Universität, wenn auch damals schon ausgedünnt und durch einen Akademismus verfälscht (aber großbürgerlich-historisch tradiert und kultiviert) gegeben waren, sind nach 1968 endgültig abgewandert. In Hinkunft kann die Universität mitnichten, wie gelegentlich noch in den frühen 50er Jahren, mit einem Kloster verwechselt werden.

Die Studentenrevolte verlieh dem Jugendbegriff eine neue Dimension; sie leitete gleichzeitig aber auch ein Zeitalter ein, welches einerseits durch die soziale Ausbreitung der Bildungsgesellschaft, andererseits durch die Verbreitung des Bildungsvorganges auf den ganzen Lebenslauf und die Verpflichtung zu kontinuierlichem Weiterlernen und **Ver**lernen (un-learning) eine Relativierung des Jugendbegriffes mit sich bringt.

In dem Maß, in dem Universität als Universität sich auflöst, entstehen als neue Subkulturen neue Anonymitäten und „Enklaven". Wolf Dieter Narr hat dies aus einem Text von Lönnendonker in der „*Zeit*" anschaulich zu machen versucht:

„Der Durchschnitts-Stadtteilindianer wacht in der Wohngemeinschaft auf, kauft sich die Brötchen in der Stadtteilbäckerei um die Ecke, dazu sein Müsli aus dem makrobiotischen Tante-Emma-Laden. Liest zum Frühstück **Pflasterstrand, Info-BUG, zitty**, geht – falls er nicht Zerowork-Anhänger ist – zur Arbeit in einen selbstorganisierten Kleinbetrieb oder in ein ‚Alternativprojekt', alle fünf Tage hat er Aufsicht in einem Kinderladen, seine Ente läßt er in einer linken Autoreparaturwerkstatt zusammenflicken, abends sieht er sich ‚Casablanca' im off-Kino an, danach ist er in der Teestube, einer linken Kneipe oder im Musikschuppen zu finden, seine Bettlektüre stammt aus dem Buchladenkollektiv. Ärzte und Rechtsanwaltskollektive, Beratungsstellen für Frauen, Frauen- und Männergruppen gibt es im Getto. Der gesamte Lebensbereich ist weitgehend abgedeckt . . . Dabei ist die Kommunikation intensiv, verglichen mit der, die durchschnittliche Bundesbürger untereinander pflegen. Mit diesem unterhalten sich die Stadtteilindianer, antiautoritäre Studenten und Spontis nur, wenn sie müssen, bei einer Razzia z.B. mit Polizisten. In West-Berlin und in Frankfurt gibt es Angehörige der Szene, die stolz darauf sind, seit zweieinhalb Jahren kein Wort mehr mit einem von denen, die draußen sind, gewechselt zu haben."

9. Die Ergänzung der Erziehung durch Sozialorganisation für die Jugend und mit der Jugend

Wie soll man diese Enklavenbildung verstehen? Ist sie nicht vielleicht die Frucht der Sehnsucht nach einem Moratorium, einem Schonraum, dessen sich die Jugend mit ihrem Anspruch auf Partizipation begeben hat? Und kann man überhaupt Verbindungskanäle wie Röhren zu diesen Isolierten treiben? Ich möchte hier einige Andeutungen an den Schluß stellen.

Wenn wir einen Blick zurück werfen, so sehen wir, daß vieles in unseren Verhaltensweisen der Kindererziehung wach geworden ist, was vor einem Jahrhundert undenkbar gewesen wäre. Pädagogische und psychologische Ideen haben einen großen Lernprozeß eingeleitet. Ich glaube, daß die Fähigkeit angestrebt werden sollte, Werte im Sinne einer „principled flexibility" zu vermitteln. Es müßte Modelle geben, die eine solche Erziehung auf der Basis der gemeinsamen Erarbeitung ermöglichen.

Bestimmte Probleme der Jugend kann man nicht verbessern, ohne die Einstellung der Elternpersonen, der Institutionen und Organisationen zu verändern, von denen die Jugendlichen abhängiger sind als andere Altersgruppen.

Der alle Bereiche umfassende soziale Wandel und die Krisen der Institutionen haben vielfältige Verunsicherungen zur Folge. Hieraus ergibt sich die Notwendigkeit zur Schaffung neuer Beratungsdienste, nicht nur der Schul- und Berufsberatungsstellen. Die Erziehung, die man jungen Leuten angedeihen läßt, komme der Vermittlung einer zweiten Selbstachtung gleich, schrieb La Rochefoucauld[13)] im 17. Jahrhundert. „Erziehung" im herkömmlichen Sinn genügt heutzutage nicht mehr, um das nötige Selbstvertrauen für die Aufgaben der Daseinsbewältigung zu gewinnen. Mit Instrumenten der Psychotherapie muß ein ins Detail gehendes und gezieltes Verständnis der Probleme der Jugend geschaffen werden. Die Reflexion über die so komplex gewordene Welt ist notwendig und die Mittel, um mit der eigenen Reflexion fertig zu werden, sind der Jugend in die Hand zu geben. Erziehung muß um jene Bewußtheit und um die Fähigkeit zur Selbstgestaltung erweitert werden, von deren Belastungen das 18. Jahrhundert in seinem Enthusiamus für Aufklärung noch keine Vorahnung besaß.

Ich möchte hier eine konkrete Anregung geben; ich glaube, daß auf verschiedenen Gebieten der Sozialarbeit gerade die Modellversuche aus dem sozialwissenschaftlich-psychologischen Bereich eine außerordentlich wichtige Funktion als Meßfühler dessen besitzen, was in einer Gesellschaft möglich und nötig ist. So würde sich ein Jugendzentrum empfehlen, das von Sozialarbeitern, der Jugend selber und von verschiedenen Wissenschaftlern als eine Art Modellversuch gestaltet werden könnte.

Ich schließe damit, daß ich sage, daß **Erziehung nicht mehr genügt.** Gerade die Alternsforschung und die Lebenszyklusforschung, die heute die Jugendforschung zu umgreifen und zum Teil in eine Lebenslaufforschung umzuwandeln beginnen, zeigen, wie wichtig die Aufrechterhaltung von aktiv erlebten Inhalten ist. Die Fähigkeit zur Wiederbelebung oder Wiedervergegenwärtigung von sinngebenden Inhalten in den späteren Lebensphasen ist unmöglich, wenn nicht in früher Jugend für Grundlagen gesorgt wurde, auf die zurückgegriffen werden kann. Die Gesellschaft wird an die Alten zahlen müssen, was sie den Jungen nicht zu erfüllen bereit ist.

1) Vgl. dazu Leopold Rosenmayr, Schwerpunkte der Jugendsoziologie, Band 6 des Handbuchs der empirischen Sozialforschung, herausgegeben von Rene König, Stuttgart 1976.

2) Jugend in Europa. Ihre Eingliederung in die Welt der Erwachsenen. Eine vergleichende Analyse zwischen der Bundesrepublik Deutschland, Frankreich und Großbritannien – 7. Shell-Studie zur Situation der Jugend, durchgeführt vom EMNID-Institut, bearbeitet von Viggo Graf Blücher, 3 Bde: Vorstudie; Tabellenteil; Kommentar. 1977.

3) Richter, Horst Eberhard, Eltern, Kind, Neurose, Reinbek 1969

4) Hill, John P., Adolescence, in: D. Allen und E. Seifman (Hrsg), Teacher's Handbook, Chicago 1970, S. 113

5) Rosenmayr, Leopold, Familienbeziehungen und Freizeitgewohnheiten jugendlicher Arbeiter, Wien 1963

6) Scheuch, Erwin K., Die Jugend gibt es nicht. Zur Differenziertheit der Jugend in heutigen Industriegesellschaften, in: Jugend in der Gesellschaft. Ein Symposium mit Beiträgen von H. v. Hentig, H. Lübbe, E.K. Scheuch, München 1975

7) Kaase, Max, Die politische Mobilisierung von Studenten in der BRD, in: K. Allerbeck und L. Rosenmayr (Hrsg.), Aufstand der Jugend? München 1971, S. 168ff

8) Jugend zwischen 13 und 24 – Vergleich über 20 Jahre – 6. Shell-Studie zur Situation der deutschen Jugend im Bundesgebiet, durchgeführt vom EMNID-Institut, bearbeitet von Viggo Graf Blücher, 3 Bde: Vorstudie; Tabellenteil; Kommentar, 1975

9) Jennings, Kent und Richard Niemi, The Political Character of Adolescence, Princeton 1974

10) Yankelovich, Daniel, Changing Youth Values in the 70's, New York 1974, S. 23

11) Coleman, James S., The Adolescent Subculture and Academic Achievement, in: American Journal of Sociology, Bd. 65 (1960)

12) Eisenstadt, Shmuel, Cultural Settings and the Adolescence around the Year 2000, in: J.P. Hill und F.J. Mönks (Hrsg.), Adolescence and Youth in Prospect, Guildford/ Surrey 1977, S. 119

13) La Rochefoucauld, Maximes et Memois, no. 98

Arbeitsgruppe Rosenmayr

Leitung: Inge Blatt

Blatt:

Ich glaube, daß Ihr Referat als Grundlage für unser Gespräch dienen sollte, und daß wir mit Fragen oder Meinungsäußerungen dazu beginnen. Bitte Themenvorschläge!

Rosenmayr:

Für mich sind nach allen hier angesprochenen Themen zwei Problemkreise sichtbar: Einmal Theorie des sozialen Wandels und damit verbunden die Frage: Ist dieser Wandel beeinflußbar durch die Jugend selber oder durch Jugendarbeit? Das andere war die Frage der Notwendigkeit, mobiler zu werden; was heißt das, und worin besteht das?

Darf ich mit der Notwendigkeit beginnen, mobiler zu werden? Ich hatte versucht, eine Formel zu beschreiben, die Principled Flexibility. Dies ist ein Begriff, der wichtig ist und der besagen soll, daß nicht in der reinen Anpassung, in der ich eher Opportunismus sehe, und auch nicht in dem Verharren auf Prinzipien, die sich immer wieder in der Produktion der gleichen sozialen Formen manifestieren – das wäre Traditionalismus –, die Lösung liegt. Denn weder im Traditionalismus oder reaktionärem Verhalten noch in opportunistischen Anpassungen oder in einem blinden und unreflektierten Progressivismus sehe ich die Möglichkeiten, sondern in der Suche nach grundlegenden, aber auf die Wandlungen beziehbaren Handlungsideen.

Flexibilität oder Mobilität heißt für mich, sich im Intellektuellen oder in den Überzeugungen sehr lange mit irgendwelchen Grundwerten wirklich auseinanderzusetzen, aber zu diesen Grundwerten so viele Zugänge zu suchen und für neue Zugänge so offen zu sein, daß selbst das, was ganz festgelegt scheint, wieder in einem neuen Licht auftaucht.

Ich habe gesagt, man muß lernen, sich zu ändern. Das meine ich. Dann hat Prof. Deutsch gesagt: mobiler werden. Was Wittgenstein die Überzeugung genannt hat, das muß allerdings berücksichtigt werden – mir scheint, es geht gar nicht anders, als sich auf dem Boden bestimmter Überzeugungen zu ändern, die Überzeugung in diesen Änderungsprozeß mitzunehmen und sich selbst zu transformieren.

Blatt:

Diese Notwendigkeit, mobiler zu werden, die Sie beschrieben haben, ist eigentlich etwas für die Erwachsenen, nicht für die Jugend. Denn die Jugend ist doch bereit, mobil zu sein.

Teilnehmer:

Ich sehe es aus der Praxis. Wir sagen z.B. einem jungen Mann, der Schlosser gelernt hat: Als Schlosser können wir dich im Moment nicht gebrauchen, aber du kannst bei uns Chemiefacharbeiter werden; wir können dich umschulen, du kannst mit deinen Fähigkeiten etwas anfangen, aber du mußt andere Dinge dazulernen.

Dann kommt das Problem: Warum hat man eigentlich den jungen Menschen nicht sehr viel früher jemand gesagt, daß das, was sie lernen, eventuell nach ihrer Lehre überholt ist. In diesem Zusammenhang sehe ich das Problem der Mobilität: das Erkennen, daß man eingeschlagene Wege früher als vor 20 Jahren ändern muß.

Blatt:

Das war ein sehr konkretes Beispiel aus der Praxis. Vielleicht sagt jeder kurz, woher er kommt.

Teilnehmer:
Ich bin bei der Shell und bin zuständig für Ausbildungswesen und Personalplanung.

Teilnehmer:

Ich bin Diplom-Pädagoge und arbeite im Moment hauptsächlich mit arbeitslosen Jugendlichen. „Mobilität" war mir auch zu diffus; Mobilität kann Verhaltensweise sein, kann sein, Modetrends mitzumachen, kann aber auch heissen, Mobilität im Beruf, im Wohnort.

Mobilität im Beruf muß zumindest für die Gruppe, mit der ich arbeite, konkret definiert werden. Sie glaubten, Jugendliche seien mobiler. Das mag für Modetrends gelten, aber nicht für den Wechsel des Wohnsitzes, um eine Lehrstelle zu bekommen. Dabei spielt auch die Frage eine Rolle, wie frei Jugendliche sind, sich so mobil zu verhalten, wie sie es möchten. Daher sollte jeder, der „Mobilität" sagt, hinzufügen, welche er meint.

Teilnehmer:
Ich bin Schulleiter einer berufsbildenden Schule. Was eben angesprochen wurde, war die berufliche Mobilität. Wir haben das Thema aber weiter gespannt: es geht allgemein um die gesellschaftliche Mobilität, die Fähigkeit, sich entsprechend der Wandlung der Gesellschaft und der Umwelt umzustellen. Ich glaube, wenn man Mobilität in diesem Sinn erreichen will, kommt es darauf an, daß die Menschen Methoden lernen, wie sie sich ihre Umwelt erschließen

und sie verstehen können, wie sie sich mit dieser Umwelt auseinandersetzen und an ihrer Neugestaltung teilnehmen können.

Teilnehmer:
Auch ich empfehle, sich den Begriff der Mobilität näher anzusehen, ihn zu strukturieren. Er wurde in diese Diskussion von vornherein ein wenig aufwertend hineingebracht. Das hing mit der Empfehlung von Prof. Deutsch zusammen, daß die Mobilisierung der Kräfte das Heilmittel gegenüber den Bedrohungen der globalen Entwicklung auf längere Sicht sei.

Ob man eine Verhaltensweise aber Mobilität oder Labilität nennt, ist in bezug auf die äußere Erscheinung zunächst einmal das gleiche. Eine Interpretation wird man erst dann finden, wenn man weiß, wie Mobilität funktional wirken soll. Sie kann bei der Jugend zu Unsicherheiten und zu Entwicklungen führen, die in keiner Weise wünschenswert wären. Man könnte auch den Begriff Labilität anwenden, wenn nicht vorher klar ist, auf welcher Plattform die Mobilität beginnt.

Rosenmayr:

Es ist ausgedrückt worden, daß Mobilität ein vieldimensionaler Begriff ist. Sie waren etwas unsicher. Sie haben gefunden, der wichtigste Zugang sei der vom Beruflichen her. Darüber ist schon Einigkeit erzielt worden. Ich habe versucht, den Mobilitätsbegriff auch von den Überzeugungen her zu erläutern, weil ich so beglückt war, daß sowohl von Deutsch als auch heute früh von Daniel Bell die Fragen der grundlegenden Wertorientierung des Menschen in die Diskussion einbezogen wurden.

Wie verschiedener Meinung man auch über diese Werte sein kann, ich halte es für richtig, es nicht bloß bei der Anpassung oder den unendlich wichtigen Fragen der Veränderung im Beruflichen zu belassen, sondern auch die anderen Elemente einzubeziehen. Ich bin sehr froh, daß Blücher zum Schluß gesagt hat: bei aller Betonung der Notwendigkeit, schon den jungen Menschen eine Fähigkeit zu vermitteln, die er vielfach anwenden kann, ist es auch notwendig, gewisse Festpunkte zu vermitteln, Hilfen bei der Wertsuche zu geben.

Als Kind hat man mehr oder weniger mechanisch etwas gelernt. Dann stehen die Werte im Vordergrund. Dann kommen Spannungen mit den Eltern, Entdeckung der Sexualität, Freunde, eine neue Umwelt-Auseinandersetzung. Da dient es, wenn bei dieser Erstellung eines Wertgefüges irgendwelche Hilfen gegeben werden. Das ist manchmal sehr schwer. Die Erzieher wissen, daß man, je mehr man hilft, um so mehr abschrecken kann.

Ich hielte es für außerordentlich wichtig, wenn Sie noch weiter etwas über die Beschränkung der Beweglichkeit bei arbeitsuchenden Jugendlichen sagen könnten.

Teilnehmer:

Ich bekomme die Jugendlichen dadurch, daß es in Nordrhein-Westfalen die Pflicht gibt, ein zehntes Schuljahr zu machen, wenn man keinen Ausbildungsplatz hat. Wir machen einwöchige Lehrgänge, um auch das Sozialverhalten zu schulen. Wir vermitteln Kontakte mit Berufsberatern oder mit Personalchefs und Ausbildern von Firmen.

Wir haben z.B. von der Firma Demag Personalchefs zum Einstellungstest eingeladen, weil sie gewerbliche Lehrlinge brauchen. Wir haben das mit einer Klasse getestet. Von den ca. 30 Schülern hätten zwei Drittel halbwegs ihren Wunschberuf ergreifen können. Dann wurde bei den Eltern angefragt, und nur zwei durften schließlich weg. Das war eine Mobilität um 60 km. Allein 20 km Weg ist schon ein Hemmnis. Das kann man mit dem Mofa nicht ganz schaffen, und da ist vor allen Dingen keine Unterstützung vom Elternhaus da.

Das Problem ist, daß die Eltern sich nicht in die heutige Lage hineindenken können. Ich glaube, daß da auch die allgemeinbildenden Schulen zum größten Teil versagt haben, daß sie die Bereitschaft nicht unterstützen und die Jugendlichen allein lassen. Wer hat denn schon mit 15 oder 16 den Mut, in eine wildfremde Stadt zu ziehen, wo er keinen kennt, und damit seinen Bezugskreis zu verlieren? Das muß man bedenken und nicht einfach sagen, Jugendarbeitslosigkeit ist eine Frage der Statistik.

Blatt:

Da kam die Problematik der Mobilität heraus. Es ist im Grunde eine Frage der Erwachsenen; in diesem Fall sind die Eltern nicht mobil genug.

Teilnehmer:

Man muß sich einmal klarmachen, daß eine der Voraussetzungen für Mobilität eine Dimension ist, die sich Bereitschaft zur Mobilität nennt und die in den Jugendlichen oder Erwachsenen angelegt sein muß. Das heißt, daß offensichtlich die Bereitschaft zur Mobilität in frühester Kindheit anerzogen werden muß wie ein Persönlichkeitsentzug. Das kann man sich ganz praktisch vorstellen. Die Bereitschaft zur Mobilität entsteht auf dem Hintergrund dessen, was in der Wissenschaft offene Persönlichkeit heißt. Dafür sind z.B. Erziehungsstile kennzeichnend, in denen ein Kind für irgendwelche Experimente nicht gleich bestraft wird, sondern die Eltern das Kind dafür loben; wo das Kind viel selbst machen darf und wenig vorgeschrieben bekommt. Wenn die Lehrer sich darüber wundern, daß die Jugendlichen sich nicht mehr rühren: Es könnte wirklich daran liegen, daß solche Erwachsenen- oder Jugendbildungsmaßnahmen zu spät einsetzen. Man müßte bei den Eltern beginnen.

Teilnehmer:

Ich möchte dagegen sprechen. Hier wird die Mobilität als positive Einstellung oder Persönlichkeitsqualität dargestellt. Ich möchte die These aufstellen, daß die Weigerung, Mobilität zu zeigen, heutzutage auch eine Notwehrmaßnahme des Jugendlichen ist. Man sollte bedenken, daß die Sozialstrukturen im Laufe der Veränderung unserer ganzen sozialen Umwelt mehr und mehr zerstört werden. Das geht bis in die Familien, wo die Bindungen immer brüchiger werden. Man braucht sich nur die Scheidungsquoten anzusehen. Diese Verunsicherung führt notwendigerweise zu einer Reaktion. Die Reaktion ist die Weigerung, Mobilität zu zeigen.

Sicher ist viel Wahres an dem, was Sie gesagt haben: Erziehung zur offenen Persönlichkeit, Erziehung, die Wachstum ermöglicht. Aber man darf nicht vergessen, daß eine stabile Persönlichkeit nicht möglich ist ohne ein stabiles soziales Netz. Ich habe einfach keine Lust, wenn ich an einem Arbeitsplatz bin – ich bin beim Deutschlandfunk in Köln –, wenn ich in Köln gearbeitet und gewohnt habe, mir einen Bekanntenkreis aufgebaut und Freunde gefunden habe, nach kurzer Zeit diesen Arbeitsplatz wieder zu verlassen, nur weil die marktwirtschaftliche Situation es von mir verlangt.

Ich habe das einmal gemacht. Ich weiß aus eigener Erfahrung, was das für Identitätsprobleme mit sich bringt. Das möchte ich dagegenstellen.

Rosenmayr:

Ich sehe hier eine Konfliktsituation, aus der es keinen einfachen Ausweg gibt. Es ist festzustellen, daß die Eltern die Mobilität der Kinder einschränken. Das ist zu korrigieren. Auf der anderen Seite haben Sie erwähnt, daß ein Netzwerk von Fremden Sicherheit gibt, stützt und gezielter anzuregen vermag als vieles Andere. Ich bin sicher der Meinung, daß es viele Probleme mit sich bringt, einen Menschen aus seinen Bezugsgruppen – Gruppen mit denen er irgendwie ein Selbstgefühl entwickelt und mit denen er sich identifiziert – herauszureißen. Man will nicht das Schicksal der Wanderarbeiter und Emigranten ab dem 18. und 19. Jahrhundert. Das ist wohl ein Wertkonflikt.

Graf Blücher:

Ich möchte Ihnen für zweierlei danken: erstens, daß Sie den Wertbegriff noch anschaulicher hereingebracht haben, zweitens, daß Sie so deutlich davon gesprochen haben, daß jetzt in der Diskussion die horizontale Mobilität gemeint ist. Wir hatten die horizontale Mobilität schon im Zusammenhang mit der beruflichen Mobilität erwähnt: 60 km entfernte Arbeit aufnehmen, ebenso die Abhängigkeit von der personalen Mobilität: einen neuen Kreis suchen.

Wir haben jetzt drei neue Begriffe von Mobilität. Es fehlt noch die vertikale und die personale Mobilität ganz allgemein, d.h. die Offenheit für Veränderungen. Mobilität als solche ist weder gut noch böse. Die Bewertung entscheidet sich erst daran, wenn man die Folgen sieht. Wenn damit die Welt gerettet wird, dann ist sie gut. Wenn damit eine Person so hin- und hergerissen wird, daß sie kein Zuhause mehr hat, dann ist sie schlecht.

Wäre es nicht besser, einen Begriff auszuwählen, z.B. das angeschnittene Problem der beruflichen Mobilität, weil es am einfachsten zu diskutieren ist und die Probleme am deutlichsten sind? Ich weiß nicht, ob man sich entschließt, die Diskussion so zu beschränken, aber damit ginge nicht alles so schrecklich durcheinander.

Für das, was Sie wollen, sind Ihre fertig Ausgebildeten falsch ausgebildet worden. Sie sind nicht fürs Lernen ausgebildet worden. Sie sind beruflich festgelegt. Das kann gut sein, wenn man so lange sucht, bis man ein entsprechendes Ziel gefunden hat. Das kann schlecht sein, wenn es bewirkt, daß sich auf die Dauer ein unglückliches Berufsschicksal entwickelt. Horizontale Mobilität von 60 km, Wechsel des Freundeskreises ist wahrscheinlich nicht so schlimm wie ein verfehltes Berufsleben.

Blatt:

Ich wäre schon dafür, daß wir uns auf die berufliche Mobilität beschränken. Aber in allen Beiträgen ist zum Ausdruck gekommen, daß die personale Mobilität die berufliche Mobilität wesentlich mitbestimmt. Wir müssen beide sehen.

Teilnehmer:

Sie haben gesagt: ich habe keine Lust, mich zu verändern. – Das ist richtig und verständlich. Aber die Frage ist doch, ob man den Jugendlichen mit einer solchen Antwort wirklich hilft. Es ist nichts Neues, daß Jugendliche mobil sein müssen, gerade in der Ausbildung. Mit der Trennung vom Elternhaus muten wir dem jungen Menschen nicht mehr zu, als wir ihm immer zugemutet haben. Man sollte auch den erzieherischen Wert sehen, der darin besteht, daß der Jugendliche sich in einer neuen Umgebung durchboxt und auf diese Weise mit seine Persönlichkeit bildet.

Rosenmayr:

Sehr gut ist durch den letzten Diskussionsbeitrag der Gesichtspunkt der Familie herausgekommen. Früher hat den Eltern das Herumwandern ihrer Kinder in anderen Haushalten zum Lernen gar nichts ausgemacht, das war selbstverständlich. Erst die starke Mutter-Kind-Bindung, die ein neues Produkt des 18. und 19. Jahrhunderts ist, hat die Abschirmung gegenüber der Mobilität aufgebracht.

Nun ist es die Frage, ob wir bei dieser bürgerlichen Abschirmung des Kindes unbedingt verharren müssen. Aber ich glaube, wir können die Geschichte nicht zurückdrehen. Doch muß sowohl Festigkeit vermittelt als auch Mobilität ermöglicht werden.

Arbeitsgruppe Rosenmayr

Teilnehmer:

Es wurde gesagt, die Jugendlichen sollten sich damit abfinden, daß sie womöglich umlernen müssen. Ich glaube, es ist eine große Gefahr, das als Mobilität zu bezeichnen, was im Prinzip Anpassung ist. Wir verlangen von den Jugendlichen Mobilität und meinen, daß sie sich an die Verhältnisse anpassen, die die Gesellschaft oder die Wirtschaft ihnen aufzwingt. Ich glaube, daß man Mobilität in Verbindung mit Freiheit, und zwar nicht Freiheit, die von oben aufgedrängt ist, sehen sollte. Sondern ich sehe darin die Chance, daß Jugendliche die Möglichkeit haben müssen, Perspektiven zu erkennen.

Für dieses Symposium besteht eine Aufgabe darin, zu überlegen, inwieweit ein Mobilitätsbegriff formuliert werden kann, der ausklammert, daß man sich Mobilität von oben aufzwingen lassen muß, und vielmehr den Jugendlichen die Chance gibt, von sich aus Mobilität zu zeigen.

Teilnehmer:

Ich finde das sehr wichtig. Heute morgen ist immer von den objektiven Prozessen gesprochen worden, davon, was sich verändern wird: Bevölkerungszahlen, Verstädterung usw. Man ist geneigt, stillschweigend davon auszugehen, der Jugendliche hätte sich diesen objektiven Prozessen anzupassen. Was wichtig ist: Wie reagiert der Jugendliche auf sie, wie weit kann er ihnen einen Sinn abgewinnen?

Prof. Rosenmayr hat davon gesprochen, daß die Wertprävalenz oder Sinnprävalenz bei Jugendlichen oft nötiger geworden ist. Der Jugendliche wird sich zunächst einmal den Herausforderungen der objektiven Verläufe nicht so stellen, daß er sich ihnen anpaßt, sondern daß er versucht, ihnen einen Sinn zu geben, daß er seine persönliche Identität in allen Veränderungen bewahren kann. Daher wäre es notwendig, die Frage der subjektiven Identität und des Sinns anzusprechen.

Wenn Mobilität darin besteht, sich diesen Prozessen anzupassen, lehne ich sie ab. Es muß auch die Wahlfreiheit bestehen, sich auf gewisse Mobilitätsanforderungen negierend zu verhalten. Das wäre eine Erweiterung der Mobilität im Sinn geistiger Ablehnung.

Teilnehmer:

Ich glaube, daß die Immobilität auch Ausdruck eines in unserer Gesellschaft weit verbreiteten Symptoms ist, nämlich der Trennungsangst.

Ich meine, wir müssen erst eimal als Faktum akzeptieren, daß wir mit Menschen zusammenleben, die nicht diese offene Persönlichkeit besitzen, die Sie in Ihrem Beitrag als so erstrebenswert angesehen haben, diese offene Persönlichkeit, die in der Lage ist, immer wieder neue Kontakte herzustellen. Wenn wir sehen, welche Probleme Studenten in psychologischen Beratungsstellen vortragen, sind es immer wieder Kontaktschwierigkeiten.

Es ist heutzutage notwendig, soziale Beziehungen, soziale Strukturen zu schaffen, die es dem einzelnen ermöglichen, seine Identitätsschwierigkeiten, seine Trennungsängste nicht als derart bedrängend zu erleben, daß er nicht mehr in der Lage ist, seine eigenen Interessen zu sehen und sie auch durchzusetzen. Wenn man erkennt, daß berufliche und personale Mobilität in einer komplexen Gesellschaft notwendig ist, und wenn man diese komplexe Gesellschaft bejaht, dann muß man sich auch Gedanken darüber machen, wie man die sozialen Strukturen bereitstellt – nicht nur für die Jugendlichen, aber vor allen Dingen für die Jugendlichen –, die Sicherheit bieten.

Teilnehmer:

Überspitzt formuliert: Wenn man bestimmte Mobilitätsforderungen stellt, dann soll man gleichzeitig für die Kommunikationsformen sorgen, in denen diese gesteigerte Mobilität im zwischenmenschlichen Bereich kompensiert werden kann.

Teilnehmer:

Es sind mehrere Forderungen gestellt worden, was man den Jugendlichen vermitteln soll. Dazu müssen wir aber auch klären, wer das macht und wie das gemacht wird.

Ich will ein Beispiel aus meiner beruflichen Praxis bringen. Ich bin bei der Friedrich-Ebert-Stiftung. Wir haben auch mit Jugendlichen zu tun. Wir haben in der Jugendbildung in Heimvolkshochschulen, wie wir sie betreiben, in den letzten Jahren einige neue Methoden und Formen entwickelt, die darin bestehen, daß man den jungen Leuten nicht mehr im schulischen Sinne etwas beibringt, sondern daß man auf ihre eigenen Bedürfnisse und auf ihre Lebenssituation eingeht und versucht, sie selber ihre Probleme erarbeiten zu lassen.

Nur haben wir in letzter Zeit beobachtet – ich habe mich mit Kollegen öfter darüber unterhalten –, daß diese Art der Seminare mit Jugendlichen sehr viel schwieriger geworden ist. Vor etlichen Jahren sprudelte noch Aktivität. Es war überhaupt kein Problem, die Jugendlichen zu motivieren. Jetzt beobachtet man, daß es unwahrscheinlicher Anstrengungen bedarf, damit sie überhaupt aus sich herauskommen. Da sitzen Jugendliche, die zweifellos in vielen Bereichen desorientiert sind. Sie scheinen unsicher und nicht in der Lage zu sein, ihre eigenen Probleme zu artikulieren. Was machen wir, wenn wir einen Ausweg finden wollen? – Das einfachste wäre, ihnen die Sicherheit wiederzugeben, indem wir wieder Werte und Normen vorgeben.

Sie haben gesagt, im Prozeß des Erwachsenwerdens ist ein Zeitraum, wo die Jugendlichen ihre Werte suchen. Da müssen wir ihnen etwas anbieten. Ich würde gern von den Wissenschaftlern hören, welche Möglichkeiten es gibt.

Arbeitsgruppe Rosenmayr

Rosenmayr:

Ich habe keine Zauberantwort. Mir fällt auch auf – und zwar von der Beobachtung der Studenten –, was Sie über das geringe Aus-sich-Herausgehen gesagt haben. Ich bin nicht sicher, ob das nur der Leistungsdruck und die Angst ist, sich als nicht ganz qualifiziert zu erweisen. Es sind auch andere Faktoren, die dazu führen.

Teilnehmer:

Ein anderer Übertragungsmechanismus: Da man unbedingt etwas lernen muß, um überhaupt eine Arbeitsstelle zu finden, hat man sich daran gewöhnt, in jeder Schul- oder Lernsituation nach Effektivität zu suchen. Vielleicht sind diese Seminare, wo man sitzen und etwas aus sich heraus erarbeiten soll, den Jugendlichen zu zeitaufwendig.

Rosenmayr:

Es ist heute sehr wichtig, in der Lehre mit Methoden zu arbeiten, die sich nicht aufdrängen. Ich habe gruppendynamisch fortschrittliche Lehrer erlebt, die nur herumquatschen. Die große Hoffnung, die auf die an sich richtigen Gruppengespräche gesetzt wird, zerbricht, wenn das von Seiten der Pädagogen nicht gekonnt ist.

Teilnehmer:

In der Schule z.B. kann ein Gruppengespräch auch nicht funktionieren, weil es abgebrochen werden muß, wenn es läutet.

Rosenmayr:

Eine Erfahrung, die ich anbieten kann, ist, miteinander zu arbeiten, aber auch miteinander etwas zu tun und zu erleben. Ich weiß, wie das Zweier- und Dreiergruppen zusammenbindet. Dort lassen sich Überzeugungen, wenn sie mit dem Leben selbst ausagiert werden, geben und vermitteln.

Teilnehmer:

Daniel Bell hat eine ähnliche Definition gegeben: Dinge gemeinsam tun, daß man sie für verbindlich hält; Werte finden, die sich in gemeinsamem Handeln herausbilden.

Rosenmayr:

Ich verweise auf die These des Kinderpsychiaters und Kinderpsychologen Fritz Redl, der aufgezeigt hat, daß zwei extreme Typen überzeugend in Jugendgruppen arbeiten können: der, der radikal gewisse Werte leugnet, und der, der sehr strenge Werte setzt. Sie finden Gefolgschaft in den Gruppen. Aber woher bekommen wir diejenigen, die Werte wirklich überzeugend weitervermitteln? Ich glaube, daß man Persönlichkeiten stützen muß, die eine gewisse selbstreflektierende Radikalität in ihrer Existenz haben, und versuchen, sie in die Arbeit mit der jungen Generation zu involvieren.

Blücher:

Ich möchte warnen, ein solches Programm ohne psychologische Fachkenntnisse anzupacken. Der Soziologe sollte sich mit dem bescheiden, was er kann: feststellen, wo die Probleme liegen und dann dem Psychologen überlassen, die Dinge in Ordnung zu bringen.

Teilnehmer:

Ich möchte Graf Blücher widersprechen, daß man diese Dinge einfach ausblenden soll. Wenn ich Prof. Rosenmayr richtig verstanden habe, gehört zu einer Wertbildung so etwas wie Vorleben, aber auch in aller Radikalität und Konsequenz. Das erinnert mich an Ihren Diskussionsbeitrag gestern abend. Sie sagten, daß es heute leider sehr wenige erwachsene Menschen gebe, die den Jugendlichen etwas vorlebten, was akzeptiert und nachgeahmt werden kann. Ich glaube, das ist ein wichtiges Problem.

Teilnehmer:

Es geht um das eigene Verhalten. Man muß nicht permanent konsequent sein, allerdings glaubwürdig.

Teilnehmer:

Wir müßten dafür in größerem Maße Methodenlehre vermitteln, weil Inhalte sehr schnell veralten. Wie kann ich in vernünftigen Bahnen Auseinandersetzungen führen und zu einem eigenen Standpunkt gelangen? Die Methoden dafür gilt es zu vermitteln.

Teilnehmer:

Es kommt nicht so sehr auf Methoden an, sondern darauf, menschliche Zusammenhänge zu gestalten, die dem einzelnen als wachstumsfördernd erscheinen, die für ihn wirklich eine emotionale Qualität haben. Es geht um eine emotionale Qualität, die man am Arbeitsplatz findet. Das bedeutet, daß der einzelne sieht, daß er sich im Beruf, in seiner Arbeit verwirklichen kann. Solange das nicht möglich ist, helfen auch die besten Methoden nicht.

Rosenmayr:

Ein Beispiel einer sehr erfolgreichen Methode, das ich gerade gesehen habe, ist das System der Bewährungshilfe, wie es auf Grund eines Gesetzes in Österreich eingeführt worden ist, nach vielen Jahren Kampf und langer Vorbereitung. Es besteht darin, daß der Jugendrichter einen jugendlichen Delinquenten statt zu Freiheitsentzug zu Bewährungshilfe „verurteilt". Das heißt, daß der Jugendliche die Pflicht hat, sich einmal oder zweimal in der Woche mit einem Bewährungshelfer oder einer Bewährungshelferin zu treffen, und daß die gesamte Rehabilitation, z.B. Finden einer Lehre oder Anstellung, von dem Bewährungshelfer betreut wird. Das setzt weiter voraus, daß der Bewährungshelfer trachtet, in das System der jugendlichen Persönlichkeit Werte einzubringen, und versucht, in Anlehnung an sozialpädagogische Ideen von Freud gewisse Ersatzprozesse in Gang zu setzen. In gewisser Weise findet ein Übertragungsprozeß des Delinquenten gegenüber dem Bewährungshelfer statt, der vielleicht eine Bezugsfigur ist oder eine Vaterrolle einnimmt. Hinzu kommt – das macht die Methode erst gut –, daß der Bewährungshelfer in regelmäßigen Abständen mit einem hierfür spezialisierten Psychiater spricht und damit Supervision hat. Er berichtet über Lebensprobleme, die aus Übertragung und Gegenübertragung im Verhältnis zu dem Probanden herauskommen, und arbeitet auch seine emotionalen Probleme ab, so daß er nicht allein mit diesen oft schwierigen und konfliktreichen Persönlichkeiten dasteht, sondern eine Kontrolle hat.

Solche Methoden sind zu bejahen und notwendig.

Teilnehmer:

Ich glaube, daß vieles nur in Teamarbeit geht, mit gegenseitiger Kontrolle. Aber es dürfen keine neuen Abhängigkeitsverhältnisse aufgebaut werden. Methoden kann man nur erleben und erlernen im Team.

Teilnehmer:

Bei Jugendlichen liegen die Schwierigkeiten oft in ganz einfachen Dingen. Sie müssen im politischen Unterricht lernen, wie man überhaupt eine Sendung im Fernsehen analysieren kann, welche Schlüsse man daraus ziehen kann, wie man sich überhaupt informieren kann, über Telefon, Presse usw. Diese Methoden erst können zu einer Selbständigkeit führen.

Teilnehmer:

Zu der Bewährungshilfe: Wir haben es praktiziert, daß eine Patenschaft eingerichtet wird, wenn ein Mann durch Versetzung oder Neueinstellung in einen anderen Betrieb kommt. Das heißt, in den ersten Monaten kümmert sich ein Mitarbeiter persönlich um ihn, bis er sich voll eingelebt hat; nicht nur um seine Arbeit, um das ganze soziale Umfeld bis hin zur Wohnungssuche oder Freizeitgestaltung. Das sind Ansatzpunkte, mit denen Hilfestellung geleistet werden kann.

Blatt:

Da scheinen Ansätze von dem vorhanden zu sein, was hier gefordert wurde. – Wir haben noch nicht über die Formulierung eines Menschenbildes gesprochen, was ebenfalls vorgeschlagen wurde.

Teilnehmer:

Ich bin noch ein bißchen unzufrieden. Hier sind aber vielleicht Soziologen, die auf meine Frage eingehen können: Wie können in einer Welt, die im Fluß ist, in der Sozialisationseinrichtungen sich verändern, Verwandtschaftsbeziehungen nicht mehr die frühere Bedeutung haben, Nachbarschaftsstrukturen mehr und mehr zerstört werden, wie können da Alternativen geschaffen werden, und wie sehen sie aus?

Eine Vision, die so aussieht, daß wir ein Volk von Nomaden haben, die von einer Stadt zur anderen, von einem Arbeitsplatz zum anderen hüpfen, sich nur in Diskotheken aufhalten und nur fähig sind zu einem Small Talk an der Kneipentheke, finde ich nicht besonders schön. Eines scheint mir jedenfalls sicher: daß Alternativen angeboten werden müssen.

Graf Blücher:

Wir kommen nicht darum herum, den sozialen Kontext zu interpretieren. Es gibt gute Methoden, das genauer zu ermitteln; sie werden angewandt, wo es gelingt, sie zu finanzieren.

An sich sieht es mit den Gesellungsformen, den Gesellungsmöglichkeiten und den informellen Möglichkeiten, zueinander zu kommen, in der Jugend gar nicht so schlecht aus. Es hat über die Jahrzehnte Veränderungen von sehr intensiver, lebenslanger Bindung über eher freie Bindungen zu einer Form gegeben, die charakteristisch modern ist. Fast jeder hat einen Freund, wenn er gefragt wird. Es ist nun wieder Aufgabe vertiefter Untersuchungen, festzustellen, welcher Art diese Freundschaft ist. Fast jeder hat von einem bestimmten Alter an eine Freundin. Es gibt auch Möglichkeiten, informelle Gruppierungen zu erfassen, Beziehungen in Gruppierungen, die momentan fest sind. Es gibt an jedem Ort bestimmte Treffpunkte von Jugendlichen. Da versammeln sie sich eben, da ist ihre Domäne.

Die horizontale Mobilität eines jungen Menschen ist im allgemeinen in der Bundesrepublik durch eine Grenze eines Landkreises ausgedrückt. In bestimmten Altersklassen sind sie hochmobil. Sie sind nicht so fest gebunden, daß das Zerbrechen einer Freundschaft einen lebenslangen Schock bedeutet, sondern sie sind in der Lage, neue Beziehungen zu knüpfen. Das entspricht den Anforderungen und Voraussetzungen der mobilen Gesellschaft. Im grossen und ganzen haben sie schon ganz gute Kommunikationsformen entwickelt die der Lage durchaus angepaßt sind. Wir werden nicht gefragt, ob wir als Gesellschaft mobil sein wollen, die Gesellschaft schreibt uns das vor.

Rosenmayr:

Mich überzeugt nur teilweise meines Kollegen Blücher Hinweis darauf, daß bei Befragungen Freunde angegeben werden usw. Es gibt diesen Zwang, Freunde zu haben, der sich auch bei den Fragebogen-Auskünften niederschlägt. Aber ich glaube, daß irgendwo doch, zumindest unter gewissen Bildungsvoraussetzungen, ästhetischen Voraussetzungen oder Selbstproblematisierungen – das muß keineswegs nur immer mit dem Schüler verbunden sein –, durch den Zusammenschluß der politischen Jugend und des Sich-darstellen-Könnens in einem politischen Zielverständnis, so etwas wie das (versteckte) Empfinden von Gemeinsamkeit auftritt. Das ist eine wichtige, sehr schwer greifbare Sache, die weiter verfolgt gehört. Viele Menschen kommen heute viel früher in ihrem Leben darauf, wie einsam sie sind, schon lange vor der „Midlife-Crisis", deren Klischee mich nicht überzeugt.

Den Realismus des Herrn Ota Šik habe ich bewundert: Es muß Voraussetzungen geben, damit wir uns weiterentwickeln können. Aber ich bin trotzdem nicht der Meinung, daß die Veränderungen nur von dorther kommen können. Wir haben ein paar merkwürdige Daten über die Bereitschaft der Österreicher, in der Energiewirtschaft zu sparen, vom Institut für Empirische Sozialforschung. Wie nebulös das auch sein mag, ich halte es nicht für so aussichtslos, daß durch neue Lebensstile und durch soziale Bewegungen Bedürfnisse auftreten, die auch für die Politiker – aus welchen Gründen auch immer – wichtig sein mögen.

Ich war bestürzt über die Aussage: früher mit religiösen Werten, heute mit Wissenschaft. Verstehen Sie mich recht, daß es gar nichts Traditionalistisches sein muß, sich mit den Problemen der Religion zu beschäftigen. Ich habe es nur andeuten können, daß es sehr interessant war, wie 1968/69 gerade von Marcuse her der Kampf gegen den Primat der Zweckrationalität in und durch Wissenschaft gekommen ist. Diesen Kampf haben Habermas und Marcuse selber mit der Vernunft zu begründen versucht, das große Dach zu machen. Wie ich glaube, gibt es jedoch sehr verschiedene Wege. Das ist mein „Positivismus."
Einerseits glaube ich an die strengen Grenzen der Wissenschaft, andererseits an die ganz anderen Wege, menschliche Kenntnisse und Erfahrungen zu bilden. Daher jagt es mir Schauer über den Rücken, wenn die Religion durch die Wissenschaft ersetzt werden soll. Ich sage das absichtlich hart, weil das genau der Punkt von Säkularisierung ist, über den wir jetzt ein bißchen hinauszukommen imstande sind.

Graf Blücher:

Vielleicht kommen wir ganz bewußt doch zu einer mehr grundsätzlichen

Argumentation. Ich könnte mir vorstellen, daß nicht eine bestimmte Epoche gemeint war. Natürlich war es nicht nur Religion, Religiosität, es war eine Haltung: du mußt dich so verhalten, eine Form von Über- und Unterordnung, die von Spranger in seinen Untersuchungen hervorragend geschildert worden ist. Es war eine feste Ordnung, zu der die Religion als ein schirmendes Dach gehörte, das alles motivierte, aber nicht als ganz persönliche Religiosität des einzelnen.

Dann haben wir die Freisetzung erlebt, nicht nur in der Jugend, in der gesamten Gesellschaft. Es wurden überall Entwicklungen freigesetzt, es kam der Fortschrittswahn, der Wachstumswahn, ein grenzenloser Optimismus. Charakteristisch für diese Epoche ganz allgemein – das läßt sich auf viele Einzelheiten rückkoppeln – ist vielleicht das optimistische Buch „Ihr werdet es erleben", in dem ein grenzenloser Fortschrittsglaube entwickelt wird, natürlich immer unter der Voraussetzung eines ungestörten Szenario.

Dann kam die große Enttäuschung. Die Energieprognosen waren leider falsch, die Araber machten Schwierigkeiten. Gerade zur richtigen Zeit, als die Energiekrise kam, kamen die Bücher des Club of Rome. Es gab eine regelrechte Reaktion auf den Fortschrittsglauben mit all den Erscheinungen auf das, was unser Leben heute so gefährlich macht. Plötzlich wurde das Nullwachstum postuliert.

Es war eine sehr starke Besinnung auf Werte, die wir in der vergangenen Epoche schon fast vergessen hatten. Wenn jetzt gefordert wird, emotionale Bindungen vor Mobilität zu setzen, hat das mit Werten, die der Soziologe wertfrei registriert, nichts mehr zu tun. Dann sehen wir, daß zur Zeit die Grundrichtung mindestens in Form der Besinnung verläuft. Man denkt über alles nach, man stellt die bisherigen eigenen Erkenntnisse in Frage. Diese Diskussion, wie sie hier gelaufen ist, ist auch kein Zufall. Ich denke, daß über Probleme sprechen auch schon ein Schritt ist, vielleicht besser als Methoden, die rezeptartig angewandt werden.

Blatt:

Ich glaube, es war gut, daß Sie uns noch einmal den Wandel der Werte in den letzten Jahren bei uns vor Augen geführt haben.

Teilnehmer:

Was wird höher eingeschätzt, Freundschaftsbeziehung oder beruflicher Aufstieg?

Graf Blücher:

Das ist keine Alternative, das hängt von der Situation ab. Das kann man nicht generell entscheiden. Aber man kann eines lernen – das ist ein Appell an die

Arbeitsgruppe Rosenmayr

Pädagogen – : die jungen Leute müssen entscheiden lernen. Sie müssen lernen, Rangordnungen aufzustellen, in ihren Lebenszielen, auch in ihren emotionalen Zielen. Schlimm scheint mir nur die Entscheidungslosigkeit, das Sich-treiben-Lassen. Wenn man schon umzieht, weil man sich beruflich verändern muß, dann muß man wissen, was man in Kauf nimmt. Wenn man auf etwas verzichtet, muß man wissen, ob einem das soviel wert ist. Diese Entscheidungsfähigkeit kann man lernen.

Teilnehmer:

Nach der Aufsplitterung der politischen Jugend Ende der sechziger/Anfang der siebziger Jahre war wohl feststellbar, daß für die Jugendlichen die Zweierbeziehung wieder an Wert gewann und daß in diese Zweierbeziehung die emotionalen Qualitäten, wie sie gestern abend angesprochen wurden, Zärtlichkeit, Vertrauen usw., wieder einfließen. Ich glaube, das ist ablesbar. Ich sehe Tendenzen, daß persönliche Beziehungen in Form der Zweierbeziehung und aktive Besinnung wieder an Wert gewinnen.

Rosenmayr:

Ich glaube, das war das Schlußwort. Ich danke der Diskussionsleiterin.

Zusammenfassung Arbeitsgruppe Rosenmayr

Diskussions- oder Arbeitsgruppen können kaum vorherbestimmt werden. Zahlreiche Zufälligkeiten – ganz abgesehen vom Zeitfaktor – wie Mentalität oder Interessenlage der Teilnehmer, die spontan gewählte Reihenfolge der Themen, abweichende oder insistierende Gedankengänge und andere Dinge mehr bestimmen weitgehend das Ergebnis solcher Gruppen.

So kam es, daß sich die Arbeitsgruppe mit Prof. Rosenmayr in lebhafter und engagierter Diskussion den Begriff „Mobilität" im weitesten Sinn erarbeitete. Das zweite vorgesehene Thema aber, die Theorie des sozialen Wandels und die Möglichkeiten der Jugendlichen bzw. der Jugendarbeit, diese Entwicklung mitzugestalten, kam zu kurz und konnte nur in zwei abschließenden Stellungnahmen von Prof. Graf Blücher und Prof. Rosenmayr gestreift werden.

Zur Mobilität: Es wurden zwei verschiedene Begriffe herausgearbeitet, die horizontale und die personale Mobilität. Die erstere umfaßt sowohl Mobilität im Beruf, als auch damit verbunden Mobilität in der Wahl des Wohnorts. Dieser Gedankengang führte zur personalen Mobilität, der Bereitschaft zum Wechsel persönlicher Bezugsgruppen und, weiter gefaßt, der Offenheit für gesellschaftliche Veränderungen.

Es stellte sich heraus, daß Mobilität durchaus nicht nur zu positiven Ergebnissen führen muß. Besonders die personale Mobilität, untrennbar verbunden mit der horizontalen, kann Unsicherheit, Identitätsverlust und endlich Labilität zur Folge haben.

Prof. Graf Blücher: *„Mobilität als solche ist weder gut noch böse, die Bewertung entscheidet sich erst dann, wenn man die Folgen sieht."*

Aus diesem Grund betonte Prof. Rosenmayr die Notwendigkeit, den Jugendlichen neben der Mobilitätsbereitschaft auch Festpunkte zu vermitteln, Hilfen bei ihrer Wertsuche anzubieten.

„Es muß sowohl Festigkeit vermittelt als auch Mobilität ermöglicht werden."

Immobilität als bewußte Weigerung der Jugendlichen, sich wirtschaftlichen und gesellschaftlichen Zwängen anzupassen und Immobilität als Folge unbewußter Trennungsängste wurden angesprochen. Dabei erhob sich aus dem Teilnehmerkreis die Forderung nach Bereitstellung sozialer Strukturen, menschlicher Kommunikationsformen, die die Unsicherheiten gesteigerter Mobilität im zwischenmenschlichen Bereich kompensieren könnten.

Einen breiten Raum nahm die Diskussion über die Methoden ein, Mobilitätsbereitschaft zu lehren. Prof. Rosenmayr führte als richtungsweisendes Beispiel das System der österreichischen Bewährungshilfe an.

Zusammenfassung Arbeitsgruppe Rosenmayr

„Man muß miteinander arbeiten, aber auch miteinander etwas tun, etwas erleben. Ich weiß, wie das Zweier- und Dreiergruppen zusammenbindet. Dann lassen sich Überzeugungen, wenn sie mit dem Leben selbst ausagiert werden, geben und vermitteln."

Folgender Diskussionsbeitrag Prof. Graf Blüchers mag als abschließende Beurteilung des Mobilitätsproblems gelten: *„Wir werden nicht gefragt, ob wir als Gesellschaft mobil sein wollen, die Gesellschaft schreibt uns das vor."*

Zur Theorie des sozialen Wandels wurde – wie schon erwähnt – wenig gesagt. Prof. Graf Blücher führte den Teilnehmern in einem Beitrag den Wandel gesellschaftlicher Werte in den letzten Jahren vor Augen.

Prof. Rosenmayr wies für die Zukunft und in bezug auf die Möglichkeiten der jungen Generation darauf hin, daß er wissenschaftlich begründete Systemveränderung nur für eine der notwendigen Voraussetzungen hält, und daß seiner Überzeugung nach in den Menschen zahlreiche andere geistige Innovationsmöglichkeiten angelegt seien.

„Wie ich glaube, gibt es doch sehr verschiedene Wege. Einerseits glaube ich an die strengen Grenzen der Wissenschaft, andererseits an die ganz anderen Wege, menschliche Kenntnisse und Erfahrungen zu bilden."

Gedanken zum Problem der Jugendarbeitslosigkeit aus der Sicht eines Unternehmens

Johannes C. Welbergen

Bis vor kurzem noch stand im Vordergrund der Bemühungen praktisch aller gesellschaftlicher Gruppen, den Menschen von der Arbeit zu entlasten. Das Schlagwort von der „Befreiung des Menschen von der Arbeit" machte die Runde, so als ob Arbeit nur eine Last sei und nicht auch etwas Sinngebendes. Heute denken wir vorrangig darüber nach, was zu tun ist, möglichst vielen Menschen wieder genügend Arbeit zu verschaffen. Wir werden uns auch zukünftig damit auseinanderzusetzen haben, wie wir den Menschen sinnvoll von Arbeit entlasten können, gleichzeitig aber dafür sorgen müssen, daß genügend Arbeitsplätze vorhanden sind. Es kann dabei kein „entweder – oder" geben. So gesehen ist Arbeitsbeschaffung ein zusätzliches Problem, das bewältigt werden muß, besonders im Interesse der jungen Generation, denn Arbeitslosigkeit bedeutet nicht nur finanzielle Einschränkung, sondern gleichzeitig das Gefühl, überflüssig zu sein.

Die Jugend wird in den nächsten 10 Jahren mit großen Schwierigkeiten zu kämpfen haben. Sie wird mehr Hindernisse auf ihrem Weg zur Ausbildung überwinden müssen als die vorausgegangene. Es ist daher eine der Aufgaben dieses Symposiums, die Ursachen und Wirkungen zu analysieren und Wege aufzuzeigen, die helfen können, das Problem zu lösen.

Gegenwärtige Lage und zukünftige Entwicklung

Studiert man in Abhandlungen die Probleme der kommenden Generation, so findet man früher oder später die Bezeichnung „chancengeminderte Generation", wobei ich lieber sagen würde „geforderte Generation". Die starken Jahrgänge von 1954 bis 1964 mit einem Anstieg der Geburten um 34 % auf rund 1,1 Millionen pro Jahr, der sogenannte Geburtenberg, ist jetzt Schülerberg oder aber im Übergang zur Ausbildung.

Der Höhepunkt bei den Schulabsolventen der Haupt- und Sonderschulen wird im nächsten Jahr erreicht sein und damit wohl auch der Höhepunkt in der Nachfrage nach Ausbildungsplätzen im dualen Bereich.

1981 wird der Höhepunkt der Abgänge von Schülern mit mittlerer Reife und 1984 der Höhepunkt der Abgänger mit Hochschulreife erreicht sein. Mit anderen Worten: auf den Schülerberg wird der Studentenberg folgen.

Während wir dies konstatieren, stellen wir gleichzeitig fest, daß sowohl unser Bildungs- als auch unser Beschäftigungssystem von krisenhaften Erscheinungen gekennzeichnet ist: Eine asthmatische Wirtschaftsentwicklung mit rund

H.Lübbe

1 Million Arbeitslosen und einem Rückgang der Arbeitsplätze einerseits sowie übervollen Universitäten und einer zunehmenden Zahl von Erwerbssuchenden andererseits.

Nach verschiedenen Prognosen wird das deutsche Arbeitskräfteangebot zwischen 1985 und 1990 um ein bis zwei Millionen Personen höher sein als 1975. Will man Vollbeschäftigung erreichen, so bedeutet dies, daß bis zum Zeitraum 1985/90 zwei bis drei Millionen Arbeitsplätze zusätzlich geschaffen werden müssen.

Zusammengefaßt kann man sagen, daß die größten Schwierigkeiten in den kommenden 10 Jahren liegen werden.

Aber auch in den 90er Jahren wird es Schwierigkeiten geben, allerdings mit umgekehrtem Vorzeichen. Aufgrund der demographischen Entwicklung und der heutzutage sehr schwachen Geburtenjahrgänge ist nämlich ab 1990 mit einem Tendenzumschwung auf dem Arbeitsmarkt zu rechnen. Die Verknappung des Arbeitskräftepotentials wird dann erneut zur limitierenden Größe für die wirtschaftliche Entwicklung in der Bundesrepublik Deutschland werden. Die Ursache ist klar: Mitte der 60er Jahre gab es in der Spitze rund 1,1 Millionen Geburten pro Jahr; gegenwärtig sind es nur rund 600.000.

Wenn wir also heute nach Lösungsmöglichkeiten für die in den nächsten zehn Jahren vor uns liegenden Schwierigkeiten suchen, dürfen wir den zu erwartenden Umbruch zu Beginn der 90er Jahre nicht außer acht lassen. Mit anderen Worten: Die Maßnahmen, die wir heute ergreifen, müssen flexibel und umkehrbar sein; das erleichtert die Aufgabe natürlich nicht.

Ich habe eben einen Blick in die Zukunft versucht. Aus eigener Erfahrung im Umgang mit Prognosen erscheint mir hier gleich ein Wort der Warnung angebracht. Prognosen sind notwendig, aber sie sind mit Unsicherheiten behaftet. Man sollte deshalb auch die Prognosetechnik verbessern und in Szenarien denken, d.h. mehrere mögliche Entwicklungen darstellen, um so die Unsicherheiten besser in den Griff zu bekommen. Analysiert man einmal Prognosen aus der Vergangenheit, fällt auf, daß man sich oft geirrt hat. Ich denke beispielsweise an die 1964 von Alexander Picht mit dem Schlagwort vom „Bildungsnotstand" vorhergesagte Bildungskatastrophe. Aber ich könnte Ihnen auch aus meiner eigenen Branche Irrtümer nennen.

Darüber hinaus bin ich der Meinung, daß Prognosen häufig die Findigkeit und Fähigkeit des Menschen unterschätzen, mit den prognostizierten Schwierigkeiten fertig zu werden. Für mich gilt daher der Satz, daß erkannte Probleme bereits halb gelöste Probleme sind.

Neben den durch die sogenannten Schüler- und Studentenberge sich ergebenden Herausforderungen muß man auch die Konflikte ansprechen, die daraus resultieren, daß Bildungswunsch und Arbeitsmarktrealität zunehmend auseinanderfallen. Während Ende der 50er Jahre nur 5 % eines Jahrgangs Abitur machten, sind es heute rund 20 %. Zwar ist der Anteil der Abiturienten, die in die Universitäten drängen, seit kurzem rückläufig, absolut gesehen jedoch immer noch steigend. Ein neuer Berg droht, der Akademikerberg. Lösungsansätze sind vorhanden, ich werde sie später skizzieren.

Wir sehen uns heute in der Wirtschaft mit der Tatsache konfrontiert, einen gespaltenen Arbeitsmarkt zu haben. Wir haben einerseits einen Mangel an qualifizierten Facharbeitern, andererseits aber einen Überschuß an Akademikern. Das ist zum Teil eine Folge der Vorurteile gegen handwerkliche Berufe – deren Beherrschung heute oft höhere geistige Fähigkeiten voraussetzt als früher – und der materiellen Überbewertung akademischer Berufe. Sicher ist dies auch eine Folge der Tatsache, daß den jungen Leuten eingebleut wurde: je höher die Qualifikation, desto besser die Chancen.

Dies war früher richtig, trifft heute jedoch nur noch bedingt zu. Ich denke hierbei z.B. an jene Studenten, die glauben, durch Aufnahme eines Doppelstudiums ihre Berufschancen erhöhen zu können.

Dies ist ein Trugschluß, denn durch Doppelstudium und allzu langen Aufenthalt auf der Hochschule wird die arbeitsbezogene Qualifikation nicht immer erhöht. Oft verschlechtern sich die Berufschancen sogar, weil der Jungakademiker dann in der Regel zu spät ins Berufsleben eintritt und darüber hinaus zu wenig praktisch ausgebildet ist.

Eine große Zahl von Studierenden wird, wie es heute heißt, keinen „der Ausbildung adäquaten Arbeitsplatz“ finden; insbesondere, wenn der Staat seinen Bedarf an Akademikern zurückschraubt. Bisher hat dieser Bereich 60 % der Universitätsabsolventen aufgenommen. In Zukunft, so sagen die Finanzminister der Länder, sollen dies nur noch 15 % sein. Etwas anders sieht es im Bereich der privaten Wirtschaft aus, die gegenwärtig rd. 20 % der Hochschulabsolventen aufnimmt. Für den Bereich der Wirtschaft wurde ein jährlicher Zusatzbedarf über den Ersatzbedarf hinaus von längerfristig etwa ein Prozent ermittelt. Zusammen mit der drastisch auf 15 % reduzierten Absorptionsquote des Staates würde dies bedeuten, daß künftig lediglich ein Drittel aller Hochschulabgänger adäquate Beschäftigungsmöglichkeiten erwarten könnte.

Es gibt allerdings auch andere Schätzungen, nach denen in den 80er Jahren insgesamt 50 % der Universitätsabsolventen einen der Ausbildung adäquaten Arbeitsplatz erhalten können.

Wie auch immer die Schätzungen aussehen mögen, hier ist ein ernstes Wort der Warnung angebracht.

Es gibt akademische Berufe, in denen die Beschäftigungschancen bereits heute äußerst gering und die Zukunftsaussichten ebenfalls trübe sind. Ich denke hier beispielsweise an den Beruf des Lehrers, Psychologen, Politologen oder Soziologen. Wer heute ein derartiges Fachstudium trotz Warnung aufnimmt, muß sich darüber im klaren sein, daß er das stark erhöhte Risiko für seine Entscheidung später selbst zu tragen hat.

Im Zusammenahng mit dem Problem der akademischen Ausbildung und der formal überqualifizierten muß man auch gleich den Verdrängungsprozeß von oben nach unten ansprechen, der sich einstellen wird, wenn man keine Gegenmaßnahmen einleitet. Ich meine hiermit, daß Studierte bei der Suche nach Arbeitsplätzen mit Abiturienten konkurrieren und diese wieder mit Mittel- und Realschülern usw. Es sind Gegenmaßnahmen nötig, um das zu verhindern, sonst werden Haupt- und Sonderschüler auf der Strecke bleiben.

Aber es gibt nicht nur eine Akademikerschwemme, es gibt auch eine Konzentration auf nur wenige Ausbildungsberufe.

Gut die Hälfte aller Auszubildenden befindet sich in nur 20 Berufen, wie z.B. Kfz.-Mechaniker, Elektroinstallateur, Maschinenschlosser oder Verkäuferin, Friseuse, Bürokaufmann. Diese Konzentration entspricht nicht den Anforderungen der Arbeitswelt. In Berufen, in denen über 60 % der männlichen Jugendlichen ausgebildet werden, arbeiten heute nur rd. 30 % der männlichen Erwerbstätigen. Bei den weiblichen Erwerbstätigen fallen Bedarf und Ausbildung noch weiter auseinander. 90 % lassen sich in Berufen ausbilden, in denen nur 30 % arbeiten.

Maßnahmen zur Überwindung der Probleme

Was bedeutet dies alles für die junge Generation und welche Maßnahmen müssen aus der Sicht der Wirtschaft ergriffen werden, damit in der Rückschau nicht von einer „betrogenen Generation", wie dies schon heute geschieht, gesprochen werden muß. (Ich halte – wie schon gesagt – den Begriff „herausgeforderte Generation" allerdings für besser.)

Zunächst einmal: Wenn das Problem nicht gelöst wird, werden bei zunehmender Arbeitslosigkeit mehr Jugendliche Zweifel an unserer Gesellschaftsordnung anmelden. Fragen nach dem Sinn des Lebens und dem Sinn des Lernens und Studierens werden verstärkt aufkommen. „Wozu der Leistungsdruck?" – es sei dahingestellt, ob es wirklich einer ist – wird gefragt werden, wenn man das Erlernte später nicht anwenden kann.

Die positive Einstellung zum Staat und zu unserem Gesellschafts- und Wirtschaftssystem, die heute noch bei über 80 % der Jugendlichen vorhanden ist, würde sicherlich negativ beeinflußt werden.

Bei der Suche nach den „Schuldigen" machen es sich viele zu einfach, wenn sie sagen: „Die Marktwirtschaft ist schuld." Dies ist sogar nicht nur zu einfach, sondern es ist schlicht falsch. Denn es steht zweifelsfrei fest, daß die Marktwirtschaft der Prägung, wie sie in der Bundesrepublik verwirklicht ist, schon jetzt dazu geführt hat, daß die geschilderten Probleme nicht in der Schärfe auftreten wie in anderen westlichen Ländern. Dies zeigt ein Blick in die internationale Arbeitslosenstatistik.

Nun zu den Maßnahmen, die ergriffen werden müssen.

Da die Beschäftigungs- und Ausbildungsprobleme mehrfache Ursachen haben – die demographische Entwicklung ist gekoppelt mit konjunkturellen und strukturellen Problemen der Wirtschaft – müssen mehrere Maßnahmen gleichzeitig ergriffen werden. Es wird eine Aufgabe für alle Beteiligten sein, für die Jugend selbst, für die Lehrer und Ausbilder, für die Unternehmen, für die Gewerkschaften, aber auch für den Staat. Dieser sollte beispielsweise dafür sorgen, daß die Berufsberatung quantitativ und qualitativ den Anforderungen entsprechend ausgebaut wird; andernfalls wird sich die Tatsache, die ich vorhin erwähnte, daß sich 90 % der weiblichen Lehrlinge in Berufen ausbilden lassen, in denen nur 30 % arbeiten, nicht korrigieren lassen. Man muß versuchen, Neigung und Bedarf besser in Einklang zu bringen.

Aber ich will nicht von dem reden, was andere tun sollten, sondern mehr darüber, was die Wirtschaft tun muß.

Man findet immer wieder den Hinweis, daß Wirtschaftswachstumsraten von 4 % und höher das Problem weitgehend lösen würden. Aber kaum jemand rechnet mit 4 % Wachstum.

Trotzdem muß die Förderung des Wirtschaftswachstums mit an erster Stelle der Lösungsmöglichkeiten rangieren; denn im Wachstum liegt ein wichtiger Schlüssel zur Lösung der Probleme. Besonders hier erwarte ich Fragen von Ihnen.

Sicher ist ein rein quantitatives Wachstum nicht mehr erstrebenswert. Es muß einhergehen mit einem qualitativen Wachstum. Gezielter Umweltschutz, Energie sparen, Einsatz von sogenannten Soft-Energies. Bundespräsident Scheel hat kürzlich auf dem DGB-Kongress in Hamburg davon gesprochen, daß Innovationen nötig sind und neue Bedürfnisse geschaffen werden sollten.

Erlauben Sie mir, daß ich dies nur anführe und dann für die Diskussion stehen lasse.

Es gibt bei uns Sättigungstendenzen und deshalb – aber nicht nur deshalb – einen gewissen Wachstumspessimismus. Andererseits lebt die Mehrheit der Weltbevölkerung in relativer Bescheidenheit, wenn nicht in Armut. Hier liegen Aufgaben und Wachstumschancen für unsere Industrie.

Sie sehen, Arbeit ist im Grunde genommen genug vorhanden. Die Wirtschaft würde diese gern ausführen; worauf es aber ankommt, ist, die Güter und Dienstleistungen zu Bedingungen und Preisen herzustellen, daß der Markt sie uns auch abnimmt.

Referat Welbergen

Da über das Wirtschaftswachstum allein die Chancenminderung der jungen Generation offensichtlich nicht in den Griff zu bekommen ist, meine ich, daß von Seiten der Wirtschaft in den nächsten Jahren zusätzliche Anstrengungen unternommen werden müssen, wobei ich den wichtigsten Punkt gleich zuerst nennen möchte:

Es müssen mehr Jugendliche in Berufen ausgebildet werden, als dies aus heutiger Sicht notwendig erscheint. Die Wirtschaft braucht in den 90er Jahren diese gut ausgebildeten Kräfte, zum Teil auch schon heute. Diese Entwicklung hat schon begonnen und muß fortgesetzt werden.

Dabei kommt es wesentlich darauf an, dem vorhersehbaren Mangel an Ausbildungsplätzen zu begegnen, der z.T. eine Folge erhöhter gesetzgeberischer Anforderungen ist. Diese haben vor allen Dingen kleine und mittlere Firmen in der Ausbildung behindert. Aber auch große Unternehmen mußten Ende der 60er Jahre die Ausbildung reduzieren, weil sie sich wegen der erhöhten Anforderungen des Berufsbildungsgesetzes und den entsprechenden Verordnungen nicht mehr in der Lage sahen, sie im bisherigen Umfang durchzuführen. Ich möchte Ihnen dies und die Möglichkeiten einer Überwindung der gegebenen Schwierigkeiten aus der Sicht eines Unternehmens, in diesem Fall also am Beispiel der Deutschen Shell, konkret erläutern. Vorausschicken muß ich dabei gleich, daß mein Unternehmen mit weniger als 5.000 Beschäftigten nicht repräsentativ für die Großindustrie ist und alle ergriffenen Maßnahmen in ihrer quantitativen Wirkung zur Minderung der Jugendarbeitslosigkeit natürlich außerordentlich begrenzt sind. Meine Ausführungen mögen deshalb nur als Beispiel verstanden werden und sollen in keiner Hinsicht als beispielhaft gelten.

Ich sagte, daß die Ausbildung wegen der Konsequenzen aus dem Berufsbildungsgesetz reduziert werden mußte. Dies soll keine Kritik an den Ausbildungsverordnungen sein, denn diese haben in der Tat das Qualifikationsniveau der Jugendlichen erhöht. Dennoch bleibt das Faktum, daß z.B. auch wir in unseren Niederlassungen, die sonst traditionelle Schwerpunkte unserer Lehrlingsarbeit waren, unsere Ausbildungstätigkeit einstellen mußten, weil zwingend vorgeschriebene Ausbildungsinhalte, wie z.B. Personalwirtschaft und Materialwesen, dort nicht vermittelt werden können. Zwangsläufig entfielen damit viele Ausbildungsplätze. Um dennoch einen Beitrag zur Minderung des Problems leisten zu können, mußten wir neue Wege gehen.

So kam es für die kaufmännsiche Ausbildung zu einem Verbund von Niederlassungen, Raffinerien/Werken und Lagern. Die kaufmännisch Auszubildenden werden jetzt überwiegend in den Niederlassungen ausgebildet und wechseln für Ausbildungsinhalte, die dort nicht vermittelt werden können, für mehrere Wochen zu einer benachbarten Raffinerie oder einem Lager.

Dort, wo eigene Raffinerien nicht zur Verfügung stehen, haben wir eine Kooperation mit anderen Unternehmen getroffen. Sie erfolgt in der Weise, daß Shell Lehrlinge eingestellt, die Ausbildungsverantwortung sowie sämtliche Kosten übernimmt und der Partner die Ausbildungsinhalte vermittelt, die unsere Niederlassung nicht anbieten kann.

Für die gewerblich Auszubildenden haben wir mittlerweise in allen unseren Raffinerien die Plätze vermehrt. So konnte die Zahl der gewerblichen Lehrlinge gegenüber 1976 nahezu verdoppelt werden. Die Zahl der kaufmännischen Lehrlinge stieg von 1976 bis 1978 ebenfalls um das Doppelte an.

Neu ist für uns auch eine spezielle Ausbildung von Abiturienten zusammen mit der Wirtschaftsakademie Hamburg. Es handelt sich um eine 3-jährige kaufmännisch-betriebswirtschaftliche Ausbildung, die mit der Prüfung zum Betriebswirt endet. Die Ausbildung erfolgt sowohl durch praktische Tätigkeit im Betrieb als auch durch intensive wissenschaftsorientierte theoretische Ausbildung bei der Wirtschaftsakademie. Mitarbeiter unseres Hauses haben maßgeblich bei der Entwicklung der Lehrpläne für diesen Ausbildungszweig mitgewirkt und sind in den wesentlichen Gremien für die Weiterentwicklung dieses nach unserer Auffassung sehr zukunftsträchtigen Ausbildungsmodells tätig. Wir halten diesen Weg für eine attraktive Alternative zur Hochschulausbildung, der dazu führen soll, praxisorientierte und qualifizierte Mitarbeiter für das mittlere und obere Management heranzubilden. Wir hoffen, daß diese Form der Ausbildung von möglichst vielen Unternehmen und Handelskammern aufgegriffen wird. In Kiel und Stuttgart ist dies bereits geschehen.

Darüber hinaus werden wir untersuchen, wo in unserem Unternehmen noch zusätzliche Ausbildungsplätze zur Verfügung gestellt werden können, und zwar Ausbildungsplätze, die über unseren betrieblichen Bedarf hinausgehen.

Wenn wir zu dem Ergebnis kommen, daß in unseren Werken und Raffinerien die Voraussetzungen gegeben sind, werden wir dort Ausbildungsplätze zusätzlich zur Verfügung stellen, um Facharbeiter der Chemie und Chemiewerker auszubilden. Diese Ausbildung wird dann auch den kaufmännischen Bereich beinhalten, um die Auszubildenden in den Stand zu versetzen, zu einem späteren Zeitpunkt eine eigenständige unternehmerische Position, z.B. als selbständige Handwerker, aufzubauen.

Dazu gehört natürlich Mut und der Wille zur Risikoübernahme. Wir wollen dazu beitragen, daß sich wieder mehr Jugendliche dafür begeistern.

Ich bin der Meinung, daß dieser freiwillige Beitrag, der Investitionen und Kosten in Millionenhöhe bedeutet, geleistet werden muß, um auf privatwirtschaftlicher Grundlage zu helfen, die auf uns zukommenden Probleme zu lösen.

Aus der Länge meiner Ausführungen zum Thema „Ausbildung" können Sie ersehen, daß ich hierin die zentrale Aufgabe der Wirtschaft sehe, damit die

Chancenminderung der jungen Generation nicht eintritt.

Ebensolche Aufmerksamkeit erfordert dabei die Gruppe der minderbegabten bzw. behinderten Jugendlichen; denn es besteht die Gefahr, daß diese Gruppe überhaupt keinen Eingang in das Berufsleben findet, da es die Tätigkeiten, die sie ausfüllen könnten, mittlerweile nicht mehr gibt. Ich sehe die große Gefahr, daß unsere Gesellschaft glaubt, sich diese minderbegabten Arbeitslosen leisten zu können, indem sie hierfür einfach bezahlt. Für mich liegt in dieser Frage ein zumindest ebenso großer sozialer Zündstoff, wie in der Frage der Beschäftigung der auf uns zukommenden Flut von Akademikern.

Wie Sie wissen, sind von verschiedenster Seite in letzter Zeit Vorschläge gemacht worden, wie man die Arbeitsmarktsituation weiter entlasten kann:

Verkürzung der Wochenarbeits-, Jahresarbeits- und Lebensarbeitszeit. Die dazugehörigen Stichworte lauten: 35-Stunden-Woche, zweiter Erholungsurlaub, weitere Herabsetzung der flexiblen Altersgrenze, Ausbau der Erwachsenenbildung, Langzeiturlaub, wie er von Zeit zu Zeit deutschen Hochschullehrern gewährt wird. Auch der gleitende Übergang in den Ruhestand mit abnehmender Wochenarbeitszeit während der letzten Arbeitnehmerjahre ist in die Diskussion eingebracht worden. Ob dieser Lösung Modellcharakter zukommen kann, bleibt abzuwarten. Möglicherweise kann jede dieser Maßnahmen einen begrenzten Beitrag leisten.

Ich möchte aber an dieser Stelle gleich etwas zur 35-Stunden-Woche sagen, die ja gegenwärtig im Vordergrund der Diskussion steht. Die 35-Stunden-Woche mit Lohn-Ausgleich ist in meinen Augen völlig ungeeignet, da die Bundesrepublik bereits heute zu den Ländern zählt, die die höchsten Lohnkosten in der Welt zu verkraften haben. Eine Arbeitszeitverkürzung von 40 auf 35 Stunden pro Woche entspricht einer Lohnkostenerhöhung von 12,5 % und es fragt sich natürlich, wer diese Kosten tragen soll. Der Rationalisierungsdruck würde hierdurch verschärft und das Gegenteil von dem erreicht, was angestrebt wird. Aber auch ohne den Lohn-Ausgleich halte ich diese Maßnahme z.Z. für ungeeignet. Ein Blick in die Arbeitslosenstatistik zeigt, daß dieser „Beschäftigungstausch" nur auf dem Papier gelingen dürfte. Facharbeiter sind bereits heute Mangelware, arbeitslos hingegen sind vornehmlich Ungelernte, an Teilzeitarbeit interessierte Frauen und ältere Angestellte. Hier gibt es also nichts zu tauschen. Außerdem habe ich begründete Zweifel, ob eine derartige Maßnahme wieder rückgängig gemacht werden könnte im Hinblick auf den sich nach 1990 abzeichnenden Arbeitskräftemangel.

Meines Erachtens ist es ein Fehler, sich einseitig auf die 35-Stunden-Woche zu stürzen und dabei die anderen Maßnahmen aus den Augen zu verlieren.

Meine Damen und Herren, lassen Sie mich – bevor ich zum Schluß komme – noch eine grundsätzliche Bemerkung machen:

Ich habe den Eindruck, daß wir alle uns beim Auftauchen eines Hindernisses viel zu sehr darauf verlassen, daß irgendeiner ein Schild mit der Aufschrift „Umleitung“ hinstellt, dem wir dann nur zu folgen brauchen.

Sicher ist es bequem, einem ausgeschilderten Weg zu folgen. Aber Sie wissen selbst, daß es nicht immer der beste Weg ist. Die eigene Findigkeit führt häufig schneller ans Ziel.

Bezogen auf die Chancen der jungen Generation möchte ich daher folgendes sagen:

1. Es gibt Hindernisse, aber es gibt keine ausgeschilderte Umleitungsstrecke und wird sie auch in Zukunft nicht geben.
2. Was wir tun können, ist, daß wir gewisse Orientierungspunkte setzen.
3. Auch die Jugend muß ihre Findigkeit und ihren Ideenreichtum einsetzen. Sie darf und kann sich nicht nur darauf verlassen, sicher ans Ziel geführt zu werden.

Gerade den letzten Punkt – nämlich den der Selbsthilfe – halte ich für außerordentlich wichtig, denn ich habe den Eindruck, daß viele Jugendliche erwarten, daß sie automatisch ans Ziel geführt werden.

Neue Anforderungen an die Bildungspolitik?

Dr. Peter Glotz

Die Entwicklung der Bildungsexpansion ist von Herrn Zander nachgezeichnet worden. Zur Charakterisierung der Bildungsexpansion möchte ich gerade im Hinblick auf die Entwicklung, die Herr Welbergen hier analyisiert hat, auf drei Zahlen hinweisen. Es sind Zahlen, die auch in der statistisch überaus interessanten Antwort der Bundesregierung auf die große Anfrage der SPD-Fraktion stehen, die vor einigen Tagen im Bundestag diskutiert worden ist. Diese Antwort kann ich sehr empfehlen, weil sie das gesamte statistische Material der letzten Jahre aufarbeitet.

Die drei Zahlen lauten folgendermaßen: Wir haben die Zahl der mittleren Abschlüsse in den letzten 15 Jahren von etwa 18 % auf etwa 33 % in der Bundesrepublik gesteigert. Zweitens – und das ist die bekannteste Zahl – ist die Zahl der Hochschulberechtigten, also nicht nur der Abiturienten, sondern auch derer, die über Fachhochschulen und auf anderem Wege zur Hochschulreife kommen, von rund 7 % auf rund 19 % gesteigert worden.

Die dritte Zahl erscheint mir am wichtigsten. Die Zahl derer, die ohne einen qualifizierten Hauptschulabschluß die Schule verlassen, ist von rund 17 % auf etwas über 12 % gedrückt worden. Diese dritte Zahl scheint mir noch wichtiger als die beiden anderen Zahlen zu sein. Wenn man das gesamte Zahlenmaterial, das ich jetzt vorgetragen habe, ansieht, muß man feststellen: Was wir Bildungsexpansion nennen, ist nicht bloß eine Akademikerentwicklung, sondern in der Tat eine Veränderung der Qualifikationssituation der jüngeren Generation auf unterschiedlichen Ebenen und nicht nur im Bereich der Akademiker. Ich halte die These von einer zu einseitigen Entwicklung unseres Qualifikationssystems in Richtung auf die Hochschule nicht für ganz falsch, aber ich glaube, man muß die drei Zahlen im Zusammenhang sehen.

Zwei Sätze möchte ich kommentierend zu diesen Zahlen sagen. Erstens: es soll sich keiner einbilden, daß diese Entwicklung ausschließlich eine politisch gesteuerte Entwicklung war. Man muß sehen, daß dies auch eine Entwicklung war, die aus der ökonomischen Struktur und der ökonomischen Entwicklung einer sehr dynamischen Marktwirtschaft und aus den Ansprüchen der Mittelschichten in dieser Gesellschaft entstanden ist, wie Herr Welbergen gerade gesagt hat. Ein Anteil für diese Entwicklung war sicherlich politisch gewollt. Wenn es auch ungerecht ist, immer den armen Georg Picht ausschließlich zu zitieren, es gibt eine Reihe von Bildungsreformern. Dies geht auch zurück etwa auf die Politik der Sozialdemokraten und auch der Liberalen. Bloß wenn Sie im einzelnen die Zahlen analysieren, werden Sie feststellen, daß dieser Druck zu mehr Bildung auf allen möglichen Ebenen in Bayern und Baden-Württemberg, die seit Jahren konservativ regiert werden, nicht geringer gewesen ist als in anderen Bundesländern. Dort ist der Ausbau des Bildungssystems – obwohl in der Struktur eher in den traditionellen Formen gehalten – quantitativ nicht geringer gewesen als in den anders regierten Bundesländern.

Dies muß man sehen, wenn man über die Frage debattiert, wie eigentlich die Bildungsexpansion zustande gekommen ist. Eine zweite kommentierende Bemerkung zu diesen Zahlen: Ich staune manchmal darüber, warum sich so viele Leute über die Konflikte wundern, in denen wir uns befinden. Es ist doch selbstverständlich: wenn man so massive Veränderungen in einer Gesellschaft verursacht – und wenn diese im Bildungssystem durchgesetzt werden –, entstehen mit einem gewissen Zeitverzug anschließend entsprechende Konflikte auf dem Arbeitsmarkt. Für mich jedenfalls ist selbstverständlich, daß mit der Veränderung des Bildungssystems und der Tatsache, daß sehr viel mehr Leute sehr viel höhere Qualifikationen bekommen und sich deshalb auch die Konkurrenz um bestimmte Positionen vergrößert. Dieses wird nicht automatisch im Arbeitsmarkt sofort akzeptiert und hingenommen. Die spitz zulaufende Pyramide auf dem Arbeitsmarkt konnte sich nicht plötzlich von heute auf morgen und ohne Konflikte verändern. Wer sich eingebildet hat, daß dies möglich sei, unterlag einem Harmoniemodell von Politik, das mit der Wirklichkeit überhaupt nicht übereinstimmt. Ich meine, daß das aufgeregte Sich-Wundern über die Konflikte, die jetzt entstehen, zum Teil nur aus politischer Naivität erklärt werden kann. Man mußte wissen, daß diese Konflikte auf uns zukommen. Ich gebe zu – das sage ich jetzt mal selbstkritisch für die Politiker –, daß sich die Politiker aller Gruppierungen und Farben auf diese Entwicklung zu wenig eingestellt haben.

Noch auf etwas anderes haben sich die Politiker zu wenig eingestellt. Ich habe es gerade schon angedeutet. Mehr Chancen für mehr Leute bedeutet mehr Konkurrenz. Nehmen wir nur als Beispiel – Herr Welbergen hat es bereits herausgegriffen – den Arbeitsmarkt der Akademiker. Natürlich können Sie auf 7 % Spitzenpositionen nicht 20 % Leute eines Jahrgangs unterbringen, die inzwischen an unseren Hochschulen studieren. Sie können zu erreichen versuchen – das geschieht auch durch eine stärkere Angleichung der Einkommensdifferenzen –, daß mehr Führungspositionen entstehen. Aber daß dies nicht in dem gleichen Prozentsatz, wie der Staat seine Bildungspositionen ausweiten kann, gleichzeitig auf dem Arbeitsmarkt zu entsprechenden Veränderungen führen kann, wird auch jedem einleuchten. Also entsteht mehr Konkurrenz, und das bedeutet, daß auch mehr Stress entsteht.

Ich will noch darauf hinweisen, daß offensichtlich manche von uns – auch wieder unabhängig von der politischen Färbung – sich in der Tat erhofft hatten, daß durch ein stetiges Wachstum, wie wir es seit der Währungsreform in der Bundesrepublik und auch in allen westlichen Industriegesellschaften bis in die späten 60er Jahre und an den Anfang der 70er Jahre hatten, das alles zu finanzieren sei, also eine gleiche Zahl von zusätzlichen gutbezahlten Positionen aufgrund der Bildungsexpansion gleichzeitig geschaffen und aus dem Wachstum bezahlt werden könne. Dies war in der Tat ein Irrtum. Es ist zu einem Teil ein Grund für die Auseinandersetzungen, in denen wir uns heute befinden.

Zu diesen Auseinandersetzungen noch einige polemische Bemerkungen. Denn hier ärgert mich zuweilen, wie ich offen zugebe, daß versucht worden ist, diese Entwicklung auch politisch auszunutzen und unter dem Stichwort „Tendenzwende", das ja wirkungsvoll durch die Bundesrepublik gegangen ist, politisch auszuwerten.

Mehr Konkurrenz bedeutet auch folgendes: diejenigen, die bisher fest davon überzeugt sein konnten, daß ihre Kinder eine bestimmte Entwicklung vor sich hätten, beispielsweise auf die Hochschule kämen oder einen mittleren Abschluß erreichten, sind nun plötzlich in eine Entwicklung gestellt, in der sie sehen, daß ihre eigenen Kinder sehr viel mehr Konkurrenten bekommen, als dies in einer geschlosseneren und geordneteren Gesellschaft vorher der Fall war. Aus dieser Erkenntnis ergeben sich auch heftige wirkungsvolle, wie man sieht, und durchaus schlagkräftige Bürgerinitiativen und politische Entwicklungen. Nicht, daß ich sie kritisiere. Es ist das Recht jedes Menschen, Bürgerinitiativen zu gründen und entsprechend zu handeln. Ich versuche aber auch die Motive zu analysieren, nicht die Motive schlechthin, sondern einen bestimmten Teil dieser Motive.

Die Argumentation ist bekannt, die heute mit „Akademiker-Proletariat" und „Akademikerberg" und solchen Begriffen zum Teil so wirkungsvoll arbeitet, daß heute schon die Zahl derer, die die Chancen wahrnehmen wollen, bereits sehr abgesenkt worden ist. Wir haben ja seit vielen Jahren stagnierende Zahlen beim Hochschuleingang, und in den letzten zwei Semestern sind rapide absinkende Zahlen festzustellen. Derzeit wollen nur noch 70 % der Abiturienten studieren. Früher waren es immer um die 90 %. Das sind zum Teil vernünftig verlaufende Marktprozesse, zum Teil sind es auch die Folgen einer ziemlich gezielt geführten Abschreckungsdiskussion.

Nun bin ich bei der These, die auch im Referat von Herrn Welbergen vorkam: Ist nicht unser Bildungssystem allzu einseitig auf Hochschule und Akademiker ausgerichtet? Wenn Sie mich am Grünen Tisch unabhängig von Politik und politischer Entwicklung fragen, was man denn hätte machen sollen, würde ich sofort sagen: Die These ist richtig. Wäre es besser gewesen, nicht so sehr das allgemeinbildende Schulwesen und die Hochschulen in diesem Ausmaß zu vergrößern und auszubauen, sondern viel stärkeren Nachdruck auf die Ausweitung und den Ausbau der beruflichen Bildung zu legen und auf diese Weise – von praktischen Qualifikationen ausgehend – zu höheren Qualifikationen zu gelangen? Ich muß aber darauf hinweisen, daß dies in unserem politischen System nicht so einfach war. Es ist leicht erklärlich, warum es anders gemacht wurde. Der Veränderungsakzent ging von der staatlichen Politik aus, und die staatliche Politik hatte Verfügungsmacht über Schulen; sie konnte Schulen bauen, Hochschulen bauen, Lehrer und Professoren einstellen. Aber die Verfügungsmöglichkeit über die Veränderung der beruflichen Bildung war sehr viel geringer. Die berufliche Bildung ist sehr stark von der Wirtschaft bestimmt worden und wird es auch immer noch werden. In dieser Hinsicht handelten diejenigen, die die staatliche Politik verändern wollten, dort, wo sie Handlungsmöglichkeiten hatten, und nicht in dem anderen Bereich, der bestenfalls durch Gesetze hätte reguliert werden können. Die entsprechenden Gesetze, die versucht worden sind, sind ja auch gescheitert. Das ist der eine, wenn Sie so wollen, politisch-psychologische Grund.

Lassen Sie mich aus der politischen Auseinandersetzung ein Zweites hinzufügen, aus der Debatte, die wir jetzt im Bundestag um die Große Anfrage hatten, wo die ganze Bildungspolitik zur Diskussion stand. Ich hatte eine Auseinandersetzung mit dem Kollegen Dregger, der ebenfalls diese These ausgesprochen hatte. Ich möchte das, was ich dort mit Dregger ausgetragen habe, in diese Diskussion einbringen. Meine These ist die Behauptung, es wäre besser gewesen, die berufliche Bildung zu reformieren, statt nur die Hochschulen und das allgemeinbildende Schulwesen zu reformieren, ist nur dann wirklich glaubhaft, wenn derjenige, der das sagt, auch glaubhaft an eine Veränderung und Reform der beruflichen Bildung herangegangen wäre. Ich habe dem Herrn Kollegen Dregger einen Satz aus seinem eigenen Programm zitiert, aus dem hessischen CDU-Programm, in welchem steht: Eine CDU-Landesregierung wird sich auf Bundesebene dafür einsetzen, daß ausbildungshemmende Bestimmungen, z.B. Ausbildungsordnung, Höhe der Ausbildungskosten, zweiter Berufsschultag, zurückgenommen werden und die betriebliche Ausbildung vor Bürokratisierung geschützt wird. – Ich habe Herrn Dregger gesagt: Ihre Grundthese kann ich akzeptieren, aber wenn Sie gleichzeitig den zweiten Berufsschultag zurücknehmen wollen und wenn Sie gleichzeitig den Konflikt, den es um die Verbesserung der Ausbildungsordnungen dann sicher auch mit Teilen der Wirtschaft zu führen gegolten hätte, nicht zu führen bereit sind, dann dürfen Sie nicht auf der anderen Seite sagen, man hätte diesen Weg gehen müssen.

Jetzt bin ich bei der Tatsache, daß wir uns eben wirklich in einem Markt befinden. Niemand darf sich wundern, daß Leute lieber Betriebswirt, Volkswirt oder Ingenieur werden als Facharbeiter, solange der Betriebswirt in einem Unternehmen im Normalfall besser bezahlt wird als der Facharbeiter. Nehmen Sie einmal ein paar praktische Beispiele, mit denen ich täglich zu tun habe.

Ich habe in Berlin eine große Technische Fachhochschule, die sehr gut ist und auch bei der Wirtschaft einen guten Ruf hat, und ich habe eine Technische

Universität. Auf der Technischen Fachhochschule braucht man 6 oder 7 Semester, auf der Technischen Universität – nehmen wir die gleichen Fächer, z.B. Maschinenbau – rund 13 Semester, um fertig zu werden. Wenn man genau hinguckt, ist das Curriculum an beiden Universitäten nicht sehr unterschiedlich. Es ist ein bißchen mehr Konstruktion an der Fachhochschule, ein bißchen mehr Mathematik und Grundlagenphysik an der Technischen Universität. Aber sehr groß sind die Unterschiede nicht.

Trotzdem gehen immer weniger junge Leute an die Technische Fachhochschule und immer mehr zur Universität. Das liegt daran, daß die Fachhochschul-Ingenieure im öffentlichen Dienst mit A 10 eingestellt werden und die Diplomingenieure mit A 13, um einmal magische Zahlen zu nennen. In den Verdienstchancen und -möglichkeiten und der Eingangsgehälter besteht der Unterschied. Das ist im öffentlichen Dienst viel schlimmer als in der Wirtschaft, das gebe ich zu. Aber auch in der Wirtschaft ist noch ein gewisser Unterschied festzustellen, zumindest im Eingangsbereich. Auf diese Weise werden Bildungsströme gesteuert.

Wenn wir diese Steuerungsmechanismen nicht verändern, dürfen wir uns auch nicht beklagen, daß die Leute weniger praktische Tätigkeiten erlernen, weniger über diesen Bildungsweg und mehr über den allgemeinbildenden Weg gehen. Wenn wir das wirklich verändern wollen, müssen wir auch ernsthaft an diese Steuerungsmechanismen herangehen. Dazu sehe ich selten die Bereitschaft. Im übrigen warne ich davor anzunehmen, daß man diesen Prozeß steuern könne. Ich weiß nicht, wie dieses Gremium politisch zusammengesetzt ist. Aber wenn man auf der einen Seite skeptisch ist, ob eine staatliche Investitionslenkung sinnvoll ist und funktionieren kann – und ich stehe dieser Skepsis sehr nahe –, dann muß man erst recht gegenüber der Meinung skeptisch sein, diese Bildungsströme, die Studentenströme und das komplizierte Gebilde von Arbeitsmarkt und Bildungssystem seien stärker steuerbar als heute. Ich warne vor einem derartigen blinden Glauben an die Steuerbarkeit solcher Prozesse. Ich sehe keine Instrumente dafür.

Es ist sicher richtig, Herr Welbergen, daß eine Reihe von Bereichen heute Facharbeitermangel haben. Nach meiner Kenntnis ist aber die allgemeine These von Professor Hegelheimer nicht belegt. Darüber könnten wir vielleicht in der Diskussion sprechen. Auch heute kann kein Unternehmen jemandem, der einen bestimmten Facharbeiterberuf erlernt, auf 5 oder 6 Jahre im voraus seinen Arbeitsplatz garantieren. Ebenso wäre es umgekehrt ein falscher Ratschlag, jemandem zu sagen: Werde bitte nicht Betriebswirt, Volkswirt, Ingenieur, Elektroniker oder Maschinenschlosser, dann ist dein Berufsleben gesichert. Ich würde genauso sagen: Werde nicht Grundschullehrer oder Architekt. Bei den Psychologen bin ich schon skeptisch; ich glaube, die Gesellschaft hat noch Bedarf an Psychologen. Aber Architekten? Ich könnte aus meinem Arbeitsbereich nachweisen, in welchen Fächern Bedarf vorhanden ist. Bei den

Architekten und den Grundschullehrern läßt sich in der Tat der Bedarf absehen. Ich würde sagen: Studiert nicht auf Grundschullehrer und Architekten! Ich könnte noch eine ganze Reihe von Bereichen hinzufügen. Insofern, glaube ich, können Patentrezepte und Antworten nicht gegeben werden.

Ich möchte meine kleine Einführung für unsere Diskussion mit zwei Forderungen abschließen, die die Politik selber an sich stellen und verwirklichen muß. Erstens bin ich fest davon überzeugt, daß wir das allgemeine Szenario unserer Bildungsentwicklung nun lange genug beschworen haben und daß es jetzt notwendig ist, die Arbeitsmarktprobleme, von denen wir ständig reden, konkret anzupacken. Ich will das an einem Beispiel erklären. Alle Politiker laufen seit Jahren durch die Gegend und sagen: Es ist gut, daß mehr Leute mehr lernen können, aber sie müssen auch bereit sein, im Zweifelsfall einen Arbeitsmarkt zu akzeptieren, der nicht automatisch 3000 DM Anfangsgehalt bringt, der nicht automatisch im öffentlichen Dienst die A 13 als Eingangsstufe bringt. Dies ist eine richtige These.
These.
Ich freue mich, daß der Bundeskanzler in der letzten Regierungserklärung auch darauf eingegangen ist. Man muß das in der Politik offen sagen. Aber man muß auch die Voraussetzungen dafür schaffen.. Es ist heute eine Banalität, daß jemand im öffentlichen Dienst unter A 13 mit großen juristischem Examen keine Eingangsstelle findet. Wenn man da Wandel schaffen will, muß man eine Änderung des Bundesbesoldungsgesetzes, des Beamtenrechtsrahmengesetzes und anderer Gesetze verlangen. Darüber reden viele, aber keiner will den Anfang machen. Es ist Aufgabe der Bundespoltik, dies zu ändern und in dieser Richtung wirklich etwas zu tun.

Dasselbe gilt für die Fragen der konkreten Arbeitsmarktpolitik. Ich könnte Ihnen Beispiele aus meinem Arbeitsbereich nennen, wie man ein Trainy-Programm machen kann. Mancher findet heute lange keinen Job, weil er keine Berufserfahrung hat und weil der Sprung von der Hochschule zum Arbeitsmarkt zu schwierig ist. Aber auch die Lösung dieses Problems würde Mechanismen verlangen, für die Vorschläge vorliegen müssen.

Schließlich erwähne ich die Veränderung unserer gesetzlichen Grundlage, etwa des Arbeitsförderungsgesetzes, die durch das Haushaltsstrukturgesetz kaputtgemacht worden sind. Wenn man hier die Mobilität erhöhte, wenn man eine bestimmte Bereitschaft zur Weiterbildung durch eine Änderung des Arbeitsförderungsgesetzes stärkte, wären dies alles Maßnahmen, die konkret auf unseren Arbeitsmarkt zielen würden. Wir wissen alle, daß diese Probleme da sind. Wir reden auch alle davon. Bloß sind Handlungsperspektiven und konkrete Maßnahmen zu selten eröffnet worden. Ich glaube, dies muß man kritisieren.

Meine letzte Bemerkung ist eine Forderung an uns selbst. Diese Bemerkung zielt auf den Hochschulbereich. 19,5% eines Jahrgangs sind auf den Hochschulen. Diese sind nicht mehr Ausbildungsstätten für eine kleine Elite, sondern es sind sehr große Institutionen, Massenausbildungsstätten geworden. Es ist ungeheuer schwierig, daran etwas zu ändern. Da geht es um die Änderung der alten Humboldtschen Akademie, um die großen Forschungsstätten, die die Universitäten heute sind. Daß es da um einen Rationalisierungsprozeß geht, der viele Konflikte auslöst, darf niemanden verwundern. Dieser Prozeß muß aber bewältigt werden. Man muß sich in diesem Bereich mit der Problematik auseinandersetzen, daß sich rund 19 % eines Jahrgangs in diesem System befinden. Man darf nicht den Fehler machen, den die Politik heute weitgehend macht, diesen ganzen Bereich als eine Art Irrenhaus abzutun, für das die Bildungspolitiker zuständig sind, während sich die seriösen Politiker um die Bereiche Finanzen, Verteidigung usw. kümmern.Man schiebt das so ab und sagt: Macht das mal, das ist alles recht. Aber man ist nicht bereit, sich in einen Dialog mit denjenigen einzulassen, die in diesem zum Teil ungeeigneten Ausbildungssystem häufig zu lange Zeit verbringen. Statt dessen beschränkt man sich darauf, zuweilen - wenn etwas passiert - die Hochschulen als „Brutstätten des Terrorismus" zu qualifizieren. Das fällt manchem in unserer Republik sofort ein. Man sollte sich besser überlegen, daß extremes politisches Verhalten an den Hochschulen dadurch entsteht, daß die Bereitschaft bei den Politikern zu wenig vorhanden ist, sich diesem Dialog zu stellen und sich mit diesen Leuten auseinanderzusetzen. Von den fast 1 Million jungen Leuten in den Hochschulen wird nur eine verschwindend kleine Minderheit so in eine Subkultur abdriften, daß daraus die Gefahr der Kriminalität und des Terrorismus entsteht. Es ist durchaus denkbar, daß ein erheblicher Prozentsatz dieser Leute, die eine Zeitlang in der Subkultur an den Universitäten leben, nach einer gewissen Zeit Anzüge anzieht, Schlips und Kragen umbindet, sich einen Volvo kauft und dann irgendwo in einer mittleren Etage in unserer Industrie tätig ist. Aber ob dann hinter den Statussymbolen politische Gleichgültigkeit oder „Entfremdung" bestehenbleiben, ob etwa, wenn diese Gesellschaft wirklich in einen Konflikt gerät, zu wenig Leute da sind, die den Grundkonsens noch vollziehen, oder ob zuviele da sind, denen er gleichgültig ist – dies sollten sich alle Politiker genau überlegen.

Aussprache über die Referate Welbergen, Glotz

Leitung: Rosemarie Fiedler-Winter

Fiedler-Winter:

Meine Damen und Herren, ich eröffne jetzt die Aussprache. Ich habe hier eine Frage bezüglich der Anfangsgehälter. Wenn diese erhöht werden, wird dann nicht der Drang zu höherer Qualifikation zurückgehen, und zwar mit der Folge, daß eine Bildungsmittelschicht entsteht?

Glotz:

Es ist durchaus denkbar, daß es Leute gibt, die sagen: Wenn ich mit einer erstklassigen Facharbeiterposition genausoviel verdienen kann wie ein Diplomingenieur, warum soll ich dann auf die Hochschule gehen? Diese Entscheidung wird es sicher geben. Aber ich würde sie nicht für katastrophal halten. Es bleiben dann diejenigen übrig, die ein Ausbildungsinteresse über den Beruf hinaus haben. Das würde auch eine Entlastung für die Bildungseinrichtungen mit sich bringen, die ich durchaus begrüßen würde.

Rosenmayr:

Ich habe Ihren Ausführungen, Herr Senator, mit großem Genuß zugehört. In einem Punkt stimme ich Ihnen aber gar nicht zu. Sie haben gesagt, daß es sich, was die Hochschule anlangt, um ein seriöses Politikfeld handelt. Ich habe 25 Jahre Hochschultätigkeit hinter mir. Aber ich bin nicht der Auffassung, daß die Hochschule ein seriöses Politikfeld sei. Allerdings finde ich richtig, daß die Bereitschaft notwendig ist, sich zu stellen. Das ist eine Bereitschaft, die nicht nur die Politiker, sondern auch die Professoren nicht haben.

Auch in einem anderen Punkt stimme ich Ihnen nicht zu. Sie sprachen davon, die Universität sei eine große Forschungsstelle geworden. Das glaube ich nicht. Die Forschung wandert vielmehr von der Hochschule weg, zumindest dort, wo ich bestimmte Fachbereiche habe. Deshalb geht es nicht darum, Forschung und Lehre zu verbinden. Man kann nur das eine oder das andere machen. Hier liegt der entscheidende Punkt, der mich zu meiner Frage bringt, und zwar im Anschluß an unsere Diskussion der letzten Tage.

Sollen idealistische Menschen mit sehr viel Flexibilität und Wissen von der Hochschule ausgebildet werden? Ich sehe nicht ein, daß es richtig ist, Flexibilität und Allgemeinbildung anzustreben, um dieser Entwicklung entsprechen zu können. Auf der anderen Seite sehe ich gerade als Sozialwissenschaftler, wie notwendig es ist, konkretes Wissen, verwertbares Wissen zu erwerben.

Glotz:

Zunächst, Herr Rosenmayr, möchte ich folgendes sagen. Ob die Hochschule ein seriöses Politikfeld ist, weiß ich nicht.

Sie ist jedoch ein wichtiges Feld. Es handelt sich immerhin um 1 Million Menschen und ein entscheidender Teil sind nicht Funktionäre, die in irgendwelchen Posten sitzen. Das Schlagwort von der „Entfremdung" geht weiter durch die Hochschulen. Wenn man solche „Entfremdeten" weiterhin zuläßt, kann es sein, daß da ein Raum der politischen Entfremdung entsteht. Eine solche Entwicklung wird schärfere Auswirkungen haben, als der Politik dienlich sein kann, und das Problem ist, daß sich viele dieser Situation einfach nicht stellen.

Ihrer These von der Abwanderung der Forschung kann ich nicht zustimmen. Natürlich gibt es Teile, die in Max-Planck-Institute und außeruniversitäre Forschungsbereiche abgewandert sind. Aber insgesamt ist das nicht der Fall. Ich kann es jetzt nicht mit Zahlen belegen, aber es läßt sich belegen, sowohl vom finanziellen Aufwand als auch von der Forschung her.

Nun zu Ihrer dritten Frage: Kein Institut darf sich einbilden, daß es auf einem breiten Feld Leute berufsfähig machen kann. Ich kann Ihnen das am Beispiel des Ingenieurs erläutern. Man sagt uns immer, wir sollen die Ausbildung an der Fachhochschule unterhalten und nicht nur in der Hochschule ausbilden. Aber in den Büros bekomme ich zu hören: Offengestanden ist uns das wurscht, anlernen müssen wir den Mann sowieso völlig neu, aber wir nehmen den Fachhochschulingenieur lieber, weil er jünger ist.

Man nimmt also einen 25jährigen lieber als einen 30jährigen, deswegen „Fachhochschule", aber das hat mit der Hochschulausbildung nichts zu tun.

Dieses Beispiel zeigt, daß es bei einem ständig wachsenden Arbeitsmarkt nur darauf ankommt, daß der Mann so ausgebildet sein muß, daß er am Arbeitsmarkt den richtigen Platz findet. Bis diese neue Entwicklung gesehen wird, ist für wirtschaftsorientierte Bereiche das Stichwort Universitätsausbildung die einzige mögliche Antwort.

Fiedler-Winter:

Ich habe noch eine Kartenfrage vorliegen, die ich nicht entziffern kann. Bitte unterstützen Sie mich, was das heißen soll.

Teilnehmer:

Vielleicht kann ich meine Frage mündlich erläutern. Ist es möglich, die Löhne marktwirtschaftlich zu orientieren? Ich möchte von Ihnen wissen, welche konkreten Leistungskriterien Sie sich vorstellen, und ich möchte Sie bitten, das auch einmal für den Bereich des Dienstleistungssektors zu erläutern, z.B. für den öffentlichen Dienst.

Dazu noch eine Anschlußfrage: Glauben Sie nicht, daß durch eine Orientierung der Konkurrenzdruck so stark steigen wird, daß die gesellschaftliche Stabilität dadurch in einem erwünschtem Maße gar nicht beeinträchtigt wird?

Glotz:

Zunächst zu Ihrer ersten Frage. Natürlich gibt es weite Bereiche, wo die Löhne nicht durch den Markt gebildet werden. Das betrifft beispielsweise den ganzen Bereich des öffentlichen Dienstes. Es ist kein Geheimnis, daß sich heute noch alle Verantwortlichen um eine wirklich konkrete Arbeitsplatzbeschreibung, um Einstufungsbedingungen usw. herumdrücken. Natürlich sind hier die Leistungskriterien nur begrenzt anwendbar.

In der Wirtschaft ist dies aber durchaus denkbar. Nehmen Sie als Beispiel die Postingenieure. Die Post besetzt diese Stellen vorwiegend mit Hochschulabsolventen, während die Industrie sagt: Fachhochschule ist wichtiger. In der Tat stellt man fest, daß die Post Hochschulabsolventen stärker hochzieht, daß es höhere Eingangsgehälter gibt, und dann ist die Chance größer als im öffentlichen Dienst. Da können Sie die Unterschiede sehen. Dies sind Unterschiede in der freien Konkurrenz.

Dann die letzte Frage! Der Konkurrenzdruck wird größer, je freier die Chancen sind. Ich meine, man soll die Menschen nicht in den Raum stellen, sondern ihnen eine Ordnung geben, in der sie auch lernen, zu konkurrieren. Daß diese Konkurrenz gleichzeitig große Schwierigkeiten und Streß mit sich bringt, auch nicht die Kooperation und Solidarität fördert, das ist klar. Davon muß man realistisch ausgehen.

Teilnehmer:

Ich persönlich halte es für eine gefährliche Entwicklung, die sich aus der Bildungspolitik der letzten Jahre ergeben hat, was Sie, Herr Glotz, unter „Konkurrenz“ subsumieren und abtun.

Deshalb aber muß ich die Frage stellen: was bleibt denen, die am Ende hängenbleiben? Wir wissen, daß zum Teil schon Hauptschulabgänger mit nicht allzu guten Noten keinen Arbeitsplatz finden. Da kann man mit Konkurrenz allein nichts wollen. Wenn die Arbeitsplätze für junge Menschen nicht in genügender Zahl da sind, ist und bleibt es ein Problem, und ich halte es für ein Problem mit sozialer Brisanz.

Auch zum Thema Berufsbildung habe ich eine Frage. Die Allgemeinbildung wird höher geschätzt und mehr gefördert als die berufliche Bildung. Wenn ich die Zahlen richtig im Kopf habe, sind die Mittel für Sonderschulen um 17 % gesteigert worden, im gleichen Zeitraum die Mittel für Universitäten um 150 %. Das ist für mich keine Relation.

Aussprache Welbergen, Glotz

Glotz:

Natürlich müssen wir uns vor allem um diejenigen, die draußen bleiben, ganz besonders kümmern. Selbstverständlich gibt es Bereiche, in denen uns das Wort „Konkurrenz" überhaupt keinen Schritt weiterbringt. Ich verwende dieses Wort nur gegenüber denen, die sagen, wir hätten zuviel Akademiker, und die eine Bildungsplangesellschaft fordern.

Was die Frage der Berufsschule betrifft, kann ich Ihnen recht geben. Für die Berufsschulen ist zu wenig Geld ausgegeben worden. Es ist aber keine Entwicklung aus irgendeiner gesellschaftspolitischen Ablehnung heraus. Dies ist nicht anders in konservativ regierten Bundesländern. Es liegt einfach daran, daß die Mittelschule und die Gymnasien eine stärkere Lobby hatten als die Berufsschulen. In den Berufsschulen war über lange Zeit hinweg vor allem die Arbeiterschaft vertreten, die nicht so sehr aufstiegsbewußt um Geld für ihre Kinder gekämpft hat. Heute wird gefragt: Was haben die Parlamente getan? Deshalb war die Kurskorrektur notwendig, die Helmut Rohde 1974 gemacht hat.

Teilnehmer:

Ich möchte noch einmal kurz auf die Situation der politischen Entfremdung an den Hochschulen eingehen. Da sehe ich in Ihren Ausführungen zwei Probleme. Erstens ist es nicht nur ein Problem von linken Minderheiten. Das Problem hat eine lange unpolitische Tradition auch in Deutschland. Zweitens ist es auch eine Frage, wie Praxisorientierung – nicht nur für die berufliche Praxis, sondern auch für die gesellschaftlich-politische Praxis – an den Hochschulen stärker interpretiert werden kann. Da gibt es sicher ein paar Ansätze. Welche Möglichkeiten sehen Sie, eine politische und gesellschaftliche Praxis stärker in die Hochschule zu tragen?

Glotz:

Ich stimme Ihnen vollständig zu, wenn Sie sagen, daß es an den Hochschulen in gewisser Beziehung charakteristische Verschiebungen des Spektrums gibt.

Die Frage ist: Was kann man tun? Man muß beispielsweise die Kontakte zwischen den unterschiedlichen Seiten zu stärken versuchen. Wir haben in Berlin ein Kuratorium geschaffen, in das wir verstärkt Vertreter der Arbeitgeber mit hineinnehmen. Wir müssen versuchen, konkret die Praxis in die Lehre der einzelnen Fächer hineinzubringen. Deshalb gab es beispielsweise auch die Studienreformkommission mit Vertretern der Arbeitgeber und der Arbeitnehmer. Es geht darum, diese Gedanken in die Studienpläne hineinzubringen.

Ferner glaube ich, daß wir eine in manchen Fällen an den Hochschulen gewachsene „antikapitalistische Berührungsangst" abbauen müssen. Wenn wir da das schaffen, muß es gar nicht erst zu Auseinandersetzungen kommen. Aber das muß erst der Fall sein. Da gibt es viele Hemmungen. Aber ich glaube, man kann diese Hemmungen Schritt für Schritt abbauen.

Teilnehmer:

Sie sprachen davon, man solle Trainee-Programme einführen, weil vieles, was man an der Universität lernen würde, scheinbar nutzlos sei.

Darum frage ich, warum man nicht praxisorientierte Studien einführt und Untersuchungen in dieser Richtung anstellt.

Glotz:

Die fangen schon an. Aber dies ist ein Problem, das der Staat nicht allein lösen kann. Es ist vielmehr ein kollektiver Prozeß in den Hochschulen. Man muß die Universitäten dazu gewinnen, und das scheint schwierig zu sein. Ich meine, man sollte diese Ziele nicht aufgeben, man sollte die Studienreform machen, notfalls darum kämpfen, aber auch wissen, daß das nicht von heute auf morgen funktioniert. Da sind Trainee-Programme notwendig, weil man das Problem mit der Studienreform allein nicht lösen kann.

Teilnehmer:

Herr Senator, Herr Welbergen hat die Abiturienten-Programme angesprochen. Es gibt sie in Hamburg, in Kiel und Stuttgart, und man kann auch Kritisches dazu sagen. Meine Frage: wie stehen Sie persönlich zu solchen Abiturienten-Programmen, und wie sehen Sie die Entwicklung in der Bundesrepbulik?

Glotz:

Ich persönlich sehe, daß es durchaus Sinn haben kann, Alternativen zum Hochschulstudium zu konstruieren. Nur weise ich auf zwei Dinge hin. Der Abiturientenberg rauscht an uns vorüber. Herr Welbergen hat bereits gesagt, Mitte der 80er Jahre wird es weniger Abiturienten geben. Bis dahin müssen Maßnahmen ergriffen werden, daß viele aufgefangen werden können. Aber solche Maßnahmen erfordern lange Reaktionszeiten.

Bei den Programmen handelt es sich im Grunde um kleine Modelle, an denen man ausprobieren kann, wie so etwas funktionieren würde. Aber das Massenproblem werden wir damit nicht lösen können, weil das zuviel Zeit erforderte.

Teilnehmer:

Ich möchte noch einmal auf die Studieninhalte zurückkommen. Ich teile Ihre Auffassung, daß es richtig ist, sie zu reformieren. Aber dann soll man nicht in der übrigen Zeit in der Wirtschaft mit Trainee-Programmen usw. weiterzukommen versuchen. Ich habe den Eindruck, wenn die Inhalte nicht zügig genug reformiert werden können, versuchen Sie es mit administrativen Mitteln.

Wir sind eine studentische Organisation, die sich den Praxisbezug auf die Fahnen geschrieben hat. Aber wir haben z.B. die Schwierigkeit in manchen Bundesländern, Hörsäle für Veranstaltungen zu bekommen, die wir durchführen. Wir müssen in verschiedenen Bundesländern für Hörsäle Mieten zahlen,und das halte ich für absolut unsinnig.

Glotz:

Wenn das irgendwo passiert sein sollte, kann ich es nur kritisieren. Wir haben Raumvergaberichtlinien. Ich bin froh, daß ich nicht alles erfahre, was in Hörsälen stattfindet. Aber meines Wissens wird Miete selten verlangt. Das hat es in Berlin nie gegeben. Ich weiß nicht, wie es an anderen Universitäten ist.

Diese Frage berührt aber nicht das Problem, wie die Schwierigkeiten mit der Studienreform konkret beseitigt werden können. Viele glauben und sagen, es sei alles im Rollen. Natürlich ist es im Rollen. Ich verweise nur auf die KMK, und ich bin darüber informiert, weil ich da gewissermaßen Dienstherr bin. Es sind jetzt 450.000 DM für Reisekosten ausgeschrieben worden, und zwar für eine internationale Studienreform. Das heißt aber nun noch nicht, daß diese eine Studienreform mit sich bringt.

(Heiterkeit)

Allein das Gerangel um die Studienreform z.B. von der Zahnmedizin bis zu den Wirtschaftswissenschaften, dann das Gerangel zwischen diesem und jenem Bund. Ob die zu einem Ergebnis kommen oder ob man nachher von einem ungeheuren Glaubenskrieg oder einem Reklametrick sprechen wird, ist ungewiß.

Rosenmayr:

Also doch nicht so ganz seriös!

(Heiterkeit)

Glotz:

Bloß, Herr Rosenmayr, daß es so etwas nicht gäbe – wir sprechen ja vom Anfang und nicht vom Aufhören –halte ich für ein Gerücht. Das Problem betrifft übrigens nicht nur die Bundesrepublik. Politische Projekte gelingen häufiger, als Politiker es zugeben. Bei der Studienreform ist die Gefahr besonders groß.

Deswegen, so sage ich, brauchen wir die Trainee-Programme. Aber ich streite mich nicht darum. Ich versuche auch nicht, es anderen aufzuschwatzen. Ich sage nur: die deutsche Hochschule ist stabiler, als Ihr glaubt, auch in ihren schlechten Seiten.

Welbergen:

Ich bin erstaunt, wenn Sie sagen „Wir brauchen die Trainee-Programme", – die sind doch schon da.

Zuruf:

Können Sie einmal sagen, was das sind: „Trainingsprogramme"?

Welbergen:

Trainingsprogramme und Trainee-Programme sind zwei ganz verschiedene Sachen.

Ich rede jetzt einmal von meinem Hause, weil ich das am besten kenne. Wir nehmen eine große Anzahl von Akademikern. Diese werden nicht für spezifische Jobs ausgebildet, es ist also kein „Trainingsprogramm" für den Job. Vielmehr rotieren sie durch das Unternehmen für ein Jahr, gehen in die Personalabteilung, in die Volkswirtschaftliche Abteilung, in die Rechtsabteilung, wenn es Juristen sind; meistens sind keine Ingenieure darunter. Wir lassen diese Leute rotieren. Während dieses Rotationsprozesses stellen wir fest, wo sie sich am besten eignen.

Wir versuchen, auf diesem Wege die notwendigen Einsichten zu geben, was überall vor sich geht. Es erschreckt immer wieder zu erleben, daß junge Akademiker nicht wissen, wie es in einem Unternehmen aussieht. Wenn sie es aber wissen, erkennen sie auch, wo sie am besten plaziert sind. Das nennen wir nicht „Trainingsprogramm", sondern „Trainee-Programm".

Natürlich gibt es auch gewisse Akademiker, die direkt in ihren Job gehen, z.B. Elektronikingenieure. Die bringen wir im Hause sofort an die richtige Stelle. Aber wir müssen ihnen eine Spezialausbildung zukommen lassen.

Ich wollte das nur als Beispiel anführen. Es gibt schon solche Programme. Wenn sie allerdings in größerem Stil notwendig würden, auch für die öffentliche Verwaltung, dann müßten sie natürlich vom Staat subventioniert werden. Auch der Staat sollte das tun, was andere längst schon machen. Ich verweise auf die Trainee-Programme der Deutschen Bank und könnte noch manche vergleichbaren Dinge anführen.

Weil es mir gerade einfällt, möchte ich noch auf ein Zitat eingehen. Glauben Sie kein Wort von der Prognose, daß der Staat nur noch 15 % einstellt, während er bisher 60 % eingestellt habe. Die Prognose-Studie zeigt, daß die Zahl 60 % zu hoch und die 15 % zu niedrig gegriffen sind. Die Prognose kommt vom Finanzminister. Ich will lieber nicht erzählen, wie sie entstanden ist, sonst würden wir uns wieder über seriöse Politik unterhalten.

(Heiterkeit)

Aussprache Welbergen, Glotz

Ich rate Ihnen von meinem Job her, nicht alles zu glauben, was gesagt wird. Beispielsweise hieß es in den letzten 3 Jahren, daß 15.000 Lehrstellen geschaffen worden seien, obwohl man seit 5 Jahren weiß, daß nicht mehr geschaffen werden können. Nehmen Sie deshalb bitte solche Katastrophen-Prognosen nicht hundertprozentig für bare Münze. Auch Vergleiche hinken oft, wenn dahinter andere Absichten stecken. Die muß man auch nicht als letzte Wahrheit akzeptieren.

Die wirtschaftliche Perspektive für die 80er Jahre

– Ansätze zur Überwindung der Wachstumsschwäche und der Arbeitslosigkeit

Prof. Dr. Norbert Walter

Ich darf zuerst ein Wort zu meiner Person sagen. Ich glaube, daß ich dem Anspruch, Wissenschaftler und nicht Praktiker zu sein – mindestens was die Prognosen angeht –, nicht gerecht werde. Ich bin, was die Prognosen angeht, eher Praktiker. Allerdings ist es mir meist nur vergönnt, für die kurze Frist, die Konjunktur nämlich, zu prognostizieren. Deshalb bin ich sehr froh, daß ich hier über die 80er Jahre sprechen darf, weil ich ziemlich sicher bin, daß Sie alles das, was ich heute sagen werde, bis in die 80er Jahre vergessen haben und mich nicht, wie mir das als Konjunkturforscher mit meinen Konjunkturprognosen dauernd passiert, dafür prügeln werden, was ich vorhersage.

Ich habe leider erst gestern abend die Gelegenheit gehabt, zu Ihnen zu stoßen, und das ist sicherlich sehr schlecht für Sie. Denn möglicherweise erzähle ich Ihnen sehr viel, was Sie schon in sehr viel besserer Weise gehört haben. Beim „Vorchecking" gestern abend wurde mir bedeutet – und das von einem Holländer, die das Vorchecking ja ganz gut beherrschen, wie wir in den letzten Tagen bei der Fußballweltmeisterschaft gesehen haben –, daß angesichts meines allgemein formulierten Themas wieder die Gefahr besteht, daß nicht über die Jugend und die Zukunft geredet wird, sondern über irgendwelche generellen Dinge und vielleicht sogar ausschließlich über die Bewältigung der Vergangenheit. Was das Zweite anlangt, glaube ich, kann ich Ihnen Hoffnung machen: Ich werde nur über die 80er Jahre und allerhöchstens über den Startpunkt etwas sagen, aber – und da muß ich Sie gleich von Anfang an enttäuschen – ich werde über die wirtschaftlichen Entwicklungen der 80er Jahre reden und dabei die Jugend nur als eine besondere Gruppe hin und wieder erwähnen. Ich glaube, es hat keinen Sinn, daß ich nur Jugendprobleme fixiere und damit das Ganze aus den Augen verliere und Sie keine Chance haben, die Gesamtproblematik zu erkennen. Zudem muß ich sagen: Meine komparativen Vorteile liegen nicht in speziellen Jugendfragen, sondern im Fachgebiet Ökonomie, und ich glaube, daß es deshalb gut ist, daß ich auch hier dieses Feld beackere.

Ich will Ihnen schließlich gleich zu Anfang sagen, wer ich bin und von welchem Axiom ich ausgehe, damit Sie nicht ständig auf der Suche nach meiner Motivation für irgendeine Aussage sind. Mein Axiom heißt: Die Menschen, so wie wir sie heute vorfinden, sind offensichtlich keine Altruisten. Ich als Ökonom, der sich mit dieser Lage konfrontiert sieht, muß deshalb mit **einem** Element, das menschliche Handeln beeinflußt, besonders sparsam, besonders ökonomisch umgehen, nämlich mit der Liebe. Diese Haltung beschränke ich auf den allerkleinsten Zirkel. Überall dort, wo man Lösungen für größere Gruppen auf dem Prinzip Liebe aufzubauen versucht, besteht die Gefahr, daß das Ergebnis schlechter ausfällt, als man es sich wünscht und als es sein könnte. Wenn ich also im folgenden hart erscheinende Problemlösungen vorschlage, dann betrachten Sie mich nicht als einen Darwinisten aus Leidenschaft, sondern als einen Darwinisten aus Konsequenz.

Ich möchte starten mit dem, was uns am Ende der 70er Jahre ökonomisch vor Augen steht. Die erste Feststellung, mit der wir ständig konfrontiert werden heißt: Der Startpunkt Ende der siebziger Jahre.

Die Sachkapazitäten sind nicht ausreichend ausgelastet. Seit der Rezession 1975 hat sich bei der Kapazitätsauslastung gesamtwirtschaftlich nichts mehr getan. Wir liegen heute noch immer etwa 5 bis 6 % – gemessen nach irgendwelchen klugen statischen Verfahren – unter der „normalen" gesamtwirtschaftlichen Kapazitätsauslastung. Daraus schließen wichtige gesellschaftliche Gruppen, nationale und vor allem internationale Wirtschaftspolitiker zweierlei: Sie erklären damit einerseits die schwache Investitionstätigkeit und leiten andererseits die Forderung ab, daß der Staat durch staatliche Nachfrage diese Nachfragelücke ausfüllen soll.

Es gibt aber auch eine alternative Diagnose dieses Phänomens unterausgelasteter Kapazitäten: Diese Leerkapazitäten sind ökonomisch überhaupt nicht existent. Es sind dies nur noch technische Kapazitäten. Kein Unternehmer kann sie weder heute noch in absehbarer Zeit ökonomisch, d. h. mit Gewinn wieder einsetzen. Mit anderen Worten: Diese sogenannten Überkapazitäten sind schlicht abzuschreiben.

Mir scheint, daß mehr für die zweite These spricht. Daß es zu dieser Obsoleszenz dieser Kapazitäten kam, lag an folgenden Faktoren: Da hat sich einerseits die Nachfragestruktur geändert. Wir sehen das in der Automobilindustrie, wir sehen das in der Bauindustrie; nachdem dort die Nachfrage in dem einen Fall schon länger, im zweiten erst relativ kurzfristig angesprungen ist, stößt man bereits auf Produktionsengpässe. Die Überkapazitäten dagegen konzentrieren sich dort, wo man offensichtlich nicht mit Gewinn arbeiten kann: In der Stahl- und Werftindustrie.

Ein zweites Phänomen charakterisiert die Ausgangslage am Ende der siebziger Jahre: Die eine Million Arbeitslose. Mit der einen Million Arbeitslosen ist freilich die Beschäftigungslage noch unzureichend gekennzeichnet. Die Zahl der Erwerbstätigen ist nämlich 1978 – und das scheint mir wichtiger – noch immer niedriger als am bisherigen Höhepunkt 1973. Aber auch darin wird das Ausmaß unseres Beschäftigungsproblems noch nicht voll sichtbar. Denn wir haben gleichzeitig Kurzarbeit, wir haben gleichzeitig Ausbildungsverlängerung; wir haben ja heute morgen etwas über das Berufsschulgrundjahr gehört. Würden wir die Zahl derer, die sich vom Arbeitsmarkt in die sogenannte stille

Reserve zurückgezogen haben (etwa 650.000) und die 600.000 Gastarbeiter, die wieder abgewandert sind, zur erfaßten Arbeitslosenzahl hinzuzählen, so würden wir eine Arbeitslosigkeit von 2,5 Millionen haben.

Trotz dieser hohen Arbeitslosigkeit – und das wurde heute morgen auch schon angedeutet – vermehren sich die Klagen über den Mangel an Arbeitskräften, besonders in prosperierenden Branchen, aber nicht nur dort. Der Mangel ist besonders ausgeprägt bei qualifizierten Facharbeitern.

Die ketzerische Frage, die man für die Diagnose: „Unterbeschäftigung" ebenso wie vorher für die Frage „Unterauslastung der Sachkapazitäten" stellen kann, muß lauten: Ist das, was wir heute an Arbeitslosigkeit beobachten, ökonomisch gesehen überhaupt eine beklagenswerte „echte" Arbeitslosigkeit oder ist das die „natürliche", „freiwillige" Arbeitslosigkeit? Ist die Million Arbeitslose das, was angesichts der existierenden Institutionen und Subventionen und angesichts des Verhaltens der Arbeitgeber praktisch unvermeidbar ist? Herr Glotz hat heute morgen gesagt, die Erhöhung der Arbeitslosigkeit sei zum Teil bildungspolitisch angelegt. Ich will später auf diese Frage zurückkommen.

Ein dritter Punkt, der mir für die gegenwärtige Lage charakteristisch scheint, ist die fehlende Strukturanpassung unserer Wirtschaft. Wir hatten drastische Wechselkursänderungen in den siebziger Jahren, wir hatten eine erhebliche Verteuerung des Faktors Energie und des Faktors Arbeit, das eine durch das Ölkartell, das andere durch aggressive Gewerkschaften und ungeschickt taktierende und schlecht beratene Arbeitgeber. All das hat zusammengenommen den Standort Bundesrepublik für Produzenten verschlechtert. Die Probleme konzentrieren sich in exportabhängigen und energieintensiven Bereichen und bei arbeitsintensiver Fertigung. Aber es gibt nicht nur diese Verschiebungen von Kosten und Kostenstruktur. Es gibt auch eine Verschiebung der Nachfrage. Länder, die vorher kaufkräftig waren, nämlich die Westeuropäer, sind ärmer geworden. Vor allem kleinere westeuropäische Länder sind arme Länder geworden.

In Südeuropa haben wir nahezu ausschließlich arme Länder. Aber die OPEC-Länder und einige andere rohstoffintensive Entwicklungsländer sind reich geworden. Daneben gibt es relativ dramatische demographische und soziologische Wandlungen, die zu einer veränderten Nachfragestruktur führen. Wenn jemand in der glücklichen Lage war, am Anfang der 70er Jahre ein Reisebüro gehabt zu haben, der ist heute ein gemachter Mann. Reisen erweist sich als neue Wachstumsbranche. Das Auto – dank überstandener Ölkrise und relativ starker Zunahme der Zahl der jungen Einkommensbezieher – steht ebenfalls relativ hoch in der Gunst der Konsumenten, und dieses Sich-rasche-Ändern von Nachfragestruktur wird uns auch durch die 80er Jahre begleiten. Darauf kommen wir dann später.

Bedarf für forcierten Strukturwandel ist also eindeutig in unserer Wirtschaft auszumachen, aber Produzenten und Politiker versuchen diesen Prozeß zu bremsen. Die Unternehmer in den begünstigten Branchen horten Aufträge statt zu investieren. Den Auftragsbestand zu maximieren ist, wie ich – nicht durch Dritte, sondern direkt aus dem Munde von Vorstandsmitgliedern deutscher Automobilfirmen – gehört habe, wichtiges, um nicht zu sagen wichtigstes Unternehmensziel geworden. Auch bei der Bauindustrie sieht man nicht, daß die Ausweitung der Nachfrage schon zu einem Anstieg der Bauproduktion geführt hätte. Statt dessen hat mir mein Bauunternehmer vor 10 Tagen eröffnet, daß er am 15. Juli für drei Wochen Betriebsferien macht. Im Winter Schlechtwettergeld und im Sommer in der Bundesrepbulik – und nicht irgendwo in einer klimabegünstigten Zone – Betriebsferien trotz dieses Auftragsberges in der Bauindustrie. Dies scheint mir dem Bedarf an Flexibilität und Strukturwandel überhaupt nicht Rechnung zu tragen.

Die Branchen mit Absatzschwierigkeiten rufen den Staat zu Hilfe und verlangen und erhalten Subventionen und Aufträge. Ich denke an die Landwirtschaft einerseits, ich denke an die Werftindustrie andererseits. Was uns also erhalten bleibt, sind falsche Strukturen, und statt mit moderner Technik wohlgerüstet, startet die Bundesrepublik mit einem vergreisten Kapitalbestand und mit der falschen Branchenstruktur in die 80er Jahre.

Viertes Charakteristikum der wirtschaftlichen Lage am Ende der siebziger Jahre ist die hohe Staatsverschuldung. Die hohe Staatsverschuldung – es sind ungefähr gegenwärtig 350 Milliarden DM – wird von Wirtschaft und Politikern als eine besonders schwere Hypothek empfunden. Die Hälfte dieses Defizits stammt – das macht wahrscheinlich für das Argument mehr aus als die Höhe der Gesamtverschuldung – aus der Zeit seit 1975. Von den Zinsverpflichtungen, die für diese Schuld aufzubringen sind, fürchtet man eine Einengung der Bewegungsfreiheit des Staates bei seinen Ausgaben und leitet die Erwartung ab, daß es später Steuererhöhungen geben wird.

Mir scheint, daß diese Analyse einseitig ist, um nicht zu sagen falsch. Steigende Defizite und steigende Staatsschulden müssen nämlich nicht negativ zu bewerten sein, soweit sie aus produktiven Ausgaben des Staats resultieren. Unter produktiven Ausgaben verstehe ich nicht nur investive Ausgaben. Die Bezahlung der heute morgen zitierten Berufsschullehrer ist zwar keine investive Ausgabe – sie ist Staatsverbrauch –, aber sie ist mindestens ebenso produktiv wie das Teeren von Waldwegen und das Bauen eines Schwimmbades für den Landrat XY. Was nun an den Staatsausgaben produktiv ist, läßt sich leider aus Statistiken, die wir haben, nicht sehr gut ablesen. Es ist nicht einzusehen, daß eine produktive Staatsausgabe im Jahr der Ausgabe voll vom Steuerzahler finanziert werden soll. Genausowenig, wie es dem Konsumenten zuzumuten ist, daß er, wenn ein neues Produkt auf den Markt kommt, schon im ersten Produktionsjahr für das Produkt so viel zahlt, daß die Investitionen bezahlt werden können. Die Kreditaufnahme bleibt auch dann sinnvoll, wenn sie vom Staat für produktive Zwecke benötigt wird.

Die Datenänderungen in den achtziger Jahren

Über einen Punkt, das Arbeitskräftepotential, haben wir heute morgen schon einiges gehört. Ich möchte mit einem anderen Faktor beginnen, der für die Entwicklung der 80er Jahre in ökonomischer Hinsicht ebenso bedeutsam ist, nämlich die schrumpfende Bevölkerung. Während wir von 1950 bis 1960 eine Bevölkerung hatten, die um 1 % pro Jahr wuchs, und in den 60er Jahren eine Bevölkerung, die so etwa um 3/4 % zunahm, schrumpft seit etwa 1974 die Bevölkerung, und zwar pro Jahr etwa um knapp 1/2 %. Angesichts des Altersaufbaus der Bevölkerung und speziell der Tatsache, daß die Altersgruppe, die dem Nachkriegsbabyboom entstammt, noch nicht in der Altersstufe ist, wo die Gebärquote am höchsten ist, und der Tatsache, daß – ein häßliches Wort – die Reproduktionsrate dank der Pille besonders niedrig ist, ist die Wahrscheinlichkeit relativ gering, daß bis Mitte der 80er Jahre die Bevölkerung von diesem Trend des Schrumpfens herunterkommen könnte. Erst danach steigt die Größe der Kohorte, die besonders viele Kinder bekommen kann, wieder an. Freilich nur, wenn sich bis dahin die Einstellung zu Kindern – oder der Pille – ändert, ist ab Mitte der achtziger Jahre eine erneute Ausweitung der Bevölkerung möglich. Selten freilich haben sich bislang Verhaltensweisen so rasch geändert.

Wenn man Wanderungen nicht berücksichtigt – und da muß ich allerdings zugeben, daß ich einen schwachen Punkt in der Analyse habe, denn die Bundesrepublik liegt in der Mitte Europas, und es kann relativ leicht zu Wanderungen kommen, wenn die wirtschaftliche Lage anders ist, als wir Pessimisten uns das heute ausmalen –, schrumpft die Bevölkerung der Bundesrepublik bis zum Jahre 1985 auf etwa 59 Millionen. Das Einkommen, das erwirtschaftet wird, wird also auf immer weniger Köpfe verteilt. Aber das ist nur eine der Entwicklungen, die uns Schwierigkeiten machen. Eine zweite ist die starke Änderung der Struktur der Bevölkerung, die Änderung des Altersaufbaus der Bevölkerung. Wir haben extrem wenig Kleinkinder, extrem wenig Grundschulkinder; das hat eine ganze Menge Implikationen für die staatlichen Bildungsinvestitionen, das hat aber auch Implikationen für die Privatwirtschaft. Bei solch schnellen Änderungen muß man wirklich sehr anpassungsfähig sein: Was tun beispielsweise die Produzenten, die Nahrungsmittel für Kleinkinder herstellen und noch auf den gleichen Umsatz kommen wollen wie vorher, wenn die Zahl der Babies halbiert wird und die Babies ja auch nicht dicker werden sollen?

Bei der zweiten demographischen Datenänderung kann ich mich kurz fassen: Dem steigenden Arbeitskräftepotential in den nächsten Jahren. Die entscheidenden Faktoren hat Herr Welbergen heute morgen schon genannt. Wir haben unglücklicherweise einen Knick in der Entwicklung. Bis 1985 haben wir ein steigendes Arbeitskräftevolumen, nicht nur bedingt durch die von ihm beschriebene erhöhte Zahl von Schulabgängern, sondern auch durch die Tatsache, daß die Altersgruppe, die aus dem Erwerbsleben ausscheidet, besonders klein ist. Das rührt daher, daß es im Ersten Weltkrieg noch keine geschickte Urlaubsplanung wie im Zweiten Weltkrieg gab. Daher ist die Geburtenrate so gering gewesen. Von denen, die in dieser Phase geboren wurden, fehlen jene und vor allem jene Männer, die im Zweiten Weltkrieg gefallen sind.

Ich muß sagen, daß die Schätzungen, die Ihnen Herr Welbergen heute morgen für die Entwicklung des Arbeitskräftepotentials präsentierte und die auch ich Ihnen vortrage – sie lauten ungefähr: es nimmt pro Jahr etwa um 1/2 % bis zum Jahre 1985 zu, nimmt dann weiter noch ganz leicht in der Phase 1985 bis 1990 zu und geht zurück in den 90er Jahren – eine ganze Menge ungenannter Verhaltensweisen impliziert und daß es schon im letzten Jahr Entwicklungen gegeben hat, die nicht zu den impliziten Annahmen passen. So war im letzten Jahr das Ansteigen der sogenannten „stillen Reserve" stärker, als in allen diesen Rechnungen unterstellt war. Es könnte also durchaus sein, daß das Zurückziehen oder das nicht so schnelle Eindringen der Frau in das Erwerbsleben bereits einen erheblichen Teil zur (Schein-)Lösung des Problems beitragen könnte. Ich weiß zwar nicht, ob das für die Frauen das Problem lösen könnte, aber doch zumindest für die Statistiken. In der Schätzung, daß das Arbeitskräfteangebot bis zum Jahr 1985 um etwa 1/2 % steige, wurde impliziert, daß die Erwerbsbeteiligung der Frau sich so weiter erhöht, wie das in den vergangenen 5 Jahren der Fall war. Die Frage, ob die Annahme richtig ist, ist eine Frage, die man ernsthaft stellen kann. Nach 1985 wird sich das Arbeitskräftepotential wieder vermindern, vor allem deshalb, weil aufgrund des Pillenknicks nur noch wenig junge Leute ins erwerbsfähige Alter kommen.

Neben den Datenänderungen im nationalen Rahmen sind internationale Entwicklungen von eminenter Bedeutung: Einerseits haben die Entwicklungsländer noch sehr viel drängendere Beschäftigungsprobleme, andererseits ergeben sich Fortschritte bei der wirtschaftlichen Entwicklung in den halbindustrialisierten Ländern wie Brasilien, Mexiko und Spanien. Aus diesen Regionen dürfte ein enormer Wettbewerbsdruck auf die Industrieländer und auch auf die Bundesrepublik kommen. Dies dürfte den in den 80er Jahren ohnehin schon erforderlichen Strukturwandel von dieser Seite her noch erheblich forcieren. Wenn sich diese Länder tatsächlich vornehmen, was sie auf Konferenzen sagen, nämlich ihren Anteil an der Weltindustrieproduktion bis zum Jahre 2000 auf 25 % hochzuschrauben, dann dürfte für die deutsche Industrie bald eine sehr harte Phase eintreten.

Wirtschaftliches Szenario für die achtziger Jahre

Zuerst muß man da einiges zu den wahrscheinlichen wirtschaftlichen Verhaltensweisen sagen. Vorab zur Frage der Zielsetzung: Ich glaube, daß zwei Charakteristiken des deutschen Verhaltens auch in den 80er Jahren bestehenbleiben. Das erste: Wir werden weiterhin eine hohe Priorität für die Geldwertstabilität beobachten. Das zweite: Unsere Wirtschaft wird relativ stark exportorientiert bleiben. Von diesen zwei Säulen würde ich ausgehen. Ich weiß dagegen nicht, wie das Verhalten der Gewerkschaften in den 80er Jahren sein wird, ob sie zurückfinden zu dem, was ich als gesamtwirtschaftlich verantwortliches Verhalten der 50er und 60er Jahre sehe oder ob der Konfrontationskurs, wie wir ihn in den 70er Jahren beobachtet haben, anhält und modellbildend für die 80er Jahre wird.

Eine andere Voraussetzung aber scheint mir ziemlich sicher: Die Wirtschaftspolitik wird auch in den 80er Jahren auf schwachen Regierungsmehrheiten fußen.

Ich sehe nicht, wie wir rasch eine relativ stabile Mehrheit nach der einen oder der anderen Seite bekommen könnten. Das ist günstig insofern, als die Regierung, wer sie auch immer sei, kaum große Änderungen durchsetzen kann, sondern immer vorsichtig sein muß. Das ist für die Wirtschaft immer günstig. Aber es ist ungünstig in anderer Hinsicht, nämlich insofern, als die Regierung anfällig bleibt gegenüber jeder kleinen Gruppe, die ihre Interessen lautstark durchsetzen will.

Zur Geldpolitik will ich hier nicht viel sagen. Wichtigste Aufgabe der Geldpolitik bleibt es, sicherzustellen, daß die Geldwertstabilität erhalten bleibt. Ich hielte eine 8%ige Geldmengenausweitung für richtig, nicht deshalb, weil es die 80er Jahre sind, sondern weil das Produktionspotential ungefähr um 3 bis 4 % steigt und ich nicht sehe, wie man die Inflationsrate in einer Welt, in der die Inflationsraten wahrscheinlich eher zwischen 5 un 10 % schwanken, nachhaltig unter 3 % drücken könnte. Aber dies nur am Rande.

Wichtiger erscheint mir, was ich über die Finanzpolitik sagen will. Die Erhöhung der Staatsquote – ein Phänomen, das man im Grunde seit Jahrhunderten beobachten kann – hat sich in der ersten Hälfte der 70er Jahre beschleunigt. Ich rechne für die 80er Jahre mit einer Reduktion der Staatsquote. Zwar wird sich nicht der Anteil der staatlichen Investitionen an der Gesamtproduktion vermindern, wohl aber jener Teil, der in letzter Zeit besonders aufgebläht wurde, nämlich die staatlichen Transferzahlungen. Ich glaube, die finanz- und steuerpolitische Diskussion zeigt, daß sich der Zeitgeist in dieser Hinsicht gedreht hat. Ich glaube, daß sich das niederschlagen wird: In der Rentenversicherung, der Krankenversicherung, aber auch in Beschränkungen bei den Subventionen. Damit wird Spielraum für Steuerentlastungen geschaffen. Ich glaube, daß wir in diesem Jahr erste Schritte in diese Richtung vornehmen werden, nämlich einen Abbau in der progressiven Einkommen- und Lohnsteuer. Was wir in diesem Jahr nicht tun werden, ist etwas, was in den 80er Jahren sicherlich notwendig wird, nämlich ein quasi-automatischer Ausgleich für inflationsbedingte Verschärfung der Steuerprogression.

Ich komme zum dritten Punkt, zur Frage der Lohnpolitik. Die Tatsache, daß das Lohnniveau vor allem bei weniger Qualifizierten vergleichsweise hoch ist, und die Aussicht, daß nach 1985 die Arbeitskräfte wiederum nicht mehr reichlich, sondern eher wieder knapper werden, wird, auch wenn Herr Welbergen meint, daß sich die Unternehmen sehr anstrengen werden, Arbeitskräfte einzustellen, diese Anstrengungen limitieren. Denn, wenn man jetzt arbeitsintensive Produktionsmethoden wählen würde und arbeitsintensiv investieren würde – um es drastisch auszudrücken „wieder mit der Schippe arbeiten“ – dann würde man sich Produktionstechniken aneignen, die für die 90er Jahre absolut ungeeignet sind, denn dann hat man wieder Mangel an Arbeitskräften, und dann braucht man wieder hervorragend entwickelte Maschinen und hervorragend rationalisierte Produktionsmethoden. Insofern wird es sehr schwer sein, die Unternehmen im Zeitraum bis 1985 wirklich zu einem mächtigen Push in Richtung auf arbeitsintensive Produktionsmethoden zu bewegen. Das erhöht natürlich den Druck auf dem Arbeitsmarkt. Das vermindert die Chancen der Arbeitskräfte, die bis 1985 auf den Arbeitsmarkt drängen. Von dieser Seite her glaube ich, daß der Druck durch die Löhne, d. h. die Schwierigkeit, Lohnerhöhungen durchzusetzen, zunimmt.

Wie nun könnte man angesichts der beschriebenen demographischen Entwicklung und angesichts der wahrscheinlichen Zurückhaltung der Arbeitgeber bei Neueinstellungen, wie könnte man die Verhandlungsposition der Arbeitnehmerseite verbessern? Über einige Ansätze ist diskutiert worden: Es könnte einerseits eine forcierte Mindestlohngesetzgebung geben, d. h. der Staat diktiert, daß Mindestlöhne sich in bestimmter Weise zu entwickeln haben. Die andere Möglichkeit wäre eine starke Verkürzung der Arbeitszeit, um damit das Arbeitskräftepotential zu verknappen. Dies sind alles hervorragende Ideen, wenn man auf dem Mond lebt. Wenn man aber in einer offenen Volkswirtschaft lebt und die Produkte nicht nur zu Hause verkaufen muß, sondern international und zu Hause auch mit ausländischen Konkurrenten konkurriert, dann wird eine solche Politik relativ schnurstracks statt zur Besserung der Lage der Arbeitnehmer zu mehr Arbeitslosigkeit führen, mindestens aber zu weniger Realeinkommen, weil die Menschen eben zu entsprechenden Löhnen keine entsprechende Arbeit mehr finden. Die wirtschaftliche Entwicklung in der Bundesrepublik Deutschland ist zu sehr von der internationalen Lage abhängig, als daß eine Prognose ohne Annahme über die Weltwirtschaft gemacht werden könnte.

International unterstelle ich, daß auch in den anderen Industrieländern die Wachstumsraten der 50er und 60er Jahre nicht wieder erreicht werden. Ich unterstelle, daß das, was die OECD für die 80er Jahre projiziert hat, nämlich ein Wachstum in der Größenordnung von 5 %, relativ unrealistisch ist. Meine Vorstellung für die Wachstumsraten in den 80er Jahren in den westlichen Industrieländern liegt bei etwa 3,5 %.

Was bedeutet das nun für das Wirtschaftswachstum der Bundesrepublik? Ich sagte Ihnen, es ist vom Arbeitskräftepotential her kaum begrenzt, es gibt höchstens einen Mangel an qualifizierten Kräften, es gibt einen Mangel an qualifiziertem Sachkapital, und es gibt eine Nachfrageschwäche in einigen Bereichen. Mir scheint, daß, wenn man dies alles zusammen nimmt, eine Wachstumsrate von 3 % schon relativ hochgegriffen ist. Wir haben ja in dieser Zeit einen Umstrukturierungsprozeß von einer ständig exportgetriebenen und von der Staatsnachfrage angeheizten Wirtschaft auf eine von privatem Verbrauch und Investitionsnachfrage getragene Entwicklung zu schaffen, und wir haben bei der beschriebenen Bevölkerungsentwicklung noch eine Reihe von Nachfragefriktionen bei den Verbrauchsausgaben zu realisieren. Wenn ein Wachstum von durchschnittlich 3 % erreicht wird, dürfte das, was wir statistisch als Kapazitätsauslastung messen, in den 80er Jahren genauso niedrig bleiben, wie es gegenwärtig ist. Ich glaube aber, daß wir uns dann langsam aber sicher daran gewöhnt haben, dieses unnötige Mehr an Kapazität abzuschreiben. Unternehmer, mit denen ich gesprochen habe, die die Nachkriegszeit wirklich bewußt durchlebt haben, haben mir schon vor 2 Jahren gesagt: „Was uns fehlt, ist eine ordentliche Abschreibungsrunde, damit alle wissen, was eigentlich da ist, und nicht ständig von etwas reden, was nicht mehr existiert".

Was resultiert aus dieser Wachstumsrate für die Beschäftigungsentwicklung? Würde der durchschnittliche Produktivitätsanstieg, d.h. also Produktion pro Beschäftigten, in den 80er Jahren so hoch sein wie in den 60er Jahren und 70er Jahren, nämlich 4 %, so müßte man beim erwarteten Wachstum von 3 % prognostizieren, daß die Beschäftigung in den 80er Jahren weiter sinkt und – da wir ein steigendes Arbeitskräftepotential bekommen –, die Arbeitslosigkeit noch stärker steigt, als die Beschäftigung sinkt. Ich halte diese düstere Prognose für falsch, weil ich glaube, daß der Angebotsdruck auf dem Arbeitsmarkt zu zurückhaltender Lohnpolitik führt, und weil ich nicht damit rechne, daß die Gewerkschaften glauben, ihre Interessen in einer solchen Situation am besten durch eine aggressive Lohnpolitik vertreten zu können. Aus diesem Grunde nehme ich auch an, daß der Produktivitätsanstieg in den nächsten Jahren geringer ausfällt, weil der Druck für die Unternehmen, zu rationalisieren, ein wenig nachläßt.

Man sollte sich allerdings keine Wunderdinge versprechen. Meine Erwartung ist, daß die Produktivität irgendwo zwischen 2,5 und 3 % ansteigen wird. Daraus folgt, daß ein Beschäftigungsanstieg von jährlich knapp 1/2 % möglich ist. Dies reicht aber nicht aus, um bis 1985 die Arbeitslosigkeit auf weniger als ungefähr 600 000 – 700 000 zu senken. Wir sollten uns also nach meiner Einschätzung darauf einstellen, daß die Arbeitslosigkeit bis zur Mitte der 80er Jahre irgendwo zwischen einer halben Million und einer Million liegen wird und nicht darunter. Wenn wir die eine Million als Obergrenze für die Jahre 1981 und 1982 halten können, scheint mir das im Prinzip schon ein Erfolg zu sein, weil wir in jenen zwei Jahren einen besonders großen Schub an neuen Arbeitskräften zu erwarten haben.

Ich vermute, daß ein großer Teil dieser Belastung auf dem Arbeitsmarkt auf dem Rücken der Frauen ausgetragen wird; daß man durch die verschiedensten Methoden – subtil und weniger subtil – versuchen wird, daß die zunehmende Erwerbstätigkeit der Frau eben in kleineren Schritten als bislang vorangeht.

Und ein zweiter Punkt, der mir unausweichlich erscheint: Da die Politiker und die Gewerkschaften ständig darauf achten, daß alle die, die „drin" sind, besonders abgesichert werden, wird die Anpassungslast derer, die noch nicht drin sind, die der Newcomer, besonders groß sein. D.h., wenn Ihnen jemand die Hoffnung macht, daß die Jugendarbeitslosigkeit in der ersten Hälfte der achtziger Jahre eben auch nur ein „durchschnittliches" Problem sein wird, so erscheint mir das absolut unrealistisch. Die Jugendarbeitslosigkeit wird mit Sicherheit das Problem der 80er Jahre sein. Wie Veränderungen zu schaffen sind, ist klar: Es ist bei den Politikern anzusetzen und dafür zu sorgen, daß sich der Altersaufbau in den politischen Parteien ändert. Es hat keinen Sinn, wenn die Jugendlichen auf die Lobby alter Herren setzen. Es ist ganz vernünftig, daß man erwartet, daß jemand seiner Altersgruppe gemäß denkt; das werden Sie bei sich später auch feststellen.
Um ein kleines Beispiel zu bringen: Wenn ich in der Konjunkturabteilung eine Zusammenstellung guter Prognosen für die Konjunktur und guter Empfehlungen für die Wirtschaftspolitik haben will, achte ich sorgfältig darauf, daß ich nicht nur Leute habe, die Sparer in Form von festverzinslichen Wertpapieren sind, weil das natürlich Stabilitätsfanatiker sind, sondern ich achte auch darauf, daß einer drin ist, der gerne Inflation hat, nämlich ein „Häuslebauer" zum Beispiel; das braucht man. Denn ich glaube, daß es unrealistisch ist, ständig zu erwarten, daß jemand dauernd und bewußt gegen seine Interessen agiert. Deshalb lieber eine Interessenmischung. Deshalb muß in den politischen Parteien das Element Jugend stärker betont werden. Das ist aber nur ein Element der Strategie und vielleicht nicht einmal das wichtigste.

Wichtiger scheint mir die Penetration der Gewerkschaften zu sein: Ich glaube, daß die Jugendlichen, die bislang drin sind, fast überwiegend akademisch ausgebildete Jugendliche sind, die oftmals weder gesamtwirtschaftliche Einsichten noch betriebswirtschaftliche Einsichten besitzen, sondern vor allem ideologisch angelernt sind und deshalb das, was die Jugendinteressen darstellt, gar nicht in angemessener Weise vertreten. Sie mögen zwar durchaus meinen, Jugendinteressen zu vertreten, aber effektiv verstoßen sie gegen die Jugendinteressen. Ich meine also, daß man in den Gewerkschaften von der Jugendseite her mitbestimmen muß, um dafür zu sorgen, daß die Jugendlichen nicht einen übergroßen Teil der Anpassungslast in den 80er Jahren zu tragen haben.

Was bedeutet diese nationale Datenkonstellation für die Verflechtung der Bundesrepublik mit der Weltwirtschaft? Wir haben also für die nächsten 10 Jahre zu gleicher Zeit eine schrumpfende Bevölkerung und ein steigendes Arbeitskräftepotential. Das ist eine günstige Bedingung für einen ständig steigenden Ausfuhrüberschuß, da wir ja einen höheren Produktions- als Verbrauchsanstieg haben dürften. Die fehlende inländische Nachfrage also müßte ersetzt werden durch ausländische Nachfrage.

Wenn Sie nun an den Wirtschaftsgipfel denken, der in ein paar Tagen in Bonn stattfinden wird, und wissen, was die Teilnehmer dort von der Bundesrepublik fordern, werden Sie feststellen, daß es genau das Entgegengesetzte ist. Es wird deshalb sehr schwer sein, diese von der demographischen Entwicklung her im Grunde natürliche Entwicklung in den 80er Jahren international verständlich zu machen. Ich glaube, wir können sie auch nur verständlich machen, wenn wir es den anderen erleichtern, das, was wir produzieren können, auch nachzufragen. Denn es gibt eine ganze Menge Länder – heute morgen wurde es gesagt –, und zwar Entwicklungsländer, die an Bedarf nun wahrlich keinen Mangel haben. Das einzige, was ihnen fehlt, sind die Mittel, diese Dinge zu kaufen, mit anderen Worten, wir müssen den Menschen Kredite dafür geben, daß sie Produkte bei uns kaufen können. Besser noch als Regierungsanleihen, die immer ein bißchen mit politischem Kuhhandel verbunden sind, scheinen mir Direktinvestitionen zu sein. Wenn der Staat sich daran beteiligen will, soll er sich am politischen Risiko und am Transferrisiko für diese Investitionen beteiligen.

Eine weitere Lösungsmöglichkeit für das Problem der achtziger Jahre sei angesprochen: Hier sitzen viele Jugendliche, und ich glaube, der Anteil derer, die irgendwann ihr Examen machen und damit dem Akademikerberg noch einige Höhe hinzufügen, ist relativ groß. So wie früher die Kirchen dafür gesorgt haben, daß das Arbeitsmarktproblem entschärft wurde, indem sie Missionare in die Welt schickten, sollte heute, angesichts des entstehenden Akademikerberges, darüber nachgedacht werden, ob es nicht in der Welt noch Aufgaben gibt, die durch diejenigen, die bei uns ausgebildet werden, zu erfüllen sind. Dadurch wird das Studium zwar nochmals ein bißchen länger, denn Sprache und am besten auch Kultur und Geschichte seines Arbeitslandes sollte man kennen.

Andere Lösungsansätze setzen noch näher an der Basis der gesellschaftspolitischen Basis an; ich glaube, man kann wohl unschwer sagen, daß Versicherungsdenken, speziell in der Form kollektiver Verträge, unsere Gesellschaft beherrscht. Viele Gruppen fordern und erhalten Preis- und Einkommensgarantien, die Arbeitnehmer wünschen und bekommen manchmal Beschäftigungsgarantien. Die Gruppe, die es am tollsten treibt, sind die Beamten. Sie sichern sich Einkommen und Beschäftigung.

Risikobereitschaft und eigenverantwortliches Handeln wird zur Ausnahme. Das sage ich ohne moralische Anklage. Ich empfinde es aus der Sicht des Individuums im heutigen System als absolut vernünftig, daß Risikobereitschaft und eigenverantwortliches Handeln zur Ausnahme wird.

Wenn es attraktiver ist, wenn es dem einzelnen mehr einbringt, seine Kraft dafür einzusetzen, daß er Transfereinkommen erzielt oder Steuern spart, ist nicht einzusehen, warum er die Kraft für zusätzliche Marktleistungen aufwenden soll. Und das ist nunmal zunehmend so geworden. Es gibt dafür zahllose Beispiele. Am überzeugendsten scheint mir mein eigener Fall: Ich selbst bin auch der Attraktion des versicherten Einkommens anheimgefallen. Ich wurde zu Beginn dieses Monats Beamter, nachdem ich jahrelang meinte, das könne doch kaum meiner Grundhaltung entsprechen. Es war unsinnig, das nicht zu tun. Moralisch ist das ziemlich bedenklich. Aber mit der Moral kommt man relativ schlecht weiter, denn man handelt seinen eigenen Interessen entgegen.

Ich könnte andere Beispiele nennen: Mein Vater hatte glücklicherweise am Ende seines Lebens keine steigende Einkommenskurve, sondern eine, die flacher wurde. Er hat durch seine Verrentung sein Familieneinkommen erhöht. Durch Herumhören in Pensionärskreisen ließ sich relativ leicht ermitteln, daß das durchaus nicht die Ausnahme ist, sondern daß das Nettoeinkommen sich durchaus in relativ vielen Fällen erhöht. Daß natürlich jemand, der relativ aktiv war, nach seiner Frühverrentung mit 63 weiterarbeit und seinen Arbeitsplatz nicht freimacht, sondern im Unternehmen weiterarbeitet, ist auch relativ wahrscheinlich. Die Gesellschaft hat eine schwere Bürde für die Alten zu tragen, die Aktiven zahlen mehr Sozialversicherung. Was soll man tun? Ein Vorschlag, den ich kürzlich bei einer Veranstaltung in St. Gallen schon einmal vortrug, sei hier wiederholt: Angesichts der – auch heute morgen laut gewordenen – Klage, daß die Menschen in das Bildungssystem hineinrennen, hinterher herauskommen und vor dem Markt stehen, der sie nicht aufnimmt, und der Tatsache, daß auf der anderen Seite die qualifizierten Facharbeiter fehlen – diese Ausbildung scheint nicht attraktiv zu sein –, sollte man die Ausbildung von Facharbeitern, nicht aber die von Akademikern subventionieren. Statt kostenloser akademischer Ausbildung durch den Staat – das war mein radikaler Vorschlag, so weit muß man aber gar nicht gehen – könnte es beispielsweise Ausbildung auf Kredit geben, das heißt also, die Finanzierung des Studiums wird durch den Staat geleistet und muß später zurückgezahlt werden. Ähnliche Überlegungen könnte man auch zur kollektiven Kranken- und Rentenversicherung anstellen.

Ich habe bis jetzt immer nur von der Anpassung auf der Arbeitnehmerseite gesprochen. Aber das Schnorren der einzelnen beim Staat gibt es ja nun wahrlich nicht nur auf der Arbeitsnehmerseite, sondern eben auch bei den Unternehmen. Dabei denke ich u.a. auch an unsere sogenannten freien Berufe. Wir haben eine moderne Industriewirtschaft, aber auf unserem Servicesektor, dem Sektor, der nach bekanntem Gesetz von Fourastié der Sektor der Zukunft sein soll, haben wir immer noch eine ständestaatliche Organisation, eine mittelalterliche Organisation. Dies limitiert die Effizienz ganz beträchtlich. Abhilfe könnte dadurch entstehen, daß ein paar unserer Gebührenordnungen abgeschafft werden. In Amerika gibt es offensichtlich schon Zahnärzte, die Zahnkronen für die Hälfte des Preises ihrer Fachkollegen in besserer Qualität anfertigen, weil sie sich spezialisiert haben und jetzt auch noch die Erlaubnis bekommen haben, ein kleines bißchen dafür zu werben. Das könnte vielleicht Modellcharakter für uns haben, daß Konkurrenz auch dort stattfindet, wo die Zukunft unserer Wirtschaft liegt. Es gibt viele andere Bereiche, in denen auch Gebührenordnungen die Wirklichkeit beherrschen, die Konkurrenz ausschalten. Wir sollten keine Einkommensgarantie für Landwirte geben, denn wenn wir die Entwicklungsländerhilfe wirklich ernst nehmen, müssen wir den Entwicklungsländern eine Chance geben, das bei uns abzusetzen, was sie wirklich produzieren können, wofür sie komperative Vorteile haben, wie beispielsweise bei landwirtschaftlichen Produkten.

Schließlich gibt es auch noch eine besondere Art von Einkommensgarantie für Großunternehmen, nämlich die absolute Sicherheit, daß sie nicht Konkurs gehen können, weil der Staat in Notfällen immer einspringt. Mein Vorschlag lautet nun nicht, daß der Staat die Großunternehmen „hopsgehen lassen soll", das würde politisch ein bißchen naiv sein. Aber daraus sollte man schlußfolgern, daß wir unsere Kartellgesetzgebung ernster nehmen sollten, daß wir der Konzentration entgegenwirken müssen und, wo das im nationalen Rahmen an seine Grenzen stößt, sollten wir dafür sorgen, daß es international Wettbewerb gibt, d.h. Öffnung der Märkte hilft weiter.

Zur Linderung der Probleme in den achtziger Jahren müssen wir das überhöhte Reallohnniveau reduzieren, d.h. der Lohnanstieg muß auf mittlerer Frist unterhalb des Produktivitätsanstiegs liegen. Das ist der eine Punkt. Der andere Punkt, der mindestens ebenso wichtig ist – und jetzt kommt wieder der Darwinist zum Vorschein – betrifft die Tatsache, daß das Risiko, arbeitslos zu werden, bzw. zu bleiben, nicht zufällig verteilt ist, sondern sich – wie ich schon sagte – auf Newcomer und weniger Qualifizierte konzentriert. Deshalb meine ich, daß bei jenen Gruppen eine besondere Zurückhaltung bei den Lohnforderungen angezeigt ist.

Ich habe einmal eine ähnlich lautende Kolumne geschrieben, worauf mir Jugendliche antworteten und bemerkten: „Wir waren bei den Tarifverhandlungen vor drei Jahren nicht dabei, als die Auszubildenden eine besonders hohe Lohnerhöhung bekommen haben, und jetzt stehen wir auf der Gasse und bekommen keine Lehrstellen." Und sie haben natürlich recht. Es ist zu fragen, ob es sinnvoll ist, daß die Gewerkschaften für Dritte etwas aushandeln, von denen sie nicht legitimiert sind, und deren Chancen sie verderben.

Nochmals: Wir brauchen Jugendliche, die ihre Interessen in einem sehr weit verstandenen Sinn in den Gewerkschaften vertreten. Die Frage des Eindringens in den Arbeitsmarkt sollte wieder als eine Investitionsperiode in die eigenen Fähigkeiten und die eigene spätere Karriere mit angesehen werden; das hat nichts mit Moral und Ethos zu tun, sondern schlicht und einfach mit der Maximierung des Lebenseinkommens. Jeder sollte nicht nur auf die Einkommen von heute schauen, sondern auch bei seiner Berufswahl und bei seiner Einkommensforderung eben darauf achten, wie seine mittelfristigen und langfristigen Chancen dadurch beeinflußt werden.

Ein paar der Forderungen, die an die Finanzpolitik zu stellen sind, habe ich schon genannt, soweit sie ordnungspolitischen Charakter haben. Nun noch ein paar, die zu den Subventionen zu nennen wären: Viele der heute gezahlten Subventionen waren sinnvoll, als sie eingeführt wurden. Heute sind sie funktionslos. Mir scheint es relativ nutzlos, wenn ich beispielsweise aus meinem Steuersäckel Steuern bezahle und später das Geld wieder in Form von Sparsubventionen in die andere Tasche reingesteckt bekomme und es relativ sicher ist, daß die Ersparnis, die ich tätige, durch die Subvention praktisch nicht verändert wurde. Das einzige, was dieser Prozeß bewirkt, ist, daß Bürokraten zu beschäftigen und zu bezahlen sind. Es gibt aber auch Erhaltungssubventionen, von denen ich schon sprach – Werftindustrie, Landwirtschaft –, die nicht sinnvoll sind, und dann gibt es etwas, was mein besonderes Ärgernis erregt, die Vernichtungssubvention. Wenn jemand anfängt, Pfirische und Tomaten auf die Müllkippe zu fahren, dann ist bei mir als Ökonom und als normaldenkender Mensch jener Punkt erreicht, bei dem man sagen muß, jetzt muß wohl wirtschaftlich etwas Unvernünftiges passieren. Was da passiert, ist eben die Erhaltung einer Monopolsituation für Landwirte und nicht die bessere Versorgung mit Gütern, dem Sinne allen Wirtschaftens.

Neben dem Abbau der Subventionen ist die Steuer- und Abgabenlast zu reduzieren:

Ich glaube, in einer Situation, in der die Durchschnittsbelastung mit Einkommensteuer und Sozialversicherung für jede zusätzlich verdiente Mark für einen durchschnittlichen Arbeitnehmer bei 50 % liegt – eine Belastung, die, wenn man die Inflation berücksichtigt, gar noch höher liegt –, ist das Streben nach mehr Leistung und Einkommen über den Markt erheblich gehemmt.

Ein letztes Wort zum Zeithorizont der Politik im allgemeinen: Mir scheint, daß die Politik – solange der Wähler so dumm ist, wie er zu sein scheint – aufs nächste Wahljahr setzen muß und weiter auf das kurze Gedächtnis der Wähler setzen wird. Aber ein bißchen habe ich doch die Hoffnung, daß es positive Zeichen gibt. In Kalifornien gibt es eine Bürgerinitiative, die dafür gesorgt hat, daß durch Volksentscheid die Steuerlast radikal gesenkt wurde. Vielleicht sind solche Übertreibungen, die hier und da zu beobachten sind, geeignet, so manche Illusionen bei den Wählern abzubauen und damit auch die Politiker dafür zu interessieren, Politik zu betreiben, die über die nächste Wahlperiode hinausreicht. Man kann natürlich vom Politiker nicht erwarten, daß er gegen sein eigenes Interesse, nämlich das nächste Mal wieder gewählt zu werden, handelt. D.h., solange die Öffentlichkeit nicht über den Wahlhorizont hinausschaut, sollte vom Politiker nicht erwartet werden, daß er es tut.

Als ein Beispiel für die vorhandene Kurzsichtigkeit erscheint mir in der Bundesrepublik beispielsweise die Behandlung der Rentenversicherung. Ich kritisiere nicht nur die Lösungen, die die sozial-liberale Koalition jetzt verabschiedet hat, ich kritisiere vielmehr das, was sie – die sozial-liberale Koalition – und die Opposition für die Zeit nach 1981 wieder versprechen, nämlich die Bruttolohnbezogenheit der Renten. Wenn die Bruttolohnbezogenheit der Rente wieder eingeführt wird, die wirtschaftliche Entwicklung etwa so verläuft, wie ich es beschrieben habe, und die Bevölkerungsentwicklung im skizzierten Rahmen bleibt, dann wird im Jahre 2020 jeder Beschäftigte statt gegenwärtig 18 % Sozialversicherung 40 % Sozialversicherung zahlen, und ich will Sie fragen – vor allem die jungen unter Ihnen –, ob Sie daran glauben, daß die dann Aktiven, Sie nämlich, den Rentnern des Jahres 2020 dieses Opfer – 40 % Ihrer Bruttoeinkommen – erbringen werden. Danke schön.

Statement zur Frage beruflicher Ausbildung

Hermann Rappe

Ich will die 10 Minuten konsequent nur zur Frage beruflicher Ausbildung benutzen und dazu ein paar Positionen darlegen. Zunächst einmal die Gewerkschaften: Sie sind eindeutig für die Beibehaltung des dualen Systems. Einer Verschulungstendenz reden wir nicht das Wort. Duales System zwischen betrieblicher und schulischer Ergänzung, also Berufsschule usw.. Ausgehend von dieser Position muß man zu den überbetrieblichen Ausbildungsstätten ein Wort sagen. Diese überbetrieblichen Ausbildungsstätten sind verstärkt auch durch Zuschüsse der öffentlichen Hand gebaut und eingerichtet worden, durch die Handwerkskammern, zum Teil auch Industrie- und Handelskammer; es gibt auch Mischformen bestimmter größerer Betriebe und Kammereinrichtungen. Oder aber sie sind gebaut und eingerichtet worden durch kommunale Verbände und Kammern. Diese überbetrieblichen Ausbildungsstätten sollen nach unserer Auffassung eine Ergänzung der beiden Lernorte – Betrieb und Schule – darstellen, keinen Ersatz, und sie sollen nach unserer Auffassung mehr Betriebe als bisher in den Stand versetzen, Ausbildungsverhältnisse einzugehen. Wenn sich der Betrieb Teile der Ausbildung nicht leisten kann, dann sollen diese in der überbetrieblichen Ausbildungsstätte ergänzend angeboten werden. Also: Überbetriebliche Ausbildungsstätten als Ergänzung der beiden Lernorte Betrieb und Schule.

Eine Bemerkung zur Frage der starken Jahrgänge – das ist hinreichend bekannt für die nächsten Jahre –, die einen Ausbildungsplatz haben müssen: Das ist nach unserer Auffassung vor allem auch eine Aufgabe der Wirtschaft, denn ausgebildete Jugendliche werden der Wirtschaft in den nächsten Jahrzehnten fehlen. Die Politik muß das ergänzen, aber die Wirtschaft muß hier ihre Rolle erkennen. Wenn sie das nicht täte, müßte man in der Politik über andere Entwicklungen nachdenken, aber ich sehe keine Möglichkeit in der Politik, etwa Ausbildungsverpflichtungen in irgendeiner Weise zu verordnen. Also kommt es darauf an, daß die Betriebe aus eigenem Antrieb und Diskussionen in den Arbeitgeberverbänden dazu kommen, daß es in den nächsten Jahren eine erhöhte Zahl von Ausbildungsplätzen gibt. Die Aufnahmefähigkeit des Handwerks halte ich für begrenzt. 14,6 % der Beschäftigten im Handwerk sind Auszubildende, 6 % in der Industrie und 6 % im öffentlichen Dienst. Eine Ausweisung der Ausbildungsplätze müßte es also vor allem in der Industrie geben, begrenzt auch im öffentlichen Dienst, aber vor allem in der Industrie. Mit dieser Diskussion hängt sehr konkret zusammen, ob vom Standpunkt der Personalplanung an die Sache herangegangen wird oder ob die Industrie sich mehr noch als bisher dazu durchringt, über die notwendige Kapazität hinaus in den nächsten Jahren auszubilden.

Wir haben von der Organisation, in der ich diese Fragen zu bearbeiten habe, – Chemie, Papier, Keramik – mit den zuständigen Arbeitgeberverbänden seit 3 Jahren jährlich Verhandlungen um diesen Punkt, und wir haben eine Sache, die dabei immer diskutiert wurde, sehr offen beraten; nämlich dann, wenn die Industrie, konkret die Betriebe, in diesen Bereichen ausbilden, dann muß darüber diskutiert werden, daß eine ausgesprochene oder unausgesprochene Übernahmegarantie weder konstruiert noch vertreten werden kann. D. h. also, man muß offen darüber reden, daß Ausbildung vor Übernahme in das Arbeitsverhältnis steht. Es ist keine leichte Sache, das in einer Gewerkschaftsorganisation mit den Betriebsräten und Jugendvertretern auszudiskutieren. Wir haben aber diese Position, wie gesagt, seit 2, 3 Jahren vertreten, weil wir der Auffassung sind, die Betriebe müssen die Ausbildungsplätzepotentiale erhöhen. Ausbildung ist wichtiger.

Die zweite Frage ist dann: Wieviel können davon übernommen werden oder gehen in andere Bereiche und suchen sich andere Arbeitsplätze? Wenn man diese Frage der Übernahme nicht offen diskutiert, kann man, so glaube ich, nicht erwarten, daß die Industrie für die nächsten Jahre wirklich ernsthaft die Anzahl der Plätze erhöht. Ich werde auch gleich in diese Auseinandersetzung noch zwei Punkte miteinbringen. Ich glaube nicht, daß erhöhte Zahlen der Ausbildungsplätze in der Industrie einhergehen müssen mit dem Bau von neuen Ausbildungseinrichtungen. Ehe die Neubauten alle stehen, sind von der Investitionsplanung bis zur Realisierung drei Jahre vorbei.

Wir müssen in den Betrieben darüber nachdenken, daß auch in mehr der Ecken oder anderen Teilen der Industrieanlagen Ausbildungsplätze vorübergehend geschaffen werden. Nur in Bezug auf die Qualität würde ich den Anspruch stellen, daß eben genügend Ausbilder da sein müssen – also die Betreuung durch Ausbilder sichergestellt wird.

Das ist aber nicht eine so hohe Kostenbelastung, als wenn erst Neubauten errichtet werden müßten, die man dann nach einigen Jahren zu anderen Zwecken umbauen muß. Ich würde also sagen, daß man Ausbildungsplätze in Betriebsstätten schaffen sollte, zwischen Unternehmensleitung und Betriebsrat darüber nachdenken sollte, um sicherzustellen, daß genügend Ausbilder da sind.

Eine Bemerkung zu der Frage des Verdrängungswettbewerbes zwischen Abiturienten, Realschülern, Hauptschülern: Ich glaube, daß sich in Verlaufe der letzten 2 Jahre ein gewisser Wandel vollzogen hat. Die meisten großen Betriebe der chemischen Industrie, die ich durch die konkreten Verhandlungen kennengelernt habe, gehen doch im Grunde nach einer gewissen Faustregel davon aus: etwa 1/3 Abiturienten, 1/3 Realschüler, aber auch 1/3 Hauptschüler, sicher auch aus der Überlegung heraus, daß ein höherer Teil von Hauptschülern nach der Ausbildung auch in späteren Jahren im Unternehmen erhalten bleibt und ein Teil der Abiturienten sicher verstärkt auf Weiterbildungswege geht. Dies scheint mir nicht so sehr das Problem zu sein; es ging mir in den letzten 2 Jahren mehr um ein anderes Problem, nämlich der Hauptschulabbrecher und Sonderschüler. Die Angebote, die es zum Teil von der Arbeitsverwaltung her gibt, den Hauptschulabschluß nachzuholen, wird von einem Teil der Jugendlichen nicht angenommen, weil sie ihre – psychologisch ja auch erklärbaren – schlechten Erfahrungen mit der Schule gemacht haben. Sie sind in den meisten Fällen mehr auf die praktische Seite der Berufsausbildungsanforderung angelegt. Wir haben deshalb mit dem Arbeitsring der chemischen Industrie einen Tarifvertrag abgeschlossen, der beinhaltet, daß Sonderschüler und Hauptschulabbrecher eine Art Berufsvorbereitungsjahr im Betrieb machen und in diesem Jahr – begleitet durch die Ausbildungsabteilung – beobachtet werden: Ob aus diesem Kreis der Jugendlichen Jugendliche qualifiziert werden können für den Abschluß eines ganz normalen Ausbildungsvertrages, der dann 3 oder 3 1/2 Jahre je nach Ausbildungsordnung läuft. Dies ist also ein Vorbereitungsjahr. Sie bekommen eine Ausbildungsvergütung minus 10 % der entsprechenden Gruppe oder des entsprechenden Tarifvertrages. Die Jugendlichen, die es nach übereinstimmender Meinung zwischen Ausbildungsabteilung und Betriebsrat nicht schaffen, noch einen Ausbildungsvertrag nach diesem Jahr abzuschließen, werden dann von den Unternehmen – wenn nichts besonderes vorliegt – übernommen als Jungarbeiterinnen oder Jungarbeiter. Mir kam es darauf an, einen solchen Tarifvertrag mit einer starken sozialen Komponente abzuschließen, weil ich meine, auch die Tarifvertragsparteien müssen auf das Problem von Hauptschulabbrechern und Schulabgängern reagieren. Sie kommen in den meisten Fällen aus den schwierigsten Familien.

Noch eine Bemerkung zu der Frage: In welchen Berufen sollte verstärkt ausgebildet werden? Wir reden eigentlich in den Gesprächen mit den Arbeitgeberverbänden im wesentlichen über gewerblich-technische Berufe, nicht so sehr über den Bereich der Angestelltenberufe oder Laborantenberufe, also mehr gewerblich-technische, und wir reden sehr konkret auch mit den Ausbildern und Ausbildungsabteilungen über die Frage, daß Mädchen verstärkt in früher typische Männerberufe eingestellt werden. Dafür haben wir auch größere Ausbildertagungen und Veranstaltungen mit den Unternehmern gemacht – mehr Mädchen in typischen Männerberufen –, was man auch verantworten kann, da ja im Verlaufe der letzten Jahre durch eine ganze Reihe von Entwicklungen – technische Entwicklungen, die übrigens auch durch die Gesetzgebung begleitet worden sind, die Arbeitsordnungen und manches andere mehr –, manche typischen Männerberufe von der Arbeitskraft her leichter sind als früher. Hier muß das konservative Denken beseitigt werden; da geht es manchmal um sehr interessante Dinge, wenn dies diskutiert wird, denn in einer Werkstatt, wo bisher immer nur junge Männer waren, wird ja doch das eine oder andere Mädchen, vor allem, wenn es die ersten sind, ein bißchen beobachtet oder beachtet wie ein Wesen vom anderen Stern. Aber wir sind durch Modellversuche und durch Einstellungen ein erhebliches Stück weitergekommen.

Lassen Sie mich noch zur Gesetzeslage eine Bemerkung machen, weil das auch immer eine Diskussion ist, wenn über Berufsbildung diskutiert wird. Ich war fast 3 Jahre lang Vorsitzender der Berufsbildungskommission der SPD-Fraktion im Bundestag und habe also das Leiden der Berufsbildungsgesetzgebung bis in das zweimalige Scheitern im Bundesrat mitgemacht. Ich war dann mit zwei anderen dafür verantwortlich, daß wir das Ausbildungsplatzförderungsgesetz geplant haben. Ich war sehr für dieses Gesetz, zum einen, um den Datenteil zu retten, der ja nicht durch den Bundesrat zustimmungspflichtig war, weil man eben nicht nur wissen muß, wieviele Regenschirme in der Bundesrepublik produziert werden, sondern man auch wissen muß, wieviele Jugendliche aus welchen Schulen kommen und wieviele es gibt; das ist der statistische Teil. Dann war ich sehr für das Berufsbildungsinstitut, das unter der Viertel-Parität von Arbeitgebern, Arbeitnehmern, Bund und Ländern geschaffen wurde, weil das zwischen Ausbildungsordnungen und Rahmenlehrplänen gar nicht anders geht. Ich war auch für die Verankerung der Berufsausbildungsabgabe dann, wenn Ausbildungsplätze fehlen, und ich werde Ihnen ganz offen sagen, bei nüchterner Einschätzung der Lage – der politischen Lage, der Begleitumstände auch in der Koalition –, daß ich dennoch für diese gesetzliche Regelung war. Ich will es gar nicht verschweigen: Ich war deshalb dafür, weil diese gesetzliche Regelung eine Art Wirkung eines Damokles-Schwertes an der Wand hat. Wenn die Industrie nicht genügend Ausbildungsplätze zur Verfügung stellt, dann kommt die Androhung des Ausbildungsplatzförderungsgesetzes mit der Finanzumlage. Mich stört es überhaupt nicht, wenn sie nicht angewendet wird; denn wenn genügend Ausbildungsplätze da sind, braucht sie ja nicht angewendet zu werden. Ich wollte eine solche Position in der Gesetzgebung unterbringen, weil es mir sicherer schien, für die Initiative wirklich mehr Ausbildungsplätze zu schaffen. Das Ergebnis vieler Untersuchungen ist ja, daß viele große Betriebe genügend Ausbildungsplätze zur Verfügung stellen; ich denke an den Bereich, den ich zu vertreten habe, Bayer, Hoechst und BASF, wenn ich diese nur einmal herausnehme; sie liegen bei 7 bis 7,5 %, also etwas über dem Durchschnitt der Industrie. Die vielen mittleren Betriebe – also Betriebe bis zu 3000 Beschäftigten – haben ein oder zwei Prozent oder gar keine Auszubildenden; d. h. das Kernproblem liegt in den vielen mittleren Betrieben. Die zusätzlichen Ausbildungsplätze, die geschaffen werden müssen, liegen in den mittleren Betrieben, nicht so sehr in den wenigen großen.

Eine letzte Bemerkung möchte ich anschließen. Wenn es um die Frage von ausbildungshemmenden Vorschriften geht, weiß ich manchmal nicht, was der eine oder andere damit meint, was man abbauen sollte, um mehr Ausbildungsplätze zu schaffen; Ausbildungsordnungen können ganz sicher nicht gemeint sein. Ich selbst bin für Berufsausbildung in der IG Chemie im Hauptvorstand seit 1966 zuständig, und es gibt nicht eine einzige Ausbildungsverordnung, die wir nicht übereinstimmend in gemischten paritätischen Kommissionen zwischen der zuständigen Gewerkschaft und den zuständigen Arbeitgeberverbänden – also der Fachleute auf beiden Seiten – inhaltlich beraten und gemeinsam beim Wirtschaftsminister eingereicht hätten, der sie dann erlassen hat. Das, was in Ausbildungsordnungen steht, haben immer beide Seiten beraten und niemals nur die eine, das kann es also nicht sein.

Sollte die Frage von Schwerbehindertenquoten für Klein- und Mittelbetriebe auftauchen – daß deswegen nicht genügend Ausbildungsplätze geschaffen werden –, so müßte ich sagen, daß jeder mit uns darüber diskutieren muß, daß wir etwa 45.000 schwerbehinderte Arbeitslose haben. Wenn man also an der Ecke etwas ändern will, dann steht die andere Größenordnung mit zur Debatte. Das Jugendarbeitsschutzgesetz kann nach meiner Ansicht nicht als ausbildungshemmende Vorschrift bezeichnet werden. Es gibt vielleicht ein paar Ausnahmegenehmigungen, die wir möglicherweise regeln müssen, und zwar für das Bäckerhandwerk oder ein paar ähnliche andere Handwerke. Ich würde gerne von denen, die darüber reden, hören, was damit gemeint ist.

Aussprache über das Rappe-Statement und das Referat Walter

Leitung: Rosemarie Fiedler-Winter

Welbergen:

Mir liegt folgende Frage vor: „Können Sie die Schwierigkeiten, die sich einem Großunternehmen heute durch die gesetzlichen Vorschriften bei der Ausbildung von Jugendlichen stellen, näher erläutern?“ Für einen Politiker sind Sie ja sehr empfindlich. Wenn wir als Unternehmer immer so empfindlich auf jede Bemerkung reagierten, dann wäre es für uns relativ schwer. Ich sage deshalb „empfindlich“. Ich habe mit keinem Wort die Gewerkschaft oder Ihre Partei oder das Parlament angegriffen, sondern ich habe einfach festgestellt, daß gewisse Schwierigkeiten da sind.

Die Tatsache, die mir wohl bewußt ist, daß Arbeitgeberverbände an der Ausarbeitung dieser Sache mitgearbeitet haben, heißt für mich noch lange nicht, daß sie deshalb keinen Fehler enthalten können. Fehler entstehen in unserer Gesellschaft sehr oft, wir müssen nur sehen, daß wir die Fehler wieder ausräumen.

Ich habe in meinem Referat auf gewisse Schwierigkeiten hingewiesen, Schwierigkeiten, die wir in der Zwischenzeit, so glaube ich, zum Teil überwunden haben, indem wir Maßnahmen ergriffen haben, die aber sicher zu dem Zeitpunkt, als sie eingeführt wurden, noch nicht mit ihrer vollen Auswirkung erkannt worden sind. Ich habe sogar gesagt, daß viele dieser Verordnungen sehr positiv sind, weil sie die Qualität verbessert haben. Da ich ungern über etwas rede, das ich nicht so gut beherrsche wie mein Kontrahent – und Sie haben gerade gesagt, daß Sie seit 1966 für die Ausbildung verantwortlich sind – möchte ich eigentlich von der normalen Gepflogenheit weggehen und Herrn Dr. Möller bitten, hierzu Stellung zu nehmen. Dr. Möller ist da auch mit der Materie sehr viel besser bekannt. Wenn Sie also als Diskussionsleiterin es erlauben, möchte ich jetzt das Wort an Herrn Dr. Möller geben.

Möller:

Mein Name ist Möller, ich bin bei der Deutschen Shell zuständig für Ausbildung und Personalplanung. – Die Frage, die Sie angesprochen haben, Herr Rappe, betrifft die Schwierigkeiten, die uns auf gesetzgeberischen, aber auch auf dem Verordnungswege hinsichtlich der Schaffung und Aufrechterhaltung von Ausbildungsplätzen gesetzt sind. Diese Schwierigkeiten sind verschiedener Art, wobei ich zugeben möchte, daß sie häufig nur minimal sind, aber in ihrer Summierung eben doch zu einem Hindernis werden.

Das erste, was wir gehabt haben, was aber dann sehr schnell überbrückt worden ist, war die Ausbildereignungsverordnung, die ja zunächst nicht so heiß gegessen wurde, wie sie gekocht worden ist. Dennoch hat diese Ausbildereignungsverordnung dazu geführt, daß eine Vielzahl von Meistern und Leuten, die in der Ausbildung tätig waren, jetzt zumindest verprellt waren und sagten: „Warum soll ich jetzt noch einen Abendkurs durchführen und nachher noch eine Prüfung ablegen, obwohl ich glaube, doch diese Qualifikation erbracht zu haben?"

Das zweite Problem waren die Ausbildungsordnungen. Diese Ausbildungsordnungen haben dazu geführt – Herr Welbergen hat heute morgen schon ausgeführt –, daß nicht nur in unserem Unternehmen, sondern bei einer Vielzahl von Unternehmen, die gleichstrukturiert sind – die mit einer Zentrale und mit Niederlassungen arbeiten –, daß in einer Vielzahl dieser Niederlassungen dann keine Ausbildung mehr möglich war, weil gewisse Ausbildungsinhalte einfach nicht mehr zu vermitteln waren. Wir haben das früher durch entsprechende Kurse überbrückt; wir haben also die Leute aus den Niederlassungen für 3 oder 4 Wochen zu diesen Themen hereingeholt. Heute müssen wir sie eben in der praktischen Tätigkeit ausbilden. Das konnten wir in den Niederlassungen nicht machen. Ich weiß von einer Vielzahl von Firmen, die dann von heute auf morgen Ausbildungsplätze haben wegfallen lassen.

Es gibt eine Reihe von hemmenden Faktoren. Ich möchte das Thema nennen, das Sie angesprochen haben, nämlich die Ausbildung von weiblichen Auszubildenden auch für Berufe, die bisher typisch männlich waren. Ich denke z. B. an die chemische Industrie. Wir haben, wie Sie wissen – das war eine Frage, die ich sonst an Sie gestellt hätte –, wir haben überwiegend oder zu einem großen Teil dort auch Schichtdienst, und da stellt sich natürlich die Frage, wie man also einen weiblichen Auszubildenden zum Chemiefacharbeiter macht. Warum eigentlich nicht? Denn die körperliche Arbeit ist, wie Sie wissen, ja verhältnismäßig gering gegenüber den intellektuellen Fähigkeiten, die dort entwickelt werden. Ich könnte mir sehr gut vorstellen – auch wenn es einigen alten Meistern sehr einen Schauer über den Rücken jagen würde –, ich könnte mir also durchaus vorstellen, daß in einer Meßwarte einer Raffinerie auch eine Frau sitzt. Das Problem ist nur: Ausbilden können wir dort nicht; es hat auch gar keinen Zweck, denn selbst, wenn wir ausgebildet hätten, könnte diese weibliche Ausgebildete dort nicht tätig sein, weil sie eben Schichtdienst hat und bekanntermaßen Nachtarbeit für Frauen unzulässig ist. Das ist z. B. ein derartiges Hindernis.

Ich habe jetzt nur einmal drei solcher Hindernisse aufgezählt. Es kommt natürlich noch eine nicht unerhebliche Bürokratisierung hinzu. Ich möchte noch einmal sagen, Herr Rappe, das sind alles Dinge, die keineswegs allein die Gewerkschaften zu vertreten haben und die folglich meines Erachtens zumindest im gleichen Maße für die Arbeitgeberseite zu vertreten sind. Aber in der Summe haben solche Dinge eben dazu geführt, daß Ausbildungsplätze verlorengegangen sind. Wenn es darum geht, in den nächsten Jahren vermehrt Ausbildungsplätze zu schaffen, dann geht es darum, daß beide Seiten ganz pragmatisch gemeinsam daran gehen, diese Dinge zu beseitigen. Herr Welbergen hat angedeutet, wie wir das in unseren Unternehmen begonnen haben, und ich hoffe, daß wir das auch in anderen Bereichen weiter fortsetzen werden.

Welbergen:

Die nächste Frage, die mir vorliegt, lautet: Wie stehen Sie zur gesetzlichen Einführung des 10. Schuljahres auch in der Hauptschule? – Nun, ich kann weder ja noch nein sagen, denn ich muß ganz ehrlich sagen, daß ich mir noch wenige Gedanken darüber gemacht habe. Ich weiß nicht, ob es einen Bedarf gibt. Würden es die Auszubildenden, um sie nicht Schüler zu nennen, begrüssen oder nicht? Ich glaube sogar, daß viele es nicht begrüßen würden. Könnte es eine Entlastung für den Arbeits- und Ausbildungsmarkt sein? Kurzfristig ja, indem es einfach das Problem um ein Jahr verschiebt. Sonst sehe ich eigentlich keinen weiteren Sinn in dieser Einrichtung. Könnte es für die Ausbildung eventuell reichen und für das Leben eine Entlastung sein? Ich glaube es nicht. Ist es sinnvoll, das 10. Schuljahr als Vorbereitung auf die Arbeitswelt einzurichten? Ist es besser als Berufsberatung? Ich möchte das sehr bezweifeln, weil ich nämlich glaube, daß Vorbereitung für die Arbeitswelt besser im Betrieb stattfindet, als daß man nochmal ein theoretisches Jahr einfügt, um dann die eigentliche Ausbildung im Betrieb ein Jahr später anzufangen. Das wäre ganz kurz meine Meinung zu diesen Fragenkomplexen gewesen.

Dann liegt eine Frage vor: „Sie haben ausgeführt, daß 60 % der Jugend in Berufen ausgebildet werden, in denen nur 30 % der Männer arbeiten. Ist es nicht Beweis dafür, daß das System der Verteilung der Ausbildungsplätze nicht funktioniert und die deutsche Wirtschaft außerstande ist, die berufliche Bildung zu organisieren, und welche Abhilfe können Sie sich vorstellen?“

Mir ist es neu, daß die deutsche Wirtschaft bis jetzt den jungen Menschen gesagt hat, wo sie sich ausbilden lassen sollen und daß wir irgendwie an dieser Verzerrung dieses Systems von Angebot und Nachfrage mitgearbeitet haben. Es ist einfach eine Tatsache, daß sich bei Frauen sehr viel mehr als Friseuse ausbilden lassen, als es Damen oder Herren gibt, die sich den Kopf scheren lassen. Es ist auch eine Tatsache, daß sehr viele junge Leute Autoschlosser werden. Früher wurden sie gerne Polizist oder Feuerwehrmann, zumindest was meine Jugend betrifft, heute werden sie Autoschlosser. Die Wirtschaft kann sich hier nicht einschalten. Sie kann höchstens das gängige Argument eines jungen Menschen entkräften, der dadurch beeinflußt wird, daß er sagt: „Wenn so viele Menschen schon in diesem Beruf tätig sind, dann habe ich so wenig Chancen, dann suche ich mir einen anderen Beruf.“ Ob dann dieses Problem nur durch Planwirtschaft des Arbeitsmarktes, wie es heute morgen genannt wurde, gelöst wird, und ob dieses Prinzip sehr viel besser funktionieren würde, das würde ich sehr bezweifeln. Ich weiß nicht, nach welchen Kriterien man dann die Zuweisung zu verschiedenen Berufen geben würde. Wir müssen vielmehr dazu übergehen, den jungen Leuten zu zeigen, was ihre Chancen sind. Wir müssen Rahmenbedingungen, wir müssen Orientierungshilfen geben, und wir dürfen jetzt nicht auf einmal den jungen Leuten sagen, in welche Berufe sie zu gehen haben.

Fiedler-Winter:

Um damit bei diesem speziell berufspolitisch bezogenen Problem zu bleiben, möchte ich die nächste Frage an Herrn Rappe weitergeben. Herr Rappe, es wird gefragt: „Wie steht die Gewerkschaft zu den Ausführungen von Herrn Walter, die Gewerkschaften sollten ihre Lohnpolitik mäßigen?"

Rappe:

Ich bin nicht der Auffassung, daß die Frage einer Mäßigung der Lohnpolitik – zunächst mal über den Tisch gesagt – dazu führt, daß mehr Arbeitslose einen Arbeitsplatz bekommen. Daran glaube ich nicht. Ich glaube nicht, daß das Problem der Beschäftigungslage das Problem der Lohnpolitik ist. Ich glaube auch nicht, daß mit Lohnverzicht die Frage der Konjunkturankurbelung diskutiert werden kann. Was ich glaube, ist eine ganz andere Sache: Es ist der Gedanke nach mehr Arbeitszeitverkürzung; er spielte verschiedenlich heute morgen schon eine Rolle. Es ist die Frage der 35-Stunden Woche und das Problem, von daher Arbeitsmarktpolitik zu sehen.

Hier will ich Ihnen ganz offen sagen, daß ich glaube, daß eine Zielsetzung in Richtung Arbeitszeitverkürzung auf 3 Wegen zur Debatte stehen, nämlich in der Verkürzung der wöchentlichen Arbeitszeit oder im verlängerten Urlaub oder durch die Herabsetzung der Altersgrenze. Ich bin mir klar darüber, daß jede dieser Maßnahmen finanziert werden muß. Zwei davon werden durch die Tarifvertragsparteien geregelt, während die Herabsetzung der Altersgrenze eine Frage des Parlaments ist. In Bezug auf die Tarifseite glaube ich, daß diese natürlich eine Frage der Gesamtbelastung ist. Konkret ausgedrückt, wenn in der Tarifverhandlung über Stufen der wöchentlichen Arbeitszeitverkürzung beraten wird, dann ist mir klar, daß am Ende im Bereich der übrigen Lohn- und Gehaltserhöhung geringere Spielräume und auch geringere Ergebnisse erzielt werden, wenn ein Teil davon in arbeitszeitverkürzende Maßnahmen gesteckt werden soll. Das ist mir völlig klar, und ich bin auch dafür, daß dies so diskutiert wird, wie es gehandhabt wird, weil ich der Auffassung bin, daß dies langfristig auf dem Arbeitsmarkt hilft.

Die gewerkschaftliche Position oder die Arbeitnehmerposition ist natürlich immer besser in einer guten Beschäftigungslage als bei Unterbeschäftigung. Deshalb bin ich für eine solche tarifpolitische Zielsetzung, und das Argument, daß dies die Facharbeiterlücke wesentlich erhöhen würde, zieht bei mir nicht. Ich denke, daß bei einer solchen Situation die Industrie und die Arbeitgeberverbände mehr darüber nachdenken müssen, weniger qualifizierte oder anders qualifizierte Arbeitnehmer durch innerbetriebliche Aus- und Weiterbildung umzuschulen. Ich will das einmal ganz vereinfacht sagen. Die Unternehmer haben 500.000 Türken aus Anatolien zu in der Industrie verwertbaren Arbeitskräften gemacht. Ich denke, daß sie das auch mit einem Teil des Reservoirs der Arbeitslosen machen können. Außerdem weiß ich, daß Rationalisierung weder zu unterbinden noch zu unterbieten ist – es auch falsch wäre, es zu diskutieren. – Von daher sehe ich für den Arbeitsmarkt auch weitere Entwicklungen, und ich bin der Meinung, dies muß durch die Tarifvertragsparteien durch Arbeitszeitverkürzung und Urlaubsveränderung ausgeglichen werden. Dann weiß ich, daß dies darüber hinaus auf Kosten von Lohn- und Gehaltsprozenten geht.

Welbergen:

Herr Rappe, ich bin grundsätzlich mit Ihnen einer Meinung, daß Lohnverzicht nicht unmittelbar zu weniger Arbeitslosen führen wird. Wir müssen aber doch einmal auch sehen, was die Gründe für die Arbeitslosigkeit sind, wobei ich nicht einmal so sehr ausgehen will von der heutigen Situation. Die Analyse der Zahlen würde vielleicht das Problem etwas mindern gegenüber der jetzigen Situation. Es bleibt aber eine Tatsache, daß wir die Arbeitslosigkeit – und die zunehmende Arbeitslosigkeit durch den Berg Erwerbsuchende – nur durch ein gewisses Wachstum in der Industrie abschaffen können, ein Wachstum, daß wir sicher nicht hier in Deutschland haben werden, sondern ein Wachstum, das zum großen Teil außerhalb Deutschlands entsteht, wo wir unsere Waren und unsere Dienstleistungen anbieten müssen. Ich denke z. B. an Bauindustrie in Nigeria, Saudi-Arabien etc. Diese Dienstleistungen, diese Waren können wir nur anbieten und abgenommen bekommen, wenn wir wettbewerbsfähig sind, und in der Wettbewerbsfähigkeit spielen natürlich Kosten eine gewisse Rolle.

Ich will jetzt gar nicht über Investitionsanteile in der Verteilung sprechen, sondern wir müssen einfach wettbewerbsfähig sein. Hier sehe ich ein gewisses Problem, nämlich, daß, wenn wir schon sehr erhebliche Lohnstückkosten haben, durch Arbeitszeitverkürzung – in welcher Form auch immer – zusätzliche Belastungen haben. Kommen wir nicht zu einer Überbelastung der Industrie, unserer Wirtschaft, zu einer Aushöhlung? Dies können wir beim besten Willen nicht mehr hochbeten, sondern das ist einfach ein Tatbestand. Es brauchen ja nicht nur Türken zu sein. Sie sind für mich nicht unbedingt Menschen zweiter Klasse, und sie haben ja auch eine gewisse Intelligenzquote und können daher auch ausgebildet werden. Aber Tatsache ist, daß man heute sieht, daß die deutsche Wirtschaft in einem Teil ihrer Exportgeschäfte, die von Deutschen dort gut ausgeführt werden könnten, jetzt Ausländer nimmt, weil die Lohnstückkosten niedriger sind. Das sind einfach die Realitäten. Ich will hier nicht in Ideologie reden, denn das liegt mir etwas fern. Ich bin mehr auf dem Boden der Realität, aber wir können nicht daran vorbeigehen, daß unsere Lohnstückkosten für unsere Exportwirtschaft insbesondere einfach zu hoch sind.

Fiedler-Winter:

Daran darf ich gleich die Frage anknüpfen: „Glauben Sie, daß durch die Einführung der 35-Stunden Woche zusätzliche Arbeitsplätze geschaffen werden, Herr Rappe?"

Teilnehmer:

Herr Welbergen hat heute morgen über die Lohnkosten gesprochen. Aber ich sehe da noch ein anderes Problem in der Arbeitszeitverkürzung. Es werden damit die Anstrengungen der Industrie, zu rationalisieren, noch mehr gestärkt, beschleunigt und auch in weiteren Bereichen vorangetrieben. Wird nicht die Konkurrenzfähigkeit der deutschen Industrie damit ganz erheblich geschwächt? Glauben Sie nicht auch, daß eine Firma, die statt 40 nur noch 35 Wochenstunden beschäftigen darf, also nach 35 Stunden zumacht und eben keinen neuen Mann mehr einstellt, weil sie das nicht mehr bezahlen kann, glauben Sie nicht, daß diese Firma mit Freizeitproblemen der Leute fertigwerden muß? Was machen die Leute mit diesen zusätzlichen 5 Stunden Freizeit?

Rappe:

Zur Freizeitfrage will ich mich nicht näher äußern. Ich habe die Diskussion um die Herabsetzung von der 48- auf die 40-Stunden-Woche ebenfalls erlebt, und ich hatte nicht den Eindruck, daß die Menschen nicht wüßten, was sie mit der erhöhten Freizeit anfangen sollten. Es haben den Arbeitnehmern übrigens auch andere Bereiche in der Bevölkerung vorgemacht, was man mit mehr Freizeit machen kann, und ich finde, da sollten sich andere nicht den Kopf drüber zerbrechen, das machen die Arbeitnehmer schon. Das ist nicht meine Sorge.

Nun zur Frage der Rationalisierung. Wird der Trend noch erhöht? Ich habe den Eindruck, daß sowieso rationalisiert wird und daß das auch gar nicht aufzuhalten ist. Das ist gar nicht die Frage. Wenn ein solcher Tarifvertrag bei uns abgeschlossen würde, würde das sicher nicht ausrechenbar so und so viele Arbeitslose vom Markt nehmen, aber es würde die Entlassung weiterer verhindern. Als erste Stufe für das Jahr 1979 haben die Belgier in der vergangenen Nacht einen Tarifvertrag abgeschlossen, der die Arbeitszeit auf 38 Stunden verkürzt. Schon das wäre nach meiner Auffassung eine notwendige Komponente der Arbeitsmarktpolitik in der Tarifpolitik.

Walter:

Vielleicht darf ich etwas zur Frage der Arbeitszeitverkürzung bemerken. Zuerst einmal bin ich sehr froh, Herr Rappe, daß Sie sagten, daß es im Grunde nur darum gehen kann, das Problem der Arbeitszeitverkürzung bei den Verhandlungen über Lohnerhöhungen mit zu verrechnen. Es resultiert also aus Arbeitszeitverkürzung keine Lohnstückkostenerhöhung. Damit ist dieses Instrument schon sehr viel wertvoller geworden. Aber auch dann muß man sehr ernsthaft darüber nachdenken, ob das Problem der Freizeit nicht zu generell angesprochen wurde. Ich würde nicht die Frage stellen: Wollen Sie mehr Freizeit? Statt dessen muß die Frage wohl lauten: Auf wieviel Mark mehr Lohn verzichten Sie, wenn Sie soundsoviel Stunden mehr Freizeit haben. Die Frage würde ich jeden soweit irgend möglich individuell beantworten lassen.

Ich würde weiter gehen: Ich würde sagen, wir sollten bei den Gewerkschaften wie auch auf der Arbeitgeberseite mehr darüber nachdenken, wie man vermehrt Teilzeitbeschäftigung schaffen kann, auch über die Änderung von Produktionsmethoden. Das ist im Dienstleistungsbereich leichter zu bewerkstelligen als in der Industrie. Das ist vielleicht durch Verkürzung von Schichten zu erreichen. In jedem Fall würde ich es aber eigentlich nur sehr ungern sehen, wenn Arbeitszeitverordnungen vorschreiben, wie lange man arbeiten darf oder wie kurz man arbeiten muß.

Mit Herrn Rappes Antwort auf die Frage „Kann man mit zurückhaltender Lohnpolitik die Wirtschaft wieder auf die Beine bringen?“ bin ich nicht einverstanden: Die Beschäftigungsentwicklung in der Bundesrepublik in den 50er Jahren bei Lohnabschlüssen, die ständig unter dem Produktivitätsfortschritt lagen, ist für mich ein Beweis für die Richtigkeit der These; daß ein solcher Zusammenhang zwischen Lohnhöhe und Beschäftigung auch heute noch stimmt, kann ich in den USA beobachten. Dort gibt es eine zurückhaltende Lohnpolitik seit der Ölkrise, und die Amerikaner haben nicht irgendetwas zustande gebracht, sondern seit 1975 Jahr für Jahr die Beschäftigung um 3 % ausgeweitet. Wir Bundesrepublikaner bräuchten eine solche Ausweitung in einem einzigen Jahr bis 1985 und hätten unsere Arbeitsmarktprobleme nahezu gelöst. Dieses Beispiel nur, um einmal darzustellen, wie andere Wirtschaftssysteme, das amerikanische in diesem Falle, ein Problem bewältigen.

An unsere Misere sind freilich nicht allein falsche Konzepte der Gewerkschaften schuld, sondern auch das Verlernen von unternehmerischen Eigenschaften auf der Arbeitgeberseite. Nicht nur unser Kapitalbestand, sondern auch unsere Manager sind vergreist.

Rappe:

Darf ich eine Bemerkung machen? Das Folgende sage ich deshalb zu einer Beratung zum neuen Arbeitszeitgesetz, weil ich in einer konkreten Situation –

Vorsitzender des Bundestagsausschusses – bin. Dieses neue Arbeitszeitgesetz ist die Ablösung der alten „AZO", die ja noch von der 48-Stunden-Woche ausgeht. Wenn man die Beschäftigten, die drin sind, natürlich fragt – wie Sie sagen, von liberalen Überlegungen her –, ob sie denn gerne Sonderschichten und Überstunden machen würden, dann sagen die selbstverständlich „ja", und wenn das Unternehmen eine gewisse Flaute hat, dann meldet es Kurzarbeit an, und das zahlen die Arbeitnehmer durch die Beiträge der Bundesanstalt Nürnberg. Aber das Problem ist, daß sie „ja" zu Überstunden und Sonderschichten sagen. Nur, sehen Sie, die 1 Million, die draußen steht, das ist für uns als Gewerkschaften oder für mich als Politiker genauso eine Belastungsgrößenordnung, und von daher spielt das für mich genauso eine Rolle wie die Vorstellung, daß die, die drinnen sind, mitnehmen, was es gibt.

Fiedler-Winter:

Zu dem Problem der Lohnzurückhaltung liegt hier noch eine Frage vor, die sich speziell auf die Newcomer bezieht: Ob Sie dann, wenn schon nicht generell, für die Newcomer eine Lohnzurückhaltung für interessant halten?

Rappe:

Nein, wir haben geltende Tarifverträge, und in diese geltenden Tarifverträge kommt jeder Neuangestellte nach den Fristen, falls es sie gibt, hinein und da gilt der Tarifvertrag für alle.

Fiedler-Winter:

Ferner noch eine andere Frage: „Geraten die Gewerkschaften nicht durch inneren Druck in die Gefahr, alte gewerkschaftliche Forderungen als Patentrezepte für die Verbesserung der wirtschaftlichen Situation zu verkaufen?"

Rappe:

Ich wüßte nicht, welche das wären; das müßte man in einer Diskussion klären.

Fiedler-Winter:

Wir hatten z. B. die 35-Stunden-Woche diskutiert. Ein weiterer Punkt ist die Erhöhung der Massenkaufkraft, die Bürokratisierung von Rationalisierungsentscheidungen, Fragen der Vermögensbildung in Arbeitnehmerhand, z. B. Ablehnung des Investitionslohnes; warum Sie also den Investivlohn ablehnen, oder wie Sie sich die Vermögensbildung vorstellen.

Rappe:

Ich glaube, daß es in den Gewerkschaften bessere demokratische Strukturen gibt, als Außenstehende meinen, denn wer das innergewerkschaftliche Wesen kennt, der wird sich wundern, wieviel von einer Woche zur anderen gewählt wird. Das ist nach meiner Auffassung ein sehr demokratischer Prozeß; wenn das bei allen Verbänden in der Bundesrepublik so wäre!

Ich glaube also, daß die Diskussion um die Verkürzung der Arbeitszeit eine wirklich ausdiskutierte Sache ist, daß diese Konzeption auf die 35-Stunden-Woche in der nächsten überschaubaren Zeit gut ist und diese in Stufenverträgen ausgehandelt wird.

2. Punkt! Ich glaube auch, daß die Arbeitgeber nicht der Auffassung sind, daß mit Lohnverzicht die Wirtschaft angekurbelt werden kann. Die Wirtschaft kann angekurbelt werden durch Investitionsverhalten der Unternehmer oder durch die öffentliche Hand, falls das Geld – durch welche Entscheidung auch immer – über Privatinvestition in die Wirtschaft nicht hineingenommen wird. Diese beiden Möglichkeiten gibt es, aber nicht den Lohnverzicht, denn Lohn ist ja Kaufkraft, und das ist ja wohl auch eine ganz erhebliche Antriebskraft.

Nun zur Frage der Vermögensbildung: Unsere Position zur Vermögensbildung ist ja doch seit Jahren diskutiert und auch bekannt, und wenn ich mich jetzt konkret an die Adresse des Gesetzgebers wende, sieht das so aus, daß die Gewerkschaften gerne ein Rahmengesetz hätten, ein Rahmengesetz zur Bildung betrieblicher und überbetrieblicher Vermögensbildung um auf der Basis eines Tarifvertrages solche Formen zu schaffen, damit die Tarifvertragsparteien ein solches Rahmengesetz durch Tarifverhandlungen ausfüllen. D. h. also: Der Komponente übertrieblicher Vermögensbildung – ausgehandelt zwischen den Tarifvertragsparteien auf der Basis eines Tarifgesetzes – geben die Gewerkschaften den Vorzug.

Teilnehmer:

Ich habe nicht den Eindruck, als wäre die eigentliche Frage beantwortet worden. Es sind jetzt nur Argumente für den Einbau von Forderungen gekommen. Ich hätte aber auch gerne die Frage nach dem inneren Druck beantwortet. Das ist mir etwas zu kurz gekommen. Darf ich wohl noch einen Satz dazu sagen?

Die 35-Stunden-Woche erscheint mir in der Gewerkschaft noch nicht ausdiskutiert. Die nächtelangen Beratungen um die Verstaatlichungen drehten sich ja nicht um die Verstaatlichung, sondern um die 35-Stunden-Woche, wenn ich das richtig beobachten konnte. Ich gebe Ihnen auch gerne die Protokolle von diesen Sitzungen, Frau Vorsitzende.

Aber nochmals zurück zu dieser Frage. Diese Forderung ist meiner Ansicht nach noch nicht ausdiskutiert, und es gibt einfach eine Bestrebung in den Gewerkschaften, daß jetzt in der wirtschaftlichen Krise radikale Kräfte mehr und mehr nach vorne drängen, um alte gewerkschaftliche Forderungen – und das sind die harmlosen, die ich aufgeführt habe – der Gesamtorganisation aufzupfropfen. Das meinte ich mit dem „inneren Druck“.

Rappe:

Ich glaube nicht, daß die Forderung nach der 35-Stunden-Woche eine Frage irgendwelcher radikaler Flügel ist, sondern es ist eine Position aller Tarifkommissionen und aller 16 Gewerkschaften. Eine Differenzierung gibt es nicht. Das ist aber auch eine Frage der Taktik, ob man die Maßnahmen zur Arbeitskräfteverknappung, also Arbeitszeitverkürzung, über den Weg zunächst verlängerten Urlaubs geht oder über den Weg der wöchentlichen verkürzten Arbeitszeit. Das ist in einer Reihe von Gewerkschaften unterschiedlich diskutiert worden, und es wird im Moment auch unterschiedlich vorgegangen. Es dreht sich aber nicht um die Frage, daß überhaupt auf diesem Wege – Verkürzung der Arbeitszeit oder Verlängerung des Urlaubs in den nächsten Jahren – Tarifergebnisse erzielt werden sollen. Ich habe nicht den Eindruck, daß das mit innerer Drucksituation zusammenhängt.

Welbergen:

Ich bin völlig einverstanden, wenn Sie sagen, daß Einkommensstrukturbildung Konsum ist. Sie sehen es aber meines Erachtens etwas zu einfach, wenn Sie sagen: Gebt den Leuten mehr Geld, dann werden sie mehr konsumieren. Das ist nur eine Komponente. Die andere Komponente ist: Die Unternehmen sollen mehr investieren. Nun haben Sie in der Gewerkschaft ja auch Unternehmer, ich denke an Neue Heimat und an andere, und ich glaube doch, daß man immer wieder feststellen muß, daß Investieren in neue Kapazitäten mehr bringt; wir sind noch weit davon weg, daß wir die neuen Kapazitäten ausfahren können und daß Konsum schon in bestehenden Kapazitäten überhaupt ausfällt. Ich will keinen Pessimismus; ich bin zwar auch schon ein alter Unternehmer, aber man muß ja diese Sache mit etwas Realismus ansehen. Ein großer Teil der Kapazitätsauslastung kann ja nur durch neue Bedarfsentwicklung, die wir dann auch wieder erfüllen müssen, gedeckt werden.

Aber eine Sache, die wir immer wieder nicht sehen wollen, ist unsere Wettbewerbsfähigkeit in diesem Lande. Wir brauchen ja nicht nur auf diese sehr liberalen Märkte zu schauen, was an Importen kommt und wo die Verlagerung der Märkte ist, sondern auch auf die Exportmärkte. Deshalb kann ich noch so viel investieren, wenn ich nur leerstehende Gebäude habe oder unausgelastete Destillationskolonnen; dann habe ich von diesen Investitionen ebenfalls nichts. Sicher sind hier viele Komponenten vorhanden. Sie sind nur zu geneigt, immer mit dem Finger auf andere zu zeigen. Der eine sagt: „Weniger Lohn“, und der andere sagt: „Investiert doch mehr“. Wir sollten mal versuchen – und das sage ich deshalb, weil ich verkalkt bin –, nicht mehr Optimismus zu zeigen.

(Zuruf: Vergreist, nicht verkalkt!)

Vergreisen und Verkalken ist ein so subtiler Unterschied, daß ich gar nicht weiter darauf eingehe. – Aber wir sollten mal wirklich zu analysieren versuchen, was die Gründe sind, und wir sollten versuchen, unter verschiedenen Bedingungen zu sagen: „Wenn ich daran etwas ändere, was geschieht hier?" Aber wir sollten nicht immer glauben, daß nur eine Sache dieses so verändern wird, und ich glaube, man muß fairerweise sagen, daß diesbezüglich Lohnpolitik doch etwas mit Wirtschaftswachstum zu tun hat.

Rappe:

Herr Welbergen, ich bin völlig mit Ihnen einverstanden, daß man nicht immer nur auf den einen zeigen soll. Nun will ich dazu sagen: Ich habe noch mit keinem Wort etwa von der Gewinnrate der Unternehmer gesprochen. Sondern es haben immer andere von den Löhnen gesprochen. Das ist das Problem in der Bundesrepublik. Wenn man die Gutachter hört – das fängt im Januar an und hört im Dezember auf –, so fällt ihnen nichts anderes ein, als den Arbeitnehmern zu sagen, sie sollten auf Lohn verzichten. Mit keinem Wort habe ich etwa auf den einen oder auf die anderen gezeigt und gesagt, was sie tun sollten.

Ich will nur noch einmal nüchtern und trocken feststellen: Wenn die Unternehmer – aus welcher betriebswirtschaftlichen oder volkswirtschaftlichen Entscheidung auch immer – nicht investieren, weil es möglicherweise keine Marktchancen gibt, würde ich immer noch in Klammern setzen, daß die Industrieanlagen hoffentlich nicht in einem Maße veralten, daß wir eines schönen Tages zu einem Investitionsschub kommen, der das ganze Preisgefüge über den Haufen wirft; denn es gibt ja Aufstellungen – die Sie sicher genausogut kennen wie ich –, wie veraltet einzelne Teile der Industrieanlagen in der Bundesrepublik sind. Ich würde also schon meinen, auch Reininvestitionen müßten stärker sein, als sie es heute sind. Es dreht sich nicht um Erweiterungsinvestitionen; unter diesem Gesichtspunkt meine ich es nicht. Ich würde also auch Reinvestitionen vorziehen. Wenn die Unternehmer es aber nicht tun, dann ist die Komponente Massenkaufkraft für uns eben eine um so wichtigere Entscheidung und natürlich auch all das, was mit der Investitionsentscheidung der öffentlichen Hand zusammenhängt. Nur werden wir doch als Gewerkschaften sehenden Auges nicht in Unterbeschäftigung laufen und obendrein noch in Lohnverzicht. Das ist doch wohl nicht zu erwarten.

Teilnehmer:

Eine ganz kurze Bemerkung: Der Bundeskanzler hat vor einem Jahr auf dem BDI-Kongreß in Hamburg erklärt: „Wenn der Export weiter florieren soll, dann möchten wir auf das Beispiel Japan mit mehr Löhnen verweisen." Ich weiß nicht, ob das in den Protokollen festgehalten und durchgezogen worden ist.

Aussprache Rappe, Walter

Rappe:

Wenn er die Lohnquote der letzten Jahre in Japan meint, dann bin ich damit einverstanden.

(Zuruf: Die haben bloß eine andere Inflationsrate da unten!)

Fiedler-Winter:

Ich habe hier noch drei Fragen an Prof. Walter, die ursächlich zusammenhängen und die ich Ihnen jetzt einmal vorlesen will. Da heißt es zum Beispiel, um von den Arbeitsmarkt- und -platzproblemen überzuleiten: Es ist viel über die Arbeitslosigkeit gesagt worden. Alle Referenten bedauerten diese Zeiterscheinung, auch die Vertreter der Wirtschaft. Nun scheint sich immer mehr der Trend der Verlagerung von speziellen arbeitsintensiven Arbeitsplätzen in die Dritte Welt abzuzeichnen. Unter anderem in Länder mit Niedriglöhnen, wo die Gewerkschaften verboten sind und wo die Sozialgesetzgebung praktisch noch nicht existent ist, wie z.B. in Südkorea. Wissen Sie, wieviele Arbeitsplätze der Bundesrepublik dadurch verlorengegangen sind, und wird sich dieser Trend künftig noch mehr verstärken? Haben Sie Prognosen dafür?

Auf der anderen Seite eine Frage, die in die gleiche Richtung zielt: Vielen Unternehmen, besonders den großen, wird heute der Vorwurf gemacht, sie investierten einen großen Teil ihrer Gewinne im Ausland, um beispielsweise Lohnkosten zu sparen, und wirkten damit den Bemühungen der Regierung entgegen, die Arbeitslosigkeit zu senken. Ist diese Argumentation haltbar? Gibt es Zahlen über den angesprochenen Kapitaltransfer?

Eine weitere grundsätzliche Frage: Prof. Daniel Bell sagte für die weltwirtschaftliche Zukunft eine Produktionsverschiebung voraus. Die heutigen Produktionen der Industrieländer würden danach in die heutigen Entwicklungsländer abwandern. Die heutigen Industrieländer würden nur noch Technologie liefern. Ist eine solche Entwicklung wünschenswert? Kann sie sich ohne soziale Schwierigkeiten überhaupt vollziehen?

Walter:

Ich fange mit dem Letzten an. Viele Institute haben in den letzten Jahren Thesen, die so ähnlich wie die von Daniel Bell klangen oder in der Öffentlichkeit auf diese Weise verbreitet wurden, vertreten. Wir im Institut für Weltwirtschaft haben für die Projektion, daß die Bundesrepublik zum Blaupausen-Exportland werde, mächtig Prügel von der Wirtschaft bezogen. In der Zwischenzeit haben wir uns angestrengt, herauszufinden, was an der Kritik richtig ist. Wir meinen, daß die Frage einer solch radikalen Verlagerung keine Gedanken zu machen braucht, da sie nicht durchführbar ist. Wir werden wohl nie über Autos beispielsweise nur in Form von Blaupausen allein nachdenken können. Immer wird es gleichzeitig der Schaffung von Prototypen und immer wird es der Produktionserfahrung bedürfen, weil viele Probleme erst bei der Durchführung klar sichtbar werden. Das heißt, der Prozeß der Verlagerung der Industrieproduktion in die Entwicklungsländer und der Verstärkung der Bedeutung der „Kopf-Arbeit" in der Bundesrepublik wird sich einstellen. Es wird jedoch kaum zu abrupten oder gar zu extremen Umwälzungen kommen. Die schon seit der Erfindung des Webstuhls gehegten Befürchtungen, daß Automatisierung die Menschen um ihre Arbeit brächte, werden sich erneut als falsch erweisen.

Wenn ich an die Diskussion über die Bildungsentwicklung von heute morgen denke, meine ich, daß wir eigentlich froh darüber sein müßten, wenn unsere Wirtschaft sich in diese Richtung entwickelt. Dann würden wir hier in der Bundesrepublik nicht – jetzt gebrauche ich wieder ein häßliches Wort – so viele Heloten brauchen, stattdessen vielmehr die Hochqualifizierten, die so gut Ausgebildeten – in den Gymnasien, Realschulen und Universitäten. Insofern sollte eigentlich diese weltwirtschaftliche Arbeitsteilung, wie Herr Bell sie beschreibt, von uns gesellschaftlich als erwünscht angesehen werden.

Ein Wort zu den beiden anderen Fragen bezüglich der Verlagerung von Produktion in weniger entwickelte Länder. Da scheint es mir, daß der Frager eine besonders merkwürdige Art von Solidarität als Ideal besitzt. Bei ihm hört nämlich die Solidarität justament an der Landesgrenze auf. Die Frage ist, ob die Erfindung der Landesgrenze etwas ist, was einem das Gewissen prägen soll. Wenn schon Ideale, wie die Sicherung von Arbeitsplätzen, die Überlegungen bestimmen, muß man noch einen Schritt weiter gehen und fragen, ob nicht die Hilfe für Entwicklungsländer in Form verlagerter Industriebetriebe wichtiger ist als die fünf Prozent mehr an Reallohn für den Arbeiter in Hamburg.

Ich glaube, daß man die Frage nach der Hilfe für Entwicklungsländer viel ernster stellen muß auch als Nation, nicht vor allem aus christlichen, humanitären oder anderen Bewegungsgründen, sondern insbesondere, weil, wenn wir nicht selber darauf kommen, uns die Länder, um die es geht, relativ bald über politischen Druck und notfalls über militärischen Druck klarmachen werden, daß dieses an der Zeit ist.

Mit anderen Worten: Ich halte Überlegungen, die zur Lösung der Arbeitsmarktprobleme auf protektionistischen Überlegungen begründet sind und die dem einfachen Mann auf der Straße plausibel erscheinen, für geradezu selbstmörderisch, insbesondere in einem Land, das so exportabhängig ist wie die Bundesrepublik.

Dann gab es die Frage, ob man in den Entwicklungsländern nicht Gewerkschaften gründen sollte, um die deutschen Chancen bei der Produktion in arbeitsintensiveren Fertigungen wieder zu verbessern. Ich will mich dazu nicht äußern, aber bemerken, daß ich einer Gewerkschaft in Indonesien oder in Malaysia nicht empfehlen würde, die Löhne zu fordern, wie sie ihre Partnergewerkschaften in Europa fordern, die mit denen auf dem Kontinent vergleichbar sind. Denn bei einem Produktivitätsniveau, das auf dem Kontinent beispielsweise in der Automobilindustrie etwa 2,5 Mal so hoch ist wie in Großbritanien, ist klar, daß für den Fall, daß man den Engländern den gleichen Lohn geben wollte, dafür gesorgt wäre, daß auf der Insel nur noch ein paar Rolls Royces gebaut würden, aber sonst wohl kein Auto mehr. Man sollte also durchaus vorsichtig sein beim Versuch, das Problem dadurch zu lösen, daß man überall gleich schlechte Bedingungen schafft.

Denn schließlich müssen die Produkte, auch die im Entwicklungsland produzierten, auch von irgend jemanden, nämlich dem Konsumenten, gekauft werden. Wenn wir dafür sorgen, daß für die Löhne schon so viel verbraucht wird, daß für die Investitionen nichts mehr übrigbleibt, besteht die Gefahr, daß das, was neben den Arbeitnehmern notwendig ist, nämlich das komplementäre Unternehmertum, nicht mehr hervortritt. Mir scheint, daß unsere Weltwirtschaft gegenwärtig vor allem daran krankt, daß es zu wenige Unternehmer gibt. Dies liegt wohl daran, daß es sich für die Unternehmer nicht lohnt, sich besonders anzustrengen. Ich hoffe, daß die Schwierigkeit in den achtziger Jahren, einen Arbeitsplatz als Arbeitnehmer zu bekommen, dazu führt, daß wir wieder einen Zuwachs an Selbständigen bekommen. Das scheint mir die beste Lösung zu sein: Daß Leute selbständig werden, um ihre Entscheidung selber in die Hand zu nehmen, statt jener Entwicklung, die wir hinter uns haben, mit der Verbeamtung unserer gesamten Gesellschaft.

Fiedler-Winter:

Hier ist noch eine Frage zum Thema Lohn an Herrn Rappe: „Lohn ist zwar Kaufkraft, aber auch Sparkraft. Denn derzeit werden 15 % auf die Bank getragen. Angenommen, die Tarifabschlüsse bleiben maßvoll, so müßten die Unternehmen weniger starke Kredite aus den Spargeldern bei den Banken aufnehmen, könnten infolgedessen stärker und risikofreudiger investieren. Wie stellen Sie sich zu diesem Gedanken?“

Rappe:

Natürlich geht ein erhöhter Teil in die Spartätigkeit; im Augenblick ist es etwas weniger, aber in den zurückliegenden Jahren war es so. Wenn dieses Geld nicht zu Investitionen von der Privatwirtschaft genommen wird – das Geld ist heute ja preiswert –, dann entsteht ja genau die Diskussion, die auf der politischen Ebene eine Rolle spielt: Ob die öffentliche Hand verstärkt Kredite aufnimmt und die Staatsverschuldung dann eben höher angesetzt wird, weil das Geld in den Wirtschaftskreis laufen muß.

Ich bin der Auffassung, daß eine bestimmte Rate natürlich immer in die Sparkraft gehen wird. Dies wird bei der Entwicklung unserer Löhne zumindest in den Mittelschichten immer so bleiben. Ich sehe darin auch keine Gefahr. Die Frage ist nur, daß das Geld entweder über die Privatwirtschaft oder über die öffentliche Hand wieder in den Kreislauf zurückkommt.

Walter:

Ich weiß nicht, ob ich dazu etwas sagen soll. Wir haben uns in einer Publikation, die wir gerade hinter uns gebracht haben – „Die Weltwirtschaft", eine Halbjahreszeitschrift, die Konjunkturprognosen für die Bundesrepublik und wichtige Industrieländer beinhaltet –, zum Kaufkraftargument zum wiederholten Male geäußert. Im wesentlichen kann man feststellen: Eine Lohnerhöhung, die die Massenkaufkraft stärkt, hat mit Sicherheit in Höhe der Lohnerhöhungen, die zu diesem Zweck erfolgen, Kostenwirkungen. Die volle Summe wird kostenwirksam. Über die Frage, **wieviel** innerhalb **kurzer Zeit** – beide Gesichtspunkte sind relevant – davon zu Ausgaben wird, kann man, glaube ich, die Extrembehauptung aufstellen, daß es kaum mehr sein wird als die Kostenerhöhung. Es ist aber wahrscheinlicher, daß es weniger ist. An der Kaufkrafttheorie des Lohns ist also noch nicht einmal kurzfristig etwas richtig. Ihrem Vorwurf die wissenschaftlichen Ratgeber redeten dem Lohnverzicht das Wort, trage ich in Diskussionen oft Rechnung. Wenn ich Lohnzurückhaltung vorschlage, dann bedeutet dies nicht Lohnverzicht, der deshalb gefährlich sein könnte, weil es zu Untersicherheiten kommen könnte, aufgrund der rasch notwendig werdenden Nachfrageumschichtung von den Konsumenten zu den Investoren. Das würde dann geschehen, wenn in einer Welt, in der die Inflationsrate 10 % beträgt, plötzlich die Löhne eingefroren würden. Da sehe ich auch die Gefahr, daß die Veränderung der Nachfragestruktur tatsächlich rezessiv wirken würde. Einen solchen Vorschlag würde ich aber auch nicht machen.

Wofür ich plädiere, ist, daß bei einem Produktivitätsfortschritt, wie wir ihn in den letzten Jahren hatten – von 3 % –, der Anstieg des Reallohns darunter bleibt, also bei etwa 2 % liegt. In den vergangenen Jahren kam es nicht zu solchen Lohnabschlüssen, freilich nicht vor allem durch bösen Willen der Gewerkschaften oder durch geplante Permissivität der Unternehmen bei den Lohnverhandlungen, sondern meist durch die beiderseitige Überschätzung der künftigen Inflationsraten. Solche Lohnabschlüsse haben am Ende bewirkt, daß der Reallohn stärker stieg als die Produktivität, d. h. die Gewinne zurückgingen und schließlich die Beschäftigung sank.

Rappe:

Darf ich dazu eine Bemerkung machen, Herr Walter! Ich würde sehr viel leichter über solche Entwicklungen oder solche Substanzen für die Diskussion nachdenken können, wenn es entweder von der Seite der Wissenschaft oder von der Seite der Politik oder von den Unternehmern brauchbare Vorschläge über den Komplex der Vermögensbildung an die Adresse der Gewerkschaften gäbe.

Denn wenn nicht alles in den konsumtiven Teil soll – wenn das mit eine Rolle spielt –, bleibt nur noch die Entscheidung, ob bei einem solchen Zurückbremsen der Lohnentwicklung Fragen der Vermögensbildung wirklich noch eine Rolle spielen. Oder wäre Ihr Rezept, in der Verteilung dem Unternehmer mehr zu geben als dem Arbeitnehmer? Dann wäre allerdings die Frage unter Vermögensbildungsgesichtspunkten zu diskutieren.

Fiedler-Winter:

Ich möchte diesen Lohnblock noch nutzen, um eine weitere Frage vorzutragen. Die Frage geht an beide Herren: „Hielten Sie es für sinnvoll, die Tarifbezirke kleiner zu machen?"

Rappe:

Ich persönlich ja.

Walter:

Da ich Tarifbezirke nicht so genau kenne, würde ich sagen: Branchenspezifischer und firmenspezifischer sollten die Lohnabschlüsse sein. Das erscheint mir wichtiger als die für mich willkürliche Abgrenzung der Tarifbezirke.

(Zuruf: Das ist dasselbe!)

Fiedler-Winter:

Ehe wir mit weiteren Fragen an Sie fortfahren, darf ich eine Frage an Herrn Welbergen dazwischenschieben: „Die Deutsche Shell hatte laut vorliegender Bilanz 1976 eine Gewinnausschüttung von fast 300 Millionen DM – das sind 30 % des Stammkapitals und mehr als die Hälfte der Lohnkosten. Woher leiten Sie denn Ihre Rechte ab, von mangelnder Konkurrenzfähigkeit wegen steigender Lohnkosten zu sprechen?"

Welbergen:

Wenn Sie schon eine solche Frage stellen, bedaure ich, daß Sie nicht auch die hier ausgelegte Bilanz 1977 in Ihre Fragestellung einbeziehen. Es ist furchtbar einfach, nur eine Sache zu nehmen und die andere zu ignorieren.

Wir haben in der Tat 1976 eine Dividende von 20 % ausgezahlt. Darüber hinaus haben wir eine gewisse Ausschüttung gemacht, die darauf zurückzuführen ist, daß es eine Steuerveränderung gab. Deshalb haben wir absolut legitim hier gewisse Ausschüttungen vorgezogen. Sie werden aber auch in der 77er Bilanz, die hier ausliegt, aber Ihnen leider noch nicht bekannt ist, auch unsere Dividendenzahlungen und Ausschüttungen in den letzten 10 Jahren gesehen haben. Dann werden Sie erkennen, daß 1976 ein Sternjahr war, während der ganze Zeitraum sehr große Schwankungen zeigt und wir über die ganze Zeit eine Ausschüttung von, ich glaube 15 % hatten; ich sage das jetzt aus dem Gedächtnis.

Zweitens. Ich habe hier nicht für die Deutsche Shell gesprochen. Wohl habe ich hier und da ein paar Beispiele, die mir gegenwärtig sind, zur Illustration aus dem Bereich der Deutschen Shell gebracht. Aber ich rede hier nicht für die Deutsche Shell allein. Wir versuchen ja, wirtschaftliche Fragen zu diskutieren, die größere Zusammenhänge haben als nur eine Firma.

Eingangs sagte ich schon, wir sind nicht lohnintensiv, wir sind kapitalintensiv; wir sind kapitalintensiv; deshalb sind wir für die Industrie nicht repräsentativ. Viele Sachen, die bei uns sind, sehen bei uns anders aus als in der restlichen Industrie. Wir haben Haustarife und keine Industrietarife. Auch ist bekannt, daß unsere Gehaltsstruktur, unsere Tarifstruktur sicher nicht am unteren Ende, sondern eher am oberen Ende ist. Das gibt mir das Recht, trotzdem über die Überforderung durch Löhne zu reden, auch wenn es nicht unbedingt in Zusammenhang mit meiner Firma steht.

Fiedler-Winter:

Wir haben noch Fragen an Herrn Dr. Walter vorliegen. Wir wollen in Überleitung zum nächsten Punkt des Fragenkataloges mit folgender beginnen: „Sehen Sie in der gegenwärtigen Zeit sowie in der Arbeitslosenquote der 80er Jahre eine Hilfslosigkeit des neokeynesianischen Konjunkturinstruments?"

Walter:

Ich würde sagen: Insgesamt ja. Bei der auf diesem Konzept basierenden Politik ging man davon aus, daß man mit expansiver (inflationärer) Politik die Arbeitslosigkeit reduzieren könne. Dieser Philosophie hing 1973 auch noch Helmut Schmidt an, als er für die Bundesrepublik formulierte, daß er lieber 5 Prozent Inflation ertrage als 5 Prozent Arbeitslosigkeit. Die Wirklichkeit hat gezeigt, daß mit solcher Politik auf Dauer Vollbeschäftigung nicht zu sichern war. Im Gegenteil: Inflation **und** Arbeitslosigkeit stiegen an. Und nicht nur in der Bundesrepublik. Offensichtlich brauchen wir also mehr als keynesianische Nachfragesteuerung zur Lösung unserer wirtschaftlichen Probleme.

Fiedler-Winter:

Ferner wurde noch danach gefragt, weil Sie vom Ernstnehmen des Kartellgesetzes gesprochen hätten: Wie stehen Sie zu den kürzlich wieder erhobenen Entflechtungsforderungen?

Walter:

Aussprache Rappe, Walter

Da habe ich sehr radikale Vorväter, die ich dabei sehr gerne zitiere. Es gibt die Aussage, daß man im Grunde in jeder Generation, d. h. alle 30 Jahre, eine große Entflechtungsaktion haben muß, wenn man die Wirtschaft als funktionierende Marktwirtschaft erhalten will. Wenn man die Realität anschaut, stellt man fest: Eine Entflechtungsaktion ist offensichtlich nur möglich nach einer Revolution oder bei starkem Druck von außen, wie beispielsweise durch Besatzungsmächte. Ich glaube, aus innerer Kraft diesen Kraftakt der Entflechtung zu schaffen, ist nahezu unmöglich.

Obwohl ich das feststelle, möchte ich aber dennoch sagen, daß wir alle unsere politischen Kräfte zusammennehmen müssen, um mehr Markt zu realisieren. Eine ordnungspolitische Reform tut not. Wenn man das marktwirtschaftliche Konzept retten will, muß man erkennen, daß Marktzusammenballung, wie sie sich in der Bundesrepublik in den letzten sieben, acht Jahren vollzogen hat, mit Sicherheit das marktwirtschaftliche System gefährdet und denjenigen Kräften, die es abschaffen wollen, einige gute Argumente an die Hand gibt. Dabei spielt unser Universalbankensystem, das sich wie ein dichtes Netz über unsere Volkswirtschaft gebreitet und den Wettbewerb mehr unterdrückt als es ihn fördert, eine wichtige Rolle.

Es wäre also gut, wenn die ordnungspolitische Diskussion in diesem Land ernstgenommen würde, von wenigstens einer wichtigen politischen Partei ernstgenommen und endlich angepackt würde. Hierbei sind die Sünden bei den Sozialdemokraten mindestens ebenso groß wie bei den Christdemokraten. Die Sozialdemokraten in den 70er Jahren haben aus Not Großindustriepolitik betrieben, bei den Christdemokraten ist es nicht so ganz klar, welche Gruppen dafür sorgen, daß eine Wirtschaftspolitik Erhardscher Konsequenz bei ihr gegenwärtig nicht sichtbar wird.

Rappe:

Ich wollte nur ein Wort zu Herrn Walter sagen. So richtig diese Einschätzung ist, aber der Adressat müssen doch eigentlich Banken und Industrie selber sein, nicht die Politik.

Walter:

Nein, man kann doch nicht gegen seine Interessen handeln. Ich muß das vom politischen System erwarten.

Rappe:

Sie würden meinen, daß das Politische die marktwirtschaftlichen Grundsätze wieder geraderücken muß, möglicherweise mit unmarktwirtschaftlichen Mitteln?

Walter:

Auch eine Marktwirtschaft braucht Regeln: Wir brauchen ein gutes Kartellgesetz. Und wir brauchen jemanden, der die Einhaltung der Regeln kontrolliert: Das ist die Kartellbehörde.

Rappe:

Wichtig ist nur, daß das dann nicht in der Öffentlichkeit als Eingriff in die Marktwirtschaft diskutiert wird.

Walter:

Da kann man sich dann auf Herrn Böhm oder auf Herrn Eucken berufen. Da braucht man durchaus nicht linker Ideologe zu sein. Ich stimme mit Ihnen insofern voll überein.

Fiedler-Winter:

Herr Dr. Walter, Sie sprachen von zunehmendem Versicherungsdenken. Es wir wird gefragt: Was halten Sie in diesem Zusammenhang von unserem System der sozialen Sicherungen? Jeden Arbeitgeber, der arbeitsintensiv produziert, trifft die Belastung durch Lohnkosten in Form der Sozialabgaben. Die kapitalintensiv produzierende Industrie ist davon nicht betroffen. Wird auf diese Weise, durch dieses System, die Einstellung von Arbeitskräften nicht bedroht? Muß man nicht auch Maschinen mit Sozialabgaben belasten?

Walter:

Zunächst einmal stimme ich der Analyse zu, daß es Elemente in unserer Sozialgesetzgebung und Steuergesetzgebung gibt, die die Kapitalintensität fördern. Das Problem würde ich allerdings anders hören, als der Frager suggeriert: Ich würde die Belastung mit Sozialabgaben reduzieren. Ich würde beispielsweise die Lohnsummensteuer abschaffen. Sie ist angesichts der gegenwärtigen Situation nun wirklich nicht angezeigt. Ich würde die Lohnsummensteuer abschaffen und damit Belastungen für denjenigen abbauen, der Arbeitskräfte einsetzt. Darüber hinaus meine ich, daß die Sozialabgaben insgesamt eine solche Höhe erreicht haben, daß sie abgebaut werden sollten.

Die vom Frager angebotene Lösung scheint mir sehr gefährlich zu sein. Wenn ich in diesem Land jetzt auch noch die Investitionen in kapitalintensiver Form belaste, bewirke ich, wenn ich nicht auf dem Mond bin und damit das Auswandern möglich ist, natürlich einen Exitus der Investitionen, noch mehr, als das gegenwärtig schon der Fall ist. Das Rezept kann also nur sein, die Sozialabgaben insgesamt zu reduzieren und solche Verrücktheiten wie die Lohnsummensteuer ganz sicherlich abzuschaffen.

Fiedler-Winter:

Zur Überleitung zu unserem Schluß möchte ich noch eine Frage an Herrn Welbergen vortragen, die allerdings etwas schwierig ist und lautet: „Sie sprachen einige Male von Wettbewerb und Wettbewerbsfähigkeit. Es fragt sich, ob dieser Wettbewerb im Sinne der vollkommenen Konkurrenz überhaupt noch besteht. Eine gegenseitige Tendenz macht die zunehmende Konzentration deutlich. Liegen hierin nicht Gefahren für die Bereiche der freien Wahlentscheidungen wie Konsumentensouveränität und eventuell sogar der Tarifautonomie?"

Welbergen:

Ich muß den Ausgangspunkt der Frage herausstellen. Wenn wir keine Konkurrenz haben, muß ich wirklich fragen, was wir für Dummköpfe sind, daß wir keine bessere Rendite zeigen. Wir haben in Deutschland eine Umsatzrendite, die unter 2 % liegt. Vergleichsweise sind es in Amerika 6 %. Wenn Sie jetzt sagen, daß wir keine Konkurrenz haben, ist das Sünde. Es ist sehr merkwürdig. Denn wenn wir die ganze Zeit stöhnen und keine Konkurrenz haben und dann noch 2 % Umsatzrendite, dann möchte ich Herrn Walter allerdings recht geben, daß wir eine Vergreisung des Unternehmertums hätten.

Da ich davon ausgehe, daß wir Wettbewerb haben, sogar einen verdammt harten Wettbewerb, nicht nur innerhalb Deutschlands, sondern auf allen Weltmärkten, muß ich den zweiten Teil der Frage als etwas theoretisch bezeichnen. Natürlich gibt es – nach dem Monopol-Bericht, dem Kartell-Bericht, dem Tätigkeitsbericht – gewisse Konzentrationen. Man muß aber diese Konzentrationen auch im Verhältnis zu den gesamtwirtschaftlichen Verschiebungen sehen. Wie so oft, ergeben Statistiken dieser Art nur ein unvollkommenes Bild.

Fiedler-Winter:

Jetzt kommen wir zu unserer Abschlußfrage. Da erkundigt sich jemand folgendermaßen: „Herr Professor Biedenkopf führte gestern aus, daß Konsum heute die Zukunftschancen morgen senkt. Sehen Sie in der Politik heute nicht auch die Gefahr, Erwartungen und Bedürfnisse von heute zu Lasten einer ohnehin benachteiligten Generation zu lösen?"

Walter:

Ich habe in meinen Ausführungen ein paarmal diese These vertreten. Ich meine allerdings, wenn aus dem grundsätzlichen Ja zu dieser Frage die Schlußfolgerung gezogen wird, daß wir gegenwärtig vor allem das staatliche Defizit abrupt und schnell herunterfahren müssen, die Staatsausgaben einschränken und ansonsten nichts zu tun wäre, dann würde das die falsche Implikation sein.

Wir müssen dafür sorgen, daß die staatlichen Ausgaben und das Steuersystem mehr darauf ausgerichtet wird, daß Leistung honoriert wird.

Wenn sie honoriert wird, hat man gleichzeitig auch für die Zukunft vorgesorgt. Damit ist nämlich dafür gesorgt, daß Ausbildung lohnt. Dann ist dafür gesorgt, daß es attraktiv ist, Markteinkommen zu erzielen. Dann ist es schwieriger geworden, Transfereinkommen zu erzielen, Transfereinkommen als Arbeitloser, Transfereinkommen als Landwirt, Transfereinkommen als Stahlunternehmer.

Da bin ich auch gleich schon wieder ein bißchen beim Wettbewerb. Bundesdeutsche Wettbewerbsfähigkeit in „falschen" Branchen wird gegenwärtig zu einem nicht unwichtigen Teil aus den Säckeln der Steuerzahler finanziert. Auch das sollte abgeschafft werden. Auch dort hat der Staat wettbewerbspolitische Aufgaben. Es muß also nicht unbedingt Entflechtung sein. Vielleicht ist dies viel wichtiger: Daß man Widerstand zeigt, wo die Leute einem die Tür einrennen und nach Subventionen fragen. Wenn man bei der Bewältigung gegenwärtiger Probleme, die im Grunde in der Vergangenheit hätten gelöst werden sollen, Widerstand zeigt, schafft man die beste Basis, daß für die Zukunft mehr Luft besteht, daß der Staat für zukünftige Ausgaben mehr Spielraum hat.

Insofern räume ich dem Fragesteller ein, daß gegenwärtig, weil die Politik so permissiv ist, dem Druck von Gruppen nachgibt, Zukunftschancen verspielt werden. Das betrifft beispielsweise, wie ich es andeutete, die Rentenversicherung. Dort käme es darauf an, allen Gruppen, den Rentnern und den Beitragszahlern, klarzumachen, daß es um etwas geht, was nur einmal zu verteilen ist.

Rappe:

Ich bin seit Januar 1977 Vorsitzender des Bundestagsausschusses für Arbeit und Sozialordnung. Seitdem gab es Diskussionen um das Zwanzigste Rentenanpassungsgesetz, um das Kostendämpfungsgesetz, um die Kriegsopferversorgung und um das Einundzwanzigste Rentenanpassungsgesetz. Es waren meiner Ansicht nach Diskussionen, die das Problem der Leistungsfähigkeit, das Verhältnis zwischen der aktiven Gruppe und der zu versorgenden älteren Generation, in der politischen Auseinandersetzung behandelten. Ich habe in dieser Frage ein sehr gutes Gewissen. Ich glaube auch nicht, daß wir zu solchen Horrorzahlen in der Entwicklung kommen, die Sie in Ihren Ausführungen nannten, mit 40 % Sozialbelastung. Denn dann müßte konkreter diskutiert werden, daß es hierbei um das Rentengesetz bis 1981 geht, daß wir dann 1982/1983 eine besondere Situation in der Sozialgesetzgebung haben. Ihr Ende ist 1983 mit der Realisierung und dem Verfassungsgerichtsurteil ab 1. Januar 1984. Keiner von denen, die jetzt in der politischen Verantwortung sind, denkt daran, die Beitragsbelastungen in der Weise zu erhöhen. Genau deshalb haben wir ja gegen erheblichen Widerstand – ich denke an das Kostendämpfungsgesetz und an das, was Ärzte und Pharmazeutische Industrie in ihren Wartezimmern ausgelegt haben oder in ihren Zeitungen schreiben – die

Meinung vertreten, daß wir hinsichtlich der Kostenbelastung der Aktiven auf der richtigen Ebene liegen.

Eine abschließende Bemerkung in bezug auf Sozialbelastung und Steuern. Das Aufkommen allein klärt die Frage noch nicht. Es ist nämlich eine Frage der Wiederumverteilung. In diesem Sinne will ich Ihnen sagen: Der arme Staat ist immer nur eine lukrative Sache für reiche Leute. Aber deren Gewählter bin ich nicht.

Walter:

Zur Frage der Sozialversicherung wollte ich nur konkret mal meine spezielle Kritik ansetzen, wo alle drei Parteien für die Zeit nach 1981 die bruttolohnbezogene Rente erneut versprochen haben.

Rappe:

Das gilt auch für 1982 und 1983 auf der Basis niedrigerer Lohnraten. Das geht nicht mehr ab 1984. Dann gibt es ganz sicher eine neue Diskussion bezüglich der Realisierung und es wird neue Pläne geben. Die sind auch in Arbeit. Da geht es um die Realisierung des Verfassungsgerichtsurteils ab 1. Januar 1984.

Walter:

Niemand von den politischen Parteien hat gesagt, daß dies eine Regelung für zwei Jahre wird, sondern jeder hat gesagt - - -

Rappe:

Das kann auch keiner sagen, weil keiner das Gesetz kennt, das 1984 in Kraft gesetzt werden muß. Sie glauben doch nicht, daß Sie mich als Gewerkschaftler oder auch Parlamentarier auf den Punkt kriegen, daß ich heute schon wissen könnte, wie das Gesetz aussieht, das der Bundestag, der 1980 neu gewählt wird, macht. Da geht es darum, wie er die Frage der sozialen Sicherung der Frau gesetzlich lösen will. Da gibt es Untersuchungskommissionen. Kein Mensch ist in der Lage, diesen Untersuchungskommissionen vorauszugreifen.

(Zuruf: Sagen Sie das doch mal überall!)

– Das sage ich überall. Das können Sie zitieren, wenn Sie wollen.

Fiedler-Winter:

Ich danke Ihnen, meine Herren.

Ich möchte Ihnen als Auditorium ebenfalls für die lebhafte und interessierte Anteilnahme meinen herzlichen Dank aussprechen. Sie haben gesehen, daß unter den Antwortgebern nicht nur die Gewerkschaftsvertreter engagiert sind, sondern auch die sogenannten Darwinisten. Vor allem haben Sie gesehen, daß die Unternehmer nicht nur stupide Briefe schreiben, sondern sich auch engagieren, sich 3 Tage mit jungen Leuten unterhalten können, wenn es um deren Zukunft geht.

Mit einem herzlichen Dank an alle beende ich die Diskussion.

Zukunftchancen der Jugend – Versuch eines Resümees

Wolfgang Schürer

Trotz der Vielfalt der Meinungen in der Beurteilung der gegenwärtigen Lage besteht in einem wesentlichen Punkt Übereinstimmung: Wir leben in einer Zeit des Wandels. Für jedermann offensichtlich sind die Bereiche, in denen mehr oder minder genaue Bewertungen möglich sind: wachsende Weltbevölkerung, wachsende Industrialisierung, Wissensexplosion, Verdichtung und Ausbau weltweiter Kommunikation bis hin zum Informationsüberfluß sowie zunehmende Abhängigkeiten im Bereich weltweiter arbeitsteiliger Prozesse. All dies sind sogenannte sichere Größen, die diese Entwicklung veranschaulichen. Versucht man jedoch, die Gründe für den tiefen Wandel, der unsere Gesellschaft erfaßt hat, einer Analyse zu unterziehen, kann man genauso wenig bei diesen Größen stehenbleiben, wie manche Weltverbesserer im „Zurück von der Waschmaschine" mögliche Lösungsansätze erblicken. Ein Blick in die jüngere Geschichte drängt sich auf.

Das Ende des 2. Weltkriegs führte zu einer neuen Zweiteilung der Welt in die Bereiche des liberal-demokratischen Westens und des totalitären Ostens. Sicherlich ist eine solche pauschale Beurteilung nur im Sinne eines groben Rasters zu verstehen. In Westeuropa und den USA – später folgte Japan – kamen zwei bestimmende Entwicklungen in Gang: auf der Grundlage neuer naturwissenschaftlich-technischer Erkenntnis entstand gewaltiges Wirtschaftswachstum. Die Bevölkerung, die während der Kriegsjahre durch gemeinsame Opfer aller Kreise und sozialen Schichten getroffen wurde, forderte nunmehr gleiche Anteile am neuen wirtschaftlichen Erfolg sowie vermehrte Teilhabe an der sozialen und politischen Willensbildung. In den Jahren bis 1960 dominierte das Streben nach möglichst hohen Wohlstandszielen. Ab Mitte der 60er Jahre läßt sich eine wesentliche Trendwende feststellen. Abwendung, ja Bekämpfung des westlichen Demokratieverständnisses fand und findet Anhänger. Letztlich wird die Beseitigung demokratisch-liberaler Ordnungssysteme offen propagiert. Nimmt man diese beiden Entwicklungen zur Kenntnis, eröffnet sich das Ausmaß des Wandels. Immer wieder wurden die Erfolge der ersten 15 Jahre wirtschaftlicher Wohlstandssteigerung festgestellt und gepriesen. Man scheute sich jedoch besonders in den Kreisen der Wirtschaft, auch die Konsequenzen aus der zweiten Entwicklungsphase unter anderem als Folge der ersten mit in Betracht zu ziehen. Wir behaupten, daß tiefgehende Spannungen und Erschütterungen bis in die Pfeiler der sozialen Ordnung nicht nur am Horizont erkennbar wurden, sondern sich teilweise deutlich ankündigten.

Zur Ausgangslage: Die Wohlstandsgesellschaft hängt von den Erfolgen der Neuerungsfähigkeit ab. Sie bietet breiten, früher benachteiligten Bevölkerungsschichten die Möglichkeit zur vermehrten Durchsetzung ihrer Interessen. Wohlstand und Entwicklungen zum Sozialstaat erleichtern Bürgern, die Folgen von Krankheit, Alter und Tod zumindest finanziell zu tragen. Wirtschaftliche Unabhängigkeit schafft ein Mehr an Freiheit. Die Arbeitnehmer erhalten erheblichen Anteil am industriellen Erfolg, der durch Vollbeschäftigung bzw. Austrocknung des Arbeitsmarktes bis in die jüngste Zeit vollkommen gesichert erschien. Der Trend zur Wohlstandsgesellschaft hat den Aufgabenbereich des Staates in unvorstellbarem Ausmaß vergrößert. Als Konsequenz ergibt sich eine Zunahme seiner Eingriffe in das wirtschaftliche Geschehen nicht zuletzt durch den Ausbau seiner Trägerfunktion als öffentliche Körperschaft im Bereich privatwirtschaftlich organisierter Wirtschaftsgebilde. Die Vermehrung sozialen Wohlstandes hängt jedoch von den Zuwachsraten und der Verteilung des Sozialproduktes ab. Es steigt nur, wenn sich der Output der Unternehmungen erhöht. Dieser kann nur so lange gesteigert werden wie Neuerungen, Rationalisierung und Produktionssteigerungen zeitgleich erzielt werden. Die Leistungsgesellschaft, die ihre stärkste Ausprägung immer in Nachkriegszeiten findet, basiert auf realen Wachstumsraten, geringer Inflation und besonderem Leistungswillen.

Seit Ende der 60er Jahre hat sich insbesondere bei der nachwachsenden Generation eine neue Haltung gegenüber vielen bisher nur in Ausnahmefällen in Frage gestellten Zielen und Werten ergeben. Da ich nicht Soziologe bin, verweise ich auf die entsprechende sozialwissenschaftliche Literatur. Ein Hinweis erscheint mir jedoch besonders wichtig. Die Tatsache, daß Ideologien kein offenes, sondern ein geschlossenes System darstellen, nimmt diesen eine Fähigkeit: den Zugang zu neuer Einsicht und damit die Möglichkeit interner Berichtigung, die auf Erfahrung beruht. Systemimmanent im Wesen einer Ideologie ist die Unfähigkeit, Kritik zu ertragen, im Kompromiß Verbesserungen zu finden und damit das Unvermögen, durch Integration Spannungen zu lösen. Konflikte werden vielmehr erneut aktiviert – sie sollen aktiviert werden. Der Interessenausgleich ist gar nicht sinnvoll, kann es gar nicht sein. Mir ist deswegen diese Feststellung besonders wichtig, da Kritiker mit ideologischer Position kompromißlos negieren und gleichzeitig pluralismusfeindlich agieren.

Der Begriff des Wandels steht im Mittelpunkt unserer Bemerkungen. Die ihm zukommende Bedeutung verlangt nach einer gründlichen Auseinandersetzung. Wandel bedeutet nicht Balance, nicht Ausgewogenheit, nicht Sicherheit, auch nicht Prognostizierbarkeit, sondern Ungewißheit, Risiko und Veränderung in einem solchen Maße, daß das Risiko der Ungewißheit sich selbst zur Regel erklärt. Wenn wir von der weit verbreiteten Nabelschau der Gegenwart abrücken, so wird jedermann bewußt, daß es Wandel immer gegeben hat, wobei sicherlich die Dominanz des Wandels unterschiedlich war. Geschichtlicher Betrachtung folgend, läßt sich feststellen, daß Wandel und Risiko immer dann von den Menschen gemeistert wurden, wenn sie nicht die Orientierung an den Zielen verloren haben, die den Sinn ihrer Existenz ausmachten. Die Projizierung auf die Gegenwart zeigt den fundamentalen Unterschied. Der Wandel, der die heutige Zeit bestimmt, macht nicht bei der Veränderung äußerer Bedingungen halt, sondern unterwirft auch die Ziele selbst seinem Prozeß. Der Vorgang, den ich zu beschreiben versuche, wird sehr gerne auf die Formel einer Orientierungskrise reduziert. Verdeutlichen läßt sich diese These in nur allzu offensichtlicher Form, wenn wir feststellen, daß unsere Wertordnung instabil geworden ist, Sprache, Werte und Begriffe Dissonanzen aufweisen. Kommunikationsschwierigkeiten und sich daraus ergebend das Unvermögen, durch die Sprache, die Kommunikation und die Wertordnung den äußeren Wandel zu beherrschen, ist die Folge, über deren Bedeutung wir uns alle nicht klar genug werden können. Soll Wandel nicht eine Bedrohung darstellen, kann keine Gesellschaft diesen bestehen, ohne eine Adaption ihrer Existenz an die neuen Bedingungen vorzunehmen. Erfolgreiche Adaption bedingt den Willen zur Gestaltung und zur Integration des Neuen. Ist äußerer Wandel mit dem Wandel der Werte und Ziele zeitgleich, so kommt die Gesellschaft nicht umhin, ihre Werte neu zu ermitteln und neue Zielformulierungen vorzunehmen.

Die Rolle des Unternehmers war noch vor fünf Jahren aufgrund der Bedingungen der Nachkriegszeit insofern erhaben über fast jede Kritik, weil das innenpolitische Primat aller europäischen Länder durch die Wirtschaft bestimmt wurde. Wiederaufbau und in den Folgejahren der wirtschaftliche Wohlstand waren politische Ziele, die sowohl in der Prioritätenordnung die obersten Ränge einnahmen, wie auch von der Allgemeinheit schlechthin nicht in Frage gestellt wurden. Als es gelang, diese Ziele zu verwirklichen und bis anhin unvorstellbarer Wohlstand für breiteste Kreise erreicht wurde, ergab sich eine erhebliche Veränderung des Stellenwertes wirtschaftlicher und konsequenterweise auch wirtschaftspolitischer Ziele. Es leiteten sich Ziele „jenseits von Angebot und Nachfrage“ ab, z.B. höheres Bildungsniveau, Umweltschutz, Humanisierung des Arbeitsplatzes, Qualität des Lebens und ähnliche weitere. Diese Entwicklung hat zumindest eins zweifelsfrei deutlich gemacht, nämlich die Tatsache, daß wirtschaftliche Tätigkeit nicht allein wirtschaftlichen Zielen zu dienen hat.

Wieso werden im Rahmen dieses Symposiums solche Fragen zum Schluß aufgeworfen? Es ist auffällig, daß sowohl der Unternehmer, wenn die Verallgemeinerung erlaubt ist, mit Fragen, Problemen und Haltungen der jungen Generation oft wenig „anfangen“ kann und häufig rein defensiv argumentiert. Ähnliche Beobachtungen treffen für Vertreter der jungen Generation zu, die zu oft über falsche Vorstellungen und zu wenig Kenntnisse über politische, gesellschaftliche und wirtschaftliche Probleme und insbesondere deren Zusammenhänge verfügen und ungeachtet dessen „sachkundig“ diskutieren. Die Position der Defensive und die Position der Forderung mögen als Ausgangspunkt verständlich sein. Auf ihnen zu beharren, verunmöglicht die Realisierung neuer Ideen. Wenn es in diesen Tagen gelungen ist, Entwicklungen verständlich zu machen, die Bedeutung des Wandels und der Unsicherheit zu erfassen und gleichzeitig zu erkennen, welche engen Grenzen sogenannte Planbarkeit aufweist, dann kommen wir vielleicht zu einer besonders wichtigen Erkenntnis. Hochentwickelte westliche Gesellschaften, die den Pluralismus bejahen, können die Zukunft nicht mit dem Orakel erkennen; allfällige mögliche zukünftige Entwicklungen lassen sich allenfalls in Szenarien erfassen. Wir alle werden feststellen, daß in den nächsten zwölf Monaten „viele Dinge" passieren werden, die wir heute als „unmöglich" bzw. undenkbar bezeichnen. „Was nicht sein darf, nicht sein kann." Dieses Motto ist kurzsichtig und gefährlich, trotzdem begegnen wir ihm fast tagtäglich.

Als eine der unbestrittenen Erkenntnisse dieser Zusammenkunft läßt sich festhalten, daß die Innovationsfähigkeit unserer Gesellschaft eine wichtige Voraussetzung dafür ist, unsere zukünftigen Probleme überhaupt lösen zu können. Wer Chancen verbreitern will, muß als Folge härteren Wettbewerb akzeptieren. Nur auf dieser Basis bleibt Leistung das Auswahlprinzip.

In diesem Zusammenhang möchte ich auf eine mir gefährlich erscheinende, weit verbreitete Meinung hinweisen: auf die Auffassung, daß jede Art sogenannter höherer Bildung, insbesondere die des Studiums quasi „automatisch" Qualifikation bedeutet. Manche Akademiker haben in den letzten Jahren das „Selbstverständnis" entwickelt, Studienabschluß = Qualifikation. Es stellt sich die Frage: Ist solches Zeugnis auch eine Berufs- bzw. Lebensqualifikation?

In manchem Punkt wird am Ende einer solchen Tagung bei Vertretern der jungen Generation Unzufriedenheit zurückbleiben. Ihre Frage lautet: Was wird jetzt konkret gemacht?

Ich möchte mich auf folgende Bemerkungen beschränken: Eine qualifizierte Ausbildung wird auch zukünftig der Schlüssel bleiben, aufgrund eigener Leistungen den Wandel meistern zu können. Früher reichte eine Ausbildung für ein Leben. Die ständige Weiterbildung wird bei weitem nicht nur für den Akademiker zur Existenzfrage werden. Wir können nicht absehen, welche Konsequenzen z.B. neue Kommunikationstechnologien, die Elektronik, Veränderungen der Weltpolitik, um nur drei Beispiele zu nennen, nach sich ziehen.

Diese Feststellung gilt für alle Lebens- und Berufsbereiche. Wenn wir davon ausgehen, daß die Dimension des Wandels **die** Rahmenbedingung unserer Generation bleibt – Strukturwandel, Nord-Süd-Problem, permanente Überholung bestehenden Wissens, Ressourcenprobleme lassen diese Annahme realistisch erscheinen –, dann stellt sich zusätzlich ein weiteres Problem, welches nur am Rande gestreift wurde. Es ist die Tatsache, daß wir im weltweiten Maßstab – die Interdependenz impliziert diese Betrachtungsweise – ein ungeheures Angebot an ungelernten Arbeitskräften haben. Ebenso verfügen wir über einen Überfluß an Kapital; hingegen sind sehr viel weniger gelernte Arbeitskräfte im „Markt", Know-how ist in der Tat bereits ein knappes Gut, Führungsqualität in Politik, Verbänden, organisierten Gruppen und Wirtschaft erscheint als das knappste Gut schlechthin, als Kombination aus Know-how, Erfahrung und einer erheblichen Portion von unerlernbarer Intuition. Über diese Situation und ihre Auswirkung sollten wir uns mehr Gedanken machen.

Die Zukunftschancen der Jugend sind die Chancen, so hieß es im Laufe der drei Tage, welche die heutige Jugend im Laufe ihres Lebens hat. Dieser Begriffsbestimmung kann man folgen. Wir hörten, daß der Staat, die gesellschaftlichen Gruppen und der einzelne diese Entwicklung beeinflussen können.

An Politiker geht das Ersuchen, nicht ständig neue Errungenschaften zu fordern und neue Leistungen zu versprechen, wenn diese „nach den Wahlreden" weder realisiert noch finanziert werden können. Gerade die junge Generation läßt sich nicht auf Dauer täuschen. Ich bin überzeugt, daß der Mut zu einem unpopulären Wort, welches auf der Erkenntnis bestimmter Entwicklungen und der Verantwortung gegenüber der Gesamtheit vorgetragen wird, auch akzeptiert wird. Wenn wir uns aber einen Großteil unserer Probleme selbst schaffen, zusätzlich zu den großen Aufgaben, die bewältigt werden müssen, dann reduzieren wir von vornherein unsere Fähigkeit zur Problemlösung.

Die Entwicklung von Leistungsprofilen im Bereich der staatlichen Administration erscheint als ein nennenswertes Beispiel, welches weitreichende Ergebnisse bewirken wird und jederzeit realisierbar ist – wenn man nur will.

Damit stellt sich für uns die Frage: Was läßt sich für die Zukunft tun? Ich glaube, zweierlei: Einerseits – hier möchte ich an die Ausführungen von Glotz und Biedenkopf anschließen – kann die sofortige Verbesserung gegenwärtiger Probleme und Entscheidungen nicht mit dem Hinweis vertagt werden, daß die grundsätzliche Diskussion erst einmal stattzufinden hätte. Zweitens darf der Versuch der grundsätzlichen Erörterung vieler Probleme unter dem Gesichtspunkt der Zukunftssicherung nicht mit dem Hinweis verhindert werden, was schnell alles zu geschehen habe. Was will ich damit sagen? Wir drohen einem „circulus vitiosus" zu erliegen, indem wir Probleme verschieben, statt anzufangen, sie zu lösen.

Da es leichter ist, von „anderen" die Lösung der eigenen Probleme zu fordern, sei es Staat, Wirtschaft, Verbände oder Parteien, als diese mit dem Risiko der eigenen Entscheidung zu treffen, gewöhnt „man" sich allzu leicht daran, die Problemlösung an andere zu „delegieren". Diese Entwicklung ist passiv und verhängnisvoll. Die Aufgabe des Staates ist auf die Gestaltung von Rahmenbedingungen beschränkt, welche die Hilfe zur Selbsthilfe ermöglichen müssen. Die Pflicht des konkreten Engagements zu Gunsten behinderter Menschen, ist eindeutig zu bejahen. Diese Differenzierung erscheint geboten. Entsprechende Organisationsformen müssen entwickelt werden, die Hilfe und Menschlichkeit gleichberechtigt neben materielle Unterstützung stellen, sonst erstickt Unterstützung in der Bürokratie und Anonymität. So schwer es nach einer Phase von 30jährigem wirtschaftlichen Wohlstand und Wachstum fällt, so dringend ist es geboten, die zunehmenden Unsicherheiten und Friktionen realistisch zu erkennen. Es gilt, vermehrt Eigeninitiative und Solidarität zu mobilisieren. Diese Entwicklung gibt auch die Chance, aus eigener Leistung wieder höhere Befriedigung zu empfinden und neue Dynamik freizusetzen. Diese Probleme sollten weder bagatellisiert noch dramatisiert werden. Das Erkennen, daß die bisherige Entwicklung sich nicht automatisch fortsetzt, eröffnet die Chance zur Rückgewinnung eines Stücks Identität und damit zur Zufriedenheit der Menschen.

Die Zukunftschancen der Jugend sind daher keineswegs schlechter als die bisheriger Generationen. Wenn die Entschiedenheit und der Wille zur eigenen Gestaltung nicht abnehmen, dann sind die Voraussetzungen sogar heute besser. Existentielle Bedürfnisse sind für den überwiegenden Teil der Gesellschaft erfüllt. Die Organisation des öffentlichen Bereichs, unter dem Primat der Leistungserstellung und Dienstleistung, weist enorme Rationalisierungsreserven auf. Die unternehmerische Initiative hat sich, was ihre Leistungsfähigkeit betrifft, überzeugend bewährt. Der Zugang zu Wissen ist heute im Gegensatz zu früher ohne einschneidende soziale Barrieren möglich. Je mehr Chancengleichheit realisiert wird, desto größer wird der Wettbewerb. Auf diese Konsequenz wies besonders Herr Glotz hin.

Lassen Sie mich in Anlehnung an ein Wort von Golo Mann schließen: Pessimismus ist keine praktische Haltung. Der Pessimist mag schweigen und trauern, aber nicht für seine Ansichten werben und auch damit noch Selbstbefriedigung und Selbstmitleid zu gewinnen trachten. Das Amt des Kritikers ist wichtig, ebenso die Fähigkeit zur eigenen Reflexion, keinesfalls jedoch die Pose der Kassandra.

R.Fiedler-Wint

D.Bell

Einführung in die 7. Shell-Jugendstudie *)

Prof. Dr. Viggo Graf Blücher

I. RÜCKBLICK UND AUSBLICK

1.1 Vergangenheits-Orientierung

Sucht man über das diesem Symposium gestellte Thema „Die Jugend und ihre Zukunftschancen" in der Fachliteratur Rat, so wird einem schnell die starke Orientierung aller jugendsoziologischen und jugendpsychologischen Forschung an Problemen der Vergangenheit deutlich. Es fehlt nicht an Erklärungsversuchen aus Erfahrungen mit „der" Jugend über Jahrtausende.[1]
Jugendbewegung wurde über die Jahrzehnte bis heute reflektiert.

Die bündische und die politische ebenso wie die proletarische Jugendbewegung der zwanziger Jahre bleibt bis heute Diskussionsthema. Der Bewältigung der politischen Staatsjugend des Nationalsozialismus sind Bibliotheken gewidmet, in die ein Blick zu tun heute kaum noch lohnt.[2] Heute hingegen beschäftigt man sich nahezu exklusiv mit der jüngsten exzessiven Gestaltung des Phänomens „Jugend" – eine Literaturgattung, die unter den Titel „Studentenrevolte und kein Ende" zu setzen geneigt ist.[3]

Vielen der Betrachtungen ist zweierlei gemeinsam: Erscheinungen in kleinen, oft recht kleinen Teilbereichen der Jugend werden als Reaktion „der" Jugend interpretiert; Jugendprotest gilt als Soll-Anspruch. Mit Goethe könnte man sagen: „Was Ihr den Geist der Zeiten heißt, mir scheint ist Euer eigener Geist."

Von Zukunftserwartungen wenig Spuren. Allenfalls glaubt man, aus der jüngeren Vergangenheit in die Zukunft extrapolieren zu können. Man spekuliert über die Folgen der Studentenrevolte, die „unbewältigte Vergangenheit" unserer Gegenwart.

1.2 Gegenwärtige Lage

Zwei Interpretationen stehen einander unvereinbar gegenüber. Schelsky, getreu seinen jüngsten politischen Ansätzen,[4] nimmt an, man müsse „die Dauergegenwart einer Protestgeneration in den nächsten dreißig Jahren in Rechnung stellen". Man wird gerade unter den Jüngeren damit leben müssen, daß ein großer Teil der Lehrer, die die Kinder erziehen, ein Teil

---

* Vor Beginn des Symposiums hielt Prof. Blücher eine Einführung in die Shell-Jugendstudie, die anschließend diskutiert wurde.

der Professoren, die in wissenschaftlichen Berufen ausbilden, sehr viele Pfarrer beider Konfessionen und vor allem der größte Teil der Journalisten, Medienproduzenten, Schriftsteller und sonstige Sinn-Vermittler, die moralisch-politischen Loyalitäten ihres „Protestes" einhalten und offen oder verborgen nach seinen Grundsätzen lehren, predigen, informieren und handeln werden. Die „Generation des Jugendprotestes" kann, wie alle Generationsgestalten, nie widerlegt, sondern nur überlebt werden.[5]) Rosenmayr hingegen urteilt: „Die Studentenrevolte war die bislang – und auf längere Sicht? – letzte Phase der generationsspezifischen ideologischen Verdichtungen. Die noch nicht geschriebene Geschichte ihrer Nachwirkungen würde aber vermutlich das recht geringe Fortleben und -bestehen gruppenmäßig fixierbarer Generations**einheiten** zeigen. Den Marsch durch die Institutionen haben die Individuen, viel weniger die ehemals solidarisierten Gruppen ... angetreten".[6])

Betrachtet man die Gegenwart mit ihrem totalen Ungleichgewicht im Bildungssystem, dem nur durch neue Friktionen überbrückbaren Numerus Clausus, dem wachsenden Angebot an funktionsloser Intellektualität bei absinkender Nachfrage in Wirtschaft und Gesellschaft, wodurch unerträglicher Konkurrenzdruck, wachsendes Duckmäusertum, zunehmende Leistungsanforderungen und Ausweglosigkeit und Resignation für breite Schichten der Jugend produziert wird, so könnte man auch zu einem anderen Schluß gelangen: Die Zeit geht über die Spätwirkungen des Studentenprotestes hinweg und verweist dessen Bewältigung in die Aufgabengebiete der Kriminalistik, der Psychotechnik, der Ermutigung Verzweifelter und der Disziplinierung Unbotmäßiger.

1.3 Zukunftserwartungen

Aber genug der Spekulation. Das Thema „Die Jugend und ihre Zukunftserwartungen" verlangt nach realistischeren Methoden. Es empfiehlt sich, hierzu nach sicheren Erwartungen, wahrscheinlichen Veränderungen und möglichen Tendenzen zu unterscheiden.

Sicher sind demographische Prognosen für die nächsten Jahrzehnte wie die Folgen des Geburtenrückganges, die wachsende Zahl qualifiziert Ausgebildeter, der wachsende Anteil mit Ansprüchen auf akademische Berufe[7]) und die bereits absehbare technische Zukunft, die in der Verwendung von Miniprozessoren, neuen Kommunikationsmitteln und einem steil anwachsenden Energiebedarf errechenbar bleibt.

Wahrscheinlich erscheint auch, daß die Sonderstellung von Jugend relativiert wird, wenn die Ausbildungsphase durch einen lebenslangen Lernprozeß auf Dauer gestellt wird.[8]) Fraglich erscheint für heute bereits, ob nicht der Konkurrenzdruck und die entgegen allen Prognosen spürbar wachsende Knappheit der Dinge die Verhaltensweisen und Erwartungen verändern wird. Man kann auf Restriktionen mit vermehrten Anstrengungen und ebenso mit verminderten Ansprüchen reagieren. Insofern bleibt die Entwicklung gesellschaftlicher Normen und Werte eine offene Frage.

Es ist also durchaus offen, welchen Einflußgrößen, Ansprüche, Bedingungen und Restriktionen die künftige Existenz umstellen werden.

Was wir hingegen erkennen können, sind die heute bereits meßbaren Einstellungen, Grundtendenzen, Verhaltensbereitschaften und Auffassungen der verschiedenen Gruppen von Jugendlichen und jungen Erwachsenen (von „der" Jugend möchten wir nicht mehr sprechen), mit denen auf diese Einflußgrößen reagiert werden wird.

Als Orientierungsgrundlage dient die Untersuchung „Jugend in Europa"; es ist die siebte, die im Verlauf der letzten 25 Jahre vom Jugendwerk der Deutschen Shell veranlaßt wurde. Sie ist als international vergleichende Untersuchung angelegt und ihr wurde die Aufgabe gestellt, die Eingliederung von Jugend dreier Länder in die Welt der Erwachsenen zu erfassen.

II. ANSÄTZE UND AUFRISS DER JUGENDSTUDIE

Drei vorabgestellte Bedingungen für die neue Untersuchung machten es erforderlich, daß eine Reihe von Vorkehrungen notwendig wurden, wenn deren anspruchsvolle Ziele auch nur einigermaßen erreicht werden sollten. Die Untersuchung sollte sich als „Sozialisationstudie" mit dem gesamten Prozeß der Überführung in den vollen Erwachsenenstatus beschäftigen; in Anbetracht der hierfür aufzuwenden nicht unbeträchtlichen Mittel war ein Ansatz als Kohortenstudie unter Einbeziehung von jeweils drei Jahrgängen in jedem der drei Länder vorzusehen; die Bedingung einer internationalen Kompatibilität in drei verschiedenen Gesellschaften erforderte eine Reihe von theoretischen Vorarbeiten, bevor an den Aufbau eines gemeinsamen Erhebungsinstruments gedacht werden konnte.[9)]

Aufgabenstellung, Gliederung der Studie, Zusammenarbeit und Koordination mußten solchen Vorbedingungen angemessen formuliert und angelegt werden.

2.1 Aufgabenstellung

Der Untersuchung wurde die Aufgabe gestellt, den Ablauf der Sozialisation im jeweiligen institutionellen System der drei beteiligten Länder deskriptiv zu erfassen und ihr Gelingen operativ zu bemessen. Es war im besonderen zu ermitteln, in welcher Weise die Gesellschaften die Aufgabe leisten, die gesellschaftlichen Werte einer jungen Generation zu vermitteln, welche Rolle dabei das Bildungssystem, die Familie, die Berufswelt, das Freizeitleben und gesellschaftliche Instanzen sowie das politische und das Verwaltungssystem ausüben.

Der internationale Ansatz legte hierzu nahe, daß auch Nahziele zu avisieren wären, z.B. eine potentielle europäische Arbeitsmobilität, touristische Entwicklungen, die auf eine wirksame Begegnung der Völker hinauslaufen oder den Abbau von wechselseitigen Vorurteilen.

Die Aufgabenstellung gliederte sich dementsprechend in drei Dimensionen; die erste Hälfte der Befragung galt der Klärung einer am Lebenslauf orientierten Teilnahme am Sozialisationssystem, die von Stufe zu Stufe deskriptiv zu erfassen war. In der zweiten Hälfte waren einerseits der Erfolg der Sozialisation zu bemessen unter Berücksichtigung des erreichten Wissens in den verschiedenen Altersstufen, der Internalisierung von Werten und Normen und der Indizierung einer gelungenen Sozialisation und ferner politische Nahziele im Sinne einer Meinungs- und Einstellungsmessung zu erfassen, um die Bedeutung der europäischen Integration für die Befragten zu klären.

Das Aufwachsen in Familie, Kindergarten, Grundschule, Sekundärschule, weiterbildenden Schulen, Berufsausbildung und die Berufseinmündung wurden nacheinander Gegenstand sowohl des deskriptiven als auch des evaluierenden Teils der Befragung.

2.2 Ansätze der Untersuchung

Die Gliederung der Gesamtuntersuchung entsprach diesen mehrschichtigen Zielsetzungen. Einerseits mußte der theoretische Ort für die Erhebung und deren Auswertungsmöglichkeiten gesucht werden, andererseits waren die drei Länderstudien entsprechend den institutionellen Voraussetzungen in drei verschiedenen Gesellschaften so zu fassen, daß daraus ein gemeinsames Erhebungsinstrument abgeleitet werden konnte.

Der **theoretische Ort** der Untersuchung im Rahmen der Sozialisationsforschung ist dadurch gekennzeichnet, daß auf stringente Anwendung nur einer einzigen Theorie verzichtet wurde. Die zu erwartenden Rohdaten waren offen zu halten gegenüber Alternativen oder sukzessiv zu verfeinernden Analysemodellen nach wechselnden theoretischen Fragestellungen. Vertiefenden Sekundäranalysen war der Weg offen zu halten, Anregungen für weitere Sozialisations- und vergleichende Jugendforschungen vorzusehen. Die Vorstudie enthält Anregungen hierzu.

Die theoretische Relevanz der auszuwählenden Kohorten (die Zwölfjährigen, die Siebzehnjährigen und die Zweiundzwanzigjährigen, jeweils nicht scharf abgegrenzt) wurde durch Fünfjahres-Abstände bestimmt und fand Konsensus. Sozialisationsphasen, Altersstatus, Sozialisationsziele und sozialstrukturelle Differenzierungen fanden darin ihre Bestätigung. Die vielfachen Möglichkeiten eines Kohortenvergleichs, zumal bei allfälliger Replikation der Untersuchung, waren zu erörtern.[10)]

Der theoretischen Vorbereitung einer Erschließung der Indikationstechnik für die Sozialisation widmet sich der Berner Soziologe Karol Szemkus.[11)]

Die theoretische Vorbereitung der **drei Länderstudien** verwies allenthalben auf eine hochmobile Situation, durch die viele problematische Entwicklungen möglich werden. Die Grundrichtung verlief in den drei Ländern zu egalitären Formen, gegenüber denen unterschiedliche Stellungnahmen wirksam werden.

Das Sozialisationssystem in **Deutschland** befindet sich in einer tiefgreifenden Wandlung. Die wachsende Zahl besser ausgebildeter Absolventen der unteren Schul- und Bildungsstufe führte zu Ungleichgewichten in der oberen Stufe. Numerus Clausus und fehlende Ausbildungsplätze führen in Zusammenwirken mit dem Bewußtsein der Rezession und Arbeitslosigkeit zu verbreiteten Unsicherheiten.

In dieser Situation verschärft sich die Ungleichheit der Lebenschancen in Abhängigkeit vom erreichten Bildungsstand. Daraus ergibt sich ein bedrückender Konkurrenzkampf um die formale Erfüllung der zu besseren Lebenschancen berechtigenden Bildungsplätze.

Die Sozialisationsleistung der **Familie** ist nach wie vor von grundlegender Bedeutung. Strukturbedingungen familialer Sozialisation werden markiert durch Einkommensunterschiede, Unterschiede in der Wohnausstattung, der Wohnlage, mütterlicher Berufstätigkeit und vor allem schichtenspezifisch unterschiedlichem Erziehungsverhalten. Solche Merkmale führen faktisch zu hochgradig unterschiedlichen Startbedingungen trotz zunehmend egalitärem Schulsystem.

Die Sekundärsozialisation mit den variantenreichen Möglichkeiten des Bildungssystems löst einerseits Probleme der Ungleichheit – und schafft wiederum neue.

Hierzu kommt die Tertiärsozialisation mit:

Politischem System, beruflicher Orientierung an den Zielen der Erwachsenen, altersbezogenen Gruppen und vielen anderen Faktoren wie: Freizeitinteresse, Konsumverhalten, Bildungsinteressen, der Gesetzgebung und sehr großen Aufwendungen für die Jugend in den öffentlichen Haushalten mit Bundesjugendplan und ausgedehnter Jugendpflege.[12)]

In **Großbritannien** sind vorschulische Institutionen wenig bedeutsam (weniger als 10 %); mehr „Aufbewahrung“ als pädagogische Ambitionen.

Schulbeginn ist heute mit 5 (auch 4) Jahren.

Dann das öffentliche Schulsystem: Bisher enthielt es die: grammar school, technical school, secondary modern in drei Qualifikationsstufen. Künftig dagegen nur noch die „high school". Einheitsschule 11–16 Jahre, z.T. 18 Jahre.

Das Schulsystem ist derzeit völlig im Umbruch und weitgehend unübersichtlich unterschiedlich, je nach regionaler Situation.

Erst in der 3. Stufe (18 Jahre) gibt es wieder einheitlich die staatliche Universität. (Meist: 3-Jahr-Grad; wenige länger bis M.A. oder Dr.).

Seit Anfang der 60er Jahre datieren die Bestrebungen der Labour-Regierung zu einem umfassenden generellen Bildungssystem.

Die einstweilige Folge ist, daß es seitdem ein überaus uneinheitliches Schulsystem gibt.

Die „Comprehensive School" (Einheitsschule) behält die Jugendlichen bis zu 16 Jahren, es gibt eine Möglichkeit zum Wechsel zur Erlangung der Hochschulreife.

Seit 1960 gilt formell wachsende Gleichheit der Startbedingungen; Ungleichheit ist jedoch durch Elternhaus und Wohnquartier bedingt. Denn das ungleiche Niveau bestimmt die Qualitätsanforderungen je nach dem Wohnquartier. Fleiß wird heute stärker belohnt, als Intelligenz.

Ideell dominieren walisischer und schottischer Nationalismus anstelle des Europa-Gedankens; man ist stärker an den Resten des Commonwealth orientiert als an Europa.

Auch die große Rate fremdrassiger Immigration habe dazu beigetragen, den liberalen Internationalismus zu reduzieren. Diese Grundtendenz wird vom Autor eher anomisch interpretiert und nicht als eine Rückbesinnung auf traditionelle Werte.

Im Beruf gilt Anpassung an die Firma, Aufstieg innerhalb dieser, Loyalität. Den Arbeitsplatz zu behalten sei das Ziel.[13)]

Erziehung in **Frankreich** ist allgemein zu charakterisieren durch:

- Starke Differenzierung nach Stadt und Land, regional und nach Klassen und Gruppen = „Verschiedene Sozialisationsrahmen".
- Ungleichheit des Zugangs zur Schule nach sozialer Herkunft; eine wachsende Zugangsmöglichkeit ist ungleich auf die Sozialschichten verteilt: Die Chancenungleichheit bleibt.
- Schichtenspezifische Variationen der familiären Bedingungen nach Heiratshäufigkeit, Heiratsalter, vorehelichen Geburten, Scheidungen, Berufstätigkeit der Mütter, Kinderzahl.

- Ein staatliches Zielsystem für Sozialisation, sich überschneidend mit familiären Sozialzielen. Dieses setzt sich durch in Schule und Massenmedien. Es ist in unterschiedlicher Weise erfolgreich je nach Verhaltens- und Meinungsbereich.
- Ein durchaus unterschiedliches Gelingen der Sozialisation in moralischer, politischer, kultureller und staatsbürgerlicher Hinsicht.

Für die Sozialisationsinstanzen gelten allgemein starke Veränderungen im Sozialisationssystem, so daß im Vergleich zwischen 12-, 17- und 22-jährigen deren Auswirkungen in Erscheinung treten und nicht etwa ein unterschiedliches Gelingen der Sozialisation bzw. ein Einstellungswandel.

Änderungen im Familienrecht bewirken wachsende Scheidungsraten, voreheliche Geburten.

Für die Deutung solcher Erscheinungen gibt es zwei Alternativen:

Hypothese I = Zerfall der Familie, Krise;
Hypothese II = größere familiäre Mobilität und Liberalität.

Die Schule gewinnt wachsende Bedeutung, breiteren Wirkungskreis, zunehmende Kompetenzen; sie nimmt eine längere Zeit in Anspruch, als je zuvor.[14)]

2.4 Die Koordination

Auf diese Weise wurde versucht, die theoretischen Vorbedingungen und die jeweils besonderen kulturellen Voraussetzungen für eine internationale Vergleichsuntersuchung aufzuschließen. Es sollte ein Erfassungsinstrument aufgebaut werden, das im internationalen Vergleich die Unterschiede deutlich macht und der weiteren Forschung nützliche Ansätze bietet.[15)]

Das zu verwendende Erhebungsinstrument lag in seiner Grundstruktur solchen Überlegungen bereits zugrunde.

Wir haben auf die geschilderte Weise versucht, die Kooperation der beteiligten Wissenschaftler durch ein auf Rückkoppelung reagierendes System der wechselseitigen Abstimmung zum Funktionieren zu bringen. Es entstand ein vielschichtiges Gebilde von Anregungen, Information, Rückkoppelung, Abstimmung, Kontroversen, Einigung und Kooperation, das im Schaubild in großen Zügen vorgestellt wird.

III. EINIGE HAUPTBEFUNDE IM INTERNATIONALEN VERGLEICH

Einige vergleichende Daten aus den zahlreichen vorgelegten Befunden der Untersuchung mögen verdeutlichen, daß trotz der unterschiedlichen institutionellen Situation die Abweichungen in den drei erfaßten Gesellschaften so gravierend nicht sind. Wir vergleichen einige Strukturdaten, die Daten zu Familie und Kindergarten, diejenigen zum Erziehungsstil und zu den Schulsystemen.

3.1 Strukturdaten im Vergleich

Die Darstellung der **wirtschaftlich-sozialen Struktur** des Befragtenkreises gibt Antwort auf viele aufgeworfene Fragen.[16)]

55 % der deutschen Zielgruppe sind noch in Schul-, weitere 11 % in Berufsausbildung (GB: 48–10 %, F: 59–9 %). Die deutsche Schulsituation ist dadurch gekennzeichnet, daß sich 17 % auf der Hauptschule, 20 % der Realschule bzw. im Mittelbau des Gymnasiums und 8 % auf der Gymnasialoberstufe befinden. In Großbritannien drückt sich die in der Vorstudie geschilderte Unklarheit des Schulsystems so aus: 27 % sind auf der „comprehensive school", 5 % auf der „grammar", 1 % auf der „technical" und 6 % auf der „secondary modern school"; die neue „comprehensive school" hat sich demnach bereits weitgehend durchgesetzt. Zugleich befinden sich nur 1 % auf der „public school" und 6 % in der fortgeschrittenen Schulbildung. In Frankreich sind noch 2 % auf der Primärschule, 35 % auf dem ersten Zyklus und 19 % im zweiten Zyklus der Sekundärschule. Am höchsten entwickelt ist demnach der Stand auf den französischen Schulen, am geringsten auf den englischen. In Deutschland befinden sich unter den Schulabgängern 16 % mit abgeschlossener Berufsausbildung und die übrigen mit höheren Abschlüssen. In England hingegen gibt es noch 16 % ohne formale Qualifikation, 8 % mit CSE oder CEE und 14 % mit „O"-Level. „A"-Level haben – wie im deutschen Abitur – jeweils 2 %. Über das Baccalauréat verfügen in Frankreich hingegen 10 %, wozu weitere 8 % auf der „grande école" bzw. auf der Universität sich befinden; die von J.-C. Passeron zitierte „Inflation der Diplome" dürfte sich demnach massiv fortsetzen.

Auch die Berufsdaten sind aufschlußreich. In Deutschland gibt es noch 3 % ungelernter Arbeiter gegenüber 8 % in Großbritannien und 9 % in Frankreich. Arbeitslos sind in Deutschland 1 %, in England 3 % und in Frankreich 1 %.

3.2 Familie und Kindergarten

Die Bedeutung des Elternhauses ist in Deutschland am größten, in Frankreich am geringsten. Aber überall spielt die elterliche Familie eine durchaus überragende Rolle. Auch zeigt sich, daß die Bedeutung der „Boarding school" in dem dafür typischen Land Großbritannien nicht größer ist als in Deutschland – in Frankreich jedoch – wesentlich bedeutungsvoller, wo ihr maximal 14 % eines Jahrgangs angehören. „Selbständig außerhalb gelebt" wird in nennenswertem Umfang erst vom 18. Lebensjahr an, und zwar:

- in Deutschland von 34 %
- in Großbritannien von 41 %
- in Frankreich von 37 %.

Es läßt sich erkennen, daß die Wohnvoraussetzungen in Frankreich besser waren als in Deutschland, daß aber – so ergibt die Altersaufgliederung – die Verhältnisse in Deutschland mit denen in Frankreich **inzwischen** gleichgezogen haben: Je jünger die Antwortenden, um so günstiger die Antworten (Wir haben es ja mit einer Befragung in drei Altersklassen zu tun, die gleichzeitig die zeitgeschichtliche Entwicklung aufschließen!);

Bedrückender sieht es in bezug auf den „Spielplatz" aus, hier ergibt sich nur für Frankreich eine gleichbleibend günstige Situation, für Deutschland eine deutliche Verbesserung einer ursprünglich sehr unbefriedigenden, und in England gar eine Verschlechterung.

Das Verhältnis zu Vater und Mutter ist überall bei mehr als zwei Dritteln sehr gut und gut und bei nur wenigen Prozent gibt es zu Klagen Anlaß. Auch noch bei den 23-jährigen berichten 60 % von einem guten Verhältnis zum Vater und 70 % von einem solchen zur Mutter. Wo bleibt die Generationsspannung, wenn selbst noch im kritischen Alter von 17 Jahren maximal nur 13 % von einem unbefriedigenden Verhältnis zum Vater berichten?

Auf die Fragen nach dem Besuch einer vorschulischen Institution berichteten:

- 36 % der Deutschen vom Kindergarten
- 22 % der Engländer vom Kinderhort
- 68 % der Franzosen von der Vorschule.

Wie dramatisch sich die Lage in Deutschland gebessert hat, erkennt man aus den unterschiedlichen Aussagen der drei Kohorten. Es berichten über . . .

. . . Kindergartenbesuch in Deutschland:

von den 22- bis 23jährigen	29 %
von den 17- bis 18jährigen	33 %
von den 12- bis 13jährigen	45 %.

D.h., daß die Zahlen beträchtlich angewachsen sind und die vom Bildungsministerium in seinem zweiten Rechenschaftsbericht genannten Werte fast erreicht haben, nachdem jedem zweiten Kind ein Kindergartenplatz zur Verfügung steht.[17)]

3.3 Erziehungsstil in Familie und Schule

Über den Erziehungsstil geben eine Reihe von Fragen und Tabellen Auskunft. „Streng“ geht es in der überwiegenden Anzahl der Elternhäuser aller Länder zu – aber nur für Kleinkinder.

Permissive Erziehung in den Elternhäusern gibt es am häufigsten in Deutschland. Das ergibt sich in den Antworten auf eine Frage nach dem Verhalten der Eltern gegenüber Kindern unter 10 Jahren, die „eine Dummheit gemacht haben“. 8 % der deutschen Eltern taten überhaupt nichts; in England und Frankreich waren es 3 %. 17 % der deutschen Eltern prügelten, in Frankreich waren es doppelt so viele, in England auch noch 28 %. Hier hat sich zudem in Deutschland im letzten Jahrzehnt eine Grundsatzwandlung vollzogen; über Schläge in einem solchen Fall berichten:

- je 20 % der 17- und 22jährigen
- 9 % der 12jährigen.

Rund knapp ein Drittel erzieht rational: „Sie haben mir ruhig erklärt, was ich für eine Dummheit gemacht habe“; es gibt eine hohe Korrelation mit gehobenem Bildungsstand.

In einer Fragenbatterie nach dem **Entscheidungsspielraum**, die auf eine Anregung von J.-C. Passeron zurückgeht, soll verglichen werden, zu welchen praktischen Konsequenzen die heute viel zitierte Permissivität und Liberalität in der Erziehung führt.

Zunächst der internationale Vergleich: Das permissivste Land ist mit Abstand Großbritannien. Hier ist fast nichts verboten.

In Deutschland dürfen ebenfalls 6 % keine langen Haare tragen, 15 % abends nicht allein ausgehen und 18 % nicht allein in die Ferien fahren.

Die Verbote beschränken sich fast überall auf die unterste Kohorte.

Die älteste Kohorte hat praktisch überall volle Freiheit: Über 90 % dürfen die Haare lang tragen, dürfen das gesparte Geld ausgeben, die Kleidung kaufen, die sie möchten; fast 90 % (in Frankreich: 77 %) dürfen mitbringen wen sie wollen, dürfen abends ausgehen; um die 80 % dürfen allein oder mit Freunden in die Ferien fahren.[18)]

3.4 Die Schulsysteme

Ein großes Problem in Deutschland ist der Hauptschulabgang ohne Abschluß, mit dem sich 10 % der 17- bis 18-jährigen abgefunden haben, aber nur 3 % der 12- bis 13jährigen abfinden wollen. Zu diesem Thema besagen die zusammenfassenden Gesamt-Länder-Daten gar nichts; es wird allein aus der Entwicklung im Kohortenvergleich deutlich.

Für Frankreich ist die Schulreform praktisch abgeschlossen und beginnt, sich massiv auf die Praxis des Berufsalltags und die Berufschancen auszuwirken. J.-C. Passeron spricht von einer „Inflation der Diplome".

Allein für Deutschland zeigen sich noch namhaft anwachsende Schülerzahlen im mittleren und gehobenen Bereich, die ihre Auswirkung auf das Hochschulsystem nicht verfehlen werden. Die heutige „Numerus-Clausus-Situation" dürfte erst den Beginn einer krisenhaften Entwicklung dokumentieren, wie die Untersuchung erweist.

Wenn solche Tendenzen sich verwirklichen, ist mit einem massiv verstärkten Druck auf Hochschul- und Fachhochschulsystem und entsprechendem Druck auf die gehobenen Berufe zu rechnen – wobei die Tatsache der geburtenstarken Jahrgänge stark ins Gewicht fallen dürfte.[19)]

Den **kognitiven Aspekt** einer erfolgreichen Sozialisation verfolgten wir mit Hilfe einer Testbatterie, in der der Lernerfolg in den drei Schulsystemen am Wissen gemessen werden sollte. Eine vergleichende Untersuchung, die im Jahre 1960 von der GALLUP-Kette in fünf Ländern durchgeführt wurde, erlaubt auch eine Längsschnittanalyse.

Wenn die Schulsysteme sich in den inzwischen abgelaufenen reichlich eineinhalb Jahrzehnten hinsichtlich der Vermittlung des kognitiven Wissens verbessert hätten, so müßten die Ergebnisse heute wesentlich besser sein als seinerzeit. Das ist – wenigstens für die verglichenen Fragestellungen – deutlich nicht der Fall.

Im internationalen Vergleich, der durch Übercodes festgestellt wurde, schnitten die deutschen Befragten mit Abstand am besten ab, insbesondere in ihren geographischen und mathematischen Grundkenntnissen. Nur in den Naturwissenschaften folgen ihnen die jungen Franzosen dicht auf.[20)]

IV. BEDINGUNGEN FÜR EINE VERWENDUNG ALS PROGNOSENINSTRUMENT

4.1 Möglichkeiten und Grenzen einer prognostischen Jugendsoziologie

Als die Studentenrevolte ihrem Ende entgegenging, wurde der Jugendsoziologie der ersten Phase zum Vorwurf gemacht, sie sei „von den Ereignissen, die Ende der sechziger Jahre eingetreten sind, völlig überrascht" worden:

- „Zuerst dominierten Thesen und Theorien, welche die Anpassung und Integration der Jugend, also eine Art Windstille behaupteten";
- „Als dann Turbulenzen unübersehbar wurden, kamen ad hoc – Er-

klärungen zu Hauf – in sich aber so widersprüchlich, daß sie bis heute nicht in eine komplexe Theorie einzubringen waren".[21)]

Die Basis der Prognose, so das Lexikon zur Soziologie, kann bestehen in:

- Extrapolationen bzw. Fortsetzung beobachteter Trends;
- deduktiv homologischen Erklärungen auf der Grundlage von Gesetzesaussagen.[22)]

Nun lassen sich Prognosen bei Vorliegen multivariater Wirkungsfaktoren niemals exakt in solchen Bereichen formulieren, die eine ganze Altersschichtung mit allen ihren soziologischen Differenzierungen und Varianzen umschließen. Voraussetzung jeder operativ gehandhabten Prognose ist die Einengung eines Sachbereichs auf wenige Dimensionen, die operational gehandhabt werden können, so daß man die Beziehungen im Rahmen korrekt formulierter Hypothesen formulieren und demnach messen kann.

Darum wird auch darauf hingewiesen, daß in der methodologischen Diskussion insbesondere die Beziehungen zwischen Prognosen, Retrodiktion und Erklärung eines Sachverhaltes untersucht werden. Damit ergeben sich Erklärungen für die **Form**, in der frühzeitig festgestellte Tendenzen sich durch unvorhersehbar eintretende Ereignisse und Abläufe in gesellschaftliches Handeln umsetzten.

Hierfür ergeben sich in der Jugendsoziologie einige Beispiele zu der oben erhobenen Kritik; möglicherweise wurden sie von den Kritikern nicht zur Kenntnis genommen.

4.2 Schelskys Prognose über die von ihm beschriebene und die „kommende" Jugend

Im Schlußkapitel seiner Analyse heißt es bei Schelsky über die von ihm beschriebene „Generation",[23)] der (zumeist abgegrenzt als) 15- bis 24jährigen, zu der die Felduntersuchungen in den Jahren 1948 bis 1953 gelaufen waren: „**Diese** (Spat. D.V.) Generation wird nie revolutionär, in flammender kollektiver Leidenschaft auf die Dinge reagieren". Er nennt sie die Generation der vorsichtigen, aber erfolgreichen jungen Männer. Sie setzt „auf die Karte der Sicherheit, des minimalen Risikos". Es sind genau jene Kohorten, von denen es in der Studentenrevolte hieß „trau keinem über dreißig". Die jüngsten dieser Altersklassen hatten 1968 gerade das Alter von dreißig Jahren erreicht.

Hingegen gibt es eine weitere Prognose von Schelsky über die **kommende** (Spat. D.V.) Jugend, in der dieser von der „Veränderung der vitalen Grundbefindlichkeit" mit einer „erhöhten Vitalität, einem gesteigerten Körpergefühl, verstärkter nervöser Reizbarkeit ausging". Hierzu heißt es:

„Ich erwarte eine sezessionistische Jugendgeneration, gekennzeichnet durch eine Welle sinnloser Ausbruchsversuche aus der in die Watte manipulierter Humanität, überzeugender Sicherheit und allgemeiner Wohlfahrt gewickelten modernen Welt“.[24)]

4.3 Die zornigen jungen Primaner von 1964

Zehn Jahre später gelingt es, mit im Prinzip den gleichen Verfahren, wie sie Schelsky angewendet hatte, die Tendenzen der künftigen Rebellen nicht nur zu identifizieren, sondern auch auf Bildungsschicht und sogar recht genau auf Altersschicht festzulegen.[25)]

In unserer Untersuchung, deren Feldarbeit 1964 stattfand, wird gesprochen von dem „harten Verdikt (der Jugend der Bildungsoberschicht) der offiziellen bundesdeutschen politischen Linie aller Parteien als ein lebendiges Zeugnis einer einsetzenden Politisierung innerhalb der Jugend, die sich von der bisherigen Einseitigkeit des politischen Denkens abwendet und neue Wege geöffnet wissen will“ (S. 350). In einer Untersuchung der Einstellung zu Herrschaftsformen: „Es erweist sich, daß Kritik an der Staatsform der Bundesrepublik gleichbedeutend ist mit einer härteren demokratischen Grundhaltung“ (S. 354). – „Nicht das „Was“ des politischen Gegenstandes, sondern das „Wie“ der Befassung damit prägen den politischen Stil der jungen Menschen. Wir finden eine Situation vor, die offensichtlich stark in Fluß ist“ . . . „Die Reserve gegenüber der älteren Generation entzündet sich daran, daß man sie für zu lau, zu inkonsequent, zu flexibel und zu wenig entschieden befindet“ (S. 365).

Schon jetzt erweisen sich in der Bildungsoberschicht die Altersschichten als entscheidend für die politische Zuwendung. Es wird von einer „vorpolitischen Haltung“ der 15- bis 17jährigen, einem starken Engagement der 18- bis 21jährigen und eine „in überraschend übereinstimmender Weise bestätigte geringere Interessiertheit, Engagiertheit, Bewußtheit und demokratische Bindung der über 21jährigen“ (S. 378 f) gesprochen.

Eine starke bildungsspezifische Unterscheidung ist nach Art und Intensität der Zuwendung zu sehen. Die Bildungsschicht wird als „strukturleitend für die politische Entwicklung der Jugend“ bezeichnet.

Nur wenige Publizisten und keine Soziologen nehmen es zur Kenntnis: „Die Stimme der studentischen Jugend, die sich in diesem Sommer 1967 lautstark bemerkbar macht, beweist, was Blücher als Zug zum politischen Engagement voraussagte: „Innerhalb der demokratischen Spielregeln Ruf nach Aktivität, entschiedeneren und militanteren demokratischen Formen; mit großer Unbekümmertheit Tabus angreifen; ein Freiheitsbedürfnis, das junge Menschen zu unbequemen Staatsbürgern machen könnte“ (Zitat aus dem Bericht) und inzwischen gemacht hat!“[26)]

Alle Elemente sind beschrieben, die vier Jahre nach der Untersuchung zu den spektakulären Ereignissen führen: Die bildungsspezifische Unterscheidung in Aktionismus und „schweigende Mehrheit“, das „Umschlagen“ der Verhaltenstendenzen von einer Kohorte zur nächsten – nämlich bei den bis zu 21jährigen, die dann vier Jahre später zu den Trägern der Aktion werden. Selbst der Ablauf, die Erscheinung, daß der Spuk ganz plötzlich vorüber war (natürlich nicht, ohne seine dauernden Wirkungen, Schrunden und Fisteln zu hinterlassen) läßt sich retrospektiv aus der Prognose der Daten aus dem Jahr 1964 ablesen.

Natürlich lassen sich nur Tendenzen prognostizieren, nicht aber tatsächliche Vorgänge und Anlässe. Der unglückliche Tod eines Zuschauers auf einer Demonstration, der durch eine Handvoll gut geschulter Agitatoren – 50 bis 200 je Universität, nicht mehr zu einem Fanal umfunktioniert wurde, läßt sich nicht prognostizieren.[27)] Das gilt ebenso für die Randbedingungen dieser Erscheinung; und das war nun einmal der Zustand der deutschen Universitäten. Anlässe zum Ärgernis waren reichlich vorhanden.

V. EINSTELLUNGEN UND TENDENZEN IN DER DEUTSCHEN JUGEND

Die Retrospektion sollte uns dazu ermutigen, die Befunde der neuen Untersuchung zur Charakterisierung von Grundtendenzen in den hier untersuchten drei Kohorten anzuwenden. Das Bild wird weder widerspruchslos, noch durchlaufend plausibel, weder geglättet, noch eindeutig, weder wertneutral, noch zielbestimmt sein. Es soll einfach versucht werden, einige Tendenzen herauszulesen, die als Ansatz dienen mögen für weitere Analysen.

Um dies erfolgreich führen zu können, werden klare Hypothesen vonnöten sein – so wie uns seinerzeit eine Anzahl von Schülerzeitschriften den Anstoß für eine entsprechende Aufarbeitung unseres Materials gegeben hat.

Unsere neuen Daten berücksichtigen die verbesserte kognitive Leistungsfähigkeit, beobachten die politische Partizipation, behandeln Bindungstendenzen und Solidarisierungspotential, gehen auf schichtspezifische Unterschiede ein, berücksichtigen Einstellungen zu Normen und Werten und behandeln die dominanten Sozialisationsagenten vergleichend.

5.1 Die kognitive Leistungsfähigkeit

Das gewandelte Schulsystem hat ohne Zweifel ein insgesamt höheres Niveau der Schulbildung bei den drei erfaßten Kohorten bewirkt. Ein höherer Wissensstand hat sich insbesondere sozial verbreitert, wobei jedoch das Spitzenwissen, wie der Längsschnittvergleich ausweist, im Verlauf der letzten eineinhalb Jahrzehnte deutlich unqualifizierter geworden ist. Die soziale Breite der gehobenen Bildung wurde mit einer Qualifikationsminderung erkauft.[28)]

Wir fanden nur noch wenige Prozent Hauptschüler ohne Abschluß und in der mittleren Kohorte nicht mehr so viele Ungelernte. Die formale Qualifikation hat sich ganz offensichtlich erheblich verbreitert. Tendenzen zur Sprachbeherrschung sind deutlich expansiv. Das ergibt sich aus einer Frage über die Bereitschaft zum Erlernen einer Fremdsprache, wenn „die Möglichkeit kostenlos geboten würde".

Nach den Befunden der Untersuchung und nach den bekundeten Tendenzen wird der Druck auf die Hochschulen nicht nur anhalten, sondern sich noch weiterhin verstärken. Denn indem man die höhere Bildungsstufe formal erreicht, beansprucht man auch die Gratifikationen, die in früheren Phasen dem höher Gebildeten geboten wurden. Das heißt, dem wachsenden Lerndruck auf Schule und Hochschule wird ein entsprechender Qualifikationsdruck in den gehobenen Berufen zwangsläufig folgen müssen.[29)]

5.2 Die politische Partizipation

Der verbreiteteren Bildung entspricht eine Verbreiterung der Tendenzen zur politischen Partizipation. 38 % von allen, darunter mehr als 50 % der Befragten mit gehobener Bildung, sind „sicher oder wahrscheinlich" bereit, sich in Partei oder politischem Verband zu binden. Vor etwas mehr als zehn Jahren waren es rund ein Drittel weniger.[30)]

Der Tendenz der Gesamtgesellschaft zu konservativeren Wahlentscheidungen folgt die Jugend deutlich. Während noch 1973 die Tendenz zur SPD bei weitem überwog, hat sich das Verhältnis zwischen den Parteienpräferenzen 1975 nahezu ausgeglichen. Das gilt auch für die junge Intelligenzschicht. In dieser sind jetzt mehr als zwei Drittel mit dem Parteiensystem explizit zufrieden (1968: nur 35 %); die berufstätige Jugend war es seit je und steht heute dem politischen System noch positiver gegenüber (69 %).

Trotzdem bleibt eine radikale Opposition innerhalb der jungen Intelligenz bestehen; doch während mit ihr früher eine Mehrheit sympathisierte, handelt es sich heute um kleine Minderheiten. Dementsprechend finden sich aber in der Bildungsoberschicht immer noch namhafte Reste marxistischen Denkens.

Erst der internationale Vergleich verdeutlicht die gewaltigen Veränderungen, die sich in Europa in den letzten zwanzig Jahren vollzogen haben.

Die britische Jugend, früher Nachwuchs eines politisch engagierten Volkes, stellt heute die politischen Defaitisten. Die politische Resignation der früher „skeptischen" Generation im Deutschland der Nachkriegszeit hat sich praktisch zu einer Haltung politischen Engagements in vielen gesellschaftlichen Bereichen entwickelt. Die Gesellschaftsordnung findet jeder vierte gerecht.

5.3 Bindungstendenzen und Solidarisierungspotential

Die Bindungstendenzen sind seit Jahrzehnten in außerordentlichem Masse gewachsen. Politische Orientierung, zunächst bei den Eltern gesucht, wird später weitgehend auch im Freundeskreis erfolgen.

Die Miterziehung durch „peer groups" ist deutlich. Man hat Freunde, Freundinnen, bindet sich in informellen Gruppen, und hat doch im großen und ganzen ein gutes Verhältnis zum Elternhaus. Für jeden zweiten sind die Eltern die Vertrauenspersonen, und erst später kommen Freunde und Bekannte in nennenswertem Umfang hinzu. Im persönlichen Bereich gibt es keine nennenswerte Generationenspannung.

Bemerkenswert erscheint die fortschreitend permissivere Erziehung. Die Heranwachsenden haben vollen Freiheitsspielraum und werden weder von Eltern noch von der Schule in ihrem Lebensraum eingeengt. Dementsprechend wollen sie auch in der Erziehung permissiv verfahren. Der Wunsch nach Kindern ist übrigens recht verbreitet. 1975 wünschten sich 70 % Kinder, während 8 % bereits Eltern waren.[31)]

5.4 Schichtspezifische Differenzierungen

Ganz generell kann man feststellen, daß die Unterschiede in Einstellungen, Meinungen, Tendenzen und Bewertungen, die früher von Schicht zu Schicht festzustellen waren, sich recht deutlich eingeebnet haben. Insbesondere hat sich die früher zu registrierende Gegensätzlichkeit im Denken der Bildungsschichten weitgehend nivelliert. Die allgemein stark verbreiterte Bildung hat offenbar das Auskristallisieren einer eigenen Bildungsoberschicht teilweise rückgängig gemacht. Es gibt nur noch wenig prägnante Unterschiede im Denken.

Die größte Teilgruppe hält denn auch gleiche gesellschaftliche Startchancen heute für gegeben. Andererseits glauben aber auch 60 %, daß es in unserer Gesellschaftsordnung „Menschen gibt, die deutlich benachteiligt sind".

Es gibt sie und sie lassen sich identifizieren: Es handelt sich um die Gruppe der Ungelernten. Ihr Sozialschicksal läßt sich aus den Befunden von nahezu 30 Einzelfragen der Untersuchung von 1975 verfolgen.[32)] Sie haben ihr Berufsziel nicht erreicht. 58 % von ihnen blieben überhaupt ohne Ziel. Ihre existenziellen Bedingungen sind beengt. Sie verkriechen sich in privatistische Enge, haben weniger Freizeit, weniger Mitbestimmung, weniger Reisemöglichkeiten und haben ihre Situation nach der Schulentlassung nicht verbessern können.

Zugleich fehlt ein „revolutionäres Potential" so gut wie vollständig. Sie finden sich mit ihrem Schicksal ab. Das hängt möglicherweise damit zusammen, daß die Gruppe von Untersuchung zu Untersuchung kleiner wird; in unseren beiden in Betracht kommenden Kohorten sind es noch insgesamt 9 %.

5.5 Einstellungen zu Normen und Werten

Wenden wir uns der Untersuchung der Einstellung zu Werten und Normen zu, deren theoretische Begründung im Ansatz von 1975 L. Rosenmayr seinerzeit unter der Überschrift „Jugendforschung im Rahmen der gesamten Altersstratifikation" erarbeitet hatte.[33)]

Es handelt sich um Themen wie: „Orientierung an der Leistung", „eheliche Treue", „Gemeinsinn", „Zuverlässigkeit und Pünktlichkeit", „unsere Nationalfahne", „höfliches Benehmen gegenüber Älteren" und „Sicherheit in Glaubensfragen", die in Fragestellung und Wortlaut der Vorgabe in der neuen Untersuchung wörtlich, und die Themen „Eigentum" und „Sparsamkeit", die sinngemäß wiederholt wurden.

Im Ergebnis unserer Untersuchung stellt sich heraus, daß die verwendeten Fragen valide und reliabel sind. Es gibt zwar Altersunterschiede in den Ergebnissen. Aber Jugendliche orientieren sich in der großen Mehrzahl an den Normen und Werten der Gesamtgesellschaft. Es gibt aber auch Dimensionen, in denen sich deutliche Veränderungen und Gegensätze abzeichnen.

So halten 65 % und mehr eine „Orientierung an der Leistung", das Prinzip der „ehelichen Treue" und dasjenige von „Zuverlässigkeit und Pünktlichkeit" für „unentbehrlich". Dabei steigen die Zustimmungen zu diesen Werten von Kohorte zu Kohorte und dokumentieren so eine gelungene Sozialisation im Sinne der Ziele dieser Gesellschaft. Auch das „höfliche Verhalten gegenüber Älteren" wird von 63 % bejaht – zeigt aber mit wachsendem Alter eine sinkende Tendenz.

41 % halten Eigentum für unentbehrlich, weitere 40 % für nützlich und nur 4 % lehnen es rundweg ab. Die Tendenz zugunsten einer Bejahung des Eigentums wächst mit steigendem Alter.

Andererseits wird „Sparsamkeit" nur noch von 36 %, „unsere Nationalfahne" von 33 % und „Sicherheit in Glaubensfragen" sogar nur von 17 %

für unentbehrlich gehalten, wobei die Teilgruppen, die an solche Werte glauben, von Altersklasse zu Altersklasse beträchtlich kleiner werden.[34]) Man hält demnach an einer Reihe von traditionellen Werten fest. Dennoch gibt es Einbrüche in das Wertgefüge. Beharrungs- und Wandlungstendenzen finden sich gleichermaßen.

5.6 Vergleich dominanter Sozialisationsagenten

Die interessantesten Ergebnisse erbringt die Untersuchung überhaupt im Vergleich zwischen den drei erfaßten Altersklassen. Das zeigte insbesondere das Ergebnis einer in Sozialisationsuntersuchungen bewährten Frage danach, wo die „Dinge gelernt wurden, die heute als für das Leben wichtig" beurteilt werden. Es erscheint evident, daß diese Fragestellung, gerichtet an eine jüngere Kohorte, lediglich aufgrund ihrer im Zeitpunkt der Befragung erreichten Erfahrungslage beantwortet werden kann. So ist es logisch, daß die 12- bis 13jährigen ihre dominanten Prägungen nahezu ausschließlich im Elternhaus und – in deutlich zweiter Linie – in der Schule erfahren haben. Es bleibt dabei: Elternhaus und Schule sind – in unterschiedlichem Maße – prägend.

In der Kohorte der 17- bis 18jährigen schieben sich bereits weitere Sozialisationsfaktoren nach vorne. Zwar dominiert auch hier noch das Elternhaus; jedoch kommen hinzu die Berufsausbildung und weitere Faktoren, wie das Berufsleben, die eigene Bemühung, Freizeiterlebnisse und der Freundeskreis.

Erst die älteste der erfaßten Kohorten wird langsam „kompetent" für die Beantwortung dieser Frage. Hier ergibt sich ein differenziertes Bild, bei dem aber immer noch das Elternhaus dominiert. Es kommen – in dieser Reihenfolge – die Ausbildung, das Berufsleben, die Weiterbildung, der Freundeskreis hinzu. Andere Gesellungsformen bleiben unbedeutend.

Aus dem Vergleich der Entwicklung der beiden hervorragenden Faktoren Elternhaus und Schule wird im Zeitablauf der Kohorten der Prozeß der Ablösung vom Elternhaus und der Emanzipation von der Schule deutlich sichtbar. Ebenso wird deutlich, daß alle anderen Faktoren frühestens bei den 17jährigen hinzutreten und eine konsequent wachsende Bedeutung erlangen. Die Befunde weisen auf das Ergebnis der Gesamtuntersuchung hin: im großen und ganzen funktioniert die Sozialisation und die schrittweise Ablösung vom Elternhaus vergleichsweise befriedigend. Die jungen Leute treten einigermaßen ausgerüstet ihren Lebensweg an.[35])

5.7 Jugend zwischen Stabilität und Labilität

Ob sie von sich aus zu jener Festigkeit gelangen werden, die sie zum Bestehen der auf sie zukommenden Belastungen und Krisen benötigen werden, muß man bezweifeln. Für mehr als 50 % ist „Sicherheit in Glaubensfragen" nicht so wichtig bis überflüssig. Es entsteht ein Vakuum im weltanschaulichen Bereich, in das Sekten, Aberglaube oder Ideologie einzudringen vermöchten. Denn Weltanschauung wird nicht etwa für überflüssig gehalten, sondern entbehrt.

Andere tradierte Werte wie Leistungsorientierung, Zuverlässigkeit, Eigentumsorientierung und Sparsamkeit hingegen werden von 80 – 95 % wenigstens für nützlich gehalten.

Das Bild läßt sich demnach in das von Rosenmayr entworfene Schema zwischen Reproduktion und Transformation der Werte gut einordnen. Ein Grundstock bleibt enthalten, aber die Gesellschaft wandelt sich mit jeder Generation schrittweise.

Ob die Gesellschaft mit dem Hineinwachsen dieser Generation in den vollen Bürgerstatus ihre Stabilität behalten bzw. – angesichts zahlreicher heute bereits bemerkbarer Anomieerscheinungen – wieder erhalten wird, dürfte von der Gesellschaft selbst abhängen. Wenn Uneinsichtigkeit und fehlerhaftes Reagieren, wie es zur Mitte der sechziger Jahre in die „Fast-Katastrophe" geführt hat, sich wiederholen, dann könnte entweder mit erneuten Ausbruchsversuchen oder mit Anomie-Erscheinungen größeren Ausmaßes zu rechnen sein.

Wir rechnen freilich eher mit Auflösungserscheinungen als mit Ausbrüchen, da wir vermuten, daß diese Generation zu Ausbrüchen nicht die Kraft aufbringen könnte. Der revolutionäre Schwung der sechziger Jahre gehört der Vergangenheit. Der Krisendruck der Gegenwart lähmt die Aktion, dürfte aber nicht derartige Ausmaße annehmen, daß „die Jugend" sich in eine ausweglose Lage gedrängt sieht.

Es gibt vielleicht nur einen Stabilitätsfaktor, an den die Maßnahmen anknüpfen könnten, das wäre die unverminderte Festigkeit und Funktionstüchtigkeit der familialen Erziehung. Doch dürfte die Familie die Aufgaben, die auf sie zukommen, nicht ohne Rat, Anweisung und Information bewältigen können.

Dafür spricht die Tatsache, daß die Erziehung von Jahrfünft zu Jahrfünft permissiver gehandhabt wird. Sie befindet sich damit nicht mehr auf dem letzten Stand der psychologischen und erziehungswissenschaftlichen Erkenntnis; denn extreme Permissivität, das haben die Untersuchungen aus Anlaß der Studentenrevolte gezeigt, verhindert die Ausbildung eines festen Ego und stört die Auseinandersetzung mit dieser Welt.[36)]

Ohne massiv einschneidende, weitreichende und großzügig finanzierte Intervention aber, das lesen wir aus den Befunden dieser Untersuchung, wird diese Jugend ihren Weg nicht finden.

* Jugend in Europa – ihre Eingliederung in die Welt der Erwachsenen. Eine vergleichende Analyse zwischen der Bundesrepublik Deutschland, Frankreich und Großbritannien, bearbeitet von Viggo Graf Blücher in Verbindung mit Klaus-Peter Schöppner, 1. Band: Vorstudie unter Mitarbeit von Hartmut Lüttke, Karol Szemkus, Rod Preece und J.C. Passeron, 2. Band: Tabellenteil, 3. Band: Kommentar, durchgeführt vom EMNID-Institut für Sozialforschung, herausgegeben vom Jugendwerk der Deutschen Shell, Hamburg, 1977, deren Hauptergebnisse und ihre Verwendung als Prognoseinstrument.

1. Z.B. in W. Hornstein, Jugend in ihrer Zeit, Hamburg 1966; dort eine Bkbliographie der historisch orientierten Literatur. Oder: Jugend in der Gesellschaft – ein Symposium, München 1975; S.N. Eisenstadt, From Generation to Generation – Age Groups and Social Structure, Glenwe 1956.
2. Vgl. Schelskys zeitgeschichtlichen Rückblick in „Die skeptische Generation", 3/1975, S. 46 ff.
3. Darüber orientieren die bibliographischen Anmerkungen in Allerbeck-Rosenmayr, Aufstand der Jugend? München 1971.
4. Ausformuliert in „Die Arbeit für die anderen – Klassenkampf und Priesterherrschaft der Intellektuellen", Opladen 1975
5. Vorwort zur Taschenbuchausgabe „Die skeptische Generation", Frankfurt, Berlin, Wien 1975, S. XXI.
6. Stichwort „Jugend" in: Handbuch der empirischen Sozialforschung, Hg. Rene König, Band 6, 2. völlig neu bearbeitete Auflage, Stuttgart 1976, S. 300.
7. Der Bundesminister für Bildung und Wissenschaft, Bildungspolitische Zwischenbilanz, o.J. u. o.O., (Bonn 1976).
8. Rosenmayr, Stichwort „Jugend" a.a.O., S. 299.
9. Jugend in Europa, a.a.O., Bd. 1, S. 2 ff.
10. Hartmut Lüdtke, Die Analyse von Sozialisationseffekten im Kohortenvergleich, in: Die Jugend in Europa, Bd. 1, a.a.O., S. 32–62.
11. Karol Szemkus, Sozialisation und deren Indikation, in: Jugend in Europa, Bd. 1, a.a.O., S. 63–82.
12. Viggo G. Blücher, Bern, Sozialisation und Sozialisationseinrichtungen in Deutschland, in: Jugend in Europa, Bd. 1 a.a.O., S. 83–104.
13. Rod Preece, Waterloo, Ontario, Spezifische Bedingungen der Sozialisation im Britischen Kulturkreis, in: Jugend in Europa, Bd. 1, a.a.O., S. 105–108.
14. J.-C. Passeron, Agenten und Mechanismen der Sozialisation im heutigen Frankreich, in: Jugnd in Europa, Bd. 1, a.a.O., S. 129–167.
15. Die Daten der Untersuchung werden für Weiterverarbeitung der Befunde durch Interessenten zur Verfügung gehalten durch das Zentralarchiv für empirische Sozialforschung bei der Universität Köln.
16. Vgl. Jugend in Europa, Bd. 3, Soziologisch-wirtschaftliche Struktur der Untersuchungsgruppe, S. 115 ff.
17. Jugend in Europa, Bd. 3, S. 22–27.
18. Jugend in Europa, Bd. 3, S. 76 f.
19. Jugend in Europa, Bd. 3, S. 31 ff.
20. S. 50 ff.
21. Grenzen soziologischer Erkenntnis am Beispiel der Jugendforschung, in: Soziologie, Mitteilungsblatt der Deutschen Gesellschaft für Soziologie, 2–1974, S. 46 ff, mit Beiträgen von Fr. Neidhardt, H. Kreutz, J. Friedrichs, H. Lessig, M. Liebel u.a.
22. Opladen 1973, S. 524
23. Zum hier verwendeten Generationsbegriff vgl. K. Mannheim, Das Problem der Generation, in: L. v. Triedeling (Hg), Jugend in der modernen Gesellschaft, Köln-

Berlin 2/1965, S. 23 ff (zuerst 1928).

24. H. Schelsky, Die skeptische Generation, 3/1975, S. 381 u. 385.
25. V.G. Blücher, Die Generation der Unbefangenen, Zur Soziologie der jungen Menschen heute, Köln-Düsseldorf 1966, S. 348 ff.
26. Werner Klose in der „Welt am Sonntag", 13.8.1967.
27. E.K. Scheuch, Bereiten die Studenten den Bürgerkrieg vor? In: Vorträge zur Marktforschung, hg. im Auftrag des Bundesverbandes deutscher Marktforscher – Vortrag auf der 17. Jahrestagung des EMNID-Instituts 5/1968 in Hamburg, S. 16.
28. Jugend in Europa, Bd. 3, S. 50 ff.
29. id., S. 33
30. id., S. 51
31. Die Untersuchung „Jugend zwischen 13 und 24", im Jahre 1975 vom gleichen Institut in der Bundesrepublik durchgeführt, wurde teilweise zur Charakterisierung der Grundtendenzen mit herangezogen; hier Bd. 2 (Tabellenteil), S. 195.
32. Querschnitt durch die Untersuchung von 1975.
33. Leopold Rosenmayr, in: Jugend zwischen 13 und 24, Bd. 1, Vorstudie, S. 87 ff.
34. Jugend in Europa, 3. Bd., a.a.O., S. 54 ff.
35. id., S. 48 ff.
36. Vgl. z.B. S.M. Lipset, Students and Politics in congarative Perspective, in: Daedalus, Students and Politics, 1968; R. Allerbeck, Soziale Bedingungen für studentischen Radikalismus, Diss. Köln 1970; K.E. Scheuch, Soziologische Aspekte der Musik unter den Studenten, in: Politik und Zeitgeschichte – Beilage der Wochenzeitung „Das Parlament", Heft 36/1968, S. 3 – 25.

Aussprache über das Referat Graf Blücher*

Diskussionsleiter: Wolfgang R. Schürer

Frau Roitsch eröffnet die Diskussion und trägt erhebliche Bedenken gegen die Art der Fragestellung in der Jugendstudie vor: die Fragestellung orientiert sich an Normen und Werten derjenigen, die fragen. Abgefragt werden Vorstellungen, Begriffe und Wissenskataloge der älteren Generation. Alternativen bleiben unabgefragt, sind nicht vorgesehen. Bei „Ungereimtheiten" wird nicht weitergefragt. Infolgedessen können Wertsysteme und Normen der jungen Generation nicht erfragt werden. Eine weitere Folge ist, daß die Sozialwissenschaft keine Veränderungen feststellt.

Mehrere Diskussionsteilnehmer teilen diese Bedenken. Insbesondere an den Begriffen „Religion", „Solidarität", „Liebe", „eheliche Treue", „eine Dummheit machen", nach denen in der Studie gefragt werde, könne mann erkennen, daß hier an den Jugendlichen und ihren Bedürfnissen vorbeigefragt werde, da diese Begriffe nicht nur bei verschiedenen Generationen unterschiedliche Begriffsinhalte, sondern auch im Laufe der Zeit eine Wandlung des Begriffsinhaltes erfahren haben. In Zustimmung und Ablehnung der Antworten fließen höchst unterschiedliche Erfahrungen oder Nichterfahrungen ein, die nur an den gängigen Normen der bürgerlichen Bildungsmittelschicht orientiert sind (die wollen das ja so hören, wenn sie danach fragen!), ohne daß damit eine Identifikation der Befragten abgeleitet werden könnte. Es bestehe sogar die Gefahr, daß mit dem eigenen Verhaftetsein der Forscher an traditionellen Normstrukturen man an den Jugendlichen vorbeiredet.

Diskussionsteilnehmer meinen: Ähnliche Probleme lassen sich bei der internationalen Vergleichbarkeit entdecken, hier sind es primär Fragen der Übersetzung des Fragebogens und unterschiedlicher kultureller Voraussetzungen in den befragten Ländern. Als Beispiel für eine problematische Übersetzung wird in der Diskussion die Frage 21 (des deutschen Fragebogens) angeführt: „eine Dummheit machen" wurde zum Beispiel mit „to do something wrong" ins Englische übersetzt, im Französischen heißt es „ ... quand vous aviez fait quelque chose de mal ...". Die Zweifel, einen Wissensvergleich in den drei befragten Ländern anstellen zu können, entzündeten sich insbesondere an der Frage „Wer war Mozart?".

---

* Infolge eines technischen Defektes ist die Tonbandaufzeichnung dieser Aussprache verlorengegangen. Einige Teilnehmer haben im nachhinein die Aussprache aufgezeichnet. Die folgenden Ausführungen stellen eine Zusammenfassung dieser Beiträge dar.

Aussprache Graf Blücher

Professor Blücher versuchte diese Kritik durch Angabe der Untersuchungsziele zu entkräften. Keineswegs sei beabsichtigt gewesen, zentrale, jugendspezifische Werte zu untersuchen und auf ihre Übereinstimmung mit der älteren Generation zu prüfen. Das primäre Untersuchungsziel sei gewesen: die Einstellung der Jugendlichen zu den Bereichen Familie, Schule, altersgleiche Gruppen und Beruf. Blücher betonte, daß durch die Wiederholung von Fragen eine relativ große Vergleichbarkeit mit anderen, vorausgegangenen Shell-Jugendstudien erhalten geblieben sei; ein Ergebnis, das von vielen Jugendforschern begrüßt worden sei.

Professor Szemkus machte auf den Vorwurf, daß in der Jugendstudie die jugendeigenen Werte nicht angesprochen würden, geltend, daß es jugendspezifische Werte allenfalls in Form von Reaktionen auf die Werte der Erwachsenen geben könne und sicher nicht in völliger, von der Tradition gelöster Neuschöpfung. Der Jugendliche, so Szemkus, wählt seine wertpädagogischen Vorbilder häufig aus anderen Altersgruppen als den eigenen.

Szemkus sagte, man habe beim Abfassen der Fragen eine Sprache gewählt, die von den meisten der Befragten verstanden wurde. Richtig sei, daß ein Jugendlicher mit 16 Jahren unter „ehelicher Treue" möglicherweise etwas anderes verstehe, als ein Familienvater mit 43 Jahren. Die Bedeutungsverschiebung in der sprachlichen Realitätserfassung war aber nicht das Thema der Shell-Studie. Man solle nicht im nachhinein der Studie Ziele unterstellen, die nie angestrebt wurden. Die Studie könne nicht auf alle möglichen Fragen, sondern nur auf einige Fragen Antwort geben und das sei schließlich schon sehr viel.

Die Art der Interpretation der Befragungsergebnisse in der Jugendstudie stieß auf lebhafte Kritik, obwohl Blücher in der Diskussion selbst die Schwierigkeit der Operationalisierung und der Instrumentefindung einräumte. Als Beispiele wurden unter anderem genannt: Blüchers Ableitung, daß die „permissive" Erziehung daran schuld sei, daß die Jugend von der „Religion" nichts mehr halte und Gefahr von „Sektenbildung" bestünde. Lebhaft bezweifelt wurde Blüchers weitere Ableitung, daß die Jugend offenkundig nicht sehr stabil sei, weil sie mit der Frage nach der Religion zu 50 % nichts mehr anzufangen weiß.

Auch Blüchers Feststellung, die er aus dem normierten Wissenskatalog („Kennen Sie Mozart?") ableitete, daß sich das Bildungswissen verbreitert habe, aber das Spitzenwissen deutlich verringert sei, wurde von mehreren Diskussionsteilnehmern aus unterschiedlichsten Blickwinkeln „zerpflückt":

Was heißt Spitzenwissen, woran wird „breite Bildung" gemessen, welche Aufschlüsselung gibt das Abfragen von nur kognitiven Fähigkeiten?

Die Kritik an der Untersuchung ging sehr ins Detail und hakte sich immer wieder an Einzelpunkten fest, ohne in eine Struktur einzumünden, die für das gesamte Symposium hätte wichtig werden können. Eine Überleitung zu der

Auflistung der offenen Fragen: welche Bedürfnisse und Interessen haben die nachwachsenden Generationen, wo sind Veränderungen festzustellen, wo liegen für sie selbst Prioritäten, wo „Unerforschtes" und wie könnten Antworten von Politik, Wirtschaft, Wissenschaft und Gewerkschaft gegeben werden, wurde in dieser ersten Diskussion nicht aufgestellt.

Teilnehmer

Aghina, Joseph J., Student der Wirtschaftswissenschaften, Hochschule St. Gallen

Ammann Rene, Student der Wirtschaftswissenschaften, Hochschule St. Gallen

Andrykowsky, Paul, Dipl.-Kaufmann M. Sc. E, Mitglied des Vorstandes USW Schloß Gracht

Becker, Klaus E., Bochum

Bell, Dr., Daniel, Prof. für Soziologie Harvard University

Biallas, Hans-Christian, Arbeitsgemeinschaft der evangelischen Jugend Niedersachsen, Hannover

Biedenkopf, Dr. Kurt H., Prof., Stellv. Vorsitzender der CDU, MdB Bonn

Bispinck, Ingeborg, Bund der Deutschen Katholischen Jugend, Köln

Blatt, Inge, Volkshochschuldozentin, Hamburg

Blücher, Dr. Viggo Graf, Prof. für Soziologie Universität Bern

Bölling, Gisela, Studienrätin, Kultusmin. Nordrhein-Westfalen, Düsseldorf

Bohn, Helmut, Geschäftsführer Markus-Verlag GmbH, Köln

Boltze, Nils, Amt für Jugend, Hamburg

Buchmüller, Dr. Hans-Rainer, Arzt, Heidelberg

Bussiek, Hendrik, Dipl.-Sozialwissenschaftl., Journalist, Berlin

Coors, Norbert, Student der Wirtschaftswissenschaften, Trier

Creischer, Cornelia, Studentin der Wirtschaftswissenschaften, Trier

Croonenbroeck, Hans, Dipl.-Vw. BDI Köln

Deutsch, Dr. Karl W., Prof., Direktor des Intern. Instituts für vergleichende Gesellschaftsforschung Berlin

Davids, Manfred, Student der Wirtschaftswissenschaften,Wuppertal

Döhl, Klaus, Junge Union Deutschland, Bonn

Ellerbroek, Kai, Student der Wirtschaftswissenschaften, Münster

Fandrich, Wolfgang H., Cand. Wi.-Ing., Karlsruhe

Fiedler, Hans, Unternehmensberater, Hamburg

Fiedler-Winter, Rosemarie, Wirtschafts-Journalistin, Hamburg

Fischer, Dr. Arthur, Dipl.-Psychol., Psydata, Institut für Marktanalysen, Sozial- und Medienforschung GmbH, Frankfurt

Fischer, Frank, Student der Wirtschaftswissenschaften, Gießen

Frankl, Dr. Dr. Viktor E., Prof. f. Neurologie und Psychatrie an der Universität Wien

de Frenes, Michael C., Student der Rechtswissenschaften, Freiburg i.Br.

Fritschi, Peter, Student Universität Bern

v. Goßler, Gottfried, Dipl.-Kfm., Leiter Abt. Wirtschaftspolitik, Deutsche Shell AG, Hamburg

Teilnehmer

Günther, Dr. Klaus, Rechtsanwalt, Partner der Anwaltsgemeinschaft Boden, Oppenhoff & Schneider, Köln

Graf, Hans-Werner, Student der Wirtschaftswissenschaften,Gießen

Glotz, Dr. Peter, Senator für Wissenschaft und Forschung in Berlin

Grumbein, Heiko, Student der Wirtschaftswissenschaften, Regensburg

Haarlaender, Gerd, Dipl.-Kfm., Abt. Wirtschaftspolitik, Deutsche Shell AG, Hamburg

Haenchen, Dr. Hede, Arbeitskreis LERINA, Berlin-Zehlendorf

Hänisch, Ulrich, Leiter der Staatl. Gewerbeschule Energietechnik, Hamburg

Hagen, Dr. Eckehart, Leiter des Referats für Trendanalysen des sozialen Wandels, Bundeskanzleramt Bonn

Hagmann, Beat, Student Universität Bern

Hannibal, Heinrich, Referent für außerschulische Jugendbildung, Amt für Jugend, Hamburg

Hartmann, Dr. Christine, Dipl.-Vw, Bundesinstitut für Berufsbildung, Berlin

Heimbach, Stephan, Schüler, Köln-Rodenkirchener Gymnasium, Köln

Hinderer, Michael, Student der Wirtschaftswissenschaften, Hochschule St. Gallen

Hölter, Christoph, Bund der Deutschen Katholischen Jugend, Bistum Essen

Hoffmann, Volker, Dipl.-Volkswirt, Direktor der Deutschen Shell AG, Hamburg

Jäckel, Ursula, Dipl.-Soziologin, Lehrstuhl f. Soziologie, Gesamthochschule Bamberg

Jaeger, Norbert, Dipl.-Volkswirt, Büro M. Wissmann, MdB Bonn

Jansen, Marc, Dipl.-Ing., Lic. Oec., Schlieren, Schweiz

v. John, Dr. Eckart, Abt.-Leiter Forschung und Bildungspolitik, BDI Köln

Karl, Elisabeth, Studentin der Wirtschaftswissenschaften, Regensburg

Kleimeier, Peter, Schüler, Köln-Rodenkirchener Gymnasium, Köln

Kleinwächter, Reimar, Friedrich-Ebert-Stiftung, Ahrensburg

Knepper, Dr. H., MinR. i. Kultusmin., NRW, Düsseldorf

Korte, Bernd, Student der Wirtschaftswissenschaften, Hannover

Kramer, Dr. Wolfgang, Institut der Deutschen Wirtschaft, Köln

Kreyenschmidt, Gisela, Arbeitgeberverband d. privaten Bankgewerbes, Köln

Kühn, Gunda, Hamburg

Kuklinski, Stefan, Schüler, Gymnasium Hamburg-Eidelstedt

Lebreton, Yves, Pantomime, Paris

Lennaerts, Louk, Wachtberg-Niederbachem

Loepthien, Walter, Student der Wirtschaftswissenschaften, Vorstand der AIESEC, Köln

Lübbe, Dr. Hermann, Prof. f. Philosophie und polit. Theorie, Universität Zürich

Lüdtke, Gerhard, Jugendsprecher der SIEMENS AG, München

Lukas, Dr. Elisabeth, Dipl.-Psychol., Leiterin der Psychologischen Beratungsstelle der Münchner Jugendfürsorge

Martin, Ruth Ch., Dipl.-Paed., Psydata, Institut für Marktanalysen, Sozial- und Mediaforschung GmbH, Frankfurt

Mast, Dr. Claudia, Siemens AG, Hauptbereich Bildungspolitik, München

Maus, Wolfgang, Student, Bund der Pfadfinderinnen und Pfadfinder e.V. Simmern

Maybüchen, Bernd, Student der Wirtschaftswissenschaften, Wuppertal

Merbecks, Bernhard, Stätte der Begegnung, Vloto

Möller, Dr. Gerhard, Rechtsanwalt, Direktor Personalaufbau, Deutsche Shell AG, Hamburg

Monigatti, Hans, Vorsitzender des Gesamtbetriebsrates, Deutsche Shell AG, Hamburg

Moritz, Eberhard, Haus der Jugend Steilshoop, Hamburg

Müller, Hans-Joachim, Redakteur, Deutschlandfunk

Osing, Hartmut, CVJM-Sekretärschule, Kassel-Wilhelmshöhe

Pflugradt, Michael, Schüler, Gymnasium Monheim-Baumberg

Ploss, Günther, DAG

Prach, Johann, Student der Erziehungswissenschaften, Hochschule der Bundeswehr, Hamburg

Preece, Dr. Rodney, Prof., Bramhall Cheshire, England

Rappe, Hermann, MdB, Stv. Vorsitzender der IG-Chemie, Hannover

Rieß, Christoph, Student der Wirtschaftswissenschaften, Karlsruhe

Roeben, Günther, Student der Wirtschaftswissenschaften, Trier

Rögge, Karin, Studentin der Wirtschaftswissenschaften, Gießen

Roitsch, Jutta, Redakteurin Frankfurter Rundschau

Rosenmayr, Dr. Leopold, Prof. für Soziologie, Universität Wien

Roth, Dr. Günter, Oberst, Leiter des Studentenbereichs, Hochschule der Bundeswehr Hamburg

Schmidt, Wolfgang, Student der Wirtschaftswissenschaften, Hochschule St. Gallen

Schneider, Uwe, Student der Erziehungswissenschaften, Hochschule der Bundeswehr, Hamburg

Schöppl, Heinz, Betriebswirt, Geinberg, Österreich

Schöppner, Klaus-Peter, Dipl.-Psychol., Emnid-Institut, Bielefeld

Schriever, Hans Peter, Dipl.-Kfm., Leiter Jugendwerk der Deutschen Shell AG, Hamburg

Schürer, Wolfgang, Lic. oec. HSG, Delegierter des Verwaltungsrates des MS Management Service AG, St. Gallen

Schultheiß, Michael, Friedrich-Ebert-Stiftung, Bonn

Sik, Dr. Ota, Prof. f. Wirtschaftswissenschaften, Hochschule St. Gallen

Sölter, Arno, Dipl.-Kfm., Forschungsinstitut für Wirtschaftsverfassung und Wettbewerb e.V., Köln

v. Spiegel, Christian, Student der Rechtswissenschaften, Oberursel

Stahl, Hans-Joachim, Landesoberverw.-Rat, Landesjugendamt Münster

Stark, Sabine, Studentin der Psychologie, Münster

Steffen, Frank, Juniorenkreis der Deutschen Wirtschaft, Köln

Stein, Sabine, Schülerin, Meiendorfer Gymnasium, Hamburg

Stier, Thomas, Student d. Publizistik u. Politwissenschaften, Universität Salzburg

Streithofen, Dr. H. Basilius, Institut für Gesellschaftswissenschaften Walberberg e.V.

Sülberg, Hermann, Redaktion Stern, Hamburg

Szemkus, Dr. Karol, Prof., Institut für Soziologie, Universität Bern

Teufel, Klaus-Dieter, Dipl.-Kfm., Leiter der Abteilung Arbeitsmarkt- und Bildungspolitik, Zentralvereinigung Berliner Arbeitgeberverbände, Berlin

Thum, Heinz, Reg.-Dir. i. BM für Jugend, Familie und Gesundheit, Bonn

Walter, Dr. Norbert, Prof., Institut für Weltwirtschaft, Universität Kiel

Welbergen, Johannes C., Dipl.-Chem., Vorsitzender des Vorstandes der Deutschen Shell AG, Hamburg

Wendt, Andreas, Jugendvertreter Deutsche Shell AG, Raffinerie Harburg

Werner, Jürgen, Student der Rechtswissenschaften, Freiburg i. Br.

Weyde, Martin, Schüler, Gymnasium Meiendorf, Hamburg

Wiebe-Grabicki, Sylvia, Leiterin der Wirtschaftsredaktion beim NDR-Fernsehen, Hamburg

Wittig, Manfred, Student der Erziehungswissenschaften, Hochschule der Bundeswehr, Hamburg

Wolf, Klaus-Peter, Stellvertr. Bundesvorsitzender der Jungsozialisten in der SPD, Berlin

Wortmann, Dr. Joachim, Kölner Stadtanzeiger

Zander, Karl Fred, MdB, Parlamentarischer Staatssekretär im Bundesministerium für Jugend, Familie und Gesundheit, Bonn

Organisatorische Durchführung des Symposiums:

Bormann, Klaus, Jugendwerk der Deutschen Shell, Hamburg

Gerwing, Eva, Jugendwerk der Deutschen Shell, Hamburg

Klötzke, Hans-Joachim, Jugendwerk der Deutschen Shell, Hamburg

Maeder, Jens, Jugendwerk der Deutschen Shell, Hamburg

Müller, Hans E., Jugendwerk der Deutschen Shell, Hamburg

Paulsen, Rolf, Jugendwerk der Deutschen Shell, Hamburg

Struck, Hanne-Lore, Jugendwerk der Deutschen Shell, Hamburg

Veröffentlichungen der Deutschen Shell*:

- „Jugend zwischen 13 und 24" – Vergleich über 20 Jahre
  6. Untersuchung zur Situation der Deutschen Jugend im Bundesgebiet, Hamburg 1975 (Emnid-Institut)

  Band I – Vorstudie (Beiträge: Walter Jaide, Helmut Lessing, Manfred Liebel, Friedhelm Neidhardt, Leopold Rosenmayr, Karol Szemkus)

  Band II – Tabellenteil

  Band III – Kommentar

- „Jugend 1977" – Verhaltensweisen und Werte im europäischen Vergleich
  7. Jugenduntersuchung. Diese wiederum von Emnid durchgeführte Befragung wurde anläßlich des 75-jährigen Jubiläums der Shell im Oktober 1977 vorgelegt.

- „Die Deutsche Shell innerhalb einer weltweiten Unternehmensgruppe"
  Hamburg 1975
  (Inhalt u.a.: Personal- und Sozialpolitik, Grundsätze der Führung und Zusammenarbeit, Mitarbeiterbeurteilung)

- Nur für Pädagogen: Unterrichtsmodell ENERGIE":
  Lehrerhandbuch (in Form von 8 Unterrichtsbausteinen) und Schülerheft, Hamburg, 1977

- Sozialbilanz als integrierter Bestandteil des Geschäftsberichtes der Deutschen Shell Aktiengesellschaft 1975, 1976, 1977 und 1978

- „Die Einstellung der jungen Generation zum Unternehmer in seinem wirtschafts- und gesellschaftspolitischen Umfeld"
  Hamburg, 1979

*kostenlos zu beziehen bei:

Deutsche Shell Aktiengesellschaft
Public Relations
Postfach 60 05 20
Überseering 35
2000 Hamburg 60